Aligning Human Resources and Business Strategy

Aligning Human Resources and Business Strategy

Second edition

Linda Holbeche

AMSTERDAM • BOSTON • HEIDELBERG • LONDON • NEW YORK • OXFORD
PARIS • SAN DIEGO • SAN FRANCISCO • SINGAPORE • SYDNEY • TOKYO
Butterworth-Heinemann is an imprint of Elsevier

Butterworth-Heinemann is an imprint of Elsevier
Linacre House, Jordan Hill, Oxford OX2 8DP, UK
30 Corporate Drive, Suite 400, Burlington, MA 01803, USA

First edition 1999
Paperback edition 2001
Reprinted 2002 (twice), 2003, 2004 (twice)
Second edition 2009

Notice
No responsibility is assumed by the publisher for any injury and/or damage to persons or property
as a matter of products liability, negligence or otherwise, or from any use or operation of any
methods, products, instructions or ideas contained in the material herein.

British Library Cataloguing in Publication Data
A catalogue record for this book is available from the British Library

Library of Congress Cataloguing in Publication Data
A catalogue record for this book is available from the Library of Congress

ISBN: 978-0-7506-8017-2

For information on all Butterworth-Heinemann publications
visit our web site at www.elsevierdirect.com

Typeset by Macmillan Publishing Solutions
(www.macmillansolutions.com)

Printed and bound in Great Britain

09 10 11 12 13   10 9 8 7 6 5 4 3 2 1

Contents

Preface to the First Edition

So much has been written about the changing role of HR that the reader might wonder why I have sought to add to the debate. It seems that being an HR professional is a tough proposition these days and that there are endless requirements to prove that value is being added by HR interventions. The pressures on the function are enormous and in many cases, resources are thinly stretched. The HR function is frequently accused of being reactive. Yet I believe that the situation need not be so bleak and that HR has potentially the most significant contribution to make of all the functions, if it manages to combine operational excellence with a really strategic approach.

My motivation in researching and writing this book is to find out how excellent professionals are delivering value. That is not to say that I believe that the practitioners featured in this book have a blueprint for success but some of the approaches described here are likely to provide food for thought for other organizations. Similarly, I am not attempting here to address all aspects of a strategic and operational HR agenda. I have focused on some of the performance and developmental issues which I consider key if business and HR strategies are to be aligned. This is not therefore a technical book, but one which highlights what practitioners are doing with respect to strategic recruitment, organizational development, management and international leadership development and change management. I have tried to illustrate the theory with 'live' cases where time permitted, and have included checklists which I hope will be useful to HR teams and line managers in assessing their needs and service provision.

I hope that the ways in which the HR strategists featured in this book are approaching the challenges of aligning business and HR strategies in their organizations will provide evidence that outstanding value can be added by HR and offer encouragement to practitioners who are finding the quest to add value hard going.

Preface to the Second Edition

Since the first edition of this book was published, so much has changed in terms of the employment landscape, HR theory and priorities, that simply updating the text has not been enough. HR is undergoing perhaps more rapid transformation than any other function on its journey to delivering value. In today's fast-changing economic context equipping organizations to deal with the pressures they are likely to experience calls for a truly strategic response from HR. And of all the functions HR has potentially the most significant contribution to make, if it manages to combine operational excellence with a really strategic approach. Building talent pipelines, changing organizational structures and cultures are just some of the opportunities for HR to exercise leadership.

At the same time, much has stayed as it was ten years ago. Alongside the opportunities sit the pressures. It still seems that being an HR professional can be a tough proposition and there are endless requirements to prove that value is being added by HR interventions and, in many cases, resources remain thinly stretched. As the HR agenda moves on so the nature of HR interventions continues to expand, demanding new disciplines, skill sets and behaviours, even within HR's traditional heartland. Strategic workforce planning can put organizations 'on the front foot' when it comes to optimizing the changing labour market and demographic trends. Employer branding, employee segmentation and other analytical techniques, and holistic approaches to reward enable organizations to attract and retain the talent they need for success. Organizational design and development, geared to building flexible, agile cultures are an essential part of the HR role. Continuous professional development is key to raising the game.

Similarly, the capabilities HR is required to demonstrate have also moved on significantly in the last decade since I wrote the first edition of this book. No HR professional can expect to be taken seriously if he or she is unable to understand and speak the language of business, to translate the business strategy into relevant people processes and goals which are appropriate to the context dynamics facing their organization. HR needs the ability and credibility to work collaboratively with line managers to continually push up the standards and practice of people management and development.

The evolving HR role is moving ever more swiftly to becoming a core business leadership role, in which HR's own contribution is to ensure that the organization is equipped for success, now and in the future. And in the wake of various corporate failures, particularly within the global financial services sector, there is increasingly a spotlight on HR's developing role in governance, raising questions such as what is HR's role with respect to building cultures where accountability and ethical practice become the order of the day rather than letting high bonuses form part of a culture of excess and irresponsibility? Similarly, should HR professionals more obviously have a role to play as non-executives on boards, ensuring that good practice in appointments and reward at the most senior levels in organizations reflects the very best emerging practice and encourages high standards of executive behaviour?

So in writing this second edition of the book I have attempted to update my overview of the HR landscape, agenda, skill set and challenges in the light of the changing context, theory and practice. My motivation in researching and writing the book is to find out how excellent professionals are delivering value. I have tried to illustrate the theory with 'live' cases where time permitted as well as drawing on published research. In some cases I have revisited and updated where possible case studies featured in the first edition of the book as well as adding other examples of what I consider interesting practice. That is not to say that I believe that the practitioners featured in this book have created a blueprint for success but I hope that some of the approaches described here will provide food for thought for others. Similarly, I am not attempting here to address all aspects of a strategic and operational HR agenda. I have focused on some of the performance and developmental issues which I consider key if business and strategy are to be gainfully aligned.

This is not therefore intended as a technical book, but one which highlights what practitioners are doing with respect to strategic recruitment, organizational development, management and international leadership development and change management. In this edition I have looked again at the process of HR transformation and the changing nature of business partnering. I have added a chapter on some of the key skills for HR strategists and suggested a process for developing a business-aligned HR strategy. I have included checklists which I hope will be useful to HR teams and line managers in assessing their needs and service provision.

I hope that the ways the HR strategists featured in this book are approaching the challenge of creating aligned strategies will provide evidence that outstanding value can be added by HR and offer encouragement to practitioners who are finding the quest to add value hard going.

Overview of Contents

In Part One, *The Need for Strategic Human Resources,* I raise the question about what 'alignment' means in a fast-changing context, elements of which I discuss on Chapter 2. I present my case drawing on a range of HRM theory, and suggest that HR leadership should be the preferred direction of travel if the function is to really add value. HR leadership involves embracing a strategic culture-building agenda geared to creating healthy and high performing organizations. The business context drives the HR agenda, especially as work becomes progressively more knowledge- and talent-intensive. It also drives the transformation of the HR role, organization, structures and skill sets. Delivering a value-adding agenda requires purpose, focus, a well-formulated strategy and effective methods, as well as effective measurement to ensure that the right kinds of impact on organizational performance are being achieved.

In Part Two, *Strategies for Managing and Delivering Talent*, we consider a major aspect of HR's role – that of attracting, motivating and retaining talent. I explore various aspects of talent management, a concept which for me has partly a feel of 'Emperor's new clothes' about it, including all aspects of the conventional employment cycle from recruitment, development, performance management, reward, career progression etc. What is different is the rapidly changing nature of work and the global labour market, together with changing talent requirements and various forms of talent shortfall. Hence the growing emphasis on workforce/talent planning, on developing enticing employer brands, on segmenting the talent base and personalizing employee value propositions, on 'engaging' employees at an emotional level, on creating the organizational climate where people will give of their best. Debates rage about whether talent management processes should apply only to the privileged minority of 'high flyers' or whether more inclusive approaches are appropriate. In all of this, line managers are key partners, delivering the lived reality of the brand to employees.

In Part Three, *Human Resources as a Strategic Function*, we consider the implications of the evolving HR role and structures for the skills, and behavioural competencies needed by professionals. These include a much greater emphasis than in the past on business acumen, consultancy skills, organizational design and development, as well as analytical approaches borrowed from other disciplines. We look at how these skills can be applied to specific challenges, for instance to support cross-boundary working. In particular, we look at some of the challenges facing global HR teams.

In Part Four, *Implementing Strategic Change*, we look at various ways in which HR teams are changing their organizations' cultures to meet business needs, for instance to become more customer focused or to enable greater knowledge-sharing. We consider the human dynamics of change and at what HR can do to support people through periods of change. We also consider how HR can contribute to successful integration, for instance in mergers and acquisitions, and build more change-ready cultures.

Finally we look at what the future might hold for HR, and at how HR's emerging purpose and role may well crystallize further into several key elements. For me, these include attracting and mobilizing talent, building performance capability, creating healthy and successful organizations, building effective leadership, providing coherence and ensuring good governance. With an agenda such as this, I argue, the time has come for HR to get on the front foot and lead the way.

Acknowledgements

I am extremely grateful to all the people, too numerous to mention, who have contributed to this book. From the first edition I would like to thank all the former contributors, including those whose case studies do not appear in this edition. I have tried where possible to include some of the case studies from the first edition, especially those where I have been able to gain updates. These include contributions from Dr Candy Albertsson, formerly of BP Amoco, Anthony J. Booth CBE, of Ericsson, the late John Bailey of KPMG, Roger Leek of Fujitsu Services (formerly of BNFL), Brian Wisdom and Chris Johnson, formerly of Thresher, David Waters, formerly of Whitbread, Stephen McCafferty of Standard Life, Jane Yarnell for the case study on the National Air Traffic Services and Leslie Patterson of Dow Corning for her case study. I would like also to acknowledge the kind support I received from Professor Clive Morton and the late and sadly missed Professor David Hussey.

I would like to thank my former employer Roffey Park and Valerie Hammond, Roffey Park's Chief Executive at the time this book was first written. In particular I would like to thank my former Roffey Park research colleagues and associates Claire McCartney, Annette Sinclair, Drs Valerie Garrow, Christina Evans and Wendy Hirsh, Professor Peter Smith, Michel Syrett and Jean Lammiman and John Whatmore whose research is referred to in this book. I would also like to thank Pauline Hinds and colleagues in the Learning Resource Centre for their help. I would also like to acknowledge the help given in the preparation of the first edition by *Personnel Today*, particularly by the then Features Editor Scott Beagrie.

Revising this book to produce a second edition has proved a labour – not always of love – and I am extremely grateful for all the help and support I have received, especially from my employer the Chartered Institute of Personnel and Development (CIPD). I would like to thank CIPD's CEO Jackie Orme and her predecessor Geoff Armstrong for all their help and encouragement. In particular my thanks go to those who have kindly contributed case study and other material, including Research and Policy team colleagues and external researchers who have developed work for the CIPD and on whose published findings I have drawn. I am also grateful to Rima Evans, editor of *People Management* magazine, her predecessor Steve Crabb and their fellow journalists, and publisher PPL for the use of published examples of good practice. My thanks go to Dr Jill Miller, Barbara Salmon, Annie Bland and Noelle Keating for their kind assistance and to Dr Tim Miller, Director, People, Property and Assurance of Standard Chartered Bank for his ongoing advice and support.

I am extremely grateful for all the support I have received from Elsevier/ Butterworth-Heinemann. In particular I would like to single out for special mention former commissioning editor Ailsa Marks, without whose continuing support and encouragement I would not have undertaken this revision, and her successor Hayley Salter, who has enthusiastically spurred me on to complete the work. The production team, especially Deena Burgess and Elaine Leek, who has painstakingly read and corrected the revised version, deserve a gold medal.

Above all, I shall be always indebted to my dear husband Barney, and my mother Elsie, for their constant encouragement and faith in me.

Whilst every effort has been made to contact copyright holders, the author and publisher would like to hear from anyone whose copyright has been unwittingly infringed.

Part I

The Need for Strategic Human Resources

Chapter 1

Introduction: From Business Partnering to Leadership

HR passes the wallet test when it creates human abilities and organizational capabilities that are substantially better than those of the firm's competitors – and thus move customers and shareholders to reach for their wallets.

(Dave Ulrich and Wayne Brockbank, 2005)

In the decade since I wrote the first edition of this book, the pace of change in the global business environment has accelerated, new forms of organization and ways of doing business have arisen. Globalization has produced an interwoven set of challenges affecting business, organizations, consumers, workers and society as a whole. Indeed, the nature of work and the expectations of workers have been transformed and change is now a constant feature of most organizations.

In the rapidly changing global economy, external pressures mean that businesses need to innovate and act with speed if they are to keep ahead of the competition in their chosen market. Flexibility is just one feature of this changing competitive landscape as customers increasingly demand tailored products and services available round the clock. The drive to achieve high-quality continuous supply at reasonable margins has meant that production and customer service are increasingly carried out off-shore and virtual working has become more commonplace.

'Talent' and the ability to 'engage' that talent to produce 'high performance' are buzz-words which can be heard in organizations of every sector, reflecting the growing awareness of the importance of being able to attract, manage, motivate and retain the right people. People are no passive 'human resource' and if companies want to be flexible to meet changing market requirements, they also have to meet the needs of their staff, especially those with valuable 'knowledge skills'. Just as customers are increasingly demanding, now 'knowledge workers' are in a stronger position than a decade ago to make demands of employers as their skills are in short supply, especially in industries as diverse as construction, IT and pharmaceuticals. It would appear that the days of the 'War for Talent' are back with us, despite the challenging global economy.

THE HR TRANSFORMATION JOURNEY

The HR profession too has been transforming itself, in many ways leading the way forward for other professional groups. Ten years ago, many HR teams were struggling to make more 'value-added' contributions to business success, and Dave Ulrich's (1997) thinking has had a powerful influence on the evolving practice, roles and structures of HR. The past decade has seen an explosion of HR transformation activity as HR teams in every sector have changed their roles and structures, with over 80% of HR functions having undergone some form of change in the past five years alone (Reilly, 2008).

Much of the change is to achieve greater alignment between business and HR strategy and to drive more cost-effective and improved delivery. HR teams have taken many routes to do this, such as reengineering the 'back-office' HR functions by using technology to transform service delivery and information, outsourcing administration or setting up shared services, as well as devolving HR practices to line management and acting as internal consultants in their roles as business partners. However, despite the transformation journey, to some extent HR still experiences ongoing internal and external stakeholder pressures to demonstrate efficiency and added value. Therefore, whether HR transformation in some organizations is producing the right results, or advancing as quickly as it might, is up for debate.

Structural change has also brought with it a degree of role uncertainty for HR. Typical challenges include clarifying the scope and remit of HR, working out how to maximize the performance of HR, where best to make a contribution, how to satisfy its customers and how to develop HR's own skills and resources. In addressing these challenges, organizations and HR teams have choices to make. So must HR follow the rocky road or is there a high road to success? And if so, can learning from those who have been on the HR transformation journey for some time help make the road ahead easier for those who are setting out on the journey today?

'OUR PEOPLE ARE OUR GREATEST ASSETS'

And, assuming that HR does free itself up to deal with more strategic issues, the question remains: what do 'value', and 'value-added' mean in today's organizations?

Value is what is generated by talent from which employers can derive profit or other forms of benefit. In today's information age, where knowledge-intensive work is increasingly driving economic growth and when the value of intellectual capital is becoming more apparent, the truth of organizational values statements such as 'our people are our greatest asset' has never been more obvious.

While we all may be familiar with organizational values statements such as this, there appears to be a good deal of double-speak in many organizations and the reality on the ground is often different. Short-term business priorities, bottom-line considerations and the need to generate shareholder returns tend to take precedence over employee considerations. Many executives understandably pay attention first and foremost to the bottom line and in many organizations 'people issues' are way down the agenda. Where these do appear they are often treated as short-term operational problems rather than as key areas of attention or investment.

This is ironic given that the growing reality for many organizations operating in a global marketplace is that talent – the lifeblood of competitive advantage – is in short supply. While global talent in some sectors may be abundant, local talent is not, and vice versa. There is growing awareness in global companies that business fortunes increasingly depend on an organization's ability to attract and retain key talent, while driving forward performance.

Awareness of the talent challenges is one thing; knowing what can be done about them is another. This is where HR, as the key people specialist function in organizations, should be uniquely well placed to make a difference to business success. Being able to attract and retain much-needed talent and drive performance are vital ways of adding value. There seems to be a real opportunity for Human Resource professionals to play a key role in building the organization's capability to adapt in the face of ongoing change. Indeed, HR has the potential to build organizational capabilities, such as the ability to innovate, improve customer relationships, move swiftly to market, which will lead to sustainable value. But in order to do so, HR has had to embark on a journey of self-reinvention.

Ulrich and Brockbank (2005) issue a cautionary note – HR should not attempt to assess value without regard to stakeholder perspectives:

> Value in this light is defined by the receiver more than the giver. HR professionals add value when their work helps someone reach their goals. It is not the design of a program or declaration of policy that matters most, but what recipients gain from these actions. The HR value proposition means that HR practices, departments, and professionals produce positive outcomes for key stakeholders, employees, line managers, customers, and investors.

At this point in its evolution, the HR function has the potential to develop further, moving beyond HR management to more of a leadership role, given that HR's core contribution relates to culture, processes and that most precious asset of all, people. And while day-to-day people management is mainly the responsibility of line managers, the HR function's unique selling point (USP) is its ability to develop healthy and effective organizations, with the right people, with the right skills, working in the right ways to achieve the right results. HR's primary functions include finding tailored ways to attract and retain much-needed talent, to design systems, structures, roles and processes that allow talent to be well-deployed and utilized, to develop management and leadership capability and capacity and to build organizational climates and cultures that can be a source of sustainable competitive advantage. This USP should form the basis of a proactive leadership contribution from HR – if HR is ready to take the opportunity.

Yet despite this USP, and the fact that the HR role is growing in scope and depth, challenges to add value remain.

Much of the double-speak with respect to the value of people also applies to the status of Personnel or HR professionals themselves. The terms often used to describe the function – 'back office', 'support', 'cost centre', 'internal consultants' or 'business partners' – imply something that is non-essential to the organization's business and therefore of lesser value. In such cases, the actual influence of the HR director on management team colleagues can be limited.

It is often said that the battle to get a 'seat at the board table' has been won, yet it is still rare to find main board directors with an HR background and more often than not HR professionals who reach the main board find themselves with a wide range of responsibilities, of which HR is only one.

Similarly, HR is often perceived to be a 'junior' member of the board, expected to implement the board's decisions rather than help shape them. Even in key organizational events such as a merger or acquisition, HR is often only peripherally involved in the due diligence process, let alone in shaping the emerging integrated culture of the new organization.

A Function under Threat?

Other factors that may explain why HR's contribution may be less impactful than it might be include the micro-political context within which Personnel specialists are operating and the skills and effectiveness of the specialists themselves. For instance, in a Roffey Park survey, particular criticisms of HR included HR's lack of ability to add value, poor implementation of change, with HR forced into a reactive, 'picking up the pieces' role. Initiative overload, with poor follow-through of key initiatives, were other symptoms of the function's difficulties in many organizations. In other cases Personnel professionals struggled with the difficulties of balancing pragmatic solutions with professionalism, leaving them open to accusations of being 'ivory tower' and not 'in the real world'.

So along with reengineering the HR function, downsizing the HR function has been a strong trend in recent years, often because HR is not perceived as adding value. In a CIPD research study examining the changing nature of the HR role (Reilly, 2008), it is apparent that many HR professionals perceive the function to be under threat.

This mixed picture of perceptions about the role and value of HR may reflect legacy issues arising from HR's evolution as a function. Below are some of the more significant shifts in the HR role, a number of which will be explored in this new edition.

FROM WELFARE TO PERSONNEL TO HUMAN RESOURCES – THE STORY SO FAR

What HR professionals are able to deliver appears to some extent to depend on the way their role is perceived within their organization.

Traditionally, the Personnel function has been seen more as a service deliverer and a management tool than as a strategic contributor. Since the mid-1990s, Personnel has struggled to reinvent itself, get close to the customer and add value to the business. Some of the earlier ways of thinking about the Personnel role and contribution include the following.

The Welfare Model (after Tyson and Fell, 1986)

In the early days of large organizations and organized labour, the function of pay clerk was often carried out by the same person who meted out 'tea and sympathy' as the notion of employee welfare caught on. Usually held by a woman, such posts were regarded as useful tools of management but post-holders were considered administrators and were not expected to contribute to the development of strategy.

Clerk of Works

As the Personnel role evolved throughout the 1970s and 1980s it gradually became a more active tool of management. Managing people was certainly 'line' management's responsibility, but 'staff' roles such as Personnel could provide useful specialist support on a range of issues such as pay and conditions, employee welfare, recruitment and selection, etc. To a large extent, these were largely 'maintenance' roles through which the status quo was enshrined in personnel policies and procedures. The role of Personnel was often thought of as the company 'policeman' or clerk of works, ensuring compliance with set procedures.

Compliance and the Legal Obligations of Employers

The compliance role of HR remains strong and significant. HR is the visible face of an employer's obligations towards employees. Prior to 1970, the statutory regulation of the employment relationship in the UK was limited. Individual terms and conditions of employment were stated in the contract of employment and in any collective agreements. The law's intervention was restricted to basic health and safety problems, the right to limited redundancy payment and the general requirements for employers and employees to honour the contractual terms agreed at the commencement of employment. It was only 'good' employers who chose to go beyond the letter of employment law. For instance, even today, equal opportunities are still far from achieved in the UK though the general employment picture relating to equality is healthier than 30 years ago.

But since 1970 the regulatory environment has changed dramatically with increasing amounts of employment legislation and policies designed to protect employee rights. Today the contract of employment remains of crucial importance and can be enforced in court but, in addition, a whole host of statutory rights in the areas of human rights, health and safety, equal pay, unlawful discrimination and unfair dismissal have been added, with which employers are required to comply. There has been growing recognition among many employers that in order to attract talent and get the best out of a workforce, it can be in the interests of employers to go beyond the letter of the law, such as with the Right to Request Flexible Working, which is currently restricted to parents of children under six and carers, but is under review. 'Good' employers have already extended the right to all employees, with very few negative side-effects. In any case, severe labour shortages in some areas mean that employers no longer have the whip-hand in the employment relationship.

The Industrial Relations Expert

To continue the evolutionary story, between the 1970s and 1990s international competition grew considerably and there was a great need to improve UK productivity. Without the opportunity to compete on cost, UK organizations attempted to differentiate themselves on the grounds of quality, and new skills and working practices were needed if businesses were to succeed. This was also a period of prolonged industrial unrest in the UK.

The Personnel function started to attract men in large numbers for the first time. Specialists in employee relations took on the responsibility for leading negotiations with unions and (often militant) staff groups. The tough stances often adopted in these negotiations were reflected elsewhere as organizations were reshaped to meet the needs of the changing workplace. As 'fixers' of company problems such as dealing with major restructurings, redundancy programmes and other 'difficult' tasks, Personnel professionals earned the right to be taken seriously as members of management.

The 1980s was also a golden period for the development of a new range of 'hard' personnel disciplines, such as organization design, manpower planning and pay negotiations. Many of the 'baby boomer' generation of HR directors with such skills and experiences went on to significant careers in industry. However, some of these HR skills relating to collective bargaining and organization design fell into decline in the UK after the ending of the prolonged industrial unrest and reduction in the power of the trade unions. The skills void was filled to a large extent by major consultancies who helped design and implement many large-scale reengineering projects characteristic of the corporate downsizings of the 1990s. More recently, many of the 'hard' HR disciplines, such as workforce planning and analytics, are being revived and reclaimed by HR, after a period in the doldrums.

In the Republic of Ireland a similarly challenging industrial climate in the 1980s and 1990s led to the tripartite social partnership between trade unions, employers and the government. The relative industrial peace over the past 20 years has brought much-needed inward investment from companies in high technology and pharmaceuticals and other knowledge-intensive work and provided a significant boost to the economy. As a result, Personnel practitioners in Ireland have long experienced the growth of knowledge work and recognized the need to develop talent.

Personnel as a Profession

Perhaps as a result of the significant part played by Personnel in employee relations during the period of industrial unrest, the power of the role grew beyond the original confines of the job. In large organizations specialist functions such as Compensation and Benefits were created. The more Personnel became the specialist repository of information about employees, including senior management, the more it needed to be consulted about any and every issue related to employees. Personnel began to be seen as a power in the land, even if, in most cases, the Personnel director was not a member of the board. Over time, in some cases, responsibility for managing people appeared to slip away from line managers who would refer to Personnel for everything from a minor disciplinary offence to recruitment. The primary functions of Personnel became administration and generalist service delivery and the numbers employed within the function grew accordingly.

Since the 1970s there has been a gradual move to professionalize the Personnel function and increase the value of its contribution. The UK Institutes of Personnel Management and Training and Development merged in the mid-1990s and achieved chartered status in 2000 under Geoff Armstrong's leadership. Membership of the professional body gradually came to be by qualification rather than experience alone. Now the UK's Chartered Institute of Personnel and Development (CIPD) provides chartered membership to people who combine continuing professional development with qualifications and experience.

Human Resources?

By the 1990s business survival, rather than growth, became the issue in many sectors. Much manufacturing capability migrated from the UK to parts of the developing world, and the UK gradually developed a service economy. The emphasis in many organizations was on downsizing and change, with change management becoming mainly a line management discipline.

At about the same time, many Personnel functions started to re-badge themselves as 'Human Resources', reflecting a resource-based view of the firm which suggests the link between different resources and business success. From a resource perspective, three basic types of resource are thought to contribute to competitive advantage:

- Physical capital resources, which include, for example, the company's finances, equipment, plant, etc.
- Organizational capital resources, which include the firm's structure and systems for exercising control.
- Human capital resources, which include the skills, competencies, experience and intelligence of employees.

While describing human beings as a 'resource' is curious, to say the least, the link between humans as a resource and business success has been the basis of a raft of HRM theory which continues to develop as evidence accumulates about how the link works in practice. Since, for all its limitations, the term 'human resources' does imply that people are assets, and while, as assets go, people may be a fragile and volatile resource, they have the potential to create greater value than other forms of asset. More specifically, people represent latent assets, whose value is unlikely to be realized if that latent contribution is left undeveloped. Logically then, the human resource should be treated from an investment perspective more as an asset, than as a cost. Getting the best out of 'resourceful humans' is perhaps a more appropriate way of thinking about the purpose of effective people management strategies. Links between the company's human resources and competitive advantage are explored in Chapter 5.

The Spur to HR Transformation

By the mid-1990s HR itself started to restructure and 'right size' itself. In many organizations the ratio of HR to line positions had grown significantly and the more difficult trading conditions and constant restructurings of the time brought the size and value of support functions such as HR into question. This was the period when one of the most significant theory voices on the role of HR was that of Professor Dave Ulrich of Michigan University, whose model of the HR roles in 1997 in effect accelerated the reengineering of HR referred to earlier. He described four core roles and related activities, namely:

- *Strategic partner* – whose activities involve aligning HR and business strategy; organizational diagnosis
- *Administrative expert* – reengineering organization processes; creating shared services
- *Employee champion* – listening and responding to employees; providing resources to employees
- *Change agent* – managing transformation and change; ensuring capacity for change.

This model was used by organizations attempting to realign their HR functions to meet the changing needs of their business. The shifts in the HR role were intended to be as follows:

Traditional	$\longrightarrow$	Emerging
Reactive	$\longrightarrow$	Proactive
Employee advocate	$\longrightarrow$	Business partner
Task focus	$\longrightarrow$	Task and enablement focus
Operational issues	$\longrightarrow$	Strategic issues
Qualitative measures	$\longrightarrow$	Quantitative measures
Stability	$\longrightarrow$	Constant change
How? (tactical)	$\longrightarrow$	Why? (strategic)
Functional integrity	$\longrightarrow$	Multi-functional
People as expenses	$\longrightarrow$	People as assets

Ulrich's model, since revised, remains the most influential in terms of driving thinking and practice on HR's role and scope, structure and skills. HR transformation will be discussed in more detail in Chapter 3.

MAXIMIZING THE HUMAN ASSET – HUMAN CAPITAL MANAGEMENT

Since the 1990s, various researchers (Huselid *et al.*, 1997) have emphasized the role played by technical HRM in building a company's performance, with strategic HRM creating competitive advantage by building HR systems that cannot be imitated. The desire to assess the effects of HR activity on business performance has led to a focus on measurement, though the range of measures used in different organizations tends to be inconsistent, making comparison difficult.

In more recent times the quest for increased productivity at national level and for sustainable business performance from organizations has increased recognition of the importance of the human factor to business success. Human Capital Management (HCM) attempts to define measures for valuing aspects of human performance and the various 'intangible' outputs, such as innovation, associated with it, so as to be better able to understand what this contributes to organizational performance and competitive advantage. However, hopes that companies would be required to report on their human capital in annual reports were dashed in 2005 when the UK's Operating Financial Review (OFR) did not make this a requirement, and the causal link between people and organizational performance remains poorly understood. We shall explore different approaches to measurement and assessment of HRM practice in Chapter 4.

Despite this, the 'Human Capital' movement has led to increased awareness that treating employees well is a key element of increasing performance and productivity. To some extent this has strengthened the hand of those advocating effective people management, training and development. It has also suggested that HR has a key role to play in creating competitive advantage and driving performance. It has also focused management and trade union attention on what drives employee performance, in particular employee 'engagement'.

The argument goes that in order to produce the results the organization needs to be successful, employees need to be 'engaged'. Towers Perrin (2003) defines engagement as 'employees' willingness and ability to contribute to company success … the extent to which employees put discretionary effort into their work, in the form of extra time, brainpower and energy.

The assumption behind much research into high performance is that in every organization there is a value chain to high performance which runs something like this: the right employees, with the right AMO – i.e. ability (A) and motivation (M) and the right opportunity (O) – will deliver the right performance to customers, who will produce the financial and other returns required by the organization's stakeholders (Purcell, 2002). Similarly, Towers Perrin (2003) have found 'clear links between our respondents' level of engagement, their focus on

customers, and aspects of the organization's financial and operational performance across a number of areas.

The challenge for managers and HR is to create the AMO which leads to
employee engagement and performance. HR should be developing and implementing strategies which help their organizations to attract and retain talent,
which add to the value of the human asset, which produce the conditions for
great performance and which build organizational capacity and capability.

Links between good people management practice, individual development
and performance and business results have long been assumed within assessment and measurement frameworks such as Investors in People (IiP), ISO, the
European Foundation for Quality Management (British Excellence Model) and
the Balanced Business Scorecard. These all associate 'hard' business results with
'soft' inputs such as learning, customer focus, processes, people management
and leadership.

These frameworks reflect some of the broader thrusts of strategic human
resource management theory which suggest a strong link between HRM practices and organizational performance.

STRATEGIC HUMAN RESOURCE MANAGEMENT THEORY

Strategic HRM has become topical in recent years but definitions as to what is
meant by the term vary widely. Typically, strategic HRM bridges business strategy and HRM and focuses on the integration of HR with the business and its
environment. In particular, the growing literature on the impact of HRM practices
on organizational performance is commonly underpinned by the resource-based
view of the firm with its emphasis on gaining sustainable competitive advantage
by means of effective and efficient utilization of the resources of the organization, including resources that are valuable, rare, inimitable and non-substitutable,
such as human resources.

Wright and McMahan (1992) for instance discussed the importance of human
resources in the creation of competitive advantage. However Wright, McMahan
and McWilliams (1994) further suggested that, while human resources are always
a potential source of sustained competitive advantage, not all organizations have
the ability to systematically develop these through the use of HRM practices.
Similarly Huselid (1995) and Pfeffer (1995) have used the resource-based view
as a basis for examining the impact of human resource development on firm performance, in particular, utilizing a system of management practices that gives
employees skills, information, motivation and latitude, and results in a workforce
that is a source of competitive advantage.

Control and Commitment Approaches to HRM

HRM has evolved from two distinct conceptions of the link between employee
motivation and behaviour and firm-level performance outcomes. Some researchers

distinguish between 'hard', traditional HRM and 'soft', commitment-focused HRM. 'Hard' HRM reflects a contingency approach based on the assessment of the best way to manage people in order to achieve business goals in the light of contextual factors.

Walton (1985) suggested that a distinction can also be drawn between the control and commitment approaches to HRM. Arthur (1994) argues that the control approach to HRM seeks to improve efficiency by enforcing employee compliance by, for example, basing employee rewards on some measurable criteria.

The control approach is clearly represented in Fombrun, Tichy and Devanna's (1984) 'Michigan Model', which emphasized that superior firm performance is dependent on having in place systems for the regular assessment of individual employees. Associated with, and reinforcing, these systems are performance rewards and training whose performance-related outcomes are monitored. Fombrun *et al.* argued that what was important was a tight 'fit' between the external business strategy and HRM. This contingency approach suggests that for any particular organizational strategy, there will be a matching HR strategy (Figure 1.1).

The belief that the closer the 'fit' between business strategy and organizational functions will result in organizational effectiveness has been challenged in recent times. The challenges relate to the lack of empirical evidence that this close strategic fit will automatically lead to improved effectiveness, and that such approaches do not take into account measures of organizational effectiveness. There are also criticisms that such approaches can be too simplistic in their assumption that the creation of HR strategy inevitably follows the business strategy. In contrast, 'soft' HRM focuses on a high-commitment–high-performance approach to the management of people. Commitment approaches to HRM aim to shape attitudes by forging psychological links between organizational and employee goals. Also known as the collaborative model of enhancing firm performance – aimed at promoting the goals of both employees and employer – the commitment approach to HRM is clearly apparent in Beer *et al.*'s 'Harvard Model' (1984), which emphasizes the need for management to recognize employees as significant stakeholders in the enterprise. The notion of HRM being used to develop employee commitment is also central to Guest's (1997) theory of normative HRM.

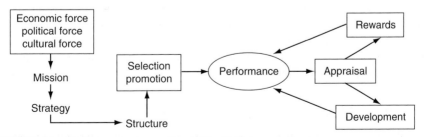

FIGURE 1.1 The human resource cycle and 'fit' with business strategy. Based on Fombrun *et al.*, 1984

At the core of this model is the notion of the centrality of employee influence and the common sense of purpose it engenders for firm performance. Employee influence is contingent on there being processes of mutual influence between management and employees that enable management to understand employee interests. Without such processes, employee intrinsic motivation is undermined, thereby giving rise to employee resentment and distrust, which results in unwillingness to take responsibility for the performance of the firm.

'Bundles of HRM Practice'

What remains unclear is how organizations can achieve consistently superior performance via HR strategy. Various researchers (for example, Delaney and Huselid, 1996) claim to have found a statistically significant link between 'bundles' of HR policies and business performance. With respect to employee commitment, for instance, Beer *et al.* found that, rather than a single system of employee involvement techniques, several approaches, such as employee briefings and work system design, may be used. These bundles of HR practices need to be internally consistent and complementary and depend on the organizational logic in that context. Thus, while individual aspects of 'best practice' are useful for benchmarking purposes, the approaches used must be congruent with the organization's state of development if the real benefit is to be felt.

Guest (1989) incorporated the HR policy goals of strategic integration, commitment, quality and flexibility into a model, whereas Purcell (1996) considers the following six elements as key to employee commitment:

- Careful recruitment and selection
- Extensive use of systems of communication
- Team working with flexible job design
- Emphasis on training and learning
- Involvement in decision-making
- Performance appraisal with tight links to contingent pay.

Similarly, Pfeffer (1998) recommends seven integrated practices that will enable organizations to 'obtain profits through people'. These are:

- Employment security
- Selective hiring of new personnel
- Self-managed teams and decentralization of decision-making as the basic principles of organizational design
- Comparatively high compensation contingent on organizational performance
- Extensive training
- Reduced status distinctions and barriers (including dress, language, office arrangements and wage differentials across levels)
- Extensive sharing of financial and performance information throughout the organization.

Again, one of the key tenets of 'soft' HRM is the internal integration of HR policy goals with each other.

Alignment?

The notion that there is 'one best' or 'universal' way to manage human resources, such as is advocated by Pfeffer (1998) stands in contrast to theorists such as Schuler and Jackson (1987) and Fombrun *et al.* (1984), who argue that what firms do depends on their circumstances and that HR strategy (HRS) should therefore also be contingent.

This contrast lies at the heart of what 'strategic alignment' means. For the contingency theorists, the best personnel policy relates to the unique character-istics and circumstances of the organization. The argument is that organizations need to achieve a fit between personnel policy choice and broader strategic con-siderations, such as market conditions and business strategy. In contrast, from a universalist perspective, alignment relates to the level of integration between HR practices that are understood to lead, for example, to employee engagement or high performance.

In my earlier edition of this book, I took the view that the best form of align-ment was one that was relevant, i.e. contingent on the organization's circum-stances and strategic aims – 'best fit'. Indeed, in many organizations, the notion of 'best fit' is attractive, especially if HR strategies are developed to meet the needs of the business in its context. Contingent HR strategies are more attractive to line managers since they can see the relevance to what the organization is aim-ing to do in the short term, and can enhance the credibility of the HR team who are seen to be business-focused.

However, I also considered that universal 'best practice' can inform local circumstances. Indeed, many measurement frameworks and competency-based standards, such as Investors in People frameworks or CMI Management com-petencies, assume a universal set of approaches that represent best practice on people management and development, regardless of context. Similarly, bench-marking processes derived from best practice can help organizations recognize choices in the way they address key issues. The danger of HR strategies built on 'best practice' is that they can seem 'ivory tower' and idealistic. Having an HR strategy that appears unrelated to the business strategy is far from useful.

While holding to my earlier view, several factors are causing me to modify it slightly. First, the body of thinking on what constitutes 'best practice' has expanded in recent times. So with respect to high performance for instance, there does appear to be a growing evidence base and broad degree of consensus, which I share, about which key ingredients are almost always present in high-performance contexts, e.g. high degrees of employee involvement. However, other less well-established factors are being added to the list of 'universalist' factors as time moves on and as research uncovers new 'drivers' of employee engagement and links with performance. For instance, work–life balance is coming to be viewed as a key factor in employee engagement, even though the link between that and high performance is not well proven. Similarly, the nature of the organization's corporate reputation is thought to be an important factor in attracting and retaining talent. For instance, with environmental and climate change issues becoming more prominent, job candidates are increasingly reported to be taking into account an organization's policies on recycling, carbon offsetting etc. when making their career choice. To the extent that major social changes affect the daily work lives and expectations of employees, and help shape their attitudes and motivations, I would argue that the nature of 'universal' factors is also always contingent on external factors.

Other challenges to the nature of strategic alignment relate to the typical time-horizon within which business goals are planned and implemented. Usually the planning time-frame is three to five years at best. Now that there is growing recognition that HR has a key role to play in building culture – to support high performance – the timeframe for developing the organization is longer than the average business planning cycle.

Similarly, some HR strategies focus on building talent from within, growing leaders for tomorrow. The development of leaders with the behaviours and capabilities to lead tomorrow's business requires HR to look beyond today's practices and business strategies and work with line managers and executives to identify what will be required in the future workforce and leadership. Activities involving growing talent and changing the 'way we do things around here' can take time, and an understanding of how to bring about change in complexity. These are issues on which HR needs to exercise leadership to produce real value for the organization but gaining the licence to focus on the longer term often depends on how effectively HR delivers in the short term.

Moreover, alignment is not always one-way and HR strategies can themselves influence business strategy. HR strategies cannot be isolated from changes in the marketplace, most specifically trends relating to the labour market. New employment legislation, shortages in the labour market, demands for greater diversity and flexibility of service provision have to be taken into account. A business strategy which requires specific types of labour that are in very short supply will prove difficult to implement.

Social Role of HR

In contrast to the notion that HR strategic alignment is all about developing the means to deliver a business strategy lies a more values-based way of thinking about the role of HR, which co-exists somewhat uneasily with the performance-based view. Michel Syrett (2007) points out that HR's role is not restricted to dealing with employees as if they are mere instruments of organizational performance. HR has a key social role to play with respect to employees, due in part to the breakdown of the traditional social contract that exchanged employee loyalty for life-time job security, and the rise of individualism more generally in society. People have increased expectations in terms of their quality of life, of which their workplace conditions and relationships form a very important part. Employees increasingly resist authoritarian management, require participation in decision-making and demand improved physical working conditions.

And HR has to address the issue of whether HR should be a business resource management function or an employee welfare facility to a much greater extent than other business disciplines like marketing or finance. The latter brings with it responsibilities and commitments which may potentially bring HR into moral conflict with business and performance-driven objectives that lead to, for example, the closure of a factory in a town with declining prospects of employment for workers whose skills base is limited.

Similarly, HR's legal responsibilities can create tensions and contradictions over the strategic business imperative to use employees as a competitive 'human resource' in highly pressured and often global marketplaces. More recent legislation, much of it originating from the European Union, includes that on working time, family-friendly rights and consultation. This is set to continue with, for example, the current focus on age discrimination.

HR practitioners need a knowledge and understanding of developments in employment law in order to both devise appropriate policies and procedures and to provide the correct advice to line managers and employers. Increasingly too there is recognition among employers that merely complying with the letter of employment law is not enough to leverage human resources for competitive advantage. A more strategic, proactive response to human resource issues is needed and should not be left to chance.

HR is at the pivot point of debates about whether the rights and needs of employees for instance for work–life balance and flexible working, should be of greater priority than those of employers who may need staff to be available for business at conventional times. The increasing quantity of regulation and law that governs the employment relationship in the UK means that HR – to a far greater extent than other business disciplines like marketing and finance – has a role as 'guarantor' or 'guardian' of employee rights as well as representing the interests of the organization. This has led to a continuing role for HR as arbiters between 'the business' and 'the workforce'. Not for nothing has Dave Ulrich's 'employee champion' now become 'employee advocate'.

Organizational Effectiveness

Increasingly, strategic HRM is coming to be understood as being about organizational effectiveness. Tony Grundy (1998) defines organizational effectiveness as: 'the capacity of the organization to adapt rapidly to its external environment and to meet market and other external demands and with good resulting business performance'. Grundy (1998) argues that integrating corporate strategy and HR matters into an 'Organization and People Strategy' more fully reflects the focus on organizational effectiveness and may prove more successful at building business performance over time. Key to building organizational effectiveness is a skilful blend of HRM practices, organizational design and development to suit a specific organization in its particular context.

Strategic HRM therefore has a clear focus on creating the right organization architecture to be more effective in the fast-changing global context. The HR role involves creating new organizational capabilities, implementing strategic change and growing the skill base of the organization to ensure that the organization can compete effectively in the future. Indeed, Stroh and Caligiuri (1998) suggest that strategic HR departments are future-oriented and operate in a manner consistent with the overall business plan in their organizations. Such departments assess the knowledge, skills and abilities needed for the future and institute staffing, appraisal and evaluation, incentives and compensation, training and development to meet those needs. This also suggests that facilitating organizational learning, both for implementing change and in helping to develop strategy, is a key element of strategic HR.

Delivering Value

Though transition to a more strategic role can be difficult, it is certainly not impossible. Several of the case studies in this book, featuring the activities of HR practitioners who are making a strategic contribution to their organizations, should offer hope and practical insights into how others have made the transition. Interestingly, as the role and contribution of HR continue to evolve, the HR function is coming to be seen as a 'player' in many organizations. In Roffey Park's Management Agenda Surveys 2000–2006 practitioners appear to see the influence of HR as strong and the function to be growing in size. Adapting the Wyatt-Haines (2007) functional value ladder, it would seem that HR is moving up the value ladder from its base, as 'follower' to at least 'enabling' the organization to maximize its performance:

Following

This is the first and lowest level, where HR follows the business and reacts to its needs, but is capable of delivering consistently and reliably, as well as managing costs, effectiveness and efficiency of HR systems. Regrettably, many HR functions fail to deliver even at this basic level. When responses are late or inconsistent, and practitioners find themselves leaping from one crisis to another, these HR functions are perceived as ineffective.

Enabling

With better organization and delivery standards, and the benefit of an understanding of the business strategy, the HR function is able to facilitate business units in delivering current business priorities.

Leading

> Looking ahead, the [HR] function is able to predict likely needs, resource priorities and
> strategic issues in order to maximize the performance of the business. In this way, [HR] has
> the role of enabling the business to enjoy strategic success. (after Wyatt-Haines, 2007)

'Leading' requires the ability to both 'enable' and 'follow' business needs, but above all requires strategic anticipation and the ability to create value. While arguably HR generally may still have some way to go before it can be said to be 'leading', the more positive views of the value of HR in some organizations may also reflect the perceived relevance of the business partnership between line managers and HR professionals, and the development of organizational strategies that deliver value.

WHAT DOES 'BEING STRATEGIC' MEAN?

One of the key challenges for the early implementers of the 'Ulrich model' who managed to free up some capacity to 'be strategic', with the intention of providing a more value-added service, was working out what 'being strategic' and 'adding value' in their context were about. Similarly, creating shared perceptions of value with line manager colleagues was challenging and measurement came to be used defensively to prove that value was being added. Consequently the HR function became seemingly caught like a rabbit in the headlights, away from the safe place of the old role at the kerbside yet unable to move forward to a new, more dynamic place. In many cases practitioners reverted to what they knew best, what they felt was expected of them by line managers, and where they gained most personal satisfaction. Inevitably perhaps, HR value and the merits of HR transformation continued to be called into question.

The Role of Business Partner

What gradually became apparent was that the role of business partner was poorly understood by all concerned. According to the theory, business partners were to see themselves as part of the business, and be capable of understanding the business drivers and implications of business strategy for people and organization. Business partners needed to be able to diagnose problems, prescribe solutions, ensure effective implementation and move out of the hamster wheel of activity to create more strategic approaches to key organizational challenges such as employee engagement, culture change, integration etc. In practice, clarification of the role largely came through doing it.

One of the critics of the Ulrich model, Ed Lawler (2006) has commented on the difficulty of HR positioning itself as a business partner. Lawler considers HR a business with three product lines:

- Administrative services and transactions with the need to use resources efficiently and provide quality of service

- Business partner services developing HR systems and providing solutions needing to know the business and exert influence
- Strategic partner role contributing to business strategy, which needs a deep knowledge of the market as well as HR.

In the early stages of HR transformation, the roles of business partners were often poorly differentiated, resulting in confusion and in many cases a reversion to generalist support activities. What gradually became apparent was that many new business partners were under-prepared or under-powered for their roles, lacking the skills, confidence or the delivery capability as consultants to ensure that value was being added over what had existed before. However, the need for higher level skills to implement strategic HRM has become increasingly recognized and addressed through HR education and development. Consultancy skills, relationship management and third party management skills, together with commercial acumen, are prerequisites for effectiveness in business partner roles, and these now commonly feature in business partner development programmes.

Similarly, while much transformation effort was focused on reengineering HR processes and structures, and the 1997 Ulrich roles of 'strategic partner' and 'administrative expert' gradually became clearer, relatively less priority was placed by those implementing the model on Ulrich roles of 'change agent' and 'employee champion'. In the first decade of the twenty-first century, it has become apparent that building organizational capabilities around change, and finding ways to grow employee engagement are key priorities. The neglected roles have therefore come to the forefront.

Towards a Strategic Contribution

We are now supposed to be in the era of HR as a strategic business partner. On the whole, this current phase of HR transformation appears to be a refinement of the earlier implementation of the Ulrich model to reflect evolving business needs and opportunities, changes in the business and organizational landscape, as well as learning from the experience of HR transformation about what works and what is required. Interestingly, even now, 42% of respondents in the CIPD study (Reilly, 2008) are still experiencing difficulty defining HR roles, perhaps because it is clear that one size does not fit all.

Ulrich (Ulrich and Brockbank, 2005) has himself broadened out and fine-tuned some of the key ideas behind his 1997 model. He advocates looking at HR roles more as mindsets and forms of responsibility deriving from the strategic needs of the business, rather than as a single structural solution. Leadership and human capital are more in evidence than in his earlier model. Ulrich recognizes that HR should not only build effective organizational leaders but can and should itself exercise leadership, especially given the importance of getting the right people strategies to meet the needs of today's organizations and employees operating in a knowledge-intensive global context.

Ulrich now proposes a new framework based on a synthesis of earlier HR roles:

- Employee advocate (ensuring employer–employee relationships are of reciprocal value)
- Functional expert (designing and delivering HR practices)
- Human capital developer (building future workforce)
- Strategic partner (helping line managers reach their goals)
- HR leader (credible to own function and others).

So what are the key aspects of the business-aligned people agenda which it is reasonable to expect HR to lead on in order to add value? This question has become more significant as scarce resources have become more tightly controlled and markets have become ever more competitive, leading to a highly commercial and hard-edged view of how to leverage 'human resources' that may potentially be in conflict with HR's welfare origins.

What do CEOs Need from HR?

Defining what being a business partner means in practice involves looking at what the 'partner' requires from the relationship. Assuming that HR's principal business partner is line management, it is important to understand what managers' view of the world is, define problems in their terms, frame what will happen in terms of results they expect and clarify what they need to do in getting there.

It can also be instructive to look at what chief executives do *not* want from HR. A small-scale research project in which chief executives talked about what they needed from the function suggests that CEOs do not place value on HR professional skills alone, though these should be of a high order and reliability. CEOs want and expect HR professionals to understand the business and its challenges, as well as to be able to translate business strategies into their human resource implications. They want HR to be able to communicate with executives in ways that demonstrate this understanding. Similarly, various studies suggest that CEOs do not appreciate too great a concern with rules and procedures that result in inappropriate 'policing' and blocking action. The quest for the 'perfect' solution or 'best practice' system is not appreciated either, if such initiatives are not owned by management or do not fit the organization. This means that HR professionals must involve line managers in the development of initiatives that make a difference to how people are managed, developed and rewarded. The well-intentioned new appraisal scheme or competency framework, if developed by HR alone, may be perceived as over-engineered or inappropriate.

What Keeps CEOs Awake at Night?

Reversing the coin, what matters most to executives is what keeps them awake at night. These, the most significant people and culture issues, should be at the heart of HR strategies. Identifying, retaining and replacing the best talent in an organization is *the* key issue most likely to keep chief executives awake at night, according to a 2006 study by Accenture. This is now a 'burning obsession among chief executives', according to Peter Cheese, global managing partner at the company's human performance practice, and affects business leaders in India just as much as those in the UK. More than 60% of the respondents to Accenture's annual survey of chief executives said that the inability to attract and retain the best talent is now a key threat to their business, outstripping the issue of low employee morale (Cheese, 2007).

The Accenture study also points out that while the relationship between HR and senior management is improving – particularly in IT, telecoms and financial services – chief executives and financial officers still need to empower and champion HR more effectively, so that people issues rise to the top of the business agenda. What chief executives require is for their strategic HR business partner to translate the organization's needs back into business language and help executives understand what must be done with regard to people if the business strategies are to be achieved. This means that HR professionals need to be able to sense the issues that count, and to have the confidence to relay some potentially tough messages to management about what needs to be done. This is the quality described by Dave Ulrich as 'HR with attitude'. CEOs also need HR to be experts in process skills, able to win commitment and influence within the organization. This requires an ongoing dialogue with the line business organization and the ability to both plan change and bring others effectively through change. Approaches to achieving this will be examined in Chapter 14.

THE AGENDA

For the HR function, the agenda becomes a simple one – the aim is to be both a contributing member of the management team as well as to create personal, functional and organizational capability.

A business strategy only has value when it is implemented and HR has a key role to play in enabling strategy implementation and business success. As Ulrich suggests, 'the successful organizations will be those that are able to quickly turn strategy into action; to manage processes intelligently and efficiently; to maximize employee contribution and commitment; and to create the conditions for seamless change' (Ulrich, 1998). For this to happen, HR managers and their teams must understand how their business strategy can be effective in the competitive and fluid environment in which today's businesses operate. This is not necessarily about analysis and planning, but about how strategy operates both as a way of thinking and acting so HR strategies and policies ensure that employees can deliver value to their customers and organizations can enjoy competitive advantage.

Of course, with the benefit of a clear business strategy on which to focus, HR teams can develop a people and organizational strategy to support the business strategy. This degree of alignment is critical to the success of the business, the effective utilization of its resources and the perceived value of the HR function. In 'steady' times it is possible to be quite specific about what and how an HR function delivers to the business and the service that it wraps around its core products and role. However, in fast-changing times, when business strategy has to adapt dynamically to new circumstances the ability to 'strategize' is all the more important. HR has to be at the forefront of creating organizational 'change-ability' and corporate agility.

This will require key capabilities across the HR function so that it can deliver consistently and reliably as well as strategically. In other words, the HR team must be able to think and act in a strategically aligned way. This is not just strategy in the sense of plans, systems and processes; it is strategy as communication, mind-set, flexibility of thought, awareness and a passion for ensuring that HR is a key strategic resource for the business, delivering value and success on an ongoing basis.

So does HR matter? Yes, HR does matter, in the three core areas of:

- Achieving competitive advantage
- Delivering greater productivity
- Transforming the organization.

Achieving Competitive Advantage

- Through *enabling* – understanding the strategic drivers for the business and implications of the competitive environment; technology in particular can help worldwide project teams to bring new concepts to market faster and respond more quickly to customer needs, while at the same time reducing costs. HR can design and implement strategies that help the organization achieve its goals in the short, medium and long term; supporting line man-agers, executives and employees to perform in ways that build competitive advantage.
- Through *linking* – building the organization's synergies through collabora-tion: by facilitating organizational learning across boundaries and helping find new and better ways of doing things. HR can help create new ways of working in partnership with other organizations and may establish a way of operating which becomes an industry norm.
- Through *attracting and retaining key talent* – in today's fast-moving context, the conventional business planning horizon is becoming ever more short-term, making workforce planning ever more difficult. Skills shortages are being felt across Europe to varying degrees. In some parts of the UK econ-omy skills gaps have been plugged by employing migrant workers for exam-ple. HR is responsible for managing talent, designing and implementing the strategies for attracting, motivating and retaining key talent, including leaders at all levels; and addressing organizational needs for flexibility and employee

needs for work–life balance. This involves anticipating not just demographic trends but readying the organization for change. The result should be that organizations have the talent they need to succeed and employees feel their needs and aspirations have been heard and taken into account.

- Through *reducing competitive pressure* – by becoming uniquely attractive to key talent which makes it harder for other organizations to compete. In particular, developing employer brands which are real and enabling employees to have work–life balance will be some of the ways HR can ensure a good supply of the 'right' talent.
- Through *growing organizational capability* – designing cultures that are supportive of innovation and performance; building the skills and capabilities of employees at all levels, including those of managers and leaders.
- *Equipping staff with the skills required* to meet changing business needs is increasingly challenging, especially since the psychological contract has become increasingly transactional rather than relational. Employees expect to be trained but may choose not to stick around to deliver on their enhanced skills once trained. Work–life balance has become a key element of talent strategies and achieving diversity has remained a major challenge for many organizations.
- *Developing pools of talent for future leadership roles* will become increasingly important and challenging. Succession planning has moved into a more consensual mode, where individual and organizational interests must be equally taken into account. More personalized approaches need to co-exist alongside the collective – being able to balance both will be a key underpinning of effective HR approaches.

Delivering Greater Productivity

- By *building high performance cultures* – organizational culture is becoming central to organizations' search for sustainable high performance and productivity. Organizational development has risen in importance and should be a key part of HR professionals' remit. Building in flexibility and the potential for innovation to structures, processes and, most of all, mindsets, takes some doing. It requires HR to be able to work effectively with organizational agents who have a key role in building high-performance work practices and cultures will be increasingly key to adding value in an HR role.
- The business context is changing so fast that speed is increasingly required for *winning and maintaining competitive advantage*. Given that change is ongoing, change management, being able to integrate cultures and create corporate agility are key to HR roles.
- By *developing good people management practice* – this includes helping managers to manage and develop their staff, many of whom will be 'non-employees' or contract workers, helping teams to work across organizational boundaries, and top management to embrace and enact their leadership roles.

- Through *organization design*. HR needs to understand the principles under-pinning operational strategy and be strong at managing the interrelated operational elements of cost, dependability, flexibility, quality and speed. From its cross-organizational perspective, HR can see how all the processes and systems within the business interlink, including where there are areas of duplication and unnecessary activities that add little to the business, and identify where improvements can be made in the light of what the business is aiming to do. HR can ensure that team roles are appropriately designed and structured; good communication processes established and ensure that cross-organizational interdependencies are identified, with teams able to share learning across boundaries.
- Through *role modelling good practice*. HR itself needs to be able to adopt good operational principles and be able to take a concept and turn it into real-ity faster than the competition to provide real advantage to the organization.
- Through *efficiency and effectiveness*. HR needs to organize its structure and delivery mechanisms to create higher levels of autonomy, accountability and performance across the business.
- HR must *understand needs of customers* (internal and external) accurately and apply their resources to projects, functions and services that customers actually need.
- HR must ensure that through its *relationship management* the quality of relationships across the business improves, preventing time being wasted on back-biting and political games.
- HR can *improve internal management processes* and systems by providing approaches and processes through which managers and leaders can direct, manage performance, develop, coach and communicate effectively.

Transforming the Organization

- Working with line managers to *design effective structures and roles to achieve business objectives*. The dimensions of strategy, people, task, struc-ture, skills and systems are closely linked.
- As the nature of work changes, skills and capabilities become redundant. As they are replaced by new performance imperatives, new cultures and behav-iours are required. HR has a key role to play in *anticipating how work will change*, and building development paths to equip people for new roles.
- HR can *develop teams and managers to be able to cope effectively* with change, since change is now the norm.
- HR can *build corporate reputation* – by ensuring that the employer brand is ethical and backed up by practice.
- HR can *build inclusive policies and practices that maximize diversity* – international labour laws are becoming ever more stringent and HR has the challenge of anticipating requirements and protecting the organization from infringement of the increasingly copious amounts of employment law.

For example, working lives are getting longer and one of the most significant pieces of European legislation to have come into effect over the past decade outlaws discrimination on the grounds of age. Not only can people work for longer, in many cases they will have to. Across Europe the growing pensions burden on companies has virtually closed access to final salary schemes or their equivalent. Developing policies that will support the recruitment, management, motivation and welfare of a more diverse age range of staff is only one facet of the evolving HR agenda.

- HR must *create employee engagement* – every organization needs employees who not only possess the skills and knowledge required for the job but are also motivated and committed to using those skills on behalf of the employer. Employee 'engagement' has become a key quest for HR teams in every sector, both during times of significant change and in relatively stable phases because the changing work environment has resulted in a loosening of the conventional emotional ties by which employees remained attached to their employer.

- How employee engagement is achieved remains open to many interpretations, but significant elements in most definitions are opportunities for employees to have 'voice', i.e. to be consulted and have a say in what happens at work, to be equitably rewarded and to have the opportunity for learning and growth. Working with line managers and trade unions to *create policies and communication practices that build effective employee relations and engagement* is another key element of the HR role.

CONCLUSION

So as the HR role continues to evolve, there is clear evidence that when operating at a level to produce cross-organizational solutions, for instance to the challenges of culture change, employee engagement or the sourcing of scarce talent, HR can play a significant enabling role for the business.

And as HR continues to develop its role, practitioners are increasingly asking themselves what HR is for. While more strategic activity is clearly bearing fruit, the latest challenge seems to be more one of defining what lies within the scope of the HR role. So should CSR, environmental policies, organizational development, work–life balance, internal communications, employer branding all be part of the HR agenda? Arguably yes: as always, the real challenge is that of making the 'right' choice of what to focus on that will deliver the greatest returns.

This is where HR leadership is the next step on the evolutionary ladder. This will make HR a function which is both proactive and responsive to business needs, underpinned by humanistic values and capable of shaping thinking and practice with respect to the management and development of people. This is the high road towards delivering value for today's and tomorrow's organizations.

REFERENCES

Arthur, J.B. (1994) Effects of human resource systems on manufacturing performance and turnover. *Academy of Management Journal*, 37, No. 3, 670–687

Beer, M., Spector, B., Lawrence, P.R., Mills, D.Q. and Walton, R. (1984) Managing human assets in a conceptual review of HRM. *Harvard Business Review*, 84: 15–38

Cheese, P. (2007) *High Performance Workforce 2006 Study*. Accenture (www.Accenture.com)

Delaney, J.T. and Huselid, M.A. (1996) The impact of Human Resource Management practices on perceptions of organizational performance. *Academy of Management Journal*, 39, No. 4, 949–969

Fombrun, C., Tichy, N.M. and Devanna, M.A. (1984) *Framework for HRM: Strategic Human Resource Management*. New York: John Wiley

Grundy, A. (1998) How are corporate strategies and human resource strategy linked? *Journal of General Management*, 23, No. 3, (Spring)

Guest, D.E. (1989) Personnel and Human Resource Management: Can you tell the difference? *Personnel Management*, Jan: 48–51

Guest, D.E. (1997) Human Resource management and performance: a review and research agenda. *International Journal of Human Resource Management*, 8, Issue 3

Huselid, M. (1995) The impact of Human Resource Management practices on turnover, productivity, and corporate financial performance. *Academy of Management Journal*, 38, No. 3, 635–672

Huselid, M.A., Jackson, S.E. and Schuler, R.S. (1997) Technical and strategic HRM effectiveness as determinants of firm performance. *Academy of Management Journal*, 40, No. 1, 171–188

Lawler, E. (2006) *Achieving Strategic Excellence: An Assessment of Human Resource Organizations*. Palo Alto, CA: Stanford University Press

Pfeffer, J. (1995) *Competitive-Advantage-through-People: Unleashing the Power of the Work-Force*. Cambridge, MA: Harvard Business School Press

Pfeffer, J. (1998) *The Human Equation*. Cambridge, MA: Harvard Business School Press

Purcell, J. (1996) Human Resource Bundles of Best Practice: a Utopian Cul-de-Sac? Paper presented at ESRC/BUIRA Seminar Series on Contribution of HR Strategy to Business Performance

Purcell, J. (2002) *Understanding the People and Performance Link: Unlocking the Black Box*. London: CIPD

Reilly, P. (2008) *The Changing HR Function*. London: CIPD

Schuler, R.S. and Jackson, S.E. (1987) Linking competitive strategies with human resource management practices. *Academy of Management Executive*, 1, No. 3, 207–219

Stroh, L. and Caligiuri, P.M. (1998) Strategic Human Resources: a new source for competitive advantage in the global arena. *International Journal of Human Resource Management*, 9, Issue 1, (February)

Syrett, Michel (2007) Commercial acumen, in: *Developing HR Strategy* (December). London: Croner

Towers Perrin (2003) *Working Today: Understanding What Drives Employee Engagement*. The 2003 Towers Perrin Talent Report

Tyson, S. and Fell, A. (1986) *Evaluating the Personnel Function*. London: Hutchison

Ulrich, D. (1997) *Human Resource Champions: The Next Agenda for Adding Value and Delivering Results*. Cambridge, MA: Harvard Business School Press

Ulrich, D., interviewed by R. MacLachlan (1998) HR with attitude, *People Management*, 13 August

Ulrich, D. and Brockbank, W. (2005) A new mandate for Human Resources. *Harvard Business Review*, 76, No. 1, 124–134

Walton, R.E. (1985) From control to commitment in the workplace. *Harvard Business Review*, 85, No. Mar–Apr, 77–84

Wright, P.M. and McMahan, G.C. (1992) Theoretical perspectives for strategic human resource management. *Journal of Management*, 18, No. 2, 295–320

Wright, P.M., McMahan, G.C. and McWilliams, A. (1994) Human resources and sustained competitive advantage: a resource based perspective. *International Journal of Human Resource Management*, 5, No. 2, 301–326

Wyatt-Haines, R. (2007) Adding value through IT. *Strategy Magazine*, June, Issue 12

Chapter 2

The Context for Strategic HR

Whiplash change, fleeting advantages, technological disruptions, seditious competitors, fractured markets, omnipotent customers – these 21st century challenges are testing the design limits of organizations around the world and are exposing the limitations of a management model that has failed to keep pace with the times.

(Hamel and Breen, 2007)

No organization is immune from the changing tides of global economic, social, political and technological trends. In the twenty-first century many of the socio-economic certainties of the twentieth century are crumbling. Strategic HR management involves keeping abreast of the times and developing organizational strategies that prepare organizations not only to respond to changing environmental pressures but proactively to seize the initiative in their various markets. In this chapter we shall consider some of the driving forces for change in the global environment and their emergent impact on the world of work.

THE CHANGING BUSINESS ENVIRONMENT

Despite strong economic growth in the UK since 2000 there is a huge productivity gap between the UK and other industrialized nations. Marketplaces are becoming ruthlessly competitive as unique technologies, unique physical assets and historic brands are challenged by new competitors, new consumers demands and changing distribution channels. In the UK, high street giants such as Sainsbury's and Marks & Spencer have had to radically change their approach to survive and thrive. Nevertheless, despite gloomy short-term economic forecasts, the long-term prognosis for the UK economy is good. With flexible labour markets and open capital markets, the UK has fewer constraints on growth than many other countries. If the UK manages to close the productivity gap it has a unique opportunity to leap ahead of competing nations in terms of overall growth (Lewis, 1999).

Globalization

Globalization continues to drive growth and wealth creation. Much manufacturing capability has migrated from the developed to parts of the developing world. The West is becoming predominantly a service economy, with the UK in particular seeing the development of high technology, financial services and travel and tourism as major growth areas. Corporations face a myriad of markets where once there were stable brands spreading across the globe. As a result, they now need to balance global scale with local responsiveness and local brand identification.

Much of the change experienced at local level, even in the public sector, is the consequence of globalization that has been made possible through deregulation of markets, availability of technology and other factors. The consequent burgeoning of customer demands, availability of new products and service, increasing competition and the need for innovative solutions and cost reduction are leading to change becoming the norm rather than the exception in organizations of every kind.

Kenichi Ohmae, author of *Triad Power* (1985), suggested that the route to global competitiveness was to establish a presence in each area of the Triad – Japan, the United States and the Pacific, and Europe – and to use each of the three Cs of commitment, creativity and competitiveness. Some would argue that to Ohmae's Triad should be added China and India, two rapidly developing economies whose potential is only now starting to be realized.

Indeed, major political shifts have opened up vast new markets for capitalist goods and services, such as China, while closing down some 'traditional' ones. China and India are developing rapidly and differently as global economic powers, as they make use of industrialization, Internet technology and increasingly skilled labour forces.

As competition in the service economy becomes more intense – and the financial services industry is a prime example of this – the trend towards market consolidation through acquisitions is often a defensive move to avoid being swallowed up by bigger players. In a *Financial Times* report, one-quarter of organizations surveyed had experienced a merger/acquisition in 2005 and there was a 39% rise in the value of mergers and acquisitions during 2005, along with a 9% rise in the number of deals (*Financial Times,* 21 December 2005). Similarly, in Roffey Park's 2006 *Management Agenda* trend data survey, ongoing consolidation of the marketplace is particularly noticeable in the financial services. In other sectors, strategic alliances seem to be the preferred option with over half the respondents predicting that their organization will develop such an alliance in the near future.

Ohmae (1985) points out how globalization will ultimately affect all aspects of a nation's economic life:

> The essence of business strategy is offering better value to customers than the competition in the most cost-effective and sustainable way. But today, thousands of competitors from every

corner of the world are able to serve customers well. To develop effective strategy, we as leaders have to understand what's happening in the rest of the world, and reshape our organization to respond accordingly. No leader can hope to guide an enterprise into the future without understanding the commercial, political and social impact of the global economy.

Change is the Constant

Against this backdrop it is hardly surprising that organizational change continues to be the order of the day, especially in large organizations. Many of the sources of trend data report similar tendencies. According to Bain and Company's Management Tools and Trends Survey (Rigby, 2007) companies are looking outside to grow. They are acknowledging the impact of globalization, especially the importance of China and India as sources of growth. Four out of ten agree that cross-border acquisitions will be critical to growth objectives in the next five years.

Similarly, according to the 2006 Roffey Park *Management Agenda*, the main challenge faced by all organizations is building company performance in an increasingly difficult market, and many are attempting to stimulate innovation and create performance cultures while simultaneously trimming costs and managing change. In the Bain and Co. survey too, executives are recognizing the importance of 'soft issues', with nine out of ten executives agreeing that they are also looking beyond cost-cutting to be successful, and that 'culture is as important as strategy for business success'.

Our increasing awareness of global interdependence is also driving concerns about some of the environmental challenges which can appear beyond ready control, such as climate change and increasing numbers of pandemics. Add to that social, economic and political trends such as the fluctuating price of energy, political turmoil in the oil-rich regions, the personal and national consequences of global politics and extremism – these are all driving perceptions of a less secure and stable world.

There is growing fear of loss of oil, of water scarcity and of the exhaustion of finite resources and a determined drive by energy suppliers to find alternative energy sources of cheap, clean and renewable energy. While low-cost air travel opens up the prospect of increasing global mobility, the cost in terms of carbon emissions is increasingly being calculated down to the level of an individual's 'carbon footprint'. Social behaviours with respect to recycling, limiting unnecessary travel and other attempts to limit environmental damage reflect a public desire to limit further potentially irreversible damage to the world's climate and eco-system.

In the West people are living longer and the working age is expanding ('from 10 to the grave'). Increasing importance is attached to living healthy lives and there is a growing interest in well-being and quality of life. Increasingly people are enjoying multiple careers and embracing the idea of lifelong learning. The growth of the 'me first' society and the cult of celebrity appear to be increasingly counterbalanced by trends such as the return to traditional values of respect for others and towards living more worthwhile lives, what Faith Popcorn has described as 'karma capitalism'. While the trend towards ever-increasing consumption continues, consumers are becoming more reflective. There is a growing awareness that not enough attention is paid to those at the bottom of the pyramid, which is reflected in the trend to purchase fair trade products.

In the UK and other developed countries there is an overstretched housing market and debt, with increasing inter-generational transfer of wealth and debt in prospect. Despite increasing medical knowledge and improvements in health, people are worried about the state of their health service, pensions, the education system and crime.

Business is increasingly required to adopt a more proactive stance to some of these issues, since these societal insecurities affect consumer confidence and the economy as a whole. This is leading to a wider questioning of the role and purpose of business with respect to society, and increasingly corporate reputations stand or fall on perceptions of the ethical nature of the brand, the product and its manner of production.

Consumer Demands and the Need for Flexibility

The global economy is driving patterns of consumer behaviour which were relatively in their infancy only a decade ago. In the UK the 24-hour shopping and service culture has taken root, with changing working patterns an inevitable consequence. Consumers now expect to buy their groceries round the clock, have them delivered at home at times to suit themselves, to access customer services via help-desks and shopping opportunities by telephone or Internet. Companies are responding to customer demands by running their operations on a 'sun-time' basis from different parts of the world. Thanks to technology, organizations are able to outsource, 'off-shore' or 'right-shore' key parts of their operations which they believe can be done more cheaply and effectively elsewhere.

Organizations are therefore becoming increasingly reliant on different types of flexible worker who can provide the cover required, whether or not these workers are directly employed by them. These less secure forms of employment may already be changing the nature of the dynamics of employer–employee relationships to more transactional than relational. Indeed, Syrett (2007) argues that it is in an organization's interest to treat 'non-employees' such as contractors or temporary staff as if they were employees, if they are to derive the most 'engaged' performance from contract workers. After all, a company's brand increasingly depends on how customers view the service they receive, which in turn can be provided by third-party suppliers whose only connection with the brand is contractual.

The Impact of Technology

In this global marketplace and thanks to technology, new services and channels abound, niche players can take on the big conglomerates and national boundaries become irrelevant.

Technology is facilitating the rise of the virtual world. Selling or buying via the Internet has become the 'normal' way to do business. Public and private sector services are increasingly provided online, communicating with customers via telephone or the Internet has become the norm, threatening the competitive positioning of conventional postal services. Call-centre-based helplines are available for most services, including round the clock health advice.

Technology is opening up ready access to market information and changing where, when and how you get information. Members of the public can now obtain seemingly limitless amounts of information and entertainment via the Internet. Information is no longer the privileged preserve of members of specialist professions, political groups or sects. Commercial service providers such as Google and Yahoo! vie for share of market with 'volunteer'-led services such as Wikipedia, where the data are provided by contributors who are also users of the service.

Technology underpins the growth in online communities and the burgeoning of social networking. Increasing use of chat rooms and services such as 'My Space', 'Face Book', 'You Tube', seems to potentially counterbalance the apparent fragmentation of society by enabling people to create their own online identities or avatars and have access to thousands of new 'friends'. Even Queen Elizabeth II has her own 'You Tube' presence featuring clips of royal videos.

People expect to get ever-higher service standards as companies reduce their costs. And as consumers access personalized services via the Internet, reducing the need to go to the shops, there are reported to be changes in society such as the increasing isolation of consumers and greater fragmentation of communities. In contrast, young people in particular are forming new online and other communities in which friendship groups augment family relationships.

Technology then is making possible choice, personalization, free and constant access to information, networking, collaboration as well as competition. As users of technology, employees are aware of what can be possible, with the result that they have growing expectations about what work can do for them, as much as what they bring to their work. As such, employees increasingly view their employer through the lens of the discerning and demanding consumer.

The Knowledge Economy

Many pundits argue that we are now in a new industrial era or at least on the verge of the Knowledge Economy, where the individual is king or queen, with corresponding freedoms of choice. Information and knowledge have become key tradeable assets for companies and individuals. These assets form the basis of the 'New Economy'.

The implications of this are significant:

- Governance of society is mutating
- The very nature of the firm, of the workplace, is changing
- Work itself, and the nature of the employment contract, are undergoing major changes.

GOVERNANCE OF SOCIETY IS MUTATING

One impact of globalization is the apparent transfer of power and influence from local and national communities into the global arena, and new forms of global governance are slowly emerging. In the global electronic economy, investors and fund managers can transfer huge amounts of capital in an instant. This can sometimes lead to the destabilization of a national or regional economy, as happened in East Asia. Similarly, the US 'Credit Crunch' and collapsing property market in 2008 has had repercussions for developed economies throughout the world. The global marketplace is indifferent to national borders and many nations have lost much of the sovereignty they once had. According to Professor Anthony Giddens (1999), 'globalization is political, technological and cultural, as well as economic'.

Conversely, there appears to be a corresponding push for greater local control of power, for 'subsidiarity' and the right to make decisions at the most local level possible, as witnessed in the UK by the devolution of some political powers to Scotland, Wales and Northern Ireland. Giddens argues that in a world based upon active communication 'political power based upon authoritarian command can no longer draw upon reserves of traditional deference or respect'. He points out the paradox and political instability inherent in the fact that while many parts of the world are making the transition to democracy, at the same time there is widespread disillusionment with democratic processes.

Giddens' commentary appears all the more relevant since the events of '9/11' 2001 and the increasing polarization of views and cultural differences within a global political landscape which appears increasingly fragmented and turbulent. Yet despite political, religious and cultural differences, collaboration can abound, especially in times of crisis, such as the international response to the Asian tsunami in 2005 or the active international control of the spread of potential pandemics such as SARs or Avian Influenza.

These twin thrusts of competition and collaboration are increasingly common features of the workplace too. What may have previously seemed improbable alliances, such as those between former competitors, are becoming commonplace. Networks of small-scale companies will increasingly form as independent producers find common interest and come to rely on cellular, self-managed teams, according to Leadbetter (2001). Of course, too much unfocused collaboration can produce the 'country club' effect, which can lead to complacency and is not very productive. In contrast, Goldman Sachs is described (in Gratton, 2007) as a powerful organization that thrives on cooperation without becoming cosy. For employees and managers, the ability to work effectively across and between organizational and time boundaries to achieve common purpose is likely to become a key capability in years to come. For Gratton (2007), the four key elements that have to be mastered are a cooperative mindset, an ability to span boundaries, productive capacity and a shared purpose.

At the same time globalization is leading to flexible labour markets and increased insecurity. The monoculture is becoming a thing of the past: diversity-driven innovation appears to be key to economic vibrancy. Technology provides new possibilities for social networks and the next wave of technology will provide pervasive wireless connectivity. This is resulting in ever greater possibilities of rapidly gaining access to information, and for shaping opinion about any organization or institution, leaving individuals and organizations potentially vulnerable to unwelcome exposure.

Trust, Ethics and Values

Opinion polls carried out in various Western countries suggest that people have lost a great deal of trust in their institutions, politicians and conventional democratic procedures, with younger people often said to be particularly disaffected and alienated. Giddens (2006) suggests that what is needed is a deepening of democracy on a global level. This, he argues, will involve active devolution of power and the use of alternative democratic procedures such as electronic referenda and people's juries. He also suggests that a strong democratized civil culture, which markets cannot produce, will be needed. Government, the economy and civil society need to be in balance.

In this context the role of business too is increasingly under the spotlight. The debate centres around the relationships between business, society and the public good. It seems that organizations are becoming ever-more aware of the need to protect their reputations through effective corporate social responsibility (CSR) policies and practices. This is hardly surprising given the various financial scandals that have rocked major corporations in recent years. There is even an 'Impact on Society' reporting website open for business to any company committed to the principles of transparency and improving their positive impact on society.

Compare this with the views of the 1970s US economist and free-market advocate Milton Friedman, who described the then-growing demands for business to have a social conscience as 'pure and unadulterated socialism'. He argued that business has a duty to make a profit first – anything else will create confusion. In contrast, Charles Handy (1997) argues that firms must see their roles as contributing to society over the long term, rather than simply increasing shareholder dividends in the short term.

Reputational Risk

But beyond debates about the purpose of business, there are strong brand drivers for addressing ethical issues. Global communications now have power to reach into even remote societies. 'News' can now be relayed around the world instantly, shaping opinions and transforming traditional family and societal values. The instant availability of news is increasingly recognized as potentially both an organization's greatest threat when the nature of the news is 'bad', and a major opportunity to enhance company brand and reputation when the news is 'good'. So many of the financial and other corporate scandals brought to light in recent years have fundamentally affected the 'licence to operate' of the organizations in question, in cases such as Enron, putting them out of business altogether. Once bad news is 'out', it travels instantly around the world. In this context company brand is synonymous with corporate reputation. Consequently, organizations are now paying serious attention to the ethics of how they treat their employees and communities, how they reduce their carbon footprint, how they deal with corruption in their midst, and how they source from suppliers who are known not to exploit their workers.

Corporate reputations, in turn, depend to a large extent on the behaviours and decisions of those who work for, or represent an organization. They can be put at risk – rightly or wrongly – by disgruntled employees who have access to company information and who make use of company intranets and the Internet to broadcast poor practice, or who exploit company data for personal gain. Similarly, corporate reputations can be put at risk by being perceived to be a bad employer. The range of employment legislation and the growth of litigation in the UK, echoing US practice, is reflected in the plethora of employment tribunals in which employees bring cases alleging that their employment rights or, in some cases, their human rights have in some way been infringed. These are just some of the reasons why addressing ethical considerations with regard to the workforce, such as addressing inequality and unfairness at work, and improving employee engagement, have risen up the business (and therefore HR) agenda.

McDonald's in the UK is one employer who knows only too well the cost of damage to reputation. A few years ago the company suffered a wave of unwelcome publicity in which the calibre of employees who were willing to accept a 'McJob' was ridiculed. David Fairhurst, People Director of McDonald's, decided to put the story straight. He commissioned Professor Adrian Furnham to carry out a survey of young employees, their parents and former head teachers. The research found that working at McDonald's, with its training, work discipline and customer focus, had a powerfully motivating effect on employees, many of whom had failed at previous jobs elsewhere. The findings enabled McDonald's to go on the reputation offensive and become seen as an employer of choice in a tough labour market with generally high turnover rates.

Corporate Social Responsibility (CSR)

From a situation a decade ago where many firms adopted CSR mainly to minimize risk, there is now a growing emphasis on responsible business as a positive source of competitive advantage. In the past decade, levels of ethical consumerism in the UK are growing steadily, and show no signs of slowing down. The Cooperative Bank's annual Ethical Consumerism report reveals a sharp increase in the sales of ethical products and services, rising from £9.3 billion in 1999 to £25.8 billion in 2004. Even though many companies still do not take CSR seriously, 78% of the UK general public involved in the poll want to hear about companies' responsibilities to their customers, employees, communities and the environment, according to a MORI poll (Ipsos MORI, 2007).

Similarly, environmental concerns about climate change and global warming have galvanized many communities in the developed world and the geo-political move towards a carbon-free world is rapidly gaining ground. In December 2006, UK Prime Minister Gordon Brown (then Chancellor of the Exchequer) issued the following statement in his pre-budget speech: 'within ten years every new home will be a zero carbon home, and we will be the first country ever to make this commitment'. Businesses are having to respond in kind and, according to Phil Hodkinson (2007), 'expanding our business measures to include our environmental and social impact will in time transform management's understanding of what makes a successful and sustainable business'.

Major businesses have already responded to the spirit of the times. In 2007 Sir Stuart Rose, chief executive of Marks & Spencer, announced a £220 m programme to make the retailer carbon-neutral by 2012. Sustainability and corporate citizenship are an integral part of the M&S brand as well as a key part of its commercial recovery. Similarly, Sir Terry Leahy, chief executive of Tesco, has introduced carbon labelling on all 70 000 of Tesco's product lines. British Airways is the only airline in the world that is actively trading its carbon emissions and also runs a voluntary carbon offset scheme for its customers in return for the carbon emissions created by their journey.

Investors too are making it clear that it is not only morally preferable to be socially responsible but a sign that a company is managing risk. Companies that fail to achieve alignment between business values, purpose and strategy with the economic and social needs of employees and customers, while embedding responsible and ethical business policies and practices, risk exposure to the harsh world of scrutiny and censure. Companies that do not keep a grip on working conditions, the activities of suppliers or pollution are likely to be prosecuted, shut down by the authorities or boycotted by the public. That broader awareness of business's responsibility to the wider community is evident in the Bain and Co. (Rigby, 2007) survey, with seven out of ten executives agreeing that 'environmentally friendly products and practices are an important part of their mission'.

Organizations are also more attractive to potential recruits if they are seen to be active in supporting their community, and in other ways practising corporate values. For example, according to Emma Schmitt of Standard Chartered Bank: 'Doing business in an ethical way is increasingly important for international companies like Standard Chartered. Half of our graduates cite our ethical approach as a reason for joining the bank. We give our employees two days additional leave each year to volunteer for community initiatives and we find it really enhances employee engagement' (quoted by Davidson, 2007). One such project involved 12 staff members helping to teach blind students interview and career development techniques.

Other non-financial benefits of responsible business practice include things like building trust in the brand, increasing customer satisfaction, improving staff morale, reducing absentee rates, strengthening community relations in addition to reducing the organization's carbon footprint. Management teams are being encouraged to take their corporate citizenship roles seriously, and in some cases, executives are rewarded on the basis of how they demonstrate corporate values, including 'community involvement'. Arguably the best leaders – in business and elsewhere – are those who are prepared to learn from others and help others learn from them. They are the people who are prepared to hold themselves and their companies to account.

Ethics from an Employee Perspective

It seems that employees too place great importance on working for ethical organizations, with 83% of *Management Agenda* respondents classing CSR as personally important to them. Interestingly, more women than men maintain that CSR is of personal importance to them and it appears to be mainly respondents from larger organizations who are most concerned about CSR.

There do, however, appear to be big gaps between the 'walk' and the 'talk' on some aspects of CSR. For instance, diversity appears to be more espoused as a concept than practised for real in many organizations. The majority of employees (63%) believe that their organization does not actively manage diversity and 31% of respondents believe that a gender pay gap exists, with men receiving more money than their female counterparts. There appear to be significantly more visible female role models within medium-sized organizations and more especially in public sector and not-for-profit organizations than in commercial organizations. However, most of these female role models are mainly in middle management roles, and tend to be in support or staffing functions such as HR rather than business leadership roles.

Diminished Loyalty and Trust

The importance of trust as the basis of a positive psychological contract between employees and employers is highlighted by these findings. The absence of trust undermines employee motivation and loosens the bonds of employee commitment. In particular, the widening gap between perceptions of workplace conditions is fertile breeding ground for employee cynicism. Corporate scandals and 'fat cat payouts' for example have led to increased cynicism and distrust (46%), and 25% of respondents report that they have lost trust in corporate leaders altogether. Senior managers are the least trusted group within organizations (only 24% trust their senior managers to a great extent), while subordinates (53%) and peers (46%) are the most trusted.

It seems that greater employee confidence in the external job market and in their own employability is leading to a reduction in effort and commitment to organizations in some cases. Only 27% of *Management Agenda* respondents classed the collective sense of purpose and commitment within their organization as 'high'. This cocktail of reduced employee commitment and trust is unlikely to be helpful to retention or to developing and sustaining high performance.

Closing the Gaps

Organizational policies and practices can make a difference to the quality of employees' working lives, but only if they can be effectively implemented.

There are reported mismatches between the importance ascribed by employees to issues such as work–life balance, and what they judge to be the level of importance accorded to these issues by their organization. It is no good having a flexible working policy if those who work flexibly must sacrifice career progression. Wide gaps remain between the practice of corporate values and what is espoused; perceptions of appropriateness of reward vary according to level of hierarchy; what people want from top management and what they get remain very different. The challenge for HR is to add value by identifying how some of these gaps can be closed.

Organizational contexts also appear to have a significant impact on whether or not policies produce the right results for organizations and employees. In the public sector, many respondents report that their organization takes the issue of work–life balance seriously, and that they are also able to achieve an appropriate work–life balance. Similarly, employees working for large organizations are more likely to report that they are experiencing more change, and are less likely to consider their top managers as leaders than employees in small organizations. Employees in smaller organizations are less likely to report that their organization actively manages for diversity or has CSR policies in place, yet they are more likely to report that they are able to work flexibly. Perhaps large organizations can learn from their smaller neighbours, such as those in our survey, how to create the sense of community and how to show more effective leadership, while smaller organizations might learn from their larger counterparts some of the evolving elements of good practice relating to corporate citizenship. Similarly, some public sector bodies may be well placed to show others how to manage for diversity and to achieve more flexible ways of working. HR networks can facilitate exchanges of learning on key organizational issues where no one sector or organization may have all the answers.

Closing such gaps calls for more active people-centred leadership. HR professionals, together with top managers, have a significant opportunity to influence workplace climates through their greater access to key levers such as communications, reward and sanctions. What appears evident from these findings is that many top managers fail to act as leaders to their employees and are therefore perhaps missing the opportunity to move the focus of attention from a purely short-term, reactive and task-focused agenda to one which is more strategic, humanistic and ultimately more effective. HR has the challenge of developing effective leadership at all levels. HR professionals need to be guardians of the development of a high-performance workplace climate, where people feel that their work is meaningful.

What is also clear from these findings is that today's employees, especially young high flyers, not only want to make a good living, they also want to make a difference. It is therefore in the interests of employers to provide opportunities for their key employees – and others – to explore how society works, to get engaged in the wider world and more obviously develop fulfilling roles. By so doing employers are more likely to retain their key talent and go some way to closing the gap between the 'walk' and the 'talk' on values. When people can have their choice of employer, the power balance in the psychological contract shifts from the employer to the employee. Employers who fail to recognize this are more likely to lose the talent they need to build competitive advantage.

Demographics: the Ageing Workforce

Due to the falling birth rate in Europe, by 2030 the EU will lose 20.8 million people (6.8%) of working age at a time when Europe will need an employment rate of more than 70%.

The so-called 'demographic timebomb' in Europe and the United States is paralleled by other social trends reflected in the phrase 'the Age of Individualism'. In Europe and the US declining birth rates generate future short-ages of both employees and consumers. In the West more men and women than ever before live in single-person households, leading to increasing numbers of small occupancy housing being built. Single women are said to be healthier and fitter than single men living alone, and though people are living longer than in the past, they are not necessarily leading healthier lives.

Throughout Western Europe the workforce is ageing. At the same time as the workforce in the developed economies is ageing, fewer young people are entering the workforce. By 2020 there will be 2.7 workers to every non-worker, compared with 4:1 in 1990. Pensions issues, and the extension of the right to work beyond the age of 60, suggest that employers and employees will need the skills of older workers while at the same time they will need to provide opportunities for younger workers. It is predicted that people of the 'baby boomer' generations will be among the last to be able to enjoy a comfortable retirement from the age of 60. Managing a multi-generational workforce is set to become a new management challenge.

In the UK labour market these demographic shifts are already evident in the recruitment pool where the workforce is becoming older, female and more diverse. According to DTI statistics (DTI, 2007), the consequence of these trends means that the UK labour pool by 2010 will be as follows:

- 20% will be mothers (50% as single parents)
- 1.3 million fewer workers will be aged 25–35 ('Generations X, and Y') and 3 million more workers, over 35 years
- 80% of workforce growth will be represented by women
- 10% of the working population will come from ethnic minorities
- 80% of 16-year-olds will stay on at school (and later, if proposals to extend compulsory school education to 18 are approved)
- Only 20% of the workforce will be made up of white, able-bodied men under 45 years in full-time work.

Talent 'Crisis'

One of the key challenges facing HR is ensuring that there are the right people in the right places with the right skills. At a time when, despite short-term recessions, many developed economies are experiencing underlying growth, there is a risk that talent shortages will become a key factor affecting organizations' ability to achieve their goals.

According to the Future of Work Organization (Grantham and Ware, 2007), the predicted 'talent crisis' will hit organizations operating globally across all sectors by 2010. The United States alone will experience significant talent shortages by 2010, with a shortfall of 10 million knowledge workers.

At entry level, many employers report skills deficiencies in young recruits, and in the UK there is a determined attempt by government to support workplace learning and development to equip young people with the vocational skills required. In many sectors, particularly those requiring higher level specialist skills, there are global shortages of talent, even if there is local abundance of other forms of talent.

Retention will be Key

In the UK at the time of writing there is the highest level of employment on record. Registered vacancies are increasing and there is an increase in proportion of employers reporting skill shortages, despite predicted downturns in the economy for the short term. The increased labour market buoyancy for those with marketable skills is reflected in a general increase in labour turnover (10% in 1992; 14% in 1996; 18% in 1998; 21% in 2005). Retention will be key to avoiding talent shortages. Turnover is highest amongst young workers and over 25% of 20–24-year-olds were working for a different employer a year before (Office of National Statistics, 2006).

UK businesses face huge staff turnover problems as links between employees and employers break down, a report has revealed. The report, *Corporate Warming*, by Adecco and the Institute of Employment Studies (Reilly, 2007), has found that 45% of employees will leave their company in the next three years, attracted by better salaries, more security and better career progression and challenges elsewhere.

Rene Schuster, Adecco Group country manager, said:

> The labour market is changing and self-starting employees are demanding more from companies and it is up to businesses to realize this and close the gaps in employee management. We know from past research that 40% of UK employees surveyed have applied for a job or registered with a recruitment agency in the past 12 months. If businesses don't start engaging with their employees on the issues central to them, they will ultimately vote with their feet and leave.

Findings show that fewer than four in ten businesses undertake employee satisfaction audits to gauge motivation and only a quarter appear to examine vital attrition data. Peter Reilly of IES argues that 'a strong labour market creates choice and freedom for employees. This leaves employers vulnerable, if people management falls through the management cracks, to increased turnover and labour costs, unproductive workers and the risk of not quickly replacing highly valued employees' (quoted by Peacock, 2007).

The challenges then to attract, motivate and retain talent are significant, especially since the Future of Work Programme (2002) and other studies report significant deterioration in worker satisfaction, and an increase in working time and stress over a decade. Moroever, what motivates and retains employees is likely to reflect perceived differences in expectations about pay and benefits, and attitudes to work, depending on class, age, sex and occupation. Stereotypically, Generations X and Y differ from each other and from their predecessors the Baby Boomers, as will be discussed in Chapter 6.

The challenges for employees of the Knowledge Revolution are generally reported as having to deal with too much information, leading to overload and ineffectiveness. In many organizations, knowledge management is still in its infancy – it's a case of working harder, not smarter. Workers are increasingly unable to escape from work, given the widespread use of sources of contact, such as mobile phones, data devices and laptops and the growing perception that accessing e-mails at any time, even on holidays, is expected. Ironically, the Future of Work Programme findings suggest that high commitment management practices are contributing to the work–life imbalance that accounts for a dramatic decline since 1990 in reported worker satisfaction levels (Nolan, 2004). On the other hand, some employees find access to information and the ability to work anywhere, at times to suit themselves, liberating.

At the same time employee career prospects will vary according to many factors. Local or specialized knowledge makes workers more attractive to (many) employers and it is predicted that complex jobs will multiply; routine work will wither away. Although economists debate whether polarization is really occurring between so-called 'knowledge work' and work that can be routinized, nevertheless it is the latter which tends to be outsourced, often dispersed to emerging economies. The so-called 'digital divide' has significant social and economic consequences for individuals. Knowledge work requires higher-level skills – and ongoing development, especially updating in new technologies. Moreover, the evidence base for the UK contradicts forecasts of the end of careers and the rise of the portfolio worker. Nine in ten employees work under full-time contracts. Organizations that provide effective development are more likely to attract and retain employees than those that do not.

THE CHANGING NATURE OF THE WORKPLACE

Thanks to technology, the nature of work and the workplace are being transformed. In recent years there has been a shift away from secure employment to outsourcing and short-term contract jobs. However, employee preferences appear not to have kept pace with the shifts in the nature of employment contract on offer. In the *Quality of Working Life Survey* (Worral and Cooper, 2006), 66% of the 10 000 managers surveyed said that the major restructurings of recent years had added significantly to their feelings of job insecurity. And Charles Handy's prediction that most people would have a 'portfolio' career is only slowly becoming reality. In practice, most employees seem to prefer continuous employment, which offers high levels of job security. Indeed, average job tenure in 2003 was longer than in 1992 when a permanent job with prospects was the most common type of employment expected and on offer.

Private Equity

Work is back at the heart of political debate. How much will the goal of building sustainable organizational success be compromised as companies are acquired by private equity firms who are not obliged to report publicly on their actions and expect to make significant gains in the short to medium term? Companies such as Boots Alliance and Sainsbury have been subject to takeover bids which take them out of public ownership and scrutiny into a more potentially hostile management environment.

Commentators are becoming increasingly alarmed that companies, private equity groups and investors are not properly controlling their growth, or ensuring that they have good risk controls. Powerful UK trade unions, such as the GMB, allege that private equity firms are asset strippers and there is a concern that the exclusive focus on balance sheets is taking attention away from issues such as pension funds, working conditions and the environment. Management teams who are ambitious to create longer-term success for their companies are increasingly buying their own companies in order to be able to realize this ambition.

At the same time, others argue that private equity acquirers are generally more alert to the drivers of growth than many other forms of investor. Many firms study carefully the nature of current leadership talent in the acquired company, and the strength of the talent pipeline, as well as the key processes that must be developed to fuel growth, including innovation. Working to short-term timeframes means that experienced management teams take speedy and effective decisions – far from being asset strippers they actually build more effective organizations for the longer term to sell on. Perhaps some private equity firms at least have a closer understanding of the value of human capital than they have previously been credited with.

Employee Relations

The Future of Work Programme (2005) suggests that the more participative and employee-friendly workplaces predicted a decade ago are also slow to be realized in the UK. In practice, in many organizations the degree of workplace employee 'voice' remains limited and family-friendly policies, such as the right to request flexible working, are limited with only the bare minimum required by law on offer.

Similarly, the Future of Work Programme (2005) predicts that international organizations will experience challenges to traditional national patterns of industrial relations and participation. In the UK it is predicted that decision-making will be pushed away from centralized hierarchies and there will be a revival of trade unionism, especially over issues such as diversity.

Throughout the UK's public sector from the late 1990s, public sector managers and trades unionists have talked of working in 'partnership', a model put under strain in 2008 by public sector pay restraint, a weakening UK and global economy and some resurgence of industrial relations disputes, albeit not on the scale of the late 1970s and the infamous 'Winter of Discontent'. 'Partnership' describes agreements between unions and company management, where the joint aim is to make a business successful and follows from the TUC's six principles of partnership agreed in 1999, because their primary interest lies in maintaining labour standards. Such partnership approaches are typically reflected in extensive meetings between trade union representatives and management and the chance for greater involvement by staff. Arguably, so significant are the challenges of creating an effective response to the changing environment that even traditional adversaries such as managers and trades unions should continue with, and extend their 'partnership' to tackle competitive challenges. HR has a key role to play in proactively providing advice and the HR support mechanisms to underpin the joint objectives. This is in effect an internal consultancy service, particularly in enlisting the support of unions with respect to change management.

As a result perhaps, less adversarial relations have been evident between employers and unions over the past decade, with only a few wildcat strikes or prolonged forms of industrial action in the UK, such as the more significant disputes involving the Transport and General Workers' Union (T&G) and Gate Gourmet (in 2005) and the threatened BA Cabin Crew strike (in 2006).

In theory, of course, effective HR management, consultation and participation could negate the need for trades unions at a local level. In theory too, employers and employees share many interests, even though not all of these are identical. Indeed, Stephen Overell (2005) described this as 'the great unheralded revolution in working life is the people-centred outlook of many organizations, bringing with it the rhetoric of mutual gains, shared interests, high commitment, teamwork, careers, development, and involvement. HR management is killing off the unions.' However, others would argue that HRM is limited in its effect on employee relations and that collective modes are being revived.

Unlike more embedded European Workers Councils, trades union memberships in the UK have been steadily dropping since 1995. By 2004, according to the *Workplace Employment Relations Survey* 64% of workplaces had no union membership compared with 57% in 1998. The same survey in 2005 suggested that workplaces are less likely to recognize unions for bargaining over pay and conditions. Collective bargaining is less prevalent and in general there appears to be a shift away from collective representation for employees towards direct consultation with management.

Changes such as these are leading in the UK to consolidation amongst trades unions, and the creation of 'super unions', which in turn will create issues for unions about representation at local level. The merger between Amicus and

T&G to form the UK's largest trades union 'Unite', announced on 1 May 2007, represents a third of the UK's union membership and could dominate the twenty-first-century workplace, according to Tony Woodley, General Secretary of T&G. Derek Simpson, General Secretary of Amicus, described the new union as 'the greatest campaigning force on behalf of ordinary people that has ever existed' (*People Management*, 5 April 2007). He argues that it is a precursor to the creation of a single global trades union movement capable of taking on the might of multinationals.

Subsequent moves to create 'Workers United' from a merger between Unite and the United Steelworkers of the US and Canada reflect the intentions of the two joint General Secretaries of Unite, Tony Woodley and Derek Simpson, to recognize the global context and tackle cross-boundary issues:

> That is why, right from the start, Unite is going to be doing two things no British trade union has done before – seeking union mergers across frontiers and devoting serious money to organizing employees outside our traditional comfort zones.
> Globalization makes the first of these objectives imperative. The challenges presented by world capitalism – outsourcing, wage-cutting – cannot be met by any union that confines its operations within one country alone. Already we have signed an agreement to seek a merger with the United Steel Workers of the US and Canada. This blazes a further trail and, when finalised, will constitute the first transatlantic trade union.

> (Derek Simpson and Tony Woodley, *Guardian*, 1 May 2007)

Employment Legislation

The plethora of employment legislation in recent years requires employers to take their responsibilities to employees seriously and provide greater protection for employees against some of the harmful effects of modern working conditions. Protection against bullying, damage to health, inequality and discrimination on the grounds of race, gender, ability and age is enshrined in European employment legislation. In some cases, company ombudsmen have been appointed to ensure that fairness is possible for both employers and employees.

On the other hand, many UK employers argue that the legislative burden is now so great that this is one of the reasons why Europe's productivity lags behind that of the United States and Asia and, according to a DTI-sponsored study *i2010, Responding to the Challenge* (Nolan and Salmelin, 2005), many EU member states, particularly Germany, France, Spain and Italy, have not had the courage to reform labour laws and superfluous regulation, making organizations rigid and unable to move swiftly enough to adapt to changing requirements.

The Need for Real Leadership

How leaders within organizations respond to the challenges and opportunities of the dynamic environment in which they operate is critical for the success of their business. According to Phil Hodkinson, board member of Business in the

Community and previously group finance director of HBOS, speaking at a BITC conference in 2007:

> Leaders take risks. They challenge conventional wisdom and have the courage to take a stand even if it means being out of step with their peers. Leaders also decide that they can change their business model without going bust. The really clever ones add value by differentiating themselves through innovation and by understanding the long-term context in which they operate. The leading companies in the future will be those that develop and implement business strategies that contribute to and harness a low-carbon economy and thus also contribute to their own sustained growth.

Top Leaders Have a Rosy View of Leadership

In the current context, it is useful to consider what 'good' leadership looks like from the perspective of followers. Employees are looking for clear direction, inspiration and effective change management from their leaders.

Employees are increasingly reporting that they expect their top leaders to be ethical and authentic, to work as teams and to lead by example. Leaders are also expected to manage the reputations of their organizations in the face of worldwide demands for higher standards of business practice, accountability and responsibility.

> *To what extent does your organization experience inappropriate leadership and management styles?*
> To some extent/to a great extent 72%
> *Management Agenda* survey (2006)

In the *Management Agenda* survey (2006) some differences of perception about the quality of leadership are evident, with senior managers viewing leadership in their organization more positively than junior managers: 82% of board directors rate 'distant' (executive) leadership as good or excellent compared to 63% of other directors/senior managers, 64% of middle managers and 51% of junior managers. With regard to 'near-by' (supervisory/managerial) leadership, 89% of board directors rated it as good or excellent compared to 67% of other directors/managers, 57% of middle managers and 34% of junior managers.

These findings have a number of possible explanations. For instance, employees may have unrealistic expectations about the roles, values and behaviours of top leaders. It would appear that many employees want their top leaders to be more visible and to practise organizational values more than they currently do. Another explanation is that top leaders are out of touch with what their employees really think and may be deluding themselves about their own leadership abilities.

The desire of followers for leaders to act as role models for organizational values has become increasingly evident in recent years in the annual *Management Agenda* survey. This is not only with respect to an individual leader's behaviour but also in the way leaders act to bridge gaps between organizational rhetoric on values and actual practice. For example, in the 2004 survey 76% of respondents suggested that management and organizational practices were very much out of sync with espoused values statements. Reward systems in particular were considered to contradict recommended practice and respondents reported few incentives or sanctions to encourage management to model the values. By 2007 the *Management Agenda* survey reports leadership development to be the most pressing organizational development issue. Succession planning is one of the most widely reported ways in which organizations are preparing for the future.

Many respondents call for senior leaders to lead a culture change to create an appropriate climate for high performance and to improve employee morale by dealing with inappropriate leadership behaviours. Several respondents reported that, where senior managers did model organizational values, individual commitment to the organization increased. On the other hand, the disconnection between management rhetoric and practice appears to be a strong reason for people wishing to leave.

Changing Organizational Structures

Structural change is one of the more significant forms of change that employees are likely to experience and the 2006 *Management Agenda* survey suggests that 89% of organizations underwent structural and system change in the previous two years. Structures are increasingly being used as a key plank of building a performance culture, as well as of saving costs. The challenge of structure change is to manage the change in a way that makes employees want to give of their best.

Operating Internationally

'Virtual' companies are appearing at the centre of loose alliances, linked together with global networks. Transnational organizations appear to be decentralizing and globalizing with the help of technology. Typical company practices linked to globalization include using global/international teams and international joint ventures. With regard to talent, global companies generally work towards creating a pool of international talent, rather than developing smaller talent pools in regions, and many establish centres of functional excellence.

Flatter Structures

Many organizations have continued to flatten management layers in recent years. The emphasis continues to be towards smaller, more flexible units with as few levels of management as possible. Delayering in the 1990s appeared strongly driven by the need for cost savings and the benefits to businesses are being felt in sustained profits. Difficulties arise when the staffing of specific units is too 'lean' to do what is required and when managers fail to provide the required forms of leadership. Equally important, flatter structures appear to highlight some aspects of the changing employment relationship, namely that such structures do not easily lend themselves to conventional promotion opportunities for employees.

This can lead to a loss of employee commitment and a turnover of staff with marketable skills who are still looking for more conventional career development opportunities.

Call Centres

One of the most significant developments in workplace organization in recent years is the growth of call centres. Particularly common in customer service operations, especially in the financial services sector, working in call centres has gained ground as a form of employment. Call centres have often been criticized as being the human equivalent of battery hen conditions, with employees encouraged to conform to rigid standards and conditions. Employees are usually grouped in large buildings where their performance is carefully monitored.

In the UK, towns such as Livingston in Scotland, and Cardiff have become call centre hubs. Indeed, over 27 000 people are employed in shared service centres throughout Wales alone. Fierce competition for the best employees in the local labour market is commonplace. Increasingly, working in call centres has come to be seen as a relatively attractive prospect by young people or 'women returners'. This can arise because there is little alternative employment in the locality, but some people, including graduates, actively choose to work in call centres and plan to make them the basis of their career, rather than a temporary phase while they are looking for something better.

Part of the reason for this is that there appears to have been a marked advance in understanding about how to manage and motivate people in a call centre environment. Typical enabling factors include a great emphasis on teamwork, strong and encouraging supervision and a high social factor, which many employees find appealing.

Outsourcing and Off-Shoring

The call centre concept is being extended to international service centres, offering a wide range of professional expertise. Service centres can be based in any geographic location and typically require employees to be multi-lingual, graduates and professionally qualified in their own field. Shared service centres (SSCs) are usually external enterprises set up to manage outsourced non-core business processes. The SSCs are usually jointly owned by partners and are tied in to ongoing business process reengineering.

These are already used by a number of international organizations to service human resources, finance and other functional needs. Early adopters included Kelloggs UK, which migrated its European financial processing to a European shared service centre in 1997, and the BBC outsourced its financial transaction processing to an SSC in 1998. It is not just technology that is driving change in the finance function. What is really pushing reform is renewed global regulatory demands for tighter internal controls, as well as an ongoing need to cut costs. Finance directors are continually being challenged to deliver higher value at lower cost.

Call centre technology has also facilitated the development of outsourcing, by which activities considered peripheral to the organization's core are delivered by third party suppliers. If work can be 'parcelled up' into outsourceable chunks, it can also go off-shore. Increasingly, customer help-desks of every sort are now provided from locations such as India and Central and Eastern Europe, where English language and technical skills are available and labour costs relatively low compared with the UK. Outsourcing overseas or 'off-shoring' is also known as 'right-shoring' and competition for business is stiff, with UK call centres increasingly losing out to cheaper suppliers.

Research by the Hackett Group (Perry, 2005) indicates that if more UK companies off-shore their shared service centres, the current dearth of skilled finance professionals will soon turn into a glut. The study found 84% of companies will bring in more staff with diversified skills, with the majority having run their operation for two or more years. But what is even more important is whether to take the step abroad at all. Hackett research suggests that those companies that do take the biggest step in developing an SSC from in-house to virtual in one fell swoop stand to make the biggest gains.

Some companies have reversed the trend on outsourcing and have taken back in-house some aspects of their operations which they had previously outsourced. In some cases this was because they found that anticipated cost savings were simply not there, and worse still, that once the outsourcing contract was in place, service levels dropped. Indeed, those with experience advise never to outsource a problem. In the long run, it will not only cost you more to fix but, worse still, it may never be fixed in the way you foresaw it. In short, don't jump on the bandwagon because it seems to be the quickest route to cutting costs.

Perry (2005) advises that unless finance directors understand the reasons why they are going down the SSC route, they should take care. Besides the obvious cost savings that an SSC eventually brings, the path is littered with stumbling blocks. Savings are rarely immediate.

The social and psychological effects such a move has on staff and customers is not to be underestimated. Communication at all levels at every step of the way is crucial for any finance director wishing to build a successful SSC. Otherwise achieving the goal of cutting costs and tightening controls remains elusive.

Managing effective delivery through third parties requires a special set of skills on the part of both the outsourcer and the provider and when customer service and other 'public face' activities of the brand are delivered by a third party, the risks involved require serious and sustained management attention. This is not simply a question of developing clear service level agreements but also requires managers, including HR, to manage relationships across boundaries, develop shared agendas as well as maintain quality to commonly agreed standards.

The Changing Nature of Work Itself

Central to the role of HR are the challenges of attracting new talent to the organization, creating the circumstances and policies supportive of staff motivation, ensuring that the organization can make the most of emerging human capital and retaining key talent.

In today's organizations, the nature of employment is changing and the notion of a 'nine-to-five' full-time role is now an anachronism for many. The concept of permanent employment as a 'right' has been replaced by employment being due to having marketable skills. The trend towards 'core' workers who remain in an organization's employ and 'peripheral' workers who are outsourced appears to have taken hold. Routine office and production work can now be exported anywhere around the world or carried out electronically. As organizations continue their quest to cut wage bills and increase quality, low-skilled workers in the West are effectively having to compete for jobs against highly skilled workers from developing countries who are willing to take on jobs at the minimum wage.

Knowledge Workers

We are now firmly in the era of, the 'Knowledge Economy' where knowledge-intensive industries are increasingly driving GDP. Back in 1999, Ian Angell, then Professor of Information Systems at the London School of Economics, suggested that the Information Age would not simply counterbalance the removal of 'old' jobs with the creation of new ones. Growth would be created from the intellect of knowledge workers, not from the labour of low grade service and production workers. He suggested that growth would be decoupled from employment, and that survival by adding value will be a new form of natural selection. He argued that what would be required in employees is 'intellectual muscle' which will be hard to develop and even more difficult for employers to track down and retain.

Indeed, Professor Angell's predictions have come to pass. A report from the Sector Skills Development Agency (the *Working Futures* report, Dickerson *et al.*, 2006) suggests that traditional jobs that have underpinned the livelihoods of generations of skilled working-class people are moving closer to extinction. The report forecasts that an additional 1.3 million jobs will be generated by 2014, with women expected to benefit most from the increases. However, it cautions that there will be a stark divide between 'old' jobs such as factory work and 'new' posts in the consumer sector. Other findings include:

- 340 000 skilled jobs in metals and electrical trades will be lost by 2014;
- 105 000 administrative jobs and 234 000 secretarial posts are set to be lost; and
- 400 000 jobs will be created in the caring personal services sector, such as beauty therapy and hairdressing.

Growing numbers of what Will Hutton, Executive Vice-Chair of the UK's Work Foundation, describes in Maslowian terms as 'Apex workers', are able to command huge salaries and to take their pick of enticing employment options. Where there are shortages of particular skills and knowledge, the balance of power swings of course to the employee.

However, while there is general acknowledgement of the importance of knowledge workers, the sharing of knowledge around organizations, which is generally considered key to leveraging that knowledge, remains problematic. The restructurings since the 1990s have broken up central teams who typically looked after corporate knowledge. The tendency within business units is for isolationist attitudes to come to the fore which can lead to wasted effort and duplication as well as untapped opportunities. The organizational issues related to the management of knowledge are examined in Chapter 17.

The Role of the Manager

A few years ago managers seemed an endangered species as they appeared to represent organizational superfluity; in an empowerment context it was argued, were 'checkers checking checkers' necessary? Perhaps the reality is that managers are more needed than ever, but that their role is changing. No longer are they expected to be the 'first among equals' or the technical expert. The current trend in management thinking is to see the manager as helper rather than as problem-solving hero. In all sectors managers are being encouraged to take on the role of coach, whether or not they have appropriate skills for this. However, the trend is firmly in place, with professionals and technical managers increasingly expected to take some responsibility for people management. There is a greater emphasis on teamworking and client relationship management skills for instance are typically required.

The role of managers is becoming increasingly complex due to the variety of forms of contract by which employees and contractors are employed. Managing a departmental team of full-time workers is becoming a thing of the past as managers are increasingly required to act as organizational 'glue' between workers of all kinds. Even the notion of 'the workplace' is open to new interpretation with the increasing trend towards virtual working. Businesses are increasingly developing new work methods to handle supervision and to counter isolation. In particular managers have to develop forms of communication appropriate to managing remote workers which increase mutual trust and high performance.

The nature of the individuals being managed is changing too. Highly skilled knowledge workers generally do not take kindly to being managed, and are very critical of management if their needs are not met. Managers then have the tricky task of managing performance, raising standards and gaining commitment from people on whom the business depends for results and whose technical skills are likely to be superior to those of the manager. They also have the task of acting as a 'shield' to protect employees from bureaucratic and other barriers to innovation.

Managers then have the challenges of communicating with, and developing, their teams, providing focus during times of change, managing more age-diverse workforces who are working in a variety of contractual relationships and improving performance at the same time! No wonder that increasing management capacity and capability is considered one of the key solutions to the challenge of building and sustaining high performance.

Changing Working Lives

Teamworking

Team working appears to be extensive, with the majority of respondents in Roffey Park's *Management Agenda* surveys working in some form of team, typically on a project basis. An increasingly prevalent form of teamworking is cross-functional or cross-boundary, with 63% of respondents in the 2006 *Management Agenda* survey working in such teams. Cross-boundary working will be explored in Chapter 13. Working in teams appears to be a major source of satisfaction and skills development for the majority of respondents, though it is recognized by many that multiple skills are required to work effectively in today's teams.

'Virtual' teams appear to be gaining ground. They typically come together around specific business issues or opportunities and tend to be project based. They rely on the convergence of a number of complex technologies and can be based almost anywhere. Virtual enterprises tend to disband when their task is finished, or relocate to areas where there is least regulation or most profit.

Demanding Work Environments

Work environments are becoming ever-more demanding. Eighteen per cent of respondents have experienced harassment to varying degrees, with the key forms reported including the 'long hours culture' within their organization, being excluded or sidelined and direct bullying. Twenty-seven per cent have experienced some kind of discrimination based upon their gender, age, ethnicity, class or religion.

Organizational Politics

Another key feature of organizational life appears to be the increasingly political work environment facing many employees. In Roffey Park's survey people report working longer hours, experiencing increased politics (56%) and conflict (46%). To some extent this can be understood in the context of more fluid organizational structures in which informal political alliances can be a means of getting the job done beyond formal reporting lines.

Cross-boundary working also appears to be on the increase. This seems to heighten the possibility of political behaviour since loyalties can be tested when reporting lines become less clear. Many respondents spoke of the importance of developing effective networks not only for getting the job done but also for personal career development purposes.

However, the majority of respondents commented on the negative features of working in a political environment, including the adverse effects on job satisfaction.

Use of Communications Technology

The fast pace and flow of information affects most aspects of working life. One British MP commented at a Labour Party Conference in 2007 that, while ten years ago people might have kept in touch using their mobile phone, now people often have a mobile phone plus two Blackberries. Rather than listen with rapt attention, conference delegates are more likely to be texting comments to others during sessions.

In Roffey Park's survey, typically, people reported that they now spend considerable periods in front of a screen working online, using e-mail, rather than talking with people, even if they are in the next office. People suggested that they found face-to-face communication the most effective means of communicating but that voice- and e-mail were now the favoured forms used at work. E-mail in particular came in for comments which suggest that the benefits of technology can easily be outweighed by their drawbacks if used ineptly. Among the positives, it appears that the more widespread use of technology is beginning to make smarter ways of working possible.

On the other hand, numerous comments suggest that much of the information conveyed by e-mail is irrelevant at best and at worst can add to the work pressures and stress which many people are experiencing. People complained about being deluged with unnecessary data via e-mail and voice-mail. A study in the UK by Gallup (see Buckingham and Coffman, 1999) suggested that individuals are interrupted every 10 minutes on average by incoming messages to which they are expected to respond. Keeping focused, and making progress towards key work targets can be very difficult in such circumstances.

Many respondents also commented on the negative impact of e-mail on people's ability to relate to others. The bluntness of some messages causes offence and there is a call from many respondents for a new form of etiquette which takes modern means of communication into account.

Career Issues

Given the shifts in organizational forms and structures in recent years, careers now take a number of forms though the dominant form of career development expected by employees still appears to involve conventional vertical progression up a hierarchy. Many staff have found their career has reached a plateau earlier than they expected. Instead of being promoted, they have to accept lateral moves in a culture that regards sideways moves as negative. In a situation where jobs are in short supply, lack of career development opportunities might seem to be a small price to pay for ongoing employment. For employees looking to move up the conventional career ladder, mergers and acquisitions and flatter structures do not just shift the goalposts – they kick them down. In a situation where there are high levels of employment, employees who want the opportunity to progress their careers are likely to move on. Rather than being a 'personnel' issue, the challenges relating to career development are now a business issue. Not least is the significant lessening of employee commitment to the organization, due to a perceived reduction of career opportunities. This is leading to turnover, especially in jobs requiring specialized skills and which can command high market rates. Career issues will be examined in Chapter 9.

Work–life Balance

The long hours culture appears firmly entrenched in the UK but is coming to be considered more unacceptable. Trades Union Congress (TUC) research (2008) found that in 2008, 15.5% of all workers in the East of England worked more than 48 hours per week, increasing from 13.4% in 2007. This means that the total number of employees in the East of England working excessively long hours leapt to 374 000. And the rate of increase of long hours working in the East of England was the sharpest increase in the UK. Many surveys highlight the widespread stress among employees caused by long hours, uncertain employment prospects and unclear expectations. Indeed, TUC research also showed that 45% of employees wanted to work fewer hours and more than two million people in the UK – one in ten employees – would give up pay for a better work–life balance.

In Roffey Park's *Management Agenda* survey, 83% of respondents work consistently longer than their contracted week (Holbeche and McCartney, 2005). Increasingly stressful work environments and the lengthening of the working week are taking their toll upon the work–life balance of many employees. Seventy-eight per cent of respondents reported suffering from stress as a direct result of work and 49% suggest that they do not have a satisfactory work–life balance. They report ongoing heavy demands made on them by employers with regard to both the quality and quantity of output, as well as a requirement that employees will learn new skills and do more with less. Despite these demanding conditions, the majority of respondents report themselves as still being relatively committed to their employers. Professor Cary Cooper (2006) argues that job insecurity is one of the key drivers of job-related pressure and stress and issue a challenge to directors to take a leadership stance to these issues:

> As directors, we must attempt to provide people in our organizations with a sense of continuity, some sense of security and an environment that values and rewards their contribution. Let's not allow technology, and the unremitting clamour for change to control us.

Interestingly, although these conditions appear to be general, regardless of sector, the way in which people are responding to them appears to polarize into two broad reactions. On the one hand, some people appear to thrive on pressure and do not people perceive the additional pressures on them to be stressful. Almost a third of respondents felt that the increased demands made on them had a positive aspect since they provided a developmental 'stretch'. Comments in this case suggested that individuals believe that the organization is getting the best out of them and that their own ability has been recognized. There is a sense that for some people, the increase in pressure and responsibilities is enabling them to realize some of their potential.

On the other hand, most respondents consider stress to be damaging to them personally. Ninety-one per cent spoke of increased stress affecting relationships, as well as wear and tear on the individual. A third of respondents reported that their health has suffered as a result of heavy workloads and lack of balance between work and other parts of their lives. This negative situation is compounded when there appears to be a lack of recognition of the problem, and of employees' achievements, by the line manager and the organization. One comment is typical of many: 'responsibilities are growing faster than rewards'.

Workplace stress not only affects individuals but also productivity. Several respondents refer to the way in which unreasonable workloads can result in quality being compromised. Stress is a common reason given to explain the growing levels of absenteeism in the UK's workforce. Absence costs UK employers £13bn each year and £3.9bn of absence costs are attributable to mental ill-health. The average employer spends 10% of annual paybill managing the consequences of absence and there is compelling evidence that higher absence reduces customer satisfaction and productivity, since employee absence is correlated both to declining employee commitment and to declining customer satisfaction with service, and customer intention to spend more with the company (Bevan *et al.*, 2007).

There is also wide disparity in the importance employees and employers are reported to attach to work–life balance. While 68% of employees consider work–life balance as of increasing personal importance, only 32% suggest that it is important to their organization. Work–life balance is also not supported by top managers in many organizations. Indeed 66% of senior managers are reported as 'not bought-in to the idea of balance' and only 22% suggest that their senior managers practise work–life balance values at work.

Many organizations do appear to be making some efforts to tackle work-related stress. Fifty-two per cent of the organizations sampled reported themselves to be implementing initiatives/standards to reduce stress, including Health and Well-being Strategies, Occupational Health and Health Road Shows. This range of pressures is creating a new 'stress-busting' industry. City workers can now enjoy holistic therapy treatment during lunch periods and some firms are hiring specialists in Indian head massage to provide relief to employees at their desks. However, employees report that truly flexible working is the main enabler of work–life balance – and 90% of our sample claim there is a growing demand for flexible working in their organizations. While the range of flexible working options has increased in recent years, it appears that concerns over career progression are still preventing certain groups from requesting a flexible working pattern. For instance, only 19% of fathers are exercising their 'right to request' to work flexibly and non-managerial staff appear much more likely to work flexibly than senior and middle managers.

Management style and the chance for personal development appear to be two factors that relate closely to whether people perceive the pressures on them to be positive or negative. The key role of managers is reflected in the Health and Safety Executive's (HSE) Management Standards on how employers should tackle workplace stress. In the absence of specific legislation, these standards, based on the risk assessment approach, are seen as the most useful method of tackling stress in the workplace. The extent to which people feel able to grow and 'empowered' to do their jobs appears to be closely linked to job satisfaction and resilience to extra pressure. In a 1998 study people who considered the added pressure on them to be negative spoke of inappropriate command and control management styles still preventing empowerment from being a reality. On the other hand, many of those who perceived the pressures to be positive spoke of the stimulus provided by increased challenge, broader roles and the opportunity to develop others. These they found helpful to their personal development. This may be linked to the fact that 86% of respondents stated that their role has changed in the past two years, bringing greater variety, responsibility and a more strategic focus than before. The changing roles were not necessarily brought about by skilful management interventions or by succession planning but by organizational growth and structure change in many cases (Glynn, 1998).

On the whole, the respondents agreed that the extra work pressures called on employees to make sacrifices, particularly with respect to their home life and spending time with their children. However, many admitted that their own ambition was a key driver and that they were to some extent prepared to collude with their employers over such conditions in order to make career progress.

Arguably, this is an area where responsible employers can provide clear and unequivocal support for better balance, rather than appearing to endorse the principle of work–life balance but do nothing to make reality match the aspiration. Where a combination of lack of recognition, increased workloads, poor management and lack of career opportunities exists people are most likely to contemplate changing their jobs. If pressures remain constantly high and people are expected to continuously raise standards and output levels, and do more with less, they may in some cases, voluntarily 'downshift', i.e. step off the career ladder, or in some cases leave paid employment altogether, in order to 'get a life'. In a survey by recruitment company Select Appointments (2006), people who most want to downshift are in education and financial services. In both, nearly one in six employees wants to reduce their hours – even if it means taking a pay cut. Where the pressures on employees undermine their performance, the real impact of such stresses will be felt on business results and many organizations are now beginning to address the question of enabling employees to have balance. Offering people the chance to balance work and personal life therefore makes good business sense.

What Can HR Do About Balance?

HR has a significant role to play in ensuring that their organizations are enabling employees to have some form of balance. Developing employee-friendly policies is part of the solution, but such policies need to be owned by employees and senior managers if they are to become a reality. Some of the more interesting practice on this front comes from the United States. In America, stressed-out employees of Boston City Council have an automated phone system which screens calls for depression. Callers listen to recorded descriptions of how they feel ranging from 'I get tired for no reason' to 'I feel others would be better off if I were dead'.

They punch the appropriate number and hear a recorded diagnosis that urges severe cases to seek counselling (*London Evening Standard*, May 1999).

In the UK, organizations such as Watford Borough Council have developed clear family-friendly policies that are supportive of flexible working and provide childcare vouchers. Littlewoods recognizes that employees have a life (and dependants) outside work. The company policies allow people to change conditions as their circumstances change, for instance with elder care arrangements. Job-shares are encouraged and time off for emergencies is considered normal so that people do not have to resort to subterfuge to deal with a family crisis. Business Express, which is part of the Littlewoods group, offers employees five days' paid leave for family reasons each year. Fathers have ten days' paternity leave as a right. Having this as a right means that employees are more likely to be open about their needs rather than simply taking 'sick' leave. This means that the organization can plan for the leave and avoid unexpected downtime.

In the United States, casual-lifestyle retailer Eddie Bauer uses its work–life programmes to help employees lead more productive and balanced lives. The firm has won many accolades for its approaches to employee support, including being named as one of the 'Best Companies to Work For' by *Washington CEO* magazine. A flexible work environment plus offer, an exceptional benefits package, make Eddie Bauer an employer of choice in the US. HR has produced a package of benefits that covers routine and non-routine challenges of work and home. The firm's management believes that the investment more than pays for itself because many of the programmes reduce health-care costs. The Employee Assistance programme offers a Child and Elder Care consulting and referral service, referrals for personal counselling and legal and financial assistance to both employees and their family members.

Among other initiatives introduced are:

- Balance Day, a free day once a year when employees can 'call in well'. This is in addition to normal time off
- As well as the usual array of benefits, extras include a casual dress code and alternative transport options such as preferred parking for carpools
- Its Customized Work Environment programme offers options such as job-sharing, a compressed workweek and telecommuting
- It offers a plan that allows employees to enjoy group buying power for mortgage loan discounts
- Emergency child-care.

Employers with employee-friendly policies argue that these policies are helping the business, as well as employees. In the case of Eddie Bauer, the work–life programmes have led to fewer sick days, less absenteeism and lower health-care costs. LloydsTSB's policies are based on the belief that by offering employees peace of mind they are more likely to see greater productivity. By encouraging an overt and planned approach to leave for family issues, the company can also plan and arrange appropriate cover.

Retention is also improved since people appreciate working for a supportive employer. At the UK City of Bradford Council, staff appreciate council efforts to promote a good work–life balance, including its investment in services such as life coaching, cognitive behavioural therapy and alternative therapies. Staff can carry out voluntary work during council time if they match it with the same amount of their own time.

Flexible Working

Flexibility has been a buzz-word since the 1990s referring to both the need for organizations to structure themselves so that they are highly responsive to the changing environment and the effect this has on the nature of employment. Although flexible working is on the increase, many employees still work traditional hours with a commute at either end of the day. However, new technology at the office, such as wireless Internet and video conferencing, makes work more varied for the 'nine-to-fiver'.

Currently around 29% of UK employees work part-time or in some other form of flexible working pattern. To date, flexible working has appeared to be driven by organizations to help them respond to the changing business environment, rather than to meet employee needs.

Part-time and shift working is, of course, well established in the manufacturing, retail and leisure industries. The number of part-time jobs is increasing faster than full-time ones. People working part-time (mainly women at the time of writing) can arrange their schedule in a variety of ways (working mornings only for example).

Firms may be reluctant to let staff go part-time but may be more willing to accommodate job-sharing. The Internet means that jobs can be shared across the globe. Flexi-workers tend to have a range of options: they can work annualized hours where an employee's workload is calculated over a whole year, or compressed hours, where work is condensed into fewer days.

Charles Handy's 'portfolio workers' create their own career profiles by juggling several roles. The term 'sunlighting' is used to describe people who take time off from their regular work to do paid work elsewhere. Contractors, consultants and freelance workers enable organizations to call upon a body of experts when they are needed rather than keep them on the payroll all the time. Contractors can juggle other jobs while maintaining a relationship with a company. This change in the employment model towards a more flexible one, with an increasing proportion of short-term contracts, has been given added impetus by a raft of employment legislation, such as the 2002 Employment Act, which introduced the 'Right to Request' flexible working for parents of children under six years of age and the Work and Families Act of 2006. Making flexible working possible in ways that support the needs of the business as well as of employees is a challenge which HR and line managers are starting to face.

However, the management of a flexible workforce will mean more accurate planning and corresponding changes in HR systems and thinking. In the Roffey

Park surveys, the most common form of flexible working on offer was part-time work, working from home, combined office and home working, and job-shares, followed by fixed-term contracts. Less common are term-time-only working, 'key-time' working, voluntary reduced hours, associate schemes, etc.

Over half the people in the Roffey Park *Management Agenda* survey (often employees of long standing) would like to work flexibly. These included people returning from long-term sickness, staff who have to travel long distances to get to work, individuals wanting to give more time to interests outside work and single people with a need for more time than money. The majority of people wishing to work flexibly were working mothers or individuals wanting to take time out to study. Working fathers and people with caring responsibilities, especially for elderly relatives, were also keen to work flexibly. Typically, respondents from larger organizations (1000–5000 employees) were more likely to want flexible working than employees from small organizations of 50 or fewer, and technical workers were the group most likely to want to work flexibly. But enthusiasm for flexible working is growing in organizations of every size, creating different types of challenge for employers. In a study of small and medium-sized organizations (CIPD, 2007) significant numbers of employers were offering part-time or variable working hours and even home-working. Extended leave arrangements are common as is study leave, demonstrating that employers are keen to support the needs and aspirations of their staff while also keeping the business operationally efficient.

Flexible working can be requested by anyone at Nationwide where more than 5000 staff work reduced hours while a number job-share, work from home or have term-time-only contracts. Staff can take a career break of up to six months during which they continue to receive all benefits, except pay. Other benefits include private health-care, concessionary mortgages, quarterly rewards and a long holiday entitlement. Employees can choose to retire at any time between 50 and 75. Everyone should have a decent pension to look forward to, as the company pays 23.8% of salary into a scheme, with staff contributing 5%.

The idea appears to be gaining ground that a much wider range of jobs can be based away from an office environment, thanks to technology. Working from home is increasing in some sectors including IT and employees are generally well equipped with the relevant technology to make teleworking feasible. Laptops, fast Internet speeds, mobile phones and other devices enable people to work from home, avoiding long commutes and heavy transport costs. People in sales roles are also able to stay out on the road spending time with customers, rather than having to come into the office to file reports.

Companies such as BT, who supply the electronic infrastructure and are introducing other technologies such as Solstra to enable people to work from home, have seen this side of their business grow significantly in recent years. Telecommuting produces a number of benefits for organizations. It allows office buildings to be disposed of and their capital released. It also means that people are more likely to focus on their job when they are meant to be working since there are fewer 'social' distractions. However, there is some evidence that, despite the benefits to many telecommuting employees, such as being spared the physical commute to the office, some feel a sense of loss of the community aspect of organizations.

Many respondents predict the ongoing outsourcing of non-core activities. Managing intellectual capital is becoming a key priority in many organizations. For managers, to the challenge of managing a more flexible workforce which includes greater numbers of contractors and temporary staff, will be added the need to manage knowledge when staff have no strong loyalty to the organization.

Realizing the Benefits of Flexible Working

Some pointers about how HR can realize some of the benefits of flexible working for their organization can be found in research on flexible working in small firms by the CIPD for the British Chambers of Commerce (2007):

Understand your business. Flexible working arrangements that work well for another business won't necessarily work in yours. Some jobs can be done from home, while in others, being there all the time is essential. Consider both what is right for your organization and where your employees' needs lie. How can flexible working improve the service to your customers?

Communicate effectively. Making your people aware of the opportunities for flexible working can be built into induction programmes, and reinforced by training. Having a clear set of organizational values can also help in selling the benefits of flexible working.

Define roles and responsibilities. It's important that managers and individuals understand their responsibilities for making flexibility work. People need to see it from the organization's point of view as well as their own. It's about give and take – not just individuals getting what they want. When there is a well-understood culture, teams can often sort out their own issues.

Try it out. You don't have to do it all at once. If there are concerns about whether flexible working is feasible, it can be helpful to have a trial period of the proposed working arrangement. But think in the longer term about the effect on others whose jobs may be more difficult to do on a flexible basis. Ask people to come up with their own ideas.

Make flexible working acceptable. You may have comprehensive written policies, but bringing these to life can be challenging. If you and your managers are not seen to 'walk the talk', flexible working won't be taken seriously. Explaining how flexible working benefits the business as well as employees is crucial. And senior staff need to lead by example.

Measure and evaluate. Remember: if you can't measure it, you can't manage it. And be open to ideas for improvement. Large organizations are not always good at evaluating the effectiveness of their flexible working practices. Our research shows that small firms are perfectly capable of monitoring the impact of flexible working on business outcomes.

LOOKING TO THE FUTURE

In the first decade of the twenty-first century the struggle for business survival in a fiercely competitive global environment is being superseded by the search for sustainable business performance. 'Maintaining excellent results' and 'growing the business' through expanding into new markets, improving existing products or developing new ones are just some of the goals which companies are embracing.

Aligning HR and business strategies involves taking into account key present and future trends, building specific goals with stakeholders and working towards these. One of the commonest reported future trends suggested by *Management Agenda* respondents is business growth through strategic alliances. HR can play a significant role in ensuring that employees working in such alliances have the skills they need for success in these complex arrangements, including influencing, political and strategic thinking skills.

Trends towards flexible working, outsourcing, using contractors, part-time and temporary staff appear to be well established. HR and managers may need to review how well they currently manage their flexible workforce and identify ways to create mutual commitment and benefits. Efficiency and tight budgetary controls are not enough to guarantee competitive advantage. Organizations will need creativity, innovation and continuous renewal if they are to sustain success. Those which are likely to be successful will be companies that continuously produce new products and services and where innovation is a 'natural' ingredient of every role. Globalization is driving the need for effective and efficient cross-cultural collaboration. HR can play a key role in designing structures, roles, processes and practices that facilitate creativity and enable knowledge to be captured and disseminated, so that wheels do not have to be continuously reinvented.

The steady change in the nature of work, the rising demand for new skills and the rise of the knowledge worker are making business success ever-more dependent on the skills and commitment of employees. The importance of learning for both the organization and the individual is greater than ever and it seems clear that the implications of the management of 'intellectual capital' in the 'post-industrial age' have not yet been fully grasped by some managers.

Leadership and management capacity will be of great importance in establishing environments where innovation can flourish. Transformational leadership, as exercised by senior management, will be a key ingredient in engaging employees, harnessing employees' initiative and achieving innovative solutions to business problems. The 'turn-off' factor of inappropriate management styles will become a major risk factor for organization since it is a primary reason for people wishing to leave their organizations.

HR has a key role to play in actively monitoring the practice of leadership, improving the quality of current and future leaders, and enabling the development of distributed leadership. In particular, HR has a key role to play in ensuring that an ethical approach underpins business practices, leadership behaviour and decision-making.

Issues relating to talent management will continue to be central to the HR agenda. Delivering on recruitment and staffing, especially as skilled labour becomes harder to find and as employees' loyalty to single companies decreases suggest that workforce planning, recruitment, retention, talent identification, skills development, management and succession planning, as well as enhancing skills required to respond to an ever-changing environment, will all grow in importance. Attracting the best new talent in today's candidate-driven market, will require employers to develop an employer brand offer which distinguishes the company from its competitors.

Retaining key players is likely to become a major challenge in many organizations. Employees are making themselves increasingly employable, with or without the help of their organizations. Their enhanced skills, including strategic thinking, and their recognition of the importance of managing their own career suggest that people recognize that they have a choice. HR will need to be at the forefront of building a new psychological contract with employees and ensuring that their organizations become employers of choice for employees – current and potential – will be a likely strategic goal. This will mean developing effective policies to deal with the unprecedented pressures placed on many parts of the workforce by the ongoing demands for improved speed, quality and productivity. The long hours culture and demanding roles may be unsustainable and cause many employees to experience a lack of work–life balance, whereas for others this is a price they are prepared to pay for career advancement.

Organizations wishing to retain their knowledge workers will need to address the issues of balance, flexibility, learning, careers as well as management development. They will also need to find ways of maximizing the knowledge present in ever-more fluid organization structures and turn that knowledge to competitive advantage. The question of whether and how this can be achieved will be explored in Chapter 17.

CONCLUSION

Organizational change is, ironically, here to stay; rather than being the exception, it is the norm. In this changing context, the strategic HRM contribution is essential. Managers will need help in managing complex change and making both the formal and informal aspects of organization adapt effectively to a rapidly shifting environment. HR will need to ensure that they effectively manage restructuring processes, and build good employee relations. The HR professional should be in touch with the effects of change from the employee angle and be able to anticipate some of the priorities that will need to be addressed if organizations are to attract and retain a knowledgeable and committed workforce.

Building an organization that is capable of change and high performance, that has the structures, systems and processes with sufficient flexibility to allow them to adapt, and, most importantly, whose employees are committed to making a difference, will require HR to have vision, skills of organizational design and development, the ability to understand and use organizational psychology, and to influence others. Engaging the workforce through developing a culture of participation and empowerment will call on HR to be able to operate both tactically, to address the needs of today, and strategically to build the organization that can succeed over time.

CHECKLISTS ON ORGANIZATIONAL DESIGN

Globalization

Globalization research carried out for the International Personnel Association in 1998 suggests that the three critical aspects of people management to the success of multinational companies in the global arena are as follows:

- The adoption of flexible management policies and practices worldwide
- The inclusion of the HR function as a strategic business partner in global business
- The development of global leaders.

Similarly, an article by Linda Stroh and Paula Caligiuri (1998) suggests that 'successful multinational corporations recognize the value in having global managers with the expertise to anticipate the organization's markets and to respond proactively. These organizations have learned that leaders who are flexible and open to the demands of the global market have made possible the organization's international business success'.

- How does your organization manage across borders, i.e. is your organization predominantly:
  Domestic?
  Multi-domestic?
  A simple export organization?
  Using local agents?
  International?
  Truly globalized with a complex web of businesses, joint ventures and alliances across most of the world's economies?
- What is the impact of globalization on HR organization, i.e. should HR be centralized, decentralized or a combination?
- How are international employees deployed and global leaders developed, e.g. on short-term assignments, expatriate postings, etc.?

Dealing with Ethical Dilemmas

- What ethical dilemmas exist at, and between, the following levels – corporate/organization, business unit, managerial, individual?
- What differences in values exist between those organizational levels?
- What potential conflicts exist between local and corporate cultures?

- How is authority held – formally/institutionally/informally?
- How can differences between local and corporate cultures be worked through?
- What is the role of HR in dealing with ethical dilemmas?

Flexible Working

- What types of flexible working will enable the organization to meet its needs? What types are requested by employees and can we accommodate these?
- What help will managers need in managing the flexible workforce?
- What form of training is received and how will this be carried out?
- How will communications and HR processes be tailored to ensure that flexible workers feel fully involved and committed to the organization?
- What team building will be required when new forms of team, especially 'virtual' teams, are set up?
- How can we enable employees – full-time or 'flexible' – to manage the new generation of knowledge through learning?

Balance

- How will we find out what 'balance' means to different groups of employees?
- What role will senior managers need to take in changing a 'long hours' culture?
- What innovative approaches can we use to create an employee-friendly culture?
- What other forms of reinforcement need to be in place within HR systems to ensure that employee-friendly policies are implemented?

REFERENCES

Angell, I. (1999) Brave new world. *Tempus*, Issue 15

Bevan, S., Passmore, E. and Mahdon, M. (2007) *Fit for Work: Musculoskeletal Disorders and Labour Market Participation*. London: The Work Foundation

Buckingham, M. and Coffman, C. (1999) What is a great workplace? A weekly summary of Gallup's discoveries about great managers and great workplaces. The Gallup Poll – Managing. *Labour Market Skills and Trends, 1997–8*. London: DfEE

CIPD (2007) *Flexible Working. Good Business: Guide to How Small Firms Are Doing It*. London: Chartered Institute of Personnel and Development

Cooper, C. (2006) The age of insecurity. *Working Life*, August

Davidson, A. (2007) Doing the right-on thing. *Sunday Times magazine*, 1 April

Dickerson, A., Homenidou, K. and Wilson, R. (2006) *Working Futures 2004–2014*. London: Sector Skills Development Agency

DTI (2007) *Delivering i2010: Ensuring the Right Conditions for an Innovative, Inclusive and Competitive UK Knowledge Economy*. London: Department for Trade and Industry

Evans, C. (1996, 1997) *Managing the Flexible Workforce*. Horsham: Roffey Park Management Institute

Garrow, V., Holbeche, L. and Sinclair, A. (2006) *The Management Agenda*. Horsham: Roffey Park Management Institute

Giddens, A. (1999) The BBC Reith Lectures, 1999, BBC Radio 4

Giddens, A. (2006) A social model for Europe, in Giddens, A., Diamond, P. and Liddle, R. (eds), *Global Europe, Social Europe*. Cambridge: Polity Press, pp. 14–30

Glynn, C. (1998) *Work–Life Balance*. Horsham: Roffey Park Management Institute

Grantham, C. and Ware, J. (2007) Closing the talent gap: companies and communities team up. *The Leader*, Sept/Oct: 12–16

Gratton, L. (2007) *Hot Spots: Why Some Teams, Workplaces, and Organizations Buzz with Energy – and Others Don't*. Harlow: FT Prentice Hall

Hamel, G. and Breen, B. (2007) *The Future of Management*. Cambridge, MA: Harvard Business School Press

Handy, C. (1997) *The Empty Raincoat*. London: Hutchinson

Hodkinson, P. (2007) Companies that count. *Sunday Times*, 6 May

Holbeche, L. and McCartney, C. (2005) *The Management Agenda*. Horsham: Roffey Park Management Institute

Ipsos Mori (2007) Green Britain' Survey, 11 July, Ipsos Mori publications

Leadbetter, C. (2001) Welcome to the knowledge economy. *Environment and Planning C: Government and Policy*, 19: 903–926

Lewis, J. (1999) Mind the gap. *Personnel Today*, 1 April

Nolan, P. (2002) The ESRC Future of Work Programme. *New Technology, Work and Employment*, 17: 150–151

Nolan, P. (2004) Shaping the future: the political economy of work and employment. *Industrial Relations Journal*, 35, No. 5, 378–388

Nolan, J. and Salmelin, B. (2005) *Collaboration@Work Report: New working environments research unit, i2010, Responding to the Challenge*. ec.europa.eu/information_society/activities/atwork/hot_news/publications/documents/collabwork2005.pdf

Office of National Statistics (2006) *Labour Market Trends*, June

Ohmae, K. (1985) *Triad Power*. New York: Free Press

Overell, S. (2005) Twilight of the brotherhood. *Personnel Today*, 23 August

Peacock, L. (2007) *Personnel Today*, 24 April

Perry, M. (2005) Shared Service Centres are not a Panacea. *Finance Week*, 23 November

Reilly, P. (2007) *The Work in Progress: Corporate Warming Report*: Adecco

Rigby, D.K. (2007) *Management Tools 2007: An Executive's Guide*: Bain and Co

Select Appointments: www.personneltoday.com/articlesbytopic/199/work-life-balance.htm

Stroh, L.K. and Caligiuri, P.M. (1998) Increasing global competitiveness through effective people management. *Journal of World Business*, 33, Issue 1

Syrett, M. (2007) The rise of the non-employee, in *Developing HR Strategy* (December). London: Croner

Worral, L. and Cooper, C. (2006) *The Quality of Working Life*. Corby: The Chartered Management Institute

Chapter 3

Transforming HR into a Strategic Partner

For many functions, HR transformation is currently one of their critical deliverables.

(Reddington, Williamson and Withers, 2006)

In Chapter 1 we looked at the evolution of Human Resources from its earliest stages to today's era of 'the strategic business partner'. The current period of HR transformation has been profoundly influenced by Dave Ulrich's thinking. In this chapter we shall examine in more detail some of the ways in which HR is being transformed, and look at the role of business partner in particular.

REINVENTING HR

We may be getting beyond the point where HR has to 'earn a place at the table' (Brockbank, 1997), although in many organizations this has still not been achieved and, rightly or wrongly, HR still suffers from a bad press. An article about HR in *Fortune Magazine* asked: 'why not blow the sucker up?' For Neil Hayward, formerly HR Director for Booker PLC, 'it is not enough to redesign, restructure or reposition HR. A re-invention is necessary'. That reinvention usually involves reengineering to improve the effectiveness of HR while reducing cost. Approaches to reengineering are considered later in this chapter. Reinventing HR means looking at new ways to deliver services and answering the question 'What is the purpose of HR in this organization?'

The 'Three-legged Stool'

Since the late 1990s, Dave Ulrich's thinking about HR roles (1997) has been highly influential on theory and practice of HRM in global companies. Indeed, of the 80% of organizations which have changed their HR function in the past five years, 57% have introduced some form of 'Ulrich model' (Reilly, 2007). The assumption behind the Ulrich model is that, in order to free up HR to do higher value activities, different delivery models of 'transactional' administrative work should be found, leading to greater efficiency, higher quality and lower costs.

Where it has been introduced, the 'Ulrich model' has usually been interpreted literally as a functional design, though Ulrich himself insists that he was not describing a set of HR roles, in the sense of jobs, but a set of functions to be carried out. Nevertheless, when it has been implemented in structural terms the 'Ulrich model' has led to the splitting out of integrated HR teams that carried out the full range of HR activities, from administration to strategic direction and the creation of a structure based on the so-called 'three legged stool'. This comprises a (small) corporate centre, with service delivery via business partners, centres of expertise and shared services.

Corporate HR, usually a small team, is responsible for the strategic direction and governance of the function. The term 'business partner' is used to describe the business-facing role through which relationships with key business units are built and maintained. Business partners act as internal consultants to leaders of business units and contract with former colleagues as suppliers. Centres of expertise provide professional support to business partners in specialist areas such as resourcing, employee relations, reward and training. Administrative functions are supplied through shared services, or through external or outsourced provision.

The widespread adoption of the 'Ulrich model' is evident in CIPD research (Reilly, 2007) which has found that many central HR teams in large organizations in the UK have decreased in size. There has been a noticeable shift to consultancy-type roles with many HR responsibilities devolved to the line. To some extent, these consultancy-type relationships have left HR with less direct power since the line manager becomes the 'client' to HR's 'supplier'. Service level agreements can reinforce these respective expectations. Operational HR roles have been the most endangered, with parts of the operation outsourced, such as pay and recruitment.

Many organizations have experienced problems with the quality of outsourced provision and the current trend appears to be to take back into the centre the areas of operations that leave HR most exposed if they go wrong. The most common HR structures appear to concentrate the strategic roles in the corporate centre, leaving operational support to the line being provided through divisional support units. Where such devolved support units exist, they sometimes report back to the head of HR, and are therefore clearly maintaining a strong professional link, while other units report to the divisional director, maintaining only a dotted-line relationship with the head of HR.

Shared Services

Administration service centres, providing shared services that deliver low-cost, highly automated transaction processing to employees (internally or externally), are replacing junior personnel officer and administrator roles. In some cases, call centres and help-desks have been established to ensure that operational HR support of some kind is available to line managers who may not have a regular HR contact.

The CIPD research into the changing roles of HR (Reilly and Tamkin, 2007) found that shared services is a large-organization phenomenon. For instance, Unisys has established an international online service centre which provides solutions to HR issues in a way that meets 'local' as well as corporate requirements. In terms of tasks, they carry out the transactional activities one would expect.

Overall, the structure of shared services varies by organization, especially in a global context. Only 4% of the CIPD survey respondents said that they wholly outsourced their HR shared services operation and around a quarter outsourced part of their shared services activities. There were other examples where shared services was insourced, and included multi-functional, as well as mono-functional cases. Call centres may or may not be part of the shared services operation. The important thing is to gain a track record of keeping basic HR processes in order. CIPD survey respondents reported positive experiences of call centres, although there are still challenges in terms of managing customer expectations.

Centres of Expertise/Excellence

Turning to centres of excellence or expertise, CIPD survey results (Reilly, 2007) indicate that nearly two-thirds of those organizations that have introduced shared services have also created centres of expertise. HR centres of excellence are typically made up of experts who focus on specialized consulting services providing mission-critical HR disciplines such as change management, executive compensation and bonus arrangements. In addition, rapid response teams are ad hoc groupings formed to provide services for specific needs such as a major acquisition or divestiture. Learning and development is the commonest centre of expertise, thereby helping to integrate learning and development and HR. In some organizations expertise is held within the business unit, not performed corporately, so that it aligns with specific unit needs.

Where problems with centres of expertise were reported, they mostly concerned interfaces with the rest of the HR organization. As units devolve there can be tensions which the function attempts to resolve in different ways. The centre can come to be seen as increasingly peripheral as most strategic decision-making takes place in the business units. This can be particularly challenging when HR attempts to take a corporate perspective on the development of high potential talent, for instance, since business heads can be reluctant to share information with the centre that might cause them to lose a 'star' employee to another region. One organization's approach to resolving such tensions is described in the case study about Dr Candy Albertsson, formerly of BP Amoco, in Chapter 11. Similarly, the market nature of relationships within which some HR teams operate can prove a barrier to a meaningful relationship with line managers. Some organizations are overcoming this difficulty by avoiding internal charging systems.

GETTING HR TRANSACTIONAL WORK 'DONE DIFFERENTLY'

The process of transition to a new form of service delivery can be difficult. The challenge is to ensure that transactional work is delivered accurately, efficiently and cost-effectively, or else it undermines HR's ability to be seen to add value through more strategic work. If the basic HR administrative processes are not in good order, especially on sensitive issues such as executive pay, no strategic contribution is likely to be considered of value until the administrative problem has been fixed. If the problems recur, the credibility of HR teams can be at stake. Conversely, HR teams who concentrate on administration tend to be criticized as being 'reactive' and are regarded as a cost. Processing paperwork, addressing employee concerns and administering personnel policies are time-consuming and energy-hungry. Since a key aim of HR teams must be to improve cost-efficiency, business competitiveness and customer service (Ulrich *et al.*, 1995) the paradox must be resolved.

However, finding ways to get HR transactions done differently can have something of a catch-22 flavour to it for the HR function. The expectations of many internal customers/business partners and of some personnel specialists themselves about what HR can and should contribute may vary considerably, and line managers often still expect HR to deliver HR administrative services in conventional ways. It is understandable then that many HR teams choose to concentrate on delivering the core processes right without attempting to develop a more strategic contribution.

Looking at the relationships of the HR function with stakeholders, CIPD research into the changing roles of HR (Reilly, 2007) found that in the opinion of CEOs, HR's weakest area is the quality of HR processes. In terms of the relationship between HR and the line, CIPD found that the division of people management responsibilities between HR and the line has remained largely unchanged since 2003, despite HR's wish to have more work transferred to line managers.

The Early Challenges of HR Transformation

Early adopters of the Ulrich approach often lacked the infrastructure for HR to deliver on its value-adding promise. Devolving back to line managers the responsibility for routine aspects of HR delivery and supporting them via information technology with HR information systems and help-desks appeared one way of resolving the paradox.

Devolving to the Line

Devolution to the line was frequently hampered by poor or missing technology (e.g. self-service systems), limited HR technology skills, the extent to which line managers considered people management to be a key part of their role, and the skills and time available to them for people management tasks. Typically, little support was available to line managers to help them develop the skills needed to carry out the devolved HR activities now expected of them if the new HR model was to work.

Even today, devolving to the line may not work if line managers are unwilling, unable or under-prepared for what is now expected of them with respect to personnel activities. Some managers feel that they lack the skills required and prefer the idea that there is a function they can turn to, or blame, if problems occur.

Devolution of HR activities to the line is often unpopular with line managers, who tend to reject the notion of internal consultancy unless they are also continuing to receive service delivery support. Line expectations about what Personnel is meant to deliver may well be rooted in the 'tea and sympathy' or the service delivery phase of evolution. As one line manager in a pharmaceutical company announced to his Personnel colleague when she came to tell him about her change of role; 'Don't tell me you're an internal consultant and here to solve my problems. Since you're leaving me to do my own recruitment, you are my problem.'

And even where responsibility for many aspects of people management has largely passed back to the line, a vicious circle is often evident which can be hard to break out of. Because line managers sometimes appear to lack the skills or the will to do what is required well enough, HR tends to lack trust in line managers, and therefore does not give them enough discretion. As a result, HR ends up focusing back more on administration than on strategic activity. Occasionally, too, HR professionals are reluctant to devolve responsibilities to the line for fear of losing professional control and consistency in the way procedures are being implemented.

What emerges from CIPD research into the changing roles of HR (Parry et al., 2007) is that the 'value-add' of HR comes from two sources: its service delivery and facilitation roles. It has been easy over recent years, with the obsession with HR's strategic contribution, to overlook the fact that many managers value HR doing the bread and butter of people management work. Indeed, when HR devolves mainstream activity to line managers in order to focus on more strategic issues, HR is often criticized for failing to add value in the here and now.

In smaller organizations in particular the recruitment and retention of staff, and ensuring that they have the requisite competencies to do their work, are vital processes. HR has a key role in both supporting line managers with these processes directly and by enabling, encouraging and coaching managers to get the most from their staff.

If devolution to the line is to work effectively, line managers need to be upskilled for their key roles and the process of devolution needs to be well thought through and planned. For instance, it may be better to phase the devolution of some activities to the line rather than simply making line managers responsible for all aspects of 'transactional' HR. It is reasonable to expect that all line managers have responsibility for some core 'people' processes – such as managing performance, communicating well with their teams and developing employees they manage. Preparing line managers well for these tasks may involve management development, providing user-friendly tools, learning groups and manager help-desks to ensure that managers can be reasonably expected to play their part.

ALIGNING HR STRUCTURES TO BUSINESS STRATEGY

Even where HR manages to free itself up to carry out a more strategic role, the HR function still struggles to focus on strategic matters beyond immediate business planning cycles, even though many of today's challenges in the competition for talent require longer-term solutions. Roffey Park and other research carried out in UK and multi-national organizations since the mid-1990s has consistently found that HR is still perceived as too reactive, producing piecemeal initiatives that go nowhere or solutions that do not match the need, and is constantly 'on the back foot' when dealing with key issues.

HR transformation is increasingly coming to be seen for what it is: a means to an end, rather than an end in itself. That end must be to build successful organizations which are able to compete effectively, as well as address short-term demands. It is crucially important that HR is able to identify and address some of the people issues that will affect their organization's success beyond the short-term. Today's global trends suggest that competition for scarce talent is going to increase, that competitive advantage can only be sustained through the skilful deployment and performance of highly talented and engaged employees; therefore today more than ever should be the era in which HR can make its mark as a contributor to business success.

Issues to consider when restructuring include:

- What sort of service do clients need as opposed to want?
- What do you believe are the strategic priorities?
- How can these be delivered, and by whom?
- What are the relative costs and benefits of different structures?
- If parts of the service are to be outsourced, how will you maintain service quality?
- If HR services are separated in this way, how can HR professionals develop the experience and skills to make transitions between different types of HR role?

Reengineering HR

A relatively radical approach is to reengineer the HR function. Hammer and Champy (1993) define reengineering as 'utilizing the power of modern information systems to radically redesign processes in order to achieve dramatic improvement in critical performance measures'. Reengineering can target the whole function or just a key HR process.

Reengineering HR typically happens when organizations restructure their central functions in order to encourage diversification within the business. Corporate centres are often thought to hold back individual businesses because of their desire for a common culture, or for system compatibility. Corporate centre staff often see their role as managing the concerns of a range of stakeholders, including customers, suppliers and employees and community interests. Though these contributions are real they are hard to quantify and the trend to demerge or decentralize functions appears well under way.

Reengineering HR involves assessing how work is performed and how processes can be improved. Then processes that have the greatest potential for improvement and cost savings need to be identified. Internal customers' needs must be clearly defined and the people rearrangements for improving business fundamentals determined. The basics involve asking:

- Why is an activity done?
- Why is it done when it is done?
- Why is it done where it is done?
- Why is it done the way it is done?
- Who does it and why?

HR programme delivery can then be revamped accordingly. However, many HR teams have found that reengineering HR in a dramatic rather than incremental way is less effective than recreating the HR function to help an organization build and maintain the capabilities needed to execute business strategy better than competitors.

Arthur Yeung of San Francisco State University and Wayne Brockbank of the University of Michigan (1998) have identified two main ways of reengineering HR. One is technology-driven, where an 'off-the-shelf' system package is used and HR processes redesigned accordingly; the other is process-driven, which starts with a process redesign and then has systems custom-built to support the process. The most effective way of reorienting HR to make a more strategic contribution is when the HR team itself reviews what it would contribute as a function, and how it would structure itself, if HR operated in a 'greenfield site'.

Brockbank and Yeung advocate the technology-driven approach because:

- It allows suppliers to provide the technical support available from previous systems
- Since it builds on existing systems, costs should be lower
- Time-consuming technical hitches can be eliminated.

THE ROLE OF TECHNOLOGY IN HR TRANSFORMATION

Other theorists agree about the potential of technology to transform HR's capability. Mohrman, quoted in Weatherley (2005), describes the contribution of technology to different HR roles:

- A personnel services role: transactional self-service processes
- A business support and execution role: HR systems administration; employee and manager tools
- A strategic partner role: data analysis, modelling and simulation capabilities.

Technology is playing a very large part in HR transformation, supplying much of the infrastructure through which transactional work can be done differently and in value-for-money ways. Technology enables choice – to retain processes in-house or to use some form of external provision via outsourced solutions that need take no account of geographical location. With a strong technology platform help-desks and free access to HR information systems can be provided to managers and employees. Work that lends itself to being parcelled up as a process is typically a target for being delivered differently, for instance through outsourcing. However, the 'total' outsourcing of HR administration pioneered by BP, Accenture and BAE Systems, appears to have failed to take off on a major scale.

HR Information Systems (HRIS)

Many UK organizations now have some form of HRIS in place. Not surprisingly, companies in the advanced technology sector, such as Apple Computers and Hewlett–Packard, have led the field on this form of delivery of operational HR. Human Resource information systems are usually built on People Soft and SAP packages.

Cost reduction is a main driver behind HR reengineering efforts. The use of advanced information technology in order to transform the delivery of routine but important administrative activities is leading to greater efficiency and reduced HR-to-employee ratios. US-based IT networking company Cisco Systems developed a sophisticated intranet system for its own staff which saved about £1.75 million in 'headcount avoidance', or about 30 HR jobs. HRIS can help to improve processes and empower line managers. This, of course, brings down the cost of service delivery and should allow professionals to concentrate on adding value through knowledge-based, problem-solving activities.

However, the effectiveness of such systems is also open to debate. Reengineering can itself be costly, since the hardware, communications infrastructure and applications software need to be appropriate and require a heavy time commitment from staff involved (consultants, HR and IT staff). They can also be subject to poorly implemented software and spiralling costs.

Another driver for reengineering efforts is improving the quality and consistency of HR services. Yet in many companies, decentralized decision-making about IT systems has led to a plethora of HR systems being used which do not talk to each other, causing duplication and lost opportunities, especially when carrying out internal talent searches, for example. In situations such as this, IT systems can seem more of a constraint than a help.

Where they work well, HRIS do produce the intended benefits. One company has completely revamped its separate, people-related systems within a single shared system architecture. People management information has been streamlined, automated and integrated. This means that continuous HR process improvements can be easily incorporated, ensuring that the systems continue to be relevant and supportive to managers. Another company has been able to radically reduce the cycle time in salary planning while increasing accuracy. Other organizations use IT to cope with the process of filling management positions, from forecasting needs to identifying suitable candidates. Increasingly, companies are using telephone and e-mail help-desks to answer and process routine enquiries about pay and benefits, medical and retirement plans and other issues where a 'human' response is required.

Reengineering HR processes, and providing user-friendly tools to acquire information on demand, can be helpful to managers who now have devolved responsibility for addressing employee issues directly, without the intervention of HR. Some companies make available online self-sufficiency tools such as internal job posting systems, directories of all employees and their locations/contact details, training courses and other important information.

Self-service

Employee Self-service (ESS) is one of the fastest-growing trends in the delivery of HR information. For instance, Unisys and IBM have found innovative technology-based solutions to providing an effective administration service to the line while freeing up HR specialists for more strategic work. According to the solutions architect for Cisco Systems, 'the concept of self-service frees up HR to concentrate on the value-added aspects of the business – analysis, leadership development and so on' (*Personnel Today*, 29 April 1999). The ESS at Nationwide allows employees to select their own benefits within the total value of the job. Nortel are also using Manager Self-service (MSS) to drive responsibility and decision-making further down the organization. It provides managers with a variety of HR tools, such as access to information about their subordinates, and the opportunity to analyse information in order to improve their effectiveness.

So HR information systems are part of the transformation story and a number of key messages about how to use them to advantage emerge from a CIPD/Cranfield report *HR and Technology* (Parry *et al.*, 2007). This report argues that the use of technology is more likely to lead to cost savings when used in conjunction with other changes to the HR function, such as the move to a shared services function. Nortel's shared service for instance ensures that transactional HR services are delivered consistently and that any change request approved by the line manager is within company guidelines.

Making the Most of HRIS

Another key to making the most of HRIS is appointing an intermediary to bridge the gap between HR and IT teams. In the UK, the National Health Service (NHS) is in the process of implementing the 'electronic staff record' (ESR), a national, fully integrated HR and payroll system to be used by all 600-plus NHS organizations from the end of 2008. The senior management team from IT contractors McKesson meet the NHS project staff working on the electronic staff record on a daily basis. In Nortel, a special HRIS team manages the relationship between HR and IT to avoid the communication gaps which can lead to delays in developing and implementing the system.

Once the processes have been reengineered, additional training is generally required to help staff, line managers and HR professionals use the new processes effectively. Training can overcome one of the commonest pitfalls, which is that users do not understand the new system. Some resistance can be anticipated since reengineering can also present risks to existing systems and threats to jobs. The level of psychological resistance should not be underestimated. In the NHS, training for ESR users was designed in consultation with staff whose preferred method of training was classroom-based. Training was designed on that basis but a blended approach was also adopted, including an element of e-learning, to overcome transport difficulties for some staff. E-learning is also evolving with training packages moving away from long videos to shorter clips, viewable via mobile technology.

Various organizations evaluate the impact of technology on HR processes using customer satisfaction ratings as a measure of success. Norwich Union examines the accuracy of data entry in order to assess improvements and at Transport for London (TfL), HR services have set service level agreement targets (such as response time for answering calls, and the time it takes to close a case), which are measured daily using the new technology.

Technology is a key element of enabling a change in HR structure. In TfL business partners have found their roles have changed from 70:30 administration:strategy to 30:70 since the move to an HR service centre. Assuming that the new processes are correctly targeted, championed from the top and add value, this allows HR professionals to focus on areas where their contribution can significantly move the organization forward.

HR Outsourcing

Reengineering the transactional functions is one solution to the challenge of freeing up HR to focus on more value-adding activities. Outsourcing is another. The potential benefits of outsourcing are also wide-ranging and include:

- Cost reduction
- Increasing administrative efficiencies
- Access to updated technology
- Reducing risk
- Providing expertise not available internally
- Moving HR up the value chain.

Outsourcing can potentially deliver administrative efficiencies, for example by taking advantage of the streamlined, simple proven processes that an outsourcing provider has in place. Indeed some pundits argue that outsourcing most if not all the HR function's delivery is the future of the HR profession.

For instance, SPV management, a UK-based entity, decided to outsource the entire UK HR function following its acquisition by a large US company in 2002, avoiding the need to recruit or train people internally to understand and deal with UK employment law issues.

Another potential driver for organizations to consider HR outsourcing is access to up-to-date technology. As the use of technology generally, and HR information systems, in particular, continues to accelerate, organizations might look to replace fixed costs associated with technology investments with variable costs associated with an outsourcing arrangement. In this way, they reduce the capital they have tied up and the need to re-invest in these capital costs as technological advances dictate.

I think that total outsourcing of HR is an unlikely prospect. Indeed, there has been some media hype about the transformational business process outsourcing arrangements that various multi-nationals have embarked upon over the past five to ten years. This might lead organizations to believe that outsourcing is growing fast and is the preferred option to service provision in every circumstance.

However, research (WERS, 2004) indicates otherwise, suggesting that outsourcing is specific to certain activities and limited in extent – training, payroll and resourcing of temporary positions are most commonly outsourced. Similarly, a 2003 CIPD survey of HR practitioners concluded that the outsourcing market was broadly static, with some organizations increasing their use of external providers and others cutting back. In addition, most of the publicity surrounding outsourcing focuses on large organizations that may lead those operating in the small and medium-sized enterprise (SME) market to believe that outsourcing is of more limited relevance to them. Smaller organizations might not believe that they have sufficient volume of activities to benefit from these, though linking with other organizations to pool their administrative activities into one shared service or outsourcing centre might enable smaller organizations to gain the benefits of outsourced arrangements.

For those organizations that do decide that outsourcing is an appropriate way forward for them, the transition from in-house provision to outsourced solution requires careful consideration. Appropriate choice of outsource provider to reflect a good cultural fit, together with carefully articulated requirements, agreed performance measures and effective contract management are important to ensure that the arrangement delivers the maximum desired benefits. The typically long-term nature of outsourcing arrangements means that, as important as these contractual arrangements are, it is even more important to build good working relationships with the outsource provider.

Preparing for HR Transformation

For organizations that are considering reengineering their existing HR service provision, it is important to first consider it in detail, and then ask whether you need to change the way you currently operate. If you decide that changes are appropriate, two further questions arise. First, what is the extent of the changes that you need to make? Do you need to introduce wide-ranging transformational changes, for instance, or are you actually looking at more minor tweaks? (See Figure 3.1)

The next question is whether retaining internal capability is important, or whether entering into an outsourcing arrangement will be the most appropriate solution. Alternatively you might realize that you can deliver the changes internally or with the help of an external consultant.

Winning support for such changes is essential if they are to succeed. When planning to reengineer HR, therefore, it is important to be clear about why it is needed and how reengineering fits with the overall strategy to achieve business goals. Typically, reengineering is triggered by problems with existing systems and the need to address specific goals. It is important to think through the sources of problems and pick the right HR process from the outset rather than launch programmes that are too complex and never get completed.

Setting clear and realistic goals can help achieve buy-in from top management. Clients need to perceive the benefits to them of supporting the development and implementation of new systems. It is important to develop a centralized system that can flex to allow local autonomy and meet the varying needs of the business. Ideally, forming coalitions with internal clients who are champions of change can help create a culture supportive of change within the organization.

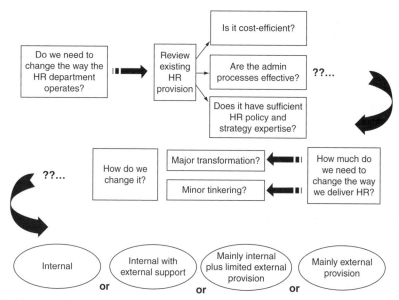

FIGURE 3.1   HR transformation process (after Reddington *et al.*, 2006).

A steering team, usually consisting of senior HR managers, line and MIS managers, is formed at an early stage. This team helps to find out the key concerns of users of the proposed process, works out the problems with the current process, sets new targets for the process and develops an implementation plan. Implementation teams are formed to provide solutions to each of the proposed processes and action plans and milestones are established. Implementation teams need to be held accountable to clear and measurable targets. Monitoring the processes and communicating results helps maintain support for the change.

INTERNAL CONSULTANCY

By devolving some responsibility for operational personnel issues to line management, many Personnel functions have freed themselves up to add more value. Moving up the value chain requires new approaches, such as formally acting as internal consultants to line managers and business unit leaders, the aim being to ensure that the business can benefit from focused solutions, delivered in a timely and effective way. This requires HR to develop consultancy skills, including relationship management, diagnostic and problem-solving skills which enable them to identify causes and appropriate solutions. Some organizations prefer to retain a 'rump' of the core Personnel function to provide generalist service delivery while other team members provide internal consultancy.

Early implementers of the internal consultancy approach typically experienced a number of challenges with working it through in practice. Of course, effective consultancy is a highly skilled process and consultancy skills are now a vital part of an HR professional's toolkit. Yet success as an internal consultant is not always easy and in some ways can be harder to achieve than working as an external consultant since you have a longer-term set of relationships to maintain and perhaps a set of client expectations of your function which can help or hinder what you can achieve.

THE ONGOING CHALLENGES OF HR TRANSFORMATION

However, despite the potential benefits of freeing up time through automation, functional transformation does not automatically mean that HR will spend more time on 'value added' activities, as research by Lawler and Mohrman (2003) concluded.

Too Internal a Focus

Ironically, CIPD research suggests that it may be the very process of HR transformation itself which runs the risk of creating something of an 'own goal' phenomenon for HR with respect to effectiveness. So much time, effort and expenditure is typically put into transformation that HR can become too internally or overly focused on 'ideal' HR processes and roles with the effect that become 'cleverer at being HR'; as a result they run the risk of losing sight of client needs and business relevance. Pragmatic and gradual shifts of role may be more effective than leaping into complete restructuring in pursuit of an 'ideal' delivery model. As one respondent advises: 'do not worry about the theory, worry instead about what the business needs and what you currently have'.

What Happens to HR Careers?

Another issue for HR functions that have separated out into different roles – 'business partners' whose role is to act as internal consultants to leaders of business units and to contract with former colleagues as suppliers through shared services or centres of excellence, or else look for external solutions to diagnosed needs – is the question of what an HR career looks like. For HR specialists who may find themselves in only one 'leg' of the 'three-legged stool', for instance managing an outsourced call centre/help-desk, career development may look very different from that of a business partner for whom progression may more obviously be towards HR director roles. We return to the skills implications of HR careers in Chapter 12.

Lack of Teamwork

Similarly, the move to transform HR by creating business partner roles and using various 'arm's length' solutions, such as outsourcing, shared service centres and help-desks may be restricting the amount of real teamworking across the function as a whole. In the early days, for instance, debates raged between HR colleagues about who 'owned' the 'client' – business partners acting as internal consultants, or those who supplied the service? If excellence is being developed in each of the channels, the challenge for the HR function is to act as organizational role model of cross-functional learning and sharing of good practice.

Short-term Agendas

While internal consultancy does provide value at local level, it alone is not enough to enable HR professionals to really add value to the organization. Part of the problem is that the more highly client-focused you are, the more likely it is that you will be delivering solutions that fix that particular client's immediate problem, perhaps at the expense of corporate needs. Typically, internal clients of HR are interested in solving problems that affect them in the short term; they are less interested in what they fear will be the over-engineered corporate solution which is delivered too late to be of real use. There is also the human tendency to reject solutions that are 'not invented here'.

Consequently, internal consultants can often find themselves chasing local issues where the business head has seen a 'people problem' and tried to fix it. It can be hard to challenge a powerful player who perceives you to add value only if you do what they say. The focus on short-term issues then gets in the way of being able to produce the bigger wins for the organization in equipping it for its future challenges because you are too busy focusing on, or repairing damage in, the short term.

The vicious cycle of lots of activity without clear strategic goals can lead to ineffectiveness. The real value that can be added through HR, including work-force planning, the development of effective talent management and succession strategies, and strategic recruitment for the organization as a whole, can get dissipated at business group level, and make it difficult to create breakthroughs on significant issues. Indeed, Dave Ulrich challenges HR professionals to distinguish between the 'do-ables' that represent day-to-day activity without reference to more strategic goals and the 'deliverables', or activities with a real purpose, which will make a real difference to the business and organization.

Heavy Price to Pay

With respect to transactional HR, the cost of new supply arrangements, including outsourced or off-shored solutions, has often been greater than anticipated; line managers have frequently been under-prepared for what has been required of them, and the loss of what many HR professionals have considered their heart-land has been a source of regret for some.

AND YET ... THERE ARE BENEFITS

Despite the 'growing pains' of HR transformation, the benefits of change are beginning to come through more obviously, and much learning has taken place about what works in real contexts. For instance, there is growing recognition that higher-level skills are required for HR roles today than in the past, though 40% of CIPD respondents still report shortages of resource and 38% describe skills gaps within the HR function. These days, the early implementers of the 'three-legged stool' have tended to put in place training and development to help business partners understand their role and equip them for it. Typically, the number of business partners has been trimmed down to focus on key internal business relationships and challenges. 'Strategic business partners', usually HR directors, manage the most senior relationships and take an overview role about where value needs to be added. Some HR functions have retained or reinstated a rump of HR generalist support provided directly to business units in the traditional way, or via shared services. Better preparation of line managers for their role is helping free up business partners to add value.

Building HR Strategic Capability at Microsoft UK

Of course, creating the HR organization that can add value does not happen over-night or in a vacuum. Dave Gartenberg, HR Director of Microsoft's UK organization at the time of writing, has a clear vision for HR. He believes that HR should be a driving force in the business, helping it hit its potential through its employees and leaders. For Dave, critical success factors include:

- Exploiting (getting the best from) talent
- Reducing the need for external hires
- People being able to grow and have work–life balance
- People feeling they have made a difference.

Dave values the Ulrich model but recognizes that when he arrived at Microsoft UK in 2005 even the transactional work was not being done well. Drawing on his previous experience in the chemicals industry, Dave introduced a deep process orientation, using principles from Total Quality Management and Six Sigma. Having mapped key transactional HR processes, the team improved them, and thereby managed to reduce some of the dissatisfaction with HR. This was a stepping stone to higher value-added contributions. An HR shared service centre was formed which pulled much of the administrative work off the generalists' plate so it could be redeployed to higher value-added spaces (as well as improving the cycle times for employee requests for the administrative support).

The next stage was to find out how HR could help the business to grow. Dave introduced the role of Organizational Development Director to the team and created roles for Business Partners whose roles were to understand the business drivers and goals, identify the barriers to success and use HR levers to help the business achieve success. At the same time Dave introduced an ongoing programme of formal and informal on-the-job development for the HR team, helping them to develop business acumen and consultancy skills.

Even so, Dave recognized that as the team developed, the organizational design for HR was still not right. For business partners, being an end-to-end generalist for the client groups meant that the ability to focus on any one part of the HR agenda was seemingly random. Too much effort was still being put into transactional and generalist HR, with the effect that more strategic initiatives were being starved of time and attention.

Dave recognized that demand for the work of the HR consultants can at times be a bit unpredictable. Similarly, there was no easy way for resources to flow across businesses when there were seemingly random (but consistent) spikes in HR issues in the businesses since in the 'intact' team design it was very difficult to move resources from one business to others. As a result, there was not always consistent alignment between what the client's needs were and the Career Stage Profile (level) of the generalist on that business. Nor was HR consistently challenging managers and business leaders to establish and help drive a strategic HR plan that is aligned and supports the business. For HR professionals, the levelling and career path within HR was seemingly random.

Accordingly, Dave's new design takes both the needs of the business and the career development needs of HR professionals into account. He and his team came to the conclusion that they needed to divide the HR work into two areas. In terms of responsibilities, a simple way to describe the split is that the 'consultants' will drive front-line manager capability and resolve employee issues, and the 'business partners' will work with the leadership teams on the overall HR agenda and strategy. Responsibilities look like this:

HR consultants	HR business partners
The focus of the role is to work with employees and front line managers – the kind of activities that tend to be more immediate in nature, and very problematic if not done exceptionally well:	The focus of the role is to work with managers and their leadership teams – the kind of activities that tend not to be as urgent in nature, but critically important to the longer-term health and capability of the organization
Front line manager induction and onboarding	Leadership team (LT) induction and onboarding
Manager coaching	Leadership coaching
Employee relations and performance issues	Leadership team effectiveness
Trends and statistics in employee relations	People review
Initiating the recruitment process for information technology positions	Talent management
Redundancy situations	Work with leadership teams to define HR priorities/agenda

Shared responsibilities
- On interview loops for all people manager openings. Providing feedback on manager competencies
- Review model implementations

The second change is how the team is organized. The consultants were formed into one team, which allowed for many benefits but the most significant are (1) giving one team line of sight to the manager capability issues which can help the team identify root causes, and (2) allowing for a critical mass under one manager who can easily see where the peaks and troughs in demand are, and flow the resources accordingly. So the consultants have a primary alignment to organizations, but know they'll receive back-up when peaks hit their business, and conversely they will back their peers up when they are in a situation of having 'bandwidth'. As a result, HR and line managers have the benefit of deep understanding of given business areas but the capacity is available in the design to ensure a high degree of flexibility and responsiveness.

The generalists who were switching client groups and/or roles met with the people taking over the responsibilities. During these handovers they covered issues like:

- Key business issues facing business units (BU)
- A walk-through BU organization chart

- Key people in the organization
- Any employee relations issues in the works
- Which managers are either new and/or not (yet) strong.

Business partners are a ring-fenced resource to help drive BU HR plans and constructively challenge BU leadership teams with respect to discussions about people, organization and culture. This should allow for a more strategic approach to a variety of key talent and organizational issues. For Microsoft this should prove a very useful model, and has the potential to be applied elsewhere.

In many organizations, shared services have developed so effectively that they are now able to operate, as in the case of Fujitsu Services, as a profit centre, providing outsourced HR solutions to other companies.

HR Transformation at Fujitsu Services
(based on Reilly and Tamkin, 2007)

In Fujitsu Services (formerly ICL) HR is emerging from a period of major transformation which has resulted in HR being at the top table. In the six years since Fujitsu ceased to be a manufacturer of computer mainframes and moved to being a professional services company there has been a clear recognition that the company's only real asset is people and that margin is to be gained through the intellectual property they represent. Therefore being able to identify, develop and retain talent is right at the top of the CEO's priorities and is at the heart of business strategy. Resourcing and talent management are therefore central to HR strategy.

During those six years of transformation, the company has been almost completely reengineered, roles have changed and the skill-sets required for success have changed too – yet the overall headcount remains at 18 000. Role distinctions between technical and programme management are breaking down and a key requisite therefore for anyone working in Fujitsu Services is the ability to adapt and potentially be mobile. At the same time the organization has a strong task culture which can sometimes cause teamwork and relationships to break down and potentially lead to employee relations problems. In such circumstances, HR has a key role to play in coaching senior managers, building effective relationships and leveraging expertise. In particular HR has to 'walk the talk' through facilitating and acting as beacons of expertise within the business.

In common with many organizations, the HR team at Fujitsu Services concludes that HR's contribution to business is hard to quantify and assess, but that does not stop HR paying attention to what appears to matter most. Typical measures of HR contribution include:

- Attrition
- Failed recruitment
- Benchmarking, e.g. costs of recruitment, rewards, ratios HR : line
- IIP accreditation – which is seen as key to access to government bids.

In transforming HR, Fujitsu's business partner model is based on demand-pull. So HR operates principally as an internal consultant. Acting as internal consultant involves having to deal with ambiguity in order to find the right solution for the client. This has required a mindset change, with the business being treated as a customer rather than a partner, and where the business strategy is translated into the HR agenda. It has also required a change of language for HR professionals, away from HR jargon to 'business speak,' underpinned by a deep understanding of what the business is about and where it is going.

HR transactions are user-friendly and there has been a deliberate simplification of processes following a major review of all services from the user perspective. Employees can access Internet-based forms for calculating their pensions, for example. They can also update their own personal information so that employees can guarantee its integrity.

To achieve this transformation has required training for all HR practitioners, resulting in customer-friendly teams. The HR Academy training programme has included a series of modules covering the whole employment cycle. The role of business partner is understood by all as being about distilling best practice in HR and 'finessing' it in the way the organization can understand and use it. The business partner role is seen very much as protecting the organization from HR, making sure that HR delivers to tough service level agreements, as well as delivering on internal projects. The focus is on identifying problems, aligning initiatives, focusing on the benefits to be delivered to the organization as well as on direct interventions, in the client's language and focused on their problem.

Given the ongoing growth of Fujitsu Services through acquisition, change management is a key responsibility of business partners and a range of tools and methods are applied to achieve effective integration. Use of a change network map helps clarify key roles and responsibilities for sponsors and change agents. Force field analysis and behavioural profiling are just two of a range of other tools in regular use which help focus effort appropriately. These help all concerned take a strategic approach to organizational design and development. Behavioural profiling, for instance, is a means of creating culture audits. It is then possible to decide the target profile of the new organization and the initiatives required to achieve that.

HR's other key focus is on directly supporting business development. As a provider of professional services to other companies and public sector organizations, Fujitsu Services is active globally providing near-shoring, off-shoring and outsourced solutions. As a result of supporting bids the HR team has amassed a wealth of experience of the Transfer of Undertakings (Protection of Employment) or TUPE and business transformation which it is putting to good use not only within Fujitsu Services but as an external consultancy in its own right providing HR business outsourcing. HR operates as a profit centre and external consultancy is becoming a major part of senior HR practitioners' roles. Andy Montrose (2007), Fujitsu's Head of HR, UK Public Sector, for example spends about 80% of his time being externally facing and is supported by a team providing the resources required.

In switching from a product-based economy to a people-based economy, Fujitsu Services is at the forefront of knowledge-intensive organizations in coming to grips with a new business model fit for the twenty-first century. The people-based economy has greatly enhanced the importance of HR to the business. HR's ability to effectively manage change and to build talent strategies that work puts it rightly at the top table. As HR's evolution continues, business partners will be contributing directly to the bottom line. Being demand-led and equipping HR and its clients for success clearly works!

HR COMPETENCIES

HR practitioners can and do carry out a range of roles, variously described as strategist, mentor, talent scout, architect, builder, facilitator, coordinator, champion of change. The art is to have the awareness of, and flexibility for what is needed in different situations. Many an HR strategist takes up a new role in an organization that is apparently ripe for change but has deeply embedded practices that are difficult to shift. The strategist usually experiences great frustration as he or she sees their attempts to bring about change wither away. The pragmatist works within this context to make change happen at the pace which is likely to lead to the embedding of new approaches, rather than seeking to bring about widespread initiatives in order to make their mark.

The skills of the HR specialists are key to the effective development and implementation of people strategies. First and foremost, professionals need to be credible, demonstrating good understanding of the business and able to translate business needs into their organizational implications. Credibility is often gained or lost on the ability to both shape strategy and implement it.

While line management is responsible for the growth and operation of the business, HR has a key role to play in partnering with the line to prepare the organization and its employees for future challenges. This is where HR operational effectiveness is enhanced by a strategic perspective. Strategic thinking is clearly essential if HR professionals are to be capable of making the decisions to drive the organization forward. This requires developing a tolerance of ambiguity and a willingness to take risks.

Winning the right to contribute strategically comes from delivering results. HR functions need to systematically assess and improve all basic HR processes. This requires focusing on improving administrative services and separating them from strategic tasks in order to increase efficiency and effectiveness. HR Operations should then be managed, monitored and measured in the same way any other business process would be.

If HR is to truly act as a business partner, specialists need to really understand the business and be able to reflect that understanding in their actions. For example, for Ulrich and Brockbank (2005) an HR perspective that is both unique and powerful is one that establishes the linkages between employee commitment, customer attitudes and investor returns. Basic consultancy skills, such as gaining entry and diagnosis, should be part of the professional toolkit. Being able to use data effectively to make a convincing case is part of the HR toolkit. Good analytical skills are also important, so that HR can use relevant metrics and understand the implications of trend data. While HR generalists do not need to be experts, they should be able to use creative approaches to designing HR processes that really meet needs.

Similarly, part of the art of the HR business partner is knowing when to take the lead in initiating a new people-related process and when to begin by building line ownership; how to build the corporate from the local and vice versa. This means that HR has to be on the look-out for useful initiatives that have begun elsewhere in the organization which can be built on in order to create greater coherence and avoid 'death by a thousand initiatives'.

More importantly, HR professionals need to be able to manage culture, recognizing what needs to be maintained, strengthened or changed, as well as to manage change. The skills of bringing about change extend beyond being able to take a longer-term view. Project management skills and the ability to work successfully in cross-boundary teams can be essential to effective delivery of outcomes. They need to be able to cope well with change and help others to do so. They need to understand their organization's cultures and be able to work out – with others – what needs to be strengthened, because it supports what the organization wants to do and what does need to be changed.

Perhaps the core expertise for strategic roles lies in managing ongoing change and working with managers to develop a robust and resilient workforce able to thrive on change. Project and programme management skills are essential. Bringing about change requires HR specialists to be able to influence key players and to have the confidence to challenge. This means being politically aware and being prepared to use various forms of influence, including power, to get the job done. Of course, the most easily available form of power is personal power, which stems largely from an individual's personality. This kind of power is reflected in being respected as a professional, being a team player and being the kind of person who is trusted and to whom people at all levels can turn. We shall return to the subject of HR skills in Chapter 12.

Prioritizing the HR agenda does require stepping out of the vicious cycle of constant delivery in order to choose the key areas of focus if value is really to be added. Radical choices may or may not be the consequence, but you do not know until you try. According to Keith Walton, a member of IBM's management consulting unit, 'HR is traditionally seen as a cost. If you can separate the operational from the strategic, you can see that the strategic side adds value.'

CHECKLISTS ON THE ROLE OF HR

From Operational to Strategic

The following questions are intended to offer the basis for an HR team self-assessment:

Expectations of the Role of HR

- What business are we in? What should we be in? Who are our customers?
- How do our customers perceive our services?

- What are managers' and employees' expectations of HR?
- In reengineering processes, what are the implications for roles and responsibilities of HR professionals?
- In what ways can managers and HR specialists work more closely to link strategy and personnel practice?
- If we had fewer services, do we know what trade-offs our customers would be willing to make?

Adding Value

Test Question:
Would you manage HR differently if your personal circumstances were impacted upon directly by bottom-line performance?

- What current organizational or managerial issues, if resolved, could result in substantial business improvement?
- Where do we add value? Proportionately how much time do we spend on value-adding activities?
- What is the relationship between cost and value of the work we perform?
- (How) do we invest in HR practices that deliver business results?
- What does our organization need from HR currently – and in the next few years?
- What changes could we make to increase the effectiveness of HR in our organization?
    How will we measure the success of reengineering efforts?
    How will we let people know?
    How should we structure HR to add value?
    What should be the ratio of HR to the line?

Changing the Focus of HR

- Where are we now in terms of our HR function?
- How much does IT play a part in our overall HR strategy?
- Who will champion reengineering efforts?
- In what ways will reengineered processes be superior to existing ones?
- In moving from operational to strategic, how should the gap be filled, and by whom?
- If we devolve aspects of HR to the line, how do we maintain consistency?
- How should line managers be prepared for their role?
    What should we offer?
    What new competencies and skills do we need?
    What flexible practices will enable us to shift from operational to strategic?

The Influence of HR

- Is HR represented on the management board or involved in actually devising the HR strategy?

- Which body makes the strategic decisions in practice?
- How does that body receive information about, and take decisions on, managing people? How is HR involved?
- Will the organization give a higher or lower priority to managing people in the next five years?
- If the priority will be lower, what impact will that have on retention of key people?
- If we change what we do, which process would we begin with?
- How will we minimize resistance to change?
- How shall we deal with managers who cannot make the transition?

REFERENCES

Brockbank, W. (1997) HR's future on the way to a presence. *Human Resource Management*, Spring 36, No. 1, 65–69

CIPD (2005) *HR Outsourcing: The Key Decisions*. London: Chartered Institute of Personnel and Development

Hammer, M. and Champy, J. (1993) *Reengineering the Corporation: A Manifesto for Business Revolution*. New York: Harper Business

Lawler, E. and Mohrman, S. (2003) HR as strategic partner. *Human Resource Planning*, 26, No. 3, 15–29

Montrose, A. (2007) *HR Business Partner Conference presentation*, 19 October: Roffey Park Management Institute

Parry, W.E., Tyson, S., Selbie, D. and Leighton, R.K. (2007) *HR and Technology: Impact and Advantages*. London: Chartered Institute of Personnel and Development

Reddington, M., Williamson, M. and Withers, M. (2006) *Transforming HR: Creating Value Through People*. Oxford: Butterworth-Heinemann

Reilly, P. (2007) *HR Roles in Transition*. London: Chartered Institute of Personnel and Development

Reilly, P. and Tamkin, P. (2007) *The Changing HR Function: Transforming HR?* London: CIPD

Ulrich, D. (1997) *Human Resource Champions: The Next Agenda for Adding Value and Delivering Results*. Cambridge, MA: Harvard Business School Press

Ulrich, D., interviewed by MacLachlan, R. (1998) HR with attitude, *People Management*, 13 August

Ulrich, D. and Brockbank, W. (2005) *The HR Value Proposition*. Boston, MA: Harvard Business School Press

Ulrich, D., Brookbank, W., Yeung, A.K. and Lake, D.G. (1995) Human Resource competencies: an empirical assessment. *Human Resource Management*, 34, No. 4, 473–495

Walton, R.E. (1985) From control to commitment in the workplace. *Harvard Business Review*, 63, No. 2, 77–84

Weatherley, L. (2005) *HR Technology: Leveraging the Shift to Self-service: It's Time to Go Strategic*. Alexandria, VA: Society for Human Resource Management

Yeung, A.K. and Brockbank, W. (1998) Reengineering HR through information technology. *Human Resource Planning*, 18, No. 2, 24–37

Chapter 4

Measuring the Impact of Strategic HRM

The only HR actions which have value in any organization are those which contribute to the achievement of its goals.

(Phelps, 1998)

For many Human Resource practitioners, it's an act of faith that people management is a key factor in determining profitability and HR practitioners are under pressure to prove that value is being added by HR activities. Implementing effective people management and knowing which approaches are working is difficult enough; assessing how much effective people management impacts on the bottom line is even more difficult. Even during talent shortages, the great debate about how to measure human capital and what to measure rumbles on, somewhat inconclusively.

Amongst investors there appears to be a self-fulfilling prophecy at work: since there is little evidence of comparability, consistency or predictability in workforce metrics, these are easily discounted. Even when well-meaning executives are sincere in their belief that employees count, they are often at a loss as to how to translate this belief into policies and practices which work well, both for the business and for individuals. People-related metrics are easily dismissed.

Part of the problem is that the dominant means of measuring and assessing organizational success are quantitative and financial. After all, what is valued, or seen as critical, tends to be what is measured and reported. So much of what is reported as 'fact', i.e. financial performance data, fails to explain how the figures have been achieved. Since so many people management practices are intangible, and are therefore treated as invisible or 'soft', evidence of the link between these practices and business results often appears indirect and non-explicit. Without 'hard' proof of the link with business results, belief that good people management is critical can remain at the 'hunch' level. Should all investment in training for instance be required to produce a measurable return on investment (ROI)?

Even though strategists often condemn the narrow focus on financial data as 'driving with the rear-view mirror', the general trend among management teams and boards is to use measures which track familiar sorts of data. These may seem to offer fewer risks than those which appear unproven, especially when the only company results that tend to be publicly reported reflect the short-term bottom line. Of course, setting measures based solely on 'lag', i.e. retrospective performance, is unlikely to lead to business success in changing times. The real challenge is to identify and report on the 'lead' measures – parameters for future success as well meeting the need for control in the here and now.

THE BUSINESS CASE FOR ADDRESSING EMPLOYEE NEEDS

The growing recognition that financial performance is based on various other forms of performance – almost all of which are carried out by human beings – is evident in the growth of performance-measurement models. Acceptance of the business case for investing in the 'soft' employee issues, such as communications and training, appears to be accelerating. In the UK, the Investors in People (IiP) movement has long highlighted the importance of employees to business and social success and the number of organizations seeking to achieve or maintain their IiP status is growing. IiP has become a prestigious accolade and many of the leading organizations in all sectors can now claim to have achieved IiP status. Indeed, the UK Labour Party has achieved IiP accreditation and government departments are being encouraged to gain IiP status. This is to be achieved against a backdrop of ongoing change and the reshaping of public services to achieve a key feature in achieving the UK government's objectives.

Arie de Geus, the world-renowned strategic planner, contends that 'economic' companies whose focus is predominantly short term and bottom-line driven are likely to be outpaced by so-called 'living' companies which base their decisions on the company's and employees' potential as a living entity (see Chambers, 1997). He argues that if managers wish to extend a company's lifespan they must focus on developing brain-rich companies that can adapt to a changing environment. This involves forming relationships with employees and using conservative financing to govern their growth.

Indeed, Professor Jeffrey Pfeffer (1995) of the Stanford Graduate School of Business argues that the basis for competitive success has changed. In a rapidly changing marketplace deregulation of industries such as the airlines, telecommunications and the financial services has led to a proliferation of competition from many quarters. Protected markets are disappearing and the technologically-driven demand for ever-more innovative products makes many products quickly obsolete.

Traditional sources of competitive advantage such as investing heavily in capital equipment or aiming for economies of scale have become less important in this era of mass customization. Customers want goods and services which are tailored to their needs but they do not wish to pay premium prices for those goods. For Jeffrey Pfeffer 'what remains as a source of competitive advantage, in part because it is difficult to imitate and in part because other sources of success have been eroded by competition, is organizational culture and capability, embodied in the workforce'. If Pfeffer's assertion is correct, the importance of strategic Human Resource activity should not be underestimated. In the UK there is also increasing research evidence that there are substantial returns to managing the workforce effectively.

Ulrich and Brockbank (2005) also highlight the role of HR as a source of competitive advantage. Competitive advantage exists when a firm is able to do something unique that competitors cannot easily copy. And what it does better than its competitors must be highly valued by its customers, owners, employees, or managers. The creation of competitive advantage can be simplified as the 'wallet test', i.e. what customers will willingly pay for because they perceive value and what subsequently adds value to investors. Ulrich and Brockbank argue that HR passes the wallet test when it creates human abilities and organizational capabilities that are substantially better than those of the firm's competitors – and thus move customers and shareholders to reach for their wallets.

The UK's CIPD (Patterson *et al.*, 1997) commissioned research that was carried out by the Institute of Work Psychology at Sheffield University and the Centre for Economic Performance at the London School of Economics. The findings suggest a strong link between good people management practice and business results. The research, carried out in more than 100 medium-sized UK firms, found that people management is not only essential to the success of an organization but also that it outstrips technology, quality and competitive strategy in its impact on the bottom line (see Pfeffer, 1995).

The CIPD findings suggest that good personnel policies and practices can improve productivity and performance by enhancing skills and giving people responsibility for making the best use of their skills, but the combination of policies and practices which produces these effects varies by context.

WHAT TO MEASURE?

There is widespread confusion about what measures should be used for what kinds of analysis. For example, some studies, including Brewster, Hegewisch and Lockhart (1991), have suggested measures for assessing the strategic importance of HRM, such as whether there is an HR specialist in the top management team, the role of the line in HR responsibilities and the contribution of HR to the development of business strategy. Other studies have focused much more on specific aspects of human resource management and development.

Level of Impact?

Various theorists, including Boudreau and Ramstead (2003), suggest that, whatever the 'content', the focus of measurement should be on efficiency, effectiveness or impact. Reilly and Williams (2006) propose a balanced approach to assessing performance which combines both efficiency and effectiveness, both from the people management and from HR's functional perspective. Key for them is measuring both what is within the domain of management (such as retention and engagement) and what is within the domain of HR (such as policy formulation and execution).

CMI suggests a three-tier model of different levels of metrics which provides a useful framework for understanding the value and application of workforce and Human Capital Management (HCM) measures:

- Basic measures – quantitative data and employee profile statistics
- Standard comparable analytic measures – comparable quantitative data indicating contribution to performance
- Strategic measures of workforce capability – capable of reflecting alignment of workforce capability to business strategy.

These are not comparable and depend on an organization's life cycle and strategic context but it is these measures, CMI argues, that are of the greatest value to stakeholders. At the same time, the quest to find some common measures which establish the link between good people management and organizational performance continues.

Human Capital Indicators and their Underlying Factors

CIPD research confirms strong ties between attitudes and performance and highlights two areas of HR practice which above all relate to improvements in productivity and profitability. These are the acquisition and development of skills (through induction, training, selection and appraisal practices) and job design (as assessed by the degree of teamwork, flexibility, autonomy, responsibility, problem-solving and variety). In the firms studied it became evident that enabling employees to use their creativity in practical ways, leading to business innovation and improvements, was a feature of the more successful companies. Ironically, the average cycle time in many organizations is so short that employees' roles are constrained, preventing the realization of some of the capability of employees.

The CMI highlights five key areas of HCM which directors, stakeholders and investors agree are most likely to affect the future performance of organizations:

- Leadership
- Employee motivation
- Training and development
- Performance improvement
- Pay and reward structures.

Leadership, training and development and employee motivation appear to be the three most important measures of workforce in indicating future financial performance of organization by sector, geographical market and size (Scott-Jackson *et al.*, 2006).

Similarly, Bassi and McMurrer (2005) recommend a set of human capital indicators which they consider to be central to the management of a knowledge-based workforce:

Leadership practices
- Communication – managers and executives
- Inclusiveness – managers and executives
- Supervisory skills
- Executive leadership
- Systems – for identifying and developing the next generation of leaders

Employee engagement
- Job design
- Commitment to employees
- Time – does the workload allow employees to do their jobs right; make thoughtful decisions; and achieve an appropriate balance between work and home?
- Systems – and processes to retain good performers by continually evaluating trends in employee engagement and using this information to determine the key drivers of productivity and customer satisfaction

Knowledge accessibility
- Availability
- Collaboration and teamwork
- Information-sharing
- Systems – that collect and store information and make it available to all employees who might need it

Learning capacity
- Innovation
- Training
- Development
- Value and support – i.e. the behaviour of leaders which consistently demonstrates that learning is valued and managers make learning a priority
- Systems – i.e. a learning management system that automates the administration of all aspects of training/learning events, provides reports to management and includes features such as content management or competency management

Workforce optimization
- Processes – well-defined and that help get work done; where employees are well trained on these processes and efforts made continually to improve processes
- Conditions – where employees have the materials and technologies they need to be effective
- Accountability – where employees are held accountable for producing quality work; promotion is based on competence; poor performance

    appropriately handled and employees trust their co-workers to get the job done

- Hiring decisions – selection is based on skills requirements; new hires receive adequate induction
- Systems – and processes are in place for managing employees' performance and talents. These help employees realize their full performance potential in their current jobs; identify development opportunities for those experiencing performance difficulties and prepare motivated employees to progress their career fields.

Of these various factors, Bassi and McMurrer's (2005) research suggests that leadership practices are often a 'binding constraint' on other aspects of human capital management and development. The absence of leadership practice may be limiting both the use of, and the return to, employee skills-building. The negative effect of lack of leadership is particularly noticeable with respect to learning capacity and knowledge accessibility measures. This is then something of a vicious circle, since without effective leadership there tends to be an under-investment in employee training and vice versa. These authors argue that investments in leadership skills would lead to improved human capital management and yield an exponentially high return for organizations that have a deficiency in this regard.

Other research, by performance development consultants Lane4, focuses more specifically on return on investment (ROI) around key HRM practices. However, they too found that the top three areas that HR directors wanted to measure in terms of ROI were improved leadership, skills development and employee engagement. Again, the same research suggests that 68% of HR Directors and business leaders surveyed found difficulty translating the benefits of training into financial figures and many considered attempting to do so was both costly and time-consuming. Indeed it might be argued that restricting the measurement of ROI to finances is too narrow and that achieving improved scores for customer service and employee engagement are desirable ends in themselves.

Moreover, employers are still often inconsistent in how they measure human capital and use systems and methods that are too complicated and confusing, according to the CMI study. A clear gap emerged between what was valued by Directors and Analysts and what was actually analysed:

- Only 68% measured the contribution made by the whole workforce and fewer still (53%) focused on the impact of senior management.
- The survey explored 45 different workforce factors, but while more than eight out 10 respondents claimed to examine static measurements such as 'total employment cost', just two out of 10 measured dynamic indicators such as 'evidence of absence management' or 'talent management'.

These low levels of measurement were admitted despite respondents believing that each issue had strategic importance to future performance.

Measuring the Success of a Talent Management Programme

The fact that it is difficult to link changes to profitability should not prevent measurement providing an understanding of what has been achieved by, for example, a talent management programme. The important thing is not to focus only on data related to the activity and the process, but on what is being achieved by these with respect to the HR objectives for the organization as a whole.

According to Likierman (2007) it is important to first define the differences between talent management and what HR does anyway; establish how this links to corporate objectives, not those of HR; then break down 'talent management' into its constituent parts (e.g. proportion of posts covered by the programme, choices available for vacant posts etc.) to form the basis of effective measures. It is also essential to consult with senior and line managers to shape their expectations, avoiding the temptation to overstate what can be achieved by the talent management programme.

The next task is to improve the data, which starts with ensuring that your database provides the right variables in the right timescale – i.e. that these link with the organization's strategy. New measures could arise for instance from surveys and exit interviews. In any event, the data needs to be targeted and at the right level of detail to ensure that the right conclusions can be drawn.

Comparisons can then be made between similar internal divisions or units, as well as externally as a result of swapping data on other talent management programmes or elements, such as selection criteria and the definition of high potential. It is useful to set up a series of 'monitorable' (i.e. not necessarily quantitative) milestones which will show comparisons with the original plan.

The focus should be on outputs and outcomes, not activity. Output measures will generally be interview-based and could include interviews of employees and their line managers and the results of exit interviews. They could also come from regular reporting and feedback on issues such as retention and employee engagement. Indicative outcome measures include the numbers of candidates available for internal posts, how easy it is to make internal appointments to identified key posts and how the programme contributes to organizational success compared with competitor organizations over time. Measurement should be accompanied by a commentary to explain any gap between what was hoped for and actual performance. Likierman suggests that the commentary should take into account external factors such as the competitive environment so that the changes in the employment market can be taken into account when discussing the results of the programme.

Auditing Organizational Capabilities

Ulrich and Smallwood (2004) argue strongly that what organizations should be measuring is not specific approaches to management or individual HR practices but organizational capabilities, such as the ability to innovate, or respond to changing customer needs. These 'intangibles' are what drive growth. These authors suggest that an organizational capability is a bundle of activities, rather than a single factor to be measured. They offer the following capability framework as the basis for audit:

- *Talent* – do our employees have the competencies and the commitment required to deliver the business strategy in question?
- *Speed* – can we move quickly to make important things happen fast?
- *Shared mindset* – do we have a culture or identity that reflects what we stand for and how we work? Is it shared by both customers and employees?
- *Accountability* – does high performance matter here to the extent that we can ensure execution of strategy?
- *Collaboration* – how well do we collaborate to gain both efficiency and leverage?
- *Learning* – are we good at generating new ideas with impact and generalizing these ideas across boundaries?
- *Leadership* – do we have a leadership brand that directs managers on what results to deliver and how to deliver them?
- *Customer connectivity* – do we form enduring relationships of trust with targeted customers?
- *Strategic unity* – do our employees share an intellectual, behavioural and procedural agenda for strategy?
- *Innovation* – how well do we innovate in product, strategy, channel, service and administration?
- *Efficiency* – do we reduce costs by closely managing process, people and projects?

The audit allows leaders to focus in on a few targeted capabilities with the aim of making these world class. Ulrich and Smallwood recommend gathering data from multiple groups on current and desired capabilities. The data should then be synthesized, patterns analysed to identify the most critical capabilities requiring managerial attention. The three most important capabilities required to deliver strategy goals should then be brought to the attention of leaders, identifying which will have most impact as well as which will be the easiest to implement. Then an action plan should be put together, with clear steps to take and measures to monitor, preferably within a ninety day timeframe.

PREDICTORS OF BUSINESS RESULTS

Employee Satisfaction

The CIPD research highlights the predictive nature of employee satisfaction for business results. Satisfaction was based on many aspects of working life, such as recognition for good work, pay and conditions and relationships with supervisors and team members. This indicates that effective people management is about more than traditional HR practices such as training and has to take into account a wide range of aspects of employee satisfaction, including employee needs for growth and development. While the job satisfaction of individuals is typically a poor indicator of performance, the researchers found that it is the overall levels of satisfaction across staff which seem to affect business performance.

The Organization as Community

Another predictor of business success is how employees see their company as a community, where people feel socially included rather than alienated. In particular, the more successful organizations in the research were ones where there was a positive 'human relations' climate brought about by concern for welfare, the removal of status barriers, good communication, high-quality training and respect for employees. Kwik-Fit, for example, enjoys a high reputation within the motor repair industry for honest dealing and excellent customer service. The company's substantial sales and profit growth reflect the customer reaction to Kwik-Fit and its services. Employees are encouraged to delight the customer and have the freedom to respond to immediate customer requirements. Each Kwik-Fit location builds links with the local community and has a high degree of delegation of responsibility so that small groups can make a difference. It remains to be seen whether the 'community' feel of Kwik-Fit's operations can be maintained since its recent acquisition by Ford.

Research by the Gallup Organization about Great Managers and Great Workplaces (Buckingham and Coffman, 1999) also suggests that measures linked with employee satisfaction, such as turnover, are predictive of profitability. Gallup's research had a focus on four outcome variables: employee retention, customer satisfaction, productivity and profitability. Researchers noticed that organizational excellence was based on high-performing workgroups, rather than the organization as a whole. They found that a number of situational factors such as pay, parking, etc. which are often elements of an organizational strategy, do not make a difference to the most productive workgroups in the companies studied. What did matter were a number of factors which are more firmly the responsibility of managers, with HR support.

The Right Roles and Recognition

These factors included employees being clear what is expected of them through the setting of explicit expectations by the manager. However, individuals need to find their own way of achieving these expectations if they are to feel ownership of their job. Managers therefore need to be able to judge how to help each employee take responsibility and be able to get the best out of the different members of their teams. Employees also need to have access to the resources and equipment to do their work effectively. They need to be offered roles which make the best use of their talents. Matching the right person to the right job is a challenge for many managers, and the support of HR to enable managers to make the best use of talent can be vital. This is particularly the case with another key factor – helping people to develop. The researchers also found that praise and recognition are critical: 'the new knowledge-based worker relies and depends upon praise and recognition as the means of defining what is valued by the organization'.

HOLISTIC FRAMEWORKS – THE BUSINESS EXCELLENCE MODEL AND THE BALANCED SCORECARD

Recognition that effective performance management is key to the achievement of business results has been popularized in two influential models which have been adopted by many organizations to good effect. The Business Excellence model suggests clear links between business outputs (results) and organizational inputs, such as leadership and effective people management. The model provides a means of measuring and tracking the impact of employee-related initiatives on the bottom line.

Measures should be set around both the 'outputs' and the 'enablers' so that progress can be tracked. The Business Excellence model can be used to measure all aspects of a set of integrated HR processes, including training and development. The balanced scorecard advocates a top-down approach to business performance management, starting with business strategic intent expressed through the organization down to operationally relevant targets. It 'translates an organization's mission and strategy into a comprehensive set of performance measures that provides the framework for a strategic measurement and management system' (Kaplan and Norton, 1998).

Very widely adopted by major companies such as BP, BAT, Sainsbury, Microsoft, the scorecard typically shows how the financial bottom line of an organization is not obtained as a simple accounting exercise but that performance is needed in each of several perspectives if financial success is to be achieved. First and foremost, all these key areas need to be pulling in the same direction – that of the vision and strategy of the organization. Strategic goals, critical success factors and measures need to be established in all scorecard areas.

The Scorecard perspectives are:

- Customers, and the activities required to ensure that service matches customer needs as well as the vision
- Learning and growth, and the activities required to build sustainable growth
- Internal business processes and the careful prioritization of key business processes at which the organization can excel
- Financial, and the activities required to succeed financially in the eyes of shareholders.

The Scorecard is dynamic and should reflect the specific needs of an organization at a point in time. Indeed, different parts of an organization may have different scorecards depending on their circumstances and priorities. In some organizations, the scorecard notion is used to develop real-time personal scorecards. Some parts of the corporate scorecard may have greater priority at some times more than at others.

The process for developing a balanced scorecard is as follows:

1. Establish the vision
2. Determine strategic goals
3. Analyse each goal – what critical success factors (CSF) influence the goal
4. Assign at least one measure per factor
5. Assign a target for the current budget exercise.

When organizations establish a 'vision', 3–5 strategic goals are set to focus the organization's efforts over the next 3–5 years. With the Balanced Scorecard, there can be 3–5 goals per focus area, each broken down into a number of factors that influence that area. Business objectives need to reflect the critical success factors (CSFs) which are internal or external features of the organization's environment which have a major impact on achieving the organization's aims and are vital for a strategy to be successful. According to Jack F. Rockart (1979), there are four basic types of critical success factors:

1. Industry
2. Strategy
3. Environmental
4. Temporal

Then key performance indicators (KPI) need to be set. KPIs are measures that *quantify* management objectives and enable the measurement of strategic performance in meeting their CSFs.

An example:

- KPI = Number of new customers
- CSF = Installation of a call centre for providing quotations

The measures used to manage the performance of a business typically comprise the following:

- **Strategic measures:** market attractiveness (industry structure, growth, concentration, innovation, customer power, logistical complexity) and competitive strength (relative market share, relative quality; intellectual property, customer coverage).
- **Organizational measures:** culture, leanness, incentives, training and development, structure, purpose, process.
- **Operational measures:** customer satisfaction, product or service excellence, capacity utilization, capital intensity, productivity, outsourcing.

Depending on the emphasis placed on different measures in an organization, its information and performance measures can vary between operational fixed (for example, the 99% replenishment rate on the shelves of a Sainsbury's store) and strategic flexible (for example, Microsoft's goal of standards ownership on the information superhighway). According to this method, an Objective (tactical aim) is composed of a CSF plus a KPI plus a target.

The key message behind these models is that financial success does not occur in a vacuum and that all areas of the Scorecard have to be attended to if success is to be achieved. They therefore need to be carefully measured, tracked and potentially require investment.

THE EXECUTIVE SCORECARD

This scorecard has been devised by Saratoga Europe, part of Saratoga Worldwide, to examine the same perspectives as the Balanced Scorecard but viewed from an HR focus. Saratoga has amassed a databank of human resource measures and benchmark data from its client group. The assumption is that 'anything we do with people in any organizational setting ought to have some output and eventual impact upon results'. Data are gathered against some ninety human resource measures to assess impact on:

- Improved production
- Cost reduction
- Quicker cycle times
- Improved quality
- Positive reactions from human beings.

The Saratoga measures, both quantitative and qualitative, are grouped under the following categories of key human resource activities in which there are clear measures of success:

- Organizational effectiveness (revenue, cost, profit and added value per employee)
- Compensation and benefits
- Recruitment
- Absenteeism and turnover
- Training and development
- Occupational health and safety.

The assumption is that if employees are working effectively, they will add value through their positive effect on customers, who will in turn purchase more and produce a positive impact on the bottom line and, where appropriate, improved shareholder value. These can be measured through increased revenue growth, customer retention, etc. Conversely, where employee commitment and competence are low, there is likely to be a negative effect on the bottom line. Indicative measures would include negative customer reaction, absenteeism, turnover, etc. The Saratoga approach is to develop a strategic improvement cycle using researched people criteria incorporating internal performance trends and external benchmarks. Client organizations can then benchmark themselves against other organizations to assess their relative positions. Typical target positioning includes revenue per employee – top 25% – and cost per employee – bottom 25%.

AVOIDING MEASUREMENT FRENZY

The pressure on HR departments to prove that they add value tends to push practitioners into a measurement frenzy. One way to avoid becoming lost in a bureaucratic muddle of measures which are difficult to make sense of is to use a tool such as Activity Based Costing of the HR function. This approach focuses on identifying the key activities to be measured and checking the potential knock-on effects on other aspects of HR provision of measuring only certain activities in order to avoid 'skewing' the data or causing unintended consequences.

For example, in the UK the East Sussex Police Force, like all other UK police forces, was subject to government-imposed targets and measures on response times to emergencies. What the East Sussex police noticed was that, in order to comply with response targets, they were having to drive faster than was advisable and the number of accidents involving police vehicles rose. The police took the decision to revise the government targets at local level so that they could achieve an acceptable response time with far fewer accidents.

HR activities regarded as key should be linked with other organizational functions to develop clarity about how HR contributes to performance in other parts of the organization. These measures are then integrated to produce a holistic picture of how HR's contribution is integral to the success of other parts of the business. The emphasis should be on measuring the impact of HR-related policies and actions using business language.

Calculating the return on investment from HR is extremely difficult, even with a superficially straightforward equation such as:

$$ROI = \frac{Benefit - Cost}{Cost \times 100\%}$$

This kind of equation is usually applied to apparently discrete areas of HR activity such as the evaluation of training. The difficulty with trying to prove the real and longer-term differences which training and other HR activities can make to an organization's effectiveness is that there are so many other variables to take into account. Therefore, making firm claims about the value of an individual activity can seem specious to people who need to be convinced by numbers. That is not to say that measuring activities and trying to assess the effect of HR interventions is a waste of time. However, measurement should ideally be used to help HR select the functions and processes for action which are real priorities for the business and where there is the maximum possibility of creating a direct impact on the bottom line.

Take a notoriously 'loose' concept such as empowerment, for instance. Effective empowerment initiatives are aimed at improving an organization's bottom line by giving employees the freedom to make decisions and by treating employees as partners. Unfortunately many organizations do not achieve this goal because they fail to measure empowerment and link it to their costs and profit (Ettore, 1997). HR has a key role to play in ensuring that management understands what empowerment is really about and that measures are set which are linked to strategic goals and processes as well as to individual accountability. HR also needs to identify and set in place ways of tracking the impact of other elements known to be essential to the success of empowerment programmes such as stable leadership at the top, few redundancies, profit-sharing and power-sharing schemes and emphasis on innovation at all levels.

WORKFORCE MEASURES

The following are adapted from examples of workforce measures identified as useful by Scott-Jackson and Tajer (2005):

Corporate values
- A vision, mission or values statement
- An HR/People Management strategy that is demonstrably linked to the organization's vision, mission and values and business plan
- Objectives within the People Management strategy that are SMART, project managed and evaluated

Organizational profile
- Pay bill for the organization (as a proportion of capital employed/turnover)
- Head count
- Workforce expressed as full time equivalents (FTEs)
- Workforce expressed as % full- and part-time
- Workforce expressed by age band

Leadership
- Overall cost of leadership development – evidence of competencies, evaluation, benefits etc.
- Evidence of leadership pipeline and succession planning

Performance improvement
- Commitment to EFQM, Investors in People etc.

Recruitment
- Number recruited and at what levels
- Overall cost of recruitment
- Number black and minority (BME) ethnic groups recruited

With respect to recruitment, consultants SHL argue that the next-generation recruiting solutions, e.g. outsourcing, will offer consistent and effective measures that link recruitment directly to contributions of individuals and the company overall. They consider that there is a value pyramid with regard to recruitment processes, with different metrics applied to each level of value. For example, at the lowest level – *processing applicant data, sifting out unsuitable candidates and identifying the best candidate(s)* – metrics can be applied to 'traditional savings' to demonstrate streamlining, reduced time (therefore staff costs) and less paperwork. Medium-value tasks that are clearly measurable can be tied to savings in terms of reduced churn and recruitment costs, although they still relate directly to the bottom line. High measurable values are those which focus on people, jobs and organizations at every level, and show improved performance, an increased top line and demonstrable enhancements directly related to people (higher sales/greater potential revenue/productivity) and value (profitability/share price). SHL argue that such sustaining organizational value metrics will lead organizations to a long-term Human Capital Management programme.

Training and development
- Overall costs of training and development activities
- Average spend per employee
- Access of staff from minority groups to training and development activities
- Evidence of performance needs analysis against competencies, training design and evaluation
- Personal Development Plans (PDPs) which comply with the business plan
- Training evaluated for impact post event

Performance appraisal
- Percentage held on time
- Succession plans
- Personal development plans achieved

Retention
- Overall percentage of leavers and hard numbers (including trends in specific business areas/departments)
- Percentage of leavers by BME, gender, sexual orientation, disability as a percentage of their numbers within the organization
- If available, cost of turnover overall and per employee
- Average length of service and standard deviations

Staff motivation
- Headlines on staff opinion survey
- Number of grievances, Employment Tribunals

Pay and reward structures
- Details of incentives, to include work–life balance
- Employee support statistics, e.g. health provision/employee facilities

Diversity – percentage of workforce
- From BME groups, by gender, with disability/impairment (as per Disability Discrimination Act), by sexual orientation (where disclosed)
- From each of these groups by organizational level

Absenteeism
- Number of days lost per employee (average)
- Percentage of days lost as a result of stress-related absence

- Total cost to the organization of such absences
- Clear evidence of management of absence
- Provision of occupational health facilities
- Evidence of health and safety and stress management strategies

Ideally, all HR activity should be classified according to the level of importance and impact on the organization (Figure 4.1). This will allow practitioners to determine which activities are core, which are administrative and which are critical. Taking a hard look at which activities must remain an essential part of the HR portfolio and which might be outsourced is a first step. Working out the relative costs and payback periods for the investment made is a next step. Of course, much strategic HR activity, whether it is change management, succession planning, or training and development, has much longer payback periods than the normal business cycle. Nevertheless, the payback of HR activities should result in significant competitive advantage for the organization. Maurice Phelps (1998) of Saratoga Europe suggests that 'payback means measurable improved performance, and for your people that payback can only show through in improved organizational performance'. This means demonstrating an improving performance relationship against others competing in the same markets and servicing the same customers.

This is where HR practitioners who feel obliged to justify their existence need to master the art of collecting and presenting people-related data in a way

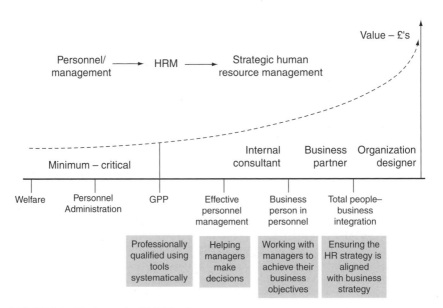

FIGURE 4.1 Moving up the HR ROI scale.
Source: Paul Kearns, *The Bottom Line HR Function* (Chandos, 2001)

which makes clear the business benefits of investing in longer-term returns in order to secure the organization's future viability. Employee behaviour needs to be measured in output terms, so that the links with hard business performance can be understood.

Similarly, HR needs to be able to apply risk management techniques to the different aspects of HR strategies. What would happen if recruitment were not carried out strategically, but dealt with in a stop-gap way? What would be the cost of failing to retain groups of key workers during a period of organizational turbulence? What would be the dangers to the organization of not developing individuals with the organizational knowledge as well as the skills to be the future business leaders? A key area of business partnership for HR is to translate employee-related policies into practice in a way that really makes a difference to the business and its employees. These policies need to help establish the link between what the business aims to achieve and the way in which employees are managed and enabled to achieve those aims. The policies should reflect the organization's strategy at the highest level, with detailed HR goals, targets and measures cascading from this.

BENCHMARKING

Part of the business of data gathering is to know how well your HR provision compares with the 'best' HR practices elsewhere and for this, benchmarking can be a useful tool. Benchmarking gains a bad press when organizations use it for the purposes of copying 'best practice' from one organization and try to apply the ideas wholesale in another. However, benchmarking can be a means of finding out what exactly is meant by 'added value' in different contexts, how this is measured and HR's role in adding that value.

Benchmarking is, in general terms, the comparison of aspects of one organization's business or practices with those of other organizations. It should be an ongoing process of measuring products, services and operating practices against competitors or those considered as market leaders and is very much linked to a philosophy of continuous improvement. Benchmarking is often specifically aimed at comparing product quality so that improvements to one's own processes can be identified and implemented. In some cases, comparisons are made with firms whose products may not be the same. So a computer firm, for example, might compare its indicators with those of a biscuit manufacturer. Aspects of the organization's processes are compared to find where other firms gain speed, efficiency, quality or cost savings from their process.

Benchmarking allows organizations to identify where in their own processes there is duplication, waste or superior practices. Typical areas for benchmarking operations include:

- Customer service levels
- Inventory control

- Inventory management
- Quality process
- Purchasing practices etc.

International companies often benchmark on their perceived company image, especially the value of the brand and the place it occupies in the minds of customers. Benchmarking usually focuses on existing products and services, so at best it might be described as helpful in enabling organizations to catch up with good practice.

If HR and line managers are trying to understand how other firms run their operations, a benchmarking audit can provide useful insights into 'good' practice. Typically, such an audit is based on finding out:

- What does the organization do?
- Who are its customers?
- Where is it located – national, regional, international?
- What is its corporate strategy?

Then explore its operations by looking at:

- Supply-chain linkage
- Quality and just-in-time philosophy and policies
- Forecasting procedures
- Inventory management
- Work environment, physical organization and layout
- Technology used
- Financial status
- Customer relations.

However, benchmarking rarely gives insights into planned future developments which might be modifications of what you are being shown. Despite this, information provided by other companies can often seem impressive to busy line managers. Benchmarking HR services allows you to identify how appropriate your HR provision is to the needs of your business relative to other HR providers, and to position your HR service along a sliding scale. This can then steer you towards useful targets for improvement, and/or supply information which can be used to justify what you propose.

With respect to benchmarking the Human Resource function and activities, it is important to identify the key HR drivers and performance indicators so that a meaningful set of measures can be developed. By gathering internal client feedback about existing HR processes, performance and practices, and documenting these, the critical success factors within the HR function can be prioritized and the appropriate focus for benchmarking can be selected.

The area for benchmarking should be chosen with care. Pick a specific aspect of the HR organization or operation which needs improving. This may be internal client relationships and satisfaction levels, delivery time for a service etc.

Review your own process to fully understand how the current procedures work and choose another organization which excels at that specific aspect. The people who are going to be involved in implementing improvements should be involved in the benchmarking visits. Visits should be short and reciprocal – you should at least be willing to answer questions which you wish to ask the other company. The data provided through benchmarking should be used for internal purposes only and treated as confidential.

HR benchmarking often focuses on issues such as:

- Ratio of HR to line staff
- Management levels of HR staff
- Involvement in management decision-making and types of decision on which HR contribution is sought
- Relationships with line management
- How HR processes operate
- How HR is structured – centrally, decentralized etc.
- Roles of HR staff, e.g. consultancy, administrative – numbers and skill levels of those in roles
- How HR operates as a team, especially in an international organization
- Accuracy rates for aspects of operational HR, e.g. monthly salary operations
- Retention rates for key worker groups
- Percentage of new recruits who are still with the organization after six months
- Forms of succession planning
- Use of technology by HR
- Training provision – types of training provided, percentage of salary bill spent on training, how training budgets are controlled
- Evaluation practices.

Although generally carried out with external organizations, internal benchmarking can also be helpful in large companies for spreading awareness of how good results can and are being achieved in different parts of the business. This can be very relevant to specific areas of HR interest such as spreading good practice on team communication, for example. The use of such internal benchmarks can be motivating for those identified within the organization as having a 'world-class' approach to some aspect of people management.

THE SERVICE–PROFIT CHAIN

The link between investment in people, providing technology to support front-line workers, improved training and recruitment practices and profitability is most apparent in service organizations. The 'new economics of service' are perhaps most evident in a number of US companies such as Taco Bell and MCI, where a radical shift has occurred in the way they manage and measure success. This involves making customers and employees paramount. The techniques used assess the impact of employee satisfaction, loyalty and productivity on the value of products and services delivered. This in turn is calibrated against building customer satisfaction and growth of customer loyalty. It has been estimated, for instance, that the lifetime value to a fast-food retailer of a loyal pizza eater can be $8000. These techniques put a 'hard' financial value on 'soft' measures.

According to a *Harvard Business Review* article by Heskett *et al.* (1994), the service–profit chain clarifies the links between the following:

- Customer loyalty drives profitability and growth
- Customer satisfaction drives customer loyalty
- Value drives customer satisfaction
- Employee productivity drives value
- Employee loyalty drives productivity
- Employee satisfaction drives loyalty
- Internal quality drives employee satisfaction
- Leadership underlies the chain's success.

Leaders of successful service companies emphasize by their words and actions the importance of each employee and customer. In the UK, Julian Richer (1995) has turned Richer Sounds into the biggest and most profitable hi-fi retailer in the country, with the highest sales per square foot of any retailer in the world. Richer's recipe is to recruit the right people, motivate them and provide them with the training they need to provide excellent customer service. He suggests that good management is 'all about achieving the right balance between control and motivation'. In other words, staff are set clear standards and robust procedures. All staff are engaged in continuous improvement through learning. Reward systems are aligned to behaviours which the organization values and wishes to encourage, such as innovation and outstanding customer service. Richer argues that it is possible to achieve a happy balance between strong central control and empowerment – and have both.

So clear is the mandate to staff that customer satisfaction is key to business success that employees are given a degree of freedom in using their initiative to ensure that customers' needs are met. Bureaucracy is kept to an absolute minimum so that speedy action can delight customers. Richer also consults staff widely on business and employee issues. As he tells staff: 'It is your responsibility to tell us what you think. We want to improve the business continually, and we can't do so unless you tell us where we are going wrong.' Employees also have the satisfaction of seeing many of their suggestions implemented.

Performance is measured weekly against a range of criteria including obvious ones such as sales and customer service. Julian Richer and members of his management team personally go though the figures each week with store managers in a third of the shops. Other measures include both positive matters such as whether staff met for suggestion brainstorming sessions, and the number of suggestions from individual employees put through, as well as negative aspects such as absenteeism. Central departments are also measured on their (internal) customer service and problems must be tackled immediately.

In the United States, companies such as Xerox are attempting to quantify customer satisfaction. Xerox has polled customers annually regarding product and service satisfaction using a 5-point scale from 5 (high) to 1 (low). They have found that providing excellent service (gaining a 5) was significantly more likely to lead to repeat business than giving good service (scoring a 4). Xerox aims to create 'apostles' who are so delighted with the service they have received that they tell others and convert sceptics. They also want to avoid 'terrorists' or unhappy customers who speak out against a poorly delivered service. Other organizations have also calculated that the real 'cost of quality' is more dramatically linked to the lost opportunities caused by an unhappy customer spreading bad news about the company than to the loss of that customer alone. Xerox recognizes that the key to customer satisfaction involves ensuring employee satisfaction and giving people the behavioural and other tools they need to do their job.

Human Resource processes and activities can and do affect every element of the service–profit chain. Employee loyalty has a direct cost to businesses when employee turnover is the consequence of a lessening of loyalty. These costs are not only the losses incurred by the cost of recruiting and training replacements but also the loss of productivity and decreased customer satisfaction when valued employees leave. The impact on customer relationships can be huge. Members of the Harvard Business School faculty have put a cumulative loss of at least $2.5 million in commissions on the unscheduled departure of a valued broker from a securities firm.

Many research surveys, including my own, have suggested that dissatisfied employees are more likely to express the intention to leave a company. Conversely, satisfied employees are more likely to stay. At Sun Microsystems UK employee turnover in a highly competitive labour market was cut to 4% due to imaginative career and other development opportunities and correspondingly high levels of employee satisfaction. Another key factor which drives employee satisfaction is internal quality which links with employees' perceptions of their ability to meet customer needs. This is where employees have the systems and other resources they need to do their job and where thought is put into identifying how to help employees to provide the most professional service. In some companies dedicated phone lines are used to answer employees' questions, remedy situations and alert senior managers to potential problems to be addressed.

MCI carried out a study of seven telephone customer service centres and found clear relationships between employee satisfaction, customer satisfaction and customer intentions to continue to use MCI services. Factors relating to job satisfaction included:

- The job itself
- Training
- Pay
- Advancement fairness

- Treatment with respect and dignity
- Teamwork
- Company interest in employee well-being.

All these factors are areas for strategic HR intervention and a shared responsibility between HR and the line.

Another American Company, Taco Bell, a subsidiary of Pepsi-Co, has integrated measurement data about profit by unit, market manager, zone etc. with the results of customer exit interviews. They found that those stores which were the top performers on customer service also outperformed the others on all measures. Consequently, managers' compensation in company-owned stores is now closely linked to both customer satisfaction and profits.

Above all, perhaps the single biggest element underlying the chain's success is leadership commitment to developing a corporate culture which centres around service. Such leaders make their priorities evident in their behaviours, such as spending time listening to customers and employees, and by the attention paid to selecting, tracking and enabling employees to provide excellent service. Corporate value statements about customer service are not enough – senior managers' behaviour and their focus on employees and customers appear to make the difference.

THE SEARS TURNAROUND

Perhaps one of the most well-known examples of a business turnaround using the employee–customer–profit model is that of the US retailer Sears Roebuck and Company, which is documented in a *Harvard Business Review* article by Rucci *et al.* (1998).

In 1992, following a period of steady and serious business losses, the new head of the merchandising group, Arthur Martinez, instituted a turnaround plan which benefited from the willing support of employees who were keen to make the business successful and from the residual loyalty of customers to the Sears brand, despite low levels of customer satisfaction. The company's service strategy was revamped, store operations were reengineered and there was a heavy emphasis on training, incentives and the elimination of unnecessary administration for sales staff. A range of other business initiatives, including Sunday deliveries, contributed to the superb results achieved by 1993 (a sales increase of more than 9% in existing stores and market share gains in a number of major goods).

The initial business turnaround was used as the springboard for more fundamental change so as to avoid the dangers of complacency identified as a primary source of failure of so-called 'excellent' companies by Peters and Waterman (1982). While the turnaround strategy had been implemented in a conventional 'top-down' way, Martinez saw the need to engage managers' and employees' hearts and minds in developing the company's future. A strong driving vision to achieve world-class status was established. The team at headquarters in Phoenix created an algorithm *work* × *shop* = *invest*. This emphasized the point that for

Sears to succeed financially, the stores had to be a compelling place to work (i.e. that employees would be highly motivated) and to shop (that the best merchandise alone would not ensure the company's success). This became known as the three Cs – 'to be a compelling place to work, to shop, to invest'.

Task forces were established to explore issues relating to financial performance, innovation, values, customers and employees. The innovation group did external benchmarking. Employees in the Values group were involved in gathering the views of all 80 000 of their colleagues to identify the six core values which Sears employees felt strongly about. These included honesty, trust and respect for the individual. The customer task force studied customer surveys going back several years and found that, broadly speaking, customers wanted Sears to succeed. The employee group conducted a survey and found that employees were generally proud to work for Sears.

The data gathered by all the task forces was used to establish goals, including to build customer loyalty and to provide excellent customer service by hiring and holding on to the best Measurement was a key feature in ensuring that the turnaround was not a flash in the pan. The task force data provided preliminary measures within each of the three elements of the vision. So, under *a compelling place to work* were measures relating to personal growth and development, empowered teams etc. Under *a compelling place to shop* were measures relating to customer needs being met and customer satisfaction. Under *a compelling place to invest* were financial measures linked to revenue growth, sales per square foot, inventory turnover etc. The Phoenix team wanted to see if there were any links between the three areas of measurement. During 1995 metrics of every kind were gathered and causal pathway modelling applied to establish cause and effect.

The result of this analysis was that clear links were established between employee attitudes and customer service, employee turnover and the likelihood that employees would recommend Sears to their contacts. A key discovery was the positive impact of an employee's ability to see the connection between his or her own role and the company's strategic objectives. Managers began to see how a change in training or business awareness could have a direct impact on revenues. Another key finding was that attitude towards the job and towards the company had a greater effect on employee loyalty and service to customers than all the other dimensions measured. These became the main focus of subsequent ongoing employee surveys which are based on a revised model of the employee–customer–profit chain. The measurement of Total Performance Indicators or TPI has become embedded in the Sears culture.

Having isolated the 'soft' issues which make a difference to the 'hard' business results, Sears can now see that a 5-point improvement in employee attitudes will drive a 1.3-point improvement in customer satisfaction which in turn will lead to a 0.5% improvement in revenue growth. The TPI model has proved sufficiently accurate for Sears that it can be used for predicting business performance – based on employee attitudes.

Measures alone were not sufficient to maintain high performance. A major training and learning initiative was launched to change the perceptions and attitudes of the workforce, help employees understand how the business worked and to improve their own approach to customer service. 'Learning maps' were used which informed employees of the changing economic and social context of retailing. The goal was economic and business literacy. Town hall meetings built on the learning and converted it into action.

Sears management recognized the importance of leadership to the development and maintenance of a high service culture. A leadership model was developed which incorporated every aspect of the transformation, including operational competence. The 15 top executives identified the skills and qualities they looked for in appraising their direct reports and from this data, 12 leadership skills were agreed, to be used as the basis for promotion, recruiting and selecting future leaders. The skills are assessed using 360-degree feedback and form the basis of leadership training. All courses at the Sears University are linked to one or more of the 12 leadership skills and more than 40000 managers have now been trained.

In a further move to align managers' behaviour to the direction of the company, the rewards and compensation of executives have been altered so that long-term incentives are now based on non-financial as well as financial measures. This is based on the reliability of the TPI as a leading indicator of business performance. These combined efforts to create customer satisfaction through improving employee satisfaction are paying off through handsome increases in revenues and vastly increased market capitalization.

HOW DOES THE ROYAL BANK OF SCOTLAND USE EMPLOYEE ATTITUDE DATA?

The Royal Bank of Scotland (RBS) has built up a powerful reputation for its sophisticated use of employee attitude data to build human capital. I am grateful to Greig Aitken, Head of Human Capital Strategy at RBS, and also to the CIPD, for the following case study which appears in CIPD's *Change Agenda: Reflections on Employee Engagement* (2006).

The RBS Group has over 140000 staff based in 30 countries. Its brands include NatWest, Direct Line, Tesco Personal Finance, Coutts and Ulster Bank. In an organization of its size, understanding the effectiveness of its people strategy and employee proposition is a strategic imperative. RBS has developed a human capital strategy that provides its business leaders with a detailed understanding of how effective the group is at attracting, engaging and retaining the best people and how its people strategy drives business performance.

At the heart of this approach is RBS's 'human capital toolkit', a comprehensive suite of online resources that provide HR staff with desktop access to a range of diagnostic tools, benchmarking resources, employee research and measurement tools. Together these resources provide RBS businesses with a deeper understanding of the links between effective people management and superior service and financial performance. This is a sophisticated, business-focused strategy within which employee attitude surveys play a key role.

The human capital toolkit provides consolidated information on the global employee base of RBS and is split into six core elements:

- *Surveys* – these provide access to analysis tools, presentations and action planning support across the group's entire range of employee surveys. This includes joiner, leaver, pulse and employee opinion surveys as well as acquisition surveys and management/leadership effectiveness surveys.
- *Benchmarking* – RBS has developed tailored benchmarking information for each business and function (for example, IT, call centres and head office departments). Forty human capital measures have been benchmarked against RBS's competitors in all their markets (for example, insurance, US credit cards, UK retail banking etc).
- *Research* – this resource provides access to internal research across the group on topics such as call centre performance, performance measures and organizational development. It also offers direct access to external research and employee research partners. HR staff can commission custom research across any HR topic from their desktop – and researchers in Washington and London are used to ensure their questions are answered quickly. Staff can discuss the findings with the researcher.
- *Measurement* – HR staff can investigate the links to business performance themselves by first accessing key metrics derived from HR's global data warehouse. Metrics can be delivered in seconds at a range of levels, from the whole group down to individual cost centres and business units.
- *Reporting* – this gives access to human capital reports on a variety of topics such as absence, staff turnover and diversity. It includes reports to the group's board, executives and senior HR staff, giving a deeper understanding of how key HR issues relate to business performance. Access to all external reports is also provided.
- *Business intelligence* – this is a 'one-stop shop' for business information relating to RBS's competitors and links to RBS business information. It's aimed at keeping HR staff updated with business context and competitor analysis.

A key resource in RBS's human capital strategy is its annual survey of employee attitudes. The 'Your Feedback' survey is delivered to over 140 000 staff in 30 countries in nine languages and is completed online and on paper (depending on business access). RBS conducts this survey anonymously through its survey partner, ISR, to get direct employee feedback and to compare their results to peer. The results are compared to ISR's financial services sector and global high-performing benchmarks, which tell RBS how it is performing against its competitors and provides managers with a powerful tool on which to base decisions. At 86% RBS's response rate for its employee survey is 20% higher than the market average.

The survey results are communicated to internal and external audiences in various ways:

- The chief executive communicates to all staff the group's results and each division delivers local presentations.
- Managers receive online reports relating to their area.
- The results are reflected in continuing employee communication and engagement.
- Results are reflected in discussions with financial analysts and in an annual corporate social responsibility (CSR) report.

Findings on employee engagement can be used to monitor business perform-ance, alongside those on, for example, communication, diversity, leadership and work–life balance.

Managers are also provided with an online survey results toolkit and an action planning booklet so that, at a local level, tangible actions are agreed and targeted:

- This includes the report for their individual business unit, bank branch and so on, as well as broader business results.
- There is detailed analysis, for example, of their top and bottom ten scores and data on how they compare.
- The toolkit provides a capability to automatically generate a tailored PowerPoint presentation for the meting expected to take place with the manager's team.

As part of its human capital strategy, RBS is an enthusiastic user of peer benchmarking – internal and external – across its employee surveys:

- Managers are able to compare their results against other parts of the group (for example, their call centre compared with the RBS call centre norm and the external call centre norm).
- RBS has pre-selected 24 benchmark groups – by geography, market and business type – to use for external comparison.

Key to the company's success has been cross-business executive support. RBS has established a human capital board to manage its work in this area. Chaired by the Head of Human Capital Strategy, it consists of business executives, HR direc-tors and the group's deputy chief economist. Under the governance of the group's HR leadership team, this board is responsible for prioritizing human capital initia-tives based on human impact. The strong support from the group director, HR and his leadership team has been instrumental in setting the human capital agenda, and ensuring the approach continues to receive strong business leadership.

RBS publishes human capital measures in its annual accounts and in its cor-porate responsibility report. This includes a review of performance, workforce demographics and the results from its global employee survey, together with how RBS is positioned against its peers in each category. The detail that RBS reports externally is extensive and is audited under the ISAE3000 assurance standard by Deloitte, who also audit the group's financial reporting. By reporting how the people strategy drives business performance, and by sharing the approach to developing a highly rewarding and productive workplace, RBS Group differentiates itself as a great company to work for, invest in and bank with.

STRATEGIC PLANNING IN DOW CORNING

This case study is prepared by Leslie Patterson, HR Director, Dow Corning. Leslie describes how a strategic HR planning framework is used to align business and organizational strategies in Dow Corning.

Dow Corning Company Profile

Created in 1943 by Corning Glass Works (now Corning, Incorporated) and The Dow Chemical Company, Dow Corning was organized to explore the potential of silicones, materials that combine the temperature and chemical resistance of glass and the versatility of plastics. In little more than a half-century, that exploration has resulted in over 10 000 products and speciality materials used by about 50 000 customers worldwide representing virtually every major industry. Headquarters are in Midland, Michigan, USA, with area headquarters located in Brussels, Belgium, and Tokyo, Japan. Dow Corning has 8300 employees worldwide with 1800 in Europe. In 2000 revenues were $2.75 bn with a net income of $104.6 m.

Strategic HR Planning Process

Description

Strategic HR Planning (SHRP) was developed by Professor Wayne Brockbank of the University of Michigan. It looks at the linkages between business strategy and human resource management and assesses the degree to which these are in alignment. The closer the alignment, the better the organizational responsiveness will be and hence the ability to adapt to customer needs and maintain competitive advantage (see Figure 4.2).

Desired Outcomes

- The articulation of the culture, behaviours and competencies which are necessary to ensure successful execution of business strategy.
- The development of a plan of HR initiatives to enable the desired culture, behaviours and competencies to become more prevalent in the organization (see Figure 4.3).

Case Study

In 1993, Dow Corning restructured into three geographic areas (the Americas, Europe and Asia) and two business groups:

- Core Products Business Group (CPBG), to produce the backbone technology, dimethylsiloxane, and deliver fluids, rubber, sealant and silicone at the lowest possible total cost.

- The Advanced Materials Industries Group (AMIG), to grow current sales and profit while focusing on the acceleration of long-term growth of silicon-based materials.

In 1997, the European CPBG general manager approached HR for help with what he believed was a communications problem. He explained that he was

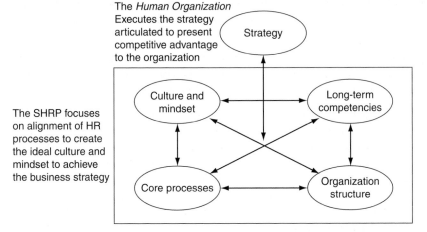

FIGURE 4.2   The components of the ideal human organization.

FIGURE 4.3   The strategic HR planning process.

concerned about the poor perception of CPBG as compared to AMIG and felt the time had come for the CPBG board to take some action to reverse the situation. Examples of what he wanted to change were:

- The AMIG business had a much more positive culture; they called themselves the 'amigos', turning their AMIG acronym into an appealing name. How could CPBG do the same?
- CPBG was losing good employees to AMIG and it was becoming difficult to attract high potentials to CPBG. How could CPBG reverse this trend?

In checking whether the same phenomena were occurring in the other geographic areas, several differences were noted. In the Americas, for example, there were more employees leaving AMIG and going to CPBG than in the other direction. Further probing uncovered the following:

- Although CPBG was a global term, the scope in Europe and the Americas was different. The Americas CPBG also included the semiconductor business, the highest growth sector at the time.
- CPBG and AMIG had different measures linked to variable compensation plans: AMIG goals were linked to sales of new products and CPBG's to manufacturing site quality goals. Pressure from AMIG to get new products out faster had resulted in some manufacturing problems. CPBG 'blamed' AMIG for under-performance on CPBG targets while AMIG targets were being met.
- AMIG was generally perceived as the 'place to be if you want to get on in Dow Corning'. The perception was that AMIG was outperforming CPBG yet the business results did not reflect this.

The main conclusion from the research was that while communications were going to be part of the solution they were not the real problem. It was agreed that it was time to check that the CPBG culture was aligned to the needs of CPBG's external customers and that the HR processes were providing the appropriate reinforcement and reward. The process used to do this was the HR Strategic Planning Process developed by Professor Wayne Brockbank of the University of Michigan which had already been used with some success with several groups in Dow Corning.

Over the course of several sessions with the CPBG board in 1997–8, the following three organizational characteristics for the CPBG culture and mindset were identified:

- Honest winners
- Confident change agents
- Customer maniacs.

These characteristics were the distillation of many long hours of reflection and discussion. However, not all were unanimously accepted. For instance, the use of 'maniacs' caused much debate. For some, this was too strong a word and had negative overtones. For others, it was good because it sent a strong message and attracted attention.

For each characteristic, we then did a gap analysis (on a scale of 1 to 5) of the extent to which it was aligned with the current culture and the impact (high, medium, low) it would have on the key business strategies if it were fully aligned. Table 4.1 is a summary of this assessment.

The next step was to assess the three characteristics against HR practices using a quality function deployment (QFD) analysis to check:

- The degree of alignment *today* (1 = aligned; 3 = not aligned)
- The potential impact if the HR practice were fully aligned (1 = low; 3 = high).

The results are shown in Table 4.2.

At this point in the CPBG process, Dow Corning announced a new corporate direction: to become a customer-driven company. External research showed that key drivers of customer satisfaction were employees who displayed the following behaviours:

Able to build relationships
- Listen, learn and work together with our customers to anticipate their needs

Act with a sense of urgency
- Our customers' priorities are ours: speeding up internal processes is a must

Display a can-do attitude
- Focus the full force of our talents on our customers and 'make things happen'

Act with integrity
- Inspire long-term trust in line with our values.

TABLE 4.1   Integration of organizational characteristics with business strategies

	Organizational characteristics		
Business strategies	**Customer maniac**	**Honest winner**	**Confident change agent**
Business strategy #1	H	H	M
Business strategy #2	H	H	H
Business strategy #3	H	H	M
Business strategy #4	M	H	H
Business strategy #5	L	H	H
Gap analysis	0 – CPBG-wide	2	1
(1 = low; 5 = high)	3 – some parts		

The closeness of the research findings to the three CPBG characteristics did not go unnoticed by the CPBG board and it gave them added confidence that they were on the right track! Indeed, initial discomfort with the use of 'maniac' turned into positive acceptance. However, before going into detailed action planning, the CPBG board felt it was time to do a reality check and share their thinking with CPBG employees. These sessions provided useful input on the content but, more importantly, they served as an essential step in change management by engaging CPBG employees in the process and by role modelling the leadership's interactive approach to communications. Feedback was very positive and typical comments included: 'These sessions are an indication that the process has started' and 'I feel like we are participating in our customer-driven company program'.

The output of the process was a project charter entitled 'Creating a Customer-Driven Organization in CPBG–Europe' with the purpose of developing a culture of unswerving devotion to customers and their satisfaction. Specific initiatives covered the HR practices of leadership, appraisal, development and reward and recognition. The subsequent restructuring of the corporation in late 1998/early

TABLE 4.2 Assessment of organizational characteristics against HR practices

HR practices	Impact – honest winner	Impact – customer maniacs	Impact – confident change agents
Recruitment	4	4	6
Promotions	6	9	6
Outplacement/redeployment	9	4	9
Appraisal	6	9	6
Rewards and recognition	9	9	9
Training	6	9	2
Developing	6	9	6
Benchmarking	6	6	3
Communications	9	6	6
IT systems design	?	6	3
Organizational structure	4	6	9
Reengineering	6	9	6
Physical setting	2	4	6
Leadership	6	9	6

Notes
•*Rewards and recognition were the only HR practice with '9' in all cells.*
•*Outplacement (redeployment) which had a '9' for two characteristics.*
•*Customer maniacs has highest number of '9's (seven versus three for the other two characteristics) which reflects and reinforces the gap analysis where customer maniacs score.*

1999 resulted in the disbandment of the CPBG and AMIG businesses but the pioneering work started by the CPBG board members has continued in the new organization.

Case Study Summary

The work with CPBG provided many benefits and learning at different levels:

- Professor Brockbank's process provided a structured methodology for making tangible and clear to management the linkages between external customers, business strategies, company culture and HR practices.
- CPBG understood that they were not competing with AMIG for the same resources.
- The CPBG board accepted that creation of the appropriate culture to achieve their business goals was a leadership responsibility.
- Completing the Brockbank process was in itself an excellent team building exercise for the CPBG board and illustrated the key role of sponsorship in change management.

Update

In the years following the writing of this case study, the strategic HR planning process became fully integrated into the annual corporate planning and budgeting process at Dow Corning. All business units now complete a critical review of the alignment of business strategy with their human organization and the projects resulting from this SHRP process are prioritized as part of the overall planning process. While the model used is no longer Brockbank's but Noel Tichy's Ideas–Values–Emotional Energy–Edge model,[*] the fundamental point remains: a key determinant of balanced growth for any organization is its human resource system. For HR, the challenge is to ensure that the HR processes for staffing, performance management, rewards and development which make up the human resource system are mutually reinforcing and aligned to the business direction.

Material in this case study © Leslie Patterson, Organizational Effectiveness Europe, Dow Corning.

CONCLUSION

HR is under pressure to demonstrate a payback from HR activities, whether these are team building, innovation or family-friendly initiatives, culture change or total quality management. The extent to which this pressure is felt in any organization is a reflection of the organization's culture. Senior line managers too are under pressure to achieve outstanding performance measured in bottom line terms. The partnership between line and HR needs to result in a workforce with the skills and motivation to help the organization survive and thrive in an increasingly competitive environment.

Senior managers have a vital role in creating an organization which views investment in talent and people management as a source of competitive advantage. In service organizations in particular, managers need to manage their investment in people – both customers and employees – and set both qualitative as well as quantitative measures to assess the impact of that investment. Employee commitment and confidence are key determinants of employee behaviour. Research suggests that these can be measurably improved if managers focus on enabling skills development and creating a community in which employees feel able and willing to give of their best.

HR needs to focus their activity on areas that are critical to the business in the short and medium term. Though I shall argue later that many of HR's critical interventions do not lend themselves to easy measurement in the short term, the extent to which unmeasured activities will continue to be seen as justifiable in the long term is questionable. HR practitioners need to prioritize the areas that will make a difference to their organization and identify, measure and track the effect of the initiatives they put in place to address these. Whichever measurement framework or guiding principle is used, HR should be in a position to identify the few things that must be managed in order to produce the biggest benefits. Profitability depends not only on assigning financial value to 'soft' measures but also on linking those different measures into a complete service–profit picture.

Collaboration between HR and other managers is extremely important. A shared vision and an agreed set of bottom-line objectives are starting points. A joint belief in the vital nature of people-related activities is imperative to an organization's success. Both parties need to recognize that HR activities are crucial to achieving their mutual objectives and ensure that both are involved in the setting of the strategic business, and therefore HR, agenda at an early enough stage. Perhaps then the value of HR's contribution can speak for itself.

*For more detailed description of the model, refer to *Leadership Engine – How Winning Companies Build Leaders at Every Level* by Noel Tichy (Harper Collins 1997), and *Every Business Is a Growth Business* by Noel Tichy and Ram Charan (Times Books 1998).

MEASUREMENT CHECKLISTS

Customer Value

- How does your organization define loyal customers?
- How do you understand changing customer demands and why customers defect?
- Are customer satisfaction data gathered in an objective, consistent and regular way?
- Where are the listening posts for obtaining customer (and employee) feedback in your organization?
- How is information concerning customer satisfaction used to solve customer problems?

- How is information about customers' perceptions of value shared with those responsible for designing a product or service?
- How will changing customer needs affect the competencies required of employees?
- How do you measure service value?

Employee Value

- How do you measure employee productivity? How well does the company deliver on its value proposition to customers?
- How do you create employee loyalty and what is the right level of employee retention?
- Is employee satisfaction measured in ways which can be linked to similar measures of customer satisfaction sufficiently frequently that trends can be established for management use?
- Are employee-selection criteria and methods geared to what customers as well as managers believe to be important?
- Do employees know who their (internal or external) customers are?
- Are employees satisfied with the support (technical and personal) they receive to do their job?
- To what extent are your organization's leaders energetic, participative, good listeners, motivational and able to walk the talk by personally demonstrating the organization's values?
- How much time and effort is put in by senior managers to creating a culture centred around service to customers and fellow employees?

Use of Measurement

- In order to survive, what must your organization do over the next three years?
- How clear are the strategic challenges to the HR team, and employees as a whole?
- Do you use measurement to challenge assumptions, check health or to cause compliance?
- Are the measures used 'lag', i.e. based on standard operating data which assumes the status quo, or 'lead', i.e. are you measuring the areas which you believe will make a difference to the organization in the future?
- To what extent are measures of customer satisfaction, customer loyalty and the quality of service output used to recognize and reward employees?

REFERENCES

Bassi, L. and McMurrer, D. (2005) Developing measurement systems for managing in the knowledge era. *Organizational Dynamics*, 34, No. 2, 185–196

Boudreau, J. and Ramstead, P. (2003) Strategic HRM measurement in the 21st century: from justifying HR to strategic talent leadership, in Goldsmith, M., Gandossy, R. and Effron, M. (eds), *Human Resources in the 21st Century*. Hoboken, NJ: John Wiley & Sons

Brewster, C., Hegewisch, A. and Lockhart, J.T. (1991) Researching Human Resource Management: methodology of the Price Waterhouse Cranfield Project on European trends. *Personnel Review*, 20, No. 6, 36–40

Buckingham, M. and Coffman, C. (1999) What is a great workplace? A weekly summary of Gallup's discoveries about great managers and great workplaces. The Gallup Poll – Managing, *Labour Market Skills and Trends, 1997–8*. London: DfEE

Chambers, N. (1997) Does the bell toll for your living company? (interview with Arie de Geus). *HR Focus*, 74, Issue No. 10, (October)

Chartered Institute of Personnel and Development (CIPD) (2006) Reflections on Employee Engagement: Change Agenda, London, CIPD

Ettore, B. (1997) The empowerment gap: hype vs. reality. *HR Focus,* 74, Issue No. 7, (July)

Heskett, J.L., Jones, T.O., Loveman, G.W., Sasser, W.E. and Schlesinger, L.A. (1994) Putting the service–profit chain to work. *Harvard Business Review*, 72, No. 2, 164–170

Kaplan, R.S. and Norton, D.P. (1998) Using the Balanced Scorecard as a strategic management system. *Harvard Business Review*, 74, No. 1, 75–85

Kearns, P. (1998) Moving up the HR ROI scale. *Financial Times*

Likierman, A. (2007) How to measure the success of talent management. *People Management*, February 22

Patterson, M., West, M., Lawthorn, R. and Nickell, S. (1997) *The Impact of People Management Practices*. London: Institute of Personnel and Development

Peters, T. and Waterman, R.H. (1982) *In Search of Excellence*. New York: Harper Business

Pfeffer, J. (1995) People, capability and competitive success. *Management Development Review*, 8, No. 5, 6–10

Phelps, M. (1998) The Executive Scorecard: Achieving competitive advantage through HR benchmarking. *International Journal of Business Transformation*, 1, No. 4, (April)

Reilly, P. and Williams, T. (2006) *Strategic HR Building the Capability to Deliver*. London: Gower

Richer, J. (1995) *The Richer Way*. Emap Business Communications

Rucci, A.J., Kirn, S.P. and Quinn, R.T. (1998) The employee–customer–profit chain at Sears. *Harvard Business Review*, 76, No. 1, 82–97

Scott-Jackson, W.B. and Tajer, R. (2005) *Getting the Basics Right: A Guide to Measuring the Value of Your Workforce*. London: Chartered Management Institute

Scott-Jackson, W.B., Cook, P. and Tajer, R. (2006). *Measures of Workforce Capability for Further Performance, Vol. 1: Identifying the Measures That Matter Most*. London: Chartered Management Institute

Ulrich, D. and Brockbank, W. (2005) *The HR Value Proposition*. Boston, MA: Harvard Business School Press

Ulrich, D. and Smallwood, N. (2004) Capitalizing on capabilities. *Harvard Business Review*, 82, No. 6, 119–127

FURTHER READING

Institute of Personnel and Development (1999) *Training and Development in Britain, 1999: The First IPD Annual Report.* April. London: Institute of Personnel and Development

Kirkpatrick, D. (1996) Revisiting Kirkpatrick's four-level model. *Training and Development*, January

Peters, T. (1992) *Liberation Management*. London: Macmillan

Chapter 5

Aligning Business and HR Strategy

While the HR challenges are greater than ever before, so too are the opportunities for companies to excel through people strategies

(Strack *et al.*, 2008)

The main focus of this chapter is on exploring the links between corporate strategy and HR strategy.

In the past decade, alignment of HR strategy with business strategy has been the holy grail of HR teams. The idea that HR strategy should be directly relevant to business requirements, an integral element of business strategy and delivering value has led to an intense focus on measurement, proving 'value added' and structural realignment for HR teams. More recently, what 'alignment' means and the idea that alignment should be the main aim of HR strategy is coming to be questioned, as I shall explore in this chapter.

We will start by looking at different approaches to developing and implementing business strategy, and the implications for organizational strategy. We will then look at a variety of ways in which HR can create 'alignment' to strategy in ways which add value.

BUSINESS STRATEGY

Organizations must inevitably make choices about how they pursue competitive advantage and the business strategy of an organization reflects the intentions of managers about how they expect to achieve results over a stated period of time. Conventional corporate planning work on three- to five-year cycles and annual business plans are formed within this. Typical strategies include innovation, cost reduction, quality leadership, cost leadership, value added, customer focus, growth through acquisition, joint venturing etc., and organizations can be pursuing various strategies simultaneously. In the broadest terms, corporate planning should provide answers to the following questions:

- Where are we now?
- Where do we want to get to?
- How shall we get there?

Any business strategy should provide answers to some basic questions:

- *What* are we going to do? (vision, mission, goals)
- *How,* where and by when and with what resources are we going to do it? (functional and business unit strategies, organizational design, resource and cost allocation, budget requirements, planning)
- *Who* is going to do it? (workforce planning and enabling, performance management, development)

And most importantly,

- *Why?* (higher purpose, rationale)

Business strategy takes account of:[1]

- **Strategic intent:** What are we trying to accomplish?
- **Strategy:** Intent, plan focus, drivers etc.
- **Customers and market:** Who are we trying to serve? Which customers (and markets) should we target? Value added?
- **Products and/or services:** What should we sell to these customers? What operations will support us delivering to customers?
- **Environmental context:** Regulation, economy, PEST factors (see below)
- **Core competency:** e.g. technology
- **Organizational resources:** Such as people, processes, structure, and systems
- **Finance:** Both working capital and long-term capital. How much money will be needed to make the strategy happen and to achieve corporate objectives?
- **Measures**: return on investment, value created.

In addition, risk factors must be identified and risk adjustment should be part of the strategy framework.

ATTUNEMENT

Business strategies should take into account the changing needs of external stakeholders such as customers, the changing business environment, including markets, and the critical resources needed to carry out the strategic aims. These critical resources include such factors as capital and technology, and increasingly

---

1. Adapted from *The Essential Guide to Managing Small Business Growth* by Peter Wilson and Sue Bates, 2003, Wiley and Sons.

rely on people – their brain power, access to information and ability to learn new approaches.

Of course simply telling people what needs to be done may not be enough to produce action. The process of aligning people's behaviour to implementation usually involves *attunement*, whereby employees become engaged at an emotional level with what they are being asked to do. Providing answers to the questions above, especially the 'why', is key to attunement. Typical leadership processes for answering these questions include *visioning* (the 'what?'), *designing the organization/roles* (the 'how' etc.), *enabling the people* (the 'who') and *valuing* (the 'why'). The answers to these questions need to be reflected in people's jobs, so that they have a clear line of sight in their daily work with the higher-level goals and purpose their organization is pursuing.

Taking External Factors into Account

Strategies should also take account of the context – especially external factors that represent threats and/or opportunities for the business. In conventional corporate planning, management teams often carry out an environmental analysis using a tool such as the PEST model (an analysis of the changing Political, Economic, Sociological and Technological factors currently or potentially affecting their organization and its stakeholders). Typical factors relate to the economy – local, worldwide or specific to particular geographic regions; or to the political climate, such as key international events. Other factors might include social and industry trends, changing demographics, emerging technology and shifting competitor behaviour. The potential impact of these changes on existing strategy as well as potential threats and business opportunities can be assessed.

One international construction company, for instance, had a small sub-business involving the reclamation of poisoned land by removing the spoilt earth to landfill sites. The company recognized that the Green movement was becoming highly influential in Europe in the early 1990s. They were able to see opportunities for a more environmentally friendly operation using bioremediation. This has become a useful and profitable part of the company's portfolio. An environmental analysis is often followed by a look at the strengths and weaknesses of the organization in relation to these threats and opportunities (a SWOT analysis) so that the potential impact on the organization of possible changes in strategy can be gauged. Such an analysis should take into account the impact of changes on customers, shareholders, management, employees, suppliers, unions and the financial community. Potential risks and ways of mitigating these are identified.

Planned versus Emergent

Models of strategic processes are often linear, sequential and apparently rational. Some classical planned approaches to strategy tend to assume a three-pronged approach – that having carried out an analysis, strategic choices are made which are then implemented. Others involve more stages. Thompson and Strickland (1998), for instance, suggest the following five phases:

1. Defining the business and establishing a strategic mission
2. Setting strategic objectives and performance targets
3. Formulating a strategy to achieve the target objectives and performance
4. Implementing and executing the strategic plan
5. Evaluating performance and reformulating the strategic plan and/or its implementation.

These classical planned approaches to devising and implementing strategy are based on fairly mechanistic models of organization and assume that the future can be known, predicted and to some extent controlled by managers. The emphasis is on intention, or strategic intent, stability and return to equilibrium. Success is thought to depend on extensive planning and design, often using external consultants, accurate anticipation of resistance to change and skill at overcoming this resistance.

Several conditions need to be in place for a planned approach to strategy to be realized. There needs to be a relatively predictable or stable environment where economic conditions, competitors or government actions are unlikely to significantly affect the organization's ability to achieve its plan. There also needs to be a consistent adherence to the vision or plan within the organization over a long time. The organization needs to have sufficient resources (e.g. money, skill, time, technology) and leadership to deploy these resources effectively in order to achieve the plan. This implies that the critical mass of the organization is aligned and working to achieve the same future state.

This is often where planned approaches break down due to a combination of internal rivalries between business units, different time spans among 'support' functions such as Personnel and IT and lack of integration of objectives across business units. All too often there can be poor communication amongst the management team and between that team and the rest of the organization. Business units then claim that they have no clear direction and are therefore unable to implement the strategy, or else they pursue strategies which are independent of each other. Communication and control methods need to be sufficiently robust to prevent re-interpretation of the planned future state within the organization.

Similarly, the nature of strategic planning itself can sometimes be too rigid to cope with a changing marketplace, and in some cases organizations fail to take the risk of following the wrong path; rather they take no path at all. Such conventional shortcomings of strategic planning are exacerbated in a fast-changing business environment.

The Need for Flexible Planning

Where there is constant flux, a more emergent strategy may be called for. Leaders need to manage their organizations as dynamic, real-time entities, not as bureaucratic systems. In a complex adaptive system such as an organization, planning needs to be flexible and ongoing to reflect changing circumstances. In practice, most organizations revise their assumptions and their plans significantly in the light of progress and changes in the business environment, resulting in re-forecast budgets and reallocated resources. Indeed organizations that are open to changing plans to meet changing situational needs typically create more value than those which adhere rigidly to targets and objectives agreed in the annual plan.

In particular, industries working in the global marketplace need a strategy framework that can adapt flexibly to many cultures and countries. Sequential approaches to planning can become restrictive and portfolio management approaches may be more suitable. Communication needs to take place between portfolio managers on a well-defined and regular formal basis so that strategy-making becomes a living process.

Flexibility therefore provides the organization with the ability to adapt to the environment. Strategic flexibility requires a proactive planning system, aware-ness of changing customer needs and competitive trends built in to the organi-zation's DNA so that managers can quickly change the direction and execution of strategy, and also be supportive of experimentation and innovation. To build an adaptable, agile organization also requires flexible structures, together with a cooperative culture to allow for cultural change. It means that organizational units should be kept as small and focused as possible. It requires intelligent tal-ent management and labour relations, customer-focused policies, processes and technologies conducive to speed and effectiveness.

Typical Challenges of Implementation

Having a strategy alone does not automatically produce results; people have to be willing and able to implement the agreed strategy. If employees are to be able to contribute their skills in the most effective way in order to realize business aims, it helps if people know what these aims are, what they are expected to do and why. It might be argued that in changing times there is an even greater need for clarity of business direction than in more stable times, and that one of the main tasks for the leaders of any organization is to provide a sense of direction and a focus for the organization's activities.

In practice, implementation of strategy can be problematic and the following are typical of the issues that have been experienced by many organizations with regard to strategic implementation:

- Implementation took more time than originally allocated
- Major problems surfaced during implementation that had not been identified beforehand
- Coordination of implementation activities was not effective enough
- Competing activities and crises distracted attention from implementing this decision
- Capabilities of employees involved were not sufficient

- Training and instruction given to lower level employees were not adequate
- Uncontrollable factors in the external environment had an adverse impact on implementation
- Leadership and direction provided by departmental managers were not adequate enough
- Key implementation tasks and activities were not defined in enough detail
- Information systems used to monitor implementation were not adequate.

The benefits of planned approaches are apparent clarity and the ability to monitor progress. The downsides are that the plan can become paramount, even when circumstances change and the strategy should change. Similarly, the relatively top-down approach generally used with such approaches often leaves those who are left to implement the plan feeling that they have had no say in creating it. The cost is a potential loss of employee ideas and commitment to the plan.

In many organizations, the day-to-day reality of the strategic process is somewhat messy. When everything is in flux, change, rather than being seen as linear, can appear cyclical, especially to employees who have worked with the organization for any length of time and may have 'seen it all before'. Often, in the absence of strong central direction, small project groups or business teams start to introduce new practices and initiatives, many of which relate to the customer. There is often real enthusiasm and commitment to what they are doing among members of project teams but the downside can be that such activities are not coordinated and can lead to duplication or political clamp-downs.

Such emergent approaches arise from the irrational side of organizations, such as political processes and other elements of the informal system. New order typically emerges rather than being designed or externally driven or hierarchically controlled. When smoking was generally banned in public places and places of work it might have been assumed that smoking would die out. Instead, some of the most firmly established and collaborative networks (which include people at all levels in an organization) are now to be found among smokers who have found themselves relegated to taking their smoking breaks at the doorstep.

The assumptions behind emergent approaches to strategy and change is that the future is inherently unknowable and that key organizational results often occur through the enhancement of random or unexpected events. Based on ideas from complexity and chaos theories, emergence involves seeing organizations as networks of multiple feedback loops which are so complex that no individual or small group is likely to see the 'whole picture'. The benefits of such approaches are that, if tapped for the benefit of the organization, the ideas of small groups and individuals can contribute vastly to keeping corporate strategy in touch with the needs of customers and the changing marketplace. Of course, because these seemingly ad hoc activities are driven by people who have a sense of ownership of their ideas, levels of motivation in such groups are usually high. Front-line staff in particular usually have a range of insights into changing customer needs and the subtle shifts in the market but their ideas and input may not be sought by management.

A classic example of a strategy that emerged as the result of learning by listening to the customer, paying attention to the reasons for success and failure, reinforcing success and thinking creatively about different distribution channels is the Honda Motorcycles' entry into the US market (the Honda case study is described in Pascale, 1995). The strategy that emerged, of selling their small motorcycles through general stores, was very far from Honda's original intention of selling large motorcycles through established dealers.

However, emergent change is not the polar opposite of planned change, i.e. random action, but rather reconciles the two. Organizations need both planned approaches that are sufficiently flexible and adaptable that they can cope with changing circumstances and the seemingly haphazard proliferation of activities in which employees are developing new ideas.

Involving Employees

Combining planned and emergent approaches is best achieved through involvement of staff. For instance, NHS workforce director-general Clare Chapman has pledged to change the culture of the health service by engaging more with frontline staff. Chapman, speaking to MPs on the Health Select Committee as part of an inquiry into workforce planning in the NHS, said: 'If what you are striving for is efficiency [in the NHS], then I am absolutely sure [an important piece] is about engaging staff. Inevitably, the people who know how to redesign the NHS so that it is most efficient are the staff themselves. As part of the leadership challenge, I am completely sure that engaging staff to find those efficiencies is absolutely the right way to get at them fast.'

As well as engaging staff in the 'how' of strategy, it is important to be clear what is going to help drive successful implementation. For Clare Chapman, achieving culture change in the NHS will depend on raising the standard of management and leadership, which in turn will require capable managers to be able and willing to do what is needed to deliver success. For Chapman, a key focus therefore is on identifying individuals who can be developed into managers: 'One would assume that among more than one million people [that work for the NHS] there are some extraordinarily good managers or people who have got the capability to be good managers,' she told the committee. 'The issue is spotting them. It is also pretty critical to make sure that it becomes a priority not just to engage staff, but also to do some very active talent-spotting' (Berry, 2007).

The challenge is to get the best of both approaches, perhaps by coordinating apparently disparate initiatives and helping people to see where linkages may occur. Where there is no clear organization vision, a sense of direction can emerge from creating coherence among different initiatives by increasing the flow of information between project groups. This coherence can provide a guiding framework for further activities. Where there is a clear business direction, helping task groups to see how they are contributing to the whole can create a sense of momentum, purpose and involvement.

Creating the Conditions in Which Change Can Occur

The role of the manager then is to create conditions in which change can occur. Managers need to pay attention to their environments and the threats and opportunities they contain, as much as to their own plans. They need to raise their awareness of how they interpret events – particularly the assumptions they use – as a key feature of their own and organizational learning.

Managers can encourage the creation of fluid, adaptive organizations through increasing information flows, improving processes, changing structures and enabling people to develop the skills required to work in them. In the same way, managers should be sensitive to the people processes they use such as the extent to which they involve people in decision-making, delegate work etc. Managers should communicate their long-term intentions in terms of broad purpose and principle, rather than detailed plans, as only broad principles will stimulate the creativity, learning and adaptability of those in closest contact with the environment.

Whichever approach is used to provide clarity about the future direction, the real challenge is trying to ensure that all aspects of the organization, especially employees, are working in the same direction. Alignment involves knowing how to connect the organization's purpose to every employee's performance.

ORGANIZATIONAL STRATEGY

The success of any strategy begins with skilful recruitment and human resource policies and works through internal debate and effective communication.

(Strategy Magazine, March 2007, Issue 11)

Organizational strategy draws out and acts on the implications of achieving both the short-term and medium-term business strategy. It can be the key to successful implementation of the business strategy. It also recognizes the requirement to build organizational capability for sustainable success. Competitive advantage can be achieved by allowing people to make things happen with the speed and flexibility the markets demand. Improving speed will require identifying organizational speed traps, resistance and other barriers to effective implementation, and then unblocking these. Organizational strategy therefore focuses on building the cultural capabilities and addressing the talent requirements for the organization to succeed.

In many organizations, the centrality of talent to business success is so clear that the HR strategy is no longer described as such but more often as the 'people strategy', 'people and organizational strategy', 'talent strategy' or simply the 'business strategy'. Critically, HR must engage the minds of leaders in the planning process by preparing them to make real-time decisions in the future with full information, especially around the assumptions on which they craft their strategies. HR must ensure that policies and processes enable knowledge-workers rather than constrain them. Indeed, various researchers have suggested that the most effective HR strategy is when HR strategy as such disappears and is more fully integrated into other resource strategies supporting the operational management process.

Planned or Emergent Approach to HR Strategy?

In Lewis Carroll's *Alice in Wonderland* Alice asks the Cheshire Cat:

> 'Would you tell me please, which way I should go from here?'
> 'That depends a good deal on where you want to get to,' said the cat.
> 'I don't much care where,' said Alice.
> 'Then it doesn't matter which way you go', said the cat.

HR strategy may be planned, emergent or some combination of these. Tony Grundy (1998) defines HR strategy as 'the plans, programmes and intentions to develop the human capability of an organization to meet the future needs of its external and internal environment'.

On the whole, researchers tend to agree that planned approaches to HR strategy may be preferable. For example, both Tyson and Witcher (1994) and Grundy suggest that emergent HR strategy may be damaging to organizational effectiveness. Other research projects also suggest that the more planned and timely the implementation of HR strategies, the more politically acceptable they are to line management and the more value is perceived to be added to the business. HR planning is therefore a key tool for aligning HR and business strategies.

There are many reasons why some HR teams may choose not to take a planned approach. Some HR teams may prefer working in an emergent way and would rather wait until there is a clear business strategy on which to model the HR strategy. This may be a long wait and opportunities for adding value may be missed. Some teams fear criticism of being seen to create their own policy in the absence of business strategy, on the one hand, or being seen to drive business strategy, on the other. The sheer complexity of the links that need to be managed between HR strategy and organizational effectiveness may mean that the overall focus of the delivery is diffuse and therefore not appreciated. Similarly, periods of ongoing change and active organizational politics can cause the links to be undermined. This may be a question of ownership of the HR strategy and where it sits in the organizational structure. However, Lam and Schaubroeck's (1998) research suggests that leaders in firms with relatively highly formalized HR planning are more likely to perceive its usefulness compared with those firms where the HR strategic objectives are less clear. In strategic HRM, planning needs to go beyond being focused on operations and control.

Whether a formal or informal approach is used, the important thing is to keep the plan simple. As HR teams adopt a strategic HRM approach, the need for integration among the different HR practices increases. These clear objectives are then likely to be useful in strategic planning activities, helping the organization to enhance organizational performance, rather than simply being a means of making the case for more resources.

HR Planning

HR planning is therefore critical to the effective development of strategy since it should identify gaps and surpluses in capabilities as well as issues of utilization of talent. At any stage in the strategic cycle, it is important to find out about the skill levels required by the business and where these currently reside.

Especially in times of change, questions HR teams should be asking themselves include:

- Do we know when and how to spot material impacts to the business and immediately make critical talent decisions?
- Do we know our pivotal roles, top performers, and current bench strength throughout the organization?
- Do we have processes in place to adapt the business and make decisions quickly?

A skills audit, handled carefully, can help take a 'fix' on the readiness of the organization for market shifts, in preparation for a merger or simply to guide recruitment. Lam and Schaubroeck (1998) suggest three different kinds of HR planning objectives:

- **Operational** – which seek to identify current capabilities and trends with short-term requirements in mind
- **Traditional** – which attempt to incorporate forecasts about the numbers of employees and their skill types to meet longer-term demands. This type of planning needs to take account of career development, succession planning, external recruitment and appraisal data. It can establish whether it is possible for the organization to achieve its strategic objectives
- **Strategic** – which is where HR planning provides valuable data and is carried out as an integral part of the overall strategic planning process. This involves line managers in developing and evaluating HR practices since this approach recognizes that those who are most knowledgeable about the workforce should be involved in building commitment to the strategy across the organization. Often the main thrust of strategic HR planning is finding ways to establish and maintain core competencies.

Indeed, so central is this identification of organizational capability considered by some researchers that they argue for an enhanced role for HR planning in overall strategic planning.

FACTORS TO TAKE INTO ACCOUNT IN ALIGNING THE ORGANIZATION TO THE BUSINESS DIRECTION

In an ideal world, the organization's mission and goals should be translated into its business and strategic organizational plan. The principle of alignment is that every aspect of an organization's activities should be integrated and pull together to achieve corporate goals.

Cultural Alignment

Achieving the strategy or vision relies on the performance of people within the organization which in turn calls for high levels of motivation and commitment among employees. Employee performance needs to reflect the mission, goals and values and, if excellent performance is required, there must be opportunities for employees to gain ownership and satisfaction from what they do. Alignment needs to happen at an organizational, team and individual level. Systems and structures need to reflect the organization's values at a very detailed level to prevent employees from being pulled in different directions.

Within the overall business strategy there may be some broad cultural objectives. For instance, if teamworking is desirable to achieve business goals, people management systems need to be revised to reflect teamworking. This means not only managing performance at individual but also team level, and setting team objectives. Team performance guides need to be developed and complemented by team development plans. Similarly, team rewards and performance measures need to reinforce messages about the importance of teamworking. The argument goes that if you don't measure desired performance such as teamworking, it won't happen.

In reality, it is usually employee behaviours that make the difference to strategy implementation. HR needs to think through the behavioural characteristics desired of employees. These include both behaviours the company wants to encourage or improve and those it wishes to discourage or stop. HR also needs to think through the HR processes that are aligned to that behaviour, such as recruitment, training, resources, location, working environment etc.

Management and employee styles may need to be adjusted. Command and control styles of management may seem out of place if the business strategy and a lean structure call for empowered employees. In an ideal workplace, skilled and motivated employees should be directly involved in determining what work is performed and how it will be carried out. More participative styles of management may therefore be more appropriate.

Addressing Alignment 'Gaps': Desired Cultures and Behaviours

Ignoring some of the key internal contradictions between different elements of an organization can lead to poor performance. Information systems and reward systems may undercut one another if people are paid only for what they know, removing any incentive to share information with others. People infer what is expected of them from the organization's culture, by the way people are treated and by what management appears to value and reward.

Employees often perceive big gaps between the 'talk', i.e. visions, values and other direction-setting messages and the 'walk' or what people really get their steer from – the behaviour of people around them, especially that of senior managers. When there is a mismatch between what is espoused, such as teamwork, and what is practised, people will believe what they see. Similarly, if the only way an organization symbolically rewards people is by promoting a privileged few, people who are not promoted are unlikely to believe feedback that they are doing a good job. Management practices which are at odds with espoused values cause employee cynicism and eat away at motivation. Similarly, a competitive strategy based on innovation but a culture that is inclined to 'blame' and risk-averse will not bring about the employee behaviours required to deliver the strategy.

At every level, gaps between organizational rhetoric and reality need to be identified and addressed. In other words, barriers to performance need to be identified and acted on if performance is to be improved.

Alignment Frameworks

There are many conceptual models which suggest how different aspects of an organization interlink with others. One of the best known is the McKinsey framework, also known as the 'Seven S' model. This and other frameworks allow a gap analysis to be made at any point in time to ascertain whether all aspects of the organization are pulling in the same direction.

An interesting distinction is drawn between the so-called 'hard triangle' of strategy, systems and structure and the 'soft square' of staff, style, skills and shared values. Typically, it is the hard triangle which excites executives and around which most money is spent on consultants. Redesigning the organization's structures is not enough if change is to be really embedded, since it is usually the 'soft square' factors that have a strong bearing on employee behaviour.

Therefore each of the seven S's needs attention, individually and in relation to the others. People need to be helped to develop the skills and the motivation to work in new structures and with changed working practices. They need to understand why they are being asked to do these things, which is where change without a clear rationale can be so demotivating for employees.

Alignment frameworks are particularly useful when change is being implemented in one aspect of the organization. Inevitably there will be knock-on effects on other parts of the system and, if these can be anticipated and dealt with proactively, difficulties can be lessened. Importantly, when an organization's mission or strategies appear to change course, this can cause conflict with previously shared values. My previous research into careers (Holbeche, 1997) highlighted how bitterly some employees resented the apparent shifts in the culture of the UK National Health Service over the previous decade. Rather than adjust to what they considered a more managerial culture, many employees left and joined the private sector where there were fewer mixed messages about the organization's mission as well as better pay.

BUILDING AN EFFECTIVE ORGANIZATIONAL STRATEGY

With many factors to consider, the choice of where to focus HR activity to deliver value is potentially vast. The aim should be to narrow effort down to priority areas, some of which will have different resource implications and may be delivered over different timescales. However the process of strategy development counts too, in particular engaging with key stakeholders, including line managers and executives in the identification of priorities.

Engaging Line Managers

Of course, in setting business strategies, line managers need to be fully in tune with what their customers say they want from the organization. The same is true of HR strategies.

What makes a difference to the delivery of business strategy is people's behaviours. HR and line managers need to think through the kind of culture needed in each unit if the people in that unit are to be able to deliver the business strategy. They also need to think through the behavioural characteristics desired of employees, if the business strategy is to be implemented successfully. So, for instance, all the 'customer focus' in the world is no use if clients perceive that the company's representatives are rude to them over the phone. HR also needs to think through the HR processes that are aligned to that behaviour. This will include issues such as recruitment, training, resources, location, working environment etc. Working through these issues with line managers in a systematic way helps line managers to see the link between managing the cultural aspects of the organization and achieving business goals.

Tony Grundy argues that the key role of a strategic HRM function is to facilitate Organization and People strategy, together with joint coordination with line management of strategic programmes such as management development and succession planning. The role of HR then would be to facilitate the development of an organizational strategy that is directly linked to the business strategy, and owned and developed with line managers.

Process for Developing HR Strategy

HR planning should be focused on helping the organization achieve its strategic intent, which derives from the vision. HR strategies need to both service the short-term (business planning cycle) and the slightly longer-term (corporate planning) cycle. For Dave Ulrich, a typical process for developing HR strategy, which should be an integral part of both corporate and company business plans, is as follows:

1. Define the business context and market dynamics
2. Articulate an HR vision
3. Specify deliverables, capabilities
4. Invest in HR practices
5. Create an HR governance structure
6. Prepare action plans
7. Assure HR competencies.

Borrowing from Ulrich's process structure, I will explore some of the factors to take into account at each stage.[2]

1. Define Business Context, Market Dynamics and Organization Stage

In addition to the external and internal factors described earlier in the context of developing business strategy, particular factors to take into account when linking business and HR strategies include:

Growth Phase

Is the organization's market share shrinking, or going into a growth phase? Several general avenues of growth have been identified by Gertz and Baptista (1995) as follows:

1. Firms may grow within existing markets: *implication* – HR's capacity to create business cultures through which revenue-enhancing strategies are implemented can be a major source of competitive advantage.
2. If a firm purchases a competitor: *implication* – HR's challenge is to identify the culture which is required for both companies.
3. Firms may grow through existing products in new markets e.g. global: *implication* – HR's role is to facilitate growth, selecting the right local leadership and balancing local and corporate demands.
4. Firms may grow through new products within existing markets: *implication* – HR needs to create a business culture which emphasizes radical innovation and continuous improvement.
5. Firms may grow through new products and new markets: *implication* – HR's role combines the approaches in (3) and (4).

Stage of Organization Life Cycle

Strategies geared to the life cycle of the organization need employees and especially management styles to be adapted to changing conditions. For example, Kochan and Barocci's four life cycle stages (1985) outlines HRS requirements at each life cycle stage (Table 5.1).

Type of Business Strategy

Similarly, different forms of business strategy require different forms of structure, HR policy and practice. For example, strategies that focus on competitive positioning through differentiation are likely to place a greater emphasis on process innovation and specialization of distinctive skills and competencies that help the organization to compete effectively.

Schuler and Jackson's (1987) three competitive business strategies and related HR policies are summarized in Table 5.2.

---

2. Adapted from D. Ulrich, *Human Resource Champions* (Harvard Business School Press, 1997).

TABLE 5.1   HRS requirements during organization life cycle

Stage	Key features of the organization/HRS
Start-up	There is a need to attract high-calibre employees, partly by paying market or above market rates, and partly by establishing skill requirements for future development and a suitable organizational culture
Growth	Various categories of part-time, temporary or sub-contract labour may be used to create labour flexibility
Maturity	A large internal labour market, and the emphasis shifts towards manpower retention. Accordingly, wages tend to be based more on grade definitions than profitability or skills
Decline	There is less employee participation, and downturns in profitability may result in layoffs.
	A focus on restructuring, cost control, redundancies and outplacements.
	Downward pressure on wages and a need to agree criteria on which to base redundancy decisions. In such a crisis situation, the future of the organization is clearly uncertain

TABLE 5.2   HRS policies related to different business strategies

Strategy	HR policies and employee behaviour
Cost reduction	Structures that emphasize control and low investment in training. Usually with narrow job descriptions and career paths.
	Short-term, results-oriented performance appraisals and close monitoring of market pay levels for use in making compensation decisions
Quality enhancement	Fixed and explicit job descriptions.
	High levels of employee participation in decision-making relevant to work, short-term and results-oriented appraisal.
	Extensive and continuous employee training and development
Innovation (product differentiation)	Structures that encourage cooperation and creativity e.g. an emphasis on project-based team performance appraisal, which recognizes developmental and team-based activities.
	Considerable investment in training and career development.
	Compensation that emphasizes internal equity

2.   Articulate an HR Vision

More recently there has been a strong emphasis in much management literature on the search for sustainable high performance, so an HR vision could be
to become a high-performing organization. Of course, there may be immediate
short-term problem areas that need to be addressed, but an effective strategy will

aim to deliver solutions that produce positive impact in the short-term and also build the organization's capabilities to become a high-performing organization over time. So typical ingredients of a high-performance HR vision may well include the basics of alignment, i.e. people knowing what their job is, having the resources and the motivation to carry it out. For more detail of high-performance elements, see below.

3. Specify Deliverables/Capabilities

The organizational strategy needs to focus on building organizational strength, agility and competitive advantage. Ulrich (1998) is careful to distinguish between the 'do-ables', i.e. activity and outcomes, or deliverables that produce value. He suggests that organizational success will spring from capabilities such as speed, responsiveness, agility, learning capacity and employee competence.

To identify specific deliverables, Ulrich poses questions such as these:

Talent

What forms of talent do we have, need now, and three years from now? Where are our critical talent shortages? How should we plug these? How can we leverage talent more?

Organizational Capabilities

What are the organizational capabilities we require? How should we organize our business to get these products/services to our customers?

Culture/Shared Mindset

What do we want to be known for by our customers?

Leadership

Leadership development and increasing management capability: what is the quality of our leadership, given our strategy? What is the mix of attitudes, skills and experience which will deliver results? What needs to be done to build the quality and effectiveness of leadership at all levels? How well developed are our leadership capacities? How well do they fit together and support each other? How appropriate are they in the new contexts in which the organization finds itself now and is likely to find itself in the future? What is the transition required to get there?

4. Invest in HR Practices (People, Performance, Information, Work)

Staffing

Who is hired into the organization? Who is promoted? How can we become an organization of choice for the best recruits?

Training and Development

Learning and development. Given our business strategy, what training and development should be provided?

Competencies

Given the rate of change, investment in core competencies may prepare employees better for any given strategy they need to implement than just addressing current organizational needs. What are the competencies we require to accomplish our strategy? Where are we now on these competencies? Where can we obtain them? How can we build them quickly?

Performance Appraisal and Rewards

What are the performance standards for individuals, groups and departments in this organization? How effective are existing performance appraisal systems?

Capacity for Change

How engaged are employees? How can we ensure that staff are involved and committed to change?

Organizational Structures, Policies and Employee Communications

How do we create flexible structures and deploy talent effectively to enable the organization to rapidly adapt to emerging challenges? What should be the shape of the organization, e.g. levels, roles, reporting relationships etc.? How do we make appropriate decisions? How do our policies support the strategy? How do we make sure that employees have line of sight to objectives, organizational purpose and the customer?

Work-Process Improvement, Change Processes

What types of initiatives should we offer to make sure our processes work well (e.g. quality, reengineering)? What are the critical processes for making change happen? How can we share ideas across the organization?

5.   Create an HR Governance Structure

What is the organization we need to accomplish our strategy? Where does decision-making currently reside? How can we achieve speed, efficiency but manage risk and stimulate innovation at the same time? How can we ensure that the organization is acting ethically at all times? What are the standards and consequences required to accomplish our strategy? Where are we now on these? What will need to shift?

6.   Prepare Action Plans

Action planning should ensure that the key elements are integrated into a focused plan for building competitive advantage through people. These plans need to be developed with the management team and delivery time-frames can be both short- and long-term. Changing the structure, for instance, can be a short-term target while changing the culture can take a very long time.

Objectives within the strategy should be SMART (specific, measurable, achievable, relevant and time bounded). These objectives should be reflected in the annual targets for individuals and teams as a whole. For details of measurement, see Chapter 4. Typical objectives associated with different areas of HR responsibility (after Lam and Schaubroeck, 1998) include:

- **Maximum strategic impact**
  Align HR practices with business objectives
  Conduct development programmes to support strategic changes
  Carry out job analyses for long-term objectives
  Improve HR adaptability on changing environment
  Enhance workforce capability and motivation
- **Coordinate**
  Improve coordination between various HR functions
  Improve team effectiveness
  Improve HR project management
  Develop compensation and benefit programmes
  Coordinate any potential HR problems
  Integrate diverse HR functions and operations
- **Communicate**
  Communicate HR policies inside the organization
  Improve management acceptance of current HR policies
  Improve employee involvement and understanding of HR
  Conduct job analyses for long-term objectives
  Communicate HR policies outside the company
- **Control**
  Clarify budget and resources availability
  Manage personnel-related costs
  Improve HR budget control
  Improve HR resource procedures and control
  Review HR operations procedures.

Specific action plans for these objectives should be coordinated into an overall plan that can be tracked. Project management disciplines should be applied, including team development and processes for ongoing engagement with stakeholders. Progress should be carefully monitored and objectives should be evaluated as action is completed to assess value added and next steps.

7. Assure HR Competencies

For more detail see Chapter 12.

ALIGNING HR STRUCTURES TO BUSINESS STRATEGY

Sparrow *et al.* (2008) argue that 'jumping to off-the-shelf structures on the assumption that they will fit the challenge of business model change can be dangerous'. They argue that HR can contribute value in the following ways:

1. *Value creation:* ensuring the organization has the ability to build and acquire talent and in turn develop the value proposition inherent in the business model. This requires understanding the new organizational capabilities central to the business model; managing immediate and sustained talent challenges; and developing HR processes that engender requisite performance outcomes such as innovation, customer service, efficiency or effectiveness.
2. *Value improvement and leverage:* enhancing the business model as it develops and learning how best to execute the business strategy. This requires: the HR function to be involved in transferring knowledge; to know how to optimize policies and practices; to manage the learning that results from any change or execution process associated with new business models; and to have multiple channels that ensure engagement of the business with such issues.
3. *Value protection and preservation:* making sure that any value that has been created does not then get lost. This requires: the design and maintenance of effective governance processes; constructive surfacing of the risks inherent in a business model and appropriate mitigation strategies; ensuring that the organization has a strong reputation across a range of stakeholders; and that it is able to retain its best capabilities (both people and systems).

These principles should drive decisions about what is the most appropriate HR structure to support the business. For more details of HR structures see Chapter 3.

Choosing HR Goals to Conform to 'Best Practice' or 'Fit'?

However, finding the best way to contribute to the creation, improvement and leveraging of value remains a challenge, even though similar HR challenges affect many organizations. For example, research carried out in 2007–8 with HR Directors across Europe, and subsequently globally by Boston Consulting Group (in partnership with the European Association and then the World Federation of Personnel Management Associations), has highlighted common human resource challenges in all the countries surveyed:

- Talent
- Demographics
- (Culture) change
- Leadership
- Work–life balance (Strack *et al.*, 2008).

Arguably then, these should form the basis of organizational goals. However, knowing how to go about addressing these issues can be difficult. Partly this may reflect the divided opinion about the best approach to adopt. Theorists and consultants who favour universalist approaches argue that groups of elements or 'bundles' of HR policies and practices represent 'best practice', and that each of these elements is interrelated to the others. If one element is at odds with the others, no matter how clear the strategy, mixed messages will get in the way of implementation. Such approaches underpin many consultancy diagnostic tools and solutions.

Other theorists argue that the effectiveness of HR strategy very much depends on the organizational context and make it highly unlikely that a best practice approach will work in every situation. This 'contingency' approach is therefore more akin to strategic alignment since it claims that the best HR policy is one that depends on, and 'fits' the different competitive strategies and the unique characteristics of individual organizations.

While a degree of flexibility of planning may be appropriate to ensure flexibility and relevance to changing demands, conversely, unless the HR strategy objectives are clear, building commitment to the strategy among line managers and employees can be difficult. Alignment may in reality be a case of achieving overall coherence between HR and business strategy rather than an absolute 'fit'.

Contingent Approaches

The contingent nature of many HR strategies is highlighted by Rebecca Fauth (2006), who reports that HR objectives appear to vary according to the different contextual pressures organizations are experiencing. The nature of the contingency will drive different forms of HR strategy, according to Mabey and Salaman's (1995) 'open approach' contingency model. The operating environment requires a corporate strategy, which in turn requires desired employee behaviours. The HR outcomes pursued through an HR strategy require three 'levers': structure, culture and personnel practices and policies. For the HR strategy to be considered successful, two forms of integration must be achieved: 'external' (alignment of business and HRS) and 'internal' (where structural, cultural and personnel strategies are integrated with one another).

In the Fauth study (2006), organizations facing greater external pressures including labour market competition, new developments in HR policy or practice and governmental legislation were more likely to possess employee-related HR objectives aimed at improving employee performance, knowledge and well-being. These were more typical of business services and public sector organizations, the latter also focusing on building partnerships with trade unions.

Organizations experiencing internal pressures, such as restructuring, changing working practices and trade union pressure issues were more likely to promote cost-control HR objectives, including labour costs and workforce reduction. These were more typical of HR objectives in manufacturing environments. Not surprisingly, organizations with employee-related HR objectives tended to promote communications, pay, well-being and training practices relative to organizations with primarily cost-control HR objectives.

Even if contingent approaches to HR strategy may be more common than 'best practice' approaches, there is something to be said for drawing on best practice once a diagnosis has been made about the specific needs of the organization in its context. Such approaches may highlight possible solutions that can be tailored to ensure relevance and provide useful clues as to where HR can best focus time, attention and effort in the quest to build high performance and create value.

HR Priorities Geared to Building Competitive Advantage

A key aim of HR strategy is to create value by building competitive advantage. A major worldwide survey conducted under the auspices of IBM and Towers Perrin, entitled *Priorities for Gaining Competitive Advantage* (1994), has identified several key groupings of HRM policies and practices which have been linked to competitive advantage.

- Culture
  Promoting an empowerment culture
  Promoting diversity and an equality culture
- Organizational structure and control
  Emphasis on flexible organizations/work practices
  Emphasis on utilizing IT to structure the organization
  Emphasis on horizontal management
  Emphasis on increasing and promoting customer service
  Emphasis on rewarding innovation/creativity
  Link between pay and individual performance
  Shared benefits, risks and pay for team performance
- Resourcing
  Emphasis on external resourcing
  Emphasis on internal resourcing – training and careers
  Emphasis on internal resourcing – managing outflows
- Communication/corporate responsibility
  Emphasis on communication
  Emphasis on corporate responsibility.

Similarly, firms in the Fauth study (2006) who were striving to build high-performance organizational cultures and to create employee engagement viewed flexible working, training, communication, bonuses and appraisals as the practices with the greatest influence on organizations' productivity. High-performing private sector organizations (assessed via profit and market share increases) typically had recently experienced acquisitions, endorsed competitive (speed and efficiency focused) business strategies, were influenced by external HR pressures, supported employee-related HR objectives and used pay and incentives HR practices.

Other practices with an impact on productivity and considered as central to HR strategy include:

- Encouraging greater teamwork
- Improving employee commitment
- Controlling labour costs
- Enhancing employees' understanding of the business
- Improving health and well-being
- Encouraging innovation and creativity
- Improving work–life balance
- Strengthening the pay and performance link.

Promoting an Empowerment Culture

Empowerment is a well-recognized feature of a high-performance culture. However, empowerment has become something of a cliché and a discredited one at that in some quarters. The main reason according to Barbara Ettore (1997) is the myths surrounding it. If empowerment is defined as an employee's ability to solve problems, make decisions and take actions based on those decisions, management has encouraged the first two but has failed to allow the third. Often the real dilemma for executives is whether to trust employees. The management assumption is that workers cannot fully understand the impact of their actions on the organization's bottom line. This assumption is based on the relative lack of information received by workers which would give them a clear insight into how their actions affect the whole operation, stretching from the business strategy and work processes to customers, shareholders, suppliers etc.

This is where empowerment without alignment with strategy and information is likely to backfire. Yet the benefits of empowerment can outweigh the risks. Empowered organizations are more likely than others to respond quickly to ideas and suggestions, enable managers to make their own decisions without having to rely on headquarters and put customers' needs first.

Empowerment needs to be aligned to the strategic aims of the organization so that employees can direct their solutions to real business issues. Typically, employees need to be clear about what the customer wants, the part their own role plays and what shareholders are looking for. Characteristically, in empowered organizations, good ideas are rewarded effectively and authority is appropriately delegated as far down the organization as possible. Systems are a supportive framework rather than a set of constraints and employees work to broad principles rather than rules. Companies like Levi-Strauss, Yahoo!, Hewlett–Packard and Nordstrom are among high-performing organizations that practise aligned and informed empowerment. However, as Ettore (1997) points out, 'as with all initiatives, if management is not committed and if HR is not a strategic function, it will fail'.

ALIGNING TRAINING AND DEVELOPMENT TO BUSINESS STRATEGY

Research carried out in the UK (Poole and Jenkins, 1996) suggests that core elements in the development of competitive advantage in respondents' organizations were:

- Management development
- Career development
- The development of high-potential employees
- Support for continuous training and retraining.

Clearly, human resource development as well as management is an essential part for building sustainable competitive advantage. Training can help in the creation of a more productive, skilled and adaptable workforce.

Benchmarking is often used to identify organizations considered to be 'best in class' on particular aspects of their strategy or implementation. Benchmarking, though useful in some ways, is not enough. For a start, what works in one organization may not work elsewhere. Second, following what others are doing is not a way to build capabilities that are unique and difficult to imitate. What is needed is a detailed understanding of competitive dynamics and being able to translate these into the people and culture implications.

Training and development (T&D) benchmarks often focus on the amount of money invested in T&D activity. These figures vary widely among employers but US surveys during the past decade suggest that a disproportionate expenditure, i.e. those who spend more than 1.5% of their payroll on T&D, is made by just 0.5% of all US employers. These few organizations recognize that having a workforce with high skill levels is a primary source of competitive advantage. In these exemplary organizations, T&D is strongly aligned to the strategic leadership and planning processes of the business. The primary focus of training supervisors, managers and executives is on creating readiness and flexibility since it is these individuals who set the tone for the rest of the organization.

Typical of the 'best practice' benchmark organizations is that they:

- Create a systematic link between business strategy and the T&D system. T&D targets are reviewed at least annually to ensure that they are still on track with changing business requirements.
- T&D executives take a full part in the strategic planning process, ensuring that strategic goals take into account the availability of the talent needed to carry out the goals.
- Information support systems are also integrated into the strategic planning process. Links between training and development activity and the business strategy depend very much on whether training is an integral part of the HR strategy and whether this too is fully aligned to business needs.

STRATEGIC ALIGNMENT THROUGH COMPETENCIES

General competencies are a means of ensuring consistency across the organization through the creation of a common language to describe performance. In addition, professional and functionally specific technical competencies make up the typical competence framework. A competency framework is a useful way of aligning HR processes to the business strategy. In this section we look at some processes for defining and using competencies. Practical examples follow later in this chapter, and also in Chapter 8, where the focus is on developing talent within an organization.

Competencies are often defined as 'a particular attribute that people have that collectively helps to develop the capability of the individual and the organization'. They are a means of describing the kinds of behaviours and approaches which should enable the organization to achieve its business objectives and should draw employees' attention to things that need to be commonly applied. Ensuring alignment relies on excellent performance management so that people are clear what their roles are, what is expected of them and how that might change. If you adjust competencies so that they are continually aligned to the business strategy, the likelihood of people's behaviour being in line with what the business needs at any point in time is high. If these are reflected in the performance standards the organization is seeking to achieve, the link between skilled behaviour and outputs is evident. So, for instance, as organizations require people to work across boundaries, there is a need for clarity on what effective cross-boundary teamworking looks like. Defining the competency can help those involved become more aware of the implications for the way they work. By definition, competencies are temporary and need a review process built in to check that they are still linked with current business strategies.

Competencies should be a means of defining where the 20% of effort needs to be put in order to achieve an 80% return. However, if competencies are used mechanistically, or are not 'owned' by the people for whom they have been defined, it is unlikely that they will produce the benefits of clarity since they will not be used. There is an increasing awareness that people's needs must be taken into account if they are to be motivated to carry out activities to a high standard. A competence framework needs to be a means of addressing both organizational requirements for performance and individual needs for development, achievement and recognition.

Defining Competencies

Ideally, a competence framework should enable employees to understand what the organization as a whole, what teams and individuals need to be good at to achieve the organization's objectives. Defining competencies can be a developmental process for those involved. For instance, in most organizations managers are required to manage change, even though they may not relish change much themselves. Involving managers in defining or reviewing competencies can be a useful way of acclimatizing them to change and help them to recognize the ways in which they can enable others to succeed by the 'new rules'.

Competencies can be identified in a number of ways and to a number of levels. Typical techniques used include repertory grid and critical incident interviews. In defining competencies it is important to start with what customers expect, create plans to give the customers what they expect, define which activities are required to achieve those plans, and then identify the skills, knowledge and behaviour needed to carry out these activities. Standards and measures can then be applied so that performance can be more closely managed.

Competencies should ideally be tailored to the organization and relate to the things the organization is trying to do or must protect, and those things which are critical to moving the organization's culture in the desired direction. Typically, the first level is to interpret the organization's purpose or values into competency statements. Another level is where the focus is on a few key or core competencies which are essential if the organization's business strategy is to be realized. A third level, identified by Prahalad and Hamel (1995), is the way in which the organization's core competence differentiates it from competitors.

Competencies should ideally be defined in terms of knowledge, skills and experience. Behaviours should be defined in simple and relevant language so that people are aware of what really effective behaviour looks like. Typically, competencies include some descriptor statements or 'anchor points' so that the graduation of skilled behaviour is obvious. Another common element in many competency schemes has been the emphasis on standards. In the UK in particular this approach has been evident in the range of government-backed initiatives in competency-based schemes such as NVQs.

Using Competencies

Defining competencies is not enough, however. What really matters is how people use their ability in the workplace – it is their actual behaviour which counts. People often need help in becoming effective at them. Ideally, the competency framework should enable development plans to be created for all three levels: organizational, team and individual. The competencies of individuals and teams create the capabilities of organizations – for speed, customer focus and innovation. At an organizational level, competencies can be a means of ensuring that the values are really lived if they are integrated into other HR processes. The trend towards competency-based pay systems is not yet well established in the UK but various organizations such as Barclays Bank have experimented with them in recent years as part of their contribution pay system. At an individual level, having the clarity afforded by the competencies should in theory allow people to be clear about how they can add value through their role.

For managers, performance management should also be easier, as should targeted recruitment against competency-based role descriptions. Role profiles can be developed at an individual and a team level. These can then provide a focus for development, performance management and recognition. Self-assessment and feedback processes such as 360 degrees can be developed around the competency-based profiles. These are increasingly used for appraisal and development purposes such as personal and team development. Typically, they are used in leadership training and subsets such as training managers to be coaches. Development can then be focused on things that matter: the organization's strategy and teams and individuals.

The Balanced Scorecard can be a helpful means of identifying appropriate measures taking into account the needs of various stakeholders. Good management information is important, as is continuous improvement and a learning culture.

The following case study illustrates one company's approach to integrating organizational and business strategies.

CASE STUDY: STRATEGIC ORGANIZATIONAL ALIGNMENT AT JAGUAR AND LAND ROVER[3]

Jaguar and Land Rover (J&LR) were at the time of writing part of Ford's Premier Automotive Group. The core activities revolve around the design, manufacture and sale of premium cars and 4 × 4s. There are six UK locations – five in the Midlands, one on Merseyside – with several smaller support organizations around the globe.

The Link Between People Development and Company Aims

For any business to thrive in the modern automotive sector is challenging in itself and the competition is exacerbated in the premium sector, which both traditional and new manufacturers are targeting like never before.

UK-based businesses cannot compete on a pure cost basis, so it's vital that Jaguar and Land Rover capitalize on the inherent value of their brands to deliver unique products and services that command a premium. The strength of the brands and their heritage are the source of that uniqueness, but it is only the people working within those brands that can bring this uniqueness to life, turning potential into reality.

Jaguar and Land Rover were brought under a common management structure at the start of 2002 in an attempt to realize potential scale and resource-sharing benefits in the face of increasingly intense international competition. This brought with it a host of complications, ranging from unaligned policies and processes through to confusion about the required 'culture' and behaviours in the new combined structure.

A thorough review of the business identified six strategic priorities if J&LR were to develop in a sustainable, profitable manner into the future. J&LR had been

---

3. I am grateful to Peter Wall, formerly Education, Training and Development manager at Jaguar and Land Rover for this account of how business success can be achieved when people management and development strategies are aligned to the business goal of achieving sustainable results.

under-performing on several key business measures, prompting a re-examination of its strategic direction and structure, in order to produce significant Return On Sales by the end of the decade.

Six critical strategic priorities were identified as:

1. Deliver outstanding quality/customer service
2. Build the brands/grow revenue
3. Develop great products that deliver the brand promise
4. Achieve a competitive cost base
5. Create the winning team
6. Build a sustainable business.

One of these 'vital few' – *Create the Winning Team* (CTWT) – is essentially the people strategy for the business and is an *enabler* for the other five. It's key to creating a performance-oriented culture, increasing personal accountability and enhancing teamworking.

One of its main focus areas is improving overall leadership effectiveness. One of the ways this is measured within J&LR is the Employee Satisfaction Index (ESI) score from the PULSE attitude survey, which had been on a consistent downward trend. Reversing this trend was targeted as an excellent indicator of progress towards longer-term success.

Approach to People Development

It is clearly recognized that without employee engagement and development and at the top of the agenda, the overall strategic plan is unlikely to succeed. J&LR adopts a holistic approach, with some of the mechanisms used to underpin the CTWT philosophy including …

Business Transformation and Policy Deployment Cascades

In order to clarify the J&LR *business transformation* strategy, and explain the Vital Few priorities, standardized communications packs were designed to engage employees in *dialogue* about what *transformation* meant to them at a practical level. All staff attended half-day workshops, delivered by local management, using a mix of video, presentations and discussion exercises. Comprehensive 'leader guides' helped inexperienced managers get the most from the process. These initiatives helped drive the improving trend on objective alignment (see later).

People Development Framework (PDF)

PDF draws together the key people development processes into a single, easy to understand model (see Figure 5.1). Introduced to improve understanding and transparency, it is reinforced by clearly defined, documented supporting processes, freely available on the company intranet.

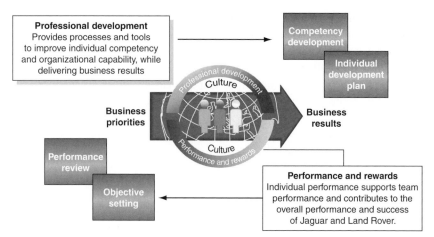

FIGURE 5.1   People development framework.

Accelerating Our Progress Workshops

To bring PDF to life, all staff participated in interactive 3-hour workshops, rein-forcing the *business transformation* messages, whilst placing specific emphasis on the importance of personal development and increasing personal accountability. These were pivotal in launching the web-based competency assessment tool, and encouraging engagement in the Individual Development Planning (*IDP*) processes.

Individual Competency Assessment

All employees are expected to demonstrate an appropriate level of competence against seven generic J&LR Business Behaviours, plus additional competencies directly related to their specific role. These focus on the vital skills, behaviours and knowledge required to transform the business, achieve quality performance and deliver superior business results. They incorporate and reflect the values identified by the J&LR Board as being critical to sustainable business success.

Automated Gap Analysis

A web-based competence assessment tool enables employees to conduct a self-assessment against these competencies which are then reviewed and adjusted, if necessary, with their immediate supervisor. The tool then automatically high-lights key competence gaps against the expectations of someone in that role, and suggests potential corresponding development opportunities.

Individual Development Plans (IDPs)

Each year, as part of the *policy deployment* process, every employee receives focused feedback on their performance against their objectives in the previous 12 months and agrees their objectives for the forthcoming period. This process may identify some business-related development needs, which when combined with any personal development aspirations and output from the web-based assessment provide the basis for a discussion on priority personal development objectives.

The resultant IDP summarizes the planned developmental activities to be undertaken to support the achievement of personal objectives, improve competency and performance levels and, where appropriate, prepare the individual for future job opportunities.

Over 80% of staff have now completed an IDP, with very positive feedback being received about process effectiveness:

'I think it's excellent. It gave me confidence that I'm working in the right way and achieving what's expected of me. Gaps were highlighted and what I needed to do to develop further. I've no negative feelings at all about the process.'

Priority Skills Gap Closure

With limited resources available, it is crucial that any development work is focused effectively on areas of maximum impact and return. J&LR operates a 'Balanced Scorecard' approach to business planning, with one of the high-level objectives on the company scorecard being *'Deployment of plans to address priority competence gaps'*. This ensures each function adopts a robust, planful approach to the identification and prioritization of key training requirements and takes proactive steps – supported by the Education, Training and Development team – to deliver measurable improvements in these areas. One of the web-based tool's key features is its ability to automatically highlight consistent gaps at department/functional level. Line management are now more able to make objective, quality decisions on where to focus training and development interventions for maximum impact.

Desk-Top e-Learning

With release to attend training courses increasingly difficult, a range of e-learning packages have been introduced that can be taken on demand direct at the employee's work station. Critically, the packages link intelligently to the J&LR on-line training administration system, providing the flexibility for people to stop and come back later to the same point in the programme. This facility is now amongst the top 5 most visited websites on the company intranet.

People Development Committees (PDCs)

PDCs are made up of functional line managers who represent the development interests of a number of 'constituent' employees. Assisted by their local HR business partner, their role is to ensure that J&LR has the right people with the right competencies for the right jobs at the right time. They use multiple inputs to assess employees' development needs and potential, and then collectively agree appropriate development plans. These include prioritizing places on nominated-access training programmes, allocating mentors and planning 'rotational' job moves to broaden experience.

Performance Management and Measurement

The annual *performance management* and *employee development* processes are explicitly connected within J&LR to ensure that both are given full and equal attention. Expanding on some key steps …

At total company level, the corporate scorecard objectives are reviewed and updated from mid-year so that the following year's version is ready by end-November. Each function constructs its own local scorecard in parallel, with 'fish bowl' sharing events to ensure cross-functional alignment.

By no later than end-January (December for senior managers), all employees agree and document their objectives for the year, with overt links to the score-card, on formal Performance Management documents using SMART methodology. This process also provides opportunities to identify business-related development needs for the coming year.

Supervisors are encouraged to have regular one-to-one reviews with team members, making performance feedback a continual process. As an absolute minimum, however, there is a mandatory requirement for two formal reviews of progress against objectives – an *interim* review at mid-year, and final at year-end. Employees are required to conduct a personal self-assessment of their own performance as part of this process, with their supervisor required to gather third-party customer feedback.

Following this process, supervisors produce recommended performance ratings for their team members, which are then moderated through facilitated *related work group* discussions within each department to ensure consistency and equity – critical given that compensation is based on the output from this process.

The final rating is then shared with the employee in a formal feedback discussion, providing further opportunities to discuss relevant development needs to enhance performance.

There is clear evidence that this *integrated* process is increasingly stimulating value-added discussions on personal development, focused on performance improvement (see Figure 5.2).

Reward and Recognition

J&LR operates a comprehensive range of reward and recognition schemes, some of which are described below …

Annual merit-based pay awards are made to managers and senior staff, based on the *related work group* output. Additionally, *individual performance payments*, annual bonus schemes and stock option programmes are used flexibly to reflect both past performance and potential future contribution.

Line managers can give vouchers worth up to £60 which employees then exchange for company merchandise. This scheme can recognize team or individual contribution – the only limit is that individuals can only receive two awards per year, and vouchers cannot be used to recognize attendance, long service or retirement.

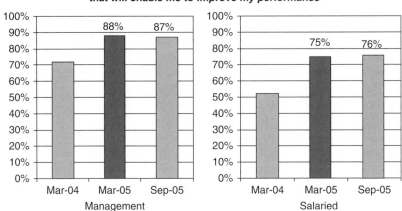

FIGURE 5.2   Value-adding personal development discussions.

There is formal long service recognition at 25 and 40 years, with celebration dinners and gifts. Certificates are also provided at 30 and 35 years.

A new attendance improvement scheme for manufacturing employees has recently been introduced at Land Rover. Depending on overall attendance patterns each quarter, a Land Rover product might be donated to the community and a Ford car could be won by an employee with a perfect attendance record. The scheme can also trigger payments into a community fund, administered jointly by management and employee representatives.

Extensive use is made of internal communication forums (e.g. management conferences, departmental meetings) to allow staff to present the results of successful projects or to receive recognition in front of their peers.

The Chief Executive presents a number of awards to PDC members at the annual conference in recognition of the part they play in the overall people development process.

Company magazines and departmental newsletters feature extensive coverage of employee successes, ranging from graduation on degree courses to community projects initiated by employees.

The company intranet also features a website giving advice and guidance for managers on non-financial reward and recognition opportunities.

Leadership and Management Development

The strategic review identified improving leadership capability as one of the 'critical success factors' for J&LR to achieve its long-term business objectives. Reflecting this, a comprehensive framework of leadership and management skills development programmes has been implemented, spanning all grades and business functions. Although some are nomination-based (through PDCs), many are available for people to view and book direct through an on-line training catalogue.

The Winning Mindset Programme

Several ground-breaking leadership development programmes have been introduced to stimulate behaviour change within the organization. The primary example is *The Winning Mindset,* initially for the Board and their direct reports and subsequently for the most senior 150 managers in the companies.

Initially, 20 of these senior managers were interviewed to discuss their strengths and weaknesses and what they would find most valuable if they were to invest time in their own development. Whilst they each identified a number of individual development needs, *all* of them said that they wanted to improve their 'soft' relationship skills. They wanted behaviourally based interventions which would make them more impactful personally.

The resulting three-day leadership programme – 'The Winning Mindset' – is very different from the more traditional, classroom-based approaches that had been used in the past. It combines both personal and team development elements with innovative reinforcement processes (e.g. DVD diaries). The programme includes a strong emphasis on self-reflection about patterns of behaviour and uses transactional analysis, drivers and other ways of deepening participants' self-insight. A mix of internal and external facilitators are used and the programme is independently evaluated by Warwick University. Unusually for a 'soft skills' programme, evaluation reveals that effective leadership development is increasingly considered as critical to business success:

- 81% believe the programme directly or indirectly meets the core business priorities
- 85% believe it will help meet future business challenges
- 90% believe it will strengthen working relationships.

Corporate Social Responsibility (CSR)

J&LR has a formal *sustainable development* policy and fully complies with all relevant employment, business and environmental legislation. In addition, it is accredited to externally-assessed quality and environmental standards (TS16949 and ISO14001).

Conscious of the potential environmental impact of its products, J&LR continuously focuses on developing and introducing new technologies to make its vehicles lighter, safer and more fuel-efficient, with these attributes now carrying equal importance to other more traditional elements such as styling or equipment levels. Each of the J&LR manufacturing facilities also deliver a high degree of environmental efficiency with continual focus on reducing energy, water and waste. The need to operate a *sustainable business model* is now formally recognized through the inclusion of cluster of actions on the 2006 company-level scorecard. These then flow through to departmental and individual objectives as previously described.

In addition, J&LR has a published *corporate citizenship* policy, and actively supports the community through a wide range of activities – from formal support for charitable organizations (e.g. *Arts and Business*) and membership of/participation in external bodies (e.g. *Advantage West Midlands*) through to operating *Education/Business Partnership* centres and hosting school visits at each site.

Individual employees are encouraged to support the community at a personal level, whether through formal positions such as school governors or by volunteering to assist with a range of centrally coordinated community projects which are promoted through a dedicated company website.

Employees are able to spend up to two paid days per year supporting such projects. In many cases, groups of people from the same teams come together to work on a community activity which doubles-up as a team building event. For example, members of the sales planning department recently worked together to renovate a community play area.

Overcoming Barriers to Success

Given the size and complexity of J&LR, and the challenging business situation it finds itself in, one of the greatest barriers to effective deployment of the People Development strategy was undoubtedly the very tight resource constraints it faced, especially in the early stages.

Convincing people that their employer takes people development seriously is often difficult, but becomes even more challenging when there is a strong emphasis on avoiding 'discretionary' spend. The unwavering support of the HR Director and the Finance Director was essential, though one of J&LR's key achievements has been to demonstrate that commitment to development is not purely a function of money spent.

The fact that CTWT has remained clearly positioned as one of the top six strategic priorities has helped keep the topic in the foreground. The J&LR Board have also actively reinforced its importance to them personally through formal processes such as the bi-monthly People Committee, and informally such as when joining employees at training programmes.

Restricted financial spend has stimulated some innovative approaches to training, ranging from the delivery of internal 'masterclasses' by subject matter experts on a wide range of topics through to collaborative working and joint funding with other businesses – both inside and outside of Ford Motor Company – on the development and delivery of new programmes.

The dissemination of good practice in personal development has been actively encouraged by processes such as network meetings for PDC chairs and facilitators and an annual PDC conference.

The end result is that J&LR is increasingly being recognized as a leader in people and skills development despite its challenging financial environment.

Measuring Business Impact

In the three years since CTWT was initiated, there have been marked and consistent improvements in the majority of key business metrics. Whilst it is very difficult to prove a direct correlation between people development processes and the business 'bottom line', there is a strong belief within the J&LR senior leadership team that the two are closely linked. This position is reinforced by clear evidence of the business impact of those elements of the CTWT strategy that *can* be directly measured, for example …

Policy Deployment

One of the main thrusts of J&LR's people development strategy has been to build increased understanding of the key strategic and operational priorities of the business, and then aligning individual and team objectives directly to the delivery of those goals. This *'Policy Deployment'* process ensures that people's efforts are focused on delivering quality products and improving business results, and that personal development is centred on increasing personal effectiveness and impact.

The effectiveness of Policy Deployment is actively monitored through a twice-yearly e-survey, and there have been steady year-over-year improvements in the number of employees stating that they have formal objectives, and a consistently high level of understanding of the links to the business scorecard (see Figures 5.3 and 5.4).

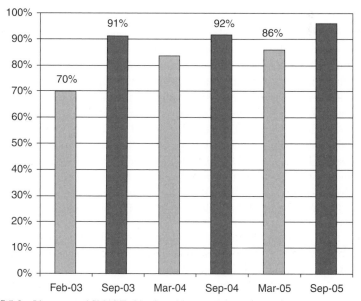

FIGURE 5.3   I have agreed SMART objective with my manager.

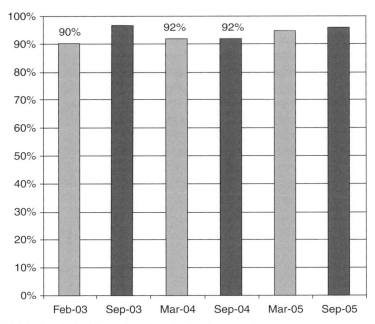

FIGURE 5.4   I understand the content of my functional scorecard.

Employee Satisfaction

It is also generally acknowledged that motivated and engaged employees are likely to make a more positive overall contribution to the business. The primary way in which employee satisfaction is measured within J&LR is through the annual PULSE survey. There has been a striking change in the overall Employee Satisfaction Index (ESI) trend over the past few years, suggesting that the various strands of the CTWT strategy are positively impacting on employee morale (see Figure 5.5).

The ultimate measure, of course, is the overall profitability of the J&LR business. Whilst there is still some way to go before the long-term profit aspirations are realized, there has been a consistent year-over-year improvement since 2004, and the forecast looks set for this trend to continue.

Not surprisingly, Jaguar and Land Rover were named as winners of the 'Outstanding Workplace of the Year' in the 2006 UK National Business awards.

CONCLUSION

HR professionals must be able to translate business needs in HR strategies that count – and these are likely to focus on building individual, team and organizational capabilities. Talent will be at the heart of business success in

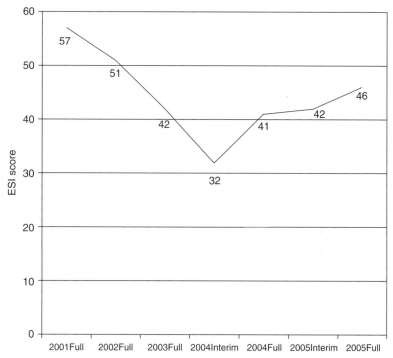

FIGURE 5.5　Employee satisfaction index.

knowledge-intensive firms. The organizational strategy has to both address talent issues and help realize business opportunities through the development and deployment of talent. What is needed is a profound conviction among HR professionals, line managers and executives, that people really matter and that leaders must develop the capabilities of employees, nurture their careers and manage the performance of employees. This includes building the cultural context within organizations which is conducive to attracting and retaining talent, and stimulating high performance. The HR strategy is therefore also a human capital strategy, an organizational development strategy and a business development strategy.

But the challenge is not HR's alone, even though HR must show leadership of this agenda. Developing effective human capital strategies requires active partnership with, and engagement of line managers. This engagement is complex and evolutionary in nature. It requires grappling with competing agendas, perspectives and values. It involves meeting stakeholder needs for respect and ownership. This requires HR widening the focus beyond senior management and better addressing the needs of line managers. It may involve learning new behaviours, changing attitudes and processes. Above all, it will involve discovering how to use the process of developing and implementing HR strategy as a means of moving an organization to a new place while mobilizing people to address the strategic agenda.

ALIGNMENT CHECKLISTS

Managing the Business Environment

How does the way we interact with the external environment add value to the management of our workforce?

- How aware are we of the business environment in which we are operating? What are the economic/political, social, demographic, technological, competitor and consumer trends? Where are the risks/opportunities?
- What is the potential strength of the impact of these trends on our organization?
- What influence do we exercise in the local business environment through lobbying and communicating in the local language?

Defining and Analysing the Organization

Does the organization enable us to build a sustainable competitive advantage?

- Is the organization's purpose linked to the structure and the roles and is the purpose evident in all aspects of goals, plans, measures?
- Is there a clear 'arrival point' when we can declare a 'victory'?
- To what extent do corporate values drive behaviours and guide decisions?
- How well aligned is the organization design to what we are trying to achieve?
- Does the shape of the organization – its size, the numbers employed, the numbers at each level or grade, the types of hierarchy and spans of control – support what the organization wants to achieve?
- Flexibility – how do our structure and contractual arrangements enable us to respond to change and integrate with the marketplace?
- Retaining talent – does job design offer employees scope for development? How do we measure motivation and morale? How do we interpret turnover and absence indicators?
- How well integrated are leadership, values and behaviours? HR practices and policies?
- How well have staffing practices, training and development as well as performance management been aligned to culture and strategy?
- How well aligned are communications to culture?

Productivity and Labour Costs

How are we ensuring the highest possible rate of return on our investment in people?

- Workforce investment – what are the options, costs and short-term/long-term payback we can expect?
- Are the costs of running the organization – the HR, distribution, and productivity measures – clear and controlled?

- Productivity measures – what are the ratios, measurement and controls we can use?
- Budgeting and control – what workforce planning and budgeting methods, headcount control and other key indicators can we use?
- Incentive scheme development – what should we take into account in designing these schemes? What measures of effectiveness are appropriate and how will we calculate the cost versus the benefit to the business?

Workforce Planning

Do we have the workforce to implement the business plan?

- Workforce planning – how do we evaluate existing human resources against future requirements (numbers, abilities, skills, experience)? How do we identify gaps and surpluses? What retention indicators can we use?
- Resourcing – how will we ensure that our strategy addresses the needs of the external environment, internal talent and retention policies?
- How will we make up gaps in the workforce – through (re)training, recruitment, development or a combination? What are the key short- and medium-term gaps we will need to fill?
- How will we deal with surpluses of employees – through retraining, relocation, redundancy?
- Career planning – how will we provide assessment (of abilities, skills, competencies), counselling and development?
- Succession planning – what forms will we use? Focused on a minority or building up a cadre? What processes will support these plans?

REFERENCES

Berry, M. (2007) *Personnel Today*, 27 February

Ettore, B. (1997) The empowerment gap: hype vs. reality. *HR Focus*, 74, Issue 7, (July)

Fauth, R. (2006) *Workplace Trends: 2003–6*. London: The Work Foundation

Gertz, D.L. and Baptista, J. (1995) *Grow to be Great, Breaking the Downsizing Cycle*. New York: Free Press

Grundy, A. (1998) How are corporate strategy and Human Resources strategy linked? *Journal of General Management*, 23, Issue 3, (Spring)

Holbeche, L. (1997) *Career Development: Managing the Impact of Flatter Structures on Careers*. Oxford: Butterworth-Heinemann

IBM Corporation and Towers Perrin (1994) Priorities for gaining competitive advantage. *Management*, 22, Issue 2, (Winter)

Kochan, T. and Barocci, T. (eds) (1985) *Human Resource Management and Industrial Relations*. Boston: Little Brown

Lam, S.S.K. and Schaubroeck, J. (1998) Integrating HR planning and organizational strategy. *Human Resource Journal*, 8, No. 3, 5–19

Mabey, C. and Salaman, G. (1995) *Strategic Human Resource Management*. Oxford: Blackwell

Pascale, R.T. (1995) The Honda effect, in Mintzberg, H., Quinn, J.B. and Ghoshal, S. (eds), *The Strategy Process*. Englewood Cliffs, NJ: Prentice Hall

Peters, T. and Waterman, R. (1982) *In Search of Excellence*. New York: Harper Row

Pfeffer, J. (1995) People, capability and competitive success. *Management Development Review*, 8, No. 5, 6–10

Poole, M.J.F. and Jenkins, G. (1996) *Back to the Line?* London: Institute of Management

Prahalad, C.K. and Hamel, G. (1995) The core competence of the corporation, in Mintzberg, H., Quinn, J.B. and Ghoshal, S. (eds), *The Strategy Process*. Englewood Cliffs, NJ: Prentice Hall

Schuler, R.S. and Jackson, S.E. (1987) Linking competitive strategies with Human Resource Management practices. *The Academy of Management Executive*, 1, No. 3, 207–219

Sparrow, P., Hesketh, A., Hird, M., Marsh, C. and Balain, S. (2008) *Reversing the Arrow: Using Business Model Change to Tie HR into Strategy*: Lancaster University Management School

Strack, R. Francoeur, F., Dyer, A., Caye, J.M., Minto, A., Leicht, M., Ang, D., Böhm, H. and McDonnell, M. (2008) *Creating People Advantage: How to Address HR Challenges Worldwide through 2015*: Boston Consulting Group

Thompson, A.A. and Strickland, A.J. (1998) *Strategic Management Concepts and Cases*. New York: Irwin/McGraw-Hill

Tyson, S. and Witcher, M. (1994) Human Resource strategy: emerging from the recession. *Personnel Management*, August

Ulrich, D. interviewed by MacLachlan, R. (1998) HR with attitude, *People Management*, 13 August

FURTHER READING

Devine, M., Hirsh, W. and Holbeche, L. (1998) *Mergers and Acquisitions: Getting the People Bit Right*. Horsham: Roffey Park Management Institute

Johnson, G. and Scholes, K. (1993) *Exploring Corporate Strategy*, Third Edition. Hemel Hempstead: Prentice Hall

Tyson, S. (1995) *Human Resource Strategy. Towards a General Theory of Human Resource Management*. London: Pitman

Wright, P.M., McMahan, G.C. and McWilliams, A. (1994) Human Resources and sustained competitive advantage – a resource based perspective. *International Journal of Human Resource Management*, 5, No. 2, 301–326

Part II

Strategies for Managing and Developing Talent

Chapter 6

Recruitment and Retention Strategies

Ask leaders what their biggest challenge is, and you get the same answer: identifying, retaining and replacing the best talent in an organization is the key issue most likely to keep chief executives awake at night.

(Peter Cheese, 2007)

The 'War for Talent' can no longer be dismissed as just another management cliché despite global economy downturns. Identifying, retaining and replacing those people who breathe life into an organization is now a 'burning obsession among chief executives', according to Peter Cheese, global managing partner at Accenture's human performance practice, and affects business leaders in India just as much as those in the UK: 'More than 60% of the respondents to our annual survey of chief executives said that the inability to attract and retain the best talent is now a key threat to their business, outstripping the issue of low employee morale' (in Matthews, 2007). Other studies confirm similar messages. Two McKinsey Global Surveys (2006 and 2007) revealed that business leaders are deeply worried about finding talented people and expect the increasingly global competition for talent to have a major effect on their companies in the next five years. The result has been increased competition to attract and retain individuals who demonstrate the most potential.

Similarly, ask talented people what their biggest career challenge is and you will hear the same refrain: finding good people to work with – and the right organizations to work for. Given that skilled workers appear to have many employment choices available to them, employers are increasingly having to compete hard for the best candidates. In the new 'War for Talent' employers have to come up with innovative and potentially far-reaching solutions if they are to attract the candidates they need to fuel their business success.

But while attracting new talent to the organization is a key challenge, especially when the talent in question is globally in short supply in sectors and industries such as pharmaceuticals, construction and information technology, retaining talent represents another set of challenges. Though recruitment and retention are often spoken of in the same breath, as here, the factors driving them are not necessarily the same. Employees increasingly want the same kind of personalized attention that customers receive, and skilled workers can and do exercise their options if they are not happy with their lot. And while companies increasingly develop 'employer brands' to attract potential employees, in common with other forms of branding, if the lived reality of the brand is different from the promise, the customer–employee goes elsewhere.

In this chapter we shall explore some of the issues related to recruitment and retention and consider what a strategic approach to recruitment and retention needs to involve. It will incorporate a wider set of policies, such as reward, development and job design, none of which is enough in isolation. We focus specifically on the inter-related strategies of developing people in Chapter 8, and the creation of effective career paths in Chapter 9. These must reflect an understanding of employee motivation and be closely linked to trends in the changing labour market, as well as to the organization's needs.

DEFINING 'TALENT' AND 'TALENT MANAGEMENT'

However, what do 'talent' and 'talent management' mean? A CIPD sponsored research project (Tansley *et al.*, 2006) looked at how a variety of organizations understood these terms and found several variations on a theme. Where there was coalescence between these variations was in the following definition of 'talent':

> Talent consists of those individuals who can make a difference to organizational performance, either through their immediate contribution or in the longer term by demonstrating the highest levels of potential.

And while various theorists argue that talent management is nothing new, but a re-labelling of old processes, nevertheless talent management looks here to stay. It is defined as:

> The systematic attraction, identification, development, engagement/retention and deployment of those individuals with high potential who are of particular value to an organization.

The need for HR to develop new approaches to talent management for their organizations has rarely been greater. These approaches are likely to include both talent strategy and the execution of that strategy and include as talent acquisition, development, management and retention. Furthermore, as Guthridge *et al.* argue (2008), talent management is very much a business issue: 'demographics, globalization and the characteristics of knowledge work present long-term challenges that reinforce the argument for putting workforce planning and talent management at the heart of the business strategy and for giving those issues a bigger share of senior management's time'.

THE TALENT 'CRISIS'

The days when employers could pick and choose among a wide selection of excellent candidates may be becoming a thing of the past. Throughout Europe there are growing skills shortages at all levels. The changing demographics of the UK workforce, its increasing diversity and the work–life balance agenda have led to a very tight labour market resulting in increased competition from organizations for individuals who are capable of making the greatest difference to perform-ance. While in the UK many skills gaps at lower levels have been plugged through employing migrant workers, the situation is not stable and employee turnover is also increasing. In the CIPD's 2007 Labour Turnover survey it was estimated that average staff turnover in the UK is between 18 and 20%, and 84% of organiza-tions surveyed for CIPD's *Recruitment, Retention and Turnover Survey* (Fernon, 2007) were experiencing recruitment difficulties. The key reasons for recruit-ment difficulties were a lack of the necessary specialist skills (65%), followed by higher pay expectations (46%) and insufficient experience (37%). According to headhunters, there is a much wider calibre of people applying for jobs than in years gone by. As employees develop their marketability and 'knowledge-based' skills are a prized asset, employers are having to compete for the best candidates.

Industries and sectors whose image may seem less attractive to candidates are struggling to find new recruits. The construction industry, for instance, which once had a steady flow of candidates for jobs that involved difficult working conditions now experiences competition for candidates from employers who can provide office-based roles using computers. Similarly, the insurance indus-try suffers from a (probably unjustified) sedentary image that may not appeal to young candidates. Where employers are looking for specific skills and experi-ence, especially where these have a high market value, such as in the IT sector, competition can be intense.

Given global talent shortages, sourcing scarce talent is going to be an ongo-ing challenge. Another study, by Deloitte (2004), suggested six questions CEOs need to ask their HR Leaders:

1. Which segments of the workforce create the value for which we are most rewarded in the marketplace?
2. Which areas of our business will be most impacted by impending waves of retirement? What are we doing to prepare successors? What impact will anticipated retirement have on the skills and productivity necessary to meet future demand?
3. In what areas is the talent market heating up (i.e. demand will outpace sup-ply)? Which segments of our workforce will be most impacted? What are the potential top-line and bottom-line implications?
4. What skills will we need over the next five years that we don't currently possess? How will we create that capacity? What happens to our business if we don't?

5. What is our turnover within critical areas? How much is it costing us? In customers? In productivity? In innovation? In quality? What are we doing to resolve the root causes?

6. Are we actively developing talent portfolios or workforce plans that will help us to understand and communicate the financial consequences of talent decisions on our business?

STRATEGIC RECRUITMENT

Of course recruitment is only one means of getting the talent organizations need to succeed. Getting the right focus and blend of approaches for capability-building is important. For example, what should be the right balance between developing current staff and external recruitment? If recruitment from outside is the only means by which senior positions are filled, internal candidates soon realize that they must leave the organization if they want to be promoted. Conversely, with too little external recruitment an organization's processes and staff can start to stagnate.

Making the right choices requires a long-term intent and perspective on capability-building, allied with pragmatism to take into account specific short-term business needs and the state of the labour market at the time.

For those organizations looking to recruit talent, recruitment is a strategic opportunity but strategic approaches to recruitment are rare; most are tactical and short-term. Recruitment is part of an integrated set of HR practices, including staff development, which play a part in building the organization's capability in a changing marketplace. Managing talent means being clear about which of the different elements of the talent process, such as recruitment and selection, are more important at any particular time, including being aware of where the pressure points are. Are we recruiting satisfactorily on the one hand, but losing people further down the pipeline at the same time?

Recruitment should be part of an integrated talent management strategy which is driven by the business strategy. The key elements of such a strategy are as follows:

1. **Understand the implications of the business strategy**
   - Where is the organization going? How are needs changing?
   - Is growth anticipated?
   - Are we becoming international/global?
   - How much change and innovation do we wish to inject into the system?
   - What costs are we expecting?
   - How much flexibility will be needed in servicing customer needs (e.g. 24-hour retailing)?

2. **Work out what is required to support the business strategy:**
   'Stocktake' current staff
   - How many people do we have? What are their skills, knowledge, experience, attitudes to change?

- What do our current staff want in terms of career development? Are these expectations realistic?

Assess future needs

- How many people will we need in the short-term future (e.g. 2–3 years)? What will their skills be?

Identify gaps

- Who has particular talents which we wish to nurture?
- Who do we especially want to retain?
- Who is at risk of leaving?
- What key skills areas are we likely to be short of?
- Where have we too many of the 'wrong' skills?
- How much will people be willing to retrain?

3. **Develop an integrated set of processes to sit alongside development plans**
   - External – develop hiring plans
   - Internal – develop retention strategies, removal plans
   - Set measures of effectiveness and identify costs

4. **Create an infrastructure for development**
   - Develop HR policies that support development and learning
   - Ensure that organizational values, feedback processes, senior management behaviour, reward mechanisms and development all align
   - Create mechanisms for self-development such as 360-degree feedback, development reviews, development centres, learning resources, career workshops etc.
   - Ensure that line managers are trained to help others with their development.

Recruitment should rarely be about straightforward replacement or gap filling. Every recruitment process is an opportunity to bring into the organization the kind of skills and experience that cannot easily be built from within. Every decision not to recruit externally is an opportunity deliberately to grow internal talent.

In the late 1990s Thresher, the UK drinks retailer was aiming to transform attitudes and behaviours among staff in its operations, a number of ways were found to involve staff. As a result, many employees became energized and revitalized by the change. The then operations director, Brian Wisdom, and HR controller, Chris Johnson, however, recognized that change needed to be embedded at all levels and that relying on the goodwill generated would not be sufficient. They deliberately recruited external 'architects of change' who would bring a different perspective into the workforce. These were people in line management roles whose experience of other change processes caused them to act as the 'grit in the oyster'.

Recognizing that these people would be under pressure to conform to the status quo rather than pursue the change required, Brian and Chris acted as mentors to the newcomers, offering a 'hotline' service when the going became difficult. The result was that the majority of newcomers stayed and had the desired effect of bringing about change from within. Many have since moved through the organization, their change agent skills recognized and valued. For more details of the change project in question, see Chapter 16.

How are Organizations Responding to the Talent Crisis?

In many organizations the link between talent and business success is now so visible and direct that the need to source scarce talent is high up amongst board priorities. Leaders are increasingly looking within for the critical skills and knowledge required to carry out the company's most important jobs. Some companies are experimenting with potentially costly solutions such as locating work where skilled employees prefer to live, rather than where other logic might dictate, and flexible role design to take talent shortages into account.

Rethinking Jobs

Cheese (2007) argues that closing talent gaps requires new levels of innovation in thinking through the design of working processes and jobs themselves:

- Jobs or tasks can be redesigned to reduce the level of skills proficiency (i.e. downskilling)
- Jobs can be moved or relocated to access different talent pools (i.e. near-shoring or off-shoring)
- Jobs can be moved to another organization better equipped to find the right talent (i.e. outsourcing or partnering)
- Technology can reduce the need for some jobs completely and provide many opportunities to change job and skill requirements (i.e. automation)
- Jobs can be structured to be carried out virtually to allow people to do the work from anywhere (i.e. restructuring)
- Particular tasks may be thrown open to the free networks and talent now available on the Internet (i.e. the 'wiki' economy).

Introducing Talent 'Puddles'

The pool of talent Nestlé is seeking to tap into is from a candidate-driven market. Recruitment services is one of several HR centres of expertise, the others being learning and development, the information and administration centre, and policy, remuneration and reward. The recruitment services team have worked with a number of functions to develop a multi-channel approach to filling their recruitment needs. Supported by the HR business partners, the function identifies its talent shortfalls and recruitment services subsequently devise an attraction strategy to fill the specific talent gap.

One initiative to help overcome the shortage of skilled applicants is Nestlé's 'talent puddles'. This is a targeted pool of talent that is easier to access and manage than a broad generic talent database, which after time grows too unwieldy to identify the appropriate candidates.

Earlier efforts to implement talent pools failed due to poor IT systems – recruiters were unable to find suitable people as the search facility was inadequate. However, the talent puddles are much smaller and contain potential talent for each function rather than the whole company.

The first talent puddle was set up in September 2006 with a £5000 budget. Creating micro-sites for jobs the department need to recruit for was the first step. This was followed by a targeted online campaign to generate candidates who were then interviewed and kept warm until an appropriate opportunity arose. This candidate relationship management strategy allows the company to have candidates who are 'offer ready' and interested in Nestlé when a vacancy becomes available. This attraction strategy is designed to fill specific jobs and 'difficult to fill' roles. Because of this the company is upfront with people that there are no jobs in existence.

According to Fionna White,[1] Head of Recruitment at Nestlé, 'Persuading senior management was not difficult. Our business case highlighted a £56000 cost of placing 13 people within the organization via agencies versus the talent puddle and candidate relationship management concept, which generated 14 offers from just £700.' Reducing time to hire and fill vacancies and the cost of recruiting are just some of the business benefits. One vacancy filled via this method led to an offer being accepted in 24 hours. White believes this approach has encouraged the organization to become better at its resource planning by turning line managers' conversations to focus on identifying their talent gaps and on 'what we are doing proactively as opposed to reacting "once the horse has bolted" as we have done in the past'.

Employer Branding

One of the key strategies for attracting candidates is developing a strong employer brand, though debate still rages as to whether or not the notion of employer branding is a passing fad or here to stay. Employer branding is how an organization markets what it has to offer to both to potential and existing employees:

> An employer brand is a set of attributes and qualities – often intangible – that make an organization distinctive, promise a particular kind of employment experience, and appeal to those people who will thrive and perform to their best in its culture (Walker, 2007).

There is growing evidence that the criteria used by younger workers in particular to select their future employer include the chance for learning and growth, respect for them as individuals, company ethics and values, even more than the pay on offer (see later in this chapter). Employer brands which imply that this is

---

1. Featured in CIPD's Recruitment, Retention and Turnover Survey, 2007.

the nature of the employee value proposition on offer are likely to be attractive to potential recruits.

Probably the first commercial organization to take the notion of employer brand seriously was British Airways back in the 1980s. According to the CIPD survey *Recruitment, Retention and Turnover* (2007), the employer brand approach has now caught on, with almost seven in 10 organizations of all sizes and sectors describing themselves as having an employer brand (69%). Attracting the people you want to recruit is cited by 80% of respondents as the main resourcing objective for investing in employer branding.

There are other reasons too for adopting the notion of employer branding, as the CIPD research suggests. Fifty-seven per cent of respondents say they are also keen to improve the external perceptions of the organization and 41% are hoping to differentiate themselves from the competition.

In conventional marketing, developing a company brand is used to gain customer awareness and loyalty. A successful brand is part of the distinctiveness of the product. The brand implies a 'promise' and creates customer expectation, the consumer 'buys' that promise and is satisfied or otherwise. As a result the customer continues to buy the product, or not; speaks well or badly of the product and, if disappointed, goes elsewhere. When a brand is closely identified with its 'product', for example as a prestige item, every element of the design, production, quality of finished goods and after-care service need to be aligned with the brand promise.

The company's mission, culture and values are noted as the main elements of the employer brand to be communicated (85%) and many employers also use their employer brand to promote their career and development opportunities (71%). The attempt of organizations to differentiate themselves through employer branding is evident in one example from a job advertisement for a commercial manager. There is tacit acknowledgement that employees are attracted by more than pay and the work itself:

> What does success mean to you? It could mean having a major say in a FTSE 100 company, a truly global organization where you enjoy real influence. That is what you will get here without question. But you will also gain so much more. You will find an atmosphere of change, growth and innovation; where the IS department is recognized and rewarded as a key driver in our business development; and your ideas will be heard throughout the entire organization ...

When it comes to delivering the reality of the promise the danger is that HR teams focus mainly on what is required to bring candidates into the organization; less on delivering the promise to existing employees. As the CIPD research suggests, recruitment advertising and communication materials are most likely to be shaped by the employer brand (76%), which also tends to influence the design of induction training. So at 'entry' a candidate's expectations are being shaped by a clear employment promise implicit in the employer brand. However, if the organizational reality does not match the implied promise of the employer brand, the effect can be disappointing to say the least for all concerned. It is therefore important to have some understanding of the likely expectations of potential candidates and how these might be met, or not, by your employment offer and employer brand.

Values

It is commonly assumed that people born between 1980 and 1994 ('Generation Y') are likely to be concerned about the environment, ethics and other aspects of a company's corporate social responsibility (CSR). However, a TalentDrain report (Eldridge and Miles, 2008) suggests that it is older workers who are more likely to be concerned about CSR and having a modern working environment than younger workers.

One firm that does have an ethical employer brand is KPMG, who provide audit, tax and advisory services across the UK. The company believes it differentiates itself from its competitors for potential recruits by its culture. This is reflected in strong working and social relationships among teams and with managers, together with career development, stimulating work and the flexibility to enjoy a rewarding home life. Departments have a strong social identity and company values have been formalized into the 'KPMG way'. A 'management for excellence' scheme has embedded the KPMG values through personal development. Progress is supported with mentoring and training. 'Out of the box' assignments are given to those who have been at the firm a number of years and are moving up to partner level. These usually involve working for a client company or for KPMG abroad.

And the company's profit share pool is divided among employees. A flexible benefits package includes the chance to buy up to 35 days' additional holiday per year, on top of the regular 25. Unpaid leave of between three months and three years is available to those with at least two years' service, making it possible to realize personal ambitions without compromising on professional ones.

Recruiting Older Workers

With Age Discrimination legislation in force throughout Europe and organizations experiencing key skills shortages, employing older workers is becoming more common, even though in practice there appears to be a continuation of subtle age discrimination in many organizations, with older workers often missing out on promotion or development opportunities.

However, legislation has made it illegal to exclude candidates on the basis of their age and recruitment advertising, job specifications and the recruitment process as a whole have to be 'age-proofed'.

Role of Technology in Recruitment

The challenge of attracting the right candidates is being made easier by the use of technology. Online recruitment is now commonplace and opens up the potential field of candidates for any given job to those with access to a computer. Recruitment and search agencies are themselves undergoing something of a transition thanks to the impact of technology. Search organizations are increasingly providing website-based recruitment services, where the value added by the consultancy is in the quality of candidate assessment and in their systematic closing procedures. Candidates, typically mid-level professionals, are encouraged to complete a set of questionnaires and instruments which produce a profile. They can place their CV on the web which means that they become available through the search consultant's website to employers around the world. Internet-based recruitment is a major trend for junior/middle management posts.

Graduate Recruitment

The trend towards online recruitment is strong, especially in the graduate recruitment arena. Technology can speed up and streamline the process of recruitment as well as expand a company's graduate outreach programme, since technology breaks down geographic barriers. UK employers are increasingly using online recruitment networks featuring portals that are designed to help employers and graduates to find each other. The main features of such portals are their databases of students and graduates from across a spectrum of UK universities. These databases provide a pool of talent that employers can tap into online via portals which become the means whereby employers can contact graduates, such as hosted chat rooms or e-mails to targeted candidates.

Employers want to be able to target specific groups of candidates and demand is high for personalization of communications between employer and candidates. Candidates want to work for employers who share their values and who are interested in investing in them to help them reach their goals. Once the graduate applies to the employer online, the portal service may provide the online application form (under the employers' own identity), screen it to ensure the candidate is suitable for the role, and be further involved in seeing the application progress online. However, such tools cannot replace a company's presence on campuses; they mainly serve to increase the size of the talent pool available to the company. Graduate recruitment websites offer diversity zones, where candidates can look for jobs that encourage applications from specific groups of people such as women and ethnic minorities.

Well-designed career websites and mobile Internet sites, such as the one PricewaterhouseCoopers launched in 2007, boost firms' profile with high-calibre graduates. Social networking sites, such as My Space and Facebook, are now online employers' and candidates' tools and employee blogs on company websites are designed to explain what it is like to work at a particular company. However, it is thought that there are cultural differences in the way these are accepted, with UK candidates being less likely to believe them than candidates in the United States.

Networking and Recruitment

According to a CIPD study (Swart and Kinnie, 2003), the process of attracting human capital in knowledge-intensive firms (KIFs) has distinctive characteristics.

Typically, informal processes such as networking are embedded in organizational practices. Networking for talent is a key theme. Recruitment is seen as a continuous process, one in which knowledge is exchanged by developing 'talent networks'. Talent networks are characterized by continuous interaction and conversation about cutting-edge skills.

Many KIFs forge relationships with universities, competitors and professional bodies in order to have access to a pool of relevant talent, or knowledge workers. A formalized way of developing networks for recruitment is the placement system – graduates and postgraduates are given the opportunity to work for the KIF for a fixed period. During this time the student is encouraged to develop organization-specific skills and knowledge while other employees learn cutting-edge skills from the placement employee through shared practice.

THE RECRUITMENT AND SELECTION PROCESS

Increasingly, employers are recognizing that the very process of recruitment may itself be as powerful an incentive to candidates to join as generous pay and conditions. The interview process should help candidates to understand the brand, culture and the company's commitment to graduate recruitment.

A well-designed recruitment process can attract good candidates and give the employer useful indications of future performance. Candidates are usually more positive about the organization if they can see a clear link between the recruitment process and the job. Structured interviews, using behavioural and critical incident interviewing, can be helpful as they allow specific job-related areas such as team leadership and customer service to be explored. Psychometrics that are relevant to the work content and realistic simulations can also be useful.

Simulations in particular allow managers to see a candidate's performance at first hand. They also provide the candidate with a chance to assess the role and to gather information about the company's approach to doing business. Flexibility is also important in ensuring that excellent candidates can be seen at times which are possible for them, rather than to a fixed interview schedule. This conveys the message to candidates that they are considered an important part of the organization's future. Decisions should be conveyed early and feedback offered so that even an unsuccessful application becomes a development opportunity. Disappointed candidates can still become advocates of the company if they feel that they have had a useful experience and been treated with respect. The professional image created by the recruitment process can therefore be an important part of attracting quality candidates in the future.

For senior management and other key positions, search agencies are often used, though it is thought that 40–50% of top appointments are filled by contacts. Increasingly, search agencies are adding a suite of activities to their portfolio which should ensure that the successful candidate becomes effective in their new role. Typically, services for the candidate include the usual follow-up counselling sessions with the search consultant. In addition, several agencies are offering one-to-one coaching and specific accelerated skills training.

Getting the Right 'Fit'

In essence, the successful attracting and recruiting of new talent means that the needs and offers of both the organization and the individual need to marry up. The 'fit' has to be right – in terms of skills and experience as well as values and needs. It is therefore important that both parties are as open as possible throughout the recruitment process. There will inevitably be a process of negotiation around those respective needs, usually over pay or the type and level of work on offer. Increasingly, individuals wish to ensure that the organizations they are thinking of joining can offer some form of ongoing development and CV enhancement. Organizations that recognize this and put concrete plans in place to enable development are more likely not only to attract but also to retain good candidates.

So important is getting the 'fit' right at the supermarket chain Asda that all colleagues, including checkout staff, are selected according to a rigorous procedure, which includes a half-day assessment process to ensure that the candidate's attitudes will match the company culture of customer service. Every new recruit is carefully inducted so that there is commonality of purpose and a level of generic skills development. Similarly, with around 400 applicants for every vacancy, Google applies a robust hiring process which ensures that incoming staff will add something to the culture. As HR Director Liane Hornsey speaking at CIPD's annual conference in 2008 said: 'Everything you do in HR should be about making sure you've picked the right people from the beginning. I will not compromise on quality.'

Delivering the 'Promise'

When the successful candidate joins the organization, each side will be monitoring the situation to ensure that the other party is living up to their promises. There is plenty of anecdotal evidence that the more help and support provided to candidates in the first few months, the more likely it is that the candidate will be able to perform satisfactorily. Similarly, candidates often feel more inclined to stay in an organization where support and interest has been offered. After all, recruitment is an expensive business. With up to 30% of jobs vacated again within months of recruitment due to disappointment on either side, ineffective recruitment is the source of unnecessary expense.

This is where another marketing concept is increasingly applied to HR practices: that of employee segmentation.

Employee Segmentation

Just as companies segment their customer base to be better able to target their products and services, so organizations are increasingly attempting to segment their employee base into various categories, such as by age, professional group-ings etc., so as to be better able to devise the most appropriate employee value propositions to meet their employees' needs. So in reward terms, for example, companies that previously introduced broad banding are increasingly super-imposing 'job family' or 'professional community' approaches to ensure that reward matches the market for the particular type of talent. Employee segmen-tation can therefore help both develop a better understanding of who, or which groups of employees, are considered 'key' to the organization's success, and help devise specific employee value propositions for these groups which are tailored to their needs. For instance HR professionals at Southwest Airlines treat front-line staff as internal customers by using employee segmentation approaches to research their needs and preferences as energetically as the company's marketing team investigate those of its external customers.

Employee segmentation approaches are driving a more 'scientific' approach to the use of organizational data in order to devise and deliver more tailored and specific forms of employment offer. Large HR functions now often employ ana-lysts to identify from employee data what seems to drive employee engagement in different segments of the workforce, so as to better target initiatives that meet both current and potential employee needs. In turn these human capital data are also being used to understand in detail the causal links between employee engage-ment, performance and business success. Organizations such as the Royal Bank of Scotland and Standard Chartered Bank are at the forefront of such developments.

With respect to recruitment, UK retailers are leading the field in the use of employee segmentation to better tailor employee value propositions to attract old and young employee candidates alike, according to Guthridge *et al.* (2008). Tesco explicitly divides its potential front-line recruits into those joining the workforce straight from school, students looking for part-time work, and graduates. The company devotes a separate section of its careers website to each of these groups and addresses each of them with specific recruiting materials designed for that group. Typical target 'segments' of current and potential employees are those from 'Generations X and Y' (see Candidate Expectations, p. 178).

Candidate Expectations

The importance of understanding what potential recruits expect, what motivates employees and what retains them is all the more evident when talent is in short supply. During the 1980s many employers were concerned at what was seen as the impending demographic 'timebomb' – that there would not be enough 18-year-olds and graduates entering the workplace in the 1990s. As things have turned out, the nature of the problem is not so much the shortage of individuals as the mismatch between what young employees expect and what organizations deliver. This may be because a broader shift in social values and expectations of work may also be occurring, and the old certainties of work and family life have been crumbling. By the 1980s time-honoured values such as security, authority, tradition and a rigid moral code had been eroded and replaced by more out-ward directed values of status, image and consumption. In the 1990s these were replaced by the inward directed values of empathy, connectedness, emotion, autonomy and ease.

Generations X and Y

Social values are reflected in a changing work ethic. Research carried out by Demos in the UK examined how lifestyle aspirations affect the attitudes of these young people to life and careers (Cannon, 1998). Cannon describes the work ethic of Generation X (generally described as people born between 1974 and 1980), in which a decline in trust and loyalty to organizations, together with a fear of boredom, leads young people to view employment in transactional terms: What's the deal? Why get saddled with a difficult job? This raises the question of how jobs can be redefined to engage employees in ways that are satisfying and also provide for flexible career development? Work and jobs are being redefined to include flexibility: new working practices include planning for career-long self-development, being able to switch focus rapidly from one task to another, working with people with very different training and mindsets, and working in situations in which the group is the responsible party.

One of the characteristics of people in the Generation X age group is their high educational attainment. The numbers of young people entering further or higher education have increased dramatically in recent years bringing young peo-ple in the UK more in line with their counterparts in other European countries, especially Germany, where higher qualifications have traditionally been valued.

There are some important differences, however. In Germany there has been a tradition of making good use of skills and higher education when the individual enters the job market (and indeed many qualifications are vocationally oriented). In the UK, by way of contrast, many of the jobs on offer to graduates have not changed from those that might formerly have been offered to school leavers. Employers who might once have recruited A-level students for management trainee positions are now becoming graduate recruiters. Job literature produced for university 'milk rounds' continues to imply early opportunities and the rapid promotion of yesteryear. In practice, graduate recruitment is followed by quiet streaming as genuine high flyers are selected from the rest. Unrealized expecta-tions about exciting careers can lead to disillusionment and cynicism among young employees.

Other stereotypical characteristics of Generation X are highlighted by the Demos research. Generation X has been exposed to more information than its predecessors through TV and other media and are used to receiving information in simple form at a fast rate. They expect things to happen at high speed. They are also accustomed to travel and are considered the first truly 'global' genera-tion, even if the links are only through a common currency of consumer prod-ucts. They are heavy users of technology, including the Internet, and are able to see some of the potential applications of transformational technology.

These experiences have potentially shaped their attitudes in a number of ways. There is a perceived lack of trust, especially in employers since they do not provide secure employment, and a wariness about commitment to anything long term. The shadow side of this generational stereotype, explored by Stuart Coupland (1992) in his novel *Generation X*, is the extended adolescence experienced by 'twentysomethings' in America and their inability to make long-term commitments or imagine a future. Underemployed, overeducated and unpredictable, they settle for low paid work in service industries with poor prospects. Loyalty to an employer is not an appropriate concept. They expect honesty from employers, especially with regard to career opportunities and dislike feeling manipulated. Organizations that promise international assignments, for instance, and then fail to deliver may produce cynical employees who leave when they are at their most valuable to their current employer.

'Generation Y' alludes to people born between 1982 and 2000. One of the apparent differences between Generations X and Y seems to be what they want from work. While Generation X is said to be enticed by freedom and independence, Generation Y is more money- and lifestyle-oriented. Young people want money, greater control of their time and the chance to use some of their intellectual potential. It also suggests that young people are attracted to join 'winner' organizations in which they can look good in the eyes of their peers. These are organizations that are future-oriented and developing and using new technologies. They are places of work where people apply their minds to adding value, such as consultancies, and where employees are involved in exciting projects. 'Loser' organizations are those where people's intelligence and individual contribution are perceived to be of only limited value, such as primary manufacturing.

There are differences in the way the generations view technology. Generation Xers mainly use technology for convenience purposes, such as online banking and shopping, but it is not central to their social lives. In contrast Generation Y see technology embedded in and integral to their life. Generation Yers are truly a 'technology native' generation, and want to use social networking and instant messaging productively. HR professionals need to keep up to date with technology if they are serious about getting the most from their staff and potential employees. For instance, BT has embraced modern technology in an effort to nurture its best young talent and increase productivity. Apprentices are given Blackberries and social networking helps create vital bonds between employees, with over 10 000 members of the BT Facebook group. Encouraging collaboration plays a significant role in improving organization wide communication.

A study by Michel Syrett and Jean Lammiman (2004) suggests that managing and getting the best out of Generation Y, whom they describe as 'Millennials', will pose particular challenges. Management and leadership styles in most organizations are predicated on how to motivate and manage the performance of the generation of workers that grew up in the 1980s and entered the workforce in the 1990s.

Yet young people entering employment today are different in a number of respects, firstly with respect to the nature of networking. They embrace new technologies for socializing. Millennials are likely to build intimacy using mobile phones and the Internet to initiate as well as maintain friendships. Social networks built up by most Millennials by the time they are young adults owe far less to mainstream corporate culture than those of their parents or elder siblings at the same age. Indeed, their loyalty is likely to be to friends rather than to mainstream corporate culture. A far higher proportion of these networks are likely to be made up of peers who are home-based free-agents, who regard old-fashioned brand image building with suspicion and whose social (as well as professional) lives do not revolve around a constant, all-encompassing workplace. Other specific characteristics of 'Generation Y' include:

- **They welcome change**. Young adults are by nature well-suited for the unpredictable workplace of the future. They have less baggage and can therefore afford to take risks.
- **They think differently**. Where years of education, training and experience were once necessary to succeed, the emphasis is now on high energy, fast thinking and quick learning. Young people value their freedom and appear to look for control over their worklife so as to be able to enjoy other aspects of their lives. This generation appears to learn and absorb information quickly, particularly about areas of interest to them such as consumer products and services. Being self-taught is no longer a barrier.
- **They are independent**. Today's twentysomethings came of age as the social contract between employers and workers was dissolving. They have never expected loyalty from a company, nor have they expected to give it. They define themselves by their skills, not the firm they work for. If they have reached this point, what about the kids right behind them?
- **They are entrepreneurial**. Margaret Reagan, a consultant with Towers Perrin which studies workforce trends, predicted in 1999 that barely a third of young people entering the workforce in the coming decade would take steady jobs with companies, most opting to freelance, work under contract or take on part-time employment.
- **They want opportunity more than money and security**. They would rather take a cut in salary or work from home in poverty to build up the enterprise they want and are able to control or influence than sign up for a well paid job that leaves them powerless.
- **They demand respect in ways their predecessors could not**. They are much likely than predecessor generations to know their own rights and demand them.

Meeting the needs of, and getting the best out of new recruits and younger employees presents employers with a distinct challenge and a need for greater flexibility. Given that many young people defer their entry into the job market, graduate recruitment may need to be seen as an ongoing activity rather than one linked purely with the 'milk round'. This may mean devising graduate development schemes along flexible lines and different entry points to accommodate people with different levels of experience.

MOTIVATION AND RETENTION

While attracting and recruiting talent presents one set of challenges, managing and retaining talent presents others. Recruitment is of little use if an organization cannot retain key employees. After all, human motivation is extremely fragile and capable of being damaged by a range of factors. Typically these are factors that have a bearing on employees' security needs, motivation, morale and sense of worth. And even if employees do not wish to leave the organization, their performance can be sub-optimal if they perceive their job to be under threat. Roffey Park research into the impact of mergers on employees, for instance, suggests that in times of major change, many employees simply 'hide' their best ideas until they sense that the time is right to market those ideas. While this may be a sensible stratagem for the employee in the short term, organizations that are looking for innovative solutions may fail to capitalize on the potential of employees.

Therefore gaining insight into what seems to motivate and retain employees is critical. Research by Leadership IQ (2008) suggests that Generation Yers in particular are even more motivated by praise than previous generations. Similarly, while Generation X may be happy with regular feedback, Generation Y demands constant and immediate feedback. They are likely to be turned off by micro-management and view flexible working as a positive thing. Holiday entitlement is considered one of the most important job factors. They also believe that financial security is very important. HR therefore needs to help them understand the importance of their work and what benefit there is for them and the company. In particular, focus on the short-term benefits, like reducing long-term fixed pay in favour of increasing variable pay for performance.

Loyalty

Some of the biggest changes in the increasingly fragmented job landscape are the shifts in employee attitudes. Loyalty to the employer is becoming a thing of the past and many organizations are urgently reviewing ways of securing the commitment of people whom they do not want to lose. According to Douglas Hall (1998), psychological contracts are judged by employees according to:

- The extent to which the organization has kept to its promises
- Trust in management to look after employee's best interests
- Fairness of treatment, especially of reward allocation.

It is hardly surprising then that a main contributory factor to the reduction in employee loyalty is the way many employees feel that their career prospects have been damaged by organizational restructurings. In today's uncertain economic climate, large-scale restructurings and layoffs may once again become a feature of the landscape. It is as well to look back to the 1990s, and the last period of major restructurings to avoid repeating mistakes from the past.

Perhaps understandably, in the changing economic climate of the 1990s, many organizations abandoned career planning initiatives, continued to shed jobs and told employees that they should take on responsibility for managing their own career. Arguably this could be interpreted as a sensible approach and a shift away from the paternalistic employment practices of many large organizations. After all, the idea that an organization, even a large one, is a static entity has been seriously challenged as companies that are household names merge, reshape or disappear.

Judging from Roffey Park's earlier research findings, few employees continue to believe that the organization will manage their career. For people who have amassed a great deal of experience in one organization but whose skills are not transferable elsewhere, the possibilities of managing their own career may actually be limited and may lead to some frustration.

The implications of career self-management are rather different for employees who have transferable skills, who know their own worth and now lack trust in their employers. Knowing that they are employable increases employees' choice and confidence. This means that employers are no longer having things their own way. There have been a number of well-publicized examples of employees refusing to comply with their employer's bidding even though they effectively close the door on major career opportunities.

This more adult–adult relationship between employer and employees is based on the increasing power of the knowledge worker to make demands of the organization which go beyond pay and rations. This is particularly clear in the IT sector where the success of several organizations relies on the product development skills of a few key individuals. It is also marked in the oil industry where filling overseas assignments as part of a broad career route for high-calibre employees is becoming increasingly difficult. This is partly explained by the rise in the number of dual-career families as well as by the increasing unwillingness of employees to make sacrifices if they are not guaranteed promotion on return from the assignment.

The truth of corporate value-speak such as 'our people are our greatest assets' is a lesson that has been painfully learned in some cases when individuals move on. There is already a good deal of anecdotal evidence that employees with transferable skills and experience are more confident of being employable and less tolerant of the frustrations of poor management, inappropriate reward and few growth opportunities. Ironically, the very skills that many employers are looking for – such as the ability to get things done, be innovative, customer-oriented etc. – are precisely the skills that will help people get jobs elsewhere.

Why do People Leave?

Retention problems are usually a symptom of other things going wrong in an organization, such as ongoing change or poor management. In many cases, the main reason for people leaving is that they do not like the way they are managed. In retention strategies, it is important to identify why people tend to go, using exit interviews and other information as valuable hints as to what needs to be done. Exit interviews conducted some six months after someone leaves, often by a third party, can yield very rich, and more objective data. Analysing turnover statistics by business unit, department, or team can add further insights. In some organizations, careful research is carried out to answer the question 'Why do people turn us down?' at the recruitment stage. This, linked with the exit interview data, provides a useful steer as to where improvements need to be made. Then, HR and line managers need to work on those problems and delay people from leaving for a while at least.

In the Roffey Park Management Agenda surveys, major sources of dissatisfaction included the increased workloads and lack of work/personal life balance alluded to earlier. Other sources of frustration included the slow pace of change within some organizations and the increase in organizational politics. These were seen by many as regrettable facts of life, leading to job dissatisfaction but essentially to be endured. If these factors are common sources of dissatisfaction to many people, as our findings suggest, enlightened leadership may well be called for to address these sources of dissatisfaction.

However, what many people said would cause them to leave their organization was poor management and a lack of appreciation and recognition. This points once again to the importance of training line managers in the skills of feedback and coaching. Other triggers for people to leave their organization include a lack of opportunity for promotion. The vast majority of respondents recognize that they are responsible for managing their career and 57% of respondents are currently grappling with the dilemma of whether to stay or leave their organization. This is where career management becomes a key priority for HR professionals. Simply telling people that they are responsible for managing their career is not enough. The irony is that the people most capable of doing this do not need help from the organization. If they become too frustrated, they simply go elsewhere. Effective career management can offer hope that development is possible, which in turn may encourage people to stay.

Findings from other research projects, such as the Roffey Park study of Work/Life Balance, reinforce the importance of management being seen to do something to address employee concerns such as the issue of long working hours. Another important social shift needs to be taken into account when planning employee-friendly policies – that is, the growing implications of eldercare. The changing pressures on employees throughout their working lives can be relieved somewhat by the sensitive provision of appropriate flexible conditions. Staff turnover at US-based retailers Eddie Bauer Inc. has dropped significantly since a range of work–life programmes were introduced which recognized the changing priorities of employees at different stages of life (see Chapter 2). Management needs to set a clear priority on introducing effective policies and practices which are more than just window dressing.

Why do People Stay?

Career management is critical too for the majority of employees who are likely to stay. Unless there are regular opportunities for personal or professional growth, people's performance is likely to peak and decline. In the *Management Agenda* surveys, money appears to be considered the main way in which people expect to be rewarded, in addition to recognition from the line manager. However, the main motivator for the majority appears to be a challenging job, rather than money alone. This corresponds strongly to Roffey Park research into the motivations of 'high flyers' (Holbeche, 1998), where only 4% of respondents reported being motivated by money.

For this group, personal achievement and challenge were primary motivators (Figure 6.1). Other motivators include variety, autonomy and good interpersonal relationships within teams.

The opportunity to use personal drive to good effect seems to be an important motivator for many respondents. A key source of satisfaction appears to be gaining influence at strategic level, regardless of one's position in the hierarchy. Enriched roles and the opportunity for significant personal development appear to be important retention factors.

Motivating and Getting the Best Out of Graduates

Similarly, motivating and inspiring performance from young people requires managers, executives and HR to work together. Employers can engage the potential commitment of young people by redefining work in terms of projects which offer variety and learning. More flexible working patterns may be attractive and this may involve restructuring work processes.

Organizations can benefit from making good use of young people's ability to develop specialized forms of knowledge. Young people want their ideas to be taken seriously and need speedy and appropriate feedback about their performance.

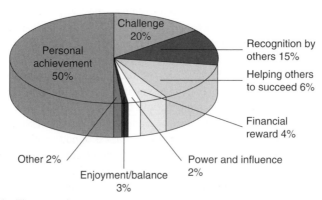

FIGURE 6.1 The top motivators.

This can be difficult to achieve in lean organizations where managers and supervisors are often thinly spread, but is essential if young people are to feel that their contribution has been noticed and valued. Managers need to take on the role of enabler and project leader and may need training and other support if this is not their 'natural' style.

They also want the chance to build marketable expertise. Some organizations assign young people a mentor who is experienced in the company's approaches if not at a higher level in the hierarchy. Where the mentor and young employee are involved in a community-based project, for instance, there are opportunities for the young person to experience being an organizational representative. Organizations that invest in training young people but also put them into project roles where their expertise can be used to good effect may benefit from making good use not only of available talents but also from increased employee commitment.

TOWARDS A STRATEGIC APPROACH TO RETENTION

Responsibility for retention is shared between line managers and HR and real partnership is needed. Specifically, the line should be responsible for recruitment and retention, with facilitation by HR. There are often tensions around this issue due to a common paradox – retention, though critical to business success, is not treated as a strategic issue. Line managers often want a 'quick fix' when a key employee threatens to leave or is about to be poached by another company. HR, on the other hand, has to consider the integrity of the pay system – doing a 'deal' in one case could set a dangerous precedent. Line managers then accuse HR of going back on the 'empowerment' idea with which they were sold devolved HR responsibilities. All too often, HR then reverts to type.

Elements of a Retention Strategy

Of course people are different, and rather than a single approach to employee retention, organizations need to be more flexible. Eldridge and Miles (2008) suggest that organizations need to be tactical in their approach to retention, and recognize the more personalized expectations of employees. They should provide a shopping list of commitment factors, such as salary, career progression, personal growth and work–life balance, and discuss these with the employee.

A more strategic approach is to put efforts into prevention, rather than crisis management. This involves doing a risk analysis on the target group. What is the likelihood of them leaving and what would be the impact of their departure? HR and line management can then have an informed dialogue about the priority areas for action. Employees can be ranked to identify who falls into the 'danger zone'. These can be given special attention. Planned actions can be put in place for other groups.

Do Not Oversell the Organization in the First Place

Many people in our surveys felt that the job or the organization had been over-sold to them at recruitment. They had been led to believe, for instance, that there were opportunities for rapid promotion, which turned out not to be the case. Graduates who were most disillusioned on this front were people who had been recruited after being wined and dined during the university 'milk round'. Many of these employees were actively looking to leave their organizations by their mid-twenties. Of course, recruitment is a mutual selling opportunity, but it should be honest.

Help People to Become Aware of their Own Career 'Derailers'

Research suggests that there are a number of common causes of career derailment which include changes in technology, personal life or one's boss. HR can pro-vide career workshops which can help people become more aware of what these factors are for them, so that they can do something about them. Many organiza-tions now use 360-degree feedback for this purpose. When the instrument is avail-able online, the whole process is easier to manage. Helping people to become aware of their own strengths and development needs can spur them on to further development.

Manage Down Employers' Expectations About How Long They can Keep People

It is unrealistic to expect a complete career lifetime commitment from any employee, yet employers continue to act as if this is what they expect. Employers must expect to see the new employment relationship as one of ongoing negotia-tion as needs change. This means that retaining key employees is both a strate-gic and a tactical issue in which the day-to-day interactions between managers and employees can undercut the best-laid retention plans or, conversely, retain an employee because of the strength of the relationship.

Consider Paying Retention Bonuses

This is very much a short-term measure and should be considered a pre-emptive strike. Various City firms specialize in offering 'golden handcuffs' to key employees especially during mergers and other major change situations. It is important to recognize that not everyone is motivated by pay and that, in most cases, you can't buy loyalty. It is also important to be realistic about what pay can do with regard to retention – at best it is a hygiene factor. Perhaps more effective is the 'lock-in' effect of generous share options and other benefits. One high technology company was concerned at the numbers of key employees who were going to work for the opposition. The main reason given was that com-petitors paid more. Some fact-finding by HR revealed that although competitors did appear to pay more, their company had a better overall benefits package.

By producing and communicating this 'benchmark' data to the target groups, people in the 'danger zone' were able to make a more informed decision and many who had been contemplating leaving chose to stay. Moreover, some of the people who had left did not enjoy their new work environment and returned within a matter of months. The company wisely chose to welcome them back.

Give People a Chance to Have Variety

This can take many forms, including attending conferences, representing their company as members of consortia etc. Ideally all employees should have the chance to learn new things, meet new people and be stimulated by external input. Without the opportunity to try new opportunities, sit on challenging committees, attend seminars and read and discuss ideas, they feel they will stagnate. A career-oriented, valued employee must experience growth opportunities within your organization. HR can work with line managers to build up development options which provide a relevant and tailored 'stretch' for individual employees and teams.

Consider Supporting People to Update their Qualifications

In the High Flyers Survey, over half of those interviewed have updated their qualifications since joining their present employer. Proportionately slightly more women than men have done this (62% compared with 56%). Most of the people who have updated have gained an MBA. Of these, half had a degree when joining and just over a quarter had professional qualifications, 40% have obtained a professional qualification and 20% have gained a job-related qualification. Indeed, many of the respondents who joined their organization in the last two years had already achieved postgraduate or professional qualifications before joining.

Interestingly very few employers seem to consider supporting qualifications as part of a retention strategy. Employees, in contrast, seem to value highly the opportunity to do an MBA, for instance. Given that the average part-time course lasts two years, and that if the course is chosen so that the individual can work on projects for their employer as part of their coursework, this seems a sensible way of retaining experienced staff for the duration of their course at least. The peak age for gaining an MBA and a professional qualification appears to be during the thirties in the Roffey Park respondent group. Gaining a first degree seems less age-specific, with small numbers taking degrees in their early thirties and another small group in their early fifties. As one managing director who recently completed an Open University degree said, 'I just wanted to see if I had it in me'. People with first degrees alone were most likely to take an MBA, a postgraduate or professional qualification or to seek professional membership. Those who joined with a professional qualification are most likely to have upgraded their qualifications with a first degree, HND, professional membership, other job-related qualifications or an MBA.

Why do People Update their Qualifications?

People were asked why they had updated their qualifications and nearly half stated that they wanted to be more effective in their current job. Verbatim comments include:

'Better financial skills'
'Lack of management qualifications'
'To cement experience'
'To keep myself up to date'
'To bring together current skills and perfect new ones'
'To gain a greater understanding of the business'.

Only one person stated that he wanted to earn more money as a result. Another main motivation for updating qualifications seems linked with career development: 47% of those who updated said that they could see their qualifications would be useful to them in the future. Several respondents from the public sector in particular where there is ongoing restructuring stated that they want to improve their CV and marketability. Comments include:

'I've reached the ceiling'
'To prepare for the next career step'
'To remain competitive, widen knowledge'.

In other cases, especially in the more regulated financial services industry, professional qualifications have become a requirement. Many respondents were extremely cynical about continuing professional development (CPD) and the requirement to document development. Others were not interested in pursuing training and education courses because they were accredited to a degree or other qualification. Largely the key considerations in choosing a course were relevance and interest.

For other people, especially by their mid-thirties, pursuing a qualification course seems to be in response to a need for a developmental stretch which they may feel they are not getting from their current job. With promotion opportunities more restricted than in the past in organizations with flatter structures, many people see gaining an MBA, for instance, as a means of developing their ability to operate strategically. Over a third (39%) say that they have updated their qualifications for personal interest reasons. One person specifically turned down the opportunity to do an MBA at a well-known business school because the interviewer had insisted on assuming that the candidate's motives for taking the course were to get himself promoted, which was not the case. Typical reasons given include:

'To develop myself'
'Academic interest'
'I wanted to experience self-managed learning'
'Hands-off challenge'

'I wanted a different experience'
'To gain an understanding of management theory'
'Part of my own philosophy of lifelong learning'.

Several respondents were in the fortunate position of having so much money as owners of their own companies that they need to take a tax break. 'Broadening the mind' seems to be preferable to spending a couple of years in some tax haven.

Company Support for Qualifications

The survey asked respondents who had obtained further qualifications (58% of the total) if their company had supported them to do this. A significant majority (92%) said that they did receive support. This was primarily (86%) in the form of financial sponsorship and two-thirds also obtained time off for study. Few people reported receiving support or encouragement from their boss or an internal mentor.

Other support included job placements and the provision of an external mentor. Only 8% believe that they did not receive any form of support whether in terms of finance, time off to study or simply encouragement. For all the people who took qualifications, the biggest obstacles appear to be lack of time to study and a sense that the learning was not valued by their employer since it was usually not directly used in the business. What therefore appears to be particularly valued is the combination of time to study, financial support, moral support from the boss, recognition of achievement and the chance to apply the learning.

Never Threaten People's Security

Some HR Directors argue that if you know redundancies are in prospect if the company fails to meet production or sales goals, it is a mistake to talk openly about this information with employees. It makes them nervous; no matter how you phrase the information; no matter how you explain the information, even if you're absolutely correct, your best staff members will update their CVs.

Getting People to Want to be Members of Your Organization

The main retention factor is when people believe in the organization and want to contribute to its success. Professor Robert B. Reich (1998) has identified what he calls the six 'social glues' of the company of the future:

1. Create a sense of ownership through financial rewards, in particular, stock options. The perception of fairness is an important retention factor. Employees must feel rewarded, recognized and appreciated. Frequently saying thank you goes a long way. Monetary rewards, bonuses and gifts and understandable raises, tied to accomplishments and achievement, help retain staff. Commissions and bonuses that are easily calculated on a daily basis, and easily understood, raise motivation and help retain staff. Give individuals an

opportunity to work on projects that make a real difference and where the goal aligns with personal goals and values. Ensure that people have interesting, challenging work to do. If challenging work is a motivating factor for many people, it follows that most people will gain satisfaction from having some sort of 'stretch' in their job. Sadly, in many organizations that have shrunk their workforce to the core, some of the most interesting projects do not get offered to internal staff but to contractors. In addition, contractors tend to be paid more than existing staff, which can rub salt into the wound.

2. Create a culture that values learning. This links with the first 'social glue' – money – learn more now and earn more in the future. Creating a learning culture is explored in Chapter 17.

3. Make work fun; if it isn't fun it won't attract the best talent. Increasingly people choose to work for a company on the basis of the image portrayed of what the workgroup and working atmosphere will be like. Good people want to work with good people. In many cases, the long hours' culture means that people will not always have the time or energy for a social life. Particularly in stressful situations, having a light-hearted but professional atmosphere can be conducive to good teamwork and to people being prepared to 'go the extra mile'. When work can also be fun, the fact that one is working long hours becomes less of a problem.

4. Create a sense of pride in the organization. One high-flying City broker was offered the chance to double his salary if he were to join a start-up firm in the United States. The broker decided against the move on the basis that he still had plenty of work challenges where he was, and he enjoyed these. Furthermore, he was proud to work for the long-established firm with its unblemished reputation. He was pleased to say which company he worked for at social gatherings. In some organizations there is a strong sense of community. This is engendered in many ways by little things can make a difference. In one organization, the chief executive makes a point of remembering the birthdays of staff and their partners. The CEO reflected on what had happened over time: 'it's just been a collection of things over the years which I thought were important and we've ended up with a strategy.'

5. Value and facilitate balance with the organization. Issues concerning balance are explored in Chapter 2. Where flexible working would be valued by employees, it should ideally be introduced. This could include establishing core time and developing contracts which include working from home or on shifts. Employees of any generation are likely to value work–life balance, not only younger employees.

Helping Managers to Make the Difference

Above all, many surveys suggest that managers make the biggest difference to people wanting to stay. People leave managers and supervisors more often than they leave companies or jobs. Starting with clear expectations of the employee, the supervisor has a critical role to play in retention. Anything the supervisor does to make an employee feel unvalued will contribute to turnover. Frequent employee complaints centre on these areas:

- lack of clarity about expectations
- lack of clarity about earning potential
- lack of feedback about performance.

Every manager is likely to be involved in setting targets and making improvements. It is possible that some managers, especially if they have been promoted from a technical role, may lack the skills required to manage people. They may need help in understanding how to set stretch targets which keep people motivated. Guidelines can be produced to make performance appraisals a positive experience for all concerned. Continuous improvement and learning targets should be features of the process of managing for high performance.

HR can and should ensure that line managers receive the support they need to develop their teams and to set clear goals and manage performance effectively. HR can help by using attitude surveys and multi-rater feedback processes to find out the facts. These can identify what the problems are, where they are and how deep they are. Some managers may need help in developing their management style to be more appropriate to the needs of their teams and HR can provide a valuable role by providing feedback and coaching line managers in how to bring out the best in their teams. Teamwork should be encouraged and team targets set which encourage cross-departmental cooperation. In particular, managers should be encouraged to identify and get rid of the daily frustrations which sap the morale of their teams, making it easier for everyone to do a good job. Managing and rewarding employees will be explored in Chapter 7.

CONCLUSION

Finding good people is becoming so difficult that one HR director of a rapidly growing telecommunications company said: 'losing people should be a criminal offence'. Similarly there is no single panacea for retaining people. Using reward alone as the main means of motivating people is likely to be a waste of time. The euphoria attached to pay increases usually lasts only a few weeks, whereas the impact of a manager on the morale and motivation of his or her team can be long-lasting. Moreover, applying blanket solutions to individual needs tends to backfire. A more tailored yet strategic approach is most appropriate to the management of recruitment and retention.

Approaches to developing talent will be explored in more detail in Chapters 8 and 9. However, the starting point in the development of a talent management strategy or a talent management intervention, is to identify how the organization defines talent. Communicating what is seen as talent, especially where the approach to talent management is inclusive rather than elitist, is essential, as is developing a language for talent management activities that is understood by all the parties in the employment relationship. Support for talent management must flow from those at the very top of an organization. The value of their visible support for talent management initiatives is pivotal to how these are regarded and valued.

After all, people don't leave organizations where they get good development.

RECRUITMENT AND RETENTION CHECKLIST

Making Excellent Appointments

- Is our job analysis underpinned by the organization context, our resourcing strategy and a candidate specification?
- What would make our organization attractive/unattractive to the candidates we want to reach?
- In our recruitment strategy do we have adequate sources of candidates, effective recruiters, appropriate methods of recruitment and selection, a budget and action plan?
- Do we use the most appropriate methods of attracting candidates, e.g advertising, search, word-of-mouth, etc.?
- What do we know about the interests and needs of candidates we would like to attract, and how well does our employer brand promise match these?
- In managing the candidate relationship do we manage or raise expectations with regard to the job, career prospects, etc.?
- In assessing candidates do we use relevant and effective methods, e.g. assessment centres, behavioural interviews, psychometric testing, references?
- In making the decision, how do we handle the process internally?
- In integrating the new recruit into the organization, what support do we provide, e.g. induction, mentor, 'buddy'?
- In following up with the candidate after several weeks, how do we assess how well they are integrating and what their needs might be?
- In evaluating our recruitment strategies, do we take into account cost, time, effectiveness and longer-term value-add?

Managing for Motivation – What Motivates People in our Business?

- In assessing the needs and expectations of employees do we focus on the individual, the group, the department, the organization as a whole?
- How do we measure morale and satisfaction?
- What kind of management style dominates – one which restricts or shares communication or one where decision-making is top-down versus participative?
- What kinds of reward systems are in use – formal (e.g. pay, benefits, bonus, promotion, other incentives), psychological – status, the nature of the job (e.g. interest, challenge)?

- What kind of work environment do we provide – physical, community, etc.? Do we provide challenging and satisfying roles?
- What opportunities do we provide for people to experience personal growth and progress their career?
- Is there a sense of community in this organization – and are people pleased to belong?
- How well do managers provide recognition?
- What help can HR provide to help managers with their role in retention?
- Which groups of employees are 'at risk?'
- What do we know about what motivates them?

REFERENCES

Cannon, D. (1998) *Generation X and the New Work Ethic*, Working Paper. London: Demos

Cheese, P. (2007) Strategic talent management. *Strategy Magazine*, Issue 14, December

Coupland, S. (1992) *Generation X*. London: Abacus Books

Deloitte Research (2004) It's 2008: *Do You Know Where Your Talent Is? A Deloitte Research Study*

Eldridge, R. and Miles, A. (2008) *Generation Y* . TalentDrain

Fernon, D. (2007) *Recruitment, Retention and Turnover Survey*. London: CIPD

Guthridge, M., Komm, A.B. and Lawson, E. (2008) Making talent a strategic priority. *McKinsey Quarterly*, January

Hall, D. (1998) *Careers In and Out of Organizations*. London: Sage Publications

Holbeche, L. (1998) *High Flyers and Succession Planning*. Horsham: Roffey Park Management Institute

Leadership, IQ (2008) *Motivating Generation Y vs Older Generations*. Employmentguide.com

Matthews, V. (2007) *Personnel Today*, 22 May 2007

Reich, R.B. (1998) The company of the future. *Fast Company*, November

Syrett, M. and Lammiman, J. (2004) Young consumers: Insight and ideas. *Responsible Marketers*, 5, No. 4, 62–73

Swart, J. and Kinnie, N. (2003) *Managing People and Knowledge in Professional Services Firms*. London: CIPD

Tansley, C. *et al*. (2006) *Talent Management: Understanding the Dimensions*. London: CIPD

Walker, P. (2007) *Employer Branding: A No-nonsense Approach*. London: CIPD

Chapter 7

Managing and Rewarding for High Performance

The scarcest resource in most organizations is not money; it is time and attention.

(Pfeffer, 1998a)

In today's fast-changing economic environment, globalization and technological advances are leading to significant changes in the competitive challenges facing businesses. As we considered in Chapter 2, there is a requirement for greater flexibility and speed to respond to significantly increased global competition, and delivery of products and services which are more responsive to customer needs. Furthermore, organizations are seeking to exploit global networks. Traditional thinking is that countries in the 'developed West' are the innovators and outsource administration and manufacturing to India and China. The reality is that these countries display a much higher level of entrepreneurship and innovation and are quickly moving into higher value-added service industries, precision engineering and design.

Simultaneously there is a global trend towards a 'Knowledge Economy', with rapid growth in the number of employees engaged in 'knowledge work' – for example, in professional services and new product and service development. In knowledge-intensive firms the basis of ongoing competitive advantage and sustainable business performance is intellectual capital – knowledge, information, intellectual property, experience – that can be used to create wealth (Stewart, 1997). According to a report from Microsoft, by 2010, over half the GDP for the UK will be generated from knowledge.

As a result of these shifts, the nature of work is changing too, with implications for the nature of skill and aptitude required from employees. There is an increase in customer-facing roles involving some form of 'emotional labour' – with the requirement for employees to express positive emotions in the way in which they interact with customers. In today's and tomorrow's organizations, sustainable business performance is going to require ever-greater discretionary contribution from people. Knowledge-intensive work requires higher-level skills, yet demographic shifts, growing skills gaps and the aspirations and commitment of the 'new workforce' suggest that global pipelines for key talent may be under threat.

And the old management models cannot do enough to ensure sustainable success. As Hamel and Breen (2007) propose; 'Management is out of date. Like the combustion engine, it's a technology that has largely stopped evolving, and that's not good.' And the nature of the traditional links between work and reward may be evolving too, given the changing expectations of today's workforce. In this chapter we will look at how organization structures and roles are being designed to enable strategic flexibility and high performance in this changing context. We will also consider how individual performance can be managed and rewarded in ways which are conducive to employee motivation and discretionary contribution.

THE CHANGING WORKPLACE

Workplaces are changing and the forms, structures and work practices which were familiar a few years ago are undergoing a serious, longer-term appraisal. Traditional organization design theory and practice centres on a process-driven approach to designing roles and interactions within the workplace. Increasingly workplaces will be characterized by nimble or 'agile' production, knowledge-intensive work and high labour flexibility. Organizations will focus on their core competencies, rather than just their current processes. Rather than being a fixed entity, the organization will be a task-oriented organic structure. Organizational designs are likely to be characterized by a small core centre and alliances with suppliers and customers.

The flexible and the informal will need to co-exist with formal, integration mechanisms. The challenge here will be to create organizations, however decentralized, which are completely unified and coordinated, and where employees experience high levels of participation and commitment. Matrix structures have now become well-established integration devices though in many organizations matrix structures are also increasingly being simplified to make them more effective. In sectors where there is intense competition, such as the financial services or the hospitality industry, the trend towards amalgamation, through mergers and acquisitions, prior to dispersal or demerger, seems well-entrenched.

Furthermore, the shape of roles and work patterns is changing to reflect the needs of the changing workforce. There are significant shifts in the demographics of the workforce, namely an increased proportion of women, greater ethnic diversity, more educated employees and an ageing workforce. There is also a significant increase in the number of employers that an individual employee expects to work for during his or her career. Arguably where job design is neglected it is likely that employee turnover will increase. Increasing demand from employees for work–life balance is likely to become as important a driver for extending flexible working practice as 24/7 operational business needs (CIPD/CapGemini, 2008). At the same time, the development of Web 2.0 and other new technologies reveals a society where the traditional hierarchies are being challenged and employees from diverse organizations can share their knowledge via peer-to-peer networks, online blogs, Facebook communities etc.

Employee Engagement

Getting the right balance between employer and employee needs will be critical to success. A three-year study by ISR (2006) found a gap of almost 52% in the one-year performance improvement in operating income between companies with highly engaged employees versus companies whose employees have low engagement scores. High engagement companies improved 19.2% cent while low engagement companies declined 32.7% cent in operating income over the study period.

If employee engagement drives employee performance there is a solid business case for investing in activities designed to improve employees' engagement levels. Towers Perrin (2003) identify the following as drivers of employee engagement:

- Senior management's interest in employees' well-being
- Challenging work
- Evidence that the company is focused on customers
- Career advancement opportunities
- The company's reputation as a good employer
- A collaborative work environment where people work well in teams
- Resources to get the job done
- Input in decision-making
- A clear vision from senior management about future success.

While pay and benefits can motivate workers, simply raising compensation does not drive employee engagement. Managers play a key role in boosting engagement levels, by coaching employees to build their work skills and providing career development opportunities. Aligning individual and organizational values is also important. Corporate cultures characterized by teamwork, good working conditions, fair treatment and the chance for learning and growth are common to most situations. And while the drivers of employee engagement may vary from one work context to another, nevertheless, these insights represent significant opportunities to enhance employee engagement.

Job Design for 'Smart Working'

Job design, and the way people are managed, must enable knowledge workers and those involved in 'emotional labour' to give of their best. So how can firms respond to this constantly evolving landscape, and design roles that meet changing business needs and also attract, motivate and retain the best employees? The CIPD, working with CapGemini, have been exploring how work and organizational design can evolve to create a win–win situation for both employers and employees and have termed this 'Smart Working', elements of which I describe in this chapter.

The pace of change is so fast that job descriptions, which create tight boundaries, are inappropriate. Important responsibilities fall between the gaps and most job descriptions are not current for more than a few months. Boudreau and Ramstad (1997) cite Disney as one organization that has understood the need to go past traditional static job descriptions and think intelligently about how roles need to differ according to what the business strategy aims to achieve:

> We suspect that … some minority of jobs (perhaps 20%) will require significant changes in the traditional job system to capture and exploit their pivotalness … one implication of effectiveness is that the organization must become more adept at identifying how to conceive and manage these new roles, which will be constantly changing and not easily captured in traditional job descriptions … a maturing talent decision science will undoubtedly mean more pressure for flexibility in traditional job descriptions.

Conventional job design has approached the challenge of reconciling employer and employee needs by considering both required job characteristics and psychological drivers of employee performance. Hackman and Oldham (1975) identified the following five 'core job characteristics' which should be taken into account in job design:

- Skill variety
- Task identity
- Task significance: the degree to which the job outcome has a substantial impact on others. The meaning of 'task significance' in the context of many roles involves –
  - Autonomy: the degree to which the job gives an employee freedom and discretion in scheduling work and determining how it is performed
  - Feedback: the degree to which an employee gets information about the effectiveness of their efforts – with particular emphasis on feedback directly from the work itself rather than from a third party (e.g. manager).

What is needed is a broad role description, with some 'fuzzy' boundaries to allow for growth, yet not so loose that needless confusion and duplication occur. Such roles are more likely to lead to 'smart work', as CIPD defines the dynamic interplay between organizational elements such as role design, leadership and management, and employee elements such as an individual's motivation and willingness to deploy his or her discretionary effort to the benefit of the organization and its customers.

Impact on Employee Engagement

Taken together, the core job characteristics are said to produce three 'critical psychological states':

- Meaningfulness – the employee perceiving the work as worthwhile or important

- Responsibility – the belief that the employee is accountable for the outcome of his or her efforts
- Knowledge – of whether or not the outcome of the employee's work is satisfactory.

Designing jobs in a way that maximizes the probability of all three of these 'critical states' being present is, in turn, believed to drive four positive outcomes:

- High internal work motivation
- High-quality work performance
- High job satisfaction
- Low absenteeism and voluntary staff turnover.

There is a large volume of literature on the 'job characteristics' theory alone, some of it disputing the link between employee satisfaction and performance, but it would seem that, by and large, these factors still seem relevant, even though the nature of work is changing for many.

The CIPD/CapGemini research (2008) suggests that a job system that will meet both employer and employee needs is likely to be characterized by:

- A higher degree of **freedom to act** than traditional roles, frequently characterized by **self-management, a high degree of autonomy** and a **philosophy of empowerment**
- Management interventions that focus on **outcome-based indicators of achievement** (role descriptions, performance management processes, strong processes to cascade corporate objectives to individual level)
- Work location that is (to a greater or lesser degree) **flexible** (working hours/location)
- **Physical work environment conditions**; hot-desking, working from home, mobile communications technology (e.g. laptops with ability to remotely connect to network, Blackberries, mobile phones, online application and portals, teleconference facilities
- **Cultural conditions** that enable smart working to align with business objectives to create a 'triple win' for the organization, its employees and its customers.

Implications for Flexibility

Job design has to take into account the changing nature of the physical work environment, especially the growth of flexible working on a significant scale. Partly this is in order that organizations can maximize the use of space and resources through approaches such as hot-desking and drop-in zones. Partly this is also because new technologies, ranging from Blackberries to 3G and new social networks, are creating an environment in which many people, especially so-called 'knowledge workers', are able to work in a much more mobile fashion.

We are also beginning to see the advent of virtual organizations which have no corporate centre. The need for different shift systems and other contractual arrangements for getting work done, such as outsourcing, is driven by the burgeoning requirements of customers worldwide for round the clock service. Partly too, flexible working is intended to meet the needs of employees. According to the TUC (Carvel, 2008), long hours are on the rise in the UK, reversing the slow but steady 10-year decline in the number of people working more than 48 hours a week. More than 1 in 8 of the workforce now works more than 48 hours each week. This increases to 1 in 6 in London. Many employers recognize that overworked staff are unproductive and have introduced more flexibility aimed at better work–life balance. In the UK there is increased take up of home-working, and a report by the Equal Opportunities Commission (EOC) in January 2007, entitled 'Working outside the box: changing work to meet the future', notes that half the working population (52% of men and 48% of women) say they want to work more flexibly. It calls on employers in highly skilled areas of business and industry to adopt more flexible patterns of work, such as home-working and mobile working, to fit around highly skilled individuals who want to have a life outside work as well as a challenging career.

Introducing flexible working hours for employees is an effective route to smarter commuting, allowing journeys either to be made outside peak periods or reducing the number of journeys altogether. There are several ways this can be achieved which are simple to implement.

- Flexitime – flexibility can be introduced on how the employee works his or her weekly or annual hours
- Flexihours – allowing employees to leave early or later in the day enables staggered commuting outside peak periods
- Condensed working – the number of commuting journeys can be reduced through the practice of condensed hours, where the employee works the required weekly hours in just four days, taking the fifth day off. Alternatively, staff could take a half-hour lunch break each day and then be allowed to leave at 3.00 pm on Friday, before the evening peak journey home (Work Wise, 2007).

Implications for Learning

Several pieces of research focus on how organizations provide people with the flexibility and environment that provides increased opportunity to learn from situations in their jobs. Wall and Wood (2005) for instance looked at the impact of job design on knowledge and skill acquisition and concluded that the organization of work and the ability of the individuals to manage this is a significant driver of discretionary performance and have identified a strong correlation to an individual's ability to learn. The idea of the connection between work organization and learning is also explored by Leach *et al.* (2005). They have focused on the effect of autonomy and teamwork on Knowledge, Skills and Abilities (KSA),

concluding that KSA mediates the relationship between autonomy and performance and between autonomy and job strain.

Benefits of 'Smart Working'

Flexible or 'smart' working is credited with other benefits too:

- Boosting productivity and profits
- Increasing a company's skills base
- Freeing up travelling time (it is estimated that by 2010, flexible working
  practices will have saved the British economy £1.9 billion in congestion
  costs)
- Saving on accommodation costs
- Improving employees' quality of work (and life)
- Lowering absence rates
- Increasing an employer's reputation as a good company to work for – hence
  attracting talent and consequently reducing recruitment costs.

Despite the benefits, flexible working is not a panacea to all problems.
Flexible working can be difficult from a management perspective. However,
some of the remaining constraints to smarter working are those placed upon
employees by their firms but also they are sometimes self-imposed. The concept
of 'presenteeism' is demonstrated in many professional services and financial
services environments, for example, where employees still feel the need to 'be
seen' in the office, even when this means they are not working productively.

Similarly, for all its benefits, technology has its downsides. While use of technology has made it possible to 'e-mail on the go', for many employees, the ability to log on via secure intranets from any personal computer may have created
a different working style and effectively increased their working day. For some
the flexibility is welcome and the additional hours are not perceived to be a problem but for others the loss of a strict division between work and leisure time can
increase stress and drive a suspicion that they are being asked to do more for less.

Of course flexible working is not available to everyone; smart working means
different things to different groups of employees. Oil rig workers are very different from mobile sales force workers and again, doctors are very different from
lawyers and accountants. Some professions are tied to their location but in all
cases there are changes in ways of working which affect roles and responsibilities and pose a challenge to HR and businesses in how they manage their people.

In manufacturing, according to MacDuffie (1995), flexible and just in time
production implies a more central role for workers in the design of jobs and a
more flexible approach to work organization. Flexible production systems are
commonly associated with high commitment HRM policies such as employment security, compensation linked to performance and reduction of status barriers. This aids the psychological contract of reciprocal commitment between the
worker and the employer. Research carried out by David Guest (1998) amongst

others hints that this is leading to a different type of 'psychological contract' between employees and their employers which has profound implications for organizations. Guest argues that this contract is important because it supports the market view of the 'employee as a rugged independent individual offering knowledge and skills through a series of interactions in the labour market'. This is reflected in the shift from a job-for-life approach to one of a 'career portfolio' which better suits the employee life cycle.

JOB FIT AND JOB DESIGN – WHAT ROLE CAN HR PLAY?

The role of HR, then, in this context will be to create the space for individuals to take greater ownership of their jobs, whilst delivering within agreed role parameters to higher levels of performance and quality, in line with the organization's view of the role requirements.

HR can help managers to understand how to define roles in the light of business drivers and how to identify the capabilities required to do the job. The key performance indicators for each role should derive from the business drivers and strategy and translated into role processes. This makes each job role more responsive to the changing business environment. Roles should be designed so that there is a clear 'line of sight' between the business strategy, the deliverables required and the end-user or other 'customer', regardless of sector. Customer focus is key to stimulating higher levels of performance, especially when there is a regular feedback loop built in such that employees understand the difference they are making to the customer experience. Information and processes should be synchronized to the line of sight so that people receive the data they need to do their job well, rather than being bombarded with unnecessary bureaucracy.

Similarly, HR can help line managers design roles with employee needs in mind also. To give employees chance to achieve, roles should provide employees with 'stretch' yet be achievable and not compromise the employee's ability to achieve work–life balance. This may mean that the role should be designed in a way that it reflects employees' different life stage needs and can be delivered through flexible working for instance. Role design should also take into account the social environment in which work needs to take place. If the employee is based at home for instance, thought should be given to how relationships can be built and maintained, communication needs and requirements met, as well as the health and safety aspects of the physical environment.

Line managers should also be encouraged to review workloads to ensure that people are not being overloaded, especially if workload distribution across a work unit is uneven. Performance management should recognize contribution and achievement, not simply effort expended. Empowerment and accountability should be characteristic criteria for role design. Employees should be given the right levels of freedom and autonomy with respect to decision-making, and appropriate training and information to ensure that they can be trusted to deliver to the standards required.

The Role of HR in Creating Integration

If the trend is towards integrated but agile structures, HR has a key role to play in enabling the integration needed to optimize the business model. Shaun Tyson (1995) suggests that the HR department itself will be an integrating device since its remit usually operates across organizational boundaries and often carries responsibility for corporate communications. The internalization of corporate values, through major communication programmes and the organizational culture as a whole, are other major sources of integration.

For example, W. L. Gore & Associates is a regular winner of UK's *100 Best Companies to Work For* award. Technological accomplishment is at the heart of all its products, which range from bagpipes to dental floss. Its most famous product is Gore-Tex, a pioneering fabric which is both breathable and watertight. The firm's internal structures reflect its approach to innovation. Staff are all 'associates', not 'managers' or 'secretaries'. The organizational culture is based on a belief in the individual. John Kennedy, who is responsible for all UK associates, states that:

> We try to let people do things they are good at as opposed to forcing them into things they are not good at. A lot of why we are successful is down to the way we treat people and how people react to that. It works for us and makes us a good place to work and a productive place at that (The 100 Best Companies to Work For, *Sunday Times*, 2006). Teamwork is considered so important that colleagues' rating of each other is one of the factors pay is based on.

High-Performance/High-Commitment Work Practices

Many studies have shown the substantial economic benefits of adopting high-commitment or high-performance work practices in contrast to conventional 'scientific' management typical of 'modernist' organizations. Often described as 'Japanese' management practices, the case for implementing such approaches is strong. Jeffrey Pfeffer (1996) cites the MIT investigation of the worldwide motor vehicle assembly industry reported in the book *The Machine That Changed The World* by Womack, Jones and Roos (1990). The assembly plants which had adopted flexible or lean manufacturing methods and associated employment-relation practices far outperformed others using mass production methods.

Other studies of the textile industry (Dunlop and Weil, 1996) have found that companies which operate team-based work and compensation as well as training for multiple jobs experienced 22% higher growth in gross margins in the period 1988–1992 than other similar companies. In another US study, Mark Huselid (1995) explored the impact of high-commitment work practices using measures of financial performance. He produced a sophisticated index which showed that a one standard deviation increase of high-commitment work resulted in an annual increase in sales of over $27000 per employee. What was interesting about this study was that it was found that the effectiveness of these work practices was not contingent on a firm's strategy but consistently led to performance improvements.

These high-commitment work practices are characterized by the following:

- Suggestion schemes, Quality circles, problem-solving groups or other forms of employee participation in idea generation
- Employee participation in decision-making
- Freedom of expression
- Extensive teamwork, including self-managing teams
- Reformulation of work to make best use of upgraded skills.

Participation and involvement mean that power shifts from middle managers to those further down the organizational hierarchy – those closest to the customer or the production process. Lawler *et al.* (1995) also report on the effectiveness of employee involvement and TQM, specifically focusing on involvement practices such as information-sharing, developing knowledge, reward strategies and power-sharing strategies. Companies operating such approaches include Levi-Strauss, Motorola and Honeywell.

Employee Relations

What is common about high-performing companies is their agenda to create relationships with employees which support their business objectives. Employee relations are therefore a priority, to be clear about the kind of relationship the business strategy required, and 'to push the execution of employee relations policies down to the lowest level possible, compatible with the corporation's overall values' (Tyson, 1995). Similarly, MacDuffie's (1995) study of HR practices in the automotive industry found that reducing status barriers aids the psychological contract of reciprocal commitment at work. For example, at W.L. Gore, innovation is a key characteristic of the workplace. There is a non-hierarchical environment created by Bill Gore, one of the firm's founders, who believed this would encourage creativity. This is a title-free organization and all staff are associates. Careful selection involves would-be associates spending up to eight hours being interviewed over as many as three days. Workmates help decide their colleagues' pay.

Despite the evidence from organizations which practise Total Quality that these practices work, diffusion seems to be slow. The main barrier appears to be that traditionally the focus of management has been on the financial and strategic aspects of the business, rather than on employee relations. Since high-commitment work practices require major up-front investments, such as in training and higher rates of pay, a willingness to take a risk that these measures will pay off is required; and many management teams are risk averse. Pfeffer (1998a) points out that managers' own perceptions of their role can interfere with effectiveness. If managers believe that they should be the people leading the organization and coming up with ideas about how things should be done, they are not likely to welcome that idea that the organization's success actually depends on many other people, often more junior, throughout the company.

Political and power barriers can also get in the way of implementing high-commitment work practices. Managers may not wish to accept that previous approaches introduced by them may not have yielded such good results as these methods. Similarly, middle managers whose roles are usually most affected, if not removed by high-performance work practices, often resist their introduction. The relative power of advocates of high-performance work practices (usually Human Resource professionals), measured in part by relative salary levels, is often lower than that of the chief critics of such approaches (often finance directors). Interestingly, one research study found that in Japan, different priorities meant that Human Resources and manufacturing were tied to the highest pay levels of functional heads.

HOW CAN HR HELP TO IMPLEMENT HIGH-PERFORMANCE WORK PRACTICES?

By Creating a Culture of Participation

High performance does not occur in a vacuum. The organization's culture must be conducive to productivity and quality improvement. HR can prepare the ground for high-performance working by creating a culture that is supportive of these practices. In recent years, various studies have indicated strong links between employee engagement and business success.

Employee engagement is an important component of talent management and has significant implications for organizational practices, especially employee communications since employee participation, or 'voice', is assumed to be one of the key ingredients leading to employee engagement. At one level of participation, employees can be relatively passive, i.e. the company consults with employees on decisions the company wishes to implement and is seeking ideas from employees about how best to implement these. To create greater engagement, organizations can deliberately build constructive employee relations, especially with staff and trades union representatives, working in proactive partnership on key items of the HR agenda. Organizations can also more obviously attempt to involve large numbers of staff in decision-making within parameters that make sense. Staff polls, blogs, chat rooms and other online channels of communication are means of not only listening and responding to staff but also of being seen to do so.

Employee Consultation

Since April 2005, employees in UK firms with a staff of 150 or more have a right to be informed on a regular basis about issues in their business. These regulations set minimum standards, but encourage voluntary agreements to be reached. They are designed to create more effective workplaces, enabling success and helping the UK respond to the challenges of globalization. The former Department of Trade and Industry (DTI, 2006) found in a survey that 95% of staff in such companies found that involving and consulting staff on a regular basis was of benefit.

The most frequently cited benefits by employees were: an improved work environment; boosted motivation and morale; and improved communication within the company.

A higher level of participation occurs when employees are genuinely involved in decision-making to some degree. In the following case, employee participation is a significant feature of high-performance working. A South African construction company, Neil Muller (Pty) Ltd, has managed to improve profitability and the amount of repeat business by instigating a culture change to support improved productivity. Management introduced what became known as Total Company Renovation to address a number of known problem areas, almost all of which related to human resources, i.e.:

- Communication between management and the workforce was fragmented and relations between the management and trades unions were not positive
- There was a lack of trust between management and the workforce
- Measurement and monitoring of productivity on-site was limited
- There was no long-term career planning
- Employees were not involved in any preplanning or decision-making
- Supervision on-site was inadequate.

Interestingly, the company saw providing job security and a career path as the foundation of the quality-improvement plan. These were considered revolutionary ideas in an industry which has a poor record of providing job security. Another key priority was building trust by improving communication and encouraging interaction between management and the workforce. Ten goals were set, including developing effective participation by all, improving every employee's lot in life, improving profitability and introducing a profit-sharing scheme.

Training played a large part in changing attitudes and skill levels. All company workers attended two-hour sessions covering five days to explain how a company works. Workshops were held for senior managers and supervisors and new ideas were brought into the company by visiting speakers. Workers were not confined to their small piece of a construction. Models were created to allow workers to see how their work was contributing to the whole building. Work targets were introduced as well as daily work measurement systems. These measurement systems are very practical, incorporating data that is already available, such as quantity surveying data, and provide the basic data for costing a job.

The achievement, or otherwise, of daily work targets is discussed by the quality control circle meeting which takes up the first 15 minutes of each day. Problem areas are openly discussed and workers are told what is going on at their site, how the work is progressing financially and why they are doing certain tasks. In addition, each level of supervision has regular meetings to help create effective communication. Social events help create team spirit and the firm's owner and his fellow-directors are actively involved. Good on-site facilities have been provided for workers and site safety is a paramount consideration. The company is no longer unionized but has created an in-house workers' committee known as the Unity Forum. This forum appears to work because of the new levels of trust and communication within the company and a more adult–adult relationship between workers and management (Robinson, 1997).

Corporate Values

Aspirational corporate values statements tend to have little impact on employee behavior without reinforcement. What is really valued in an organization is most evident in management behavior and HR practices, especially reward systems. According to CIPD/CapGemini research (CIPD, 2008), High Performance Workplaces tend to manifest the following:

- 'High Trust' management culture and organizational beliefs – a belief that people will generally strive to perform
- A philosophy of collaboration between employer and employee: participative decision-making and open communication
- A high degree of individual freedom to act, discretion and autonomy in work practices
- Employees managed by outcome.

The John Lewis Partnership has an ownership structure which allows its partners (employees) to share the responsibility of ownership as well as its rewards – profit, knowledge and power – which help create job satisfaction and engagement. The Group has developed six elements of behaviour that it believes define the way it deals with all its stakeholders, including partners. These are: honesty, respect, recognition of others, working together, showing enterprise and – as a result – achieving more.

For Nationwide, the world's largest building society, *pride* in what an organization does is a key retention factor. It is also the acronym for the company values of Nationwide:

*P*ut members first
*R*ise to the challenge
*I*nspire confidence
*D*eliver value
*E*xceed expectations.

As a mutual organization, the company is owned by its customers rather than shareholders. The 16 000-strong workforce find working for a firm with a conscience rewarding; they think it is run on strong values (78%) and believe in those values (85%).

Similarly, formal communications transmit values, though usually more is understood by the behaviour of the people conveying the message than by the words used. At Nationwide a wide range of practices ensures that staff remain engaged, even the third who have more than 15 years' service with the company.

Senior management try to be accessible, with talk-back events held at the Swindon and Northampton administration centres, while intranet feedback to staff questions is returned within 24 hours. All individual areas of the business have a fixed budget of 0.5% of their salary bill to spend on awards and this contributes to an environment where staff feel their contribution is valuable and that they make a difference.

Researching What Matters to Employees

Employee research can play a useful part in transforming businesses and keeping the workforce happy and motivated. Gathering employee opinions, seeking out what drives engagement, linking findings to business results, is increasingly bearing fruit in companies such as the Royal Bank of Scotland and Standard Chartered Bank. The starting point for successful employee research is honest feedback and it should not be launched as just another HR initiative. Ideally set clear objectives about what you want to achieve and carefully research the best methodology to use. Then consider how to structure the information so that it is easy to access, such as capturing data online, where it can be analysed in detail. Ideally the survey should allow you to benchmark your company's results against others in your or other business sectors so there are merits in adopting a similar process to theirs if you want this capability.

Simply identifying and reporting on the issues unearthed through the research is not enough. Follow-up is just as important, as it quickly demonstrates that the company has listened, is not complacent and is keen to unlock the potential of the organization. The research process may produce surprises and uncover blind spots. These should be addressed by assigning project teams to focus on each specific issue or finding, starting on a small scale, perhaps working with one or two departments to begin with. Skilful use of data can stimulate the need for change among executives. One HR team, for example, used data from employee-attitude surveys and turnover statistics and the related costs to make the case for change. Deloitte, the tax and auditing firm, acted on the results of its annual survey, prompting the enhancement of a number of benefits in 2006, including stakeholder pensions and increased flexible working options. Staff can also take unpaid career breaks of up to two years.

Influencing Attitudes

HR professionals can help bring about change by using their cross-organizational influence, ability to design structures and processes which support the business strategy and creating the culture changes through values and communication which support new ways of working. HR can expose managers and employees to new approaches by helping set up benchmarking visits to organizations that are achieving outstanding results through people.

Designing and Implementing HR Processes that Support the Business Strategy

At a practical level, to create the conditions for high performance, HR processes need to be aligned to the new ways of working. These are likely to include reward, benefits and performance management systems that drive higher performance; support for high performing teams and a key focus on building and sustaining employee engagement. These should all be underpinned by investment in skill enhancement and talent development.

Talent management has clear links with performance management: the question is how to manage talent and ensure that talented individuals stay with the organization after the investment in them? According to Jim Collins author of *Good to Great*, the secret of high performance is getting the 'right people on the bus'. HR can develop assessment processes to ensure that the 'right' people are selected for roles. It can also help employees to see for themselves if they have the capabilities for new roles. HR can work with the line to develop self-assessment processes.

The following HR processes are typical of 'vanguard' companies described by O'Toole (1985):

- Highly selective recruitment
- Extensive training and skill development
- Contingent or performance-related pay, at high rates
- Employee share ownership
- Benefits tailored to individual needs
- Providing some degree of employment security
- Sharing information about a firm's goals and results so that people know what to accomplish and how they are doing
- Reducing status differentials, if teamworking is to be a reality.

Career processes also need to be aligned to new ways of working. If multi-skilling is a requirement of employees, they need to be given opportunities to develop those skills and forms of knowledge to which they may not have previously been exposed. Employees need to know that they can access learning and development beyond their current job. Procter and Gamble, for instance, which is known for its innovative approaches to work teams, tends to put line managers into human resource positions, then rotate them back to line management positions. This ensures that HR is fully integrated with the business, that HR is seen as a credible function and is therefore highly influential.

Supporting Line Managers

It is often said that people don't leave their jobs, they leave their managers. While this may be somewhat exaggerated, a variety of surveys suggest that poor quality leadership and managers' inability to get the best out of people contributes to organizational under-performance and organizational stagnation. Increasingly too, employees expect managers at all levels to behave in ways that are consistent with organizational values and any major gaps between the 'walk' and the 'talk' on values is likely to engender employee cynicism. HR has a key role to play in coaching line managers to lead their teams in ways that are consistent with the organization's values and policies, for instance with respect to diversity and equality.

HR can provide valuable training and other resources to ensure that managers have the skills to coach and develop other people, as well as appraise performance. HR also needs to be willing and able to challenge inappropriate practice, including examples of unjustifiable prejudice for or against employees. This means that HR needs to be role-modelling ethical leadership behaviour that is recognized by others.

PERFORMANCE MANAGEMENT

Managing performance is perhaps *the* key responsibility of line managers and an area where a partnership between line and HR can be most beneficial. The four key elements of performance management are:

- A common understanding of the organization's goals
- Shared expectations of how individuals can contribute
- Employees with the skill and ability to meet expectations
- Individuals who are fully committed to the aims of the organization.

In managing performance, managers must be able to ensure that employees are appropriately focused into roles, developed and managed. There should be an enabling environment and a focus on performance improvement and feedback.

Designing Effective Appraisal and Development Processes

Appraisal requires excellent interview and counselling skills if the process is to be motivating for those involved. It relies on managers and employees having a relationship in which discussing performance is not seen as a burden or a threat. In many cases managers do not make the time to appraise people's performance well.

The Roffey Park *Management Agenda* research suggests that performance appraisals are becoming more complex. The annual review of performance is now generally supplemented by an integrated objective-setting and development planning process. The use of the 360-degree feedback processes is increasing but many of our respondents expressed some distrust of using this in assessing performance. The consensus was that different forms of feedback, such as team-, peer-, or upward-feedback, should not replace the one-to-one discussion with the line manager. Many respondents wanted more regular feedback from their line manager and some would welcome feedback from internal and external customers.

Importantly, there were many comments with regard to how performance was assessed. In particular, it was felt that only results (outputs) are really taken into account and that inputs are taken for granted. There was commonly a lack of the 'soft' measures so useful in bringing about changes in behaviour and culture. Where such measures did exist they appeared to have little bearing on how performance was assessed, with hard measures being the only factors taken into account when bonuses were awarded. Some appraisal schemes in our respondents' organizations therefore appear to be complicated but not necessarily helpful in moving the organization or individual performance forward.

An example of an effective performance management system is the competency-based process at Bayer Pharma's R&D division. The competencies on which the scheme is based were derived from the overall company vision and the strategy for R&D. Performance is managed using clear definitions of the competencies which the company believes will bring success.

The performance management scheme is very future-oriented, rather than being simply a review of past performance. The new R&D system puts individuals in control of their own performance and development since the individual is expected to take the lead when meeting with their boss to review performance. The Annual Performance Review assesses performance against last year's objectives and a competency assessment identifies areas of development which may have had an impact on performance. The individual prepares examples of work to refer to and is responsible for documenting the discussion. The manager acts as facilitator. Several weeks later a Development Review assesses what might be development priorities from the organization's perspective. The individual identifies their own personal development priorities in the light of their aspirations and a detailed development plan addresses both sets of needs.

In many organizations the link between personal development and the business strategy is weak, with appraisal being used as an annual administrative chore, which means that employees fail to take personal development seriously. HR can help by designing user-friendly processes which focus both on job training for the current position but are also future focused, thus giving employees a strong message about the value they bring to the organization and also preparing them for changing work demands.

In one financial services organization, strategic imperatives to achieve loyal and satisfied customers have been translated into key performance indicators in which all business units and managers are expected to deliver results. Objective areas include leadership, management of process quality, operational results and customer focus and satisfaction. Each of these is supported by behavioural dimensions, together with resources to help people develop effectiveness in these results areas. The HR team has developed a list of ways of developing these behaviours, based on the work of the Center for Creative Leadership. They include suggestions such as:

- Take part in a task force on a pressing business problem
- Plan an off-site meeting, conference, convention

- Integrate systems across units
- Business trip to a foreign country.

Appraisal discussions take place annually, while objective-setting and development planning are separate processes which are carried out more frequently.

Helping Line Managers to Set Appropriate Measures

The old management dictum 'if you can't measure it, you can't manage it' is starting to be turned on its head. Success criteria should be those that make a (positive) difference to the organization. While measures undoubtedly send strong symbolic messages about what is valued, the question of what is being measured and therefore considered important is increasingly being called into question. Targets need to be set for the deliverables that are required but not at the expense of how the deliverables are to be achieved.

Conversely, if measures are set around 'soft' targets such as behaviours, these need to be taken seriously or employees will soon understand that only performance which has a direct impact on the bottom line counts. In many organizations 360 degree feedback processes have been introduced as part of culture change initiatives and senior management development.

Some organizations claim that the feedback is incorporated into decisions about pay. In most cases, the link with pay has been almost entirely with bottom line performance with the achievement of other 'soft' behavioural targets being regarded as very secondary.

Helping Managers Deal with Poor Performance

In some organizations, poor performance is handled by simply passing on the underperformer to another department. Sometimes, managers find difficulty in confronting aspects of poor performance because they lack confidence in their ability to handle the conflict which might arise. Similarly, some managers find it hard to delegate, and others are so thinly stretched that there is no one to whom they can delegate. Some managers are managing teams of contractors rather than full-time or permanent employees. HR needs to be able to support managers in understanding how they can achieve high standards with slim resources. They can help establish networks of peer coaches amongst line managers, coach managers directly and provide 'rehearsal' opportunities for difficult conversations, help managers think through the options available to them, as well as advise on disciplinary procedure as appropriate.

REWARD STRATEGIES

The dynamic link between performance and reward has been much debated and since the 1990s there has been a period of major change in reward management. According to Hay Group (Heneman, 2002), if employees are to feel that they are being fairly treated, pay needs to be competitive, and benefits should reflect what matters to different segments of the employee population. There should be incentives for higher performance, and the opportunity for share ownership. Recognition awards are also important in ensuring that employees feel their work is being assessed and valued.

Pensions have also been in the news since the Pensions Commission reported in 2005, drawing attention to the looming pensions crisis. Half of salary-related pensions were closed to new entrants between 2000 and 2003, and by 2007 most were also closing to current staff members as organizations sought to manage their pensions commitments for the future. Many employers have replaced salary-based schemes with new money purchase schemes. However, some employers differentiate themselves by maintaining their commitment to final salary pensions. At the Royal Bank of Scotland (RBS), for example, benefits include flexible working hours, a final salary pension, share options and profit-related pay.

Of course, reward should be the exemplar of alignment and provide a direct line of sight for employees between the organization's goals and strategy, the individual's role and how well they perform in their role (see Figure 7.1). It is not the only aspect of organization that provides this line of sight, but it is perhaps the one aspect that most clearly represents to employees, both symbolically and practically, what is really required of them and how much they are valued.

All human resource systems, especially pay, need to reinforce the forms of skilled performance the organization requires of individuals. Implementing any new business strategy is meaningless unless there is a degree of consistency between what is expected of employees in terms of working practices and the systems, processes and resources needed to do the job. Similarly, reward strategies should help reinforce the sorts of behaviours and other aspects of performance the strategy calls for. For example, if the business is following an innovation-led

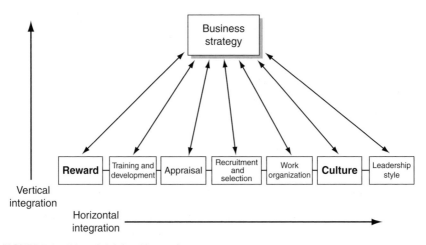

FIGURE 7.1 'Line of sight' and integration.
Source: S. Bevan, © The Work Foundation

strategy, the thrust of reward policy should reflect this and encourage appropriate employee behaviours, as identified by Stephen Bevan of The Work Foundation (see Figure 7.2).

Employee role/behaviour	Reward policy thrust	Other HR policies
• Creativity: seeking new solutions	• Mix of individual and collective rewards	• Broadly defined job roles
• Risk-taking behaviour	• Use of 'soft' performance measures, periodically monitored	• Cross-functional career paths to encourage the development of a broad range of skills
• Medium-term focus		
• Collaborative and cooperative behaviour	• Emphasis on medium-term performance	• Appraisal focusing on medium-term and collective achievement
• Concern for quality and continuous improvement	• Use of learning and personal growth opportunities as a 'soft' reward	
• Equal concern for process and outcomes		• High investment in learning and development
• High tolerance of ambiguity and unpredictability	• Broad-banded and flexible pay structure	• Frequent use of teamworking
• Encouragement for learning and environmental scanning	• High relative market pay	

FIGURE 7.2 Innovation-led strategy.
Source: S. Bevan, © The Work Foundation

On the other hand, when the business strategy is principally one of cost-reduction, reward policies will typically reflect this focus and reinforce something of a law of diminishing returns (see Figure 7.3).

Employee role/behaviour	Reward policy thrust	Other HR policies
• Repetitive and structured tasks	• Focus on individual rewards	• Narrowly defined job descriptions
• Risk-averse	• High proportion of earnings at risk	
• Predominantly short-term focus		• Appraisal focused on short-term results
	• Emphasis on short-term performance	
• Reliance on individual effort		• Task-focused training with short-term pay back
• Concern for quantity	• Narrow and rigid pay structure	
• Primary concern for results rather than process		• Limited opportunities for progression and development
	• Moderate relative market pay	
• Need for predictability and standardization	• Use of 'hard' performance measures, frequently monitored	
• Focus on productivity improvement		

FIGURE 7.3 Cost reduction-led strategy.
Source: S. Bevan, © The Work Foundation

Reward and Employee Segmentation

So, whilst reward schemes need to meet both the organization's needs for managing its salary bill and for ensuring that it is getting good performance from its employees, they must also be designed to meet employees' needs to be appropriately recompensed for their efforts. And when it comes to designing reward systems from the employee perspective, it is clear that 'one size' does not 'fit all'. Here, the importance of employee segmentation cannot be over-emphasized. This is the marketing and sales discipline applied to the workforce. On the one hand employee segmentation should take into account the organization's needs and the relative importance of certain employee segments, as defined by the nature and criticality of the work to the organization's success; and also by the skills involved and the scarcity of those skills. Those key employees should also be defined by their needs, life cycle stages, aspirations and expectations. Reward and other HR processes should then be designed to meet the needs as far as possible of key segments of the workforce, without unduly disfavouring others.

The Symbolic Power of Reward Systems

While they are usually logically designed to meet strategic requirements, reward schemes carry enormous symbolic significance for employees. They are a powerful means of teaching employees what is actually valued in the organization, as well as what is not. Typically this is achieved by incentivizing particular types of performance, such as increased sales, and by punishing employees who appear to be underperforming. As such, they have a greater impact on employee attitudes and behaviour than corporate rhetoric or values statements which encourage teamworking, for example. So if the organization encourages teamwork but continues to award significant bonuses for individual achievement alone, teamwork is less likely to be taken seriously.

In theory, reward schemes are designed to be motivating, offering appropriate incentives for, and recognition of, desired performance. Whether schemes that focus exclusively on the financial aspects of reward achieve this aim is open to debate.

While money is sometimes thought to be a motivator, and it certainly appears to be for some people, at least at some stages of their career, Herzberg's (1966) well-known motivation theory suggests that money is just as likely to demotivate. Take the example of someone who is told by their manager that they are going to get a 10% pay rise in recognition of superb performance. The employee will no doubt be very pleased unless he or she finds that other members of the team are going to get a 15% pay rise. This is where the principle of equity – or at least what feels fair – becomes paramount to employees. Similarly, once the employee has grown used to the level of pay, no matter how large the initial rise, money in itself ceases to be motivating, according to Herzberg. Losing money, on the other hand, continues to be universally demotivating.

There are numerous examples of people whose jobs have been effectively downgraded during delayering, and so have their pay and benefits. The 'running sore' effect of such organizational decisions can cause people to see themselves as victims. Almost inevitably, loyalty to the organization suffers as a result. Changing reward arrangements therefore is likely to be as much a source of concern for the organization as it is for employees.

Talent Management and Reward

CIPD talent management research found that reward systems can have a significant impact on talent management initiatives, particularly in terms of retaining talent. A study carried out by Innecto Reward Consulting (2006) found that:

- Cultural, economic and technological changes in the past 10 years have made financial reward a greater motivator than challenging work or personal pride.
- Nearly three-quarters of the 690 'career-oriented' UK executives under 40 years old who were polled said they now expected a pay rise every year.
- Two-thirds claimed that financial reward is now the number one career motivator.
- Yet just 15% of the 189 HR professionals surveyed believed financial reward to be a key motivator.

These findings suggest that unless there is a joined-up approach to rewards and talent management, an investment in talent management activities may just not be worthwhile – but it also indicates that HR must be far more alert to the problem – particularly as 75% of those surveyed admitted that their businesses had lost at least five talented staff in 2005.

Reward is clearly a major area for attention at the design stage of talent management strategy. And while other factors matter, unless reward is taken into account, increasing investment in talent management does little to retain key individuals.

THE NEED TO REVISE REWARD STRATEGIES

In times gone by, when organizations had relatively stable hierarchical structures, pay schemes were apparently clear-cut. Job evaluation was used to decide how much each job was worth in terms of its contribution to the organization. Jobs were defined and allocated according to a clear set of job grades, each of which had a salary range. The majority of staff would be on a fixed pay arrangement and pay was often linked with seniority and subject to almost automatic increases regardless of performance. Of course, this made managing the salary pot relatively straightforward.

Arguably, such schemes were acceptable to many employees, especially people working for bureaucratic organizations, since some kind of pay increase could be relied upon, even if the increase was not dramatic. For many HR specialists too, such schemes had advantages since they often appeared to have power in negotiations about pay and promotion. They were the organization's gatekeepers and saying 'no' was part of the job.

However, as organizations' needs changed, such schemes seemed to offer fewer advantages, apart from familiarity. A system that reinforced the status quo was increasingly out of step with the need for greater and more flexible outputs from employees.

In an attempt to move towards a performance culture, many organizations have introduced pay schemes over the last two decades which are intended to

reflect performance in the job more than the job grade itself. Yet a large proportion of UK companies have still not developed reward schemes that link pay and
benefits to a team's performance and their contribution to corporate values in
a flatter structure. Instead, paying market rates remains the preferred model for
many organizations alongside schemes that recognize individual short-term performance but not long-term development.

In these changing times, reward schemes quickly become sources of
employee discontent. Indeed, research carried out by Roffey Park found that people who are dissatisfied with their career development are likely to consider that
their organization's reward scheme and leadership are inappropriate. It seems
that when people are reasonably happy with their jobs and career prospects, the
reward scheme is seen as less of an issue. In organizations that have delayered
significantly, traditional job evaluation-based pay structures are beginning to
seem outdated and inappropriate. With flatter structures, the reduced number of
management levels usually means that people's job responsibilities have grown
way beyond the original job description. Because organizations can no longer
guarantee vertical promotion they are actively looking for ways to promote and
introduce the idea of lateral careers. However, fixed grading schemes often deter
people from making 'sideways' moves since they will actually lose pay in the
bargain. New skills are called for in a job environment, which typically includes
large cross-functional teams often managed remotely and pressures to create new
and different relationships with a changing customer base. Allocating a 'pricing' value to a job description in such changing circumstances seems restrictive.
Above all, reward systems need to be able to provide people with a real sense of
progression, or at least not demotivate employees when promotion opportunities
are fewer.

While many HR professionals are keenly aware of the need to reshape reward
strategies, the difficulty lies in identifying what needs to change and what the
organization wishes to reward. Sadly, introducing revised schemes can raise as
many problems as leaving the current system, however inadequate, in place.
According to Jeffrey Pfeffer (1998b), 'The successful investment in new reward
practices involves a great deal of effort, commitment and expertise. And it is
probably the most difficult task facing HR managers.' He suggests that there is
no such thing as a perfect pay system, but that good systems are about customization and tailoring, rather than off-the-shelf solutions.

More Flexible Approaches to Reward

As CIPD Pay and Benefits surveys have reported, many employers are revising
pay mechanisms to reflect the broad shifts in the competitive marketplace. Many
organizations have responded to competitive pressures by focusing their business
strategies on customer needs and securing customer loyalty by developing more
flexible, innovative products and services. The need for flexibility and cost-
effectiveness has led to organizational restructurings of various kinds, including

flatter structures, with their focus on teamwork, broader roles and non-traditional work arrangements.

If organizations require high levels of flexibility of employees, reward systems may also need to be flexible. Job grading, reward and development systems must be linked up with future opportunities. These will still need to evaluate relative contribution but they must also allow assessment of competence and skill progression. At the same time, no system can allow its costs to escalate out of control. The challenge therefore is to find a flexible and tailored alternative, or set of alternatives, which allows for a better match between organizational needs and constraints and employee needs and aspirations.

Many organizations are experimenting with more flexible packages, which include elements of variable pay, linked to job performance, competence, skills development and desired team and leadership behaviours. The new systems include a greater element of discretion for the line manager, feedback processes and a degree of individual choice in benefits.

From the employee perspective, job security and career progression up a clearly defined hierarchy are becoming things of the past. Full-time employment is increasingly being replaced by various forms of flexible work arrangement including fixed-term contract working, part-time and temporary arrangements.

Reward systems should take into account the needs of employees for whom pay may have replaced promotion as a means of making career progress in today's increasingly diffuse organizations. Reward systems are about more than merely paying people for work done. Increasingly, employers who are looking at strategies to recruit and retain the best people are viewing reward as part of the package – see Chapters 8 and 9 for examples of this.

Performance-Related Pay

Incentive schemes and performance-related pay continue to provoke debate. There is assumed to be a link between productivity, individual and team performance and reward. In the United States variable pay systems are growing rapidly. In the UK performance-based pay has been relatively well established for a number of years, especially in the private sector where it is the norm. Such schemes need to be responsive to the business drivers, the changing technology, the new skills needed and the fact that to be successful in a new environment, people need to do different things. Performance-related pay is now increasingly commonplace in public sector and not-for-profit organizations, and there is often a variable pay element in clerical roles, even though individually job-holders may have only small effects on overall organizational performance.

Public Sector Pay Reform

One in five workers in the UK is employed within the public sector, which has an overall pay bill of £135 bn. Public sector reforms under way represent a significant cultural shift on several fronts. The emphasis now is strongly on achieving performance outcomes with a major focus on the customer or consumer of services, and moves away from a model whereby individual departments, agencies and authorities deliver specific outcomes independently of one another. The shift too is away from direct delivery toward commissioning, with much 'traditional' public sector delivery now outsourced to commercial or not-for-profit agencies.

Pay is a key plank of public sector structural reform strategies, with a continuing drive on performance and productivity and in a context of greater public scrutiny and demands for accountability. The government's view is that public sector pay rises drive inflation and therefore pay restraint is needed. And against a straightening employment environment, with 80 000 fewer public sector jobs in 2007 compared with 2005, and a pay bill for local government alone topping £3 bn in 2008, Prime Minister Brown's 'Golden Rule' of 2% annual increases represents the slowest growth rate of public sector for a decade.

At the same time, performance-related pay is now widespread across the public sector and, despite various public sector unions contesting its introduction, the trend seems set to stay. In 2006, 87% of public sector bodies gave clerical and manufacturing workers annual general cost of living increases together with some form of performance-related pay (CIPD, 2006).

Despite the extent of the reforms, employment relations remain rooted in earlier negotiation and collective bargaining models. Pay and reward models in particular need revising in line with the reforms, to recognize broader elements of reward and contribution, and a platform of good employee relations is needed to allow for greater reform. Amongst the more innovative approaches, West Midlands Police, for instance, has adopted a reward and contribution framework for police staff which includes more flexible job design, better performance and review processes, which puts the emphasis back onto line managers. Part of the deal is that what is expected of staff is clear and the nature of support provided to employees relates to managing capacity as much as holding people to account.

In some government departments variable pay has met with a mixed response since, for some employees, performance-based pay effectively constitutes a demotion in terms of their pay packet. One of the main consequences of introducing variable pay in place of a wholly fixed pay system is that what is considered as 'core' to the job may assume a lesser importance in the mind of the job-holder than any aspect of the job which is singled out for variable pay. Therefore if short-term bottom-line performance is the basis of the bonus, employees are likely to put their efforts into this, perhaps at the expense of other things that the organization is trying to achieve in the longer term.

Equal pay is another key feature of the public sector, with maintenance of the equal pay infrastructure being considered as important as the desire for performance return, although in 2007 there was still an average gender pay gap across sectors of 17%. It used to be thought that public sector pay may lag behind the private sector, but the index-linked pensions representing financial security in old age were a compensation for lower lifetime earnings. Perhaps for that reason, pensions reform is progressing slowly in the public sector and final salary pension schemes have largely survived the reform process to date. However, the Local Government Employers' *'Delivering a Rewarding Future'* highlights the intention to start to manage pay and pensions more closely. A key challenge for public sector pay in the future is the question of pay parity across sectors when public, private and not-for-profit organizations work in partnership to deliver performance outcomes. The question will be how to develop cross-sector reward strategies to avoid significant anomalies.

Ironically, at a time when performance-related pay has become 'the norm', it is itself coming to be called into question – is it the panacea for encouraging excellence that the theorists thought would be the case? Some of the main proponents of the link between performance and reward are now thinking again. Unilever, a consumer goods multinational employing 300 000 people in more than 60 countries, has been an exponent of performance-related pay for almost three decades. But since a board review in 1994, the company has rethought its practice in the context of corporate restructuring and will continue to do so for the foreseeable future (Ashton, 1999).

How Effective is Performance-Related Pay?

The effectiveness of performance-based pay remains hotly contested. Indeed, research by Scholtes (1995) lists five reasons why performance-based reward, recognition and incentive systems generally do not work:

- There are no data to show long-term benefits
- They set up internal competition
- Reward systems undermine teamwork and cooperation
- They often reward those who are lucky and pass by those who are unlucky
- They create cynics and losers.

This highlights a danger with variable pay. With today's increased spans of control, variable pay risks becoming a proxy for performance management. The more performance is rewarded through variable pay, the greater the disappointment of the individual who feels that his or her talents have not been recognized if the bonus is small.

The managing director of a small consultancy decided to introduce a new form of performance-related pay which singled out the achievement of a number of business goals for special reward. Junior staff had relatively less access to the resources needed to achieve these targets. Nevertheless, one junior consultant put in a major effort to achieve the targets and succeeded in achieving the performance threshold required for a bonus. Her reward turned out to be £10, accompanied by a letter from her boss encouraging her to try harder next year! Not surprisingly, the consultant decided to test her fortunes elsewhere.

Developing merit-based pay systems may be one of the most challenging areas for human resource specialists, since there are many factors to be taken into account when revising a compensation system to make it reflect performance.

Since reward is one of the most visible signs of the 'contract' between employers and employees, it is important that every aspect of the pay system should be transparent, and that what is being rewarded should be clear.

This raises tricky questions such as how clear is 'transparent': should the pay system reward for instance only the outputs of individual performance, or how these are achieved as well? Should individual 'stars' who have shone thanks to help from their team be singled out? Should higher levels of skill be reflected in performance, or should developing new skills, albeit at a more basic level, be incentivized? Simply unpacking the diverse aspects of behaviour, skills and experience which lead to the sort of performance organizations require can be complex. Typically, problems can occur, for example when work processes are supposed to be underpinned by teamwork, but individual bottom-line performance is the only thing that is taken into account when determining pay.

Broadly speaking, any reward system needs to reflect the key drivers for future organizational success in the short and medium term. In developing reward strategies that respond to these business drivers some basic questions need to be answered. What, for instance, are the critical roles, tasks, skills which should be rewarded? What are the new working practices that the organization wishes to encourage? Will teamworking be more critical to achieving business goals than individual performance? Is having one system the only way of thinking about a revised system?

The question of what constitutes performance continues to be debated. Organizations are demanding more from their staff, not only in terms of 'output', in other words, performance against agreed targets, but there is now an increasing emphasis on the 'input' or how targets have been accomplished. Inputs include the new skills which people are required to use in their jobs and the cultural targets which the organization wants to encourage in terms of attitudes and behaviours. Many organizations want people to be keen and willing to take on broader responsibilities, learn new skills and develop wider competencies. In addition, technology is bringing about a more fundamental change, switching the nature of the way work is carried out from directive tasks to process-driven activities.

In some organizations only outputs are assessed for bonus purposes while in others inputs are also taken into account. Typically, the new areas of incentivization include 'soft' areas such as making creative suggestions, receiving positive feedback from customers, teamworking and demonstrating leadership. To support this approach there is usually an emphasis on competencies and various feedback mechanisms are used.

WHAT REWARD STRATEGIES ARE APPROPRIATE IN CHANGING ORGANIZATIONS?

The move towards more flexible reward strategies reflects the need to attract and retain key employees. An increasingly mobile workforce is going to require that there is at least parity in pay and benefits wherever they are working geographically.

Expatriate conditions that guarantee a level of secured income are becoming less frequent. A number of organizations are beginning to consider paying the difference between the total compensation in two locations by way of a cash supplement. Given that most European countries are likely to continue to have different approaches to reward, the use of total compensation packages is set to increase.

Similarly, the shift away from state benefits in many European countries is likely to put pressure on employers to provide basic benefit programmes including pensions. Employees in years to come will no doubt become adept at comparing the overall value of such packages. Competitiveness in the labour market may well depend on employers thinking ahead about how their compensation package can be used to attract and retain the best talent.

Long-Term Incentives and Share Ownership

There seems to be a growing use of long-term incentives (LTIs) and the practice of retaining key people through the use of incentives has long been popular in the United States. In the UK and other parts of Europe where the incidence of such schemes is much lower, there appears to be a trend in multinational companies such as Shell and Total towards extending these incentive schemes to European senior employees. Employee share ownership appears to be also on the increase. Companies such as Procter and Gamble are giving all employees share options to encourage continued commitment to the organization.

Broad Banding

Many organizations are introducing broad banding, where a small number of wide salary bands encompasses many varied roles. This should make job enrichment and lateral moves easier, as long as opportunities to make those moves exist. In practice, the process of introducing broad bands is fraught with difficulty. The new bands are often viewed with suspicion by employees, as reflected in a well-known cartoon sketch in which the boss says to the character: 'We're introducing broad banding. . . . which means that not only will you have the opportunity not to be promoted you will also earn less for more work'.

Increasingly, 'job families', or 'professional communities', are being added to broad bands to ensure market fit and relevance to employees. These approaches allow different professional and business groups to be rewarded differently and reflect market conditions. These have the advantage of specifically addressing the needs of different groups of key workers, but can be difficult to implement in an organization which has strong centralizing tendencies. Job families are not simply reflected in rewards but also in new roles and other HR processes such as recruiting, training, organization, management style and internal communication.

Ideally, for the job family system to work, the required capabilities are established and combined into roles. The key performance measures are then directly cascaded from the measures of business performance. The focus is on 'total pay', which includes both benefits and pay as well as taking into account employees' perception of the package. The notion of individual value and capability is crucial, with increased value reflected in earnings. Since it is recognized that both employee inputs and outputs are different from in the past, the need to create an employment environment which meets employee and business needs is a prime consideration.

Other Trends

Many organizations are experimenting with competence-based pay (CBP), also known as knowledge- or skills-based pay, which takes the notion of performance-related pay in a particular direction. CBP works on the basis of rewarding the skills an individual possesses and actually uses. Typically, completion of a training unit relating to a particular competency or skills unit usually results in a pay increase. The downside of such schemes is that they tend to be very complex. The emphasis on individual competence can lead to a failure to reflect sought-after cross-organizational business goals such as teamworking and quality.

Team Pay

Many organizations are now trying to encourage teamworking and want to see this reflected in their pay schemes. Team-based pay schemes provide financial rewards to individual employees working within a formally established team. Payments are linked to team performance or the achievement of agreed team objectives. Team pay has not yet been proved to be effective for white-collar workers and research carried out by the CIPD has shown that team pay is often more talked about than practised. One of the drawbacks of the wider spread of team pay is that every scheme is unique. It is not possible to simply adopt some broad recommendations from other organizations, nor are such schemes easy to design or manage. The CIPD found that team pay works best if teams stand alone with agreed targets and standards, have autonomy, are composed of people whose work is interdependent, are stable, are well established and make good use of complementary skills.

Some companies see little need for team incentives while others recognize that flexible working with individuals sharing responsibility implies greater pay equality. The three basic elements of a team-based reward package (assuming that the basic pay is right) are:

- The individual element, i.e. the basic salary but varied in relation to performance or skills/competence
- A team element related to the achievement of team targets
- An organizational element related to business performance measured as profit, or added value.

These may be in the form of cash or shares. Some companies are devising incentives such as coupled team and individual bonuses while others are flattening pay differentials and putting little emphasis on incentives. Hierarchical pay structures are not conducive to teamworking. It is difficult to foster team spirit if individuals are concentrating on promotion. Nor should performance be the sole criterion for rewarding success.

FLEXIBLE BENEFITS

Given the way the work environment is changing, continuing to offer benefits that are based on the 'job-for-life' assumption is unrealistic. More flexible workforces may not wish to see their deferred benefits accruing in small ways in a variety of employers' schemes. The important thing is to find out how people perceive their benefits and whether these are valued and appropriate to both company and employee needs.

In the UK, Cable and Wireless has developed a cafeteria-style benefits system. Items in the scheme include pensions, health-care, childcare vouchers, annual leave, life cover and dental insurance for employees and their partners. Their HR team emphasizes the importance of good communication about the nature of the scheme. At Cancer Research UK, employees have online access to self-service benefits from which they can choose options to the value of their entitlement.

Changing social needs are creating the need for more innovative approaches from employers. In the United States some companies, such as Lotus Development and Apple Computers, are now extending benefits to domestic partners as well as spouses. Hoechst Roussel was formed during the 1994 merger of the two pharmaceutical companies and both companies had offered generous and expensive benefits packages. The company took the opportunity to revise, rather than simply integrate the two reward structures. Hoechst Roussel HR team ran a staff attitude survey to find out what people actually wanted in the way of benefits. Ninety per cent of staff said that they wanted more choice over the benefits they received; 80% said that some benefits should be cut back and others expanded; 70% said they would like to swap some benefits for cash; 60% said that they would be prepared to make extra contributions to improve certain benefits. No one wanted to see benefits abolished in favour of a pure cash equivalent. It was clear that the company needed a flexible benefits system.

The HR team realized that choice is an important benefit in itself. As the HR director, Richard Baker, said:

> In the past we'd approached benefits from the company's standpoint, not the employees', but even so there was no link to the company's corporate goals. Now we had an opportunity to use employee benefits to reinforce the culture of the new company, giving employees the same responsibility for determining their benefits that they were being given in other parts of their work.

Benefits clearly have to be relevant if they are to be valued. Managing a flexible benefits scheme is not easy since it is a dynamic situation, people's needs change. Some pundits advise adjusting one or two benefits, rather than revising a complete scheme. Sophisticated software is needed to support a flexible benefits scheme. Introducing a flexible benefits scheme is not a panacea but it should allow for a closer matching of individual needs with the organization's goals.

HOW DO PEOPLE WANT TO BE REWARDED?

The past few years has seen the introduction of a range of extrinsic rewards such as:

- Profit (gain) sharing
- Flexible benefits
- Bonuses payable in terms of extra leave rather than pay
- Bonuses payable towards prestigious qualifications
- Long-term incentives (LTIs)
- Deferred incentives
- Extending private health schemes to all employees and their families
- Longer holidays
- Sponsored holidays
- 'Free' family holidays in company-owned cottages
- Enhanced early retirement.

However, our research suggests that intrinsic motivators such as the chance to do something worthwhile, to have a development stretch, to increase job satisfaction are all as important as the financial package and represent 'psychological' rewards. Many people want to feel that their skills and contribution have been recognized by others, especially their boss. Ironically, the more inflexible the formal reward scheme, the more people appear to rely on other forms of recognition to reward individuals.

Many of the people who took part in the *Management Agenda* surveys suggested that some of the best rewards were linked with new opportunities rather than pay alone. They enjoyed the respect and recognition of peers and managers. Some see development as the route to promotion in the future and that work opportunities come from having higher-level skills.

Total Rewards

Looking ahead, the notion that reward should be thought of more holistically, rather than as just a package of pay and benefits, is becoming widely accepted. Zingheim and Schuster argue that by understanding how extrinsic rewards such as pay need to sit alongside sources of deeper motivation, such as the opportunity for growth, designers of reward processes can more obviously meet employee needs to be treated fairly, and organizational needs for a manageable pay bill by adopting a total reward philosophy. They suggest that six key principles should be adopted if the approach is to be effective. The aim should be to:

1. Create a positive and natural reward experience
2. Align rewards with business goals to create a win–win partnership
3. Extend people's line of sight

4. Integrate rewards
5. Reward ongoing value (i.e. skills, consistent performance and value relative to the market) with base pay
6. Reward results with variable pay.

They describe four categories of tangible and intangible reward which make up Total Rewards. These are:

1. Individual growth
- Investment in people
- Development and training
- Performance management
- Career enhancement
2. A compelling future
- Vision and values
- Company growth and success
- Company image and reputation
- Stakeholdership
- Win–win over time
3. Positive workplace
- People focus
- Leadership
- Colleagues
- Work itself
- Involvement
- Trust and commitment
- Open communication
4. Total pay
- Base pay
- Variable pay, including stock
- Benefits and indirect pay
- Recognition and celebration.

Cambridgeshire County Council introduced Total Rewards in 2006 as part of the new People Strategy. In terms of tangible rewards, equal pay and final salary pensions are available to all staff, performance-related pay is available to executives and managers. Benefits include childcare vouchers, BUPA membership, flexible working, an employee housing scheme, a 'green' travel scheme and careful workload management. Annual Reward Statements reflect the monetary value of the total reward package received by individuals, which helps employees see how the different elements contribute to their overall compensation.

What is clear is that organizations which are contemplating introducing some form of Total Reward system are focusing their attention most on the employees they most want to recruit and retain, which is where employee segmentation is a vital tool in understanding what different employee groups want and need. The question frequently asked is: 'Do we need to make our different offerings meet the needs of our current and future key staff?' and the answer has to be 'Yes'.

RECOGNITION

In many organizations the scope for modifying the reward system may appear limited. Recognition schemes take on a special significance since they are a symbolic way of reinforcing the 'new' behaviours and performance needed in the organization.

Research suggests, however, that formal recognition schemes rarely motivate people in the long term and can be laborious to administer. Despite this, there are many examples of recognition schemes which are perceived to be successful since they are linked to the business strategy, are imaginative and regularly modified and offer individuals a degree of choice in how they wish to be recognized.

Supporting Culture Change through a Reward and Recognition Process

In establishing a TQM process within a company, a transition to a corporate culture in which there is a continuous improvement philosophy is a basic requirement. One scheme that has been well received by employees and includes elements of recognition with financial reward is run by an Australian pharmaceutical company. This annual quality award aims to endorse a culture of continuous improvement by recognizing the following types of contribution:

- Exceptional teamwork
- Excellence in normal key tasks
- High achievement in a special project.

Since this company values its role as a community leader, individuals can be nominated, for instance for activities that lead to an improvement in the environment. Nomination forms provide a review of the important attributes of a quality employee. These include:

- Attitude to quality
- Teamwork
- Commitment to their department
- Attitude to company and co-workers
- Consistency with work performance
- Attendance and punctuality
- Enthusiasm
- Accuracy
- Use of initiative and knowledge of customer requirements.

The nominations are reviewed quarterly by the quality committee, which consists of eight representatives of each area of the business and includes the general manager as chairperson.

Recognition of successful nominations takes place at a company meeting which all employees are invited to attend. Each successful nominee receives a certificate from the quality committee, thanking them for their contribution. Successful nominations are reviewed and awards made consisting of:

- A monetary component such as a package at a prestigious hotel
- A framed certificate from the company
- An individual and group photograph used for publication in the company newsletter and placed on a notice-board in the staff canteen.

Quarterly winners of each category also qualify for the Annual Quality Award, the eventual winner of which receives a large cash prize in the form of a travel voucher.

Recognition is increasingly being given for the practice of organizational values, especially those relating to community service. At Cadbury–Schweppes, for instance, an informal award scheme recognizes outstanding employee contributions in community-based activities. Overall winners receive £2750 for their cause, as well as the chairman's award trophy. The firm also recognizes staff efforts as volunteers through its Big Heart award. Seven winners receive a certificate and a cash donation to charity.

Reward and recognition schemes are obvious areas for active collaboration between Human Resource professionals and the line. In theory, pay structures are really just elaborate ways of recognizing people and providing a fair exchange for their labours – an actual income. In practice it is probably unrealistic to expect any pay structure to provide all the answers to the question of how to motivate people.

An arguably more important means of motivating people is often underestimated since it does not lie in one system-wide approach. Research suggests that ongoing recognition by line managers and peers has a greater impact than any company scheme. Recognition by other people of what an individual or team has achieved can be very reinforcing, confidence building and supportive. As such it can form part of an individual's 'psychological' income or what makes coming to work really worth while. Given the need for people to work in new ways, including in teams, formal recognition processes are a means of encouraging people to focus on what the organization really needs, in both the long and the short term.

CONCLUSION

In producing a high-performance organization, HR has a key role to play. Working with line managers, HR can devise structures and work processes that should enable the organization to achieve its goals. HR processes, especially reward systems, need to align with other management practices in moving the organization forward. Pay cannot make up for unpleasant or difficult working conditions or poor management, and addressing some of these sources of frustration is likely to be more rewarding in the long term than simply changing the way people are paid. According to Jeffrey Pfeffer (1998b), it is important to recognize that 'pay is just one element in a set of management practices that can either build or reduce commitment, teamwork and performance'.

With reward systems, it seems that the more impersonal and corporate the scheme, the less employees find financial reward motivating. It's as if there are too many external factors that have a bearing on the pay decision, reducing the importance of individual achievement. If excellent performance is required, people need to see the link between what they have achieved and what they are paid. Producing excellent performance then becomes a matter of individual pride and motivation.

Of course, the more 'individual' the package, the more difficult the reward system becomes to administer, but this in itself should not deter the HR strategist who wishes to develop reward systems which are more likely to meet current and future needs. And reward strategies should not focus solely on pay and tangible benefits. No matter how rigid the pay system appears to be, the importance of recognizing the unique contribution of each individual is obvious. This is where line managers and peers have such an important role to play. If an organization is able to revise its reward systems, it may be useful to ask employees what are the important considerations that need to be taken into account in developing the 'Total Reward' approach which matters most. The more employees feel a sense of involvement and ownership of the scheme, the more they are likely to find it motivating. The more choice, flexibility but transparency that can be built in, the better.

The main criterion for a successful reward scheme is that it motivates, rather than 'turns off'. Some of the more satisfying reward systems from the employee perspective include a large element of collective reward, so that employees are not competing against one another. Money is not the main motivator for many people. People need to know that they are valued by their employer and learn to value themselves. When people feel valued and confident, they are more likely than not to release their potential to the benefit of the organization. Reward strategies which take a holistic perspective of what people consider to be rewarding and include a range of rewards in the design of any new system are more likely to motivate and retain skilled employees who are keen to help the organization achieve its short- and longer-term aims.

When this happens, the virtuous cycle of motivation is under way.

CHECKLIST FOR PERFORMANCE AND REWARD STRATEGIES

Managing Performance

Is the performance of individuals managed effectively for successful business performance?

- Are business goals and individual objectives aligned?
- How do we define standards in terms of behaviours and outcomes?
- How clear are performance requirements?
- How fair is the distribution of work?

- Are objectives clear and specific? Are performance measures business related?
- Do people have the skills required to achieve their objectives?
- Do appraisals include a review of past performance, an assessment against agreed standards and targets, as well as feedback?
- How consistently is performance monitored and rated? What scales are used?
- How honest is communication about performance? How are poor performers dealt with? What performance counselling is available?
- How clear are the links between financial/non-financial rewards and performance?

Employee Relations

How strong is the commitment between the workforce and the business?

- What degree of employee participation exists?
- How well do employees understand business objectives?
- Is there a sense of acceptance of the organization's philosophies and values?
- Do employees feel a sense of belonging and identification with the organization?
- How well are organizational and employee needs integrated?
- How well is information communicated? Is it two-way? How do managers and employees receive information and how well do they share information?
- What forms of employee representation exist?
- What regulatory issues must be taken into account?

Developing and Managing Reward Strategies

Does the organization's reward strategy achieve the right results?

- Does the reward strategy reflect corporate goals?
- Are the messages sent by the pay system aligned to other management practices?
- Has the organization been sharing its profits in a way that creates a sense of fairness at all levels of the company?
- How do you find out what people value with regard to pay and benefits?
- Do quantifiable measures help managers to make compensation decisions?
- How competitive are salaries for different groups? Is our reward strategy market-driven? Does it reflect industry 'best practice'?
- How segmented is our pay structure? How transparent is it?
- What are the criteria used in job evaluation, e.g. knowledge, problem-solving, accountability?
- What job-evaluation method, if any is used? How do we ensure equity?
- How are hourly paid roles evaluated compared with salaried roles?

- How is reward managed, e.g. performance-related, incentives, benefits?
- Does it include fixed and variable components, as well as short- and long-term incentives?
- What other methods, apart from pay, can be used to build commitment to teamwork and performance?
- How well are these aspects of the reward strategy working? Is it flexible enough to cope with change?
- What innovative approaches might add value?

REFERENCES

Ashton, C. (1999) Company links HR to business strategy. *Personnel Today*, 1 April

Boudreau, J. and Ramstad, P. (2007) *Beyond HR: The New Science of Human Capital*. Boston: Harvard Business School Press

Carvel, J. (2008) Long hours on the increase warns TUC. *Guardian*, 6 June

Cheese, P. (2007) Strategic talent management. *Strategy Magazine*, Issue 14, December

CIPD (2006) *Annual Reward Survey*. London: CIPD

CIPD/CapGemini (2008) *Smart Work*. Discussion Paper. London: Chartered Institute of Personnel and Development

Collins, J. (2001) *Good to Great*. New York: HarperCollins

DTI (2006) The Information and Consultation of Employees Regulations 2004, DTI Guidance (January). www.berr.gov.uk/files/file25934.pdf

Dunlop, J.T. and Weil, D. (1996) Diffusion and performance of human resource innovations in the US apparel industry. *Industrial Relations*, 35, No. 3, 334–355

Guest, D. (1998) Is the psychological contract worth taking seriously? *Journal of Organizational Behaviour*, 19: 649–664

Hackman, J.R. and Oldham, G.R. (1975) Development of the job diagnostic survey. *Journal of Applied Psychology*, 60, No. 2, 159–170

Hamel, G. and Breen, B. (2007) *The Future of Management*. Boston, MA: Harvard Business School Press

Heneman, R.L. (2002) *Strategic Reward Management: Design, Implementation, and Evaluation*. Charlotte, NC: Information Age Publishing

Herzberg, F. (1966) *Work and the Nature of Man*. New York: World Publishing Co.

Huselid, M. (1995) The impact of human resource management practices on turnover, productivity, and corporate financial performance. *Academy of Management Journal*, 38, No. 3, 635–672

ISR (2006) Effective execution – how leadership impacts the bottom line, www.isrinsight.com. 1 June

Lawler, E.E. III, Mohrman, S.A. and Ledford, G.E. (1995) *Creating High Performance Organizations: Practices and Results of Employee Involvement and Total Quality Management in Fortune 1000 Companies*. San Francisco: Jossey-Bass

Leach, D.J., Wall, T.D., Rogelberg, S.G. and Jackson, P.R. (2005) Team autonomy, performance, and member job strain: uncovering the teamwork KSA link. *Applied Psychology*, 54, No. 1, 1–24

MacDuffie, J.P. (1995) HR bundles and manufacturing performance: organizational logic and flexible production systems in the world automotive industry. *Industrial and Labour Relations Review*, 48, No. 2, 197–221

O'Toole, J. (1985) Employee practices in the best managed companies. *California Management Review*, XXVIII: 35–66

Pfeffer, J. (1996) When it comes to Best Practices, why do smart organizations occasionally do dumb things? *Organizational Dynamics*, 25, No. 1, 33–44

Pfeffer, J. (1998a) *The Human Equation*. Boston, MA: Harvard Business School Press

Pfeffer, J. (1998b) Rethinking reward practices: myth and reality. *Reward*, July

Robinson, J. (1997) Productivity: a case study. *Management Services*, March

Scholtes, P.R. (1995) Do reward and recognition systems work? *Quality Magazine*, December: 27–29

Stewart, T.A. (1997) *Intellectual Capital*. London: Nicholas Brealey

Towers Perrin (2003) *Working Today: Understanding What Drives Employee Engagement*. The 2003 Towers Perrin Talent Report

Tyson, S. (1995) *Human Resource Strategy*. London: Pitman

Wall, T.D. and Wood, S.J. (2005) The romance of human resource management and business performance and the case for big science. *Human Relations*, 58, No. 4, 429–462

Womack, L.P., Jones, D. and Roos, D. (1990) *The Machine that Changed the World*. New York: Simon & Schuster

Work Wise UK (2007) *Don't Be in the Dark this Winter, Commute Smart*. Employers Guide

Zingheim, P.K. and Schuster, J.R. (2007) *High Performance Pay Fast Forward to Business Success*. Scottsdale, AZ: WorldatWork

Chapter 8

Strategies for Developing People

To manage talent successfully, executives must recognize that their talent strategies cannot focus solely on their top performers.

(Guthridge *et al.*, 2008)

As we have already discussed, talent management is increasingly seen as a critical element of helping organizations achieve competitive advantage. The growing economic importance of knowledge-based services and products is driving the need for higher level skills in industries as diverse as construction, pharmaceuticals, defence and high technology, which are already experiencing serious shortfalls of available global talent, with even greater shortages predicted thanks to the growing impact of demographic trends. Similarly, skilled workers expect to carry on developing their skills. If organizations are to successfully attract new talent, they have to provide growth opportunities.

In such a context 'the war for talent' is once again with us and growing the skills of the existing workforce has to be a key plank of any talent management and organizational strategy. So central is talent management to business success that the Boston Consulting Group global study of HR Directors and Executives (Caye *et al.*, 2008) found that 'managing talent' is the most critical challenge facing HR. And CEOs as well as HR directors are now likely to number talent management among their key priorities.

Yet despite widespread recognition of the importance of having an effective, organization-wide talent management process in place, only 38% of organizations surveyed in CIPD's (2006) Learning and Development survey had a formal talent management strategy and of those 74% had no well-developed plan to implement the strategy! This is particularly the case in the UK's public sector where there appears to be no systematic and coordinated approach to developing the next generation of leaders and judging talent is still a more intuitive than systematic process. Short-termism is reported to lie at the heart of the problem. What is really needed, according to Guthridge *et al.* (2008), 'is a deep-seated conviction, among business unit heads and line leaders, that people really matter – that leaders must develop the capabilities of employees, nurture their careers, and manage the performance of individuals and teams'.

LIFELONG LEARNING AND DEVELOPMENT

Young people entering the job market these days should not expect to have finished learning when they complete their formal education. People are increasingly expected to demonstrate a wide range of skills and continuous learning and development is the order of the day. More to the point, because the range of skills required of employees will continue to expand, the ability to know how to learn will increasingly be required for career success.

The need to keep on growing the skills of the existing workforce is seen as vital to national success too. On-the-job training is one of the most critical factors affecting UK competitiveness, according to Lord Leitch in his review of skills in the UK (2006). Seventy per cent of the 2020 workforce have already completed their compulsory education. If the UK is going to improve its competitiveness and productivity, it has to teach people already in work.

Furthermore, skills development alone may not automatically lead to improvements in performance or productivity. The quality of people management is a key success factor in translating improved skills into performance, and the old adage about people leaving their managers appears to hold true. A CIPD focus group of HR Directors confirmed that improving the quality of leadership and management is central to employee engagement, performance and retention. For these HRDs, talent management, employee engagement, leadership development and business success are inextricably interlinked. A strategic approach to development is clearly needed.

TOWARDS A STRATEGIC APPROACH TO DEVELOPMENT

In creating a development strategy, it is important as ever to start with where the business is going and what that suggests in terms of the skills that will be needed. HR teams are often criticized for developing training and development strategies that do not match business priorities. Sometimes the problem lies within the HR team itself. If the person who attends board meetings is the HR director and he or she fails to discuss strategic imperatives with the professionals charged with Human Resource development (HRD), it is not surprising that the HRD team will do what they think is appropriate.

But simply focusing on what the business needs without taking account of individual needs is unlikely to be effective. Paradoxically, the pace of change and the demanding workloads of most employees may act as a deterrent to intentional and formal development. Employees will often claim that they are too busy to attend training courses and too exhausted to undertake part-time education out of work hours. Development strategies need to take into account the reality of most people's working lives and the fact that conventional training is only one way in which people can develop. Development solutions can take many forms, not least using technology, and strategies should ideally be as innovative as employees are now required to be.

The development strategy should be guided by a vision, philosophy and set of values. What is the philosophy which will underpin development – do you want people to be self-sufficient or do you see development as a partnership between the individual and the organization? Will development be demand-led or provider-led? This should provide the rationale for decision-making and can be communicated to employees.

More Inclusive Approaches

In Chapter 6 we used the following definition of 'talent':

> Talent consists of those individuals who can make a difference to organizational perform-ance, either through their immediate contribution or in the longer term by demonstrating the highest levels of potential.

But this still leaves the question: does 'talent' apply to the many or just the few?

In the early years of the current century, McKinsey raised the flag about the 'War for Talent' and made the case for emphasizing recruitment and retention of the 'A' players – the top 20% or so of managers. More recently there has been a growing recognition that the 'B' players – the capable performers who make up the bulk of the workforce – are also crucial. Often people in quite junior roles, such as front-line staff and technical specialists are often as vital to overall success as the 'A' players.

Therefore more inclusive approaches to talent development are a good idea. The question development strategies need to answer is 'how do we ensure that all employees are developed to their full potential and maximum effectiveness'? For instance Aviva, the insurance company, has a strategy of managing the 'vital many' rather than risk alienating the bulk of the workforce by focusing exclusively on high flyers.

Development should ideally be focused on areas that are relevant to both the individual and the organization. One employee, for instance, might need a rapid injection of job-related skills due to a change in technology. Another may have reached the stage in his or her career when a development stretch is required, such as a major new responsibility or an MBA programme might provide. While a development strategy should be sufficiently flexible that it can adapt to individual needs, organizational priorities may take precedence. This is where having a guiding framework and criteria for decision-making can be helpful.

In any development strategy there are likely to be three areas of focus:

- Organizational level, where corporate requirements such as Induction, Quality Improvement, Leadership, Customer Care and Culture Change Programmes are addressed

- Departmental/Business Unit level, where job-related training and development is likely to take place
- Individual level, where people are usually motivated to close the gap between their current and desired capabilities.

Some areas of development, such as the identification of talent, high-flyer schemes and succession planning, usually involve all three levels.

It follows then that to ensure an optimum return on the time and other resources invested in development, that those activities are well targeted. This means ensuring that development activities address real needs, that appropriate solutions are offered and that these make a positive difference.

Needs Analysis

One way of finding out what is needed is to carry out some form of development needs analysis based on the current skills of the workforce. There are many ways of doing this, which include surveys, using existing data such as appraisal information, sampling of specific groups, benchmarking with 'world-class' organizations to identify obvious gaps etc. Clearly since development activities, especially job-related skills acquisition, should lead to enhanced performance, managers need to be involved in the process of identifying needs and providing follow-up. The analysis should provide answers to the questions:

- What is needed and why?
- Where is this needed?
- By whom?
- How will this best be provided?
- How much will this cost?
- What will the expected return look like?

Evaluation

Making a difference can be measured at a number of levels. Donald Kirkpatrick's (1996) evaluation framework suggests four levels:

1. Reaction – what do participants think about the activity at the time?
2. Learning – how have skills, knowledge or attitudes improved as a result of the activity?
3. Behaviour – how does participants' changed behaviour affect their constituents, e.g. their workgroup?
4. Results – how do these improved behaviours, skills and knowledge translate into bottom-line impact?

This last point is perhaps the most critical from the business perspective. Increasingly 'hard' measures of the impact of development activities are required. These are always notoriously difficult to distinguish from a host of other variables.

Kirkpatrick suggests the following guidelines to implementation when trying to assess the impact of training on business results:

- Use a control group, if possible
- Allow enough time for results to be achieved
- Measure both before and after training, if feasible
- Repeat the measurement at appropriate times
- Consider the cost of evaluation versus the potential benefits
- Be satisfied with the evidence if absolute proof isn't possible to attain.

The link between the objectives of the individual, the development activity and the individual's performance needs to be strong if Level Four evaluation is to be credible. In one financial services organization in the early 1990s, poor business results meant that there was a freeze on promotions. There was also a squeeze on management development and any spend needed to be fully justified. The HRD team, in partnership with some of the business heads, argued that the company would lose some of its 'star' employees unless some form of development was offered. The question was, where should limited investment be focused?

The HRD team had been engaged in the identification of leadership competencies and it was decided that these could be used as the basis of a development centre for an identified group of 'at-risk' high flyers. The outputs of the centre were to be information which individuals could use to drive their personal development plans with their managers. To ensure that these plans could be relevant, managers were involved before and after the event in identifying individual objectives and in providing on-the-job coaching. Managers clearly needed, and received, careful briefing about their role.

Individuals and managers needed to discuss and agree, prior to the event, what the individual's main development needs were relative to the competencies. Various tools were provided, including 360-degree feedback, to help them to prioritize objectives. They had to be quite specific about how addressing that need would help. So they had to answer questions such as:

- If you were to learn to deal better with that situation, what difference would that make to you, to other people and the business?
- How will you know that you are making progress on that objective? How will you deal differently with the situation?
- How will people respond differently to you? What difference will that make to you, to others and to the business?

Participants came with very clear objectives and measures of success in mind. They were therefore active partners with the HRD and Management team who were delivering the activities to ensure that the centre met their needs.

Immediately following the centre, individuals met with their manager and agreed a practical action plan to build on the outputs of the centre. The participants were followed up over the next 18 months at three- and six-monthly intervals. The results were impressive. In addition to the 'soft' targets of the centre, such as making people feel valued, boosting morale etc., there were many examples of the impact on the bottom line of improved performance as a result of people taking part in the centre. One participant was able to pinpoint how, by changing his own leadership style as a result of the feedback and coaching he had received, he was managing his own team more effectively (and the team agreed). Nothing else had changed – it was the same team, and the market conditions were just as tough. However, within a year of the centre, that team had outperformed all other comparable teams, producing millions of pounds' worth of extra sales revenue.

Pressure to prove that development activities add value is usually at its worst when business results mean that every item of expenditure needs to be justified. However, carrying out evaluations on this scale can be time consuming and costly too, except that the costs are likely to be hidden. This is partly because salaries of trainers and trainees are usually excluded when costs are calculated except in sectors such as local government where the purchaser/provider accountability split still focuses minds on true costs. Marilyn McDougall and Angela Mulvie (1997) carried out a study of how companies measure the impact of HRM to the bottom line. They found that many organizations make access to management knowledge and skills available to employees on a general basis as part of a philosophy of continuous learning. Participants are therefore not expected to prove how the training has helped them produce improved bottom-line results, though the researchers predict that this situation might change.

PRIORITIZING DEVELOPMENT NEEDS USING COMPETENCIES OR 'CAPABILITIES'

Over the past two decades the use of competency-based development processes has become commonplace. Competencies are increasingly coming to be thought of as too instrumentalist and, in extreme cases, as bureaucratic hindrances to performance if they lie at the heart of over-engineered HR processes. Nevertheless competencies can provide a common language within organizations to describe both desired skills and behaviours required to achieve desired organizational outcomes. Increasingly, competencies are being described as 'capabilities', or 'characteristics' (see Standard Life case, Chapter 15) since they reflect what at individual and team behaviour level contributes in aggregate to the building of organizational capabilities. For clarity therefore I shall refer to 'competencies' as being those capabilities which at an individual and team level contribute to organizational capabilities, such as customer focus.

Competencies should ensure that development opportunities are targeted to meet specific objectives for the relevant individuals. Competencies can be used to develop self-assessment questionnaires and other feedback processes to ensure that individual needs are understood. Some organizations are offering managers 360-degree (or multi-rater) feedback based on a range of competencies. One software company, for instance, provides feedback from skilled facilitators followed by a range of optional workshops which managers can choose according to the needs identified through the feedback.

Ensuring that development opportunities are appropriately targeted may prove more difficult. It is useful to identify shortlists of priority areas of management development for the short, medium and long term. In the medium term competencies can be used to define the skilled components of each role and build generic skills relating to standardized role descriptions. In the short term, management development effort should produce best outcomes when it is tightly linked to specific business objectives and targeted at relevant groups or individuals. Criteria for prioritizing management development needs include:

Business Needs

- The current short- to medium-term business strategy. If the management team wishes to prepare the organization for ongoing change, change management and leadership competencies become priorities.
- The biggest obstacles in terms of management skills or behaviour to achieving the overall business goals, i.e. does the lack of certain competencies prevent the organization from maximizing opportunities or actually cause operating problems?
- The specific priorities of different business groups
- Cultural priorities
- What managers would like to develop.

Typically, priorities include areas that are broadly perceived to be key competencies and which are also seen as development needs.

Building to Strengths

Focusing development on areas that people consider strengths may seem contradictory. However, there is a reasonable amount of research evidence to suggest that people are usually motivated to even higher levels of performance when they are working on areas in which they feel they are effective. Strengths-based approaches are used by Standard Life as part of a business recovery strategy (described in Chapter 15).

Case Study: Talent Management and Development at Malmaison[1]

Organizations going through rapid growth, especially through acquisition, can risk losing key employees. In 2005, the Marylebone Warwick Balfour group, which already owned the Malmaison hotel brand, acquired the Hotel du Vin brand as part of the group's aim to become the largest boutique hotel chain in the UK. Sean Wheeler, group director of People Development, helped manage the merger. The merger provided the opportunity for greater investment in hotels

---

1. This case study is drawn from Emma Clarke, Enjoy your stay, *People Management*, 5 April 2007.

as well as opportunities for training and development, annual salary reviews and incentive schemes that a smaller company could not offer. Retaining and motivating existing staff is crucial since the company plans to double its staff within four years and succession planning is central to the talent strategy.

Initially the two brands were kept separate, but Wheeler started to bring the staff together more, through an exchange scheme, awards, management training, a staff newsletter and cross-brand meetings. Though the two hotel groups shared similar values, including teamwork and a can-do attitude, Hotel du Vin was better at retaining talent than its sister company since staff did not necessarily consider Malmaison an employer of choice. Indeed, many senior managers in this brand had come in from outside, whereas Hotel du Vin tended to promote from within.

Wheeler wants to grow staff from within and has developed a holistic strategy to do that. He recognized that staff were unaware of the opportunities available to them. He therefore introduced an online 'talent toolbox' which asks individuals about their aspirations and helps managers develop action plans. This toolbox also acts as a staff survey and findings from 2006 highlighted concerns about pay, benefits and internal communication. Accordingly the company introduced an annual salary review, incentive and bonus scheme for Hotel du Vin staff. Lifestyle benefits for all staff have been introduced, such as discounts for hairdresser's and gym membership.

Training is a key element of the strategy. Wheeler has initiated new forms of hands-on development, such as new staff attending food, wine and bar schools at their hotels, where they are given the opportunity to cook some of the dishes. Such training is also proving helpful in enabling staff whose first language may not be English to learn. Personal development plans and a management development programme help build supervisory skills.

Other developments include improved communications, with a company-wide newsletter and 'Your Voice' sessions where representatives from every hotel come together to express staff opinions. The CEO Robert Cook also makes regular tours and has set up quarterly 'Ask the CEO' events where staff can come along to ask questions. Wheeler has also developed a talent team who will build up a pipeline of external recruits through better relationships with key schools, colleges and universities throughout the UK. These various initiatives are starting to show signs of bearing fruit, with 23% of staff promoted in 2006 and the company winning a place in the Caterer and Hotelkeeper's Best Places to Work Hospitality award in 2007.

WHAT PEOPLE PERCEIVE TO BE THEIR DEVELOPMENT NEEDS

How do the strengths and development needs of managers, high flyers and directors differ? Two Roffey Park surveys carried out in 1998 highlight the skills employees perceive they need to do their jobs. One survey, the *Management Agenda*, was completed by a cross-sector population of managers mainly based in the UK. The sample was a good mix of junior, middle and senior managers as well as people who were running their own companies. The other survey was a focused look at the needs of high flyers in 400 organizations.

The surveys asked both groups about their current skills and strengths. In both surveys the information supplied was a self-assessment and may be viewed differently by people reporting to the individuals surveyed. The top skills of the *Agenda* group reflected the broadly 'people management' aspects of their role and were as follows:

- Interpersonal
- Communication
- Flexibility
- People management
- Organization/planning
- Analytical
- Presentation
- Motivational
- Leadership
- Coaching.

The high flyers had a similar range of skills and strengths but there were some different priorities in terms of job focus. For nearly half of this group, developing strategy is their key priority with other responsibilities for managing a team, building and maintaining relationships with clients and managing the financial side of the business. These priorities reflect the business focus and direction-setting so often associated with high flyers.

Similarly, the emphasis given to managing a team and managing relationships with clients suggests that people-related activities are important. However, the high-flyer group as a whole placed little priority on issues relating to customer satisfaction and quality management or training and development.

Not surprisingly, the current skills and strengths of the high flyers reflected their priorities to a large extent as follows:

- Communication
- Managing people
- Strategic thinking
- Interpersonal
- Business
- Financial
- Political/influencing.

Organization/planning skills, analytical and leadership skills were seen as strengths by a small percentage of the high-flyer sample. Interestingly, although almost half the group saw strategy as their key priority, only 35% of the group considered strategic thinking to be a strength. Many more people reported that they knew they should be operating strategically, but that day-to-day work pressures and the 'comfort factor' attached to doing an operational role meant that in reality many senior managers were failing to take a leadership role with regard to developing the organization. The probability that these individuals were failing to delegate appropriately was high.

The survey asked both groups what they believed were the skills they needed to develop to equip them for their current role (i.e. short term). The Agenda group's needs were as follows:

- Political/influencing skills
- Strategic thinking skills
- IT skills
- Financial
- Entrepreneurial
- Leadership
- Business
- Change management.

This group appears to be mainly in implementation roles, with an emphasis on raising or maintaining quality. Ideally, these managers should have opportunities to improve processes across their organization. Without making this overly complex, senior managers can improve the efficiency of services while developing themselves at the same time. They may need help in project management skills, including dealing with third parties as work is increasingly put out to tender. The art of managing a flexible workforce is somewhat more challenging than managing a directly managed staff.

DEVELOPMENT NEEDS OF HIGH FLYERS

The high-flyer group perceived some short-term development needs in IT, although 17% of the total sample felt that they needed no more skills to do their current job. People saying this tended to be older and/or to have been in their current role for some time. While this is no reason to assume that people are stagnating, there is the possibility that people are in roles which have become too 'easy' for them. New business skills may also be needed to continue to be successful in today's changing organizations. Peter Cochrane (1998) suggests that in the twenty-first century:

> ... the big bucks will be earned by 'data gurus' – specialists who can navigate their way through the information overload with ease and tell you what you need to know. At the very least, you're going to have to be computer literate to earn a living – or even get in your front door. But you don't have to become a nerd.

The skills people felt would equip them for future success were diverse. The main areas were as follows:

- Business
- Political/influencing
- Managing people
- Communication

- Leadership
- Interpersonal.

Interestingly, rather at odds with current management trends, this group does not see the ability to coach and develop others as crucial to future success. This may reflect the pragmatic reality that in many organizations promotion to senior positions has not depended on a manager being an effective 'people person'.

However, as many organizations are attempting to integrate culture change objectives with succession planning, this may change. A number of the organizations referred to in Chapter 11 are now screening candidates for senior roles on the basis of how they demonstrate leadership behaviours.

How Do High Flyers Learn Best?

The majority of high flyers in our survey considered their biggest learning experience to be having been 'thrown in at the deep end'. This was backed up by remarks about needing to 'achieve against all the difficulties'. In many cases, their learning had occurred by being given special projects, often without fully adequate resources and being left to get on with it. This suggests that some of the best forms of development for high flyers are to give them specific responsibility for challenging projects, especially if they need to negotiate for some of the resources required.

However, what also came across strongly was that people only considered the effort worthwhile if their achievement was recognized by others. Lack of recognition of a major achievement can be disheartening for anyone but is particularly damaging to a high flyer.

Other ways of learning involved one or a combination of the following:

- Studying, especially MBAs
- Training, though mainly linked with other interests than work
- Dealing with office politics
- Dealing with people generally, but managing a team in particular
- Doing the job, as long as the job has plenty of challenge and variety
- Learning about yourself, often through personal development groups or simply reflecting
- Risk-taking, often involving a change of personal direction
- Learning from hardships
- International experience
- Family/life experiences.

People who were studying for MBAs seemed to find most value in the kinds of courses where their studies related directly to their own work. MBAs are particularly useful for developing strategic thinking ability as well as general management knowledge, but the real challenge for the HRD team is to ensure that the learning is transferred to the workplace. One of the main causes of disillusionment in fact was where people felt that there was no opportunity to put their enhanced skills to good use in the workplace.

Supporting the Development of High Flyers

For the majority of high flyers in the survey, having the chance to achieve was of paramount importance. This suggests that job roles should provide opportunities for significant challenge, but that managers of high flyers and others need to be able to give effective recognition to keep the high-flyer feeling valued. Qualifications were seen to offer a useful 'stretch' by many people and they are a means of retaining people while they are studying.

The challenge for organizations, especially HR professionals, is to understand how better use can be made of higher-level skills. To some extent, the choice of qualification or course programme can make a difference as to whether the skills are seen to be useful to the organization. Some MBA programmes focus more obviously on applied project work based on participants' own work rather than relying largely on case studies.

Organizations are likely to benefit from this approach during and beyond the period of study and individuals are also likely to gain the opportunities to apply their skills. Indeed, some companies such as British Airways sponsor their own MBA programmes to ensure that outputs are geared to the business and that assignments are work-based. Managers who have been through the programme form a network providing support to new cohorts of students.

Although most of the high flyers in the survey considered that they were 'self-starters', many acknowledged that other people had been influential in their development. One of the biggest forms of help was supportive (senior) management. This often took the form of senior management involvement in young high-flyer schemes as well as the attention paid by senior management to project work being carried out by high flyers.

Almost a third said that supportive colleagues had helped them. There were many examples of networks of individuals who have developed a collegial relationship, despite individual differences and rivalries. One group of (female) chief executives of NHS trusts formed such a network following a leadership development programme. The group provides mutual support and encouragement as well as practical sharing of ideas. However, what several members of such groups suggested was that it was important that such networks be exclusive in terms of level, so that people of roughly the same seniority would be sharing ideas.

Some people acknowledge help from a mentor other than their line manager, but for the majority, recognition by the line manager was crucial. Younger high flyers particularly valued the coaching and feedback provided by helpful line managers. In short, the most effective organizational support appears to be provided by people who are interested in the high flyer's development.

Similarly, the biggest blocks to development appear to be other people, especially unhelpful management. When compounded by an atmosphere of rampant organizational politics, many high flyers felt unable to achieve. In some organizations, a blame culture acted as a disincentive to risk-taking, one of the main sources of learning for high flyers.

Ideally human resource managers should have a conversation with each of the high flyers in their organization to find out what really motivates them and to see to what extent their needs can be accommodated. Through such individual attention it may be possible to give people at different stages of their career the chance to move into more challenging roles which do not necessarily involve promotion. In some cases this may require the organization to display greater flexibility. More details of approaches to developing high flyers can be found in Chapter 11.

WHERE IS LEADERSHIP GOING?

Of course, there is no shortage whatever of leadership theory, but the impact of globalization and technology has to a large extent reframed the environment in which organizations create value. This has also created a new leadership challenge. An increase in complexity, ambiguity and uncertainty, and an increased potential for anxiety and mistrust are all key elements of the new leadership terrain.

A key theme therefore is the need for new or evolved forms of management and leadership, more suited to the demands of a complex, fast-changing knowledge-based economy, whose focus is on engaging employees in ways which produce discretionary effort. As Gary Hamel states: 'Management is out of date' (Hamel and Breen, 2007). 'Old' management and leadership styles, based on a convention of low-trust/high control sit uneasily against a paradigm of 'volunteer' knowledge workers, who are expected to be accountable and empowered, willing and able to create shared learning and intellectual capital. Hamel argues convincingly that 'what ultimately constrains the performance of your organization is not its operating model, not its business model, but its management model' and that 'management as currently practised, is a drag on success'.

'As a Scientific Concept, Leadership is a Mess' (Augier and Teece, 2005)

Quite what is required to lead successfully in today's organizations is less clear. However, one key theme emerging from the literature is that managers are now being encouraged to act as leaders both individually and collectively. Leadership is *'shared'*, *'we'*, or *'distributed'* according to various theorists. Spears (2004) suggests, 'We are seeing traditional and hierarchical modes of leadership yielding to a different way of working – one based on *teamwork and community*, one that seeks to involve others in decision-making, one strongly based in ethical and caring behaviours.' There is a strong emphasis on employee development and on managers creating the environment to allow staff to release potential.

Indeed, a strong sub-theme is about building communities of leaders at every level who can proactively shape some of the context around them, and deliver successful implementation through high-performing, highly motivated and committed teams. Raelin (2005), for instance, argues that 'leaderful' organizations see leadership as concurrent, collective, collaborative and compassionate, in contrast to more traditional leadership which tends to be thought of as serial, individual, controlling and dispassionate.

Another key theme in recent leadership literature is about the need for individual business leaders to have strong values and to exercise moral leadership, perhaps not surprisingly in this post-Enron age. For Tubbs and Shultz (2006), the leader's values strongly shape behaviours of people around them. Forms and styles of leadership are variously described as *'moral'*, *'grown-up'*, *'versatile'*, *'differentiated'*, and *'prosocial'* leadership. A leader's authenticity is a very strong theme in the literature. Goffee and Jones (2005) amongst others argue that leadership demands the expression of an authentic self. People want to be led by someone real. People associate authenticity with sincerity, honesty and integrity.

And, given the context of almost constant change, various authors argue that authentic leaders must learn to embrace paradox and be versatile: strategic and operational, forceful and enabling. The emphasis is as much on emotional intelligence as on intellect. The literature suggests that leaders handle uncertainty by reflective conversations, that they must find sources of advice they can trust and that the first step of any leadership development journey requires leaders to look at themselves intensely and critically, i.e. leaders have self-insight and grapple with their shadow sides; that leaders need moral codes that are as complex, varied and subtle as the situations in which they find themselves.

Jim Collins (2001) is not alone in pointing out the almost altruistic nature of 'great' business leaders. Collins suggests that the 'level five' leaders he describes in *From Good to Great* work for others and themselves; they recognize the intrinsic worth of employees and other stakeholders, support the development of associates, and bring both hope and pain by the changes they bring about.

Moreover, such leaders fully embrace their role as organizational leader, whose focus is on building a culture which is sustainable. They develop the culture consciously, using symbols and dialogue to create moral solidarity and enriching the culture by telling stories. Effective behaviours include understanding the bigger picture, demonstrating a compelling and achievable vision, inspiring others, active listening, reframing, encouraging others to be creative, creating transformational change, developing a team-oriented culture. According to Sujansky (2003), the leader must share vision, encourage employees to take risks, set the right example, stretch employees, provide work–life balance, recruit and retain winners, celebrate victories.

However, leaders need to strike a balance between the needs of the business and the organization – that one should be a means to the other. As Covey (2004) suggests, in business you need to focus on mission (purpose) and margin (profitability) – one without the other doesn't work. Dave Ulrich (Ulrich and Smallwood, 2006) suggests that leadership is about getting the results organizations need, in the right way. Ulrich also promotes the idea of creating a leadership brand as an identity throughout the organization. For Ulrich what is required is an appropriate blend of leadership roles – organizational strategist, organizational executor, talent manager, human capital developer – underpinned by high levels of personal proficiency.

DEVELOPING LEADERS AND MANAGERS

But how to develop such managers and leaders? HR should lead the process of identifying and developing leaders, using employee survey and other data if need be to reinforce the business case for developing managers and leaders. In creating a management and leadership development strategy, development should be focused at the right level – conventional skills alone are unlikely to equip managers for their roles in years ahead and leadership and management skills need to be advanced in order to provide the vision, culture and change necessary.

And there is no shortage of opportunity to make a difference through development. A large DDI survey (Pomeroy, 2006), found that only 61% of global business leaders feel that they have the skills to 'bring out the best in people'. The strategy should also focus on what can realistically be developed. Tubbs and Schultz are not alone in arguing that some aspects of leaders are more or less fixed (core personality), while others can be developed (behaviours). Moreover, leaders and managers may need ongoing development if they are to acquire the entrepreneurial mindsets required for success.

Ulrich argues from a 'leadership brand' perspective that connecting leadership development to business, organizational, individual performance is essential. The leadership skills and behaviours required should be deduced not from some ideal competency template but from the results leaders will actually have to achieve.

A typical 'leadership brand' succession planning process involves first anticipating changes in markets over the coming five- to ten-year period, then to envision where the organization wants to be in those markets. From that, it should be possible to envisage what potential leaders will need to deliver in five years and start to identify and develop leaders with the qualities and abilities to operate in the ways that will deliver success.

Looking ahead from a results perspective, managers will typically be required to manage more diverse workforces, including age diverse, to manage at a distance, across different time-zones and cultures. These will be leaders who can develop flexible structures and roles with a line of sight to the customer, coach and develop their teams, create a shared sense of direction in the face of ambiguity, be credible and demonstrate their values through their actions and behaviours.

LEADERSHIP DEVELOPMENT STRATEGY

Crafting a leadership development strategy involves making choices. HR teams may find the following questions helpful in clarifying both the options and potential implications of the choices they make:

- In making our talent management decisions how much should we put the business needs first above the individual context/requirement?
- How do we spot talent (given that people do not come wearing badges); should we grow our own?
- Should we favour internal versus external talent?

- Should we be aiming for the development of the many versus the high potential few?
- What do we need to emphasize more – long term/strategic thinking versus short-term operational excellence?
- And how do we ensure that we are operating to high standards with respect to equality and diversity when identifying and developing our leaders?

An effective management and leadership development strategy will include HR developing the skills to coach managers and will create genuine development opportunities – and encourage risk-taking. Methods of management and leadership development appear caught in a time-warp and alternative forms of development through technology remain in their infancy. Using the best methods to achieve the right outcomes means that a blend of opportunities may be needed. While training is still the most common development practice, leaders in the DDI study find special projects, mentors and personal coaches more effective. Other methods may include job shadowing, secondments, coaching as well as off-the-job development, networks and visits. Developing communities of leaders will require great communications, strategic conversations and the creation of cross-organizational networks united by shared purpose.

Assessing impact is also important; in particular, ensuring that leaders are operating more effectively as a result of development is important. It is therefore helpful to set outcome targets that reflect what should be expected of managers as a result of development, such as developing their own staff to their full potential, and then rewarding leadership excellence.

DIRECTORS

Many high flyers, if they are not already directors, aspire to 'high level positions'. In a separate and ongoing study of the development needs of directors, known as The Strategic Leader as Learner (Holbeche, 1994), a number of chief executives, managing directors and directors have been interviewed since 1994. In this brief extract from one interview, the Chief Executive of an arts organization was asked about his current skills, as well as those required for the future:

Q: What skills, knowledge, experience etc. are required in your current role?

A:
- A thorough understanding of the processes of the (business) at all levels.
- Wide management experience covering a range of activities.
- Experience of dealing with unions, human resources, health and safety.
- Knowledge and understanding of profit-making activities, e.g. catering and bookshops.
- Good negotiating skills, communication skills and the ability to persuade and influence people at all levels.

Q: What areas of skill would you like to develop beyond their current levels?
A:

- The ability to think really creatively about the problems which present themselves and then achieve a logical and systematic resolution to those problems. Very often these are not new problems and I would like to be able to think creatively about the best long-term solutions. This will prevent what happens at the moment which very often feels like firefighting.
- The need for more detailed future planning particularly in the area of communication will also become increasingly important. As strategies/policies change, people need to understand why.

This survey suggests that many directors need an:

- Injection of creative thinking into their current work
- Understanding of how other organizations deal with similar issues
- Ability to take a longer-term view of situations and problems that are going to arise
- Ability to provide improved leadership
- Ability to help managers develop.

Interestingly, on the last point, management trainers had been called in to assist a large PLC to train managers in coaching skills. The last group to go through the workshop were the most senior. The trainers reported the experience of working with this group as 'odd'. Of all the groups who had been through the programme, this was the least skilled at helping others to develop. They needed plenty of coaching before they were able to drop their 'arrogantly fearful' mask of not taking the issues too seriously. The HR director who took part in this workshop found the process illuminating and worrying: 'it's given me an interesting insight into how our senior managers work – they don't bring people on'.

Innovation

Arguably one of the key priorities for directors should be to provide a strategic direction for the organization. This is likely to require them to be innovative or at least to recognize and nurture innovative ideas in others. In Innovation at the Top, a survey of 120 CEOs, main board directors and senior managers was supplemented with focus groups and interviews with directors who were known for their innovative approaches. The research focused on two issues: what informs decisions of senior managers and directors and what inspires creative decisions.

The findings revealed that for many directors the pace of change can drive out the ability to innovate. For the majority, their flashes of inspiration occur outside work on the whole, while carrying out innocuous and seemingly unrelated activities such as listening to Radio 4 or taking the dog for a walk. In addition to the amount of work and the pace of change, it seems that the weight of Western tradition with its preference for structured, analytical thinking can militate against the more radical and innovative thinking so often required in the development of strategy, new products etc. According to Jean Lammiman and Michel Syrett (1999), authors of the report:

> Right brain thinking, which exists on a metaphorical and spatial plane, is the stuff of which new ideas are made. It sits uneasily in the context of a management culture founded on a rational process of thought that is presumed to result in informed and effective business decisions.

How Can Directors Be Developed?

Directors have a primary leadership role and represent role models to other senior managers. It is therefore essential that they are seen to take the lead in any development. Some of the most effective development takes place when directors have the opportunity to meet informally for off-site sessions to address strategic issues, focusing on major topics to the exclusion of mundane tasks. Sometimes short, issue-based events such as conferences are a means of exposing directors to ideas from outside the organization. Some companies have formed consortia who create an agenda for a series of 'masterclasses' provided by a management guru or leading business figure. These are often supplemented by visits to consortia members' sites so that directors can come to understand other companies' issues and ways of handling them.

Given the importance of directors developing fresh ideas for their organization, the relationship between time and creativity appears to be a key issue according to the Innovation at the Top research. The workplace is likely to be the main forum for idea development and a routine that encourages creative thinking would be an asset. Many directors are keen teamworkers and prefer to develop strategy with a colleague and speak regularly with non-executive directors about broad business issues. Similarly, while the research suggests that directors tend to shy away from formal programmes like a benchmarking group, it may be helpful for directors to join or establish an informal development network with groups of peers from other organizations. It may be possible for visits to other companies to take place which can be used both as informal benchmarking and as a means of bringing back different approaches to management and leadership.

Key Skills for Directors – Leadership, Strategic Thinking and Change Management

In numerous surveys, these competencies appear to be areas of relative weakness within the senior management across all sectors.

Ideally, these related competencies can be addressed through a strategic leadership programme of some sort.

The problems in developing senior managers often lie in getting them to sign up to the need for some development. This may be because they consider development of any sort as remedial, or because they believe they should be 'good' at everything because they are senior. It may be the case that they have not received direct feedback from constituents and are therefore unaware of how they affect the organization. Senior managers need to be willing to open themselves up to new learning and to own the output of development programmes.

Given the learning preferences of directors, a development programme is likely to be a relatively short, e.g. a three-day module which introduces some key ideas, followed by a number of follow-on meetings on specific themes. These meetings could take the form of seminars or 'content-free' learning groups where the emphasis is on managers' own learning objectives. Ideally, such a process should be linked to an actual change initiative or set of activities to provide a context and rationale.

Ideally, all senior managers within an organization should experience a similar programme so that the benefits of shared messages and experiences build up in a way which reinforces good practice. Typically, some of the most effective ways of developing leaders involve the use of feedback processes, such as upward or 360-degree feedback. The design of such a programme should have a practical focus and lead to action. Ideally, senior managers should work in teams to undertake real organizational or business projects after the training programme which allow them to transfer the benefits of their shared learning directly to the business.

SUPPORTING MANAGERS' DEVELOPMENT

Creating a Self-Development Culture

Development should be seen as primarily the individual's responsibility but encouraged and supported by the organization. A newsletter that regularly focuses on development achievements will convey the message that development is taken seriously, especially when directors contribute. Similarly, where people set themselves development targets they should be encouraged to identify the organizational benefits (including bottom line) of what they are planning to do. That way, people's development can be more clearly understood and celebrated in terms of its contribution to organizational effectiveness.

In the medium term, reward systems should be enhanced to reflect development. Managers should be rewarded on the achievement of people development targets and individuals should ideally be offered a small bonus, or a slightly higher salary if their improved skills enhance their contribution. The appraisal scheme can be supplemented, if this has not yet happened, with a development planning process. This again calls upon line managers to be willing and able to hold development discussions with individuals.

Enabling Development Through Competencies

People should be encouraged to move jobs around the organization, acquiring different forms of experience. Competencies can be helpful in facilitating this process in that job requirements can be defined in ways which enable people to undertake a realistic self-assessment. Job profiles can be updated and specific technical competencies defined. This way, a data bank of people requiring specific forms of development can be matched against available options. There may also be opportunities for job swaps and secondments if resourcing is a problem. The increased mobility of staff can also be supported by greater awareness of the roles of different business groups. This can be encouraged by briefings hosted by different business groups at their place of work.

Training

Training is still the most common main form of off-the-job development in many organizations. Indeed, the CIPD Learning and Development survey (2006) found that traditional classroom-based training is still popular and is expected to grow. The survey found that the main strategic business objectives for investing in training were:

- Organizational development (89%)
- Increasing returns on investment (77%)
- Improving market share and increasing the levels of product innovation (66%).

Training can be helpful for both awareness-raising and skills development. At PricewaterhouseCoopers (PWC) employees typically spend more than 50 days in off-the-job training during their first three years. PWC trains more than 20% of the chartered accountants in the UK and its business diploma – a four-year development programme – is run in association with the London Business School. At Ernst and Young, the international financial consultancy, staff receive detailed industry training as well as coaching in people skills. Everyone is allocated a counsellor and is also informally mentored. People take responsibility for their careers, with programmes in place to ensure they can achieve success quickly.

Training can be helpful in raising managers' awareness of the strategic issues for their organization through briefings and networks. There is a growing emphasis on clear objective-setting, contracting between participant and line manager before programmes, flexible programme design and rigorous evaluation, including attempts to establish return on investment (ROI). However, the majority of respondents in the CIPD survey considered that most of their development took place on-the-job, or outside work. Typical of a number of criticisms of training provision is the following comment:

> I'm concerned about the lack of structure in my development (which has led to poor timing in some events), a lack of personal involvement in decisions and I feel that some of the formal training was too general in character and therefore did not relate specifically to my needs.

This lack of tailoring to individual needs is perhaps inevitable if a 'sheepdip' approach to training is still taken. There is also the danger that managers will resort to training as a remedial solution to a 'people problem' rather than thinking more creatively about how a person might be developed. Ideally, any training should help people to come up with solutions themselves, rather than simply forcing them through hoops. There is often little awareness about how people can be developed on-the-job. In many organizations, cultural and staff surveys highlight the same issue with monotonous regularity: line managers do not know how to help other people to develop. They are often perceived to be too busy, unsupportive, have inappropriate management styles or simply do not see developing others as part of their role.

Other Off-the-job Learning and Development Processes

- *Action learning:* Group sessions to problem-solve on real life issues. These can enable individual needs to be met in the work context. Helps develop self-reliance for solving future problems. Learning groups are increasingly being used in a number of organizations such as Pfizer and Fujitsu.
- *Attachments (or shadowing):* Becoming a temporary assistant to another person in order to gain an understanding of their job.
- *Brainstorming or 'mind-showering':* Having an ideas communication system – like a suggestion box, and rewarding the best idea(s) on a regular basis.
- *Case studies/Case histories:* Examples of the experiences of other industries or managers that might be examined. Broadens horizons, gives ideas for different ways of doing things.
- *Contact developing (networking):* Encouraging membership of/attendance at professional or local business groups. Builds a network with other managers' industries to gain new insights and create ideas.
- *Counselling:* Recognizing where an individual's behaviour indicates a personal or work-related problem, or giving guidance on how to solve a problem. 'Unblocks' people who are in difficulty, builds good communication.
- *Conferences:* To help people see the 'big picture' or buy in to corporate objectives. To share the experience of other people and organizations. Increases sense of belonging, heightens commercial awareness.
- *Distance learning:* Encouraging further study or education which can be done at the person's own pace. Need not be directly related to current role. Broadens knowledge and increases skill base.
- *Exposure to senior management:* Observes and perhaps becomes involved in more strategic issues and decisions. Strengthens natural ability in this area and builds confidence.
- *Learning resources – films/videos/DVDs/podcasts:* Wide selection available for a variety of techniques and skills. Aids learning by presenting information in a memorable way.
- *Modelling:* Having team members observe another individual who displays outstanding performance. Illustrates best practice in a practical way.

- *Networking:* A powerful way of expanding relationships, knowledge, business and career opportunities.
- *Non-executive director/Trustee appointments:* Supporting high potential managers to take up non-executive director appointments. Assigning an individual to a committee, along with managers from other departments or externally. Broadens horizons and increases confidence.
- *Outdoor team development:* Outdoor team building and training events. Not directly related to current job, but can be enjoyable and build team spirit.
- *Presentations:* Short presentations (10–15 minutes) using visual aids or simulations (see Simulations) to impart skill or knowledge.
- *Role playing:* Trying out difficult situations in relative safety. Offers opportunity for feedback and coaching.
- *Secondments:* Individuals spend a period of time working in a different part of the organization. Widens their viewpoint and experience.
- *Self development and self analysis:* A variety of techniques exist to aid this process, including: keeping a personal journal, creating a learning log recording new experiences, doing value exercises, personal skills and management style audits.
- *Seminars/team briefings:* Conducted by internal or external facilitators for specific groups. To distribute knowledge or brainstorm (pool ideas) on problems. Encourages team spirit, opens up creativity and communication, increases learning.
- *Simulations:* Can be done in seminars or team briefings. Recreations of the job environment or a specific job situation. Enhances problem-solving and skill in real situations.
- *Volunteering:* Growing in usage as both a development opportunity for individuals and teams and also for carrying out an employer's corporate social responsibility commitments. Timberland is amongst a number of companies who commit company time and money to collective projects to assist community projects.

Google is one company which does not struggle to attract potential recruits. In fact, so attractive is Google as an employer that Liane Hornsey's team receives 3000 job applications every day (Liane is Google's Director of People Operations, EMEA). In Google, employees (known as 'Googlers') are given a chance for both personal development and a taste for the wider business. Examples include a job shadowing programme and an 'ambassadors' programme, where European staff can undertake a job swap with a Googler from the Asia–Pacific region. Personal and skills development are also reflected in the GTG (Googler to Googler) learning initiative, a series of training sessions given by Google staff for their colleagues. Sessions can cover skills as diverse as coding, mathematics or salsa dancing.

Giving staff time not only to learn but to innovate in their jobs is enshrined in Google's working practices. The most notable manifestation of this is the company

'70–20–10' policy for engineers, which prescribes that each programmer should spend only around 70% of their time doing their core job. Twenty per cent should be spent on related activity or a project that will help them do their core job better while the remaining 10% can be spent on less focused 'blue sky' thinking, such as dreaming up new products. The fruits of this policy are evident in the ongoing streams of new and innovative products.

Technology-Based Learning

There has been a real explosion of interest in the use of technology to stimulate learning with the advent of Web 2.0 and the era of social networking. Podcasting, social networking, various forms of blended learning combining face-to-face with e-learning have gained currency. While initially e-learning failed to take off in any substantial way, the new technologies are stimulating real interest and more accessible learning materials and many pundits predict a huge growth in online learning in the next few years. This is driven by shortage of time to attend training and the increasingly global spread of organizations which makes training solutions costly. Increasingly blended learning, including some element of off-the-job and e-learning, is becoming popular.

Prudential Portfolio Managers is the investment-management arm of the Prudential Corporation, which employs 1000 people in various global locations. The challenge is to provide development opportunities without requiring employees to be constantly travelling. Nick Holley, formerly director of Prudential Portfolio Managers UK and now Executive Director of the HR Centre of Excellence, Henley Business School, says: 'The biggest issue is time. Personal development is seen as important but not urgent, so it is easy to put off.'

A new online system which allows for just-in-time training has been launched, called 'I'. This is described informally as a global virtual university and covers 11 technical areas such as portfolio management, and generic skills such as delegation and performance management. Knowledge management has been built into the system. When an employee enters a particular learning area, the first page supplies the names and contact details of other employees with expertise in the area who are willing to provide support. Each learning area provides information on training courses, including a wide range of externally run courses, and lists other development resources available from the company's open learning centres. There is also a list of recommended reading which was created through a deal with a bookshop which supplied a list of the best books on a given topic.

The system gives employees online access via the intranet to a management training system operated by a UK management centre. This gives people the resources they need to manage their own learning following an assessment of their skill needs. The system covers topics such as teamworking, strategic awareness, leadership and financial awareness. Various toolkits allow people to apply management models to their own circumstances.

On-the-Job Development

It seems that most senior managers learn best by experience. On-the-job learning is therefore likely to be the primary source of development. Given the importance of this form of learning, it is essential that managers are able to support people with their development as well as their current performance. At Cadbury–Schweppes, development opportunities include a variety of programmes as well as 24-hour e-learning facilities. Staff belong to teams, which maintains a family feel and ensures that individuals have a voice.

- One of the key sources of development on-the-job is having some challenge, without being 'stretched' to breaking point. Job enrichment is achieved by making job content more challenging, either technically or managerially. It could be thought of as *deepening* the job and develops ability in current role. Challenges come in various forms and have greater or lesser motivational effect depending on the individual. Typically, a rewarding form of development occurs when someone is given responsibility for a venture whose outcome is not guaranteed, where the outcome is important and noted by others. It is important that achievements should be recognized by others, especially managers, and appropriate rewards (even if only a show of esteem) be given.
- Another key source of learning is *variety*. This can also take many forms, including the chance to try new things, meet new people, develop new work interests. Again, imaginative problem-solving between manager and direct report can assist in identifying opportunities for variety in any job, however mundane. Having the opportunity to represent your employer at a conference, for instance, can be useful.
- Ironically, *hardships* are apparently a major source of development, providing that people are able to recover some learning from the experience. Some people may find the ongoing cost-cutting approach represents a form of hardship. Focusing on how to overcome difficulties can generate positive and creative solutions. Having a (peer) mentor can help in this process.
- *Other people*, especially bosses, are a major source of development. The role-modelling effect is strong and emphasizes the importance of training senior managers to act consistently with organizational values.
- *Career counselling*. A few major corporations have trained directors to be career counsellors for other people. This is an organization-wide responsibility, rather than being restricted to direct reporting relationships. Each director takes on a small 'caseload' of people who are regarded as key to the future, but for whom there may be no immediate prospect of promotion. The benefits in the form of improved morale and retention of key people can be great.

Other on-the-job methods of development include:

- *Delegating:* Either temporarily or permanently. Giving a person part of your job to do as a development exercise. Stretches the person and develops management ability.

- *Feedback:* Gaining regular performance feedback from colleagues (peer assessment), managers and subordinates. Gives more rounded information to person, builds internal communication.
- *Research assignments:* Short-term study with report back. Keeps people informed of developments in their field; is a good refresher for the person.
- *Reading/reviewing:* Circulating links to journal articles or snippets from newspapers and publications. Keeps people up to date with the latest techniques and issues.
- *Self-assessment tools:* In many organizations, tools are now provided to encourage self-development, including the use of development centres and learning resource centres. These can often include skills inventories, behavioural instruments and provide routes to relevant learning resources.
- *'Sitting by Nellie' or pairing:* A traditional method of learning involving one individual partnering a more experienced person and having them explain what they are doing. Trains the person in the detail of the job – can be part of coaching.
- *Task forces:* Groups of people from different parts of the organization asked to examine a specific issue, as a team, from a variety of perspectives. Improves inter-department communication, helps solve real work problems.
- *Team building:* Events run with small specific team to promote understanding of individual roles and contribution. Helps to play to people's particular strengths.
- *Visits:* Arranging a tour for small groups or individuals to other organizations or parts of the group to observe processes. Broadens knowledge, creates exchange of ideas.

Coaching and Mentoring

This involves spending time with individuals to improve their skills and knowledge. It increases the skill base and strengthens communication. One manager described the benefits she had gained from skilled coaching:

> When I first joined the NHS I expected that success meant promotion every 18 months. One-to-one coaching from my manager cured me of this blinkered, black and white approach.

Many organizations, such as British-American Tobacco, have trained managers in coaching skills and the trend towards the 'line manager as developer' is well established.

Mentoring involves providing skilled support to an individual who is usually not in a line reporting relationship with the mentor, who is generally at a more senior level in the hierarchy than the learner. It can increase the learner's understanding of how the organization operates, and be useful in exploring career development issues. Mentors may not work in the same organization as the learner, and increasingly relationships formed through networking are a primary source of contacts and development advice. Coaching and mentoring can be helpful but line managers generally need training in relevant approaches. In some companies, managers' ability to help others to develop is now taken into account in performance management and reward processes.

Peer Mentoring

Some organizations are introducing peer mentoring to address both organizational needs for teamwork and greater collaboration and individual needs for support. Peer mentoring involves two, three or more individuals agreeing to have a development relationship with one another with the clear purpose of supporting individuals to achieve their job objectives. HR can help such relationships to be established through creating a mechanism whereby peers can identify likely peer 'resources'. Often this is through the use of a database on which information is stored about people who have specific expertise and are willing to act as peer mentors. These can be matched against people who express specific needs. Sometimes people are looking for a mentoring relationship with someone who can help them increase their understanding of how another part of the business operates. Other people wish to link up with individuals who have developed their careers in particular ways within organizations. HR can help people to think through their objectives and give some guidance on how to approach peers with a view to forming a formal mentoring relationship. Sometimes organizing a café-style kick-off event helps to get peer mentoring underway.

Ideally the relationship should offer reciprocal benefits for it to work. One example is a training manager and a human resources manager from the same organization who were called on to work on the same major project for a period of several months. There was a history of some hostility between the two departments which they represented, and, as individuals, they did not warm to each other's styles. However, they took the decision to go through a formal contracting process to see if they could help each other. The project proved to have benefits for both individuals and for their departments. The individuals concerned now have a much greater understanding of one another's needs and what they can offer.

In the following case study, drawn from the CIPD report *Talent; Strategy, Management, Measurement* by Professor Carole Tansley *et al.* (2007), mentoring is a key feature of the firm's talent development strategy.

Case Study: Talent Development at PricewaterhouseCoopers LLP

PricewaterhouseCoopers LLP (PWC) employs more than 140000 people in 149 countries on industry-focused services in the fields of assurance, tax, human resources, transactions, performance improvement and crisis management. It provides solutions to the problems facing businesses and the capital markets today through its lines of service and 22 industry-specialized practices for a variety of clients. Its aim is to continue to be the UK's leading professional services firm by investing in its people, supporting local communities and helping to shape its industry and rebuild public trust in corporate reporting.

With 14 000 partners and staff in offices around the UK PWC draws on the knowledge and skills of its people in the UK and other countries in the global network of firms. Its strategy includes being the leading professional firm in the markets it decides to serve and being a great place to work for all its people.

Key Drivers for Talent Management Within PWC

Key drivers are both the need to address development requirements of all staff and the demand from clients for consultants with the right skills. Because the organization is divided into different businesses, the possibility of having human resources in 'silos' of different disciplines is recognized. Efforts are therefore made to have an enterprise-wide view of the business and encourage the mobility of staff which is so important for both individual experiential learning and organizational development. Taking this approach matches what its clients want, which is having people at a senior level in client accounts who have experience in a number of sectors. This is so much more meaningful and useful to a client than having someone who has been in one sector all his or her life.

How PWC is Approaching Talent Management

PWC has around 1000 graduates, 650 of them in its assurance business. As a leading employer in the UK professional services sector, PricewaterhouseCoopers recruits highly educated junior professionals in the creation of its Level 1 talent pool. Its carefully targeted selection systems place new entrants on a structured orientation, training and education programme, undertaken over a period of four years. In subsequent stages, projects, secondments and work assignments aid experiential learning, develop required skills and enable the participants to gauge which areas of work they would like to settle in.

PWC presently has a global framework of seven core competencies which are the benchmark against which employees are measured for a variety of roles as they go forward. It is using those partly as definitions of talent and future leadership potential and partly as a statement of what might be called 'price of entry'. In the early stages its talented people have to have a relatively good level of expertise against these competencies, but when seeking leadership later on, PWC is looking for something that is not particularly embodied in the generic competencies used across the business.

The Issues and Challenges of Talent Management in PWC

Because of legislative requirements built into PWC's recruitment policies and graduates' subsequent educational development, technical competency is taken as a given. Other attributes are then majored upon, such as adaptability – but finding evidence of such qualities is one of the talent management challenges. Its traditional way of training graduates has been by time-fixed movements through career stages, but it is beginning to develop more radical approaches within the constraints of legislative requirements and the required pace of movement through the pipeline. This involves the creation of work placement opportunities to build individual development through movement around the organization. In this it is attempting to be responsive both to the individual and his or her personal desire for experiential learning and satisfactory pace of career development, while at the same time addressing organizational needs in terms of meeting job requirements and encouraging mobility to develop breadth of skills. At the more senior level, mentors and coaches are perceived as important elements of executive development. As James Chalmers, assurance partner recounts:

> The mentor role varies across our business. Some people will have structured mentor schemes, which can be less effective. Everyone should have the opportunity to have a mentor: they should explore who the right mentor is and they should be self-starting. It is not necessarily one mentor. I have four or five mentors, depending on the circumstances or the situations I am in. They are a disparate group. I could list the people I talk to today but they might not be the same people I would talk to later on this year or next year.

Finally, PWC is aware of the necessity of gathering the right sort of talent management data and making it more readily available to those involved in the talent management process at all levels – not only to business leaders but also to its 'stewards of talent', who are senior partners from various parts of the business whose responsibility it is as part of a talent review group to look at the talent pipeline and report to the business leaders.

What the Benefits Have Been So Far

The essential element which helps PWC align organizational and individual needs is a structured performance management process which allows regular feedback and enables, when appropriate, speedy mobility between businesses, roles or tasks. The importance of including training in the development of emotional intelligence is also highlighted, and here different kinds of qualities are sought, such as listening empathetically, understanding one's own feelings, being emotionally stretched, and relating effectively. Openness and transparency about people's potential to progress in the organization is appreciated by PWC employees.

CONCLUSION

The need for employees at all levels to be involved in ongoing development – of new skills, exposure to new experiences and learning to learn – is apparent. Developing talent relies on a blend of informal and formal methods. The mix will depend on the needs of both the business and of individuals, but a planned investment in developing coaches and mentors throughout an organization will pay dividends in providing a supportive culture for talent management.

HR can work towards creating a culture in which learning is valued and supported, and where the enhanced skills of the individual are put to good use. In such a development culture the pressure to measure a return on every development activity may be less strong than in a culture that believes that any offline activity is a cost. Individuals can take responsibility for managing their development. After all, it is in their interest to do so, but the organization can help 'kick-start' the process by providing people with the opportunity to understand what to develop and how. This will be enhanced in organizations where personal development planning is a core element of a performance review process.

Ironically, pressure of work in some cases is so strong or the company ethos so 'macho' that people are not always prepared to learn, especially through training. Various innovative approaches such as 'just-in-time' training, using on-line resources, can help, but sometimes the best form of development is when individuals take themselves to a residential training programme and find time to reflect. Senior managers in particular are important role models in both learning and valuing learning. They set the tone and ironically need to be willing to exercise some old-fashioned 'command and control' with regard to development. This is all the more the case when a planned approach to talent development is combined with a commitment to utilizing and progressing individuals who have participated in talent management programmes. They will have built up expectations. If their talents are not put to proper use, the risk is that they will lose commitment to the organization and, having been developed, have an increased attraction to another employer. Encouraging people to prioritize development, whose returns to the business may not be immediate, over short-term business demands, at least occasionally, may well produce larger returns in the long run.

CHECKLIST FOR DEVELOPMENT NEEDS

The Changing Nature of Work and Implications for Development

- Will there continue to be a demand for the types of service or product we currently offer?
- What will this mean for the kinds of skills and competencies which will be required of those providing the service or product, e.g. will they need more/less specialist knowledge, greater flexibility etc.?
- How buoyant is the employment market for these kinds of skills? What will these mean in terms of ease of recruitment?
- How many alliances or joint ventures does the organization currently operate? How well are they working? Are there some alliances which the organization should be forming to deliver a better service to clients?
- Will people be required to work in various forms of alliance in the future? What will this mean in terms of training needs, working practices and HR policies?
- How often do we review the nature of people's work tasks?
- What proportion of employees is working on areas where their knowledge and competencies are best used?
- How will work be distributed? What will HR's role be in redistributing staff rather than recruiting additional staff?

- How are the roles of specialists changing? Will they need to function at a higher level in several areas, rather than one? What will be the priority areas for professional/technical training and development? How will people be counselled about possible role change?
- How will 'knowledge workers' work with 'service providers'?
- To what extent does the organization's current structure work well? What could be done to improve it?
- With which management systems is our organization most comfortable?
- Are these still effective, or do they need to be changed?

Development

Is this organization developing its staff and securing employee commitment?

- What are the current top development priorities for the organization?
- How will addressing these help the organization to move forward?
- How will we resource the top priorities? Will we use external support?
- What costs will be involved in addressing the top priorities?
- What should we focus on in training and development?
- How wide a choice of development methods do we currently use?
- How do people in our organization prefer to learn?
- How flexible is learning design to meet different learning needs?
- How much do we/should we use technology to help people to develop?
- Are people encouraged to attend training and other forms of development in work time?
- How well selected and trained are people who act as mentors on formal programmes?
- What mechanisms are in place to encourage peer mentoring?
- What practical tools are provided to ensure that people can manage their own development?
- How easy is it for people to access information about development opportunities?
- Who are the best role models of line managers as coach? How can they help their peers to improve their skills?
- What help can be given to ensure that line managers provide effective follow-up after training to help transfer learning to the workplace?
- What cost/benefit analysis is carried out on development opportunities?
- How effective are our evaluation methods?

REFERENCES

Augier, M. and Teece, D. (2005) Reflections on (Schumpeterian) leadership: a report on a seminar on leadership and management education. *California Management Review*, 47, No. 2, 114–136

Caye, J-M., Dyer, A., Leicht, M., Minto, A. and Strack, R. (2008) *Creating People Advantage: How to Address HR Challenges Worldwide through 2015*. Boston: Boston Consulting Group

CIPD (2006) *Annual Learning and Development Survey*. London: CIPD

Clarke, E. (2007) Enjoy your stay. *People Management*, 13, No. 7, 34–37

Cochrane, P. (1998) Quoted in Parrish, J., Just the job. *Evening Standard*, 20 April

Collins, J. (2001) *Good to Great: Why Some Companies Make the Leap and Others Don't*. London: Random House Business

Covey, S. (2004) *The 8th Habit: From Effectiveness to Greatness*. London: Simon and Schuster

Goffee, R. and Jones, G. (2005) Managing authenticity: the paradox of great leadership. *Harvard Business Review*, 83, No. 12, 87–94

Guthridge, M., Komm, A.B. and Lawson, E. (2008) Making talent a strategic priority. *McKinsey Quarterly*, January

Hamel, G. and Breen, B. (2007) *The Future of Management*. Boston, MA: Harvard Business School Press

Holbeche, L. (1994) *The Strategic Leader as Learner*. Horsham: Roffey Park Management Institute

Institute of Personnel and Development (1999) *Training and Development in Britain, 1999*, IPD Survey Report. London: IPD

Kirkpatrick, D. (1996) Revisiting Kirkpatrick's Four-level Model. *Training and Development*, 50, No. 1, 45–49

Lammiman, J. and Syrett, M. (1999) *Innovation at the Top: Where Do Directors Get Their Ideas From?* Horsham: Roffey Park Management Institute

Leitch, S. (2006) *Prosperity for All in the Global Economy – World Class Skills: Final Report: Leitch Review of Skills*. London: Stationery Office

McDougall, M. and Mulvie, A. (1997) HRM's contribution to strategic change: measuring impact on the bottom line. *Strategic Change*, 6, No. 8, 451–458

Pomeroy, S. (2006) *CIPD/DDI Survey UK Highlights: Global Leadership Forecast 2008–2009*. London: CIPD

Raelin, J. (2005) We the leaders: in order to form a leaderful organization. *Journal of Leadership & Organizational Studies*, 12, No. 2, 18–30

Rogers, A. (1999) Desktop menus offer quick training snacks, *Sunday Times* Financial Appointments, 30 May

Spears, L.C. (2004) Practicing servant-leadership. *Leader to Leader*, 34: 7

Sujansky, J. (2003) 20 keys to leadership. *Healthy, Wealthy n Wise*, September

Tansley, C., Turner, P. and Foster, C. (2007) *Talent: Strategy, Management, Measurement*. London: CIPD

Tubbs, S. and Shultz, E. (2006) Exploring a taxonomy of global leadership competencies and meta-competencies. *Journal of American Academy of Business*, 8, No. 2, 29–34

Ulrich, D. and Smallwood, N. (2006) *How Leaders Build Value: Using People, Organization and Other Intangibles to Get Bottom-line*. Hoboken, NJ: John Wiley

Chapter 9

Developing Effective Career Strategies

The overall message is ... the need for organizations to urgently address the issue of career management by discovering their own and their employees' career needs and negotiating equitable career deals with them. Only if they do so, and abide by the deals struck, will they recover the trust and commitment of their employees.

(Peter Herriot and Rob Stickland, 1996)

When I wrote the first edition of this book in 1999, 'careers' was the word on people's lips – what had happened to classic white-collar careers? After all, the previous decade had seen some of the old 'truths' about the nature of employment in the West being fundamentally shaken. These 'truths' or expectations have been described as the 'psychological contract' between employer and employee. It used to go something like this: as long as the employee was doing a good job they might expect continuing employment and be able to contemplate promotion up the career ladder. In return, the employer expected high levels of performance and loyalty from employees.

However, ongoing organizational change and uncertainty during the 1990s seriously challenged key aspects of this 'psychological contract' between employers and employees. 'Jobs for life' became a thing of the past. However, much of the reality of working life differed from this mythical psychological contract, when flatter structures came along they challenged the expectation about career development being 'onwards and upwards'. Instead, organizations were simultaneously telling employees that they were responsible for managing their own career, while shedding jobs and abandoning previous career management practices which maintained the myth that careers could be planned. Employability was supposed to have replaced job security as part of the 'new deal'. As far as promotion goes, the common message given by many employers has been 'manage your own career' and make yourself 'employable'.

In the early years of the millennium, during the so-called 'War for Talent', the balance of power in the employment relationship swung in favour of skilled employees. During a prolonged period of growth and full employment, the discussion has moved on to less of a focus on 'careers' and more on 'talent management' (from the employer perspective) and 'lifestyle' (from the employee perspective). Balance and capability-building have become the new mutual expectations. Fun and enjoyment at work has been a regular theme in management literature in the first few years of this millennium and Lord Layard's 2005 book *Happiness: Lessons from a New Science* shows that there is a paradox at the heart of our lives. While most people want more income, he argues, yet as societies become richer, they do not become happier. All the evidence shows that in general, people have grown no happier in the past fifty years, even as average incomes have more than doubled. This paradox is true of Britain, the United States, continental Europe and Japan. The search for a better lifestyle, and for greater balance between work and the rest of life, is becoming the dominant issue for most employees regardless of age.

Now the tide is turning again, and in the early stages of a potential recession towards the end of the first decade of the millennium, the power balance in the employment relationship appears to have swung back in favour of the employer, at the apparent expense of the employee. Job security is once again no longer a given in exchange for good performance and flatter structures have reduced the career options for many employees. In such a scenario, the psychological contract of 'mutual development' is in danger of being breached, with trust a likely casualty and the danger of creating a conforming rather than committed workforce. This in turn may create damage to both employee well-being and organizational performance and learning.

The changing psychological contract has various implications for HR and in this chapter we shall focus on careers, looking first at how employee expectations may be changing. We have already looked at balance issues in Chapter 2, and will return to issues of organizational learning in Chapter 17.

HAVE CAREER EXPECTATIONS REALLY CHANGED?

Interestingly, many employees perceive messages about 'manage your own career' to be abdication on the part of the employer and they no longer trust in the mutual benefits of the employment relationship. Judging by Roffey Park research findings, few employees now believe that the organization will manage their career. On the one hand the idea that even a large organization, is a continuing entity has been seriously challenged as companies which are household names merge, reshape or disappear. On the other, the increase of confidence in employees who know their own worth and who no longer trust in their employers has led to some well-publicized examples of employees refusing to comply with their employer's bidding even though they effectively close the door on major career opportunities.

The extent to which employees have adjusted their ideas about careers is open to question. The Roffey Park research has looked at whether people are adjusting their career aspirations to consider lateral growth a viable alternative to the vertical progression implied by fast tracking. We have certainly found that for some people the opportunity to broaden their job role, albeit at the same level, has represented a form of career development since they have had greater challenge, visibility and a chance to learn new things.

On the whole though, we have found few people who seem prepared to abandon ideas of conventional career progression in favour of lateral growth. In our survey of high flyers we asked people what their ultimate career goal was and the most frequent response (38%) was a 'high-level position'. On the face of it, employers who are offering fast-track development may well be able to tap this market of ambitious individuals.

THE EFFECT OF FLATTER STRUCTURES ON EMPLOYEES

So how have flatter structures affected people? In the first stages of the Roffey Park research (1994–96) an overwhelmingly negative picture emerged. People complained of continuing uncertainty, lack of career development, overwork, long hours, stress and increased political behaviour. The effect on roles was dramatic: many people were unclear what their role was or how to succeed and managers were frequently described as not walking the talk of empowerment. Senior managers, on the other hand, complained that people were not willing to become accountable, that there was little innovation and risk-taking, and that 'plateaued performers' were unwilling to rise to the challenges of developing the new skills and attitudes required.

The Growth of Flatter Structures

In the 1997 research phase and the return of growth in many countries, the author was interested to find that talk of flatter structures was as widespread as ever, even in organizations that appear to retain up to 14 organization layers from the bottom to the top of the hierarchy. Why should this be? It's almost as if organizations are expecting employees to adopt the mindset that goes hand in hand with flatter structures. In other words, to be flexible, willing to learn new things and to develop at the same organizational level even though many of the structures, processes, management styles and rewards are firmly rooted in the old hierarchy.

It is easy to understand why organizations should want to have their cake and eat it. Flatter structures seem to offer the potential of a wide range of benefits since they should make possible greater teamworking, customer-driven processes and the elimination of waste. After all, who needs checkers checking checkers? Flatter structures should also make it possible for 'more' to be truly achieved by 'less' if people are able to work to their potential in an 'empowered' environment. The theory also suggests that employees can also have more rewarding and fulfilling jobs in such an environment. Yet it seems that the extent to which these potential benefits are actually being achieved is very patchy indeed. On the one hand, businesses are finding that flatter structures are helping them to be more profitable and that there is increased teamworking. Much of the increased profit-ability is essentially short-term, since it relies on savings achieved on headcount and accommodation. On the other hand, how much people are experiencing job satisfaction and developing new forms of career is debatable.

New Forms of Career Development?

The research found, for instance, that, contrary to the rhetoric of flatter struc-tures, promotions are still happening but perhaps for a different group of peo-ple than in the past. In the research sample, one-fifth had been promoted in the past two years, but these tended to be people who were already relatively senior. An interesting group of young high flyers also appears to be zooming through the ranks. Several examples were found of managing directors below or about the age of 30. One of the biggest super-elite involves leading management teams who are significantly older than themselves. Interestingly, many of the people who had been promoted had no intention of staying with their organization for very long, suggesting perhaps that promotion can no longer secure loyalty.

For other people, remaining at the same level appears to be becoming a real-ity, with ever-widening gaps appearing between levels. The people who appear to be most dissatisfied are those whose jobs have remained the same as two years ago, but demands on them have grown. These people spoke of lack of career development, continuing uncertainty, poor leadership and inappropriate rewards. It was almost as if frustrated career hopes caused people to be extremely dissatis-fied with the organization and its systems, although many people still claimed to be relatively loyal to their employer. Nevertheless, this group were mostly look-ing for other jobs outside their current organization.

In contrast, people whose jobs have grown in some way, albeit at the same level, seem generally happy to stay with their current employer. It was this group who reported most of the benefits of flatter structures, such as having greater autonomy, teamwork, more challenging and satisfying roles. Though still at the same level, many of these people spoke of having opportunities for career development. One woman, for instance, works for an electricity company where she was previously responsible for facilities management at one plant. As the company has grown, her role has expanded to include responsibility for all plant facilities, becoming consequently more strategic, rather than purely operational. These people tended to be less concerned about pay issues or the competence of leaders, though it is arguable that it may be only a matter of time before these energized performers also become dissatisfied if their enhanced skills are not appropriately recognized and rewarded.

The Paradoxical Effects of Flatter Structures on Roles

There are many contradictory effects on people's roles. On the one hand, there appears to be a widespread trend towards generalist roles, with people being encouraged to become multi-skilled project team members. In many organizations specialist roles are still being outsourced. On the other hand, there appears to be people who can simultaneously be experts in their fields but also think and act as business people. For many IT and Human Resource professionals, for instance, this means being able to provide credible, value-added services in a consultancy capacity.

Some of the most paradoxical effects are to be found in managerial roles. Many of the people whose jobs have disappeared during the period of the research were in junior line management roles. Arguably, increased use of technology is likely to see this trend continue. Some senior managers considered their roles to have narrowed in organizations where staff at more junior levels are 'empowered' to do things which would previously have been within the remit of the boss. Yet in other ways there seems to be more demand for management roles than ever. With continuing trends towards outsourcing and the growth of the flexible or contract workforce, many managers find themselves these days coordinating the work of people who have no formal links with the organization other than through temporary contracts. As such, managers become the 'glue' which holds teams and projects together.

Similarly, many managers have seen their spans of control expand considerably, and fashionable trends towards the line manager as developer have simultaneously applied pressure on managers to provide appropriate support to their teams, while preventing them from having the time to do this. In British government departments, for instance, many senior civil servants whose previous role was to supply policy advice now find themselves being encouraged to take on a much more obvious people-development role, enabling those lower down the hierarchy to provide advice to ministers. Ironically, many ministers, and indeed customers of other organizations, are out of step with the 'empowered' environment since they still expect to be in contact only with the person 'in charge'.

How much people are really adjusting their career expectations is questionable, which is hardly surprising given the mass of conflicting messages at large in many organizations. 'Manage your own career' sits uneasily alongside the more obvious ways in which high-flyer and 'fast-track' schemes are returning, providing rapid advancement for the privileged few. Nevertheless, some people do appear to have successfully managed to make their mark in these changing organization structures.

One piece of the research involved interviewing individuals who were considered by their organizations to be indispensable, to see if these individuals had anything in common which might provide a 'success template' for careers in flatter structures.

A 'Success Template'?

The things which these people had in common were broadly that they all viewed change as inevitable and generally had a positive and even opportunistic approach towards it, being able to take some risks. None of them thought or acted like victims and they all seemed able to learn from mistakes without reproaching themselves. They were good at making things happen and skilled at interpersonal relations. They were visible and good at networking inside and outside the organization. They all had a strong sense of what was important to them. Ironically, two-thirds of this group had left their organizations two years later, mostly because they were frustrated at the slow rate of change.

Loyalty to themselves was a higher priority than loyalty to the organization. These were people truly able to manage their career. The very skills which made them valuable also made them employable and able to exercise choice.

It will be interesting to see what happens over the next few years. Although organizational trends do seem to have a built-in pendulum effect, the shift to lean but effective structures which allow for organizational effectiveness and individual growth seems set to continue. As long as there is a good balance between both sets of needs, flatter structures may provide the longer-term keys to survival and success for organizations. To bring about that balance may require major shifts of thinking, management style and investment strategies on the part of organizations and a willingness to learn and develop new ways of thinking about careers on the part of employees. While few employees seem to be considering the kind of portfolio, freewheeling careers predicted by many pundits, flatter organization structures may yet provide the means of developing the skills and experiences which should ensure employability and job satisfaction in years to come.

THE ROLE OF HR PROFESSIONALS

Among those organizations that are restructuring, human resource and training professionals can help to enrich jobs and keep people motivated. One crucial element in this role is helping employees to develop a positive approach to lateral career development. Often there is considerable stigma attached to the idea of a sideways move and many people who have experienced such moves report a lack of support or understanding of their development needs in order to help them function effectively in their new role as quickly as possible. In some cases, Human Resource professionals have worked with line managers to create a tailored development package for the individuals concerned.

In some organizations, there is a deliberate attempt to reposition sideways moves as developmental. Examples include individuals on lateral transfers being featured positively in company newsletters and the payment of a one-off bonus in recognition of the effort and learning curve involved. Care has to be taken to ensure that the benefits of sideways moves do not seem biased in the organization's favour, since they often release bottlenecks and create opportunities for others. This is where a well-thought-out policy on lateral moves and the provision of help where necessary can be useful to make it possible for individuals to develop new skills.

Changing structures often lead to confusion over roles which can lead to stress, overwork or poorly targeted effort. Training can help, especially in providing employees with the 'new tools of their trade'. There seems to be a decided upturn in the amount of training taking place especially on job knowledge, assertiveness, decision-making and quality processes. In some organizations, competencies are being used to help employees gain a clear picture of what skills and behaviours are required in the changing organizations, and also for job-profiling purposes. This can lead to greater clarity about the role for the current job-holder as well as facilitating cross-functional moves in a way that may have been rare in the previous structure. Where this is combined with an open job posting scheme, 'surprising' moves can prove very successful for all concerned. Again, Human Resource professionals can facilitate this process to ensure that human capital is being maximized.

A common shift in role is that of line managers being expected to take on a more developmental responsibility towards their staff. Some managers find this a relatively unfamiliar role and one for which they feel ill equipped. Training for managers can help them to develop the skills and willingness to see people development as a business priority among others. Often training is offered to managers in tandem with new appraisal schemes. The trend in many organizations seems to be to separate out job review processes from development discussions.

Despite the difficulties that the Roffey Park research uncovered, the most encouraging message for Human Resource and training professionals is that, with their help, flatter organizations are working. With work practices that position lateral moves as career opportunities, honest appraisal and support for team-working (including a reward strategy that reinforces team development), human and organizational needs can converge and lead to an energizing new working environment. It seems that flatter structures can produce benefits for employees if they are willing to adjust their expectations about career development. They have to develop new perspectives on their careers, and to appreciate the value of forms of status other than traditional promotion. Most importantly, employees need to adopt an enterprising approach to their own career development.

TOWARDS A NEW PSYCHOLOGICAL CONTRACT – HELPING PEOPLE TO HELP THEMSELVES

Employees who successfully adapt to flatter structures have accepted responsibility for managing their own career. Such employees are architects of change, thriving in the flatter structure by constantly looking for new ways to improve their practices and challenge the status quo. These self-empowered individuals are motivated by teamwork and developing broader skills rather than simply achieving conventional status. Such new-style employees actively negotiate development opportunities as part of their recruitment package and take responsibility for their own learning. These employees seem to have a clear sense of what is important to them, and indeed this is a common characteristic of individuals identified by their employers as key contributors.

Some organizations are providing self-development processes to help people to manage their own careers. The National Health Service has encouraged personal responsibility through a process that helps employees to recognize the need for self-management. The Roffey Park Management Institute designed a three-day event for the National Health Service called a PEER (Personal Exploration and Evaluation Review) Centre. This is partly a development centre and partly a development planning process where the participants are trained to observe and coach each other. The PEER process allows individuals to explore the issues relating to structural change. They can also get feedback on their effectiveness measured against the organization's own expectations. This type of exercise is going to become more common and more crucial as a vehicle for development in flatter structures that encompasses all employees, not just those on the management fast-track programme.

A key feature of this process is the emphasis on helping individuals to clarify their personal values and to use this enhanced awareness to help them find ways of increasing their job satisfaction in the here and now. This twin emphasis on the needs of the organization and those of the individual allows people to develop a pragmatic approach to development planning.

Companies in the fast-moving technology sector seem to be among the first to develop new forms of career development. For example, Sun Microsystems Europe is a computer company in a state of continuous growth. To maintain stability while restructuring, the company clarified its employees' career objectives through sponsoring the development of a tailored programme. Called Managing Your Career in Sun, the programme provided a forum for people to discuss their concerns about career opportunities. Trained Human Resource professionals were able to show individuals the alternatives to vertical promotion by expanding their current job function.

Organizations in other sectors are looking to implement similar training and evaluation schemes in which people are responsible for maintaining and taking responsibility for their own employability. In return, organizations provide the resources to assist the employee and a variety of growth opportunities. For example, work shadowing, secondments and project teams give junior employees the chance to work more intimately with others at a more senior level, while the development of community roles, such as sitting on educational governing bodies, provides an outlet for an individual's skills as well as communicating positive messages about the organization.

At another computer manufacturer, Tektronix, employees play a key part in managing their employability by monitoring their own performance. Performance management at Tektronix has been developed under the Results Management System (RMS). RMS is a competencies-based appraisal system, designed to assess individual performance in a variety of areas varying from actual 'hard' results to 'soft' ones such as communication skills and relationship development. Goals and objectives are decided through negotiation and Human Resources use job descriptions only for recruitment purposes. The personal growth process at Tektronix has ensured that long- and short-term development needs are noted and that this becomes a live document which is reviewed quarterly.

At PricewaterhouseCoopers (PWC), the career management service helps employees to write their own job description and create a more satisfying working life. This independent career counselling service helps people to recognize their development needs and work out what they must do to achieve them. People are helped to focus on their career preferences and to talk through the options, both within the company and outside. The service is self-referred and confidential. Most of the work is done in one-to-one sessions during which people can discuss career issues that concern them. Individuals are then helped to set objectives that help people develop performance in the context of matching their needs to those of the business.

One scientific-based organization has drawn up possible elements of a career framework as shown in Figure 9.1. The company has developed the tools for the individual, in response to low career satisfaction ratings in a staff survey and after extensive consultation with employees. It is up to individuals whether or not they use them. Initially, take-up of some of the tools was low. It was only when line managers were helped to take on a coaching role that the self-development tools became more widely used.

Currently the organization is focusing on the 'overlap' areas such as personal development planning processes and appraisals. Training in the new processes has been provided for both managers and individuals. Currently the focus is on creating a self-development culture. Plans are in place to develop complementary organizational processes such as succession planning, pay and benefits which will add 'muscle' to the policies.

Helping people to help themselves is not simply a question of leaving people to it. Career management and development should be a partnership between the organization and individuals, since it is in both parties' interests to collaborate.

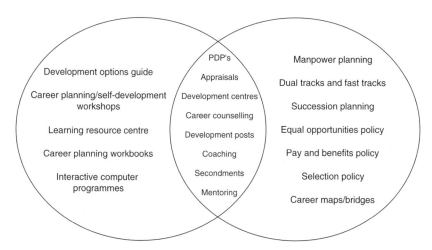

FIGURE 9.1 The possible elements of a career framework.

Job Sculpting

An interesting approach to combining individual employee and organizational needs into win–win development is the idea of 'job sculpting' proposed by Butler and Waldroop (1999). The basic idea is that if a job allows an individual to pursue their deeply embedded life interests, i.e. long-held, emotionally driven passions, they are more likely to be happy, experience job and career satisfaction, and stay with the organization. Job sculpting is the art of matching people to jobs that allow their deeply held life interests to be expressed. This can be challenging because most employees are only dimly aware of their own deeper motivations and also because the approach requires a degree of psychological insight from both a person's line manager and HR.

The researchers found only eight deeply embedded life interests for people drawn to business careers. What Butler and Waldroop describe as the 'Big 8' life interests are as follows:

1. Application of technology – some people are intrigued by the inner working of things and are curious to find better ways to use technology to solve business problems.
2. Quantitative analysis – some people excel at numbers and see mathematical work as the only way to figure out business solutions.
3. Theory development and conceptual thinking – some people enjoy thinking and talking about abstract ideas and may be more interested in the 'why' of strategy than the 'how'.
4. Creative production – some people thrive on newness and are most engaged when they are inventing something original – be it product, service or process.
5. Counselling and mentoring – some people enjoy guiding peers, subordinates and even clients to better performance, and many may be drawn to community service.
6. Managing people and relationships – some people enjoy dealing with people on a day-to-day basis and derive satisfaction from workplace relationships and focus on outcomes.
7. Enterprise control – some people love running things and feel happiest when they have the ultimate decision-making authority.
8. Influence through language and ideas – some people love expressing ideas for the enjoyment that comes from story-telling, negotiating or persuading.

Job sculpting begins when managers identify individual employees' deeply embedded life interests, ideally by bringing the process directly into the performance review process. The techniques of job sculpting are as follows:

1. Both employees and managers should prepare their thoughts in advance of the conversation. Employees might be asked to write up a couple of paragraphs about their personal views of career satisfaction, what kind of work they love, favourite activities on the job etc. These will form a starting point for the conversation.

2. Managers listen carefully when employees describe what they like and dislike about their jobs, and ask probing questions to ensure mutual understanding.
3. The next work assignments are customized accordingly to begin the process of moving the individual to a role that is more satisfying.

Job sculpting may require initially more sacrifice on the part of the employer, and some parts of the employee's role which have been left behind may need back-filling, which may be a challenge if staffing levels are tight. Nevertheless the argument goes that in a knowledge economy, talented people tend to stay in jobs they are doing well at and are fundamentally interested in, and even in challenging economic times, that is a prize worth going for.

DEVELOPING INNOVATIVE CAREER TRACKS IN A SCIENTIFIC ENVIRONMENT

In recent years, especially in organizations with flatter structures, the trend for career development to take place through a generalist route has become well established. 'Core' employees have by implication been encouraged to become multi-skilled, business-oriented individuals while specialist services have often been outsourced. Many specialists, including training and development professionals, have often therefore become business-focused external contractors. Interestingly, this trend appears to be currently somewhat in reverse in UK organizations.

In some companies, the nature of the business is specialist and technical skills remain in-house. For instance, Schlumberger, the oil services group, introduced a career path for the technical community which has proved to be a strong motivator. Recruits were promised promotions, status and compensation comparable to those of senior managers, as well as opportunities to shape research and product-development agendas. Schlumberger has also become one of the exploration and production industry's leading recruiters of women engineers by introducing flexible working practices (Guthridge *et al.*, 2008).

Another organization operating as part of a government agency directly employs large numbers of scientific and engineering staff, almost all of whom are highly qualified. On the whole, the workforce has a relatively young age profile with 44% of employees being between the ages of 20 and 30. The organization is attractive to many potential recruits because of the high-powered scientific nature of the work carried out. However, many recruits join with high expectations about rapid pay progression. Given the constraints on public sector pay awards, shrinking incomes and the ongoing uncertainty of the sector within which the organization operates, these expectations are somewhat doomed to disappointment.

The organization operates a matrix structure, with pressure to reduce bureaucracy and fixed overheads. The business requires that customer requirements are captured quickly and that a more flexible service is offered to a wider range of clients. The majority of the work carried out is project based. To achieve these objectives, the organization needs to continue to attract but also retain high-calibre staff. On the plus side, the work is challenging and rewarding but on its own this is not enough to attract and retain high-calibre staff. There are good levels of investment in training although some of this is unfocused. Technical training is widely available and there is some management training. The organization has a 'sink or swim' environment, which appeals to some of the high flyers, although some people quickly 'go stale'. However, on the whole, staff are highly educated and articulate, with high expectations. Retention is becoming an issue since many employees can see no obvious career progression.

Career Issues

Prior to reforms of UK central government, including the development of agencies, most of the civil service operated a similar pay and grading system which allowed for a degree of mobility for employees through a well-established system of promotion boards. Individuals could ask for and receive career counselling from senior civil servants. Promotion was often achieved by migrating between government departments and smaller entities, such as the organization in question. Career ladders for both management and scientific grades co-existed up to certain senior levels. Despite the many limitations of the previous system, it did have the benefit of offering clarity.

In the current set-up, obvious career ladders have disappeared. Formal progression systems such as through gradings, job titles and pay have also been disaggregated. In theory, this separation should make progression on merit easier. However, in real terms the system offers drawbacks as far as employees are concerned and indeed in terms of meeting the needs of the internal job market. Where once a person's job grade was used as a proxy for likely competence by project managers who were choosing staff for new projects, the complexity of the new system means that resourcing projects is very much a matter for the resource manager (who knows the population's skills) and project managers. This means that employees need to maintain good relations with resource managers if they wish to have their interests promoted for interesting projects.

Other problems are linked with employee needs for recognition. There can be inconsistencies in pay levels for similar jobs. Professional standing is no longer evident from employee titles which are meant to reflect qualifications, experience and competencies, rather than seniority. While in theory the new employee title system includes six stages, in practice most employees recognize only two: technician and professional. Employee titles are not yet widely perceived by all as a mark of status and recognition, nor are they used publicly. Civil service grades continue to exist as 'shadow grades', i.e. not formally part of the structure but referred to by individuals when describing where their own and other roles fit in the hierarchy in terms of status.

In terms of career progression, while technical and managerial careers do exist, there are no formal definitions. Most employees soon learn that what amounts to career advancement is through customer-facing roles such as project management. The current structure offers some limited scope for other forms of advancement. A few posts exist for technical leaders who are role models and quality monitors. Similarly, a few resource managers are responsible for allocating individuals to projects. Apart from these roles, progression to business area manager is what most employees are likely to aspire to and qualifications for these roles are largely based on having taken responsibility for managing projects of increasing size and complexity.

This leads to the problem that employees perceive that the only way to progress is through management and that the organization does not value technical work. Whereas in the past, employees would have been encouraged, and expected, to spend several years in purely scientific roles, now it is not uncommon for employees to be managing projects within their first year of employment. For people who join the organization with a strong desire to carry out scientific work, the current options are disappointing since they are obliged to leave behind the detailed scientific work if they want to be promoted. Some simply leave the organization after a few years to carry out more highly paid project management roles in industry. They reason that since they are not doing what they wanted to do, namely scientific work, they might as well be more highly paid for managerial work elsewhere. Another problem is that early access to project management roles, and the relatively quick progression this makes possible for some, means that promotion opportunities run out by the time people are in their early thirties. Again, this is a critical age for turnover.

Career Tracks, not Ladders

To address the problem the HR team, in partnership with management, has adopted a five-phase strategy for career development. Much of this strategy is in the plan/consultation phase and remains to be implemented. However, the plans appear to have met with a favourable reaction from the staff consulted (who represent at least half the workforce). The phases are as follows:

1. Research into staff aspirations and gaining ownership
2. Competency profiling
3. Developing a training framework
4. Developing a coaching culture
5. Defining career stages and developing a range of career tracks which are clear, feasible and desirable to employees.

The aims of the proposed system are as follows:

- To meet individual needs and aspirations
- To create a system which is manageable and affordable
- To provide public recognition of status
- To ensure that the new system is fully integrated with HR

- To be flexible and enable individuals to switch between career tracks
- To be consistent with the parent organization's systems and processes.

Similar issues and options exist in many organizations, as the following case study shows.

CASE STUDY: CAREER DEVELOPMENT WITHIN A PROFESSIONAL SERVICE FIRM[1]

Career Management within KPMG UK

Organizational Background

> KPMG is the global advisory firm whose purpose is to turn knowledge into value for the benefit of its clients, its people and its communities.

> (1998 Annual Report)

To achieve this purpose KPMG has an extensive and complex structure, consisting of three core disciplines: Assurance Services (Audit and Accounting, Transaction Services and Forensic Accounting), Tax and Consulting and eight lines of business. These include, for example, Corporate Finance, Corporate Recovery, Risk Management, Consulting. The firm prides itself on its reputation for being a respected professional service provider; something which it acknowledges can only be achieved through the quality and commitment of its people and through the delivery of a professional service.

The firm has recently revised its values and has introduced a Values Charter which sets out how these values apply when conducting business. Several of the statements in the Values Charter relate to the topic of career management, for example:

- We will respect all our people and the contribution they make to the firm
- We will listen to and aim to understand alternative perspectives
- We will openly and proactively share knowledge
- We will respect our own and our people's need to balance personal and business lives
- We will support our leaders, encourage our peers and develop our people.

KPMG has achieved continued growth in its business despite the recent difficulties in the global economy. However, it has found it difficult to resource this growth due to the highly competitive market for skilled professionals. Thus in addition to recruiting more high-calibre professionals the firm has continued to invest in developing and retaining its existing people. Some of the new initiatives in this area are highlighted in this case study.

---

1. I am indebted to Dr. Christina Evans Institute and the late John Bailey of the Human Resources Development team of KPMG for the development of this case study which appeared in the first edition of this book. Thanks also extend to the individuals who contributed to the research by talking about their own career experiences within the firm.

The information presented in this case study was gathered from one-to-one discussions with a number of individuals working in Audit, Corporate Recovery and Consulting. The individuals were performing different roles and at different stages in their career. Several had moved between business areas within the firm. Some had moved from a business support role into a fee-earning role. Others had chosen to combine a fee-earning role with a business-support role. Additional information was gathered from discussions with the Human Resource Development team, the latest Annual Report and the firm's corporate website.

Perspectives on the Term 'Career' and What Career Success Looks Like

While gaining promotion, either to a higher grade or further up the management hierarchy, is clearly important to individuals, promotion alone does not seem to be an overriding success criterion. Several other themes emerged from the research regarding how individuals perceive career success. Some spoke of career success in terms of personal challenge. These individuals stressed the importance of having opportunities to work on challenging and stretching assignments.

Others spoke of career success in terms of having a balance. Balance was referred to in a number of ways. First, having a balance between work and home: here the need for work–life balance to be recognized and respected by others within the firm was stressed as being important. Second, balance in terms of being able to develop a broad skills set would lead to more opportunities in the future. Some individuals spoke of how in this type of environment it is easy to get stuck in the 'expert role', which can be restrictive in terms of career development. Others spoke of career success as relating to enjoyment and job satisfaction. For these individuals having the opportunity to work on a variety of assignments and roles was stressed as being important to them. The general view from the discussions was that the firm is currently able to meet these needs.

To be successful in managing your own career in this type of environment it seems that individuals need to have highly developed skills in: networking and influencing, self-management, self-awareness, as well as the ability to manage risk at a personal level.

Career Paths and Options within the Firm

Although there is a fairly traditional career path for fee-earning staff within the firm, the research highlighted that for those who want to have a protean or more individualistic career the firm offers a wealth of opportunities. The general picture gained from the research was that the firm provides 'a land of countless opportunities, but that sometimes it is difficult to work out the terrain and best route to get to where you want to be, because of its size'. However, there was a great sense of optimism in that if an individual is interested in something, be it a particular piece of work or the opportunity to work with a particular type of client, all he or she needs to do is put their hand up and the opportunity is usually made possible. One individual commented that 'If you want something and you want it enough, then pursue it. There is usually a way to get there.'

A typical career path for individuals who have chosen a career as an accountant, for example, is that they join KPMG from university and then follow a three-year training process to qualify. This route is perceived to be a good grounding even for those who do not necessarily see their longer-term career within accountancy. There is an assumption that, once qualified, individuals will be promoted to manager position within two to three years. Thereafter, the career path is promotion to senior management, followed by partner, assuming that the individual meets the firm's performance and assessment criteria. Individuals also need to establish several sponsors who can support them with their case for becoming a partner.

The time period between qualifying and reaching manager position is perceived to be key in terms of creating opportunities for broadening one's skills and gaining exposure to different roles and projects within the firm. There is a perception that once an individual has reached manager position there is less opportunity for working in a different discipline, because of the need to keep one's professional knowledge and expertise up to date. Unlike in other organizations, managers in the firm are expected to remain technical experts, so that they can build credibility with clients and manage client projects. The perception is that time spent in another part of the business, where the manager's technical knowledge is not kept up to date, would make it difficult to return to their former role.

However, those already working at manager level do not perceive out-of-date technical specific knowledge to be such a barrier to mobility as those aspiring to manager position. Managers feel that in some cases it may simply be a case of scheduling time for individuals to get back up to speed when they return to their former role.

For those working in a business support role, i.e. a non-fee-earning one, the career paths are less clearly defined. For these individuals career development occurs more through development within the current job role, or through movement to a similar role in a different part of the firm. However, it is possible for business support staff to pursue a fee-earning career path should they choose. One way of achieving this is to study part-time to gain a professional qualification, and this would then enable the individual to move into a fee-earning role. This is something which the firm encourages and supports, both at a practical level as well as financially. Another option is to move, in a business support role, to another business area, and having developed the relevant skills become more involved in fee-earning activities. The growth in the consulting side of the business has opened up opportunities for individuals from different disciplines and with a varied business sector knowledge and/or experience to transfer into a more broad-based consulting role. Some of the individuals who contributed to the research had made this type of career move. Again this is a positive example of how individuals are developing their careers in both a lateral as well as vertical way.

Responsibilities for Career Management

The firm does not have a formal career management system as such. It recognizes the need to identify and develop talented people, but there are no separate programmes or processes for individuals who are considered high potential. The partners are responsible for managing succession planning and 'talent reviews' within their own areas. This approach means that the promotion process is perceived by some as not being as open as it could be.

Individuals are expected to manage their own careers. This is something which is made clear to them when they join the firm. At one level there is an acceptance that this is how it should be, since this is a professional community who have the capabilities to manage their own career development. However, in practice, identifying and facilitating development needs is more of a partnership between the individual and his or her counselling partner/manager.

There are two formal processes which enable individuals to receive feedback on their performance and discuss their more immediate development needs, as well as future career options. One is the appraisal system which focuses on achievements over the past year, objectives for the coming year, as well as identifying development needs. The appraisal system is values and competency based; thus it is perceived to be an equitable system as individuals know what is expected of them. The appraisal discussion is a key forum for individuals to discuss their development needs and the types of assignments which could help satisfy these, with their counselling partner/manager. Appraisals are usually conducted annually, with some areas holding them biannually.

To ensure that they get the most out of the appraisal discussion individuals need to spend time gathering feedback and information from others beforehand to feed into the process, for example from other managers with whom they have worked over the year, peers and, in some cases, clients. This gathering of evidence for oneself seems to be particularly important where an individual may not have worked directly for the counselling partner/manager over the year.

A second process for discussing performance and development needs occurs through the Engagement Review system where specific feedback on individual contributions to a client project are gathered. When conducted in a timely way individuals feel that the Engagement Review system provides another useful source of personal feedback. Again individuals need to take responsibility for ensuring that they receive the feedback from this process and that they have an opportunity to discuss it with their counselling partner/manager.

The managers who participated in the research feel that it is important for them to listen to the needs of individuals and to watch for signs to indicate that an individual is not being fully challenged, or indeed that an individual is under too much pressure. They also see it as their responsibility to act as an information source in terms of job opportunities currently available within the firm, or on the horizon, which may fit with an individual's development plans. The manager's role in supporting individuals with their development plans, even where this means transfers to different parts of the firm, is crucial for maintaining the credibility of this open career management system.

While this open and less structured approach to career management has worked well in the past, most individuals who participated in the research expressed the view that a more structured approach would be more helpful to individuals, particularly at different phases in their career. In part, this need has been recognized by the firm and several new support initiatives have recently been introduced in response to these concerns and are detailed in the next section. These initiatives have been the result of a partnership approach between Human Resources and individuals in the business.

The Role of HR in Facilitating Career Development

The Human Resources role in facilitating career development is increasingly becoming more strategic, focusing on the longer-term human resource needs of the firm. Increasingly HR is involved in discussions at the top table through the European HR director's role within the UK management team. In practice, the more recent career management support systems have been introduced through a partnership approach between Human Resources and individuals in the firm. The Career Broker role and the Career Ownership Workshops are examples of this successful partnership approach.

Support for Career Development

There are several support mechanisms in place to help individuals manage their career. Some of these operate at a corporate-wide level and some are more specific to a particular business area, unit, or department.

Corporate-Wide Support Mechanisms

All individuals who are appointed to senior manager position attend a **Development Centre** where their skills and behaviour, in relation to a known set of values and competencies, are observed. As part of the Development Centre process individuals receive one-to-one feedback on their performance from an observer. Following the Development Centre individuals may also have one-to-one coaching sessions with a Human Resources Advisor to help them take forward development needs identified during the Development Centre. Individuals who participated in the research and who had been through the Development Centre process spoke of how they had found this to be a very useful experience. In particular, they valued the support made available to them after the Development Centre, for example having access to a personal coach to help them work through their identified development needs.

Individuals who are being considered for partner position attend an **Assessment Centre**, which is also values and competency based. They also have a one-to-one session with one of the Human Resources Advisors to discuss the individual's motives for wanting to become a partner. Questions like 'Why do you want to be a partner?' and 'What will it mean to you to be partner?' are raised and discussed during this session.

The Human Resources Advisor who works most closely with individuals aiming for partner explained how initially existing partners were sceptical about this approach. However, over time they have begun to realize that it is acceptable to discuss these types of questions and that it is important to consider what the individual wants, as well as what the firm wants. Going forward, this questioning process is perceived to be crucial for individuals too, particularly as the role and demands on partners are changing. Increasingly, partners are being expected to demonstrate excellent people-management, business management and relationship management skills.

As well as the support provided for those aspiring to be partner, individuals can help their own case by identifying several sponsors who are willing to guide and support them with their case. Through experience individuals learn that it is important to have an eye for building relationships with sponsors from different business areas. In this way they maintain visibility and support in an organization which is constantly evolving and restructuring.

Individuals aspiring to partner position are also expected to have an 'out of the box experience' which is expected to last for a period of at least six months. The objective of this approach is to broaden an individual's experience prior to moving into a partner role. Individuals are involved in the discussion regarding which 'out of the box experience' would be most appropriate. It can be an international assignment, a project in another part of the business, or working within a client organization. The concept of an 'out of the box experience' is new to the firm and inevitably there have been several tensions. First, there is a concern that six months is not really enough time to get to grips with a new area and make a significant impact. Second, individuals can find it difficult at times to identify which 'out of the box experience' would be most appropriate for them given their longer-term career goals. Third, these experiences can cause personal tensions, particularly for those in a dual-career family situation.

Career Ownership Workshops, introduced a couple of years ago, were a direct response to a concern regarding the need to retain more individuals who had undergone their professional training within the firm, particularly those in Tax and Audit. Individuals who are about to qualify have several choices to make regarding their future career at this particular time. In the past individuals have found it difficult to identify what these options are and where to go for support and information, because of the sheer size of the firm. As a result many newly qualified professionals have left the firm just at the point when they qualify. This was perceived by many as a lost opportunity, as well as a drain on resources.

The decision to run Career Ownership Workshops was taken following a consultation process between partners and those newly qualified in Audit. The workshops enable individuals who are about to qualify, or have recently qualified, to find out what their future career options are. They may be half-day or full-day events. The firm has adopted an open approach to these workshops, recognizing that they are in competition with other organizations for newly qualified professionals. The rationale behind the workshop is to provide a forum where individuals can stand back and review their career options, both within the firm and outside, as well as identify people who can help them think through their decisions. Individuals who participated in the research commented on how much they valued the open attitude adopted by the firm.

During the workshop there are presentations from different parts of the business on the type of work and range of clients they work with. Individuals may also hear from external speakers who can give them insights into opportunities outside the firm. There is the opportunity for individuals to gain advice on preparing their CV from recruitment consultants. There is also an opportunity to have informal one-to-one discussions with a number of people about possible career routes within the firm. On some workshops individuals who have worked for the firm in the past have been invited back to give a presentation on how they have developed their career outside the firm.

Following on from the success of the Career Ownership Workshops, a **Career Broker** role has been introduced in some business units. The Career Broker acts as an independent advisor, as well as an information source, for individuals who are unsure about how or where to develop their career. Career Brokers network with managers and other Career Brokers in other parts of the firm so that they can put individuals in touch with the right people with whom they can have informal discussions about possible job roles and career opportunities. The intention is that this role will complement the advice provided by counselling partners/managers during the appraisal process, not replace it.

Individuals who perform the role of Career Broker are selected from the firm. Some may combine the Career Broker role with their other responsibilities. In this way Career Brokers have direct experience of working in a particular business unit and are thus in a better position to help others decide whether working in a particular area will meet their career goals. Although the Career Broker role is still in its early stages the response thus far has been positive. For individuals it has provided the independent source of advice which some have voiced as being an important additional support tool.

Performing the Career Broker role is a developmental experience in its own right. Individuals performing the role find it challenging and stretching. It is a way of developing some of the softer skills too, for example relationship building and questioning skills, as well as building up one's knowledge of the firm. Some individuals have found that the role provides them with an opportunity to work more closely with Human Resources, thus also helping to meet a personal career development goal.

Among other resources and development routes, the firm has an intranet site called **'An Ocean of Opportunity'** which provides information about current job vacancies within the firm. This is linked to other parts of the intranet which contains information regarding the range of projects being undertaken by different parts of the firm, as well as contact details. Each of these sources provide key information for individuals to help them manage their career. Individuals can also gain sponsorship for external training, particularly qualifications such as masters programmes, provided they can demonstrate how this will add value to the firm.

The firm also provides an extensive range of development activities covering technical and personal skills. Development opportunities can also occur through the firm's **Community Broking Service**. An example is the headteacher mentoring programme which operates in 40 schools throughout London. The programme involves KPMG staff mentoring headteachers in order to help them develop their financial management and organizational development skills. Secondments to other parts of the business and/or teams are another accepted way for individuals to develop their career. The opportunities seem plentiful and they can extend to any part of the firm, including internationally.

Some Local Initiatives

Several of those interviewed spoke of local departmental initiatives which have been introduced to help individuals with their development needs. These are initiatives which have been introduced following discussions within the department on what additional support would be of value to individuals to help them manage their career development. In Consulting, for example, a coaching role has been introduced. This role was introduced in response to a direct request from consultants, particularly those new to the role, as a way of helping them settle into their new role and develop their consulting skills through learning from the experience of others.

In Corporate Recovery, a manager has been assigned the role of more closely matching personal development needs with the skills needed on client project work. The perception from individuals within this part of the firm was that development needs were not always given sufficient priority when allocating staff to client projects. Individuals felt that resources were being assigned to projects on the basis of known past experience, which meant that they felt that they were being pigeon-holed in a particular role; something which was felt to be limiting in personal development terms. This appointment arose as a way of addressing these concerns. This particular manager is now involved in the appraisal process so that she has a better understanding of each individual's development needs. In this way greater alignment is being achieved between the skills required for a particular client project and the development needs of individuals.

Tensions Relating to Achieving Career Success

A number of tensions relating to career development within the firm were uncovered during the research. The key tensions and how these are currently being managed are discussed below.

Gaining Access to Information

Individuals who participated in the research spoke of how much they valued the openness and lack of formality of the internal transfer process. As mentioned earlier, known job vacancies are made public on the intranet site 'An Ocean of Opportunity'. While there is a formal job application process, individuals have an opportunity for an informal discussion with the relevant partner/manager. Assuming that there is a match between the needs of department and the individual the transfer usually goes ahead. The support of the current manager is vital in terms of making this open job posting system work.

However, not all jobs and client assignments are posted on the intranet. Thus given the size of the firm and the range of client projects it undertakes, individuals can find it difficult to gain up-to-date information upon which to make career decisions. Individuals who participated in the research commented that to manage your own career within the firm you have to be pushy and spend time networking. This is felt to be the only way of finding out what project work and opportunities are coming up and for getting your name in the frame. Several of the individuals who contributed to the research had engineered roles on projects that mapped directly onto their development goals, through personal networking. Some of these roles were on fee-earning projects, others were on business support projects, such as working on Human Resources projects. Networking with people at all levels and in different business areas is perceived as being key in terms of getting to where you want to be. However, individuals spoke of how networking can be difficult at times, particularly when working for long periods of time at a client site.

The Human Resources Development team are currently developing an on-line Career Management System which will act as an additional resource bank for individuals to draw on when exploring career options. The system will contain information such as: how to get from A to B in terms of the competencies required; profiles of individuals showing how they got to where they are within the firm, as well as a list of resources individuals can draw on to help them manage their career. The system is expected to be completed later on in the year.

Balancing a Career with Other Commitments

The nature of the work within the firm can make it difficult for individuals to gain a balance between work and their non-work commitments. Fee-earning work often involves working long hours and sometimes requires working away from home for extended periods of time. This can create tensions for individuals and their families. Although one of the firm's values is to demonstrate respect for an individual's need to balance their personal and business lives, there is a sense that the firm does not always pick up the signs that an individual is under stress as quickly as it could. It was felt that more could be done to support individuals who want to achieve greater balance in their lives.

For women wishing to develop their career within the firm the tension of achieving work–life balance is felt to be more problematic. Family commitments mean that some fee-earning roles are not feasible, which can create tensions in terms of building up the necessary experience for more senior roles. Moving to a business support role, where the opportunities for working in a more flexible way seem more feasible, is an alternative career option. However, this is perceived as taking a backward step.

The research highlighted different perceptions regarding the extent to which achieving work–life balance impacts upon career progression within the firm. Those already in more senior positions feel that achieving balance is less of a problem once one's credibility within the firm has been established. In this case it is more likely that personal preferences and commitments are taken into account when projects and workloads are being assigned. Thus should an individual ask not to be assigned to a particular project, and they have a good reason for this, this is not usually a problem and it does not create a black mark in terms of future career development. However, those who are just starting their career and are not currently in a management role were less certain of this.

While there are many existing policies relating to flexible working practices, many individuals are not necessarily aware of what these all are. In addition, there are many informal flexible working arrangements operating within the firm; as these are not widely publicized this again makes it difficult for individuals to know what is currently feasible. For women, in particular, this is perceived as a barrier in terms of future career options. This is a view echoed by Ruth Anderson, who was appointed to the KPMG board in 1998. In a news item in the *Guardian* at the time of her appointment she was quoted as expressing the view that more effort needs to be invested in helping women balance their work and family commitments so that they can reach senior positions within the firm.

Careers in the Future – Opportunities and Challenges

In response to the question 'What do you see as some of the future challenges facing the firm with regard to career development?' the following thoughts were expressed:

- Helping individuals (in particular women) develop meaningful careers while respecting their need for work–life balance. It was felt that there was an opportunity for exploring different forms of flexible career options/working practices which would ensure the continued delivery of a respected professional service, but enable individuals to have a more balanced lifestyle. One team is already championing a new working approach to help address the issue of work–life balance and have introduced the idea of a 'Quality of Life Week'. Individuals in this particular team take it in turn to have their Quality of Life Week, which means making a conscious effort not to work long hours. Making this approach work in practice requires a partnership approach between team members. Each team member needs to demonstrate sensitivity to the pressures others are experiencing, as well as offering support to the individual who is having their 'Quality of Life Week'. This has to be a reciprocal arrangement to work effectively.

- Enhancing and promoting the career development opportunities for those pursuing a career in a business support role, thus ensuring that individuals in these roles feel more valued.
- Balancing the tension between an individual's 'in demand factor' and the danger of burn-out. Here it was felt that there was an opportunity to improve the process of matching skills to assignments/situations, thus not placing individuals in untenable situations. In addition, the option of some scheduled time away from fee-earning activities was raised as a way of minimizing the risk of burn-out, as well as creating the space for individuals to work on projects which are more closely aligned to their longer-term career goals.
- Given that career success for many individuals is aligned to their need for interesting and challenging work, the continued availability of this type of work was raised as a major challenge for the firm.
- Develop a more open succession planning system so that individuals can base their own career decisions on relevant and complete data.
- More forums for individuals to gain firsthand information about the firm's future plans. Again this was felt to be a key source of data for personal career planning.

CONCLUSION

Careers remain a number-one agenda item for many employees. The idea of managing your own career has caught on, but many employees lack the time and know-how to do this. Helping people to come to terms with what careers look like in the new economy involves helping them recognize that jobs as we knew them may cease to exist. The skills of career self-management can be learnt, and the wise employer makes resources available for people to do this. Increasingly, the challenge for employers will be to retain those employees who are highly employable – and helping people develop themselves and their careers has been proved to do this. It is therefore a business imperative that organizations attract and retain talent by providing people with opportunities for growth.

In today's changing organizations this may not mean just conventional promotion. It is clear that most employees are no longer prepared to sacrifice everything for work and career structures and processes must now take into account the more flexible routes that many employees will increasingly wish to take to developing their careers. Career management will need to be much more individually tailored than the provision of blanket training opportunities. Imagination and flexibility will be needed on the part of both employees and employers if a satisfactory development route is to be found. Some of the genuine attempts described in this chapter to break out of the career straitjackets through which people have been channelled deserve success.

CHECKLIST FOR THE NEW CAREER STRUCTURES

- How do we help individuals to utilize their strengths, as well as help them to broaden their skills and experience?
- How can we help people to manage their own careers? What help do people want?
- What development tools can we provide?
- How can individuals be helped to develop their careers (by broadening their experience) in different areas?
- How can we reposition lateral development so that it is seen as a positive?
- How can we encourage individuals at all levels to become comfortable with giving and receiving feedback?
- How can we facilitate career development while at the same time managing expectations?
- What career routes can be created to stop people from being 'boxed in' to either technical or managerial roles?
- How can we help managers act as career enablers?
- How can we help people develop the skills which will enhance their employability – such as teamworking and knowledge skills?
- How can we help people at any age to progress their career development?

REFERENCES

Butler, T. and Waldroop, J. (1999) Job sculpting. *Harvard Business Review*, Sept–Oct: 144–152

Herriot, P. and Stickland, R. (1996) Career management: the issue of the millennium. *European Journal of Work and Organizational Psychology*, 5, No. 4, 465–470

Layard, R. (2005) *Happiness: Lessons from a New Science*. Harmondsworth: Penguin

FURTHER READING

Holbeche, L. (1995) *Career Development in Flatter Structures: Organizational Practices*. Horsham: Roffey Park Management Institute

Holbeche, L. (1997) *The Impact of Flatter Structures on Careers*. Oxford: Butterworth-Heinemann

Holbeche, L. (1997) *Motivating People in Lean Organizations*. Oxford: Butterworth-Heinemann

Kiechel, W. (1994) A manager's career in the new economy. *Fortune*, April

McCall, M., Morgan, W.J.R., Lombards, M. and Morrison, A.M. (1988) *The Lessons of Experience*. Lexington, MA: Lexington Books

Waitley, D. (1995) *Empires of the Mind*. London: Nicholas Brealey.

Chapter 10

Developing International Managers

The key to the great global success of the 21st century is the development and management of creative talent capable of operating across borders and cultures. IT can facilitate knowledge transfer around a worldwide business, but the critical advantage will be the human ability to manage diversity; to create the genuinely multicultural, as well as multinational organization.

(Kennedy, 1998)

As many as 25% of employees who come back from an overseas posting resign within a year, according to a survey by the Centre for International Briefing. After two years the figure rises to a staggering 40%. Some find that no new role has been defined for them and look in vain for appreciation of their new skills which often includes a second language (McLuhan, 1999). This chapter looks at some of the challenges of developing international high flyers. It highlights some of the changing organizational requirements of people in international roles and some of the dilemmas facing both companies and their employees. The skills of international high flyers are discussed and a number of approaches to development are outlined. One of the biggest challenges is ensuring that the skills of international high flyers are put to good use beyond their immediate project or assignment.

THE GROWTH OF INTERNATIONAL BUSINESS

Globalization means an explosion of business opportunities on a scale rarely seen before. Facilitated by the liberalization of trade, reduced telecommunications costs, computerization, digitalization and modern, high-speed transportation, many organizations are pushing back their operating boundaries and becoming at least 'international' players, in terms of marketplace, production or both.

In addition, increasing numbers of organizations are finding they need to expand globally in order to survive in today's highly competitive environment.

Electronic commerce has introduced new ways of customer buying, increased choice and fundamentally changed expectations about convenience, speed and price. Suppliers are finding they need global capacity to meet the needs of globalizing customers. The shift of production and customer servicing to emerging markets such as China, the Pacific Rim, Central and Eastern Europe, South America and India is evident across most sectors. Cross-border alliances and mergers create competition that spurs on the globalization of other organizations keen to survive. The challenge of maintaining margins and profitability is made even tougher as businesses make greater use of low-cost opportunities for offshoring or outsourcing, thus contributing to a global trend toward commoditization.

The economy is becoming increasingly 'boundaryless' as new markets open up and the landscape within which organizations operate changes with advances in technology and communications and the ease of travel and movement. Escalating levels of competition and global political and economic interdependence are increasing the levels of uncertainty that organizations need to confront. Events of the past few years have highlighted additional issues for global organizations. The increased scale of global terrorism, the war in Iraq and high-profile cases of corporate corruption and scandal have shaken consumer and investor confidence.

How well organizations are able to succeed in commercial and cultural situations which may be unfamiliar depends to some extent on the skills and attitudes of staff and of managers in particular. Working across a global landscape, spanning diverse countries, cultures, regulations, customers and time-zones, presents significant challenges and opportunities that are different from operating nationally.

How leaders within global organizations respond to the challenges and opportunities of the changing global landscape is critical for the success of their business (Bernthal and Wellins, 2003; Buckingham and Coffman, 1999; Hewitt, 2003; Mabey and Ramirez, 2004; Rodsutti and Swierczek, 2002). Leaders are typically the decision-makers with regard to seizing opportunities; they are pivotal in how proactively and effectively change is managed; they are instrumental in nurturing and developing talent required for future success and in creating an organizational culture that fosters high performance. Research by the Conference Board found that almost all the organizations in their study (91%) identified leadership as *the critical success factor* needed for global growth (Csoka, 1998).

Unfortunately, the global war for talent and the scarcity of leadership talent means that effective leaders are increasingly difficult to find, and the growing interest in identifying and developing international high flyers reflects these shifts. In 2007, major companies in pharmaceuticals, construction and information technology were reporting shortages of key talent needed to fuel their global growth. A study of organizations from 14 countries around the world found that almost eight out of ten organizations continue to have difficulties finding qualified leadership candidates (Bernthal and Wellins, 2003). The same research found that the majority of organizations do not have high confidence in the abilities of their leaders. The leaders themselves indicated that they lacked strength in most of the skills deemed important.

The urgent need to identify and develop leaders with global competencies and perspectives has been widely recognized (Suutari, 2002). Despite this recognized need and the shortage of leadership talent, previous research has suggested that many companies are unclear about what the development of global managers actually means. Gregersen *et al.* (1998) found that among US Fortune 500 firms, only 8% report already having comprehensive systems for developing global leaders, while 16% had some established programmes, 44% an ad hoc approach and 32% were just beginning development. Previous Roffey Park research also found that organizations recognized the importance of global leadership development but lacked coherent strategies to address it (Agyeman, 2001; Glynn and Holbeche, 1999). Reviewing more recent literature in this area, Suutari (2002) concludes that neither management research nor practice is adequately meeting the challenge of the globalization of business.

WHAT IS AN INTERNATIONAL ORGANIZATION?

What is required of international managers is to some extent determined by the degree of 'internationalism' of the company. Many organizations which claim to be international are in fact predominantly national companies which export overseas. Their main international effort may lie in the sales, marketing and customer service arenas. Management teams are likely to be largely made up of nationals and opportunities for an international career may be rather limited. A 1999 Roffey Park survey found that, while the majority of participating organizations were conducting business internationally, only 56% of respondents agreed that their organization provided the opportunity for international careers.

Other companies are more truly international in that they may be owned by parent organizations whose nationality differs from the countries in which they mainly operate. They may be based in Europe or other regions where there is a clear market for their product but the parent company could well be Japanese, American, etc. They may operate as multi-domestic organizations. Management teams are likely to be made up of a blend of nationals from the operating countries, with direction and control coming from the parent company. The national characteristics of the parent headquarters often have a strong bearing on the management styles, working practices and trading approaches which are considered appropriate.

The degree of centralization or decentralization of organizational decision-making can have a major bearing on what is required of international high flyers. Multinationals operate with relatively autonomous units, each focused on maximizing results within its territory. Local management teams may have a reasonable degree of autonomy within a clear management framework. Truly global transnational companies seek to weave their units into more flexible, web-like structures with a dual focus which is both global and local. It is argued that managers in the global corporation have to be able to work at much greater levels of complexity – in terms of geographic scope and cultural diversity and of balancing global and local agendas.

With the creation of a single currency zone in Europe, multinational companies are increasingly moving towards pan-European structures, developing centralized service centres which group together support processes such as customer services, sales or marketing. These are a way of reducing duplication, such as in IT systems, and cutting the numbers of staff and therefore cost. Specialist staff will be expected to relocate or at least seriously commute to the country in which their service centre is based. In other cases, the 'Euromanager', who lives in one country but is peripatetic and operates across national boundaries, is a reality.

Joint ventures are increasingly replacing wholly owned subsidiaries as the dominant form of overseas investment. Typically, the main problem areas are likely to lie in relations between the overseas company and the local company, especially on issues concerning communication and decision-making. Child's (1990) study of joint ventures in China found distinctive differences of approach of parent companies from different countries. In US-owned joint ventures, there was a strong tendency for the procedures and approaches of the parent company to be introduced into the joint venture partner, despite the problems this caused in the fields of informal communication, decision-making and training. By contrast, Japanese companies were found to be less likely to impose home-based Japanese management styles onto their partners, preferring instead to adapt to local circumstances. For an international manager working in a joint venture, the challenges may reach a higher level of complexity than those experienced when working for the parent company.

THE ROLE OF THE INTERNATIONAL MANAGER

The role of the international manager seems to be changing and with it the skills required to be effective are changing too. No longer is it sufficient for an international high flyer to have technical skills and to be a troubleshooting manager who can go from country to country. With barriers coming down and organizations trying new forms of international coordination and integration, the international manager is someone who can exercise leadership across a number of countries and cultures simultaneously, perhaps on a global or regional basis.

While international managers plan, direct, organize and control just like any other manager, the context in which they carry out their duties is much more complex than if they were managing purely domestic activities. For this reason, international managers should be culturally sensitive in their business practices and should learn to bridge the cultural gap that exists between their methods of management and business and those of the host country. In particular, managers must be aware that cultures vary and are learned, and that cultures influence behaviour. Increasingly, personality factors and the ability to manage local operations are seen to be critical to effectiveness.

Selecting International Managers

Identifying and developing global leaders is a key concern for international companies. In Roffey Park research into Global Leadership (Sinclair and Ageyman,
2004), leaders at the highest level were involved in identifying what leadership
capabilities were required on an ongoing basis, reviewing performance and
development plans and supporting high potential talent, for example through
mentoring. A range of methods were used to develop leadership capabilities.
Increasing self-awareness through development programmes, formal and informal feedback mechanisms are fundamental to leaders' development. Formal
training programmes were useful, not just for improving and solidifying skills
and increasing understanding of the organization, but also for providing networking and mentoring opportunities and exposure to diverse views. Interestingly, few
organizations appear to use a specific list of international competencies when
selecting people for international roles. In the Roffey Park research it was found
that the criteria used to select international leaders are often unclear. In many
organizations, functional expertise appears to be the most important criterion in
selecting and preparing employees for international work. Often the selection
process focuses on the person's willingness to go abroad, rather than on other
factors. International assignments are often used to address a particular business
problem or opportunity and their potential use as an excellent training ground for
refining the core skills of future organizational leaders is often missed. Yet arguably, the skills and competencies involved in performing effectively in an international context are of a high order and should not be left to chance.

Research (Tung, 1988) has found that the greater the consideration paid during
the selection process to adaptability and the ability to communicate, the higher the
success rate in the assignment. Other research suggests that several factors which
should be included in the selection criteria for international leaders are:

- Conflict-resolution skills
- Leadership style
- Effective communication
- Social orientation
- Flexibility and open-mindedness
- Interest in and willingness to try new things
- Ability to cope with stress.

Given the growing shortage of international managers a number of companies
are seeking to recruit employees, especially graduates, who are willing to manage abroad, rather than trying to persuade reluctant existing employees. They
market the international nature of their activities and emphasize the prospects of
early international experience to attract graduates who are specifically seeking
an international career. The recruitment of foreign students is becoming easier
and cheaper through the use of technology. Accessing on-line CVs of overseas
university students over the Internet is becoming a common feature of sourcing

for graduate entry. Mobility and the willingness to move across borders are seen as prerequisites to future success.

Capabilities Required for Effective Global Leadership

To ensure success in a global context, leaders need to understand the global business environment, manage crises, improvise and be open to continual learning as it changes and presents them with new and unfamiliar issues. They need to be innovative and responsive to stay ahead of the competition. Good cross-cultural awareness is required to understand local conditions and the environments in which they operate as well as the diplomacy and flexibility to navigate different views and the political astuteness and interpersonal skills to develop relationships with key stakeholders. The complexity and distances involved in operating globally requires effective leaders to empower and involve others and work effectively without frequent face-to-face contact. Personal character and ethics were particularly emphasized as critical for motivating and inspiring teams, projecting credibility and building relationships.

THE SKILLS OF INTERNATIONAL HIGH FLYERS

Clearly the scope of the organization's international activities will have a bearing on the skills required of international high flyers. Research by Tubbs and Schulz (2006) indicates that the skill sets of a competent manager within a localized environment differ from the skill sets of competent global managers. However, there are certain skills and characteristics which most international careers have in common. According to Professor Peter Smith (1992):

> Working effectively across cultures is not therefore simply a matter of applying skills found to be effective within the culture of one's own country or organization. It requires also that one can understand and cope with the processes of communication and decision-making in settings where these are achieved in a different manner.

Therefore, since most organizations promote from within, a major question for organizations is whether local managers can make a successful transition into international leadership roles. Stewart Tubbs and Eric Schulz of Eastern Michigan University in a 2005 study used the 'Big Five' personality dimensions (extraversion, agreeableness, conscientiousness, emotional stability and openness to experience) along with locus of control to describe successful global leaders. People exhibiting an internal locus of control feel they have greater control over events than do those with an external locus of control. Those people with an internal locus of control, Tubbs and Schulz argue, will make the better international leaders.

International leaders need to change their frame of reference from a local or national orientation to a truly international perspective. This involves understanding influences, trends, practices, political and cultural influences and international economics. They will need to understand and develop competitive strategies, plans and tactics which operate outside the confines of a domestic marketplace orientation.

Maury Peiperl of the Centre for Organizational Research at London Business School has carried out a survey in 15 countries looking at the skills of international managers. He states that:

The skills needed and the ones where chief executives see a gap are adaptability in new situations, international strategic awareness, ability to motivate cross-border teams, sensitivity to different cultures and international experience. They have less to do with the traditional talents of achieving targets (though that's always important); vision and change management are the needs of today.

Peiperl's (1998) survey found that British and German managers had the same two gaps in their skills portfolio: being able to motivate cross-border teams and to integrate people from other countries.

Being able to understand and lead multi-national teams is critical. Leaders need to be able to deal with issues of collaboration and cross-cultural variances. Merely recognizing that cultural differences exist is not enough. International managers need to be able to manage those differences if the team is to operate successfully. They need to develop processes for coaching, mentoring and assessing performance across a variety of attitudes, beliefs and standards. At the US semiconductor company Intel, the company does not try to impose a company culture on the national culture; rather, it takes for granted that these differences exist. The preferred approach to team meetings at Intel, wherever they are run, is to ensure that the meetings are structured and run in a particular way. This approach is based on the belief that having a common framework and routine provides a stability which helps overcome potential difficulties which may arise from cross-cultural differences.

Language skills are also clearly important as is being willing to continue to learn new languages if, for example, your specialist service centre is in a different location. These skills are an essential gateway to understanding and working effectively within the culture of the country in question. Being limited in language ability therefore runs the risk of missing out on the subtleties which can make the difference between business success or failure.

According to a report published by the Economist Intelligence Unit (Krempel, 1998), businesses are looking for graduates who are multi-lingual and able to understand business practice and how it differs between countries. The Peiperl study found that when it comes to language skills, British managers compare unfavourably, speaking on average 1.7 languages in contrast to their counterparts in 14 other countries who speak an average of 2.8 languages each. In the Roffey Park study, 35% of the sample recognized language skills as being the main skills required, closely followed by cultural awareness and understanding.

Some leading industrialists suggest that even these skills are not enough to ensure that future international leaders are able to lead effectively over time. According to Michel de Zeeuw, General Manager of Unisys, graduate recruits ideally have specific skills such as computing ability, as well as good communication and teamworking skills since they will be required to work with people from different countries. This is in addition to specific technical skills such as accountancy if they are moving, for instance, into a finance function. Yves Nanot, chief executive officer of Cimentz Français in Paris, suggests that, given the ongoing pace of change, managers will need a more rapid rate of thinking and making decisions and an ability to anticipate and prepare for changes. It will be important for managers to be able to 'cut through all those barriers of narrow, nationalistic thinking that for us were insurmountable'.

The traditional role of making order out of chaos will shift to one of continually managing change and chaos in ways which are responsive to customers and competitive conditions. International leaders will need to be effective well beyond traditional management practices to reflect sensitivity to cultural diversity and perspective. They need to understand different – and sometimes conflicting – social forces without prejudice.

They need to speed up business development where possible by exploiting and adapting learning between countries and markets. They also need to be able to manage their personal effectiveness and achieve a satisfactory balance between work and home.

Recruiting and Developing International Managers in BP Amoco

BP Amoco is committed to developing an internationally diverse leadership. One of the most direct ways of achieving an international management cadre is by deliberately recruiting people with an international perspective. BP Amoco has consciously attempted to develop a more multi-cultural management workforce in recent years and recruitment takes place through the worldwide recruitment network. A common set of recruitment competencies is used and these are as culturally 'neutral' as possible so as not to disadvantage candidates whose first language is other than English and whose experience of life does not include the UK, the United States or Europe. A genuine attempt has been made to devise culturally neutral selection procedures, with candidates tested and interviewed in their native language.

In addition, approximately 15 'Eurograds' are recruited each year. These are expected to be internationally mobile, to speak a minimum of three languages and be typically high potential. There are currently 60 alumni in the scheme and over time it is anticipated that this more culturally diverse graduate intake should percolate through to senior management.

In addition to recruiting international talent, BP Amoco is committed to internationalizing the current leadership. Typically this is achieved by sending senior managers to international business schools, through training and through group meetings and networks which take place in different global venues.

International experience outside work is well utilized, but the primary means of internationalizing managers is still by sending them on expatriate assignments. Given the nature of the business, expatriation is likely to be a significant part of an international manager's experience for some time to come. However, this is proving increasingly difficult for employees who have dual-career families or who are not keen for the disruption to family personal life caused by such relocations.

BP Amoco is working hard to eliminate barriers to successful expatriation. The company has devised a Partner Assistance policy to help alleviate some of the financial hardships experienced when the accompanying partner has to give up his or her job. Support is provided to help the accompanying partner to understand their career choices in the destination. Where possible, the process of finding work for the partner in the destination country is facilitated by the company. If having a job proves impractical for various reasons, partners are assisted in remaining current in their own career field. This may mean being provided with relevant trade literature, doing a distance-learning course or attending a professional conference in another location. Vocational or educational training is provided locally if possible and child-care supplied.

Help is provided to both partners prior to, during and after the assignment. Before the assignment, partners receive as appropriate a mini-severance payment to compensate to some extent for the loss of income. Career counselling is available and language lessons are offered to both partners, as is cultural training related to the destination country. During the assignment, partners are given help with CV preparation, job-search counselling, visas and work permits. Further language training is provided as well as IT support. Partner groups are established who become an active network. Partners are also assisted in re-entering the job market upon repatriation, and are offered job counselling for the UK market and help in preparing their CVs. They are given support in updating their job skills such as learning new technical or IT systems which may have changed significantly in their absence from their home country.

A number of other international companies are struggling to find creative solutions to the dual-career issue. Motorola, for instance, actually pays a percentage of their annual domestic salaries to spouses of employees on international assignments. Motorola believes that this helps partners to adjust better while overseas and to prepare for repatriation and employment on their return to their home country.

Leadership Development at Sony Europe

In 2003 Sony Europe recognized that it needed to think more carefully about leadership and succession planning. At that point management training was solely country- or function-based, rather than targeted towards building the skills Sony needs to move its managers across the business. Most senior leaders had not had access to development for many years and identifying future leaders was proving difficult.

The company responded by launching a new talent strategy, of which the senior leadership development (SLDP) is one among four strands. The others are a programme for the executive team, a European graduate programme for a handful of talented graduates with language skills and a year of previous business experience, and a leadership development programme for junior and middle managers with Europe-wide ambitions. The SLDP targets managers at MD-minus one level: the direct successors to the executive top team.

To back the talent strategy, Sony created what it calls the '3C' leadership model, coupled with a 'hugely more robust' assessment and selection. The Cs stand for competence, confidence and courage, defined by seven core competencies. Competence includes analytical and intellectual qualities. Courage covers drive, responsibility and risk-taking. However, assessment uncovered gaps in the area of confidence: that is, the ability to interact with and influence others, and to develop people.

Sarah Henbrey, divisional director of people and organizational development, reveals that Sony looked at generic management development but 'we never seemed to get much buy-in for it' – 'it didn't feel right'. It was deeper focus on emotional intelligence that was needed. The SLDP grew 'almost by chance' out of a conversation with a small company that already provided coaching to Sony. 'It was bit of leap of faith but it has worked well', Henbrey says.

The SLDP involves three modules spread over around three months. The first, entitled 'visionary leadership', focuses on the individual's motivation, life values and career path. As well as the 'lifeline', it involves using appreciative inquiry techniques to explore their understanding of 'peak' leadership performance so that they understand what good leadership looks and feels like to them. The second module, 'Leading with emotional intelligence', requires participants to keep a journal for a week to track their emotional processes at work and at home. Participants explore the energy of their emotions in ways that are helpful rather than destructive. The third module, 'Coaching for potential', involves coaching each other to learn how to use open questioning techniques (based on 'Can You Feel It?' by Rebecca Johnson, *People Management*, 23 August 2007).

DEVELOPING INTERNATIONAL MANAGERS

Many organizations appear to lack a clear strategy for developing international high flyers. So while many employees appear to want home-based short-term assignments, the dominant method of internationalizing managers appears still to be through expatriate or longer-term assignments, except where organizations have been encouraged or forced to adopt more flexible approaches. For many international companies most of the focus on training and development is based around the expatriation process. The development and training needs of host country nationals tend to take a back seat.

International Development Models

The ways in which international managers are developed will to some extent reflect their organization's preferred way of conducting international business. Typically, organizations are unclear about their strategy for internationalizing managers. For decades the dominant model has been that of the expatriate assignment. Particularly common in multinationals, this has usually meant a mobile group of high-flying executives enjoying special financial and other benefits. For some employees, an expatriate assignment has been an essential part of their career development, prior to returning to a 'home' base. For others, expatriate working has become a lifestyle of postings to different parts of the world. As we will explore later in this chapter, the expatriate model of international assignment appears to be on the decrease, with organizations and employees less happy to commit to this form of assignment.

An alternative model is the development of local managers who can understand and work with the corporate culture, but whose career is likely to be based in their home country or region. In the past, local managers have been often relegated at best to 'second in command' positions, reporting to an expatriate manager. The shift away from colonial-style relationships is evident in many parts of the world such as China and South Africa. Governments are requiring international organizations who wish to trade in their country to 'upskill' local talent who can take over the management of the enterprise over time. The challenges of this form of development include enabling the 'local' manager to develop insights into the corporate culture and to be able to influence corporate strategy in an adult–adult way.

A third 'hybrid' model consists of being primarily home-based, but with international assignments of varying lengths. These may range from a six-month technical assignment to a short business meeting with clients or team members in different locations. The Roffey Park research suggests that this is by far the most popular form of international career from the employee perspective, though organizations are slow to find new ways of carrying out their international business in ways which make sense to shareholders and their employees. Indeed, with the advent of virtual teams it is possible that an international high flyer may have no need to travel at all since technology makes possible many forms of communication, except for 'in the flesh'. However, leaders of global teams would no doubt resist the notion that all teamwork can be carried out by teleconference or e-mail.

Development Through Expatriation

Sinclair and Ageyman (2004) found that exposure to different experiences and teams was particularly useful for developing leaders' ability to deal with ambiguity and change and facilitate the transfer of knowledge. Global assignments were felt by many to be the most important development experience, increasing cultural sensitivity, broadening perspectives, and really bringing home the relevance of difference and the need for a strong focus on communications.

HOW WILLING ARE MANAGERS TO ACCEPT AN INTERNATIONAL ASSIGNMENT?

Increasingly there are signs that expatriate and longer-term overseas assignments are becoming harder to fill. An Ashridge Management College survey (Panter,

1995) found that shortages of international managers were particularly acute for British multinational companies. Two-thirds of the companies surveyed said that they had experienced shortages of international managers and over 70% indicated that future shortages were anticipated. Reasons suggested for this shortfall are that UK salary levels are uncompetitive and also that managers are becoming less mobile.

This lack of mobility can be explained by a number of factors. In a large expatriate survey conducted by Shell International in 1996, several demographic trends affecting mobility are charted:

- The increasing number of women in the workforce
- The increasing percentage of women with their own careers and who are not willing to abandon their own career in order to follow their partner to an overseas assignment. The so-called 'dual career' issue is keenly affecting industries such as oil and the utilities. Similarly, many male partners are unwilling to be parted from their families for extended periods of time
- More aged dependants
- Greater travel opportunities and chances to experience other cultures without the need to expatriate
- Reluctance to send children to boarding school.

Other factors relate to some of the major shifts in the employment relationship which have taken place mainly in the West over the past two decades. The widespread reshaping of organizations to cope with competitive pressures has had a profound impact on the so-called 'psychological contract' between employer and employee. Few organizations these days promise a lifetime's employment and, with flatter management structures, the opportunities for conventional vertical promotion have become restricted for many people. Ironically, organizations that have sought to pass responsibility for career development to employees and have told them to manage their own careers are starting to see the impact of employee choice if the employee's skills are marketable and in short supply.

The impact of ongoing uncertainty and lack of career progression has been a lessening of employee commitment in many cases. Whereas at one time employees would have been prepared to take one or two lengthy assignments in less popular locations in order to advance their careers, the link between employee sacrifice and career reward appears less clear. For some employees who have accepted overseas assignments, there seems to be a negative link with promotion, especially if they believe that they have been forgotten while overseas. Similarly, there are signs that the long-hours regime evident in many organizations is finally taking its toll. In some cases employees are refusing assignments which would upset the balance between home and work life even if they pay the price in terms of missing out on promotion.

ORGANIZATIONAL VERSUS INDIVIDUAL EXPECTATIONS

While demand for international employees seems to be increasing, the desire to accept international assignments has flattened at best. Some organizations simply do not have enough people with the skills, experience and motivation to live and work in another country. The Roffey Park International Leadership survey (Glynn and Holbeche, 1999) of 160 UK-based managers found that there was a clear mismatch between what employers were expecting of employees and what employees considered to be their needs and aspirations. There still appears to be a strong expectation from employers that if an international assignment is offered, the employee should not refuse it.

The survey found that while two-thirds of respondents were willing to accept an international assignment, 79% did not consider having an international management role as part of their individual career plan. For those people who were interested in an international assignment, the main attractions were the challenge it offered, the chance to experience another culture and the opportunities it would open up in the future. However, only 3.5% saw such an international assignment as a necessary career move.

Of those managers not willing to accept an international assignment, 52% said that this was because of a reluctance to uproot the family, and 62% of managers surveyed preferred to be given an international assignment which did not involve expatriation, even though many acknowledged that not as much experience would be gained as from an expatriate role. Over a third of the sample stated that a home-based international role involving travel is most appealing. The most popular destination was North America, which may reflect a concern over language difficulties and cultural issues. For managers who had experienced international assignments, the biggest problems they faced were cross-cultural working and language barriers.

Nevertheless, there are signs that, from the company perspective, attitudes towards international assignments are changing. The response of many organizations to the shortfall in numbers of international managers is to recruit international-minded graduates and send them on overseas assignments in the early years before other commitments make such assignments seem less attractive. Rather than being a corporate afterthought, international assignments are moving to the forefront of management and organizational dynamics. Companies are slowly realizing that well-managed international assignments are a key element in developing global corporate competencies. Expatriate postings, where they exist, are becoming interconnected with executive and leadership development as well as with succession planning. They are also being increasingly regarded as logical and required steps in career paths – and not only for those on fast tracks.

THE ROLE OF HR IN MANAGING ASSIGNMENTS

Managing assignments is therefore a key responsibility and opportunity for global HR to grow talent within the company. These responsibilities include:

- Finding employees with the appropriate skills
- Providing cross-cultural and language training for employees and their partners
- Creating career management strategies which support employee interests during and on return from assignments
- Supporting partners of employees when on assignment.

Using appropriate selection processes for specific postings or assignments is only one part of the equation. Another important ingredient is the identification of individuals with international potential long before they might be expected to take on an international role. That way, effective screening, training and familiarization can take place to ensure that individuals are ready for an international leadership task. Honeywell Inc. believe in identifying and developing potential candidates usually years before a posting. Each employee is made aware, via routine testing with specialists and consultants, of cross-cultural strengths and weaknesses.

Managers use these tests as pools to identify potential expatriates, discussing career paths with them. The aim is for them to develop a cross-cultural intellect, or what they call 'strategic accountability'. A manager may suggest that an employee begin studying a language or informally explore areas where he or she may be flexible and inflexible in a foreign culture. Honeywell managers are encouraged to pick US employees for international task teams for one- or two-day meetings abroad. Some are sent on six-month foreign assignments with no home leave to see how they will adjust to an overseas posting. Expatriates need to be aware that they will experience cultural differences in problem-solving, motivation, leadership, use of power, consensus building and decision-making.

International Mobility at Ericsson

In common with many international companies, Ericsson has to address the challenge of people working abroad for extended periods. Overall, it has a remarkable number; some 3500 long-term ex-pats living and working around the world. Team members typically have three- to four-year assignments and for some people with families this may cause considerable disruption. The shift away from the old paternalistic culture in which employees would be guaranteed a career enhancement on return from assignment means that people are now more aware that they too are responsible for managing their careers.

Ericsson is addressing the issue of employee mobility by a two-pronged strategy. On the one hand, more local managers are used wherever it makes business sense, such as in Asia-Pacific where ex-pats can be less acceptable to customers. On the other hand, the company is becoming increasingly selective about who goes on an overseas assignment. Ericsson is choosing people who are more independent and self-starting where possible. This is in addition to the high technical knowledge and the culturally sensitive customer skills they need as a member of an international sales team. Not surprisingly, finding the right people can be difficult. Internal candidates are sought and employees are asked if they would like an international career. HR also pinpoints individuals whose skills profile matches requirements.

For people who are on assignment, the challenge of reintegrating into the home base when they return is somewhat eased by the information flow from parent companies. Typically, while on assignment employees receive all local press releases and highlights of the 'home' business so that they are up to date with key issues. The company intranet is another useful way of maintaining contact. In addition, people are encouraged to be proactive in maintaining regular contact with their home base although, typically, they become consumed by current relationships and events.

Naturally, in a global business, international exposure is seen as an essential part of preparation for senior management. Typically, people move on from leading an international team to running a large division with profit-and-loss responsibility. Sometimes they are given the chance to work for a major subsidiary to gain additional experience. Ericsson has a wealth of experience in international teamworking developed over more than 100 years of worldwide operations – UK chairman, Tony Booth says it's in their bloodstream!

While effective preparation is known to be a key ingredient in ensuring the success of an international assignment, organizational support is often surprisingly minimal. A few companies have begun to use expatriated employees to coach other employees who are about to be posted abroad. The briefing works well if the returnee has recent experience in the host country. However, just the interaction with someone who has lived and worked in another country is invaluable for the soon-to-be expatriate, especially if it is their first posting.

Shell has 5000 expatriates worldwide and puts great effort into cross-cultural coaching. Those being sent to countries whose cultures are very different from the UK (about 35%) undergo a week's residential training course in the UK or the Netherlands to give them the knowledge and understanding of the social and business mores which they will encounter. At least 95% receive individual attention from one of the 'area desks' specializing in facts on every region of the world. About 1300 people receive briefings of one kind or another every year. Significantly, Shell intends that all graduate entrants will in future receive compulsory cross-cultural training, whether or not they have been earmarked for a foreign assignment.

Many companies conduct extensive international in-house seminars. These courses typically cover national cultural differences, local politics and laws when conducting business abroad, family adaptation and international finance. When training is provided it should ideally focus on three aspects of development: pre-departure, on-site and repatriation. Language training should be geared to cultural understanding rather than total fluency. Even a modest knowledge of a language can create some 'equilibrium of power' in transactions. Some European companies take a front-end approach by selective recruitment. They look harder for young men and women who already possess fluency in at least two languages, can demonstrate cross-cultural ability and have a serious interest in working globally.

Case Study: Developing International Managers at Standard Chartered Bank

Good-quality dialogue is a fundamental basis of effective talent management. Understanding and clarifying the roles of the players in this dialogue is an important part of the process. The following case study, featured in the CIPD report *Managing Talent* (2007), highlights an example of this.

Going Global with Standard Chartered Bank

Standard Chartered Bank (SCB) is a global company of almost 60 000 employees operating in 56 countries. The Bank's aim is to lead the way through sustainable business practice. With a large global footprint and significant growth aspirations, the organization perceives leadership development as essential to the future success of the business. To develop its leadership talent, Standard Chartered introduced a 'strengths-based' approach to leadership development in 2000.

As part of this ongoing initiative, the organization has a network of 200 'Strength Coaches' spanning the globe. The coaches are all HR relationship managers, who were invited to become Strength Coaches as a component of their role. To become a coach, individuals must attend a four-day training course and complete ten coaching sessions over four months, with one audio-recorded session, and they must commit to ongoing professional development.

Sarah Jones, Group Head of Leadership Development, leads the coaching network and its supervision. Jones says:

> Providing support for the coaches requires a global network of 34 'team coaches' who each provide ongoing supervisory support for three to seven coaches. Team coaches are selected from the 'cream of the coaches' with at least two years' Strengths Coaching experience. We look for people who are deeply committed to their own personal development in the area of coaching and the development of others.

The team coaches are expected to meet each coach for one and a half to two hours every three months as a minimum. If a coach would like more support, they can arrange additional meetings with their team coach. Most of these are face-to-face meetings, but they can be by telephone or video calls. Some supervisors use groups and some run 'surgeries' when they are in the country. The typical supervisory meeting includes:

- Reviewing coaching clients: what I've done particularly well and would like to repeat in my coaching; what I've done less well
- Providing support in relation to situations that have been stretching
- Challenging the coach: 'what was on your mind?'
- Reviewing the current business pressures: 'are there any themes that are emerging?'

Coaches are encouraged, within the bounds of confidentiality, to bring feedback to the supervisory session from clients they have coached. Coaches are also required to tape at least one session per year and bring it for review.

To facilitate management of the coaching initiative and coaching supervision of the team coaches/supervisors, there are seven Leadership Facilitators who provide ongoing supervision for the team coaches. The team coaches note the organizational themes discussed as part of the supervision. Periodically, these are fed back to the HR and Organization Effectiveness teams. The Chief Executive takes a keen interest in the feedback related to the organization's ongoing efforts to develop effective leadership.

Since Strengths Coaching is integral to HR, the team does not calculate the cost of the coaching and supervision as a 'separate line' item. Jones emphasizes:

> Strengths Coaching is critical to our leadership development strategy. Coaching supervision is essential to coaching; we can't afford not to do it. The supervision process helps us ensure that a coach working in 'x country' would never feel like a lost soul. Knowing that they're supported as part of an international network helps the coaches to feel confident and to know that they are key to our strategic strengths approach. This is passed on through the coaching to the leaders they work with. We're keen to ensure that employees perceive individual attention and development. This results in higher staff engagement and we see the results in stronger business performance and lower employee turnover.

To optimize the benefits of coaching, Jones recommends:

- Provide your coaches with great training – it's a challenging role.
- Be clear about the target population for coaching and the performance outcomes you'll focus on.
- Ensure you only work with numbers of 'coachees' that your coaching population can give appropriate attention to.
- Make sure both coaching and coaching supervision are part of an individual's objectives or it's unlikely to get done.

And about coaching supervision:

- Set supervision in place from the beginning.
- Pick the best of the coaches to be supervisors. Being a supervisor should hold kudos.
- Consider using external supervisors while your own coaching population gains experience.
- Ensure that both the supervisors and coaches understand what supervision is and what it's not.
- Have a clear timetable of activity that is monitored.

Supporting International High Flyers

For managers who are about to go on an international assignment, help in preparing for the experience can make the difference between an effective start to the assignment or a dismal failure. Preparatory help includes training in cross-cultural issues, setting up procedures to maintain contact with the home office and help in finding employment for spouses. Once on assignment, employees look for help in adjusting on a practical level. A mentor can be useful here: not only someone who is familiar with the local customs and who can ease the process of integration but also someone at the home office who can be a vital link for the assignee on career issues. Support networks involving communication through travel and company newsletters can also be useful.

Perhaps the main area where employees look for support from the home office is on preparing for their return on repatriation. Typically this is an area of shortfall and relocation research has shown that many employees are dissatisfied with the quality of the communication, support and advice they receive prior to, and following, repatriation. Practical help and moral support are often needed to enable families to adapt to the change. There is evidence that many returning employees suffer 'reverse culture shock' and other problems of adaptation. This often happens because of a significant mismatch between people's expectations prior to their repatriation and what they actually encounter when they return home. The greater the clarity about possible return roles before the assignment begins, the better.

CONCLUSION – BENEFITTING FROM INTERNATIONAL LEADERSHIP

The competition for effective global managers will only increase over time. It is clear that effective global leadership plays a key part in enabling organizations to compete effectively. Whatever the selection criteria used by multi-national employers, it's clear that a strategic and holistic approach to global manager acquisition is needed. Successful multi-national businesses will take the approach of attracting these key individuals by establishing a reputation for being an 'employer of choice' and by creating organizational cultures that are attractive to these distinctive leaders.

Organizations need to take a proactive and integrated approach to developing global leaders with the support and involvement of those at the top. They need to be clear about the capabilities required of their global leaders. The skill sets required in normal local managerial positions are quite different from those required in global management situations. Organizations need to carry out regular evaluation and review to ensure that development initiatives are appropriate for the needs of global leaders and encourage effective leadership practices and behaviours through all their people processes. One of the greatest challenges for both organizations and their high-flying international employees is making the most of the enhanced skills and knowledge gained by individuals through their international role. The problem is perhaps most acute on repatriation when typically the employee is expected to slot into any available role. If the individual's knowledge is not used to good effect, the employee typically leaves the organization within a short time. The phenomenon is not simply that of a bruised ego and the individual finding him- or herself to be a small fish in a big pond. It is more that there are potential business benefits in enabling the individual's enhanced skills, and knowledge of the local market with its challenges and opportunities, to be put to good use. In many cases there is not even a formal debriefing of the individual after the assignment. Frustration at having no outlet for these skills, together with dissatisfaction about career prospects, are the common reasons given for individuals leaving after an international assignment.

So this chapter suggests a potential paradox: the demand for international high flyers is likely to increase at a time when there is a growing reluctance on the part of both employers and employees to continue down the expatriate route of development. Organizations are going to have to be more creative in the ways they attract, motivate and retain people. Clearly much can be done at recruitment to ensure that people are really interested in an international career, and that travel periods are concentrated.

Better use of technology will help in the management of international teams but will not replace need for people to work together face to face. More skilful support to employees and their families who are on assignment may reduce the number of expensive assignment failures. Better use of enhanced skills may retain valued employees for longer. Giving people the chance to develop and apply the high-level skills required of international leaders is only one part of the equation. Recognizing and using these enhanced skills to the mutual benefit of the organization and the employee is the surest way to tap into the motivation and commitment of international high flyers.

CHECKLIST FOR INTERNATIONAL MANAGEMENT STRATEGIES

- What are the main ways in which international employees are deployed, e.g. on short-term assignments, expatriate postings etc.?
- How much does your organization consider 'local' managers as part of the international management cadre?
- To what extent is telecommuting replacing the need for international assignments?
- What are the implications for managers of enabling 'high touch' continuous interaction in support of international team members?
- How are employee motivation, reward and recognition currently aligned to the changing business and organizational priorities?
- How are terms and conditions for international employees currently defined? Are special terms required for expatriation, or simply reward arrangements which reflect flexibility and mobility?
- What support can be provided to help expatriate employees prepare for return from assignment?
- How can the organization benefit most from cross-cultural learning and experience?

REFERENCES

Agyeman, B. (2001) Global Leadership Effectiveness: Examining Strategies for Success. Research Paper Prepared for Roffey Park Masters Programme

Bernthal, P. and Wellins, R. (2003) *The Leadership Forecast*. Pittsburgh, PA: Development Dimensions International

Buckingham, M. and Coffman, C. (1999) *First Break All the Rules*. New York: Simon and Schuster

Child, J. (1990) *The Management of Equity Joint Ventures in China*. Beijing: The China-European Community Management association and China Enterprise Management Association

Csoka, L.S. (1998) *Bridging the Leadership Gap* [Report Number 1190-98-RR]. New York: The Conference Board

Glynn, C. and Holbeche, L. (1999) *Towards Global Leadership: Recruiting and Developing International Managers*. Horsham: Roffey Park Management Institute

Gregersen, H.B., Morrison, A.J. and Black, J.S. (1998) Developing leaders for the global frontier. *Sloan Management Review*, Fall, 21–32

Kennedy, C. (1998) Global dreams, local realities. *Human Resources*, March/April

Krempel, M. (1998) *Shared Services: A New Business Architecture for Europe*. London: The Economist Intelligence Unit

Hewitt Associates Ltd (2003) *How Companies Grow Great Leaders: Top Companies for Leaders, 2003 Research Highlights*: Hewitt Associates Ltd

Mabey, C. and Ramirez, M. (2004) *Developing Managers: A European Perspective*. London: Chartered Management Institute

McLuhan, R. (1999) The homecoming. *Personnel Today*, 4 March

Panter, S. (1995) Summary Report of a Qualitative International Research Survey. Ashridge Management College

Peiperl, M. and Coles, M. (1998) Global managers despair at heirs. *Sunday Times*, 8 November

Rodsutti, M.C. and Swierczek, F.W. (2002) Leadership and organizational effectiveness in multinational enterprises in Southeast Asia. *Leadership and Organization Development Journal*, 23, No. 5: 250–259

Smith, P.B. (1992) Organizational behaviour and national cultures. *British Journal of Management*, 3: 39–51

Suutari, V. (2002) Global leader development: an emerging research agenda. *Career Development International*, 7, No. 4, 218–233

Tubbs, S.L. and Schulz, E. (2006) Exploring a taxonomy of global leadership competencies and meta-competencies. *Journal of American Academy of Business*, 8, No. 2, 29–34

Tung, R. (1998) *Selection and Training of Personnel for Overseas Assignments*. Cambridge, MA: Ballinger

FURTHER READING

Ettore, B. (1993) A brave new world – managing international careers. *Management Review*, April

Loose, A. (1998) 'Jobs sans frontières'. *The Times*, 12 November

Sinclair, A. and Agyeman, B. (2004) *Building Global Leadership: Strategies for Success*. Horsham: Roffey Park Management Institute

Solomon, C. (1996) Expats say: Help make us mobile. *Personnel Journal*, July

Chapter 11

High-Potential Assessment and Succession Planning

Focusing on critical talent is relatively new territory for most companies and thus offers a new way to compete.

(Deloitte Research, 2004)

Despite the challenging global economic conditions towards the end of the first decade of the twenty-first century, many organizations are maintaining their faith in the future and are looking to identify, attract and grow their future leaders. Senior management development programmes, graduate entry, accelerated development, high-flyer schemes, MBA recruits . . . the return of fast-tracking appears to be under way in the UK. The promise of speedy advancement up the corporate ladder is being resurrected as a means of attracting and retaining the 'best' candidates the job market can supply.

Succession planning too is back with a vengeance, job adverts that describe development packages alongside the usual benefits are just some of the indicators of buoyancy in the market for key talent.

In this chapter we look at some of the difficulties relating to 'conventional' succession planning in the context of changing organizations and identify some possible alternative approaches from a range of organizations. Note that although I shall refer to 'conventional' fast-track and succession planning schemes in the past tense, I am conscious that such approaches are still very much with us.

THE CHANGING EMPLOYMENT CONTEXT

The employment landscape into which fast-track schemes are being reintroduced is changing in a number of ways. The increasingly international or global nature of many organizations' operations has cross-cultural implications for resourcing strategies for key positions. Another trend – the emphasis on continuing professional development – is now well established. This reflects the increasing recognition that the competitive advantage of organizations depends on the calibre and motivation of their 'knowledge workers' and their ability to stay at the leading edge of their field.

Even until relatively recently the impact of the knowledge revolution and its resourcing implications had hardly been felt. Now, employers are no longer having things their own way. This is particularly clear in the IT sector where the success of several organizations relies on the product development skills of a few key individuals. The truth of corporate value-speak such as 'Our people are our greatest asset' has been painfully evident when individuals move on. In the increasingly fragmented job landscape, loyalty to the employer is becoming a thing of the past and many organizations are urgently reviewing ways of securing the commitment of people whom they do not want to lose. This is forcing organizations to develop new definitions of who is a 'key' employee, rather than limiting the definition to those who have high potential, and the ability to reach the top jobs.

WHAT'S HAPPENING TO FAST-TRACKING?

'High-potential' or 'high-flyer' employees have long been thought of as the people with the potential to move rapidly up the corporate ladder.

> One expects achievement (performance) to be directly translated into climbing the organizational ladder: upward mobility is not only an achievement in its own right, but doubly so, since it is a negation of the alternative options: immobility (getting 'stuck' on the career ladder) or even demotion, if not dismobility (sacking) altogether. (Altman, 1997)

The assumption is that 'high-potential' people will carry on moving up the organization when those who are less able cease to progress. Most 'high flyers' are identified as such early in their careers, often at graduate entry. Other high-potential employees join organizations having obtained an MBA or professional qualification or having begun a fast-track career elsewhere.

Fast-track programmes, described by Altman (1997) as 'the conscious, purposeful process of grooming that individuals go through on their way to the top', have been a common feature of such corporate career management. Indeed the term 'fast-track' is attractive to many potential recruits to an organization and is designed to appeal to 'the best' candidates in the job market.

Of course, every organization has a responsibility to attempt to secure its future leaders and many now recognize that developing people who will supply present and future success is key. The degree to which conventional fast-tracking should be seen as the main means of achieving this remains open to question. After all, conventional succession planning generally works best when an organization's environment, market conditions and structures are relatively stable and predictable.

Until relatively recently, most organizations of any size developed succession plans for key individuals and posts in order to ensure a ready supply of individuals prepared for the top jobs in the future.

CONVENTIONAL FAST-TRACK SCHEMES AND SUCCESSION PLANNING

Until the mid-1990s when increased competition and economic turbulence led to a great deal of organizational restructuring, most large organizations were structured hierarchically, with as many as 12 management levels between the first-line supervisor and top management. Succession plans were developed to ensure that key senior positions had appropriate successors to the current post-holder, identified and groomed as potential replacements. Typically, succession planning for the top executives in many organizations is based on:

● Contingency (emergency replacement)
● Replacement (of one person by another at a certain time)
● Succession (employees who may be groomed for a post over a number of years)
● Development (of employees with high potential).

Often, certain key competencies, such as strategic vision and the ability to manage change, are regarded as differentiators for top jobs. The development of the candidates for those jobs is often carried out on an individual basis and is usually focused on remedying weaknesses and pursuing individual aspirations.

The assumption implicit in conventional succession planning is that most senior management roles can be filled from within and that growing internal talent is preferable to riskier options. The aim was, of course, to ensure that the organization had a small pool of potential successors for key roles, especially the top jobs, in the future. Consequently, alongside conventional succession planning, fast-track schemes were designed to accelerate the development of people considered to have high potential, enabling them to acquire relevant skills and experience on their way up the corporate ladder in the shortest time possible. Conventional 'fast-tracks' were available to the very small minority of employees, perhaps no more than 2 or 3% of the workforce, who were deemed to have potential for taking on general management or other executive roles. A slightly broader group, perhaps up to 10% of the population, would be developed for senior management roles.

Typically, the chosen few would be offered a series of 'broadening' moves, of real influence. Senior post vacancies would be checked with the succession plan first. Sometimes individuals were told about their perceived potential. However, such assessments often remained confidential to the Human Resources professionals and senior line managers responsible for making such career judgements.

In contrast, for most employees, advancement up the career ladder was more gradual. Promotion opportunities were often via the management rather than the specialist route, even in companies where 'dual tracks' had been developed.

Conventional succession planning was not without drawbacks. A critical issue was how potential was assessed and whether the performance of 'high flyers' was seriously monitored. Such judgements were often made early in a person's career, often at entry. Early assessment was no guarantee that people could really cope with more serious responsibilities over time. More often than not, once an individual was labelled a 'high flyer' it was unlikely that such opinions would be reviewed unless he or she seriously failed at some important activity. Similarly, people who were not classed as fast-track material early in their careers were often denied the opportunity for real advancement even if their talents later proved to be highly relevant to a significant role. If you missed the early opportunity for rapid advancement, you did not usually have a second chance.

Another common issue was the unworkability of succession plans in practice. Even in relatively stable times, roles with several identified 'successors' were frequently filled by people from outside the organization or the successors themselves were not available when the post became vacant. This became all the more apparent during the late 1980s and early 1990s with the ongoing downsizing and delayering of organizations. In many companies succession planning revolved around roles which it was assumed were critical to the organization and which were subsequently reengineered out of existence.

During mergers many roles simply ceased to exist, or individuals from the acquired company who had previously been judged to have potential were not given opportunities for political reasons. With the trend to flatter, leaner structures, many organizations gave up the attempt to plan for succession. Typically the function responsible for managing the fast-track processes, Human Resources, was itself downsized and devolved to the line. Fast-tracking became increasingly an anomaly. After all, in a 'flat' structure, where was a 'high flyer' to 'fast-track' to? With such issues unresolved, succession planning in many organizations simply stopped.

At the same time, employers are becoming more demanding and are upping the entry level stakes. The increasing requirement for most 'career' roles is a first degree at least and usually a professional qualification as well. But while it is obvious that there is increased competition for the 'best' candidates, what happens to new recruits whose expectations have been raised by the recruitment process is less clear. One government department hired a number of people with PhDs for relatively junior executive officer jobs. Not surprisingly, several of these expensively hired new recruits left months later when the reality of their employment conditions and prospects hit home.

DRIVERS FOR NEW APPROACHES?

A more adult–adult relationship between employers and employees is based on the increasing power of the knowledge worker to make demands of the organization that go beyond pay and rations. This is particularly marked in some of the oil companies where overseas assignments as part of a broad career route for high-calibre employees are becoming increasingly difficult to fill. This is partly explained by the rise in the number of dual-career families but also by the increasing unwillingness of employees to make sacrifices if they are not guaranteed promotion on return from the assignment. There is already a good deal of anecdotal evidence that employees with transferable skills and experience are more confident of being employable and less tolerant of the frustrations of poor management, inappropriate reward and few growth opportunities. Ironically, the very skills which many employers crave – such as the ability to get things done, be innovative, customer oriented etc. – are precisely the skills that will help people get jobs elsewhere.

Understandably, in times of change, the basic parameters of planning, such as knowing where the organization is going, the skills needed for the future and the resources the organization currently has, are difficult to establish. Planning exclusively around roles seems short-sighted in such circumstances.

Perhaps a more helpful model is based on identifying the skills and experiences which the broad business direction suggests will be required in the future and planning around developing talent at different levels in the organization.

RETHINKING WHAT 'KEY' LOOKS LIKE

An important question to answer when taking stock of current employees is who is key now and in the short- to medium-term future? The answer to that question may be different now from what it might have been several years ago. Similarly, organizations need to think through what they mean by potential and how to assess it. Some organizations insist that potential can only exist outside and hence rely heavily on external recruitment to resource key management positions. Often the tendency to rely on external recruitment is due to a combination of factors, including a widespread ignorance of the current skills of the existing workforce. However, such policies seem to have a largely negative effect on the morale of existing employees.

A more useful approach might be to widen access to such schemes to include internal people who might have missed the fast-track first time round if they appear to have the skills and attitudes that the organization needs as it moves forward. This is not a purely philanthropic approach. Both the cost of external recruitment, especially if the new recruit does not 'fit' and soon leaves, and the value of the often irreplaceable knowledge of existing employees suggests that fast-tracking should be a continuous, wide-based process rather than a scheme.

BUILDING THE TALENT 'POOL'

Increasingly, succession planning activities in some sectors are being extended beyond a small privileged group of 'key employees' to include a much wider group. In such organizations, succession planning is not restricted to the top jobs. The question being asked in such organizations is 'who is key?' in this era of knowledge workers and intellectual capital. This is largely driven by the recognition that, in many cases, the real assets of an organization are its employees.

Developing a Talent Pipeline in Nestlé

Nestlé focuses on building talent pipelines to meet a variety of business needs. Nestlé is a large global food and beverage manufacturer. Its aim is to manufacture and market products in such a way as to create value that can be sustained over the long term for shareholders, employees, consumers and business partners. The business focus at the moment is very much on nutrition, health and wellness and coming up with new products to meet countrywide trends, while at the same time driving down costs.

Nestlé's multi-channel talent pipeline aims to feed two broad capability requirements of the organization. First, the core capability pool is populated with employees who make up the larger portion of the workforce and have the technical skills and capabilities that are essential to keep the organization running. The second group of people is the high potential pool. This comprises employees who make up the smaller portion of the workforce who are considered to have sufficient potential to become their high performers and senior managers of the future. Each category is filled with a combination of existing employees and new recruits.

Recruiting and Developing Leadership Talent

A traditional objective of succession planning, the development of future leaders, has often taken place around specific roles. In some companies there are only succession plans and planned development for the top-level jobs and for people identified as having high potential. The trend currently is to develop leaders with a broad range of leadership competence in addition to any specific business experience they may offer. Leadership is highlighted as an area of competence in itself because of the changing requirements of business leaders to be able to provide focus and bring people with them in times of change. If the identification and growth of leadership talent is a primary objective, related objectives include the retention of talent and continuity of leadership.

Many organizations, including BP, GlaxoSmithKline and Texaco, have developed generic leadership 'competencies' which are used to define leadership potential and as the focus for executive development. Unilever uses competencies for the assessment of potential, for graduate recruitment, executive recruitment, leadership training, appraisal (performance development planning) and rewards. Texaco's Core Leadership Competencies emphasize behaviour-based leadership in addition to specifically business-related skills.

Campbell's Soups identify talent at departmental, country and global levels. This is based on an assessment of potential, not only performance. Assignments are planned to develop skills and leverage strengths. Many organizations now use assessment centres routinely to select candidates for fast-track development and competency models, together with 360-degree feedback processes are increasingly used not only for individual development but also for talent identification.

This is particularly the case in organizations that consider leadership development and succession planning as key tools in changing the organization's culture.

Global Talent Pools

Standard Chartered PLC has a structured approach to building talent pools at different levels and across many locations. There are regular business reviews on talent from Board level down to country management team and a global leadership pipeline is developed through a range of simple and effective processes. Outcome, rather than process measures are tracked. At the level of Country Management Trainees, locally tailored programmes are made available. International graduates are provided with two-year development through rotations and global programmes. Junior High Potentials are locally managed and reviewed in 56 countries. Mid-career MBAs are a strategic form of hiring which supplements the leadership pipeline. Middle management high potentials are reviewed by ten global leadership teams. Senior Management High Potentials are reviewed by the Group Management Committee. For more detail of Standard Chartered PLC's talent management processes, see Chapter 14.

When soft-drinks giant Coca-Cola was forced to look outside the organization to recruit senior marketing professionals, it decided it was time to establish a programme to identify the talent it had internally. Although the company already had a reputation for growing talent from within, in 2005 only 67% of senior roles were filled internally – a figure that rose to 93% by 2007. This was thanks to building an internal talent pipeline through the use of a development centre process.

In 2005 at a meeting of the global marketing people development forum, a quarterly meeting of marketing leaders from each of Coca-Cola's eight geographical regions, they identified a particular senior role – division marketing manager – as central to the company's succession planning in each region. The challenge was to make sure that the talent going into these roles could go anywhere.

The first step was creating a joint job description so that each region had the same understanding of what the role required. A global senior marketing leadership development centre was designed using a combination of Coca-Cola's marketing competencies and the company's core leadership competencies. Testing for this critical combination was based on reality, rather than a series of hypothetical situations. For example, there is a marketing expense exercise in which the general manager is asking the marketing manager to make choices regarding resources and budget allocation. There is also feedback based on personality preferences and 360 degree review. When participants leave the centre, they are given detailed feedback from a marketing leader and a coach.

Each event is held in a different country and brings together eight top people from across the globe in one place. As a result, marketing leaders from each area are able to see the calibre of talent internationally and there has been an increase in 'poaching' talent from one region to another, which is a positive development (*People Management*, 7 August 2008).

DEVELOPING AND UPDATING SUCCESS PROFILES

Leadership competencies are also being used to create 'success' profiles for executives, though some organizations have recognized the importance of encouraging a range of diverse talents within the organization through their 'professional community' approaches. Many organizations such as Nationsbank are using competencies as the means of developing executive success profiles for spotting potential and for development purposes. Increasingly, in organizations as diverse as Texaco, Unilever and Philips, success profiles are built on generic 'leadership' competencies as a means of bringing about culture change.

As ever, a warning note needs to be sounded: if leaders are to be capable of performing in today's and tomorrow's constantly changing environment, beware the limited shelf life of success profiles when business requirements change. Competencies must be integrated into the business planning process and updated.

CASE STUDY: THE ASSESSMENT AND DEVELOPMENT OF HIGH POTENTIAL AT BP AMOCO

I have retained this case study from the original version of this book as I think the business-ownership and coherence of the talent process described is impressive. Information is based on research carried out in BP shortly before the merger between BP and Amoco. However, numbers have been updated to reflect BP Amoco in 2001.

In a company with the size and reputation for development of BP Amoco, it is hardly surprising that the assessment and development of people perceived to have high potential should be taken seriously. Indeed, at a time (in the early to mid-1990s) when other organizations were giving up the notion of succession planning because the volatile economic climate seemed to make such exercises fruitless, BP Amoco stepped up the quality and quantity of effort spent on the identification of employees considered to have high potential. BP Amoco has long enjoyed a relatively stable workforce, with many employees still expecting to complete their whole career in the company. As such, BP Amoco has the opportunity for relatively long-range planning with regard to succession.

At the original time of writing, the person largely responsible for stepping up BP Amoco's assessment and high-potential activities at Group level was Dr Candy Albertsson, an American whose experience including working for AT&T stood her in good stead for her role in management development.

Prior to starting her own company, Candy's final role with BP Amoco was Manager, High Potential Development, where she provided the managing director with strategic support on a variety of issues including a review of BP's leadership talent pool, supply and demand for top 25 succession and the supporting infrastructure to develop world-class leadership.

Within BP Amoco, 'high potential' refers to the perceived ability to reach one of the top 100 jobs out of a workforce of 94 000. The majority of people who are thought likely to reach such roles are among the 25 000 professional and middle management employees. Before 1992, high-potential employees were principally the responsibility of a group-level committee with representatives from the three businesses (i.e. Oil, Exploration and Chemicals), the Regions and Corporate and focused primarily on deployment. Career development often took the form of a series of moves around the main businesses, acquiring different levels of responsibility and experience.

The limitations of this relatively basic way of developing future leaders were recognized but attempts to improve the process were not without challenge. One initiative was the introduction of Personal Development Planning to supplement the company-driven deployment approach to development. This introduced more of a partnership between individuals and the organization. People were given the opportunity to reflect on their career aspirations and short-, medium- and long-term goals. In some cases, people aspired to strategic, rather than operational roles and there was a 'reality check' against performance feedback to suggest whether an individual's aspirations were realistic.

The identification of high-potential employees needed special attention. Though graduate recruitment was, and remains, the main entry point for high-flying employees, formal assessment of high potential tends to take place at a relatively junior level, some four to ten years after joining the company. While talent can be spotted at this stage in a person's career, lack of line management or cross-functional experience may make it difficult to recognize undeveloped management talent. However, for employees who were not perceived at this early career stage to have high potential, the route to the top jobs was much more difficult. Candy Albertsson felt that only a junior level programme for identifying potential was wasteful of late-blooming talent. She introduced the idea and gained support for developing a senior-level assessment that would enable the identification of potential later in one's career.

Improving the Processes

Candy's objective was to ensure that the group as a whole would benefit from the effective identification and development of high-potential talent. Clearly, the challenges of winning the support of the top twenty business heads for changing processes which appear to be working well from a local business perspective required high-level influencing skills and credibility. Working with a small team of management development specialists, Candy set about creating the infrastructure for improved processes, including winning senior-level support. Key moves included the globalization of the junior-level Assessment of Leadership Potential (ALP) assessment programme to create one standard Group programme. This replaced four established regional junior-level assessment programmes. Other key moves were the introduction of a senior-level assessment programme – the

Leadership Enhancement through Assessment and Development (i.e. LEAD) –
and the introduction of a cohort review process for high potentials at Group level.

Following Project 1990 (i.e. culture change programme), an 18-month study
generated a set of nine leadership competencies which were used as a means of
providing a consistent approach to high-flyer development at group level. These
competencies were measured in a 360-degree feedback process. However, while
360 provided good individual development data, it could not be used to compare
between different people. Further data from the 360-degree process cannot be
aggregated and therefore it is not possible to assess the aggregate strengths and
development needs of the organization. It was important to build on the early
success of the new tools by building a standardized process and means of measurement across the group.

Candy believed in making these processes as transparent as possible, and the
competencies were a good start in showing people what successful performance
looks like:

> It is important to communicate to people what skills are required, and what the expectations
> of performance are in the organization. You need to provide a user-friendly way for people
> to measure. 360 is a powerful development tool, but it has its limitations.

A limitation of the use of 360 was that while each leadership competency
can be examined through a questionnaire, different raters, such as the individual's line manager, peers or direct reports, may not have had the opportunity to
observe a particular competency. Similarly, certain jobs may not provide the
opportunity for the job-holder to demonstrate that particular competency. When
views about development are being made based on incomplete or potentially
unrepresentative information, the drawbacks of the process need to be recognized. The LEAD programme addressed these limitations.

The LEAD Programme

Candy Albertsson set about introducing the concept for a new process for the
later identification of talent to supplement the junior-level assessment process
and to provide the standardized objective yardstick needed across the group. She
led the project team which started developing the LEAD Programme in early
1993. A key strategic objective of the programme was to gain quality data on
the main organizational training and development needs as well as an overview
of the talent pool within BP Amoco. Candy worked in partnership with a consultant, Joel Moses, in the design phase and the first programme was piloted in
June 1994. It was managed in-house and was once per quarter. The programme
was championed by the Deputy Chief Executive and high-potential committee. Participants in this process included employees of long standing, often with
twenty years' experience, many of whom may not have aspired to a senior level
role earlier in their career. The participant pool of about 1000 managers was
drawn from the top 1500 managers.

The LEAD programme was essentially an assessment centre in which all nine leadership competencies were assessed. It was intended to complement existing performance data rather than being seen as a pass/fail or ranking exercise rendering all other data redundant. However, the data which came from the centre in the form of a LEAD report were widely used and important. Development Groups including a line manager, a mentor and HR specialist carried out a 'reality check' on the assessment report. The report addressed each of the nine leadership competencies, plus feedback on style and approach. An important element was the in-depth feedback to individuals which went beyond the feedback typically covered in a performance review. LEAD provided participants with one and a half hours of development feedback from a line manager and there was a process in place to link feedback to action plans – the Development Group, which is described later in this chapter.

An important benefit of the LEAD programme was the development opportunity it provided for observers. It was critical that observers were able to assess behaviours as objectively as possible and to translate their observations into feedback. The observers, who were very senior line managers (i.e. the top 300), were trained in coaching and feedback skills and were required to fully understand the leadership competencies which they would be observing and evaluating. Key benefits of senior managers taking part in this skilled process were the positive impact on their own approaches to management and the further bedding down of the competencies from the top of the organization. Observers generally valued taking part in the process and this strengthened the base of support for the programme. This common approach to understanding what was required of future leaders provided a powerful tool which generated 'developmental blueprints' used by individuals, line managers and development committees.

How the LEAD Programme Worked

Each LEAD programme was run over four and a half days in two parallel teams of six participants and three observers. Delegates took part in a business simulation which reflected the environment BP Amoco leaders face in complex global markets. However, to ensure that there was a level playing field and that the simulation did not favour people with specific forms of knowledge or experience, the exercise was set outside the oil industry. The simulation contained a number of written and verbal exercises, including an in-tray. Actors were used for a situation in which participants were required to coach their 'direct report'. The simulation also contained a number of team problem-solving challenges on business, regional and group issues.

The programme was designed to measure leadership at strategic and operational levels by examining an individual's approach to decisions and problems, rather than using psychometric tests. Observers were trained for one day before the start of the simulation and then had a day's integration meeting in which they aggregated and reviewed their observations on each individual. The output of these discussions was an agreement of whether each of the nine competencies demonstrated by a participant was a strength, development need or weakness. Strengths are defined as where the individual demonstrates 'real power' in the competency; the 'development zone' is where the level of competence is 'probably sufficient for the individual's current level of responsibility but will need to be strengthened for higher levels of responsibility'; potential weaknesses are areas of limitation which could have 'significant impact' on their performance at higher level and are a priority for development. Participants received on-site feedback on Friday morning from one of the managers who had observed the process.

The written report which followed the programme consisted of a leadership competency profile and three to four written pages elaborating on each of the nine competencies, on development priorities and options. An individual's leadership competency profile could be compared against a number of development profiles identified for critical business situations such as start-ups, business expansions and alliance building. These profiles were developed from interviews with forty senior line managers and could be used to determine 'development moves' or 'ideal fits'.

Validating the Findings

One of the common criticisms of assessment or development centres is that there is a lack of follow-through when participants are back at work. Does anyone care or notice if someone has started to improve on an area of weakness? Is the information from the programme valid in the work context? Will information about strengths and weaknesses be taken into account when decisions are made about jobs? The LEAD programme attempted to provide a comprehensive follow-through from the centre, integrating with other existing processes and performance information to ensure that the data were used.

Following LEAD, all participants were strongly encouraged to establish a Development Group consisting of their line manager, an HR development specialist and a mentor. A minimum of two meetings was recommended and the aim was to enable participants to link their feedback to a written action plan back in the workplace. It is very easy for findings from a development process to be discredited or ignored if participants can say 'well, I'm not like that at work'. The development group's function was to provide the reality check for the data emerging from the LEAD programme. Ninety per cent of the Development Groups validated LEAD reports in this way, which was very powerful in strengthening the metric.

Once the findings had been validated, the reality check and action plan were permanently attached to all copies of the individual's LEAD report. The report was then available to Group and business development committees and was used for selection and development moves. The action plan was incorporated into performance appraisal objectives and personal development plans. Multiple comments could be added over time as development needs were addressed. As such, it was a living report (see Figure 11.1).

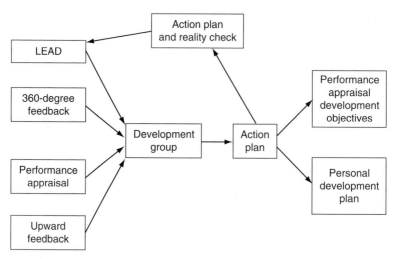

FIGURE 11.1 Linking competency assessment to development.

Identifying Organizational Strengths and Development Needs

Data on individual strengths, development needs and weaknesses were aggregated to provide a composite picture of the competency areas which needed special attention. This allowed trends to be identified and information which could be used to determine organizational training and development needs. It also highlighted areas within the talent pool where there might be issues or gaps. Candy Albertsson believes that no other tool can provide an organization with data of this quality and strategic significance, particularly since the top 300 generated the data in the first place. This information can then be used to proactively identify appropriate training and development solutions.

Succession Planning for the Top Jobs in BP Amoco – a Strategic Approach

An interesting approach to succession planning for the top jobs in BP Amoco is based on a structured, long-term assessment and development format. The 200 high-potential candidates viewed to have the capability to reach the top 100 jobs in the company are mainly drawn from the top 2500. A broader group of achievers are expected to reach the top 500 roles (i.e. Group Leadership), but development of these people takes place largely within their own businesses, i.e. Oil, Exploration, Chemicals or Global Business Centre. The supporting infrastructure for succession planning consists of a set of functional development committees within each of the businesses. These link into HR committees within each business which in turn link to the group-level HR committee (Figure 11.2).

Draft plans are initially generated by a combination of current incumbents' knowledge of direct reports and others and the HR secretariat for each committee.

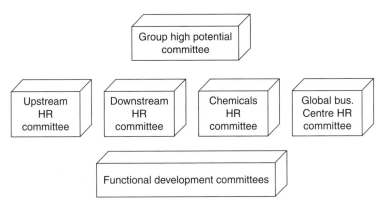

FIGURE 11.2 The supporting committee infrastructure in BP Amoco.

The committees then work to finalize the plans based on personal knowledge of potential successors and high potentials. This personal knowledge is developed through an ongoing annual review of all high-potential individuals. Each committee focuses on a different group of high potentials. Succession planning is taken very seriously by the business.

The high-potential population is divided into four groupings or 'cohorts' and these are based on:

● Stage of their development, e.g. their grade at the time
● Historical rate of progression, e.g. moving through the grades every 18 months as opposed to the norm of two years
● Longer-term potential, i.e. perceived ability to reach the top 100 or even top 20 jobs.

The four cohorts are grouped according to the approximate number of years required for individuals to reach the top jobs. Progress within cohorts is reviewed using a Development Checklist which summarizes whether a person has acquired all the key experiences for their stage of development. The checklist, prepared by the Group HR Executive support team, is easy for senior managers to understand and helps the review process to work smoothly (Figure 11.3).

The cohort analysis is done annually, with one cohort being reviewed per quarter. Only half a cohort will be reviewed at a time, with special attention being paid to those who will move in the next 12 months. Cohort membership is not static. Feedback about individuals is provided by committee members or by Dr Candy Albertsson using a structured process. Nor is the information concerning the review kept secret. Feedback on development and gaps has an impact on personal development plans and individual performance objectives. Typically, 20% move up in a cohort annually. There is not necessarily an even distribution between the cohorts. On a few occasions, a relative shortage of identified junior talent has prompted the high-potential committees to actively seek out potential

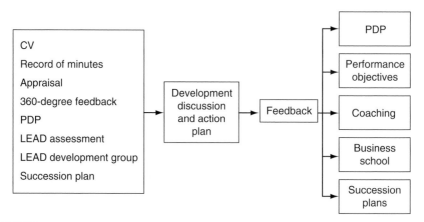

FIGURE 11.3 The cohort review process in BP Amoco.

lower down the organization. It is also recognized that telling people that they are part of the high-potential programme tends to encourage and motivate them.

However, the primary purpose behind grouping individuals into cohorts is that it enables more closely targeted development opportunities to be made available according to the individuals' stage of development. To reach the top 100 jobs it is essential that individuals are able to work across boundaries. They must have some international experience and have built up international exposure to reach the most senior roles. So for people in cohort four, i.e. 15–20 years away from a top job, it is considered important that they acquire some cross-functional experience. During their tenure in this cohort, individuals will be likely to attend a junior version of the LEAD programme, known as ALP and take part in the 'Stage 1' management development programme. Stage I offers a strategic overview of the business – the issues and deliverables within the regions. Participants meet with members of the most senior management tiers and gain a better understanding of their region. People in cohort three, 10–15 years away from the top jobs, have the opportunity to acquire international experience and cross-business exposure. They are likely to have people management and bottom-line responsibilities. They will also be invited to take part in the Stage II management development programme which has a clear group focus on business strategy and people management. For people in cohort two, 5–10 years away from a top job, there are opportunities to attend an international business school and the LEAD programme. In cohort one, with only five years before individuals are considered ready for a top 100 job, development is very individually focused. It is also expected that these senior managers will take a lead role in the development of others – by acting as mentor or an observer on the LEAD or ALP programmes. They will be invited to Group Leadership meetings and contribute to group-level initiatives. They are able to state their aspirations through the personal development planning process and their names start to appear on candidate lists. There is an internal job/people broker who networks their names with line managers and committee members, coaches high potentials on their development and builds momentum for a role change. Top 500 roles each have a candidate list of potential successors, categorized as 'possible', 'emergency' and 'preferred'.

INCLUSIVE APPROACHES – 'OUR PEOPLE ARE OUR GREATEST ASSET'

Of course the truth of organizational value statements such as this becomes evident, especially in knowledge- or skills-based industries such as IT, when highly skilled individuals who may not be considered top management material leave. This model of succession planning, focusing on people rather than specific jobs, is increasingly being adopted by British Airways. Other companies following a similar route include United Airlines and Campbell's Soups also recruits for talent rather than position. At a major insurance company, procedures vary according to level. All director-level jobs, for instance, are backed up with possible successors. Below director level, the process includes a wider population and allows for changes in roles. The aim is to build up a 'pool' of candidates who are being developed to fill positions at a given level in the organization. United Airlines has broadened the management levels included in succession planning by lowering the administrative burden through the use of client/server technology. This has enabled individual career planning and organizational succession planning to be better integrated. In the UK the Post Office has developed a succession planning system which aims to develop a broad group of people with senior management potential. This approach breaks away from the conventional elitist mould which it replaces.

One model of succession planning concentrates on identifying a discrete list of candidates who are 'ready now' to step into open positions, those who will 'probably' succeed and those who will 'possibly' succeed. The Dow Chemical Company is employing an approach that uses competencies for global leadership to blend these two models in order to have the 'best of both worlds'. The process is based on the identification of competency profiles for the top positions. The type of succession planning model used depends on the number of roles that share a common profile. The 'both/and' approach allows for both a more targeted approach to talent identification and development as well as the assurance of appropriate succession in critical roles.

Sun Microsystems UK is one company that has focused on building up a broad cadre of individuals with a range of current and potential contributions to the business alongside providing accelerated development for a few. Sun offers all employees the opportunity to carry out career self-assessments and access to a range of development opportunities. One of these, a career development workshop called 'Manage your career within Sun', helps people to gain a realistic view of their strengths and development needs, an understanding of the career options within Sun and, most importantly, a greater insight into their own values and motivations. This runs alongside high-flyer development in a conventional sense. The success of this approach in retaining employees in a highly competitive job market is evident in much-reduced staff turnover rates. Paul Harrison, Sun's HR director for Europe, Middle East and Africa, calls this 'providing career development opportunities for the top 80%'. This range of integrated activities and processes make it practically possible for employees to manage their own career, including making internal moves.

This emphasis on individuals' values and choices is very much in line with the current climate in which employees are becoming more selective about who they want to work for. Career development is increasingly becoming a more obvious arena for negotiation between organizations and employees. Fast-tracks that seem to offer rapid career development in a harsh and competitive organizational climate may be less attractive than they may at first appear. Far from seeking to whizz up a corporate ladder and take on yet more responsibility, some skilled and valued employees are now considering opting out of employment. Many companies are now offering senior employees various forms of flexible working arrangement including flexible retirement, in order to retain them. Increasingly some knowledge workers are looking for more congenial working arrangements in organizations whose ethos they can espouse. As one 'high flyer' said as she joined her new employer, 'at last I'm working for a company whose product I believe in'.

Fast-tracking then should become almost a state of mind as well as a development route. The 'fast' element should include opportunities to acquire the skills and experience needed by the organization in the short and medium term. One UK financial services organization has introduced a three-year structured development programme for a large group of existing and new employees of different levels and ages. The short-term payback to the organization is high morale among programme participants and widely applied learning. An international bank is introducing fast-tracking to accelerate the development of an international management cadre. HR staff are aware of the danger of setting up an elite and work is underway to develop career tracks for employees at all levels.

All fast-track processes need managing and individuals on such tracks need ongoing monitoring and support to ensure that they are delivering what was intended and able to make the progress implied. Some organizations make extensive use of mentors for this purpose. In Thresher, a change initiative known as the Operations Development Project, brought about shifts in working practices and job roles. New employees were seeded into the organization with the skills and experience to maintain and develop the momentum for change. Recognizing that such employees might be subject to pressure and frustrations, the Operations Director and Human Resources Controller took charge of the recruitment processes and continued to act as mentors and support to these individuals for two years or more. The individuals were not on a fast-track as such, but having the support they needed no doubt allowed them to contribute to the full. Most have now been promoted or internally headhunted.

TOWARDS A NEW FORM OF SUCCESSION PLANNING

In the days of conventional succession planning, the purpose of the process was to supply successors for key posts in the organization in the future. Often succession planning was seen as a 'stand-alone' activity which was generally considered the responsibility of a specialist Human Resource unit. The tendency was to recruit and develop high flyers in the image of existing senior managers, rather than identifying the skills and behaviours required of future leaders in line with the general business direction. In one financial services organization, the process of identifying potential through management development reviews was known as 'cloning'!

As succession planning is reintroduced, there are opportunities to learn from the past as well as to examine from scratch how to maximize the potential of such processes. It will be important to consider what is really required in future business leaders over the next three to five years and beyond, which may not be quite the same as in the past. Similarly, in the current climate of ongoing economic and organizational change, succession planning should sit within a coherent, flexible and integrated set of organizational development strategies. Just as Human Resource strategies should support the business strategy, so succession planning should be a key means of building organizational capability.

Conversely, if a holistic approach to succession planning is adopted, it is very easy to 'take one's eye off the ball' and lose sight of whether the processes are meeting the requirements. So with that warning note, an integrated approach, focused on building organizational capability to meet current and future business objectives, is the starting point for succession planning.

Recommendation One: Integrate Succession Planning with Other Initiatives

Link Succession Planning and Corporate Strategy

Among the limitations of conventional succession planning is the tendency for the planning process to be divorced from the corporate strategy and from what the organization is trying to achieve longer term. If succession planning takes place in isolation from the way the organization is going, 'successors' are unlikely to have the relevant skills and behaviours for leadership roles in the future. In devising new approaches to succession planning it is important to have a clear business imperative and be able to identify how the process must impact on the business. Of course, in times of change, developing a longer-term corporate strategy with clearly defined goals and management requirements is not always possible. Even a well-defined corporate strategy will need to flex with changing circumstances and succession planning processes will need to do the same. The Corestates Financial Corporation addresses this issue by focusing on its corporate vision, principles and core values rather than detailed corporate and business plans and so provides a focus for the development of leaders during a period of rapid change in the banking industry.

Link Succession Planning with Management Development, Leadership Performance and Assessment

Talent management activities should be developed in an integrated way with other HR policies and practice. So if what is required in changing industries are innovative, proactive succession strategies aimed at strengthening business success, it is important to tie together succession planning, employee development and the use of assessment instruments to enhance leadership performance. In Hershey Foods Corporation, assessment instruments can be used to assist in the candidate/job matching process. In the Post Office, career planning, talent review and succession planning are linked. AlliedSignal Aerospace integrates performance management, development, succession planning and reward processes. Texaco combines the use of competencies, the development of the 'talent pool', culture change and succession planning. For senior management positions in Texaco, the key to differentiating candidate readiness for advancement is through the demonstration of Texaco's Core Leadership Competencies. In Philips, leadership competencies are at the heart of an integrated set of processes which include selection, performance appraisal, development, education and training and succession planning.

Schering-Plough Pharmaceuticals review successor and high-potential talent within a three-year framework for management and organization development. Of course, in a short-term results-oriented organization, the benefits of an integrated approach to succession planning may need selling to the senior management team. Senior management attention is usually focused on matters financial, technological or concerned with market share. In a decentralized organization this task can be even more difficult, especially if the regional operations see no reason to 'share' information about high-potential individuals with the centre. In BP Amoco, the most senior levels of management are directly involved in the management of high-potential programmes, with the High Potential Committee chaired by the Deputy Chief Executive.

Recommendation Two: Be Clear About What Else You Want to Achieve Through Succession Planning

It is therefore important to be clear what objectives are being served by the succession planning process and for measures to be set to ensure that those objectives are being achieved. A few key objectives that appear to be complementary and achievable follow.

Workforce Planning and Development

A key objective of succession planning is the identification of candidate 'pools' from among existing employees who are ready for advancement. For this to happen systematically, a meaningful and effective system for talent pool review and development needs to be created. This will involve management development assessment and planning. For the process to be systematic, it will need to be against agreed criteria which are clearly understood and stem from business requirements. Data will need to be collected, analysed; decisions taken and plans made. The process will need to be monitored to ensure that the 'talent' identified is being developed and demonstrated in practice.

For the data-gathering to be effective, line managers across the organization will need to be involved, trained and taking responsibility for identifying and nurturing the organization's potential. Of course, this is easier said than achieved, especially in a decentralized organization where the benefits of business unit autonomy have to be weighed against the longer-term benefits to the organization as a whole of developing people potential as a corporate rather than local resource. As has already been stated, any planning system of this sort needs to be reviewed to ensure that it is meeting needs and moving in line with the business. It also needs to be as simple and transparent as possible. This does of course suggest an automated process to some extent but the decisions about the process should in every case precede automation considerations.

Workforce planning should highlight gaps in the organization's capability to deliver its longer-term strategies. Typically these gaps should be filled by judicious recruitment, both for specific roles and to build up the supply of new talent within the organization. Gaps in the organization's current capability can also be filled through management development. The danger in a rapidly changing environment is to assume that gaps can only be filled by recruitment rather than development, because development takes too long. This contingency approach to planning can backfire in several ways. Not only do new people usually need time to become effective in their roles, but if their 'fit' with the organization does not work, expensive mistakes can be made.

Similarly, a policy of external appointments for key roles can demotivate internal candidates, especially if they have developed the relevant skills for a key role. The challenge is to strike a balance by developing processes which aim to identify organizational and individual needs and gaps while creating short and medium-term solutions which include both development and recruitment. A happy compromise between external and internal recruitment to high-flyer schemes appears to have been struck in a UK retail bank. Their leadership development programme lasts for two years and the programme's aim is to develop the perceived potential of high flyers by exposing them to a range of learning and business opportunities. Recruits to this programme include a number of individuals in their forties, who have been with the company for a number of years and whose potential for senior roles has only recently been recognized.

Create a Lever for Critical Cultural Change

Of course, if businesses are going through change, they are likely to require different skills and behaviours of employees in general and of leaders in particular. Given the generally recognized importance of leaders 'walking the talk', succession planning can have an important role in developing leaders whose skills and values are in tune with the changing culture of the organization.

One financial services organization highlighted the problems caused by senior managers failing to practise the teamworking values which they advocated for others. The company in question attempted to bring about behaviour change by training senior management in leadership skills and using upward feedback processes. When that failed to produce significant changes in behaviour, feedback results were fed into decision-making about bonuses. Management behaviour soon shifted in the desired direction.

In Rhône–Poulenc Canada succession planning is linked to management development, organizational strategy and culture. In making these connections it is important to identify both starting points – by carrying out an audit of the current culture – and 'destination' points in the targeted culture. These should be described in terms of competencies or behaviours. The leadership competency models should be built around the targeted culture and assessment and development tools developed for 'high-potential' candidates in the succession planning pool. In Rhône–Poulenc, 360-degree models and psychometric tests are used, together with performance measurement data. The information gathered is fed into the succession planning system.

In a major pharmaceutical company, leadership planning is considered as important as succession planning. Through the Leadership and Development Review, managers are judged not simply on what they produce but on how they perform against the values of the organization. As such, the leadership planning process becomes transformational in supporting the business, not just a transactional exercise. Leadership development takes place mainly on the job and feedback from management teams is an important part of fine-tuning leadership ability. For leadership development to become a process, not an event, line Federal Express has created a Leadership Institute which conducts week-long courses where attendance is required as managers move into the various levels. Courses are also run on improving leadership effectiveness with a special emphasis on developing the 'soft' skills of leadership. A parallel process known as the Leadership Evaluation and Awareness Process (LEAP) is used to assess and prepare individuals for their roles as managers. The process allows people who are interested in formal leadership roles to put themselves forward and receive self-development tools and personalized coaching. FedEx leaders and performers are directly involved in helping other people to develop. This has produced twin benefits by increasing the readiness of managers for leadership responsibilities as well as reducing the turnover of front-line management.

Recommendation Three: Create the Processes, then Assess and Monitor Performance

Processes must be developed to track the performance and progress of those identified in the talent pool as well as systems for reviewing, refining and making changes to talent management initiatives in line with changing organizational priorities. The basic questions to ask when developing succession plans are relatively straightforward and stem from the Human Resource planning cycle as follows:

- *Selection.* Who are the right people to meet our business needs?
- *Performance appraisal.* How have they performed against their objectives?
- *Development planning.* What is their potential? What steps do they need to take to realize that potential?
- *Education, training and learning.* What learning opportunities are required to support their development?
- *Succession planning.* Who will fill our key positions now and in the future?

Ideally, a succession planning policy should take into account a number of key factors:

- The organization's external business environment and the market trends which suggest new commercial requirements and skills in the employee base
- Current and future business strategies and resourcing requirements
- Current and changing culture and values
- Defining key roles within the organization, together with the skills and competencies required to carry them out
- An assessment of the current employee base in terms of skills and competencies
- An assessment of the organization's future needs in relation to the number of employees required, their skills, training and overall makeup of the workforce in terms of background etc.
- Plans for bridging gaps.

The core processes are also relatively simple in theory, but more difficult to implement in practice for a variety of reasons. Typically these include succession planning being seen as a 'stand-alone' activity or as a responsibility of Personnel alone, processes becoming outdated or inappropriate and inadequate data flow. At the very least, succession planning processes should be developed to cover:

- Ongoing planning activity which assesses how well the organization is placed to meet replacement requirements etc.
- Individual performance and potential assessment
- Individual development planning.

Interconnected processes include:

Selection
- College recruiting – the 'milk round'
- Experienced new hire selection, including MBA recruitment
- Internal job movement

Performance appraisal
- Appraisal of job responsibilities and accomplishments
- Reviewing personal and team effectiveness
- Assessing the balance between what has been achieved and how

Development planning
- Assessment of potential
- Identification of development needs
- Career development planning
- Development action planning and review

Education, learning and training
- On-the-job development
- Educational and training programmes
- Learning groups
- Peer coaching
- Learning 'logs' and development portfolios
- Programmes to support organizational and individual development needs

Succession planning
- Identification of successors and potential successors for key roles
- Creation of development opportunities for potential successors

Effective collation of information

It is important to create a process infrastructure that enables succession planning to work effectively. There need to be simple and direct methods of assessing employee potential, for spotting opportunities to help individuals to develop and which allow for the integration of information from a range of sources including different forms of feedback. Increasingly organizations are using competencies as a means of providing a common language about performance. Information needs to be tracked and data kept up to date. Individual and job profiles must also be kept up to date so that effective opportunity matching can occur. A coherent set of processes is evident in Wendy's International. A suite of activities takes place which include ongoing disciplined job analysis, screening tools for success, assessment centres, Human Resource planning, individual development planning and outcome-based evaluation.

In United Airlines, the process of pushing succession planning down the management ranks is assisted by developing automated processes which overcome some of the limitations of paper flow logistics. This has enabled individual career planning and organizational succession planning needs to be married up more efficiently. Internal resumés are used to ensure that relevant skills are captured, together with candidates' internal/external history, future assignment and relocation interests. These can then be matched against selected management positions. Having access to the information online has resulted in streamlined reporting and improved staffing for vacancies. Many companies have a central function with a role in succession planning. In decentralized companies, the central functions typically attempt to collect information on key employees. In decentralized succession planning systems, a series of management committees takes an overview of the processes of development and succession planning within an international business group or location. These committees review the succession plans of each business unit within the international business.

The usefulness of any review process depends to a large extent on the quality of information provided by line management. Often, divisions are asked to supply the following:

- The strategic plan
- A review of the previous year
- Information about each individual, their performance, promotion potential and functions to which they are perceived to be best suited
- Details of past job and training history including current performance ratings
- Future career development plans, especially of high flyers
- Individual career ambitions
- Information on individual's cross-functional moves, including international experience
- Information on an individual's training and skill levels.

In BOC (now part of the Linde Group) additional data gathered includes what new jobs may be created in the future and who might fill them. The process is regulated by standard forms. Each business is also required to report on the strengths and weaknesses of its management, professional and technical workforce and produce an action plan to address problem areas. Companies such as Xerox use a computerized succession planning system for storing information on both staff and positions.

Succession planning systems should ideally be incorporated into human resource planning systems so that detailed planning exercises can be undertaken for any part of an organization. Employee information such as:

- Skills and performance profiles linked to overall business criteria
- Training and development profiles

Individual succession plans with alternative career/succession plans can be supplemented by data modelling to facilitate:

- Resourcing and job/skills matching
- Tracking of expertise and experience in key project areas
- Successor identification
- Identification of 'what if?' scenarios.

USING DEVELOPMENT PLANNING AND INTERVENTIONS TO ACHIEVE ORGANIZATIONAL SUCCESS

In a few of the organizations involved in the Roffey Park study, training and development planning for individuals are now more closely tied to important areas for the business. Assignments and project work arising from education and training are being taken seriously by senior management as a means of both developing high flyers and addressing real business problems.

In decentralized organizations people responsible for management develop-ment and succession planning face a number of challenges. One of these is how to identify and develop 'high-potential' employees in different regions without harming the autonomy of regional management. One of the ways of doing this is by balancing the short-term needs of individual businesses with the long-term needs of the organization. In some organizations, generic competencies are used for the identification of potential while the development opportunities are made relevant to the local business in which the individual is operating. When the ben-efits to the region's business become apparent, regional managers usually develop a cooperative approach towards taking part in 'central' succession planning.

Managing Assignments as well as Development in Place

In the case of international assignments, support may be required prior, dur-ing and after the assignment to reintegrate the individual and their learning. A number of organizations are now using mentors for this purpose, even when there is no overseas element to the assignment.

For most high flyers, development in place is likely to be the norm. Providing challenges and assignments to develop skills and leverage strengths should lead to retention. Development will involve continually 'raising the bar' and some organizations in our survey are identifying multi-sourced executive development opportunities. In some cases, organizations are collaborating on providing shared development opportunities for their high flyers. Such opportunities include secondments to other organizations in the network and joint working groups on industry-related issues.

Creating Key Management Ownership of the Process

Of course, relying on Human Resource processes alone for the identification of potential is not necessarily the best policy. It is important that line managers consider that they have a responsibility to spot and nurture talent as an organ-izational resource. Line managers are also ideally placed to assess actual per-formance and are a key partner in the objective-setting process. Engaging line managers from an early stage is critical to ensure that they are committed to organizational approaches to talent management.

Some organizations such as Schering-Plough Pharmaceuticals are now meas-uring and rewarding managers for their part in developing others. Training and feedback processes can be helpful in enabling senior managers to take on this role. Involving senior managers in assessing potential through assessment cen-tres, for instance, can be helpful in building up awareness and ownership of the process.

It is important that there is line ownership and senior management support for succession planning. Without this ownership, the day-to-day identification, development and management of high flyers may be confined to the occasional training or assessment intervention. It may be necessary to sell the importance of this to senior management and to garner support from critical constituencies.

A Partnership – Balancing the Needs of the Organization with those of the Individual

Succession planning has long been seen as an organizationally owned process aimed at securing the organization's future. Often planning processes have been held in 'secret' with the organization's judgement on employees' potential, readiness for a move and current abilities withheld from the individual. Development moves have been offered to the individual who has been expected to fall in with these plans. Our survey suggests that high flyers are becoming more discriminating about what they require from their employer and less compliant with organizational 'offers' unless these meet the individual's needs.

If the 'empowered' employee has his or her own plans, can succession planning hope to incorporate these? A number of organizations are attempting to meet a number of needs through their succession planning approaches. AlliedSignal Aerospace aims to meet the needs of individual employees, teams of employees and the organization through its integrated approach to performance management, development processes and succession planning. The NHS in Scotland aims to develop a coherent architecture of learning, experience and personal development at all stages of a manager's career, up to and including the board room. The framework includes learning support in the forms of action learning sets, mentoring and 'critical companionship' which is a helping relationship, in which an experienced facilitator (often but not always a colleague) accompanies another on an experiential learning journey, using methods of 'high challenge' and 'high support' in a trusting relationship. The overall purpose of critical companionship is to enable others to practise in ways that are person-centred and evidence-based. Some organizations are developing 'maps' of managerial careers to enable people to spot opportunities for themselves as well as gear their development to areas of interest to them.

In the Springfield ReManufacturing Corporation, employees are provided with a list of all jobs available in the organization and are asked to identify the next position they would like to hold. Training and development programmes are then built around qualification for the next position. Supervisors and managers track employees' progress and feed back results through individual annual reports. Similarly, managers are asked to provide a list of people whom they believe could fill their position. The management team then assesses whether potential candidates require further training before they are 'ready' for their specified jobs. This approach has led to the development of a pool of committed potential successors at every level in the organization.

The question of how open an organization should be about how a person's potential is perceived is often asked. The fears are that people may have expectations raised which may not be fulfilled, or that 'high potentials' will become more demanding if they know how they are perceived. These fears may be justified. On the other hand, if people are also made aware that while opportunities for promotion may be limited, other opportunities can be made available, the expected exodus may not be as large as anticipated. One FMCG company, for instance, trains its executive group in career counselling techniques. Each executive has a number of high-flying 'clients'. The objective here is not to promise rapid progression up the hierarchy but to convey the message that the organization values these individuals and is interested in their development. Being open with these individuals has not proved a problem, quite the reverse.

CONCLUSION

Increasingly, the processes used in succession planning and management development generally – such as individual development planning and 360-degree feedback – provide people with insights and information which inevitably help them to self-assess their potential. Involving employees in the succession planning process in an open and honest way may allow for more detailed, realistic career planning and lead to better retention. Adopting a 'partnership' approach with the individual should also turn succession planning into a validated process rather than a fortune-telling exercise.

Succession planning needs to be a continuous process, rather than an annual event. It should be focused on longer-term development and retention, rather than short-term replacements or emergencies. It should centre on what is needed, rather than on who is in place. It should consist of processes that overcome some of the inevitable inconsistencies in the assessment of potential. It should facilitate the removal of blockages and enable a healthy turnover in key positions. It should involve staff and create a pool of available talent at all levels in the organization. It should also lead to talent being positioned in the best place to meet both individual and organizational needs.

How can future leaders learn to both execute effectively in the short term and also develop their strategic capability? Simply moving high potential individuals around the organization at speed may not be the best way of developing them or assessing whether they do indeed have the potential to build sustained performance; in fact it may actually prevent them from developing and applying their skills in ways which put them to the test and improve business results. Members of the CIPD focus group recommend keeping high potential employees longer in development posts so that they can deliver meaningful performance before progressing on to the next experience. This not only increases future leaders' credibility with staff, it also helps to close the common gap in understanding between those at the top of organizations and those lower down the hierarchy about how to make things happen.

Even hardship can be developmental, according to previous research by the Centre for Creative Leadership. But if future leaders are to consciously learn from mistakes about what not to do next time a 'sink or swim' approach may be unhelpful. A DDI/CIPD (2008) study found that UK high-potentials are much less likely to get sufficient feedback about their performance than those in other cultures. Similarly, fewer UK high-potentials get clear communications about the importance of their development, and fewer describe their programmes as aligned with the performance management system. Some support can make the difference between success and failure and the development of multinational leaders appears to be a universal problem.

Providing deepening and broadening experiences such as participation in special projects and opportunities, linking up with international counterparts, should be part of the development mix. Development opportunities appear to be most enriching if they provide access to new, varied challenges, where there is a degree of difficulty in the task and where outcomes are important and highly visible, especially if success is by no means guaranteed.

HR specialists have an important role to play in providing support and guidance in the design and development of approaches to talent management that will fit the needs of the organization. HR will need to take on a facilitative, coordinating role as well as being able to design and monitor processes to ensure that they continue to meet business needs. To do this it is vital that they have a proper understanding of the challenges facing the organization in attracting, recruiting, developing and retaining talented people to meet its immediate and future resourcing requirements. They must also have the knowledge to advise the organization of alternative approaches to meeting its needs. This means that HR or talent management specialists must explore talent management practices in other industries to be able to advise on the best fit for their own organization. This is a significant responsibility given that the link between the quality of leadership and business success is evident in many organizations. In a real sense, the future success of the organization can depend on the way in which its leaders have been selected and developed.

While conventional succession planning and fast-track schemes may satisfy the desire for conventional career development for a few, any organization which 'puts all its eggs in one basket' is potentially leaving itself exposed longer term. Employee loyalty can no longer be taken for granted and our research suggests that promotion does not guarantee a desire to remain with an employer. More inclusive approaches to talent management can be used to enhance an organization's image: it supports employer branding in the labour market and provides a means of enhancing employee engagement to improve retention. It can also be a means of maximizing internal employee potential, which may be an even more effective way of gaining employee commitment.

A proactive, strategic approach to talent management offers considerable organizational benefits in terms of developing a pool of talent as a resource to meet identified needs. Fast-tracks can happily co-exist alongside other development routes. With respect to succession, risks can be managed and impact can be better assessed by growing a broad talent pool, and keeping high potential employees longer in development posts so that they can deliver meaningful performance before progressing to the next experience. Career processes which provide development, increased challenge and personal growth for all do seem to satisfy people and increase their commitment to the organization, for a time at least.

To be seen as credible suppliers of excellent future leaders, HR departments need to model the performance and good practices required of leaders. And the good news is, developing good leaders pays dividends. Not only does field study evidence (Barling *et al.*, 1996) suggest that leadership behaviours and effectiveness increase following training, the DDI/CIPD study (2008) found also that the companies that develop leaders well have high RoEs and profit margins. And – who knows? – by developing leaders at all levels, HR will be building corporate agility, reinforcing employer brand, creating better employee engagement and potentially winning the war on talent!

CHECKLIST FOR SUCCESSION PLANNING

Does the organization have the leadership for the future required to move it forward?

- How do we define leadership? How do we assess and select for it? How do we define the difference between managers and leaders?
- How do we define potential?
- What is our philosophy with regard to high-potential development – small or large group, or both?
- How can we develop people in such a way that they gain meaningful experience?
- What gaps do we have in our top management succession?
- How can we ensure that people with potential have a real development challenge and appropriate recognition?
- How can we ensure that the organizational needs and those of the individual are met?

REFERENCES

Altman, Y. (1997) The high-potential fast-flying achiever: themes from the English language literature 1976–1995. *Career Development International, MCB*, 2 July: 324–330

Barling, J., Weber, T. and Kelloway, E.K. (1996) Effects of transformational leadership training on attitudinal and financial outcomes: a field experiment. *Journal of Applied Psychology*, 81, No. 6, 827–832

DDI/CIPD (2008) *Global Leadership Forecast 2008–09: The Typical, the Elite and the Forgotten*. London: CIPD

Deloitte Research (2004) *It's 2008: Do You Know Where Your Talent Is? Why Acquisition and Retention Strategies Don't Work*: Deloitte Development

Some organizational references are drawn from conference inputs as follows

IQPC Conferences on Succession Planning, 5 March, 1997 and 21–22 October 1997

International Competencies Conference 15 October 1997

FURTHER READING

Grundy, T. (1997) Human resource management – a strategic approach. *Long Range Planning*, 30, No. 4, 507–517

Hamel, G. (with Breen, B.) (2007) *The Future of Management.* Boston, MA: Harvard Business School Press

Holbeche, L. (1997) *The Impact of Flatter Structures on Careers.* Oxford: Butterworth-Heinemann

Holbeche, L. and Glynn, C. (1998) *The Management Agenda*: Roffey Park Management Institute

Kaplan, R.M. (1990) The expansive executive. *Human Resource Management*, 29, No. 3, 236–247

Kotter, J. (1995) *The New Rules: How to Succeed in Today's Post-Corporate World.* New York: Free Press

Larsen, H.H. (1997) Do high-flyer programmes facilitate organizational learning? *Journal of Managerial Psychology JZ*: 48–59

Lewis, G.B. (1992) Men and women towards the top: backgrounds, careers and potential of federal middle managers. *Public Personnel Management*, 21, No. 4, 473–491

Marsh, C.B. (1992) Fatal flaws. *Executive Excellence*, 9, No. 1, 18

Oliver, J. (1997) The new look fast-track. *Management Today*, March

Phillips Petroleum recruitment advertisement, *Sunday Times*, 15 February 1998

Pomeroy, A. (2006) Executive briefing. *HR Magazine*, January

Raelin, J.A. (2005) We the leaders: in order to form a leaderful organization. *Journal of Leadership and Organizational Studies*, 12, Issue 2

Tubbs, S.L. and Schultz, E. (2006) Exploring a taxonomy of global leadership competencies and meta-competencies. *Journal of American Academy of Business, Cambridge*, Issue 2 , March

Van Gennep, A. (1960) *The Rites of Passage* (referred to in Altman, 1997). Chicago, IL: University of Chicago Press

Wallum, P. (1993) A broader view of succession planning. *Personnel Management*, September

Part III

Human Resources as a Strategic Function

Chapter 12

Skills for HR Strategists

HR professionals must have two things: business acumen and experience in organization diagnoses and execution.

Lynn Clark, VP of HR at Bristol–Myers Squibb (Strack *et al.*, 2008)

The role of HR is to help make business successful through great people and people management. Cost pressures due to increased competition, largely as a result of globalization, are driving the need for organizational capabilities such as greater speed, innovation and quality. These capabilities are delivered through people. This places HR at the heart of building a competitive culture and therefore in a leadership role. Yet many HR professionals now work at the transactional level even though they may be moving towards more strategic work.

So how can HR be more strategic? By delivering results within a strategic agenda is part of the answer. It is the business agenda which will shape HR roles and drive the need for HR professionals to continue to develop their skills and experience. The challenge for HR professionals is to decide where they are going to focus, and how to bring about change which is in line with what the business needs, even if there may be some short-term costs to the function.

In this chapter we shall consider what appear to be the key skills required to be an effective HR strategist, as well as some of the challenges posed by HR structures and careers for developing those skills.

HR STRUCTURES AND CAREERS

While HR aspires to be, and should be, a strategic function, there is not one model for the successful HR professional. HR requires many different people with different skill-sets. Over the past few years the trend towards generalist roles has gone into reverse, with areas of increasingly deep specialist expertise emerging. Many HR teams are now structured along 'Ulrich model' lines, with a small central function providing a strategic service, looking after corporate needs such as succession planning and culture change. The team at the strategic centre needs to be expert and influential, well connected with the business and the rest of the HR community.

When parts of service delivery, such as training and development, are out-sourced, HR business partners need to be skilled in the diagnosis of business needs, the selection of providers, the monitoring of quality and thorough evaluation. As business partner to the line he will require great interpersonal skills and an in-depth understanding of people issues. HR professionals also need to be skilled in the managing of supplier relationships, such as consultants and contractors, and at the same time must be fully in touch with the needs of the clients and consumers of these services to ensure that needs are being met.

HR structures are creating new dilemmas for the HR profession, and as HR roles fragment, and in many cases become more specialized, the challenge is how to develop HR career patterns which allow HR professionals to develop the experience and more strategic skill-sets required for senior roles. Traditionally the career path of an HR professional was to enter the field in some type of administrative role, gain expertise and knowledge in one of the specialist functions, such as compensation and benefits, and progress to the leadership level. Increasingly it is possible that most functional specialist areas will be outsourced and therefore it may be in consulting firms that people who want to pursue deep expertise in a given function will make their careers.

Increasingly a track record of business success, based on developing innovative and effective organizational solutions, is becoming the foundation stone for a senior HR career. However, since many HR practitioners are increasingly likely to start their career in outsourcing organizations where they will acquire a specific skill-set, they are unlikely to be exposed to broadening development opportunities. Arguably, high potential employees should rotate through HR; and the mix of experts on the senior HR team should be regularly reviewed. Developing an HR career will mean continually seeking out complex assignments, developing the innovation and organizational skill to bring all of the parts of HR together in a coherent manner to produce great results.

HR'S EVOLVING CORE ROLE AND IMPLICATIONS FOR SKILLS

Though there may be no 'one size fits all' with respect to HR skills, nevertheless there are several core skills which HR professionals, especially if they aspire to a seat at the top table, must acquire. For Wayne Brockbank (1997) HR's core role is to ensure that:

- The right people are being hired, promoted, transferred and fired
- Measures and rewards are aligned with short-term business results
- Individual employees have the technical knowledge to achieve short-term results.

These core activities alone require HR professionals to continuously develop their skill-sets. In many cases, HR is rediscovering traditional skill-sets and approaches, such as workforce planning and succession planning, and attempting to reinvent them for today's purposes.

Strategic Workforce Analysis and Talent Planning

In the light of demographic trends and as organizations continue to change size and shape, HR will need to develop new methodologies for finding the right number of employees and ensuring that they have the right set of skills. To be better able to plan for tomorrow's talent management needs, strategic workforce/talent planning is being reintroduced, especially in large organizations. BT is one company which places great emphasis on understanding the makeup and composition of its current workforce, its expected business needs and their implications for its future workforce.

Increasingly companies are also investing in analysis of key employee and customer data to be able to better pinpoint trends and identify appropriate actions for today's needs too, such as improving employee engagement and the links between engagement and business performance. The Royal Bank of Scotland, Royal Mail and Standard Chartered Bank are just some of the organizations investing in analytics to be better able to target HR initiatives to produce measurable impact on employee performance.

Employee Segmentation

In addition, being able to attract and retain the talent needed to drive success requires a deep understanding of the expectations of those talented employees. Employee segmentation techniques have been borrowed from marketing and are increasingly being applied to the HR product design process, especially with respect to employer brand approaches. This involves analysing data to be better able to understand the needs and motivations of key target groups and design tailored talent management processes. Tesco is only one of many organizations who are using employee segmentation techniques to improve their ability to attract and retain key employees. For HR, developing a marketing mindset will be helpful when positioning a company to attract talent.

HR Leadership Agenda

HR leadership is a mindset, and for senior HR professionals, HR leadership means having the vision and the skills to lead the HR function away from a 'customer service' mode to one which is more 'customer-focused'. Customer focus involves seeing the future first – thinking beyond the immediate needs – and doing it in the context of what will make the overall business more successful. HR leaders must also be able to manage and motivate a team.

However, HR leaders have the major challenge of focusing the energies of the HR team onto a strategic agenda. Deciding what should be on that agenda is where HR Directors earn their money. As we considered in earlier chapters, changes in the nature of work and the workforce, together with talent shortages, mean that the demand for skilled workers outstrips supply. Today's employees are more diverse, more demanding and less loyal than those of previous generations. Devising means to attract and retain key employees must be priorities for HR and are likely to include any or all of the following skilled activities: building new talent pipelines; tailoring employer brand propositions; creating effective work–life balance policies; upgrading the calibre and practice of leadership; improving internal communication; devising imaginative reward and recognition strategies. These will require imagination, innovation and skill on the part of HR as well as 'borrowing' insights from other disciplines such as marketing and finance.

Similarly, as organizations and their workforces change, so the nature of management will become more complex. As work teams become more multi-generational, multi-cultural and remote, managers will need to be skilled in inter-personal, strategic planning, political and alliancing skills. HR must find ways to support managers and help them develop the skills they need to carry out their roles, which in turn means that HR needs to have real business partnering skills.

WHERE TO FOCUS?

So if people are the major source of competitive advantage, where should HR focus to best contribute to building that advantage? Focusing on the 'right' prior-ities means being clear about HR's purpose. Wayne Brockbank (1997) suggests that 'if HR as a whole is unclear about its purpose, what can be expected from the rest of the company about the purpose of HR?' Brockbank suggests that the purpose of HR is reflected in the following criteria:

- Does it comprehensively cover the whole organization, thereby encouraging the corporate whole to be greater than the sum of the parts?
- Is it linked to issues which are critical to long-term corporate success?
- Does it create explicit and measurable results?

A CIPD focus group of HR directors considered the question of HR's purpose and there was strong consensus about what HR is for, and what HR needs to focus on. For them, HR leadership should be about:

1. Making a difference to the business
   - Supporting the business objectives of the firm by timely, intelligent and 'commonsensical' HR activities and planning
   - Identifying how to support implementation of business decisions across countries and business units
   - Developing integrated policies and processes
   - Making a difference to the bottom line
2. Strategic planning and implementation
   - Looking at what the organization needs to deliver (medium and long term)
   - Influencing the board and the direction of the company

- Developing the frameworks, policies and initiatives to move the business forward
- Thinking big picture
- Anything from not doing 'day-to-day' work to looking ahead three years
- Integrating future business goals/need with people issues/needs in a plan
- Clear thinking/policies/right direction/motivation of staff
3. Building the organization and talent
    - Ensuring that the organization has the right staff (skills, knowledge, motivation) to deliver
    - Creating flexible, broad business people
    - Communicating clearly to people about the things which affect them
4. Managing change
    - Creating a cohesive framework/common company language
    - Acting as internal change agent, with an eye on strategic business plans and organizational effectiveness
    - Making uncertainty manageable.

According to Brockbank (1997), a strategic agenda for HR will include building organizational capabilities for the long term that can help to create a 'broadly and powerfully defined culture which is (1) strongly customer focused and (2) capable of leap-frogging the competition through continual and radical innovation'. At the same time, the strategic agenda will set the criteria and framework for flexible HR practices in the short term which can be adjusted as conditions change. It will also have implications for the skills needed by HR.

WHAT DO HR PROFESSIONALS SEE AS PRIORITIES FOR THE FUTURE?

Strategic HR priorities will inevitably change as business priorities, the economic landscape and the labour market shift over time. The difference even a decade can make to what people consider important to focus on is reflected in two surveys gathering the views of HR professionals about future priorities. Back in 1999, a survey of personnel professionals carried out by Roffey Park and *Personnel Today* found that the following priorities were considered the primary workplace issues and challenges facing the HR profession by respondents from all sectors:

- Training and development
- Communication
- Performance management
- Aligning HR and business strategies
- Reward and recognition.

At the bottom of the list of future priorities were:

- Ethics
- Welfare issues.

Interestingly, some of the areas known to have a significant impact on employee satisfaction, such as career management, were then considered only medium priorities. The development of leaders too, especially the top team, was not considered especially important then.

How times change! More recent surveys place leadership development, talent management and corporate ethics and reputation at or near the top of the priority list. A 2002 study conducted for the Society for Human Resource Management (SHRM) found that the need for talent management has enormous implications for HR professionals. While talent management has always been part of HR's mission, a combination of demographic and market forces will bring new urgency to cultivating a workforce that offers true competitive advantage. There is also agreement that senior HR executive compensation and benefits, with the most senior HR Director often having direct responsibility to the company's board of directors for compensation, benefit and equity plans, is a key vehicle through which the HR executive can communicate their vision for the strategic role of human resources.

And in 2008 the top future challenges in HR identified by both HR and other executives in a Web survey carried out in 83 countries fall into the following categories (Strack *et al.*, 2008):

1. Developing and retaining the best employees
   Key practices include:
   - Managing talent
   - Improving leadership development
   - Managing work–life balance
2. Anticipating change
   Key practices include:
   - Managing demographics
   - Managing change and cultural transformation
   - Managing globalization
3. Enabling the organization
   Key practices include:
   - Becoming a learning organization
   - Transforming HR into a strategic partner.

So today there is much greater recognition than in the late 1990s that business is increasingly dependent on the calibre of talent and that therefore HR strategies to attract, deploy and retain talent are key to competitive advantage. There is also greater recognition that corporate ethics and reputation are significant aspects of the employer brand, and as such relate strongly to talent management. There is greater agreement that HR should be a strategic function as well as providing transactional services; that technology not only frees HR up from administration; it also provides the vehicle to leverage information about the workforce and equips HR to be better business advisers.

Credibility is also based on the ways in which HR professionals deliver organizational change – through systems and cultural initiatives – which support the business in its goals. One example of a successful business partnership is described in an article by Virginia Matthews (2007). In the article, Carolyn McCall, Chief Executive of Guardian Media Group (GMG) describes the challenges facing GMG of the impact of the digital revolution on the nature of publishing. Leadership development is considered key to organizational transformation. McCall describes how central talent issues are to business success, and what is needed for HR to make a real contribution:

> Our group HR director, Carolyn Gray, looks after the individual HR strategy of each of our four divisions and sits on our main board. She performs a strategic role with all our vital people issues. The issue of attracting and retaining talent – particularly in the digital age – is a very real one at GMG. I believe Carolyn and I have developed our succession management procedures well. We document, review and monitor succession in each of the four divisions in a highly detailed way. And that's a policy that is fairly new for this company.
>
> Aside from our transparent succession management scheme, we also have a regular leadership conference and various emerging leaders' programmes, both of which help keep us firmly focused on the issue of talent.

Similarly, there is growing consensus amongst HR leaders about the role HR must play in building organizational culture, and that the development and implementation of policy should not become an end in itself. These leadership priorities implicitly require that HR professionals can exercise the following skills and competencies:

Strategic Orientation

HR has to balance short-term requirements and longer-term organizational needs, focusing on local activities and also on corporate integration. This requires HR practitioners to be able to combine pragmatic short-term delivery focus with a more strategic orientation. As Carolyn McCall points out from her CEO perspective:

> In terms of the value of HR generally, it depends on who you get to do it. There's a danger that HR is seen as a functional department concerned primarily with procedures and processes that don't touch the business in any meaningful way. Saying your HR people are your business partners doesn't make them that unless you have HR people who are business-aware and immersed in your organization's overall business strategy. When HR people are concerned predominantly with pay or maternity leave, their skills aren't being fully used. But when they are genuinely immersed in the business as a whole, HR can work well and be highly effective.

However, there needs to be mutual understanding and trust between HR and the rest of the business for this to happen.

Organizational Design and Development

The broadening scope of the HR role and the more obvious focus than a decade ago on bringing about change has implications for HR skills development. Organizational design and development, previously part of the Personnel professional's toolkit and today more commonly 'owned' by executives and line managers, is once again being reintegrated into HR responsibilities. Building and maintaining organizational cultures which can become and remain high performing in fast-changing business environments should be high on HR's strategic agenda. High-performance cultures are characterized by highly engaged and talented workforces who provide products and services which are customer-centric, innovative and speedily delivered to ever higher standards of quality.

Culture building involves using a variety of 'levers' to initiate change, mobilize employee performance, strengthen organizational capabilities and maximize opportunities. A key aspect of culture-building involves recognizing what attracts and binds people to an organization and inspires them to do their best work. In the '100 Best Companies to Work For' Award (*Sunday Times*, 2006), high-performing companies with a strong business track record also appear to have a culture of authenticity. In the Award survey, these most successful organizations also have the best results from employee responses to questions about trust, belief and honesty. Similarly, corporate social responsibility (CSR) initiatives tend to be positively correlated with how trustworthy staff feel their company to be.

Finding how to build a culture of trust, mutual respect and engagement requires astute insight into how the organization works as a system, including its internal political dynamics, and knowing how best to intervene in the system to produce a positive impact. It means having the courage to challenge the status quo, including leadership behaviour. It requires the ability to gain insights from business, customer and employee data, and know where to implement initiatives which can unblock organizational barriers or release potential.

Global Mindset

Organizations of every sector operate in a global marketplace. HR needs to understand the dynamics of the global economy, and cultivate a workforce which is able to operate across boundaries, as well as being multi-lingual. Managing workforce diversity can be challenging. While companies may wish to leverage their global reach, issues at local country level may be quite specific and limit the capacity to capitalize on opportunities for the whole. In global companies centralized global HR staff should act as a communications hub for international staff – rather than as simply a policy or process setter. HR policies are best made at local level, especially taking account of the varying laws, practices and cultures, and within broad guidelines. For more details of Global HRM, see Chapter 14.

Business Skills

HR needs technical competence in specific disciplines such as compensation, benefits or training, but competence in these disciplines must be complemented by a deep understanding of the business and the ability to contribute on a strategic level. HR business partners can really make a strategic contribution only when they understand business goals and priorities and can create people strategies to deliver what the business needs. It is hard to be credible and relevant if you do not understand the dynamics of business – and your business in particular – operates, including its drivers and how it makes money.

HR must ensure that HR strategy is developed systematically – by analysing the business strategy, the external environment and the HR needs of the company (Strack *et al.*, 2008). HR professionals need to be aware of how the nature of their business is changing and make an honest assessment of the business challenges. There must be a good business reason for spending more on the workforce and this must be based on enhancing the top or bottom line. HR professionals need to be able to say:

- What's the business problem?
- Where can we add value?
- Here's what we'll do.

This involves understanding what's happening at top level, then working with the business to translate strategy into action, involving the line in understanding the implications of those changes for people. Above all, HR professionals need to listen to the priorities and issues in different parts of the business, and find out where people believe the business is going in the future. HR also needs to stay flexible and nimble, being prepared to continuously adapt structures, processes, roles and activities to the company's changing situation.

Developing this business knowledge may not be easy, especially if a practitioner's career has been exclusively in the human resources arena. The shortage of HR professionals with such business understanding and experience is so acute that many organizations are now looking to consultancies for strategic HR talent with the broad consulting competencies needed and also migrating operational managers into HR business partner roles, 'back-filling' where necessary with relevant HR knowledge.

For HR practitioners whose business experience may be limited there are many ways of deepening understanding of how businesses operate, such as:

- Having an internal job swap
- Carrying out a secondment in another organization (public/private sector partnerships for mutual benefit are encouraged by the government)
- Taking an MBA
- Attending management meetings or briefings
- Attending conferences
- Taking part in/leading a cross-business business initiative
- Taking part in business process benchmarking visits
- Reading industry and other trade press.

HR also needs to be able to develop practical metrics to measure their contribution to the business's strategic goals.

Technology Skills

Technology continues to reshape the workplace, as well as the HR function and the way services are delivered. Some HR roles are becoming more operational, requiring HR professionals to make technology decisions, understand process improvement and be skilled negotiators on a routine basis. HR professionals must become competent in using broad HR applications and their potential delivery systems. They must be able to apply this knowledge to the business planning process. Many HR teams now have specialists with deep technology experience; similarly some increasingly have specialists with strong financial analysis skills.

Credibility

Credibility is HR's most precious asset; hard to acquire and easily lost. HR professionals need to gain and maintain the trust and respect of their line colleagues if they are to devise and implement effective people and organizational strategies. Credibility involves knowing the business and thinking and acting as a business person first, an HR professional second. This means that the messages you are giving are more likely to be listened to and being able to use data and theories to make a case. It means being clear about how the business can build its competitive advantage through people.

According to Ulrich, credibility entails having a track record of success in HR's core role, making sure that short-term business needs and HR processes are effectively managed. HR is expected to deliver in its 'unique area of expertise' (Ulrich *et al.*, 1995). Of course, getting the basics right is what frees up HR to add more value.

Credibility is also achieved through knowing what your own values and beliefs are; having the courage to challenge and act strategically. It's about managing paradoxes and ambiguity, with integrity. Dave Ulrich (Ulrich *et al.*, 1995) describes an effective senior manager who took the risk of introducing cooperative work practices at the factory he managed, in the face of opposition from head office. The gamble paid off and performance was enhanced. When asked why he was willing to take such a risk, the manager replied, 'I've worked in other places before, and I may have to again'. This manager was willing to take a calculated risk, and take action, even though there were plenty of reasons to leave things as they were.

Ulrich also argues that credibility can be built by:

- Having earned trust
- Instilling confidence in others
- Having 'chemistry' with key constituents
- Asking important questions
- Framing complex questions in useful ways
- Taking appropriate risks
- Providing candid observations
- Providing alternative insights on business issues.

An important test of credibility is the perceived professionalism with which the HR team as a whole operates and the HR team's credibility is as strong as its weakest link. All too often HR is out of step with the rest of the organization, especially with regard to the use of technology. HR systems have often been developed in a piecemeal way over the years and very often different systems do not speak to each other, leading to duplication of effort. This potential Achilles' heel can lead to a loss of credibility within the organization, leaving the HR team open to accusations of not being able to organize the proverbial party in a brewery.

Credibility therefore involves building the capability of the HR team. HR throughout the organization needs to operate as a team and be a role model community for good communications and personal development. All team members need to be aware of the business agenda and how the HR strategy and their role contribute to achieving this. HR professionals must be equipped with the required technical and the cultural skills, including proactivity and flexibility. New technology should be quickly and effectively adopted, operating technologies improved and strategies constantly adjusted to customer needs.

Ability to Influence Others

In addition to developing a strategic agenda, HR professionals must be able to implement it. This is far less simple, since organizations as we know can have complex political dynamics that may make the implementation of what makes sound sense very difficult. One of the key requirements for successfully navigating a political landscape and effecting change is the ability to influence others. HR professionals need to build a wide range of influencing skills in order to gain cooperation without formal authority.

Professionals need to build good working relationships with different kinds of people and maintain these despite physical separation and lack of time. They must assess which are the key relationships which must be nurtured or started, whether these are at peer, management or board level. An active business partnership between equals relies on there being mutual respect and roughly equal, if different, sources of power. Gareth Morgan (1986) has identified many sources of power and influence within organizations, some of which are very pertinent to HR. These include:

- Formal authority
- Control of scarce resources
- Organizational structures and procedures
- Boundary management
- Control of knowledge management
- Ability to manage uncertainty
- Symbolism and the management of meaning.

HR may lack power in the control of decision-making processes and this area above all is where HR needs to work collaboratively with the line to ensure that decisions made concerning people are not based solely on a short-term agenda.

Even if HR is not at the top table, being able to facilitate and participate in senior management discussions, knowing what is important, using political judgement and having the confidence to say what needs to be said are all elements of influencing outcomes.

Kotter (1985) suggest four basic steps for dealing with the political dimensions in managerial work:

1. Identify the relevant relationships
2. Assess who might resist cooperation, why and how strongly
3. Develop, wherever possible, relationships with those people to facilitate communication, education, or negotiation processes needed to deal with resistance.

When step 3 fails:

4. Carefully select and implement more subtle or more forceful methods.

The political frame emphasizes that no strategy will work without a power base. Managers always have a 'power gap'; managerial jobs never come with enough power to get the work done. HR work can only be undertaken with the cooperation of other people, often large numbers of other people. Moving up the ladder brings more authority, but it also leads to more dependence because the manager's success relies on the effort of large and diverse groups of people. Rarely will those people provide their best efforts and greatest cooperation merely because they have been told to. If you want their assistance, it helps a great deal if they know you, like you and see you as credible and competent.

The first task in building networks and coalitions is figuring out whose help you need. The second is to develop relationships with these people. Kanter (1983) found that middle managers seeking to promote change or innovation in a corporation typically began by getting preliminary agreement for an initiative from their boss. They then moved into a phase of 'pre-selling' or 'making cheerleaders': peers, managers of related functions, stakeholders in the issue, potential collaborators, and sometimes even customers would be approached individually, in one-to-one meetings that gave people a chance to influence the project and the innovator the maximum opportunity to sell it. Seeing them alone and on their territory was important; the rule was to act as if each person were the most important one for the project's success.

Once you have the 'cheerleaders', you can move on to 'horsetrading', that is, promising rewards in exchange for resources and support. This builds the resource base that lets you go to the next step of 'securing blessings' – getting the necessary approvals and mandates from higher management. Kanter found that the usual route to success at that stage was to identify the senior managers who had most to say about the issue at hand, and develop a polished, formal presentation to get their support. The best presentations responded to both substantive and political concerns, because senior managers typically cared about two questions:

● Is it a good idea?
● How will my constituents react to it?

With the blessing of higher management, innovators could go back to their boss to formalize the coalition and make specific plans for pursuing the project.

The basic point is simple: as a Human Resources professional, you need friends and allies to get things done. If you are trying to build relationships and get support from those allies, you need to cultivate them. Like it or not, political dynamics are inevitable under conditions of ambiguity, diversity and scarcity.

Communicating with the Line

Churchill's statement about the British and Americans being 'two nations divided by a common language' might also be said to apply to relationships between line managers and HR. Stereotypically, line managers' preoccupations may be short-term, productivity-focused and mainly centre on their part of the business. HR, on the other hand, may be rather more concerned about longer-term or cross-organizational issues. Line managers' perceptions of the value added by HR may be influenced positively or negatively by company history, the use of HR jargon, as well as by the popular jokes made at the expense of HR, e.g. 'the department of Human Remains'.

HR needs to fully understand what the business is aiming to do and HR professionals must be able to present the business case for HR, using business language which ties in directly to business strategy and results. This means that HR professionals should be able to contribute knowledgeably to, and offer challenge in discussions about finance, marketing, sales, operations etc., and know how HR fits into the business's strategic goals.

HR needs to develop a clear view, with line colleagues, about how these translate into organizational priorities. For example, in many organizations the key priority will be relevant to develop a better talent pipeline and really effective leaders. In others the strategic aim will be to create more flexibility and build a high-performance organization. If the organization is inventing and implementing a new business model, the aim will be to change business cultures and working practices to support these. If the organization is planning to grow organically, the strategic aim will be to support the processes of creating innovative products that really sell. If the business aims to seize market opportunities and make full use of its competitive advantage, the HR challenge is to design an organization that supports the full and effective execution of the new strategy.

Similarly, HR needs to work through the implications of these strategic aims for the organization *as a system*, i.e. what will the new work processes need to be – and all the skills, resourcing and other aspects of organization which will be needed to align with the business strategy? In GE, for example, Noel Tichy and Steve Kerr reinvented Crotonville, where many innovative communication, quality and high-performance work methods such as Six Sigma had been developed. As a result, people became aligned to the GE's strategy and capable of implementing it.

If people really are the critical source of competitive advantage, getting other people to think strategically can prevent the trap of always working to short-term

agendas. For instance HR can initiate debate about some of the potential implications of external drivers on the resourcing requirements and cost base of parts
of the business:

> **HR:** *The nature of the business is changing. Government welfare reform means
> that the cost base will be heavily regulated. We will have to do things differently, prob-
> ably by reengineering processes. What do you think the impact on people will be?*
>
> **Line manager:** *We're not at that stage yet. Let's talk further down the line when
> things are a bit clearer and we're definitely going to do something.*
>
> **HR:** *I'd rather talk early so that I can influence the decision. It may be cheaper,
> for instance, to use labour based in India – do you understand the cost base and HR
> implications of using labour there?*

Consulting and Partnering Skills

Business partnering skills are really consulting skills. Whatever the longer-term
strategic direction, short-term challenges can interfere with business effectiveness if left unaddressed. Consulting skills help the HR professional identify real
organizational problems – the 'root cause' that may lie beneath a presenting
problem. They include active listening, asking the right questions and feeding
back to the management team. Using a structured consultancy approach when
working with business leaders can help HR to accurately diagnose problems
or opportunities as well as identify and implement the appropriate solution or
support.

A consultancy approach should also lead to effective delivery and enhanced
client relationships. It involves knowing how to negotiate and how to coach. It's
about developing buy-in so that a project can move through the organization and
have real impact. However, there are a few traps which are all too easy to fall
into, and one of these relates to the way people approach their respective roles in
the consultancy relationship.

Roles People Play

HR's role as internal consultant working in a client situation may vary according to the situation being addressed. Sometimes HR is the problem solver and
implementer. At other times HR's role might be 'hands off' as counsellor, coach,
facilitator or reflective observer.

Very often, in the early stages of a consultancy relationship with an internal client, the client looks to HR as technical adviser or expert for a problem
which the client has identified. Known as a 'doctor–patient' relationship, this
form of relationship, if it continues, can carry some risks. Even though this kind
of role can be tempting to fall into, since there seems to be an acknowledgement by the client of HR's expertise, one danger is that HR consultants can be

lulled into complacency and assume they know all the answers. If the client has identified the wrong cause the consultant must convince the client that their diagnosis is wrong. The client is in charge and may choose not to accept the 'prescribed medicine', causing a loss of consultant credibility. The solution itself may be implemented by the client group without further intervention from HR – occasionally, without further involvement, the solution may cause more problems than it solves. Worse still, the client blames the 'doctor' if things go wrong.

Another less than satisfactory relationship is the so-called 'purchase-sale' or 'pair of hands' where HR is used as an in-house contractor to deliver a service. In this kind of relationship the client has both defined the problem and the solution. Negotiating for a different solution may be very difficult if this is the modus operandi. Typically, in this kind of relationship, HR is treated by the client as a junior, non-strategic function.

Perhaps the most fruitful of all relationship types is the so-called 'business partner' or 'process' model. This is where both client and consultant recognize each other's skills and needs for mutual learning. Both the nature of the problem and the solutions are likely to be jointly identified. The HR partner will probably be involved in some way with the implementation of the solution. The benefits of the solution are likely to be both short and long term, not least in the nature of relationships and the trust established through partnership working.

To work effectively in this way requires good process skills and confidence to ask the kinds of questions that bring out the real needs. While there is a greater likelihood of meeting 'real needs' there may also be high risk and the process will need to be managed with integrity. Such process relationships take a lot of time and commitment and, because of the 'fuzziness' of the kinds of problems to be solved, they may be harder to budget. For clients, the process may be uncomfortable at times and will require real objectivity to recognize where the problems exist. However, clients will usually achieve a workable solution from process consultancy, as well as new skills for themselves.

The Consultancy Cycle

The classic consultancy cycle consists of:

- Gaining entry – relationship building and establishing rapport, deciding to become involved, determining who is the primary client
- Contracting – sharing expectations, defining roles and responsibilities, setting ground rules, creating trust
- Diagnosing the need – identifying the perceived requirement, collecting data, determining the client group and exploring limits
- Identifying options – determining resources and timescales, identifying a range of options and possible outcomes
- Implementing strategy – deciding on the strategy and methods, taking action, measuring, monitoring and being open to change
- Evaluating the outcome(s) – learning from experience, disengaging.

The ability to work effectively within this cycle depends to a large extent on the consultant's expertise, experience, ability to influence, and willingness to influence. In managing strategic change, the HR consultant has to be receptive to the organization's outer context, leadership behaviour and imprecise visions. The HR professional has to be skilled in the art of clarifying those fuzzy visions and providing feedback to top managers and others.

Gaining Entry

HR strategists need to talk with business leaders on an ongoing basis about what's happening and how will this affect their business. This regular dialogue helps identify when there are particular short-term issues which need to be addressed and also when and how to win support for a larger initiative which may have longer-term pay-back. In the Roffey Park/*Personnel Today* survey of Personnel professionals (1999) the ability to influence key decision-makers was recognized as important by 91% of respondents. However, only 62% of respondents felt that this was an area of strength for them.

One of the most effective ways of influencing senior managers is by exploring the people implications of business issues in business language and staying focused on business issues that matter:

- What's keeping business leaders up at night?
- What's the 'moose on table'?
- What drives the bottom line?
- How are you going to do X, given the competition?

It's about pinpointing crucial decision points and working through with executives the implications in terms of organization, e.g. what does it take to be a global company/what phase we're in/options for organic business growth versus acquisition strategies? Then it's about agreeing the focus: 'This is what you are telling me we ought to be addressing. Do you agree?'

Getting buy-in from business leaders for an HR/OD initiative can be tricky if their focus is only on short-term performance and business results, or even if they'll have job next month. The challenge then is to test business leaders' willingness to act:

- Do we have an organization that is designed to support the strategy? (If we don't change anything, results won't change.)

Using data effectively can be the most powerful means of persuading managers to a course of action, especially if you let them draw out some of the inferences from the data themselves. So, for example, when they see that there is a numerical shortfall of certain types of skills needed to implement a key strategic initiative in the short–medium term, they are much more likely to support the need for recruitment, development and succession-planning. Working in these ways helps transform relationships.

Diagnosing Needs

HR professionals need to be able to use analytical, diagnostic and problem-solving skills to help them assess correctly the perceptions, goals and stakes of different people. This is about gathering key employee, customer and other data relevant to the presenting issue. It's about using HR data and other management information in ways that get business leaders excited and not getting pulled/pushed back into old HR box. For example, how do the findings of an employee attitude survey link with business leaders' results and help them do their job better?

Diagnosis involves making sense of the data which has been gathered in order to find the best solution. The most effective way of creating an accurate picture is by working through the diagnosis with the line client.

It can be helpful to use models to structure your thinking and a range of analytical techniques such as fishbone diagrams, Pareto analysis and cause-and-effect diagrams are widely used. Some internal consultants increasingly use systems analysis tools to help make sense of the complex interdependencies within problem areas. Various congruence models such as the Seven S, Burke-Litwin and Nadler's Congruence models are useful in carrying out gap analyses.

But diagnosis is not just a purely analytical process; it is also a highly intuitive one. HR professionals must be capable of seeing the subtle interdependencies in each situation, identifying the implications of this diagnosis and then making decisions and implementing solutions effectively.

Once the system has been identified, finding both the causes and the problem's potential solutions is usually straightforward. Brainstorming and other creative techniques are used to generate possible solutions.

Sometimes clients may believe they have found the solution without the need for a diagnostic process, and indeed, this may be the case. If so, HR's role is to help the client think through any implementation or risk issues and provide support and encouragement. HR also needs to be prepared to challenge if they do not agree with the client's analysis of the problem and proposed solution. It is important to be clear about what would work better: 'Let me understand why … Help you be a better client …, What I'm concerned about as your BP is getting something that will work'; 'It's not as easy as you think'; 'It is as important as . . .'; 'We need to commit time and energy to make this right solution.'

If you meet resistance from business partners, it's about finding alternatives and making a personal investment in advocating these if you believe strongly that a better way must be found. The language used should be collaborative: 'Let me tell you why I support this idea …You have a different point of view … Let me share my reality and hear more about you.' It's about spelling out mutual responsibilities in the partnership: 'I don't think that makes sense in this setting and this is why. Let's work together to develop a solution which incorporates my view and your view.' HR also needs to be able to facilitate senior executive discussions and bring back differences of view for further discussion.

Making Things Happen

Identifying needs and solutions is not enough. Sometimes HR needs to be directly involved in implementing the proposed solution. Effective and timely delivery requires good planning and project management skills. Delivering the right solution may mean establishing one or several streams of work, involving a number of people. HR professionals therefore need to be excellent time managers, who are able to prioritize and reprioritize as need be. Project management disciplines are essential, together with good teamworking and communication with the line client. Delivering on time and within budget is key. Then it is vital to measure if the HR intervention has had the required impact or not so that we know if we're contributing to results.

As HR professionals who took part in the Roffey Park/*Personnel Today* survey suggest, implementation is hampered by the following:

HR is spread too thinly	
Agree strongly or slightly	63%
HR is too reactive	
Agree strongly or slightly	61%
HR spends too much time on trivial matters	
Agree strongly or slightly	60%

Implementation may require significant change management, especially with regard to culture change. This is one of the most important elements of the strategic HR role and will be the subject of Chapter 15. In the Roffey Park/*Personnel Today* survey of Personnel professionals, managing change and culture change ability were regarded as key by 83% of respondents. However, they were also the area of greatest perceived weakness, with only 41% feeling that they had strengths in managing cultural change.

Case Study: Building a Culture of Customer Excellence at BUPA Care Homes[1]

This case study outlines how the HR team at BUPA Care Homes responded to market intelligence, recognized critical customer needs, identified an appropriate organizational solution, delivered this in ways which were measurable, and integrated the benefits into the broader HR processes to create 'the way we (now) do things around here'.

BUPA Care Homes was the overall winner of the CIPD People Management Award in 2006. The question 'What's your personal best?' may sound as if it belongs on the sports field, but it's one that's now asked every day at BUPA care

---

1. The following case study is reproduced from *People Management*, 9 November 2006, with permission (Phillips, 2006).

homes across the country. Like athletes, care workers are rewarded with certificates and badges, but a ground-breaking experiential learning programme has also encouraged them to achieve new personal bests by improving their customers' lives.

BUPA Care Homes' customer service programme – 'Personal Best' – has enabled staff in its 298 homes to 'go the extra mile' in order to understand residents' needs. It has also helped them to develop the skills needed to offer a service that's tailored to the individual. But it was the way the programme succeeded in integrating staff development with the business agenda that made BUPA Care Homes overall winner of the 2006 CIPD People Management award, as well as category winner for Improving Business Performance through Engaging Staff.

The Need

It all started in 2003 after customer surveys started to show a decline in satisfaction levels. 'We knew we had to improve things to be ahead of our competitors but we didn't want any old training programme – we wanted to inspire our staff,' says Anne Smith, head of service development at BUPA Care Services, the subsidiaries of which include BUPA Care Homes. 'We needed something really, really powerful in order to engage our staff,' adds James Clegg, BUPA Care Services' head of people development. The challenge was not only to build a new customer service ethic, but also to embed it in people's behaviour.

The Constraints

But the round-the-clock nature of the business presented a problem: since the elderly residents of the care homes could not be left alone and continuity of carers was pivotal to their happiness, it was difficult to take staff out of the workplace for lengthy training sessions.

'When we went out for tender to training providers at first we were told it would not be able to happen if we could not take people off the floor,' recalls Julia Hurst, HR director of BUPA Care Services. 'We also had to ask: how do you join almost 300 separate homes together, and make staff feel part of the same organization and recognize the fantastic job they are doing?'

Programme Objectives

LIVE, the provider that won the tender, devised a customer care programme to meet these challenges, and to cover all 25 000 employees of BUPA Care Homes. Designed to change staff behaviour, increase understanding of what residents wanted and create a more customer-focused business, the Personal Best programme aimed ultimately to improve residents' experiences.

'Our research shows that staff attitudes and behaviours are fundamentally important to our residents. Personalized service is what the customer really wants and you can only get this through the behaviours of staff,' says Anne Smith. The research she mentions had identified empathy, reliability, responsiveness and reassurance as especially important to care home residents, and the Personal Best programme focused on developing these qualities.

The Programme

The programme consisted of three learning modules scheduled over a four-week period, followed by an implementation and review phase, all of which took place in the care homes themselves. Managers, who delivered the modules using guidance notes and supporting materials produced by LIVE, could also adjust the timetable to meet the needs of each home. Experiential learning activities proved central to the programme's success. Carol Purdy, home manager at St George's Nursing Home in Cobham, says one of the most powerful activities involved care home workers taking on the role of residents in order to see life through their customers' eyes. That gave them the chance to find out what it felt like to be fed puréed food and to be hoisted by a mechanical sling from a chair into a bed – 'quite a frightening experience', according to one care worker.

As a result of these experiences, staff now sit at the same level as residents during meal times, take their time to load the fork with a mixture of food and make sure they give eye contact. They also take residents through the hoisting procedure and do it more slowly.

While this part of the programme has taught staff to appreciate the importance of providing both physical care and emotional support, there have also been knock-on effects. These include a wider choice of food, improved team-working, and the introduction of more customer-focused 'hoisting' training.

Another of the programme's modules was designed to make staff think about what makes great service. They were told to identify three different service experiences that they had during one week, for example in shops, restaurants, banks or when making a telephone enquiry, to see what techniques they should and should not use with their own customers. 'Our staff soon began to realize the importance of things like presentation when setting the table at mealtimes and the benefits of effective telephone skills,' Carol Purdy explains. Care workers were also tasked with finding out more about their customers. Each employee had to spend a minimum of 30 minutes with a resident and ask questions about their past, present and future. 'They really got to know residents even better by finding out how they grew up and what their values are. We couldn't believe it when we found out one of our ladies was one of the first women to do a parachute jump,' says Smith. Employees also learned to identify the personal needs of their customers, as well as their own strengths and development needs.

Recognition

At the end of the programme each member of staff had to produce an individual Personal Best plan, specifying the actions that he or she would take in the future. 'The programme has given every single member of staff an opportunity to shine and feel that they make a contribution. Everyone can see where they fit in and engage with the organization,' says James Clegg. 'The programme has also created an obsession for individual service that I have never seen before.' The result of staff striving to achieve their 'personal bests' has been a stream of new initiatives.

Examples include: a resident with dementia now has her nails painted each week; another resident who had kept livestock all his life is able to keep chickens in the home's garden; laundry staff can sit and talk to residents in their rooms while mending clothes; and maintenance men have had time freed up to spend simply chatting with the male residents. Anyone within or outside the organization can nominate an employee for doing his or her personal best and that person is awarded a Personal Best badge. Three nominations result in both a bronze badge and nomination to a BUPA-wide awards scheme.

'The programme has given both us, as an employer, and our customers the ability to recognize people who do their personal best and to say well done. Our staff were unsung heroes and it has given us the ability to recognize our people for the fantastic job they do,' says Julia Hurst.

Integration with Other Key Processes

Other key people processes such as induction, supervision and performance management have also been reviewed to ensure they reinforce Personal Best behaviour. Since the success of the programme rests largely on the way in which home managers deliver its message, BUPA Care Homes has now introduced a 'managing Personal Best' programme which all line managers have to go through. This two-day training event explains how managers can launch Personal Best, how they can keep it alive and where to find support. A series of customer-service skills training modules has also been developed to complement the Personal Best programme and its behaviours and service standards. This gives staff access to training in areas such as handling concerns and complaints, effective writing and telephone skills, and teamworking.

Creating a Joined-Up Customer-Focused Organization

One of the most striking aspects of Personal Best is the sheer scale of it. The programme was designed to involve all employees, including those in central and regional support roles, as well as homes, and uptake has now reached 79% of the workforce. This in turn has created an organization that is more 'joined up' than it was and seems to have achieved that most elusive of goals – a real culture change. As Anne Smith puts it: 'The difference in the way homes feel and staff behave is most significant. Previously, we provided a more homogenous, less personalized service.' Residents appear to appreciate this change, with 69% now rating the service as 'excellent' or 'very good' – the highest score ever. In addition, staff turnover has gone down 3% in the past year, while the satisfaction rate is now 84.9% – up from 77.7% in 2004. Most impressively, 2005 saw BUPA Care Homes' best financial results to date, which were 25% up on the previous year.

One significant challenge still lies ahead for the organization, since satisfaction levels among the relatives of care home residents have not gone up to the same extent as those of the residents themselves. However, Anne Smith is confident that the next round of customer surveys will show that relatives are becoming more satisfied as they see the improvements in residents' quality of life. As Julia Hurst admits, 'Personal Best is ultimately about encouraging people to behave in a certain way to improve customer service. The programme has created an obsession for individual service that I have never seen before.'

CONCLUSION

At the current time, one measure of success for HR is whether line managers are working in tandem with HR and turning to HR for support and input when crafting business strategy. This only happens if HR as a function has established credibility through delivering operational excellence, managing change and in developing a strategic HR agenda. Looking ahead, the challenge for HR is to balance both long- and short-term agendas. Tyson and Fell (1995) have analysed several features of HR in the future which suggest that there will still be a need for the operational, largely technical role which is 'financially adequate and apolitical'. They believe that a range of specialists whose affinity is to a network rather than to an employer will emerge, leaving the client line manager as the policy interpreter. They predict that 'there will be a considerable number of HR seats at top tables' but that their occupants will increasingly be drawn from a variety of backgrounds. This means that HR professionals will need to be rigorous in raising the standards of delivery by the HR function.

They will also need to take their own development seriously and avoid the 'cobbler's child' syndrome. They will need to broaden their experience – of other parts of business and other organizations – if they are to gain the necessary experience for more strategic roles.

HR professionals must make development a continuous process, especially since HR roles and careers are changing shape. So, develop your networking skills, understand how to identify the right partnerships and alliances and how to nurture and develop them. Look outside of your own business, sector or industry type to learn good practice from others.

Then focus on building good business acumen: understand business modelling and identify the best business model for each business case. Build knowledge about key future issues in business markets by attending seminars, reading the financial press and taking part in scenario-building activities. Understand how business models and ownership structures are likely to change in nature and what this will mean in terms of business structures. Learn from successful global organizations how to cope with cultural differences. Pursue professional and business qualifications and gain exposure to other business disciplines through project work and strategic management programmes. These activities will all help achieve a well-rounded business knowledge base and skill-set. Add to that the specialist professional knowledge required for a strong foundation.

Above all, HR professionals will need the skills of conceptualizing and delivering on the agenda for the human side of the business which will build their organization's competitive advantage. For Jeffrey Pfeffer (1992), 'Innovation and change in almost any arena requires the skill to develop power, and the willing-ness to employ it to get things accomplished'. Or, in the words of a local radio newscaster, 'If you don't like the news, go out and make some of your own.'

CHECKLIST FOR STRATEGIC HR PRACTITIONERS

- Do we have the right HR structure for this organization's short- and medium-term needs?
- Is the HR team aligned to the business strategy?
- How well are HR strategies integrated with the work of other functions?
- Are HR team members measured and rewarded for their contribution to the delivery of strategic initiatives?
- Do we have a clear mandate from the management group?
- What is the quality and calibre of HR staff, both individually and collectively?
- Does HR operate as a team? What skills does the team need to develop?
- Do team members think, act and speak like business people?
- How good are we at process consultancy?
- What parts of the HR agenda do we need to get under control?
- Have we established a set of internal service standards, performance guaran-tees and ongoing satisfaction measurement programmes?
- Do we operate to total quality practices?
- With whom does the HR team need to develop relationships?
- How good are the relationships the team has developed within the business?
- How much do we involve line managers from other departments in the development of HR plans?
- How much is the HR team involved in the development of strategic HR plans?
- Do we have a regular schedule of meetings between the senior HR profes-sionals and business heads?
- Are we able to use data in a concise form to show each senior manager how HR's efforts can benefit their business units?
- Do we have plans to educate employees about the role of HR?

REFERENCES

Brockbank, W. (1997) HR's future on the way to a presence. *Human Resource Management*, Spring, 36, No. 1, 65–69

Kanter, R. M. (1983) *The Change Masters: Corporate Entrepreneurs at Work*. London: Routledge

Kotter, J. (1985) *Power and Influence – Beyond Formal Authority*. New York: Macmillan

Kotter, J. (1988) *The Leadership Factor*. New York: Free Press

Matthews, V. (2007) What keeps CEOs awake at night? *Personnel Today*, 22

Pfeffer, J. (1992) *Managing Power*. Cambridge, MA: Harvard Business School Press

Phillips, L. (2006) BUPA stars. *People Management*, 9 November

Strack, R. et al. (2008) *Creating People Advantage: How to Address HR Challenges Worldwide through 2015*: Boston Consulting Group and World Federation of Personnel Management Associations

Tyson, S. and Fell, A. (1995) A focus on skills, not organizations. *People Management*, 19 October

Ulrich, D., Brockbank, W., Yeung, A. K. and Lake, D. G. (1995) Human resource competencies: an empirical assessment. *Human Resource Management*, Winter, 34: 473–495.

FURTHER READING

Galford, R. (1998) Why doesn't this HR department get any respect? *Harvard Business Review*, Mar–Apr

Schein, E.H. (1988) *Process Consultation,* Volume 1. Addison Wesley

Chapter 13

Working Across Boundaries

Because the boundaryless organization is a living continuum, not a fixed state, the ongoing management challenge is to find the right balance of boundaryless behavior, to determine how permeable to make boundaries, and where to place them.

(Ashkenas *et al.*, 1998)

In today's global economy, working across boundaries is here to stay. Global alliances are proliferating and, according to John Naisbitt in his 1994 book *Global Paradox*, small businesses are better able to achieve success in the global economy because they are nimbler and better able to operate as dynamic networks. Mergers, joint ventures, flatter organization structures, globalization and the desire to bring the right people together to work on the right projects are just some of the other reasons why people are increasingly likely to be required to work beyond their own departmental or organizational boundaries. In this chapter we will be focusing on what it means for employees to work with people who are not part of their traditional 'functional' work team. In Chapters 10 and 14 we look specifically at the international implications of working across boundaries.

For many people, cross-boundary working may seem unfamiliar or even potentially threatening. The business press regularly features aspects of cross-boundary working, such as joint ventures or strategic alliances that appear to have gone wrong, often thanks to the 'human factor'. After all, cross-boundary working involves working with people whose culture, the 'way they do things', may be different from your own. It means working outside your own boundaries, whether these be knowledge-based, experience-based or habit-based and potentially outside comfort zones.

FORMS OF CROSS-BOUNDARY WORKING

Typically, in international organizations, people are working together across the boundaries of different national cultures. After all, in these days of the global marketplace, in which manufacturing, purchasing, customer service and other aspects of a single organization's operation may be carried out anywhere round the world, organizations are increasingly requiring employees to interact with fellow employees across geographical regions. Whether the organization's focus is European, transnational or truly global, the boundaries which many of its employees will encounter are national and linguistic and for some people, working in a multi-cultural environment presents real challenges. These challenges can be exacerbated when colleagues rarely or never get the chance to meet each other and have to rely on communicating by e-mail and other means of virtual working.

Another prevalent form of cross-boundary working is where employees of different corporate cultures are required to work closely together. Widespread competition from a range of sources is leading to greater corporate amalgamation within the marketplace. The ongoing trend for organizations to merge or at least work in some form of strategic alliance with erstwhile competitors, customers or suppliers means that increasing numbers of employees are having to develop new allegiances and be prepared to work effectively with people whose working practices may be very different. While a merger may be publicly celebrated as a 'marriage', as was the 1998 merger of jewellers Asprey and Garrard, employees may see the relationship more in terms of a divorce from all that is familiar. Nor is the public sector immune to cross-boundary working. In the UK, government pressures for greater responsiveness and efficiency are leading to cross-cutting initiatives between civil service departments and to 'Best Value' regimes in local government.

An increasingly familiar form of cross-boundary working is evident in flatter organizational structures. This is where people who may be at very different levels in the hierarchy are required to work together in ways that would be unusual in a more conventional hierarchical structure. So a first-line supervisor might be expected to understand the strategic implications of some aspect of the company's operation for which he or she is responsible when producing relevant reports for an executive. The boundaries that employees have to cross then become intellectual. They are being required to bridge different levels of attention – from an operational/technical focus to an implementational/strategic one.

In leaner organizations, the thin staffing levels often cause employees to have to cooperate effectively with other departments in order to produce work to the required standards. Sometimes, especially when work is organized along process lines, horizontal working involves working in teams of various sorts. These may be ad hoc and temporary, or more permanent. Indeed, some organizations, particularly those involved in high-tech industries, are increasingly organized along project lines with teams drawn from people with the relevant skills and expertise for the team's task. Working in such teams often requires people to work with others who have different functional specialisms and to be able to cross departmental boundaries for the good of the joint project. The case study featured later in this chapter focuses on this kind of cross-boundary working.

THE CHALLENGES OF WORKING ACROSS BOUNDARIES

So if working across boundaries is on the increase, what are the challenges for employees? Many people, working in this way for the first time realize that they need to develop a specific mindset, one in which flexibility and responsiveness to others form the basis for collaboration. One of the key features of cross-boundary working is that some employees experience mixed loyalties. This is particularly the case when project teams are seen as a 'bolt-on' to the team members' ordinary work. In a matrix structure, this often means that team members continue to have a clear reporting line back to their functional manager, with only a dotted line to the person responsible for the team. In practice, this can mean that people lack commitment to the team or that they are withdrawn from the project team before their work is done. Some employees consider that they have to become guardians of their functional specialism within the multi-functional team, putting their own functional standards ahead of the need for collaboration.

Lack of Trust

When a major change, such as a merger between two organizations, brings about the need for cross-boundary working, the differences in culture soon become apparent. When there are obvious 'winners' and 'losers' in the process, a lack of trust between the employees of the acquiring and the acquired companies may be inevitable. People become highly sensitive to signals about whether they are on the winning or losing side. In the early days of a merger these signals can include senior appointments, redundancies and whose working practices and brand dominate.

Depending on the business rationale for the merger, there are sometimes benefits in keeping operations largely separate, with collaboration at senior management level only. In other cases, the best course may be to develop a new combined culture. Of course, this should ideally consist of the best practices and aspects of culture from both organizations contributing to the achievement of clear business goals.

Unfortunately, this is hard to achieve in practice, especially when lack of employee trust can lead to a loss of commitment. Roffey Park's research into the human aspects of mergers (Devine et al., 1998) is littered with anecdotes that illustrate the dangers to the organization of this lack of trust. In a merger between two major pharmaceutical companies, some employees in the acquired company simply hid the outputs of research projects until they felt that their position was secure and that they could work in the new combined organization. This phenomenon was called 'burying our babies'.

What is particularly striking about this merger research is that many executives of organizations on the acquisition trail appear to be unaware of, or prepared to ignore, the importance of understanding the differences in culture before the damage is done. We found several examples of relatively large and bureaucratic organizations which had acquired smaller, more entrepreneurial companies. Within months, even though the acquirers were keen to retain the services of more entrepreneurial employees, the creeping introduction of the acquirer's detailed procedures caused 'star' employees to seek their fortunes elsewhere.

Turf Issues

Working across boundaries can also appear to threaten employees' sense of their own territory. This can then lead to political behaviour in which power games can be unproductive. At one level, this can appear quite trivial, but unless 'turf' issues are sorted out, cross-boundary working can be jeopardized. In a financial services organization, a new senior manager in charge of a large data-processing plant wanted to introduce new cross-departmental processes to improve efficiency and raise standards. He could not understand why various previous attempts to introduce new working practices had foundered. He gradually realized that, although the work being carried out across the plant was essentially the same, employees in one department saw themselves as being superior to the rest. They were, after all, allowed to have the radio on during the day while other departments were not. It was only after these differences were aired in an 'open space' meeting in which the employees generated the agenda that there was a gradual willingness to move towards cross-departmental working.

Territorial issues tend to be well disguised. They may emerge sounding like strong business arguments, but the underlying issues may actually be more related to the exercise of power. In cross-functional teams there can be a tendency for technical experts to pull rank, with the financial expert always having the last word. Organizational systems may well be at odds with cross-boundary working even though this may be unintentional. Working across boundaries requires people to bring their particular skills and knowledge to the achievement of a joint task for which no individual is likely to take the credit. If the reward processes reinforce the importance of individual rather than team performance, employees may consider that doing their 'day job' is what will be taken seriously when performance is being assessed and may lack commitment to cross-boundary work.

Knowledge Management

A more fundamental barrier to cross-functional working may have its roots in the ongoing uncertainty of the employment market. In the information age, there is the potential clash of employee and employer needs with respect to how information is developed and distributed. This is embodied in two apparently contradictory edicts. One is 'knowledge is power' and the other is 'knowledge is to be shared'. From the organizational perspective there are clear benefits in the pooling of information, about clients for example, and the generation of shared knowledge, thus preventing the organization from becoming dependent on any single employee's knowledge.

From the individual point of view, however, there can be little incentive to share information if by so doing you render yourself dispensable. After all, a person's expertise has traditionally been regarded as their key asset in the employment market. In these uncertain times, valuable experience and expertise are also seen to be a means of keeping your job when those about you are losing theirs.

For some people, career uncertainty is not the issue. They may simply not want to share their expertise beyond their own boundaries if it means reducing their power base as 'the expert'.

Clearly there has to be a shared platform of trust and the opportunity for employees to develop valuable new skills through the team process if people are to see benefits in collaboration. For while there is plenty of anecdotal evidence that people who develop effective knowledge management processes derive development and personal satisfaction from the new forms of learning they acquire, the barriers to being willing to collaborate can be strong. HR has a role to play in ensuring that team processes and use of information can address both organizational and individual needs. Training and appropriate rewards may be part of the answer.

Cultural Differences

Perhaps the biggest obstacles to cross-boundary working lie in cultural differences which become apparent as people work together, whether the cultures in question are for instance national, departmental, functional, age or gender related. In his extensive study of joint ventures in China, my colleague Professor Peter Smith (Smith et al., 1997) has identified a number of key areas where cultural differences become apparent. To name but a few, these include the ways in which decisions are taken and tasks are allocated, attitudes to time, including the keeping of deadlines and punctuality, the ways in which meetings are conducted, poor performance is evaluated and in which work is coordinated. There can be fundamental differences in what two groups believe to be important, and significant variations in how they expect staff and customers to be treated.

Any of these cultural differences can cause division without team members being able to identify the reason. Language problems can also lead to communication difficulties. It is essential for effective cross-boundary working to be successful, for the key differences in culture to be identified and taken into account when people are expected to collaborate. Peter Smith's work has led to a detailed understanding of ways in which people from different national backgrounds seem to experience cross-cultural working and helps to identify some of the areas where specific help, such as training, may be necessary.

Us and Them

Cultural differences of any sort can lead to an 'us and them' approach which is unhelpful in cross-boundary working. The perception of who is 'us' can change almost overnight. A few years ago a merger between two major manufacturing companies, one French, the other British, resulted in managers from each of the two national groups reverting to national stereotypes and perceiving the other as 'them'. However, when the company was later acquired by an American company, the French and British managers realized that they had more in common jointly than with the American management team. British managers found themselves acting as a bridge between the more hierarchical, long-term focus French and the more democratic, 'do it now' Americans. From our merger research, it seems that 'us and them', 'winner and loser' behaviour is more likely when people feel threatened or are acting in unfamiliar settings. This suggests that some forum, whether training, team building or other means of getting people talking with each other and better understanding each others' needs and strengths, is important.

Communication

Indeed, good communication is vital. In a large global firm such as Morgan Stanley technology is being used to bring its 53000-plus worldwide workforce together. Webcasts enable staff to access global meetings in real time, making senior management, including those based in New York, highly visible.

Similarly, in a large UK local authority, with many different service units, communication across service boundaries can be a challenge but is essential if staff are to understand and connect with the overall business purpose and strategy. The City of Bradford Council, for example, serves more than 480000 residents and provides a variety of services including education, social services, regeneration schemes, refuse and theatres. The chief executive believes that looking after staff leads to a better service for residents. In 2005 the council held 14 workshops involving more than 600 staff to find out what it is doing right as an employer and what needs to be improved. This helped staff understand the bigger picture both within the council and beyond.

Cross-Boundary Working – a Manufacturing Case Study

A major international engineering company, whose UK base has a number of sites throughout the south and west of England, has introduced some aspects of cross-boundary working in recent years through various quality initiatives. The company wants to increase the amount of project working which brings together the talents of key individuals from different sites for extended periods. Roffey Park was called in to help the company's management better understand the nature of cross-boundary teamworking so that learning could be applied to other parts of the organization. The Roffey Park researchers, Caroline Glynn and the author, were supplemented by a number of in-house researchers whom we trained in the approach used.

Our task involved studying the workings of two teams, one of which was established some three years ago and the other was formed more recently. The longer-established team (team A) is essentially working on a single major project with a very long-term deadline, while the other (team B) has a range of projects whose deadlines are shorter term. While team A, consisting of a central team of 30 people, was based at one site, team B was split between two sites approximately 40 miles apart. Both teams were considered by managers to be highly successful, though team A was felt to have greater potential than had yet been realized, and the two sub-teams within team B operated almost independently of each other. Team members also considered the teams successful. They reported a sense of pride at being part of their team and were clearly motivated by being able to contribute to their team's success.

Our research method included interviews and a survey of team members. Our aim was to draw on the experiences of team members in order to gain an understanding of the features of cross-boundary working which have contributed to its success and also to learn from those aspects which have emerged as obstacles to effective performance. We also wanted to gain an understanding of how cross-boundary teamworking differed from other forms of teamworking – if indeed it did.

THE CHARACTERISTICS OF SUCCESSFUL CROSS-BOUNDARY TEAMWORKING

Clearly it would be dangerous to generalize on the basis of studying two teams and the research base has since widened considerably. However, certain factors did become apparent for both teams. These form the basis for our ongoing study of cross-boundary working. We start with the people considerations and then look at other relevant factors.

An Effective Team Leader

One of the key features of both teams was the critical role of the team leader. This was highlighted over and over again, with one interviewee commenting 'ranked 10 on a scale of 1–10 in importance'. In this context, the team leader was the person who not only set the direction for the team but also negotiated and obtained resources, including people for the team. As such it was felt important that the leader should be sufficiently competent technically that he or she could appreciate all the functions encompassed within the team. Similarly, the leader was expected to manage the diversity inherent in the team and enhance the performance of the team as a whole by building on individual strengths.

In these two teams the leader was a senior manager who effectively acted as sponsor of the team at senior levels. An essential aspect of the role was clarifying the roles of individual team members and managing the conflicts which arise across functional boundaries. As such, having an effective leader becomes perhaps more critical for a cross-boundary team than for a conventional functional team. The leader has to manage the political interface and act as a shield for the team from the rest of the organization. In finding its own 'third way', the team may need to have the freedom to experiment and be genuinely 'empowered' to discover the best ways of working. This is usually not a problem as long as the team is seen to be successful. In the early stages, though, the team leader may find his or her credibility under strain as the team learns from its mistakes. The leader needs to be prepared to create an environment where experimentation is encouraged and team members are supported for doing so.

Given the diverse backgrounds of team members, and that there may not initially be a lot of common ground between them, the role of the leader in providing a tangible focus and direction for the team becomes all the more important. Being able to be both strategic and operational is important. They must be seen as someone who 'leads from the front', setting a strong vision and objectives for the team. They perform the important role of providing drive and determination in the face of difficulties. Within the two teams this was an aspect of leadership that seemed to be going well at the level of broad objectives, in that everybody was aware of the longer-term goals and quality/cost objectives. What was going less well was the setting of shorter-term objectives which gave people real focus in the context of a lengthy project.

The leader's role was both internal and external to the team. Both leaders were reported to be 'sold on teamworking' and were effectively acting as coach and mentor to different team members. It was widely recognized that they needed to have excellent interpersonal skills not just for communicating with the team but also for helping the team communicate effectively with each other. In terms of style, both teams felt that decision-making should be the ultimate responsibility of the leader, to avoid functional experts pulling rank, but that decision-making should be carried out in a participative way. The team leader was also seen as being responsible for communicating the team's successes to the wider organization and building up a strong profile for the team throughout the business. The team leader therefore needs to be visible, both to the team itself and within the organization as a whole.

The Team Builder

It was recognized by both groups that there was a need for someone within the team who could act as the 'spur to team excellence'. On some occasions this was carried out by the team leader, but not always. In both teams, an individual was identified as a model for good team behaviour, proving that the team can change for the better. They were seen as natural leaders who are self-motivated, confident and charismatic. They were also seen as supportive of failure and willing to try new things. As such, even without formal authority, the team builders were seen as the internal motivator of the team to better things, providing continuity, whereas the leader has to maintain both an internal and an external perspective.

More so than in a conventional team, the Belbin team role of team builder is called for. This aspect of the role is managing conflict within the team. This is an area where problems are more likely, given the complexities within a cross-boundary team. Interviewees noted that the team builder acts as the oil on troubled waters, diffusing conflict through clarifying roles and creating a 'union of individuals around common objectives'.

Facilitators

Team B used facilitators from the outset to help establish effective functioning of the team, especially in the early stages. The key functions of facilitators were described as enabling open communication, mediation and breaking down hostilities within the team. Opinions were divided as to whether facilitators would be needed over the long term and therefore whether the facilitator should be internal to the team or an external person. There was strong agreement, however, that in the early stages it was important for the facilitator to be external. It was felt that internal facilitators would not be considered impartial and would be likely to suffer from role conflict. It was also felt that an external facilitator would be more professional and expert in this role.

Team A had not used facilitators. However, the team leader recognized the importance of reviewing how the team was working and the researchers were invited to facilitate a team review which provided the team with some processes which could be used for ongoing purposes.

Team Members

Team members noted that there were a number of characteristics which were essential to working successfully within a cross-boundary team. Individuals must be committed to the team, with a real desire to achieve team goals. This means that team members must be able to balance their focus on team goals alongside functional goals. Individuals must also be willing to share success and failure with the rest of the team. Accepting their share of responsibility for both means that team members must be also prepared to confront others who fail to deliver things for which they are accountable.

Team members must be willing to help each other but they should also be able to learn from others and explore new areas outside their own environment. Simply relying on one's own functional knowledge is not enough. After all, a cross-boundary team is likely to consist of a number of people who are expert in their own field, but may not know much about other areas. It is important that members understand the broader business context within which the project is being conducted and appreciate the different elements of the project being carried out by others.

This does not entail having a detailed understanding of other people's technical specialisms, but enough of a sense of their priorities and requirements to ensure that the project plan can work smoothly, without people making unnecessary demands on others through ignorance. Members therefore have to be able to liaise across boundaries within their team and between the team and the rest of the organization, including their boss.

Adjusting to cross-boundary working involves being able to work effectively without hierarchical structures, since cross-boundary working often cuts across hierarchical levels, with senior people reporting to a more junior project leader. It was also seen as important that team members were experienced within their functional field and were not in the position of having everything to learn before they could contribute. As such, people in our case study felt that a cross-boundary team was inappropriate for someone who needed coaching or training on their functional specialism. This is one area which further research will explore.

For both teams, interpersonal relationships within the team were felt to be a strong feature of team success. In team B, strong relationships were built up within each of the sub-teams but working relationships between the two sites were not built up due to the geographical divide. There was a clear sense that team members respected each other and that the environment was one of trust and confidence. These relationships were aided to some extent by social activities outside the work environment. Although these social events were considered beneficial for team-working, the relationships within the team seemed to be developed mainly at work.

Role Clarity

Team members need to be clear not only about their own role, but also about the roles of other team members. Role boundaries and team responsibilities need to be understood to minimize the potential for conflict through role overlap, or gaps in provision which will threaten the success of the team. This is an area which is ideally addressed by the team leader in the 'forming' stage of team development when group members begin the shift from independence to interdependence. Time must be spent communicating the vision for the team and clarifying individual and team responsibilities and objectives. The research has highlighted the importance of setting a clear focus for cross-boundary teams, uniting activity around a common purpose. This is particularly important given the individual's functional ties outside the team and the danger that, without clarity of cross-boundary team objectives, individuals will fall back on functional links.

Communication and Co-location

The key difference between the two teams was about communication, which seemed to be largely due to the fact that one team (A) was co-located, while the other was not. Members of team A were very positive about the level of communication within the team. They were able to hold frequent informal discussions as well as regular review meetings. The dissemination of information was felt to happen on a regular basis which meant that information received was timely and relevant.

This was in contrast to team B, who felt that there were clear divisions between the two sites. They were united in blaming the poor communication between the two halves of the team on the geographical divide. Members in each of the sub-teams felt that they were well informed about their part of the team, but had very little knowledge of what was happening at the other site. The fact that there were very few face-to-face encounters between the two sub-teams seemed to lead to conflict which then took time to resolve.

Clearly, co-location, though ideal may not be practicable, especially in global organizations in which virtual teams become the norm. However, this case highlights the importance of at least an occasional opportunity to 'personalize' the relationship through meetings, visits, video conferencing, the use of electronic 'team rooms' and other means of helping people to establish a relationship with one another. This is in addition to the need for regular briefings and updates so that people can feel part of the larger whole.

Measures

Within the teams there was agreement that measures were important, but that what was currently measured were the 'hard' measures relating to project targets, resource usage etc. These measures were set on an individual basis. There was no conscious monitoring of 'soft' measures relating to team processes and learning; consequently there was a sense that the effectiveness of the team was judged entirely on results rather than taking into account how those results had been achieved. In a cross-boundary team where there is potential for teamworking to be seen as peripheral to individuals' main role, the use of soft measures may help keep the team focused on learning and gaining more transferable skills.

Team Learning

Although there was general agreement that team learning did occur within both teams, it was also apparent that this was very much at an informal, unconscious level than through any formal learning process. One of the problems with the informal learning was that there was no retrieval system so that the team as a whole could learn from its mistakes and successes. Team A sought to kick-start a more formal approach to reviewing learning through an off-site facilitated process while team B undertook deliberate teambuilding at an early stage.

More formal processes are now being considered and introduced. These include regular debriefing of learning events, general learning reviews of team processes as well as technical learning reviews and harnessing the expertise of more experienced team members. Where these processes have been introduced, team members have commented on the way in which trust has been built through the open approach to learning and that this is an important element of team 'bonding'. They have also remarked on the increase in job satisfaction they have felt when time has been allocated to understanding how an effective end result has been achieved.

BENEFITS OF CROSS-BOUNDARY WORKING

Clearly, when cross-boundary teams work well, they bring benefits to both the organization and to individuals. One of the key characteristics of both cross-boundary teams studied was that the people in the teams were very enthusiastic about this form of teamwork and proud to be part of teams which they recognized as successful. This success was a powerful motivating factor itself, but interviewees also valued the personal growth gained from the experience. They felt stretched within the team, commented favourably on the new insights they had gained into other aspects of the business, and appreciated their relative freedom from organizational constraints.

The only real demotivators were linked with recognition; in particular, team members resented the lack of recognition of success outside the team. They recognized that working across boundaries involves a great deal of complexity, whereas they had the sense that 'the organization does not accord enough importance to the concept of cross-boundary teamworking'.

Clearly, as cross-boundary working becomes the norm, rather than the exception, the challenge for organizations will be to ensure that these sophisticated team skills are nurtured, developed widely and rewarded. If not, people with these eminently transferable skills are likely to find a ready market for them elsewhere.

In this organization, these 'building blocks' of cross-boundary teamworking have now been applied to other teams beyond the original two. In a real sense, enabling these teams to work effectively was a joint responsibility between the line and HR. After all, line managers were responsible for the performance and outputs of the teams, while HR were able to help find ways of getting the teams working even more effectively. HR provided the teams with a mechanism for monitoring some of the important 'soft' issues which were affecting performance. With the minimum of training or other conventional interventions, HR were able to help the teams to continue to help themselves. In this next example, the cross-boundary working is across national cultures.

Case Study: International Teamworking at Ericsson

International teamworking in Ericsson, the Swedish communications multinational, is a feature of organizational life. This reflects the increasingly international nature of the business, with locations chosen according to their particular benefits within the global economy. In line with many companies, the drive for growth and increased margins means that Ericsson is moving its production closer to the main points of sale and where there is a lower cost base. Units exist in the USA and other global centres. In China alone there are five production centres.

On the other hand, though European countries such as France, Holland, Spain, Sweden and the UK are main markets, the cost of labour means that production is being phased out of the UK. The supply business is closely monitored so that change can be implemented, if need be, within a six-month period. Growth rates are driven by the global financial markets. Investors are now more sophisticated than in times gone by; so too are customers.

Sales are carried out by region, mainly to multinational customers. The importance of meeting the differing needs of an internationally diverse customer base means that the composition of sales teams must reflect the cultures of the customers. With widely varying customer perceptions of what constitutes value and quality service, international sales teams need to be competent in the 'soft' issues of customer care and be able to marry perceptions with reality. Sales teams tend to be based in the lead country of their major international clients, whether this is the operating centre or headquarters. The important thing is to be close to where the power of the customer is so that the team can fruitfully spend time applying their understanding of cultural issues.

Tony Booth, UK chairman of Ericsson at the original time of writing, believes that these sales teams need to be empowered to negotiate the sales pitch and any trade-offs within a broad negotiation margin. The desire to give sales teams ownership of the sales process has to be balanced against the need for pricing consistency across Europe. Within the Euro Zone customers can compare prices across Europe instantly. The separate teams therefore need to operate as a higher-level corporate team to avoid undercutting one another while improving their own sales figures.

The teams report to both local managers and the corporate centre. They are supported, rather than controlled, by the centre. Tony Booth believes that there is no one model of reporting which works in every circumstance. The key thing is to put people with the appropriate skills and ability close to the customer. Team members need to be credible to the customer. Credibility is often based on what the individual has achieved in their career to date, and, in some countries, their perceived power within Ericsson. The team needs to be made up of self-starting, experienced individuals who have made their mistakes elsewhere before becoming responsible for a major account.

In addition, team members have to work together as a real team, supporting each other on issues where in the past they might have expected help from HQ echelons which no longer exist. They have to work together physically and virtually and to act as their own team catalysts. Increasingly customers want to see that the whole team is credible, not just the individual sales person. The team also has to dovetail resources and skills in tough marketplaces.

The team leader, an international account manager, can be based with the team or operate in a 'virtual' way. The leader is expected to win the business and help the team deal with the challenges of delivering the business. The influencing skills of the leader therefore need to be of a high order as there are in effect two types of cultural negotiation taking place. First, the sales negotiation has to reflect the complexities of local requirements and styles. Second, bringing the business back into the corporate culture requires the leader to win support from production and other parts of the centre in order to succeed.

It is often assumed that sales people are primarily individual performers rather than team players. In Ericsson, the team aspect is taken seriously and is reflected in the bonus scheme. There is a potential team bonus of 20–30% which reflects team effort, as well as achievement. Teams would have to demonstrate, for instance, how they have taken the whole team's needs into account when bidding for resources. As a multinational supplier, teams also need to be able to negotiate with other teams when bidding for resources. This can result in conflict which has to be dealt with internally and not be evident to the customer.

ALLIANCES

While more and more organizations are developing a range of partnerships with others, the issues involved in managing alliances effectively are relatively little researched. Driving factors for alliances include overcoming the problems of growth industries. There are several telecoms alliances, such as Ericsson and Telefonica (Spain), to overcome the problems of national protectionism. Rapid technological development and innovation is leading to the need for shorter product life cycles.

In more mature industries, the concentration of players is leading to the challenging of monopolies. Redland Brick and Australian CRS are building material to challenge BPB. Governments are also creating pressures for collaboration, for instance on joint research and the transfer of technology in projects such as Airbus and ESPRIT (European Strategic Programme in Information Technologies which is half funded by the EEC). Other alliances are formed as a defensive measure to prevent other potential alliances.

Different forms of alliance are in evidence which require different forms of strategic human resource activity. These include:

- Licensing arrangements, which are typical of manufacturing industries. Strategic Human Resource Management (SHRM) input would be most likely to involve the training of local managers on-site and the development of technical knowledge
- Franchises which are typical of sectors where there is fast market entry. SHRM input is likely to involve working with franchisees to create a common set of values and behaviours with those of the 'parent' company
- Partnerships, federations and consortia which are typical of situations where organizations wish to share risks and costs. They are currently growing in sectors such as the UK Further Education sector where there is a need to increase provision and quality of programmes. SHRM contribution is likely to involve facilitating networks, and providing mentoring to create a common vision across the member organizations
- Joint ventures, which allow for specialization or shared added value. The SHRM contribution could include team building, the development of a joint venture culture and the development of flexibility among employees.

Making Alliances Work

Research by KPMG (1999) has shown that 70% of alliances are disbanded prematurely and that in two-thirds of cases interpersonal factors were blamed as the main cause of failure. Cultural differences, between companies as well as nations, were considered at the core of the difficulties. Other research suggests that common failure factors relate to partners' behaviour before the collaborative agreement is established. These include:

- Lack of clarity in defining the single firm's goals
- Poor choice of partners
- Emphasis on short-term results
- Little involvement by top management in the partnering project
- Incomplete information on potential partners.

Other failure factors related to partners' behaviour during the actual collaboration were:

- Lack of an alliance 'champion'
- Lack of trust among partners
- Lack of communication and information diffusion
- Inadequate human resources allocated to the process
- Lack of management commitment
- Failure of one of the partners to deliver their expected contribution
- Change in the partners' top management
- Conflicting culture and values of partners
- Conflicting objectives of partners
- Lack of collaboration objectives in terms of time, costs, innovative results etc.
- Inflexible people
- Loss of control on certain partners.

The KPMG (1999) research identified four phases through which alliances usually progress. These are similar to the familiar stages of team development, i.e. forming, storming, norming, performing and mourning. The first stage is the norming or 'politeness' phase when the intentions of partners are explored and attempts are made to converge toward the desired goals. The second 'conflict' or storming phase is where key players conflict with each other at a number of levels. If the conflict, especially with regard to the vision and values underlying the project, remains unresolved, the alliance is unlikely to make progress. In the next 'inquiry' phase, key players start to ask questions which explore each other's vision. If the partners come to understand and respect differences, new insights can be gained. This then leads to the performing or 'energy' phase in which the new mental models and improved trust lead to better understanding between the key players, and better outputs.

The skills required to cope effectively at each stage differ but HR professionals can support alliances through helping make differences explicit. This can be done in a number of ways, through team meetings, team building, a stocktake of working practices etc. HR can also help manage conflict and enable partners to gain positive momentum from the effective resolution of difficulties. Partners need to be helped to retain their objectivity and respect for the views of their counterparts. HR can support partners as they develop ways of understanding each other's perspectives on the underlying vision and values which they are working towards. They can also support partners as they move towards the creation of practical implementation plans to translate the vision into action.

CONCLUSION

HR can assist groups and individuals to develop effective cross-boundary working. This may mean providing team building support when new teams are established. It can also mean enabling teams to communicate effectively both within the team and beyond the team itself. This requires some understanding of the cultural differences represented and the ability to help teams make the most of their diversity. In particular, HR has a key role to play in enabling line managers to overcome some of the barriers to cross-boundary working and to make the most of the positive power of conflict. This will involve helping all concerned to identify what is different in the way they are required to work, to gain clarity about their own role and to appreciate the benefits they will gain from this increasingly common form of working.

CHECKLIST FOR CROSS-BOUNDARY TEAMS

Are we using cross-boundary teamworking effectively to meet organizational goals?

- Does the team function effectively?
- Has it a common vision and synergy?
- How clearly are roles defined? Do people understand their own and other people's roles?
- Are there complex interdependent tasks and a clear plan?
- How effective are the team dynamics?
- Does the team generate new ideas?
- If the team members are not co-located, how do they create 'human' links?
- How do liaison and coordination work?
- What training does the team need? What learning processes does it apply?
- How does the team analyse its own effectiveness?
- How does the team ensure maintained commitment to the task?
- Is there an effective team facilitator? Team champion? Team leader?

REFERENCES

Ashkenas, R.N., Ulrich, D., Jick, T. and Kerr, S. (1998) *The Boundaryless Organization: Breaking the Chains of Organizational Structure*. San Francisco: Jossey-Bass

Devine, M., Hirsh, W., Garrow, V. and Holbeche, L. (1998) *Mergers and Acquisitions: Getting the People Bit Right*. Horsham: Roffey Park Management Institute. November

KPMG (1999) The art of alliances. *Virtual Library*, April

Naisbitt, J. (1994) *Global Paradox*. New York: Avon Books

Smith, P.B., Wang, Z.M. and Leung, K. (1997) Leadership, decision-making and cultural context; event management within Chinese joint ventures, *Leadership Quarterly*, 8, No. 4, 413–431

Chapter 14

Global HRM

*Globalization is leading to – sometimes voluntarily, sometimes not – an increased trans-
fer of knowledge and insight into different national systems of management. It is leading
to a higher level and more strategic agenda to which HR practitioners can contribute.*

(Paul Sparrow *et al.*, 2004)

When it comes to business, national boundaries are eroding and whatever is
taking place in HR is now a global issue, according to Towers Perrin (2006).
Companies face a host of complex issues unimagined just 25 years ago, as they
develop a global presence. So too does HR as it attempts to move talent successfully across borders, build structures which can support business operations and
a corporate culture which binds employees together, creating a brand that is consistent across the world but which can flex to meet local requirements.

In practice, few large organizations appear able to achieve a truly global culture in which local businesses achieve a high level of global integration. Equally,
the lack of an effective multi-cultural HR strategy can potentially undermine the
organization's ability to grow its capabilities and optimize its international business opportunities. Indeed, the role HRM plays in contributing to global business success is little understood. Professor Chris Brewster, who has conducted
research into many international organizations, points out that 'although HR
forms a very substantial part of their operating costs, so far there has been very
little serious attention paid to thinking strategically about it' (quoted in Kennedy,
1998). According to Fons Trompenaars (1997), even the notion of HR management is an Anglo-Saxon concept which is difficult to translate to other cultures.

Global organizations tend to operate according to the old dictum 'think
global, act local' (or 'glocal'). From an HR perspective this can be difficult to
implement in reality. In decentralized organizations the need for a centrally
driven HR strategy may be challenged by local business and HR teams. Yet arguably certain HR matters deserve a level of collective attention which ensures that
action is taken on key issues. The major question is not about which approach to
HR policy-making and implementation – centralized or decentralized – is 'right'

but about whether anything is happening at all to strategically further the needs of the organization and its employees.

First let us consider some of the challenges facing global organizations and their leaders; then we will discuss the implications for HR strategy.

CHALLENGES FACING GLOBAL LEADERS

Global leaders face a number of challenges:

Operating in an Interconnected, Uncertain Environment

Global businesses have to deal with the challenges of operating in an interconnected, dynamic and uncertain global environment. Borders of time, distance, language and markets are being eroded. Dealing with different national and business cultures, employment market conditions, legal requirements, time-zones and languages creates significant challenges for leaders.

Business leaders also face intense and shifting global competition, technological revolution, constant change and increased exposure and pressures. Just as technology has changed the face of business, so too has it brought new threats and risks. Computer viruses, with their potential to spread rapidly across the globe, have already cost some businesses dear. Successes and failures in one region can have serious implications for others.

The interconnected nature of global business creates a complex and unpredictable environment that leaves major international businesses more vulnerable than before. What happens in one part of the world has repercussions elsewhere and global organizations are most keenly exposed to socio-political and economic shifts, as events of the past few years have illustrated. The events of September 11, 2001, wars in Afghanistan and Iraq and terrorist attacks in various parts of the world have not only had tragic and terrible human consequences but also created new levels of uncertainty and risk that have had a powerful economic effect, as has the global banking crisis and ensuing economic volatility.

Global organizations are under more pressure than most to improve their environmental, ethical and social responsibility credentials, creating additional difficulties for global leaders. The high-profile cases of corporate corruption and scandal in a number of large global organizations (Enron, Parmalat, WorldCom, Adephia, Global Crossing, ImClone) have shaken consumer and investor confidence. A survey commissioned by the World Economic Forum in 46 countries last year revealed that large corporations (whether national or multinational) are now among the least-trusted institutions (Cabrera, 2004).

These events have led to new corporate governance regulations and compliance requirements creating significant challenges for organizational leaders as well as increasing the workload of boards. Leaders also need to be proactive in managing the reputations of their organizations in the face of worldwide demands for higher standards of business practice, accountability and responsibility.

Concerns about the environment and the growing gap between rich and poor (within and between nations) are fuelling demand for ethical, responsible and sustainable business from consumers and investors alike. Global organizations are the most visible and communication technology means today's consumers are more informed. Research suggests that consumers feel that global brands have a particular responsibility to tackle social issues. Consumer pressure groups use e-mails and websites to broadcast their campaigns and boycotts to international audiences. They now talk of their ability to 'swarm', to rally many activist allies for 'direct action' against the stores and offices of a single corporation around the world on a single day. Because of their pervasiveness they are seen as particularly powerful, 'capable of doing great good and causing considerable harm' (Holt *et al.*, 2004: 70).

Scale, Scope and Complexity

Global organizations need to maximize the benefits and opportunities of operating globally, and while the increased scale of operating internationally presents opportunities it also creates difficulties. According to Sinclair and Agyeman (2004), global leaders are faced with the paradox of leveraging benefits of scale, building an integrated consistent global culture or brand and facilitating learning and innovation on a worldwide scale whilst being sensitive to local differences.

Operationalizing this sensitivity at local level remains a challenge, particularly as increased competition means that global organizations aiming to leverage benefits of scale and maximize efficiency typically do this through standardization and the reduction of what is considered unnecessary duplication. To ensure this happens effectively, leaders need to motivate people to work for global as well as local goals (Brake, 1999).

Similarly, global organizations face challenges of scope and complexity. In order to maximize the benefits of operating globally, organizations are faced with the challenge of mobilizing resources according to requirements. Varying economic conditions and regulations raise the question of what should be common and what unique? Research by ICEDR indicates that most transnational teams need to balance three concerns relating to worldwide competition. These key strategic drivers are local responsiveness, global efficiency and organizational learning. Global organizations need to make efforts to fully exploit learning acquired in one part of the organization throughout in order to facilitate learning and innovation on a worldwide scale. Dealing with constant change

Change is a constant factor in global organizations and leaders are faced with the challenges and choices of managing increasing numbers of cross-border acquisitions, mergers, partnerships and alliances (Kets De Vries and Florent-Treacy, 1999). In the process of becoming more global, organizations are forced to reengineer, redesign and re-evaluate their processes, procedures and products, as well as their workforce, services and public relations (Harris, 2002). This requires greater change management capability and adaptive strategies for gaining 'buy in'.

However, achieving 'buy-in' to change across a global workforce can be difficult. Global leaders, themselves in short supply, need to manage employees with a diverse range of cultural backgrounds and values, languages, different employment experiences and expectations. Moreover, what is considered to constitute effective leadership behaviour will differ across cultures (Dickson *et al.*, 2003).

Attracting and Retaining Global Talent

In today's business environment, where people are the key resource, attracting and retaining global talent is a key priority, and HR policies and practices need to reflect this. Research by Towers Perrin (2006) suggests that when it comes to choosing a job, people everywhere have similar needs and requirements. These will be considered later in this chapter.

Getting the Best Out of a Global Workforce

Motivating and unifying the workforce to strive for organizational success is of paramount importance and the diversity of a global organization's workforce can be one of its greatest strengths. Studies show that workforce diversity leads to superior business performance, an improved bottom line, competitive advantage, creativity, employee satisfaction and loyalty, lower absenteeism, strengthened relationships with multicultural communities and attraction of the best and the brightest candidates (McCuiston *et al.*, 2004; Ng and Tung, 1998; Schneider Ross, 2002). Yet while global companies may strive to establish consistent approaches, for instance to managing and rewarding performance, simply imposing western-style appraisal schemes and training programmes that encourage frank face-to-face dialogue can be very inappropriate in some cultures and undermine employee motivation.

Similarly, leading at a distance presents additional challenges to global leaders (Smith and Sinclair, 2003), adding an extra layer of complexity to communications. Reduced physical contact also reduces the information available for making judgements. Leaders need to learn the art of motivating, engaging, collaborating, networking and communicating with employees through virtual methods as well as face-to-face. Management mechanisms such as direct supervision as a means of coordination and control become inappropriate and new ways of cooperating to achieve tasks and meet organizational goals become necessary.

A GLOBAL HR AGENDA

HR needs to be seen to add value by supporting the strategic objectives of the organization and an aligned global HR agenda therefore must equip the organization to deal with its strategic challenges and capitalize on the opportunities of scale, scope and diversity. Opinions vary as to the best way to focus the global

HR resource. For instance Sparrow (2008) suggests that global HR coordination should focus on:

- Performance management processes
- Capability/competency systems
- Talent management processes
- Employment brand.

Research by Stroh and Caligiuri (1998) found that the three aspects of people management critical to the success of global companies are as follows:

- The adoption of flexible management policies and practices worldwide
- The inclusion of the HR function as a strategic business partner in global business
- The development of global leaders.

To these I would add optimizing the benefits of diversity, facilitating organizational learning, and enabling cross-boundary or transnational teamworking. The global HR agenda will also include a focus on facilitating international mobility. HR also has a key role to play in offshoring. This involves recruiting and building up centres, hiring in and developing managers, knowledge sharing and knowledge transfer, redefining roles to change the nature of key job roles and extending career paths.

Undoubtedly, the task of global HR at the centre is more complex and demanding than in the days when multinationals simply issued edicts from HQ which had to be implemented locally. In the global marketplace, however, such centralist approaches may not be appropriate. Striking the right balance between the corporate and the local is a vital judgement call.

Global vs Local HR Approaches?

Debate rages about which HR policies should be standardized in multinational companies and which should be left to local autonomy, and there are many variations on a theme. In recent years there appears to have been a growing trend to recentralize some core-managed processes, such as global leadership development, but the impetus for such processes increasingly appears to be 'bottom up' or from local markets and regions. The danger of too much centralization is that inappropriate policies are imposed and fail to be implemented. Equally, too much localization can mean that delivery becomes fragmented and resources are wasted with endless reinvention of wheels. Decision-making can become bogged down.

HR strategy development needs to be managed in such a way that all professionals develop a shared understanding of the overall strategic goals and direction, as well as the skills to deliver in the ways required. HR services at the 'centre' should focus on adding value through, for instance, the design of corporate processes or change programmes. Other 'corporate' needs might include top team recruitment and high-flyer development. Similarly, many companies consider that a key responsibility of global HR is sourcing talent within the company from around the world. In decentralized and federated organizations this can be difficult to achieve globally. The BP Amoco approach described in Chapter 11 shows one company's approach to integrating regional and global sourcing of talent. A key enabler of global sourcing of talent is having an effective international Human Resource Information System (HRIS) which can make a more strategic deployment of staff possible globally.

Global HR should be responsible for determining how learning can best take place in different locations and enabling the process. A number of multinationals, such as Coca-Cola, have created a position called Chief Learning Officer who is responsible on a global scale for ensuring that the company's human capital is put to good use. The challenge is to decide how learning can best take place in each country and develop appropriate processes. This requires a flexible approach by Global HR in implementing policies worldwide. Similar approaches have been taken on issues concerning employee rights. Companies such as American Express and many others now have designated 'Company Ombudsmen/women' who have the responsibility of ensuring that company and employee interests are appropriately served.

Conversely, corporate approaches which generally come unstuck at local level are in areas such as management by objectives, pay for performance, terms and conditions. Corporate values, especially with regard to diversity, when rigidly imposed may run counter to local norms. One American company takes an inflexible approach to maintaining core values, such as insisting that discrimination will not be tolerated. They have, however, allowed some flexibility in the manner in which this value is imparted in different locations. Consistency of intention is balanced by flexible pragmatism in delivery.

With respect to vision/mission/values/strategy, Paula Larson, Executive Vice President – HR Office of CEO, Invensys plc (2008), argues that employees everywhere need to have a clear line of sight and that HR and management teams should not necessarily adjust the message but recognize differences … making clear what are the big 'rules' or non-negotiables. Global leadership teams in particular need to talk with employees everywhere about what the values mean to them and model the behaviours implied by the values. Goal deployment should link directly to strategy. However, the key message is to be clear how corporate vision, mission and values translate locally. It is important to be clear about the 'what' to be delivered, but leaving room for local discretion about the 'how'.

Global HR Leadership

For Larson (2008), successful global HR leadership involves knowing your business – especially in the global context; she suggests going out and visiting customers. Larson argues that while it may be difficult to gain deep insight into every national culture within a global operation, nevertheless it is important to use a cultural 'lens' to develop understanding – be careful not to typecast but use cultural 'factoids' to start from somewhere that is probably a 'safe' place to start to deepen that understanding.

Larson also counsels against assuming that every local cultural approach should be given precedence over corporate. Having strong academic underpinnings for statements, beliefs and suggestions, for instance on global leadership competencies, offsets 'this is the way it's done around here' cultural challenges between organization culture and the country cultures. Similarly with respect to change management – it is important to know the difference between 'I'd rather not change thank you very much' and relevant cultural differences.

Global HR teams and structures

In many global companies the real challenge is not only the development of global leaders but also the raising of standards of the global HR team. It seems that there is no substitute for tough/tender team building to ensure that the global HR group welds into a team, and helping to create the global HR agenda is one way of focusing team building on an issue of real importance.

- According to researchers Linda Stroh and Paula Caligiuri (1998), 'the biggest barrier to HR units becoming strategic is their own lack of expertise of international business-related issues'. Global HR teams need to anticipate the HR needs of their organizations while coping with a range of operational issues such as staffing foreign subsidiaries and establishing compensation rates. Getting the right balance will ensure that the HR contribution is strategic rather than reactive.
- Paul Sparrow (2008) too argues that it is crucial that HR avoids getting trapped in the operational. He suggests that this is best avoided by dividing regional time between the biggest or small but important strategic units, and getting sites that are off the 'radar map' to self-manage. Decision logics need to be developed for when to parachute in HR support or not.
- Getting the HR structure right is crucial. For instance, Sparrow (2008) describes how one global organization has followed the 'Ulrich model', with shared services concentrating on administrative and transactional personnel activities separately from the main HR group through Service Centres for 'back-office' processing. HR business partners work to an 'embedded HR' model in which HR personnel provide dedicated support as generalists, business partners and account managers aligned to a business unit of the holding company. Then capability management involves clarifying organizational capabilities and crafting necessary HR investments and policies through centres of excellence or expertise that maintain the critical fields of knowledge and a specialist core HR function structure.

HR managers need to operate as a worldwide team, take into account the culture of different countries and decide which aspects of policies and systems need to be addressed locally and which are truly global. The global HR team needs to be able to share information and power with one another and with other people which requires a degree of flexibility in both behaviour and policies. Tact and compromise are likely to be hallmarks of effective HR teams who find ways of collaborating on global and local issues.

A global HR team needs to have the skills and credibility to carry out a global agenda which will further the organization's strategic mission. If, for instance, an organization is contemplating a joint venture with another company in another culture, HR should be involved in identifying and eliminating as far as possible potential 'hotspots'. This will involve analysing the differences in working practices, leadership styles, organizational cultures etc. which are likely to cause problems. Acting on this information can be vital in ensuring that the joint venture stands the best chance of succeeding. Similarly, if an organization plans to open a facility in a 'new' country, HR needs to carry out a comprehensive and early analysis of the HR system in the country, including the education level of potential workers, employment laws and national cultural norms relating to work practices. Recommendations can be made which reflect the realities of the political, economic and labour context.

Facilitating International Mobility

HR has a key role to play in facilitating international mobility. This includes enabling many forms of mobility, such as frequent commuters, employees on short-term business trips, tax-equalized or reduced package expatriates, permanent transferees, reverse or acculturation moves, virtual international employees in cross-border project teams as well as globally outsourced or insourced sites. In many global organizations HR teams divide responsibilities for facilitating international mobility across the life cycle of the international assignment (GMAC, 2008).

Case Study: Talent Mobility at Gordon Ramsay Holdings

In the following short case study (drawn with permission from CIPD — Tansley *et al.*, 2007a,b), talent mobility is a key ingredient in both business expansion and staff development.

Initially employing 80 people, Gordon Ramsay Holdings (GRH) now has over 900 staff and has witnessed rapid expansion since its first restaurant – Restaurant Gordon Ramsay – opened in 1998. The organization includes nine leading restaurants in London, consultancies in Dubai and Tokyo, new restaurants in Florida and New York, and there are plans to open new outlets in the USA and Europe in the future. The business is overseen by two chief executives, Gordon Ramsay and Chris Hutcheson (Gordon Ramsay's father-in-law). Gordon Ramsay plays a crucial role in the creative direction of the restaurants and works closely with the restaurant personnel, giving him the opportunity to identify talent in the restaurants and kitchens. This, combined with his celebrity status, has afforded the organization a high-profile reputation within the hospitality and catering industry, both nationally and internationally.

Key Drivers for Talent Management

Creative talent is key to the success of Gordon Ramsay Holdings. Gordon Ramsay, as one of the CEOs, places considerable importance on developing this talent within the organization, which means that the business can continue to expand effectively throughout the UK and internationally. When opening a new restaurant, the organization typically places a home-grown senior chef in charge of the new venture, to work alongside senior restaurant staff taken from other restaurants in the business. Mark Sargeant, the head chef at Gordon Ramsay's at Claridge's, for example, began working with Gordon Ramsay in 1998, and Marcus Wareing, the chef patron at Petrus, has worked with Gordon Ramsay for over ten years. Developing internal talent means that the organization has also addressed recruitment difficulties associated with the lack of highly skilled chefs in the labour market.

Approaching Talent Management

Gordon Ramsay Holdings focuses its efforts on developing rather than recruiting talent, particularly in terms of the kitchen staff. Formal training is offered to employees (such as increasing staff knowledge of wines and cheeses), but the talent-spotting and development of individuals is carried out by the line managers with the help of Gordon Ramsay.

The chefs asked to head up a new restaurant are offered financial incentives to ensure that the new enterprise is successful. As part of their training, up-and-coming chefs are also sent on sabbaticals to improve their cooking skills. Typically this involves working in a prestigious restaurant outside the UK for a lengthy period of time. These individuals are not obliged to return to Gordon Ramsay Holdings after they have finished their training – but invariably they do. On their return, the newly-trained chefs bring fresh ideas to the restaurant and also help to improve the skills of their colleagues.

This approach means that Gordon Ramsay Holdings are able to expand successfully, retain talent within the business and guarantee that all staff are trained in 'the Gordon Ramsay way' to ensure continuity of service and standards. Retaining an informal, nurturing approach to managing talent has also enabled the organization to remain creative – a key success factor in the competitive restaurant industry.

Talent Management

Virtually every company, regardless of its geographic scope, needs to understand its employees if they are to attract and retain them; what they think and want; what motivates and demotivates them; what causes them to want to stay and perform or leave. Towers Perrin's Global Workforce Study (2006) found that:

- People want different things from their company at different stages of their employment life cycle. Therefore a 'one size fits all' approach does not work, especially with respect to reward strategy.

- When it comes to choosing a job, people everywhere have similar needs. Three key requirements are: ensuring adequate compensation and financial security; achieving work–life balance; and having relevant learning and career opportunities.
- People care about job security, but value mobility as well, and generally remain open to considering other job opportunities. This poses a potential retention risk for companies that cannot afford to lose certain types of key skill. However a considerable number of people will stay with a company if the conditions are right, and if the company is perceived to be 'talent friendly' and progressive in terms of having leading-edge people practices and work environments. This makes it all the more important to continuously improve the employee value proposition.
- Retention has a lot to do with organizational practices around managing and rewarding talent. Employees want to work for a company that is known to seek out and retain the right type of top talent. People place a premium on being able to build their skills and have opportunities to learn. They want to work for a 'winning organization'.
- Manager behaviour in particular has a strong influence on employee retention though there are variations on the way manager influence is thought to operate. In some countries, what makes a difference to retention is managers' ability to understand what motivates people; in others it is about how they inspire enthusiasm for work or treat people with respect and trust. In other countries it is about how managers ensure access to learning opportunities, conduct effective performance reviews and hold people accountable for performance goals.

Getting the right blend of ingredients to attract and retain talent and produce enhanced performance therefore requires HR to have a good understanding of what motivates employees at any stage of their own development, of what employees need to make them effective in their job and ensure that they feel appropriately managed. In the following short case study developed for CIPD, the performance requirements of knowledge workers are reflected in both job design and HR processes.

Case Study: Managing Performance at CapGemini

CapGemini is a global leader in consulting, technology, outsourcing and local professional services. Headquartered in Paris, the organization operates in more than 30 countries with 82 000 people across the globe. In the UK CapGemini Consulting employs 800 consultants working across functional and industry sectors.

CapGemini's Consultants need the ability to work effectively from any location. Therefore, all new joiners are provided with powerful lightweight laptops with wireless connectivity, mobile phones with e-mail and Internet capability, easy access to teleconferencing facilities and the ability to access the intranet remotely for information and processes. Business applications are hosted on the intranet to enable consultants to remotely access time and expense recording, HR applications (including performance management applications), company communications and, importantly for knowledge workers, the ability to tap into the collective understanding, expertise and experience of the business through an online knowledge management system. In addition to classroom learning, experiential learning, coaching and mentoring, a significant amount of e-learning is available through the web.

The success of consultancy engagements is based on the extent to which they meet defined objectives and client expectations. Consultants are therefore performance managed against these criteria, as well as business objectives and behavioural indicators.

Consultants are provided with a great deal of autonomy in their daily work – consultants are often responsible for the planning and definition of projects in line with customer requirements and operate as self-managed individuals. Consultants refer to mentors and 'reviewers' (a colleague a grade above who is responsible for reviewing performance management) on development matters. Pastoral care is provided by a business team leader. All these roles interact within a virtual environment, rarely being together in the same physical environment or project team. As a result of this context, telephone, conference calls, e-mail, other electronic communications and frequent social gatherings are a key feature of the culture at CapGemini. Indeed, internal communications contribute greatly to the sense of community within teams and across the business.

Although taking a very much outcome-driven approach to the contribution of a role, a common set of behavioural competencies per grade aligned with learning interventions, feedback and self-analysis tools, is used to provide appropriate focus on the ways of working of consultants.

CapGemini has adopted a management style which complements this context. The business operates a flat structure, with six grades of consultants throughout the business. Leaders in capability units ensure that they are approachable and know their people on a personal level. Culturally, decision-making is delegated and it is a low-politics environment. Values of fun, modesty, solidarity, freedom, trust, boldness and honesty are celebrated and reinforced through recruitment, performance, recognition, learning and other processes, and role-modelled by leaders.

CapGemini attracts a high standard of applications for vacancies and is proud of its low attrition rates. Two CapGemini consultants were recognized at the first Consultant of the Year Awards in 2007. In addition, CapGemini receives a high standard of customer feedback and its share performance has consistently outperformed the DAC (CapGemini is listed on the Paris Bourse).

Developing Global Leaders

The challenges of operating in a global environment for organizations highlight the need for effective leadership. Operating internationally, global leaders can be presented with widely diverging socio-economic and environmental conditions.

Countries vary in terms of infrastructure, regulations and laws, levels of bureaucracy and business culture. They have different time-zones and languages. These differences create additional challenges for leaders in managing their business identity, maximizing efficiency and attempting to enforce required standards.

Many global companies want a leadership talent management process which is able to respond to the unique needs of a given market yet also able to produce the benefits of consistency and fairness. Most successful global companies recognize the importance of having senior managers with an international orientation. Stroh and Caligiuri (1998) suggest that 'successful multinational corporations recognize the value in having global managers with the expertise to anticipate the organization's markets and to respond proactively. These organizations have learned that leaders who are flexible and open to the demands of the global market have made possible the organization's international business success.'

An essential part of a strategic HR agenda is developing global leaders. This may require sending managers on overseas assignments as developmental experiences, not simply because there is a technical need for their skills. Global HR should also be involved in developing a global orientation in 'local' or host country managers, as described in Chapter 10. Typically, 'local' managers can be introduced to global leadership through visits to the corporate headquarters and other company centres around the world.

In Roffey Park research into Global Leadership (Sinclair and Agyeman, 2004), organizations used a variety of methods and innovative strategies to support and encourage effective leadership practices. In particular they focused on developing processes for consensual decision-making; managing and developing performance throughout the organization; maximizing responsiveness to survive in a dynamic, competitive environment; facilitating knowledge sharing and the flow of resources through the company; encouraging a global focus rather than local allegiances; managing global change processes; supporting diversity; and deliberate focused efforts to manage the company's reputation.

Leaders' own strategies to enhance their effectiveness included keeping up to date and broadening their perspectives though reading, building relationships and networking; seeking new experiences to build their capabilities; developing and reviewing processes for effective and regular communications; developing strategies for motivating and facilitating high performance across diverse teams and distances; taking a proactive approach to managing potential dilemmas arising from cultural difference; creating learning opportunities and developing self-awareness; and processes for effective change management. For further detail of international leadership development see Chapter 10.

Case Study: 'Conversations that Count' at Standard Chartered PLC

In the following case study, developed for the CIPD by Tansley *et al.* (2006a,b)[1], Standard Chartered Bank (SCB) set out to revamp its talent management

---

1. Used with permission from CIPD.

approach. A key tenet of this approach was 'that people perform best when they play to their strengths'.

Standard Chartered PLC is listed on both the London Stock Exchange and the Hong Kong Stock Exchange and is consistently ranked in the top 25 among FTSE-100 companies by market capitalization. Standard Chartered has a history of over 150 years in banking and operates in many of the world's fastest-growing markets with an extensive global network of over 1400 branches (including subsidiaries, associates and joint ventures) in over 50 countries in the Asia-Pacific Region, South Asia, the Middle East, Africa, the United Kingdom and the Americas.

As one of the world's most international banks, almost 60000 people are employed, representing over 90 nationalities, worldwide. With strong organic growth supported by strategic alliances and acquisitions and driven by its strengths in the balance and diversity of its business, products, geography and people, SCB is well positioned in the emerging trade corridors of Asia, Africa and the Middle East. The bank derives over 90% of profits from Asia, Africa and the Middle East.

Key Drivers for Talent Management

SCB seeks to develop the capability to respond to market changes, evolve business strategies and achieve its ambitious growth aspirations, and these are the key drivers for its talent management initiatives. The HR function (see Figure 14.1) provides employee self-service and extensive data analysis across the bank's 56 operating countries to allow all global HR processes to be consistently adopted and monitored across the bank's markets.

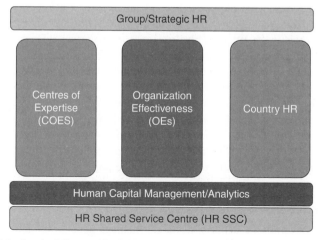

FIGURE 14.1 Standard Chartered Bank HR structure.

The Issues and Challenges of Talent Management in Standard Chartered

SCB is experiencing fast growth in the international domain, and it has a particular interest in ensuring that the talents of its diverse workforce are maximized through employee engagement and inclusivity. One way in which it is attempting to do this is through human capital management and the use of robust technologies. Data for all SCB's direct employees across 56 markets are held on one HR management information system, Peoplewise, which is powered by Peoplesoft technology. Using comparable, standardized and robust data provided through the global Peoplesoft system and the Human Resources Shared Service Centre in Chennai, India, the bank is able to provide extensive data reporting capability. This strategy enables most of its global processes to be consistently tracked across the Bank's markets, including data on core demographics, performance, reward, training, talent management, diversity, and development.

Global Processes

The global talent management processes are enabled by HR but owned by line management. At their heart these processes are strengths-based as well as data- and research-driven. Talent classification leads to quarterly Talent Reviews and succession planning. The staff engagement survey data feeds into performance review and reward, and then into individual objectives and development plans.

Appraisal is a key part of talent management at SCB, not only in its own right, but also because it is used to classify employees into five categories, ranging from high potentials (HIPs) to underperformers. This system allows the bank to manage its talent by revealing the skills and potential inside its workforce – and showing where there are gaps. '*High-potentials* (HIPs) are people with significant headroom, who would be expected to rise at least two further levels in the foreseeable future,' Geraldine Haley (Group Head of talent management and leadership development) explains. Second are *critical resources*: people who have the potential to improve and whom the bank certainly wants to keep, but who are not real high flyers. Third are *core contributors*. 'They are valuable resources who are probably doing what they do best now,' Geraldine Haley says. Fourth are *under-achievers*, who could be doing better and should be helped to do so. Bottom of the pile are *underperformers*, who are 'in the wrong job and should be moved into another role or managed out'.

All employees, from juniors to one level below the board, are assessed annually according to this system in conjunction with their interim reviews. Combining classification with appraisal has kept the burden for managers to a minimum because they see it as part of the same process. It also helps to ensure management accountability and therefore accuracy of data.

'Conversations that Count'

Alignment of different aspects of talent management is another challenge, and SCB have a number of initiatives that seek to address it. One particularly successful example is through the use of five briefings entitled 'Conversations that Count', which are short guides to quickly enable managers to have vital conversations with each member of their teams.

Conversations on performance and on development have a set schedule that involves planning in January, reviewing in July, and assessing in December. These five main 'conversations' take place on a flexible basis on engagement, strengths and career, and are related to the needs of the individual team member. It is felt that when a conversation between manager and employee is the 'right' conversation undertaken in the 'right' way, it can help increase engagement, enable people to develop and use their strengths, enable the bank to keep its best talent, encourage energy, innovation and fun, satisfy customers, and deliver better business and financial results.

Managers are advised that their HR regional manager can then help them access further sources of support if needed, including training programmes and extra information on their HR information system. These conversations are:

- *Perform* – at the start of January employees are asked to draft business and financial objectives for the year ahead and consider how they will deliver the values of the business during the year. A meeting is then arranged to discuss this, and managers will also share information that provides context – e.g. their own objectives. SMART objectives are then agreed and consideration given to what the objectives mean for the employee's learning.
- *Learn and develop* – at the start of January the employee is asked to draft a document that will set out: what he or she needs to learn – bearing in mind objectives and future career goals, and how he or she needs to learn – drawing on a wide range of learning options. A meeting is held with the manager to discuss the learning the employee needs in order to achieve excellence in the role and deliver this year's objectives. Resource constraints such as time and budget have to be considered and how to work imaginatively within those constraints. The year's learning and development priorities are then agreed, written down and signed off.
- *Build careers* – the time may be right for a career conversation when the employee has mastered the core aspects of his or her job and is ready for additional or fresh challenges and it has been 12–18 months since the last career conversation. A meeting takes place where the employee discusses his or her career goals. Tools are provided beforehand to assist with the employee's reflections.
- *Engagement review* – a 'lite' engagement review takes place once a year with existing team members already known well by the manager. Ahead of the meeting the individual is briefed, open questions are asked during the meeting, and agreed actions recorded and commitment made to follow up. A 'full' engagement review is for team members who are new to the manager. During the meeting, the manager is required to ask open, focused questions under the headings: 'Know me', 'Care about me' and 'Focus on me'.

- *Build strengths* – in order to have the 'great conversation', when the manager and the HR manager believe the time is right, the employee is asked to complete an online questionnaire called StrengthsFinder™ which is designed to identify talents and strengths. It need only be completed once because the talents it reveals are enduring; it is used to support the development of a person who performs well and has high potential.

One of the bank's Strengths coaches helps the employee to understand the talents it reveals, and how he or she can be developed towards strengths. The conversation with the manager takes place after this to explore what the employee has learned, to discuss the actions he or she will take to develop talents into strengths, to consider opportunities to use his or her talents and strengths more often, and to record agreed actions and sign off. The employee is encouraged to have a follow-up session with the Strengths coach every six months. So 'Conversations that Count' are an essential way in which different elements of talent management are aligned.

Standard Chartered PLC's approach is a highly structured and integrated one involving steps that make the process clear to the managers undertaking the reviews by focusing on the dialogue that is required to take place in various conversations. This notion of 'conversation' also appears in other areas of HR practices that relate to talent management. For example, Hirsh (2003: 237) suggests that the succession planning process also involves dialogue between key parties, and she coins the useful term 'succession dialogues'.

Global Talent Pools

There are regular business reviews on talent from board level down to country management team. Outcome, rather than process measures are tracked. At the level of Country Management Trainees, locally tailored programmes are made available. International graduates are provided with two-year development through rotations and global programmes. Junior High Potentials are locally managed and reviewed in 56 countries. Mid-career MBAs are strategic hirings which supplement the leadership pipeline. Middle management high potentials are reviewed by ten global leadership teams. Senior Management High Potentials are reviewed by the Group Management Committee.

Creating an Inclusive Culture

As well as developing leaders, SCB aims to build a high-performing and inclusive culture. SCB is a very diverse organization, with more than one hundred nationalities represented throughout the bank and more than fifty nationalities within the most senior five hundred employees. The gender balance at SCB is broadly equal, with 47% of employees being female. However, only 16% of senior managers are female and one of the bank's priorities for 2008 is to raise that percentage.

Competition for talent across many markets is intense. The bank believes its inclusive approach known as Diversity and Inclusion, or D&I, gives it a distinct advantage over its competitors, creating a much larger pool of talent for recruitment. It also provides engaging opportunities for employees to develop, both as individuals and as part of a team.

Diversity through Inclusion

SCB focuses on three strands of diversity – nationality, gender and disability (with a particular focus on visual impairment). Over three hundred people across SCB now have a D&I role, and a D&I Ambassador role was created for a number of senior employees to raise awareness of D&I across the business. Many D&I issues are market-specific. To address this, SCB appointed 50 D&I Champions across 48 markets and territories, as well as 28 Country Councils to support the Champions. In 2006 D&I Champions and Councils took part in a review and action planning process, listening to employees in order to determine local D&I issues. Examples of the issues raised include:

- Employees would welcome the opportunity to work more flexibly
- Greater opportunities to gain international experience without relocation
- Unintentional exclusionary behaviour often goes unnoticed.

In 2006 SCB piloted a D&I awareness programme in various countries to make staff aware of, and understand the role that D&I can play in helping create an inclusive culture. Awareness-raising sessions were also held with the global leadership team meetings to help deliver the message in each business area. Key priorities include:

- *Valuing employees* – employee retention is a key management priority and an integrated approach to managing employee retention is being developed.
- *Engaging employees* – effective employee engagement leads to increased productivity and revenue and lower employee turnover. SCB has measured employee engagement globally since 2001 and continues to see an increase in engagement each year. In 2006, 97% of employees completed the survey (Gallup Q12).
- *Empowering women* – the increasing size of Standard Chartered, along with the success of various global initiatives and the value these have demonstrated, have led to a programme focused on helping women to reach their full potential. The programme, known as GOAL, was launched in India in 2006. GOAL uses the principles of sports-based social inclusion to build women's self-esteem, strengthen their leadership skills and provide access to education opportunities. Participants attend coached netball sessions and undertake a modular leadership course. Best performers will be rewarded with scholarships, micro-finance opportunities and potentially, internships at SCB's branches.
- *Health and safety* – SCB is committed to creating a healthy, safe and fulfilling environment in which people can work. During 2006 SCB introduced a

zero tolerance safety process for identifying risks. All the bank's offices were inspected, and ongoing health and safety training aims to ensure an embedded health and safety awareness culture.

- *Employee wellbeing* – in 2006 SCB introduced employee volunteering on a global basis to support individuals' commitment to community initiatives. The scheme gives each employee an additional two days' leave each year for voluntary work they fund themselves. So far over 1000 employees have chosen to take this opportunity. SCB also launched a pilot of the reward level programme in five countries. This rewards employees who demonstrate outstanding business performance with an additional five days' leave, sponsored by Standard Chartered, to spend on a project that ties in with SCB's community strategy.

- There is also a global approach to flexible working and continued annual family days across the bank. In November 2006, a global Employee Wellbeing week was introduced for all employees. A variety of events were held across the bank with record levels of employees involved in talks on different topics, such as physical activities, family days, health checks, healthy food, quizzes, competitions, comedy and even massages. In Singapore, for example, more than five hundred people had health screenings, while in Korea, more than three hundred employees and customers received finger pressure therapy from visually impaired therapists.

Supporting Transnational Teams

Another vital area for HR activity is supporting transnational teams to achieve business success. Transnational teams, as defined by Bartlett and Ghoshal (1989), bring together individuals of different cultures working on activities which cross national borders. Team development involves the full range of HR activities such as selecting staff for teams, clarifying roles, developing appropriate appraisal mechanisms, enabling performance, building reward processes and career planning. Research carried out by Snell *et al.* (1998) for the International Consortium for Executive Development Research (ICEDR), however, suggests that HR teams in many multinationals are not yet in a position to fully support transnational teams. In many cases HR policies perpetuate traditional organization structures rather than the more 'web-like' structures of transnational operations. More flexible approaches to team development are needed and HR strategies need to be aligned to the business needs if effective transnational teams are to be appropriately supported. The ICEDR research indicates that most transnational teams need to balance three concerns relating to worldwide competition. These key strategic drivers are local responsiveness, global efficiency and organizational learning. In successful international organizations, HR strategies and policies support these drivers.

Local responsiveness is critical as teams need to make allowances for the specific demands of different cultures and market conditions. Variety therefore needs to be a feature of a transnational team, especially since members of transnational teams are often dispersed geographically and need to be able to deal with local issues appropriately. Some companies take a polycentric approach to staffing, with new members added only if they add value.

Training programmes can improve a team's responsiveness to local issues, but those which seem most helpful are programmes that emphasize the company's strategies and processes so that team members can understand the big picture within which they are operating. Typically, transnational teams work as virtual teams which not only need all the training and development usually made available to co-located teams but also have the added dimension of communicating mainly through technology rather than face to face. Managers of such teams may also need help from HR in understanding the implications of managing a multi-site operation.

Conversely, the demand for global efficiency means that a high degree of coordination and integration are required. HR practices need to ensure that global concerns are not neglected. In some companies this is achieved by deliberately understaffing teams in order to ensure that team members collaborate in order to make up for the shortfall. Cross-cultural awareness training can be helpful as can deliberate team building activities when a team is first formed. Teams can be trained in conflict resolution as well as being able to establish ground rules which can lead to integrated teamwork.

Some companies emphasize the corporate values as a means of blending together teams in a way that transcends national and functional boundaries. To aid integration further, team leaders can be trained to achieve decisions by consensus and individuals can be given responsibility for carrying out a task on behalf of the whole team. If the HR function is to support transnational teams it is important that the HR group itself operates as a transnational team. This may require the team to be involved in its own team development process before being able to work effectively on supporting other teams.

Teams also need to leverage knowledge continuously around the world and be able to institutionalize the learning within the organization as a whole. IBM's International Airlines Solutions Centre has developed an intelligence network which enables the knowledge generated by transnational teams to be shared. Formalized communications can be a helpful spur to organizational learning. In one company, the business planning process involves team members in researching and reporting back to the rest of the team on the needs of a range of external constituents. Improved use of technology also means that teams can gain access to talent elsewhere in the organization which might otherwise have been 'hidden' in the hierarchy.

HR information systems need to operate on an international level to include data on potential team candidates wherever they are based. Ideally such systems should allow for the storage of data which also includes individuals' preferences about where they would like to work. Clearly, reward schemes should ideally reflect these needs. However, formal reward systems are often problematic with regard to international teamwork. An international software provider achieved considerable business growth throughout the 1990s and is now operating globally. In the early days of establishing the international business, each 'local' business fought for its own business and supplied customer service locally. Rewards were heavily geared to business winning. When the business had achieved a critical mass, the sales operation was restructured so that sales were carried out by the UK team only, leaving all the 'local' operations to supply customer service only. Since rewards continued to be based on sales, rather than customer service, this change was understandably unpopular with the local teams.

The ICEDR team found that where individual goals and incentives were used, they appeared to encourage local responsiveness. Surprisingly few companies in their survey used formal team-based incentives. Similarly, few appraisal and reward schemes appeared to recognize learning even though executives acknowledged the value of organizational learning through transnational teamwork.

Case Study: Transnational Working at Jaguar and Land Rover[2]

Jaguar and Land Rover were once part of the same group in the era of BL cars, but went their separate ways for a period during the 1980s and 90s, Jaguar being privatized and then bought by Ford, Land Rover remaining with what became the Rover Group which was ultimately acquired by BMW. When Ford bought Land Rover from BMW in 2000, Jaguar and Land Rover were initially run as completely separate businesses as part of Ford's Premier Automotive Group, but they have operated under a common management structure since 2002 in an effort to realize greater benefits of scale. They remain separate legal entities, some leaders having responsibilities solely in one business, whilst others span both. Each is in a different phase of the business cycle and faces challenges unique to their own particular market sectors, all of which makes the leadership role particularly complex and challenging.

A strategic review of the Jaguar and Land Rover businesses in 2002/3 led to the identification of six key priorities for the future. One of these was the need for a significant cultural shift, with 'Creating the Winning Team' becoming the manifestation of that objective. Many senior managers were known for their outstanding technical skills, rather than necessarily for being good leaders, so it was quickly recognized that a significant investment in leadership development would be required if the organization was to achieve its ultimate long-term goals.

An additional layer of complexity has been added since that time. In the face of increasing global competition, Ford is keen to see even greater partnership working amongst the different businesses within its portfolio, which in Europe includes Volvo as well as its own European operation. In consequence, there has been a significant increase in joint working between all four brands in recent years, with employees from the different organizations regularly meeting together, clarifying the parameters within which they are working and

---

2. Jaguar and Land Rover was acquired by Tata in 2008. I am grateful to Peter Wall (formerly Education, Training and Development Manager at Jaguar and Land Rover), for this case study, which just predates the acquisition by Tata.

establishing clear boundaries around what will be done jointly and what will remain separate. As a consequence, senior leaders are also having to become highly competent at cross-boundary and cross-cultural working.

Facilitating Cross-Boundary Learning through Training and Development

Cultural issues can represent a major challenge. Simply exporting an approach which has worked well in one location may not work elsewhere. Training and development is a key enabler of this cross-boundary joint working, and the T&D managers from each company mirror the overall approach by running development collaboratively across their respective businesses. T&D is split into four broad clusters, with one business taking the 'lead' on behalf of all of the others for each particular cluster:

- Leadership
- Management, administration and business competencies
- IT and systems
- Technical skills, including technical skills for non-technical managers, according to functions.

The approach of the respective T&D managers is critical to the success of this process, not only in setting direction and monitoring progress but also in paying close attention to some of the softer enabling factors such as acting as a sounding board for the project leaders, and helping them evolve effective working relationships in a really practical way. Issues which have had to be worked through include the whole spectrum from scheduling face-to-face meetings in the early stages to build relationships, right through to how to deal with different approaches to setting budgets, who pays for development work and how the cross-charging process will work.

Achieving real tangible business outcomes from the synergies of joint working has meant breaking through many assumptions and different set ways of working. Here, the different national culture backgrounds of team members have proved a real asset. Peter Wall has first hand experience of working within a wide range of different cultures and leadership styles – including Japanese, German, American and Swedish – has enabled Peter to sensitize team members to what may be happening under the surface of their discussions, and to more easily see how to navigate successfully across cultural boundaries.

Peter's message with regard to facilitating cross-cultural learning is as follows:

- Keep your language simple, without being patronizing. It is tiring for people who are working in English if this is not their first language. Avoid idioms.
- Total listening – seek first to understand. It really helps to hone one's emotional intelligence, to feel intuitively for what colleagues are trying to say, be tactful.

- Try to propose rather than being overly directive. This is the equivalent of a reflective versus more stereotypically US action-oriented style.
- Lead discussion on HOW the work gets done as well as the physical outputs: what does consensus look like for this group? (e.g. I might not completely agree; but can I live with that?); talk about what we can do to address tensions; identify specific things we can gain from each other; what's the message we want to give to senior directors?

KEY LESSONS

In developing an integrated global business, an HR strategy that is fully integrated with the business strategy is essential. The environmental demands on global businesses have placed leadership development, talent sourcing and management, corporate reputation and leading for diversity and opportunity centre-stage. These are central to HR strategy in a fast-changing international business. It is important to identify and focus on a few critical HR practices rather than attempt a large number of initiatives that do not deliver. Finally, it is worth recognizing that global network cultures are more complex than those in 'conventional' single country organizations and require much greater coordination and persistence.

CHECKLISTS ON GLOBALIZING AND SUPPORTING THE INTERNATIONAL BUSINESS

Supporting the International/Global Business

- How does your organization manage across borders, i.e. is your organization predominantly:
  - Domestic
  - Multi-domestic
  - A simple export organization
  - Using local agents
  - International
  - Truly globalized with a complex web of businesses, joint ventures and alliances across most of the world's economies?
- What is the impact of globalization on how HR is organized, i.e. should HR be centralized, decentralized or a combination?
- Which HR practices need to be global and which local?
- How do HR practices ensure that global concerns are not ignored?
- How effectively does the global HR team operate? How does it achieve a global/local balance?
- How flexible are the HR practices in use?
- How do global 'hard' systems support HR and global management?
- How is resistance to global approaches overcome?
- How well is HR currently supporting transnational teams?

- How much does your organization consider 'local' managers as part of the international management cadre?
- What are the selection criteria for leaders of international teams?
- What approaches are used to develop international teams and leaders?
- How are managers helped to develop a global perspective?
- What are the main ways in which international employees are deployed, e.g. on short-term assignments, expatriate postings etc.?
- To what extent is telecommuting replacing the need for international assignments?
- What are the implications for managers of enabling 'high-touch' continuous interaction in support of international team members?
- How are employee motivation, reward and recognition currently aligned to the changing business and organizational priorities?
- How are terms and conditions for international employees currently defined? Are special terms required for expatriation, or simply reward arrangements which reflect flexibility and mobility?
- To what extent do current reward initiatives encourage sustained commitment, flexibility, innovation and quality among transnational workforces?
- Can Western-style pay structures and systems be successfully adopted internationally?
- What scope or expectation exists across international boundaries to develop flexible 'total compensation' initiatives?
- Despite a common governance initiative of sustained shareholder value creation, can common approaches, e.g. on cost minimization and commodity pricing, really work in a global company?
- How do international employees achieve a work/personal life balance and is it the organization's responsibility to do anything to assist this? If so, what can be done?
- How is knowledge generated in one region leveraged within the business as a whole?

REFERENCES

Bartlett, C.A. and Ghoshal, S. (1989) *Managing Across Borders: The Transnational Solution*. Cambridge, MA: Harvard Business School Press

Brake, R.J. (1999) *Oregon Business Magazine*, 22, No. 2, 36

Cabrera, L. (2004) *Political Theory of Global Justice: A Cosmopolitan Case for the World State*. New York: Routledge

Dickson, M.W., Den Hartog, D.N. and Mitchelson, J.K. (2003) Research on leadership in a cross-cultural context: Making new progress and raising new questions. *Leadership Quarterly*, 14, No. 6, 729–768

GMAC (2008) *Global Relocation Trends Survey*. Global Relocations Services

Harris, P.R. (2002) European challenge: developing global organizations. *European Business Review*, 14, No. 6, 416–425

Hirsh, W. (2003) Positive career development for leaders and managers, in Storey, J. (ed.), *Leadership in Organizations: Current Issues and Key Trends*. London: Routledge

Holt, D.B., Quelch, J.A. and Taylor, E.L. (2004) How global brands compete. *Harvard Business Review*, 82, No. 9, 68–75

Kennedy, C. (1998) Global dreams, local realities. *Human Resources*, Mar/Apr

Kets de Vries, M.F.R. and Florent-Treacy, E. (1999) *The New Global Leaders: Richard Branson, Percy Barnevik, David Simon and the Remaking of International Business*. San Francisco: Jossey-Bass

Larson, P. (2008) Presentation: HR Partnering in a Global World, National Conference, Harrogate, CIPD

McCuiston, V.E., Wooldridge, R.R. and Pierce, C.K. (2004) Leading the diverse workforce: Profit, prospects and progress. *Leadership and Organization Development Journal*, 25, No. 1, 73–92

Ng, E.S.W. and Tung, R.L. (1998) Ethno-cultural diversity and organizational effectiveness: A field study. *International Journal of Human Resource Management*, 9, No. 6, 980–995

Schneider-Ross (2002) *The Business of Diversity*. Andover: Schneider-Ross

Sinclair, A. and Agyeman, B. (2004) *Building Global Leadership: Strategies for Success*. Horsham: Roffey Park

Smith, A. and Sinclair, A. (2003) *What Makes an Excellent Virtual Manager?* Horsham: Roffey Park Institute

Snell, S.A., Snow, C.C., Canney Davison, S. and Hambrick, D.C. (1998) Designing and supporting transnational teams: the Human Resource agenda. *Human Resources Management*, 37, No. 2 (Summer), 147–158

Sparrow, P., Brewster, C. and Harris, H. (2004) *Globalizing Human Resource Management: Tracking the Business Role of International Human Resources Specialists*. London: Routledge

Sparrow, P. (2008) Global HR presentation, Annual Conference, Harrogate, CIPD

Stroh, L.K. and Caligiuri, P.M. (1998) Increasing global competitiveness through effective people management. *Journal of World Business*, 33, No. 1, 1–16

Tansley, C. *et al.* (2006a) *Change Agenda: Reflections on Talent Management*. London: CIPD

Tansley, C. *et al.* (2006b) *Change Agenda: Talent Management: Understanding the Dimensions*. London: CIPD

Tansley, C., Turner, P., Foster, C., Harris, L., Sempik, A., Stewart, J. and Williams, H. (2007a) *Research Insight: Talent Management*. London: CIPD

Tansley, C., Turner, P., Foster, C., Harris, L., Sempik, A., Stewart, J. and Williams, H. (2007b) *Talent: Strategy, Management, Measurement*. London: CIPD

Towers Perrin (2006) *Winning Strategies for a Global Workforce*. Towers Perrin Global Workforce Study

Trompenaars, F. (1997) *Riding the Waves of Culture*. London: Nicholas Brealey

Part IV

Implementing Strategic Change

Chapter 15

Bringing about Culture Change

Companies around the world are coming to the realization that the right strategy is crucial but not always sufficient. And when great strategies fail, leaders often instinctively know the reason. Their next question is, How do we fix our culture?

(Couto *et al.*, 2007)

Change is an inevitable consequence of strategic decisions. After all, planned strategy involves bringing about desired choices and usually involves stopping, starting or modifying activities. However, if the strategy is to be successful, the organizational culture, or 'way we do things around here', needs to be conducive to the change. This is likely to be a culture with a positive work climate, where work practices and employee mindsets are adaptable to changing needs; where employees are energized and committed to the change and able to play their part in achieving it. In practice, many of the 'brakes' on implementing strategy lie in the way the organization's culture operates and the lack of 'buy-in' to change by employees. So while changing strategy and structure can be difficult enough, what is much harder to achieve, and takes longer to happen, is changing the organization's culture.

HR has a key role to play in building healthy and changeable organizational cultures, but managing the process of change can be daunting. Obstacles that prevent the system from operating in this way need to be identified and eliminated. New practices and processes need to be introduced. Changes come so thick and fast that in many organizations it may be hard to isolate just one change process that needs to be managed. Yet change does need to be managed if the positive impetus for change is to overcome the forces of inertia and resistance which are common to most organizations.

WHAT IS MEANT BY 'CULTURE CHANGE'?

Organizational culture is reflected in the way organizational members behave and the beliefs, values and assumptions which they share. Some of these assumptions may be so taken for granted that they become invisible and only become visible when change threatens them. The assumptions may be apparent in the formal systems, such as the reward scheme, or may be more active in the informal or 'shadow' system in which the grapevine, political behaviour and net-works flourish.

Typically, the culture is most visible in manifestations such as the way employees treat one another, how they dress, the size and layout of office space, the appearance of the reception area and how customers are treated. Less vis-ible, but good indicators of culture are the organization's rituals and routines, the amount and nature of political activity and the symbolism of certain aspects of an organization's history.

Types of Organizational Culture

Roger Harrison (1986) has identified four broad categories into which organi-zational cultures can be classified. Any organization, he argues, has a blend of these types of culture, though some types may be characteristic of some organi-zations more than others. Each of these types of culture has its strengths and limitations, as well as its 'dark' or 'shadow' side, where a culture's strength can become a limitation. He suggests that organizational excellence is achieved through exploiting the dynamic tension between the strengths of these different culture types.

Each culture type has the capacity to empower or disempower people. A power culture empowers through identification with a strong leader but can dis-empower through fear and through an inability to act without permission. A role culture, such as in a bureaucracy, empowers through systems that serve the peo-ple and the task, reducing confusion and conflict. Such a culture disempowers through restricting autonomy and creativity and erects barriers to cooperation. An achievement culture empowers through identification with the values and ideas of a vision; through the liberation of creativity; through freedom to act. It disempow-ers through burnout and stress; through treating the individual as an instrument of the task; through inhibiting dissent about goals and values. A support culture empowers through the power of cooperation and trust; through providing under-standing, acceptance and assistance. It disempowers through suppressing conflict; through preoccupation with process; through conformity to group norms.

Organizations as Systems

Certain characteristics of organizational culture may be harder to shift than oth-ers. Complexity theories suggest that all organizations, which are essentially complex systems, act as networks of interconnections. These networks, which are basically feedback loops, are not necessarily consciously planned but spring up across the organization in ways which connect different groups of people. While some networks, such as learning groups, may be part of the formal sys-tem, the informal system where most networks operate is inherently unpredict-able and self-organizing. The way these networks operate is most obvious in the 'corridor conversations', which provide a way of bypassing blockages and act as 'safety valves' for employees. The informal system is a social, political one in which people communicate and learn.

The grapevine is a much faster means of communication than formal systems and, because the grapevine cannot be controlled, it is easy for negative ideas to be embedded there, especially in times of change when anxieties may be running high. The stories circulating via the grapevine often show that high levels of creativity exist within the organization since people will invent what they do not know. Equally, the informal system is subject to the 'ripple effect' of the stone in the pond. When positive messages are implanted there they can also spread like wildfire.

The types of stories which are told can teach employees about how they are expected to behave. In 3M the story about the invention of the Post-it note (which was an accidental discovery in the search for another product) is deliberately told to new employees to encourage them to experiment and learn from their mistakes. In another organization, the story about the appalling way in which a redundancy situation was handled made the organization notorious in the town where it was based and taught employees to expect to be dealt with ruthlessly. Not surprisingly, many 'uncontrolled' departures followed the redundancies.

Formal change programmes tend to set up more resistance than emergent change, especially if they appear to threaten values which employees hold dear. A number of years ago the new chief executive of a small consulting firm, wishing to improve the profitability of the firm, introduced a new reward system based on individual targets and performance-related pay for income generators. This was to replace the flat rate percentage of profits which previously distributed equally to all employees on a collegiate basis. The new reward system threatened to undermine the teamworking for which the consulting firm was known. For the first few years there was strenuous staff resistance and for a while there was an uneasy co-existence of the formal and informal system as employees and management tried to reason with each other.

The chief executive persisted with the scheme and gradually resistance gave way to a grudging acceptance of the scheme. Some consultants began to enjoy the individual bonuses. They became reluctant to share leads with colleagues and political games started to be played. Teamworking broke down. Profitability did increase in line with the improved market but only as new staff were brought in to replace those who left because they no longer enjoyed the culture.

Why do People Resist Change?

Many psychologists have addressed this question and have identified that change can represent a major personal transition, akin to bereavement, during which what is familiar has to be destabilized and 'let go' before people can move on to integrate new learning. For people who like the comfort of the familiar, or who are rather risk averse (which is surprisingly common among senior managers), change can threaten their comfort zones. Of course, change can bring many opportunities for individuals and organizations and there is much research evidence to suggest that people who have a positive approach to change usually manage to make opportunities for themselves during periods of ambiguity.

A qualitative survey carried out by the Spencer Stuart Organization in 1998 highlights the strong cultural resistance to change which was experienced by executives who were hired by utilities companies in the USA to champion moves to a competitive market culture in monopolies. Many of the executives brought in to implement change left within two years. The most common cultural challenges were:

- Resistance to change
- Unfamiliarity with competitive markets
- Aversion to risk
- Lack of responsiveness to risk
- Managers' and employees' sense of entitlement to resources and benefits.

The study also found that 'champions of change' felt that the following were most valuable in overcoming cultural challenges:

- Outstanding communication and persuasion skills
- Taking action to create entirely new programmes and structures
- Managing well in the face of uncertainty
- Flexibility
- Marketing skills and a customer-focused viewpoint
- Knowledge of competitive market finance and accounting.

On the whole, though, organizational change can seem threatening to employees because when the change is imposed top-down, such as in the decision to acquire another company or to sell off part of the organization, employees feel that they have no control over what is likely to happen. This is when the consequences of change can appear profoundly negative to employees. Transformation can threaten people's mental models of how their organization should act, what work should be like and what their own prospects look like. In the early phases of Roffey Park's Career Development in Flatter Structures project, some of the symptoms of employee dissatisfaction came through when people were asked about the effect of delayering on them. Comments included:

- It's unrewarding financially
- Chaos; no one knows what anyone else is doing
- We've added a tier rather than taking one away
- There's confusion about people's roles
- Ongoing uncertainty with all these changes happening
- People do not know where they are going any more
- Loss of staff loyalty
- Stress levels high

- No accountability
- Turf protection
- Same workload but fewer staff to do it.

Sadly, comments also included criticisms of the role of HR in managing change: 'HR credibility knocked – an example of what not to do'.

Ironically, while so many change projects are introduced in order to bring customer and business benefit, the effect of change on employees can actually lead to a downturn in profits, at least in the short term. One of the reasons for this is a loss of focus. Organizations can become introspective and cease paying attention to the external business environment. If political behaviour and 'turf wars' break out during the period of uncertainty, the internal focus becomes stronger. Similarly, the rate of change can be so great that employees simply stop working and spend their time in speculation. There may also be a leadership vacuum at the top of the organization because members of the management team are actively involved in managing the business deals rather than the organization.

Overcoming resistance to change is a joint effort between HR, line managers and employees. And while there may be no single blueprint for effective culture change, initiating culture change by helping employees understand the need for change – by sharing information about the business strategy and involving people in data-gathering and problem-solving – are some of the approaches featured in the case studies in this chapter. Then ensuring that people benefit from the change with new development opportunities and aligning reward systems are ways of embedding change so that the new becomes the 'way we do things around here'.

How Does an Organization Reach a State Where Positive Change is Possible?

Chaos theory suggests that while an organization can exist in a stable or unstable state, the state most productive of change and new possibilities is the 'edge of chaos'. The organization has to have the capacity to be stable, but also to change/evolve. If there is too much stability, however successful the organization, complacency can set in and the organization can become internally focused. Too much change can produce chaos, lack of coordination and waste. The edge of chaos, where there is experimentation but within parameters, is most conducive to emergent culture change since the people who are likely to be affected by the change are the ones who introduce it. Edge-of-chaos states are typified by muddling through, searching for error, brainstorming, use of intuition and agenda-building.

Factors that affect the direction in which the culture travels (towards stability etc.) are as follows:

- How richly the network is connected – do the feedback loops work across the organization and through the management levels?

- The diversity of 'mindset' of the people within the network
- How quickly, or otherwise, active information flows through the system
- How power differences are used
- How anxiety is contained.

To reach this state, you have to recognize that the formal and informal systems co-exist. Do not over-control or predetermine goals and agendas. The informal networks themselves must generate their own order and change. The role of the senior manager is to articulate ideals, open-ended challenges capable of different interpretations, umbrella concepts and metaphors. It is important to avoid power being either highly controlled or widely distributed and hardly ever use authority. Other important activities include:

- Actively promote a diversity of culture. Create forums where individuals and groups can operate in a spontaneous and self-organizing way.
- Develop group-learning skills and encourage the development of the informal organization. Provoke challenges which are ambiguous and which may generate conflict; create an environment in which senior managers are open to challenge from subordinates.

One example of a change process that began life as a 'bottom-up' initiative is that of Brighton-based Family Assurance. Facing an increasingly competitive market in the financial services industry, the company introduced a change programme through staff focus groups in 1997. But as well as this 'bottom-up' approach it became clear that 'top-down' changes were also needed. Leadership became a key issue. Time and again the message from the focus groups was that the management approach was too project-focused and was seen as not being interested in the people issues. To address these issues, directors took part in a transformational leadership workshop, using 360-degree feedback which led the directors to place greater priority on the people issues (McCurry, 1998).

APPROACHES TO CHANGING CULTURES

Management writers such as Quinn (1995) argue that most change happens in an evolutionary rather than a revolutionary way. Strategic decision-making in 'real-time' business is more akin to logical incrementalism. Quinn suggests that managers have a view of where they want the organization to be in years to come but try to move towards this position in an evolutionary way. They do this by attempting to ensure the success and development of a strong, secure but flexible business, but also by continually experimenting with 'side-bet' ventures. Managers seek to become highly sensitive to environmental signals through constant environmental scanning. They manage uncertainty by testing changes in strategy in small steps. They also encourage experimentation in the organization. Moreover, there is a reluctance to specify precise objectives too early as this might stifle ideas and prevent the sort of experimentation which is desired. This approach takes account of the political nature of organizational life since smaller changes are less likely to face the same extent of resistance as major changes.

Roger Harrison (1986) argues that different approaches to changing an organization's culture may be more or less difficult. In managing change you should intervene no more deeply than is necessary to accomplish your purposes. Strengthening the culture, for instance by doing the same things only better, is perhaps the easiest form of change to implement. This is the best approach when the organization does the 'right things' but not well enough. Balancing the culture to preserve the culture's benefits and to encourage cultural differentiation is more difficult. This is appropriate when the organization's culture is narrow, where the cultural patterns fit the organization's business but the necessary checks and balances are missing. Changing the culture, through, for instance, introducing new values and beliefs or work and leadership styles is the most difficult of all. This is necessary when needed improvements are blocked by the limitations of the current culture.

Other researchers, such as John Kotter (1995), who have made studies of why change efforts often fail, have identified the need for:

- Creating a sense of urgency and 'readiness' for change
- Creating powerful guiding coalitions who are willing to bring about change and letting a clear vision emerge
- Communicating the change continuously and in many different ways
- Coordinating efforts, measuring and communicating progress
- Keeping morale and energy levels around the change project high by celebrating progress so far, and using that energy to tackle the more important issues obstacles to change
- Consolidating improvements while eliminating remaining obstacles to change.

In all of these steps leaders, managers and HR have vital roles to play.

COMMUNICATION AND LEADERSHIP

In managing change, communication plays a vital part in building an organization that is adaptable and more than the sum of its parts. These days we are much more likely to talk about the need to 'engage' employees, especially when change is needed. Communication is about relationship building and has a major role to play in building trust and commitment. It can help create buy-in to new ways of operating. Communication should be considered a key component of change management and is an obvious area for active collaboration between Human Resource professionals and the line.

People Need to Understand Why Change is Happening

When I first started researching career issues in flatter organization structures in 1994, Europe was deep in the middle of a profound economic recession

(Holbeche, 1997). I wanted to find out why organizations had restructured by removing management layers – whether it was part of some strategic plan, such as providing better service to customers by removing bureaucracy, or whether delayering was driven by the need to trim costs, regardless of the impact on employees or customers. One of the key findings in the early part of the research was the link between the perceived reason for the delayering and the effect on employees. If people thought that the reason for delayering was simply cost-cutting, their morale and motivation tended to be more adversely affected than where there appeared to be a more 'strategic' reason for the change. It seems that failure to communicate a strategic focus for the changing organization, compounded by a failure to communicate progress towards the new business targets, leads people to question the quality of leadership.

Some of the best formal communication schemes we encountered use a wide variety of methods to convey simple messages and include two-way communication processes which are taken seriously. Attitude surveys are widely used but action needs to be seen to be taken on at least some of the findings for such processes to have credibility. Good communication leads to employees feeling 'empowered' to contribute to the development of the organization. Involving employees in decisions affecting business strategy can produce dividends. Thresher, for example, has run trial programmes on different working practices for three years. These have led to improvements in morale and performance and the business results of the trial teams speak for themselves.

Formal communications typically include some or all of the following:

- Senior management presentations, roadshows, corporate videos
- Team briefings and management cascades
- Help-desks and electronic mail question and answer services
- Staff newsletters.

Communication should be as two-way as possible, with staff being given opportunities to discuss the latest news. Key messages may need to be repeated in many different formats. Staff response to the messages about change should be anticipated and questions-and-answer sessions built into presentations.

Marion Devine (1999) suggests that, broadly speaking, formal communications should aim to:

- *Inform* – about the organizational/personal implications
- *Clarify* – the reason for the change, the strategy and benefits
- *Provide direction* – about the emerging vision, values and desired behaviours
- *Focus* – on immediate work priorities and actions, together with medium-term goals and dignity
- *Reassure* – that the organization will treat them with respect.

Communications should be honest and should involve all stakeholders. However, formal communication processes alone may not be enough to achieve buy-in. What matters more is how the message is conveyed, especially if the behaviour of senior managers in particular contradicts their verbal messages. In one financial services company, for instance, directors were expected to lead a culture change towards a focus on the customer. They spoke publicly about the virtues of the company values, especially teamwork. Since they were known as being themselves a dysfunctional management team, these separate presentations were received with scepticism by staff. It was only when the CEO threatened the directors with financial penalties for failing to model leadership and teamwork that their behaviour changed and their messages about the need for teamwork became credible.

Trust

During change, the role of leaders is paramount and motivating people to move bravely forward when the destination may be unclear is a challenging task. Leaders' credibility can be quickly lost if senior managers are out of touch with what is happening on the ground. As will be seen in the next chapter, senior managers have often been through their own personal change process having had prior knowledge of, and some control over, what is about to happen. They may well be unaware of how staff are feeling and what their needs are. HR professionals can play a key role in keeping the top management in touch with the bottom of the hierarchy and acting as listening posts for areas which senior managers should attend to. Top management needs to be seen to care, to act competently and fairly and to keep promises. Leaders should be discouraged from announcing that 'there will be no redundancies': even in good faith this cannot be guaranteed.

Leaders should communicate openly about the situation which, as long as the managers have not built up a legacy of cynicism among employees, should lead to employees trusting top management. Employees are then more likely to suspend judgement and display their trust by going the extra mile. Management teams need to speak with one voice during change since any dissent among the leadership is likely to cause trust to break down and put the change effort back. Similarly, leaders should not be seen to tolerate sabotage of the change effort, especially among their own ranks, but should deal firmly with those who seek to revert to the status quo.

HELPS AND HINDRANCES IN MANAGING CHANGE

One UK firm incorporated and became a PLC at the same time in the late 1990s. For partners, and those aspiring to be partners, the implications of the change for their own career aspirations, working practices and the way in which the organization is to be managed are significant. For people who might have expected to have a key role in decision-making as well as those who might once have aspired to 'owning' the firm, the changes initially appeared retrograde at a personal level, while being good for the business. A group of senior associates and salaried partners considered what would help them to adjust to the change. While no two change initiatives are alike, their comments hint at some relatively common line management concerns with regard to change. Their suggestions about how the changes they were experiencing could be better handled were as follows:

What people expected of senior management

- Forward planning
- Professionalism
- Conviction on delivery of the message
- Senior management should 'own' the change
- Managing expectations beforehand
- Immediate feedback
- Openness and honesty
- Having a logical process to manage the change
- Making resources available for the new business strategy
- Reward and benefits should be speedily aligned to the new approach
- Implementing change quickly

Expectations of self and peers

- Flexibility of response
- Develop a support network
- Be focused
- Work with the change
- Build up inner strength
- Create common conviction about light at the end of the tunnel.

The managers also considered what was getting in the way of successfully managing change. They found that the 'hindering' factors were as follows:

- Limited time for reflection
- Emotion
- Detachment of senior management
- No direction
- Aggressive/defensive responses from senior management
- Fudging of issues
- Lack of communication
- Uncertainty
- Dishonesty
- Lengthy deliberation
- 'Surprise' announcements with no explanation
- Inflexibility
- Systems and processes which dull the energy
- Imposed change.

Arguably, these comments highlight the importance of a strategic HR contribution to managing change. This involves 'reading' the organization and providing senior management with feedback about how employees are receiving the change. Executives often need coaching in the arts of leadership especially during major change. HR needs to be prepared to confront executives if their style is contributing to the problems experienced. Similarly, HR needs to adjust human resource processes and systems to ensure that they are aligned to the change and do not act as 'brakes' on the way forward.

Ensuring that communication processes are working well in different parts of the organization is another key contribution since typically some managers are better than others at keeping employees abreast of the changes and their implications. Helping employees and managers to cope with change and develop flexible approaches is easier said than done, but creating workshops and other forums where people can get together and contribute their ideas to the implementation of change can help. Involving and energizing people is key if people are to stop being doorstep critics and become active proponents of change.

David Waters (formerly of Whitbread) has implemented many change initiatives (see Chapter 16). He uses a hierarchy of proactivity to explain to people what the company needs from people during change. At one extreme are those who wait for guidance before they will do anything. These are the 'spectators'. At the other are people who will act without consultation and reflect on their actions afterwards. Given that there are often long periods during change when guidance is not forthcoming, the 'spectators' are unlikely to receive the instructions they need and therefore may hang on to 'old' ways of doing things, whether or not these are appropriate. People at every level in an organization can be galvanized into finding new ways forward, as in the case studies which follow, but line managers and HR may have to accept that some people will need a lot more encouragement than others before they will try anything different.

CHECKLIST – DEVELOPING A POSITIVE CLIMATE FOR CHANGE

- Understand your current culture and what can be strengthened, balanced and changed
- Link the changes in roles with the business imperative
- Define future roles
- Break established patterns
- Challenge cultural and other sacred cows
- Set new standards
- Involve people in designing their future
- Excite and enthuse people
- Support people in learning
- Give people the opportunity to exercise new skills
- Empower people.

CASE STUDY: CREATING A UNIFIED IDENTITY AT COMPASS GROUP

I am grateful to Rima Evans of *People Management* for the following case study (Manocha, 2004).

Compass Group is a large international company with a diverse portfolio. Compass is the ninth largest employer in the world and has a 415 000 strong workforce scattered across 90 countries. In the UK it serves the food in many hospitals, schools and workplaces; manages motorway services stations; provides catering for celebrated events such as the Wimbledon Tennis Championships and the Oscar awards ceremonies; and owns sub-brands such as Upper Crust and Caffe Ritazza. Yet despite its size, many of its staff admitted they had no idea how far the Compass Group reached. As Tracy Robbins, group HR Director leadership and development, who is based at the company global HQ in Surrey, says: 'we recognized that we needed to focus on building a Compass Group identity'.

Until 2002, the lack of this identity was not so crucial. Since 1987 sales have topped £11 billion, with the group growing largely through acquisition – 167 companies joined Compass between 1987 and 2000. But in 2002 the company decided it wanted to pursue a different strategy – one of more organic growth. Growing through acquisition meant a strong focus on financials, but 'we wanted to start differentiating ourselves through service. And the only way of doing that is through our people,' says Robbins.

One of the biggest hurdles to this new people-centred focus was the company's disparate nature. Not only is the company made up of myriad sub-brands, it also operates in eight different market sectors. Staff are spread across the globe in countries such as Kazakhstan and Angola, and on remote sites such as oil and gas rigs. Robbins says: 'Almost 170 different businesses from around the world have been brought together. Our challenge was to find a way to bond these businesses together, to provide a corporate "glue". But we also wanted to make sure we preserved the uniqueness of our individual businesses and brands.'

The people charged with making that happen were the operational teams, supported by their HR teams. The solution – a global HR strategy – was called 'The Journey from Good to Great'. Robbins describes this as a pathway to improved business performance. In practical terms it set out a simple, clear new vision – 'Great People, Great Service, Great Results' – and a series of values: 'Can do'; win through teamwork; embrace diversity; passion for quality; share success. These values underpinned strategies already in place: 'We had existing strategies, such as being a preferred employer and customer satisfaction. But we didn't have a framework to make that happen. The new strategy meant that we were united in a common direction,' Robbins explains.

Drawing up a global strategy is one thing, but fully engaging employees and gaining their emotional commitment is quite another – particularly if your staff span every continent in the world. Before the company embarked on any training programmes, the Compass strategy had two fundamental assets in its favour: its sheer simplicity and support from the very top. 'The focus on people was the aim of our Chief Executive Mike Bailey,' Robbins says. 'It's valuable to have a CEO so focused on staff, but having started out as a chef he has more of an affinity with the front line.'

The global training programme launched to connect staff, both front-line and senior, to this single vision and set of values was a huge task. It was the first ever worldwide devoted to it. Leaders were given training to enable them to manage change and implement the strategy, while front-line staff attended experiential, interactive modular sessions to encourage them to put forward ideas, no matter how small, on how they could improve both individual and team performance.

While the programme had at its core the same messages and content, it was tweaked to take cultural nuances into account. In some countries they had to work around the behavioural elements. For example Kazakhstan is a very egalitarian society so the concept of supervision is different from that in the UK. For these reasons it was crucial that the language used to convey the company values and messages was appropriate.

The phrase 'Good to Great' was effective because of its universality. The only exceptions were China where 'great' means 'rich', and Spain, where it's not a powerful word. Here more appropriate words were substituted.

According to the company, the roll-out of the training programme has produced positive feedback from staff, but there was also other tangible evidence of its success. The staff 'great ideas' scheme, which was launched at the same time as the vision and values strategy, became so popular that, although it is officially a global scheme (with the top 100 ideas being rewarded by 100 company shares), many countries and regions launched 'sub' schemes and collated their own 100 great ideas.

The training had a positive effect on employee engagement. A global staff satisfaction survey, carried out in 2002, was planned as part of the vision and values strategy. It found that 81% of staff enjoyed their jobs and were motivated and 70% were proud of the company. An impressive 74% said they were likely to go above and beyond their duties, far more than the 63% global average (from the Walker Information 2000 Global Employee Survey). As for the bottom line, in the year 2002–3, the company reported organic growth of 6% turnover and a 10% increase in operating profit, with the customer-focused culture playing a key part in equipping the business to succeed.

CASE STUDY: DEVELOPING A CUSTOMER-FOCUSED CULTURE IN STANDARD LIFE

The following case study is in two parts. The first (which appeared in an earlier edition of this book) describes a highly effective HR strategy underpinning a shift towards a more customer-focused culture at Standard Life at the end of the 1990s. The second part brings the story up to date and details how HR strategy has become central to business effectiveness.

Part 1

> Standard Life is a long-established mutual company operating in the UK, Ireland, Canada, Spain and Germany, predominantly in life insurance and pensions. Standard Life UK operating companies include Standard Life Assurance Co., Standard Life Investments, Standard Life Bank Ltd and Prime Health. Despite competition from banks, building societies and many other sources, Standard Life has been through a period of solid growth which has included launching its own investment house and bank in 1998. There are 9700 employees, 7500 of whom are based in Edinburgh. The head office is in Edinburgh, where Standard Life is the city's largest private employer.

During the 1990s Standard Life successfully transformed itself from being a relatively staid and paternalistic organization into one that balances dynamic business innovation with effective risk management and where there is genuine employee ownership of the culture change. The need for change was strong. The drivers for change were typical for the financial services industry at that time:

- Static market growth
- Rising unit costs
- Increased regulation
- Increased competition
- Customer requirements for customer service as well as excellent financial strength.

In the early 1990s, the board of Standard Life agreed that it was essential to increase market share, recover the competitive position as a low-cost provider and maintain financial strength. To achieve this, the board recognized that Standard Life needed to develop a genuinely customer-focused organization and created a forward strategy known as Total Customer Satisfaction (TCS). It was clear that employees were going to be key to delivering the TCS strategy and their behaviour and attitudes had to be transparently customer-focused. The quality programme underpinned by competencies became the mainspring for the new culture.

The management process is derived from the group mission and vision and these are underpinned by a set of values as follows:

From	To
Internally driven	Customer-driven
Task	Added value
Parent–child	Adult–adult
Functional	Collaborative
Uniform	Diverse

Operating principles were also established with three clear areas of focus:

- *Customer* – Customers' needs and expectations will drive our actions
- *Process* – We will deliver value through processes which we will seek continuously to improve
- *People* – We will train and develop all staff to realize their full potential to serve our customers.

Group strategies were developed, together with three-year company plans and corporate scorecards, using the Balanced Scorecard approach which enables progress to be measured. The whole process is cascaded through the organization with divisional scorecards, plans and supporting scorecards. Staff are aware of, and refer to, the operating principles in internal meetings. The competence framework is seen as essential to translating the values into action. Competencies run through all development initiatives, especially leadership development and are also key to contribution (line) management, recruitment, feedback processes, market pricing, provision of learning materials, succession management. The link between these 'soft' people processes and the 'hard' business results is made transparent through the use of the Scorecard.

The Role of HR in Supporting Change

Human Resources played an important role in bringing about this successful culture change. Initially, responsibility for managing the culture change implicit in TCS lay with the Corporate Development unit. HR took back the initiative for organizational development and training. For Stephen McCafferty, then Assistant General Manager Resourcing and Development, the challenge for HR was to get right the match between the environment, the team, the job specification and the job-holder, all within a cultural context. Training was a key plank of this strategy, with line managers encouraged to take an active performance coaching role.

HR strategic plans were created for each division so that HR could be fully aligned to the business. HR's role was to offer the line best practice, not to interfere. The HR team was organized so that 'Business Consultants' supported different parts of the business, helping the management teams link their operational functional plans and their strategic plans with how they could get the best out of their people. In the years of rapid growth, a key focus was recruitment.

With business commitment to improving customer service, an Employee Development Strategy was created which clearly focused on serving customer needs. Elements of the strategy were:

- Build the skills required to become a customer-focused organization
- Enhance the capability of our leaders
- Build 'self-directed/just-in-time' learning
- Build explicit links between employee development and business outcomes
- Create a 'feedback' culture
- Become recognized as an 'Investor in People'.

The Employee Development Strategy comprised:

- Total customer service training
- Proactive contribution management
- Reverse feedback
- Technical based training.

Some of these are explored in a little more detail as follows.

Total customer service training is largely delivered by the line and has high business credibility. Line managers receive recognition for providing effective coaching for performance improvement to their teams.

Proactive contribution management, rather than appraisals and backward-looking performance management, encourages employees to ask themselves:

- What will you contribute to the organization to achieve the goals?
- How will you develop to achieve these and your own goals?
- How will we work in partnership based on competencies to achieve these goals?

The contribution management discussions take place quarterly between employees and their managers. Development priorities are agreed on one or two competencies which are linked to the job. At the end of the year, the discussion involves taking stock and planning for the future.

Workshops offering *reverse* or 180-degree *feedback* are run for senior and middle managers. The first workshops were championed by the CEO and top 27 managers. Now into phase 5, with over 300 managers having taken part, the upward feedback process is producing desired behavioural changes in managers who now take the developmental aspects of managing people very seriously. The process has now become integrated into the cycle of management activity, rather than being seen as a one-off. As with all HR-related activity, upward feedback is timed to suit business needs in the different parts of Standard Life.

Similarly, the feedback process has to be seen to add value. The results of the feedback have to be used. Initially, the feedback forms the basis of an individual action plan which eventually becomes part of an individual's contribution plan. Then the entire team of the person who has received feedback are engaged in a review meeting to discuss the themes of the feedback in more detail, with the support of an individual adviser. There is an agreed action plan for the team which then goes into the manager's contribution plan. At an organizational level, the feedback results are used to direct training and development activity. Ultimately, the overall feedback results are reported in the Standard Life Organizational scorecard. Measurement is a key feature of the Standard Life approach to organizational change. The Organizational scorecard is used to ensure that cultural shifts, such as changing leadership behaviour, are actually happening. Three-quarters of the executive group have now experienced reverse feedback and their results are fed into the organizational action plan, as well as individual development plans. For internal purposes, the results are also broken down by business unit, with an indication of what is being done to address issues. 'League tables', though, are not made public within the organization since encouraging competition between business units and managers would be seen as counter-cultural. Currently the results are used entirely for developmental rather than assessment purposes, though eventually they could be linked with reward.

A key issue within change is trust between management and employees as a whole. The feedback process suggested that there is a perceived lack of trust between the executives and employees. The managing director has taken this issue seriously. There has therefore been a conscious attempt to build trust by consulting staff openly on issues such as the revised grading system. There is also a deliberate focus on building better relationships between managers and their teams, making better use of manager role models who can coach their peers in new behaviours, and an emphasis on dealing with performance robustly. The scorecard results have started to show the positive effects on business results of good people management practice.

Current and Future Focus

The HR team has also focused on a range of additional ways of adding value. 'People asset techniques' such as training are receiving serious investment, with 8.5% of payroll including downtime expended on training in 1998. Recognizing that culture change needs to be led from the top, one important area involves training executives. An initial workshop, which involved case studies, psychometrics and discussion groups with observers, provided the impetus for further development. This was followed by action learning sets, teamworking initiatives and a range of specific modules such as for influencing skills, strategic leadership, strategic marketing and finance. This executive programme was run in collaboration with the Management Development Network (MDN), a network established by Standard Life with other major employers in Scotland such as Scottish Power and Motorola.

Other HR priorities include the use of Open Access Development Centres (described in Chapter 17), leadership development, NVQs and the development of a new induction process. Career development has been a major area of focus and a range of self-assessment and career self-management tools have been developed for use by employees. The HR team are very clear that certain things will become more (or less) important over time as the business changes and they use a framework to keep track of where the priorities are and progress made against them. Clear areas for future focus include the enhancement of the employee brand, consolidation and welfare reform. Priorities within these will include designing the psycho-social elements of the workplace, calling on the skills of the in-house ergonomist, as well as relationship building within the evolving HR function.

Measuring Progress – and Success

Standard Life believe that investing in people development makes a positive difference to the organization, but, as always, proof is needed. Compared with other large financial institutions in 1997 (Corporate Leadership Council research) they are ahead of their competitors by spending 8.5% of payroll on employee development. The challenge is to assess whether the spend is justified. The evidence collected suggests that the investment is paying off handsomely.

The team use the organizational HR Scorecard to keep track of progress (Figure 15.1). They believe that they have been able to establish links between improved market share and where HR has made a difference. A number of external benchmarks of success reinforce the team's own assessment. An independent survey of the company's results carried out by the Independent Advisers'

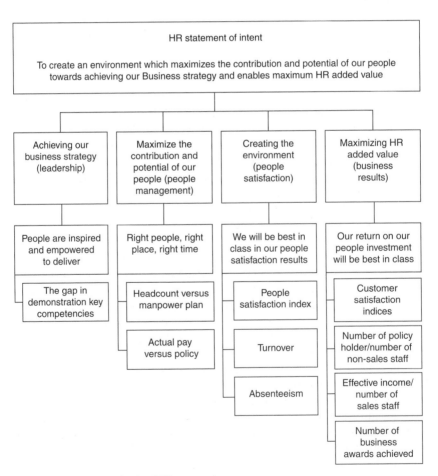

FIGURE 15.1   The organizational HR scorecard.

Strategy Group has placed Standard Life ahead of its competitors because of its changed culture. This result represents a startling improvement over the assessment made at the start of the culture-change period when Standard Life was rated 37th out of 39 companies.

On the Customer element of TCS the company won the PIMs award (the quality award for the financial services industry) in 1996 and has since won it three times more. Employees have been rewarded with bonuses to celebrate the achievement. On the Process element, Standard Life has maintained a Triple A rating for financial strength and unit costs continue to fall. On the People element, the company has won Investors in People status for the second time. The HR team are aiming to reach world class and are using EFQM measures for internal assessment purposes. The team won the 1998 Cranfield Award for linking HR strategy to business strategy.

In hard business results, Standard Life's share of the total market has shifted from 5.5% in 1995 to 6.9% in 1998, representing an increase of 25.45% (this excludes Unit Trust and PEP). This is a remarkable achievement by any standards, but the success of the business strategy has no doubt been made possible because of a well-aligned and implemented HR strategy underpinning the culture change. The link between the 'people aspect' and a good return on investment has become clear. On the 'soft' side of measures, the subtle signs of shifting culture are difficult to pin down but are real for all that. Some of the more obvious signs of shifting attitudes are evident in 'surprises'. An IS manager, for instance, who once saw anything concerning people to be HR's responsibility, is now working with HR to plan for succession, being very aware that without it he cannot succeed in the future. Measuring values about customer focus could easily concentrate on training, when in fact the processes need to feed into selection and the way people are managed and rewarded.

Measuring 'people' values highlights the potential for dilemmas if the needs of staff and customers are different. While aiming for consistency, the HR team realize that some trade-offs may be necessary between different aspects of the values at different times. Work patterns, such as a proposed 24-hour banking service, need to be determined by the needs of customers, though shift patterns may not suit the needs of existing employees who have been used to conventional working weeks. This has implications for the nature of the workforce – permanent, contract, flexible, a mix of new and existing staff – and for the way people are managed. Potentially key organizational values around fairness at all times and employee welfare will become the guiding principles for resourcing decisions. Rewarding people by contribution made is now reflected in the breakdown of a common grading system, with a greater emphasis on market pricing of jobs.

The culture change goes on … The company aspires to a culture where people at all levels deal with each other openly and honestly, where promotions are founded on consistent criteria, based largely on contribution and through demonstration of the key competencies and where career development is given prominence. The true test of whether the values are meaningful to people is when they start to relate to senior management in an adult–adult way, as they are now start-ing to, and receive an appropriate response. There is now ample evidence that the various parties concerned with managing careers, namely individuals, man-agers and the organization, are beginning to accept their different responsibili-ties. Individuals in particular are recognizing that they need to take ownership of their own careers and managers at all levels are now beginning to encourage and support that development.

Lessons Learned

The HR team believe that certain elements were vital to achieving this successful culture change. These were:

- Top team commitment and focus – and willingness to commit money to achieving culture change
- Listening to the staff – they are HR's customers
- Designing and trialling initiatives to support staff and help them to do their jobs
- Training managers how to coach
- Using competencies to provide clarity about what is needed
- 'Borrowing with pride' – i.e. looking at good practice elsewhere and adapting it to meet the needs of Standard Life.

Part 2

As with every aspect of life, organizations change too and over a decade, a lot can happen. This is the case with Standard Life, and I am very grateful to Stephen McCafferty (HR Director of Standard Life at the time of writing the current edition of this book) for the following update:

During the period 1998–2002 we continued to embed the processes described earlier. For instance in 2002 we ran another version of the TCS approach for the whole organization. We took 10 000 staff through a workshop for a day to rein-force the values and general direction of the business, together with the strategy. At the time we were well capitalized and thought that we could grow the busi-ness to four times the size of 2000. However, 2002 saw the continuation of what turned out to be a long and severe market downturn. Standard Life had a much higher proportion of its funds in equities than our competitors, and the downturn produced a significant downturn in values.

Then in 2003 we had issues with the regulator – the Financial Services Authority (FSA) – who introduced a new reporting regime called 'Realistic Reporting'. This required financial institutions to:

- Capitalize risk and reserve for it
- No longer take account of future profits of the existing business, i.e. the previous practice of projecting forward based on current results and then dis-counting back, given that future scenarios could be very different.

There were big issues with the balance sheet and serious discussions with the FSA towards the end of 2003 and at that point the previous CEO left. His Deputy was appointed CEO in his place and immediately reviewed the business model. This resulted in changes to the business model, moving away from volume to a focus on profit and cost reduction. In 2004 alone, 25% of the headcount was taken out.

As a business we were left with three choices:

1. Close the company to new business (which would have meant reducing staff numbers to 2000–3000)
2. A trade sale to a competitor (integration would have led to similar staff number reductions)
3. Demutualize to raise the capital needed for growth.

We chose the last option and 2004 saw the HR role change from enabling growth through development to enabling survival through downsizing. As a function we became invaluable to the line, creating redundancy policy and supporting the line with practice.

HR's Role in the Downturn

In 2005 the business was preparing to demutualize and HR supported putting the new organization design in place, pulling head office functions out of business units and setting up business units as companies in their own right. We created Group-wide HR policies and created the structures and disciplines that a plc would have. This was HR getting the company into shape, though we were still downsizing, exiting many executives and renegotiating service level agreements with Executives. We created retention measures for key talent and new incentive schemes which were more highly geared and based on profit for both Executives and staff. It was a manic, fantastic learning experience. The HR function was really galvanized and pulled through to be at the centre of the business.

But change of this order could not have been achieved without some damage to employee relations. When a whole organization employee engagement survey was carried out in 2005 using Gallup Q12, Gallup reported that they had never seen as big a drop in engagement from one wave to the next in any company worldwide (the previous survey had been in 2004). This dubious distinction reinforced the urgent need to re-engage staff and develop the organization.

One way of doing this was 'One Standard Life,' a 2 × one-day workshop run for all staff (in line with the company values). The aim was to pull people together and focus on making the business successful. Learning maps created by executives were used and managers acted as facilitators. The maps were pictures explaining why we were where we were – about the market conditions and regulatory environment and an admission that there had been some poor decision-making in the past. The workshop was a cathartic experience for staff who were able to express their anger, especially about the actuarial community, but then start to come to terms with what had happened.

The HR team also continued their work on organizational and structural change, as well as working with management teams on re-engaging their own teams using the Q12 action planning process and focusing on what teams could do to improve their own situation. HR itself is organized along typical 'Ulrich' lines, with a strategy group, Centres of Excellence, Business Partners and Shared Services.

Pension Issues

During this time the company was preparing for IPO. Standard Life had a defined benefit pension scheme for all staff which was in deficit. The new CEO and new Group Finance Director recognized the need to reduce the size of the deficit in order to avoid lowering the share price at IPO and therefore failing to provide value to policy-holders. If this were to happen there was a danger policy-holders would not vote in favour of demutualization. It was decided that the deficit should be eliminated with a cash injection but that from then on, pensionable pay increases would be restricted to 2.85%.

Stephen brought together pensions experts, actuaries, communications experts, people and staff associations (Standard Life is not unionized). He gave everyone the challenge: 'if you can come up with a better proposal which achieves the same outcomes, then do it'.

The pensions work took 18 months. It got off to a bad start; communications went badly and soon Amicus was demanding representation rights and recognition. It was clear that the good work on starting to build trust was being undermined. Part of the challenge in resolving the issues was that many staff did not really understand how their own pension operated so education on pensions was a necessary early step. Stephen himself, as well as other top managers, fronted up many of these sessions with the staff, with meetings sometimes involving hundreds of staff. The message was that everyone is sharing the pain and that it is an executive team decision. In the end an innovative solution was found which allowed people the choice of protecting past service or a final salary basis and future accrual via defined contributions or, converting all service career average. Ninety-eight per cent of employees voted to change, with 96% selecting for the career average option.

The first half of 2006 was spent getting the company ready for flotation and once the company had floated in July, there was time to ease off the pressure somewhat and take stock. Many people took long delayed holidays to recover from the hectic pace of the previous months.

The New Phase

The year 2007 marked something of a turning point as the now-floated company looked ahead. A new business strategy was created and Stephen supported the CEO and his executive team with the process of engaging people in its development and implementation. For instance the embryonic strategy was rolled out to the top 100 managers via a workshop which corralled their involvement and input to its development. These managers then led sessions with the top 500 managers culminating in a roll-out to all staff in a full day workshop held over a three-month period. The first exercise of the workshop was called 'A Line in the Sand', which served the purpose of allowing employees to vent their frustrations about the recent past, and then move forward in a positive way.

Alongside a new business strategy, the Board recognized that a new organizational culture would be needed if the business strategy was to be achieved. In a context of low trust and poor employee engagement, leadership is needed to rebuild trust. And if another business goal – to create an exceptional customer experience – was to be achieved, employees should also have an exceptional employment experience, so one of the six key business objectives is about being employer of choice.

Building a Strengths-Based Organization

In any organizational change active support from the top is critical. Standard Life's Group CEO Sandy Crombie helped enormously to promote the strengths-based approach. The Group-wide People and Organizational Strategy is called 'Shaping Our Future' and connects the HR function directly to enabling business success. Its aim is to build a flexible, positive and effective organizational culture which plays to, and maximizes, organizational and individual strengths and aligns them to business outcomes. This strengths-based approach represents quite a shift in terms of culture, moving away from a stereotypically arrogant management style to a 'leader-led' approach. It focuses on making the most of what people bring, rather than on attempting to develop what they lack.

Leadership is one of six work-streams within the People Strategy. In the past, leadership in Standard Life was defined through competencies and leadership development and related processes worked on the 'bridging gaps' premise. Stephen introduced a leadership framework which is based on leadership characteristics or 'what matters most'. The framework is based on the notion of authentic leadership – it's about being real as a leader. The five parts include:

- Creative leadership
- Working together
- Passion for performance
- Customer empathy
- Globally connected.

The new approach has been introduced to the top 100 managers through workshops and is embedded in a new performance management system which cover the three core elements:

- Know me – strengths, limitations, motivations
- Focus me – align through roles and targets with business outcomes
- Recognize me – feedback and remuneration processes.

The process of embedding the new approach is under way. The top 500 have been introduced to the strengths-based philosophy. By end 2008 every member of staff will have the opportunity to be profiled using the Gallup 'Strengths Finder' Tool. Fifty 'Strengths Coaches' (members of the HR team and managers) have been trained to work with other managers and managers themselves have been trained to provide effective feedback and coaching to individuals. A coach works with the top team, helping them understand their strengths and limitations. The leadership framework is embedded in HR processes such as talent reviews and assessment processes for external hires.

So while there is much still to do, the journey towards re-engaging staff and building a strengths-based organizational culture is well under way. One small measure of how much has been achieved is that employees were asked to make their choice about the new pension arrangement options in January 2008 and the process went off very smoothly despite the previous furore raised by the change of pension arrangements. Just before what could have been a very difficult occasion, the employee engagement survey was run again. The results showed that employee engagement was not only significantly up against the scores achieved in 2006 but were back at 2004 levels. No wonder HR is considered central to business success in Standard Life!

CASE STUDY: CREATING A CULTURE OF EMPOWERMENT AT PETERBOROUGH REGIONAL COLLEGE

I am grateful to Debbie Dear, HR Director of Peterborough Regional College at the time of writing for the following case study.

Further Education in the UK operates in a highly competitive market with many different providers vying to attract students. In this crowded marketplace, success breeds success and a College's reputation for the quality of its learning provision, as assessed by Ofsted inspectors, can make all the difference between succeeding or failing to attract students in sufficient numbers to be viable. At the start of the millennium Peterborough Regional College had been found to be 'average' by inspectors (with an Ofsted Grade 3) and had failed to achieve its targets for the previous four years. As a result the college was failing to attract students in the necessary numbers and funding was being withdrawn.

Peterborough Regional College started its transformation in June 2002 with the appointment of a new Principal. The HR impact on this change began in May 2003 when Debbie Dear joined the College as Director of HR and member of the college's senior management team. This was a new position which was created by the new Principal.

The new principal wanted to build a successful college and recognized that a culture change would be needed if this was to be achieved. He needed all 700 members of staff to feel empowered to do what was needed to put students at the centre of the college. In the previous period, the college staff had experienced a hierarchical structure and something of a blame culture. The new principal began the task ahead by restructuring the senior management team. Some members of senior management left and were replaced from within the college by experienced staff who were willing to adopt a different leadership approach from that of their predecessors.

The Director of HR role was created to change historical perceptions of a 'fear' culture and to play a key role in the strategic management of the college. Debbie had inherited a tiny HR team whose function was administrative – legal compliance and paying people. Even the administrative service offered was limited. For instance recruitment was a strictly amateur process – staff tended to recruit people they knew as there was no overall recruitment process. In the early days, people were unsure just what Debbie's role was about. Debbie was keen to bring a more professional approach to Personnel in the college and recognized that HR could and should be key to bringing about a more student-friendly culture. However, the HR team soon learnt that transferring change techniques learned elsewhere does not always work. They tried to restructure the business administrative support function and learned the hard way that there should have been more communication, a longer lead time and more staff involvement in order to implement change successfully.

Gaining Buy-in to Change

One of the early breakthroughs in changing the perception of the value of Personnel, now renamed 'HR', to the positive came from taking a more proactive, strategic approach to recruitment and helping solve a recurring problem for a key department in the college. The team quickly became aware that one of the departments in particular – Construction – suffered shortages of teaching staff and seemed unable to attract enough candidates of the right calibre. Despite running courses which were highly valued by students the department had to cancel many courses because of staff shortages.

HR helped the Construction department in tackling the recruitment problem. They held careers open evenings, advertising posts in new places such as the *Sun* newspaper and developing a simple and effective recruitment process. The recruitment problem was solved but it also made evident to staff the potential benefit of working with HR and seeing HR as part of the solution rather than the problem. This early example also signalled to staff the direction of the culture change – that simpler, more effective ways of working that put students at the centre were what was needed.

Supporting Change

Debbie believed, as did the college principal, that HR strategy should be about implementing good practice and be fundamentally geared to moving the culture towards one which is more open and free, and where people are empowered. The vision of the preferred culture was the 'Soft S' style – where staff have the right skills and attitude and are managed as adults, rather than a culture that favours managing through 'hard' systems). They recognize, however, that culture change does not occur overnight, especially in further education where change seems to happen more slowly than in other sectors. They considered consultation with staff as a key element of a successful human resource and business strategy, giving staff greater ownership of change. For example, getting middle managers to take on board the 'Soft S' vision was very challenging, as many managers were sceptical of what this would involve, given their experience of previous management styles. A development route was chosen to change the culture rather than restructuring. There were a large number of managers who had acquired considerable service in the college, of 15 years or more in some cases, many of whom were former teachers who had not had access to management training or development in the past. Consequently, many managers lacked basic human resource management skills and knowledge.

However, rather than just calling in the trainers, Debbie was well aware that simply setting up a training programme and expecting whole-hearted participation was unrealistic, given the relatively high levels of cynicism towards management, even amongst managers. Instead a consultation exercise was held in which managers were asked what they needed. They wanted practical hands-on tips, for instance on how to hold a disciplinary interview, rather than high flown theory.

Having consulted, the programme attendance by managers was made mandatory, an act which was unusual in further education and elsewhere. Managers needed to have the skills and behaviours required to make sure that good practice happened consistently across the college. The course received such good feedback to the point that managers themselves asked for more development and also learned approaches, which can be cascaded, such as how to hold effective team meetings.

Embedding Change

Leadership at all levels is considered to be an important aspect of the culture change. Consequently, 'Apprenticeships' were introduced to get succession planning in place and leadership opportunities were offered to a wider group, so that talented staff at all levels could have access to, and be prepared for, management responsibilities. But for lasting culture change to take place, the changes in managers' skills and behaviours needed to be embedded both within the organization and have an impact on managers' own and other people's performance. The college went on to introduce a more individualized leadership development programme involving tailored coaching.

HR also ensured that the desired behaviours were reflected in the new salary structure that has been implemented and see reward as a key means of bringing about change. Having carried out research into reward and motivation in the college, Debbie recognized that money is not the key motivator for most staff. What matters more is job security and job satisfaction, given the legacy of redundancies in the past few years, and being paid a salary that's fair and equitable. In the new salaries model – which cost £1million to sort out – the college moved away from national pay scales to a salary structure which is specifically designed to meet local needs. The system is completely transparent and available for staff to see on the college intranet. It is linked to the success of the college in terms of improvements in quality through achievement of qualifications and recognizes experience. It rewards values and behaviours linked to improving the student experience.

Once again, communication and consultation have been key factors in the widespread acceptance of the new scales. Both trades unions represented at the college were involved in the salary review and have bought in to the new salaries model. Consultation now takes place with the Employee Consultative Group set up in 2005. This consists of both union and elected non-union representatives from all areas of the college and act as a Works Council. The representative groups, though not decision-making, are a forum for genuine dialogue and provide staff with the opportunity to voice their issues and concerns on matters such as resource requirements and workload.

Staff representatives recognized that it would be unrealistic to discuss salaries without talking also about the strategic challenges. One example of changing performance requirements is the need for greater staff flexibility with regard to teaching styles in order to accommodate the needs of a more diverse range of students than in the past. Due to a variety of changes in the local economy the College is attracting growing numbers of migrant worker students, many of whom are taking courses that require a higher level of English language skills than they currently have. There is also a need to support lower level students. Consequently, teachers need to be able and willing to adapt their teaching methods appropriately. For many staff such shifts represent considerable change and potential loss of job satisfaction. To achieve staff buy-in to what is required has therefore meant involving the staff representative groups in the business strategy, making them aware of some of the drivers for change and keeping them updated of developments.

Results

The effects of culture change are evident throughout the college and good practice continues to be embedded, but increasingly this is driven by staff themselves. For instance, managers are now asking Debbie to help them carry out 'Soft S' performance reviews, i.e. to provide the right levels of support and challenge to ensure that standards are continuously raised. Training has been provided in how to deliver performance judgements in a developmental way.

HR is building on the beginnings of this performance culture by devising a performance management process which is based on the college values, providing criteria which ensure fairness and enable people who go the extra mile to be rewarded. The process will include a self-assessment element which staff discuss with their managers in their appraisal, which in turn feeds into the training and development plan for the college. Managers are more actively taking responsibility than in the past for core issues, such as managing workloads and controlling absence. The HR team has grown to include CIPD qualified professionals who can provide more expert support to the college. Rather than being feared as in the past, HR advice is increasingly sought as managers rise to the challenge of their management responsibilities.

Staff surveys over the three years since 2005 have shown steady improvement in staff satisfaction with regard to the three key areas measured – management styles, communications and benefits. The success of the salaries model is evident. Since its introduction there have been no complaints about unfair pay or lack of progression opportunities.

The most recent Ofsted inspection result was Grade 2 and the College team are aiming for a Grade 1 in the 2009 inspection. Student numbers have increased by 20% as the college's success rates rise and its reputation grows.

Key Learnings

Debbie recognizes that in order to bring about the scale of change achieved so far she has needed and received support from the top, especially when faced as she was in the early days by considerable opposition from senior management colleagues who appeared to value the status quo. She recommends that anyone embarking on culture change should be persistent, listen to people, understand their specific issues and get to understand their history, since no 'off-the-shelf' package of experience from elsewhere is likely to work in new situations. Having a high performance philosophy that can be tailored to a specific organizational context is key.

She also says that seeing change happen is in itself very rewarding and seeing managers and staff develop is very satisfying. A professionally qualified HR team with the same cultural values is essential to ensuring that the change is driven through and modern HR theories are adapted for the organization's needs. Debbie continues to contribute to the College strategy and believes that many of the improvements under way, including moving to a Total Reward model, will continue to create a culture typified by the phrase 'Success in a caring college'. When that happens, Debbie believes the culture will have well and truly changed.

CONCLUSION AND KEY LEARNING POINTS

- If you are going to carry out a change project, it must be in a strategic context, so that you can bring the people with you and they understand why they have to change.
- Changing any process in isolation is a fool's errand. There needs to be integration between process and function.
- Structured project management is crucial to the success of a change initiative. There need to be clear milestones and deliverables along the way. People need to know whether the change is working or not, and take corrective action as appropriate. If you are using an external consultant to manage the project, make sure that they 'fit' culturally.

- There has to be a strong business case for the change and measures need to be set and monitored – around both 'hard' and 'soft' targets.
- Communication cannot be overplayed. Too much top-down communication may cause people to stop listening. Find ways to get two-way communication flows and engage people in communicating the change to each other. Create motivational messages, videos and other ways of reinforcing the message when the first flush of enthusiasm wears off.
- For change to be really effective, there has to be an active partnership between the business and HR. Organization design should push decision-making as far down the hierarchy as possible and make people accountable. Delayered structures work best in this regard, as long as people have the appropriate skills and behaviours and are provided with the resources, including training, they need to do the job. Each layer should have clear areas of accountability which should be different from other levels.
- Self-managing teams can become high performing and are an excellent way of involving people and tapping into their creativity. They may need support to prevent them losing sight of the bigger picture and starting to compete with one another.
- Remember to celebrate the achievements of all those involved in the change. In celebrating current success, do not denigrate the past by implication. Motivate people for ongoing change by stabilizing what works.

CHECKLISTS ON CHANGE MANAGEMENT

Creating Future Directions

- What is the vision for the future of the organization?
- What are the values of the organization? To what extent are these values translated into leaders' behaviours and commitment?
- How much do employees believe that the lived values matched the espoused?
- What are the cultural 'gaps'?
- What is the organization's culture, and what are we trying to change?
- What are the aspects of the organization's culture that need to be strengthened, balanced or changed?
- How can we create an adaptable culture in which change is welcome?

Enabling Change

- What is our change strategy? Methods? Action plans? Who is involved?
- What are the most effective methods of communication used in the organization? How often do we review these methods to assess if they are still effective?
- What do employees like to know about in practice?
- In what areas are employees asked their views? What follow-up is offered when employees have been consulted?

- How active is informal communication, i.e. gossip, corridor conversations etc. To what extent are these a proxy for formal communications?
- What are the main communication issues stopping our organization from being more effective at the following levels – small group, departmental, business unit, whole organization? What can be done to address these issues?
- What are the main issues which currently or potentially cause difficulties between the organization and its clients, or vice versa?
- What approach to change is taken – evolutionary or revolutionary?
- Are leaders capable of leading the change? If not, how can this be compensated for?
- Is there a guiding coalition who can help drive change forward?
- Are there clear project plans for implementing change?
- Do we have any genuine change agents? How can we engage them in the change process?

Human Implications of Change

- Have we considered the human implications of change and how we will address these?
- What are the sources and types of resistance to change? How do we overcome resistance to change?
- How can we help people to cope with change?
- What is the impact of our change(s) on customers?

Becoming a Change Agent

- How can we assess sources of influence?
- Where should change start in our team?
- How well has this team effected change in the past? What has worked? What are the barriers to success?
- How well do we integrate different initiatives into an overall change framework which is coherent?

REFERENCES

Couto, V., Mourkogiannis, N. and Neilson, G. (2007) Culture change: calling on philosophers and engineers. *Strategy + Business Magazine* (Booz Allan), June

Devine, M. (1999) *A Mergers Checklist*. Horsham: Roffey Park Management Institute

Harrison, R. (1986) *Diagnosing Organization Culture*: Harrison Associates

Holbeche, L. (1997) *Motivating People in Lean Organisations*. Horsham: Roffey Park

Kotter, J.P. (1995) Leading change: why transformation efforts fail. *Harvard Business Review*, 73, No. 2, 59–67

Manocha, R. (2004) Bonding agents. *People Management*, 11 November

McCurry, P. (1998) Power transformers. *Personnel Today*, 22 October

Quinn, J.B. (1995) Strategic change: logical incrementalism, in Mintzberg, H., Quinn, J.B. and Ghoshal, S. (eds), *The Strategy Process*. Englewood Cliffs, NJ: Prentice Hall

Chapter 16

Mergers and Acquisitions

I know that what looks good on paper can easily turn sour in practice, and very many mergers have failed – why? Because a merger is ultimately more about people than balance sheets. We need to bring together two groups of people and build a new organization which is more than the sum of its parts.

(Sir Michael Bett, former First Commissioner of the Civil Service)

This chapter is based on the Mergers and Strategic Alliances research project carried out by Roffey Park Management Institute since 1997. The first phase of research focused on the human aspects of mergers and was based on in-depth organizational case studies. Organizations studied from the commercial sector include examples from the financial services, manufacturing, retail and the oil industry. From the public sector, cases include a government department, a government agency and two Further Education colleges. Each case is distinctive and shows that mergers are rarely identical. A broader group of organizations contributed information to the study anonymously.

The findings suggest that there is a business case for taking people issues seriously. The starting point for the Roffey Park research was that while many organizations claim that their mergers have succeeded, short-term financial measures of success due to rationalization are unreliable indicators of the longer-term effectiveness of a merger. A study by Hall and Norburn (1987) of the financial benefits of mergers and acquisitions (M&As) found that returns to shareholders are at best 'slight' and at worst 'significantly negative'. Mergers hold out the attractive prospect of increasing earnings per share (EPS) to shareholders. However, the risks attached to mergers are mainly linked to the Human Resource arena. Interestingly, it is perhaps because of the recognized difficulties of making mergers happen successfully that the UK government pressure on Colleges of Further Education to merge has been replaced by a requirement that colleges work in partnership to achieve many of the same ends.

It is the range of issues relating to people within merging organizations which can determine whether the merger is as successful as it might be, or indeed whether it succeeds at all. While there is increasing awareness that human factors have an influence over the success of the merger, executives are often at a loss to know how to address the different issues. Frequently, they are so absorbed with the nature of the business deal and in securing their own interests that the organizational implications of the deal are only considered once the deal has been struck.

Bungling the handling of a merger can result in losing people – who often constitute the market value which attracts the acquiring organization in the first place. People are a vulnerable asset – and the benefit of this asset can be destroyed if senior managers do not anticipate and prepare for the emotional response of employees at the outset. Meridian Consulting suggest that failure to create additional value through the combination and deployment of the intellectual property gained from the deal represents a new type of risk, known as knowledge risk. They calculate this as follows:

> The knowledge value at risk – that is the amount of shareholder value the firm stands to destroy if they fail to successfully integrate and leverage acquired intellectual property – equals the premium paid multiplied by the acquiring company's price-to-earning ratio, i.e.
>
> Value at risk = premium $ P/E ratio

They argue that if the combining organizations are to become capable of achieving shared business goals, three abilities must be grown, i.e.

- The ability to talk with one another
- The ability to work with one another
- The ability to learn from one another.

Roffey research suggests that the way the merger process is handled will have a major impact on how much people feel willing to exercise these abilities. Similarly, the roles, behaviours and attitudes of managers make a big difference to how well employees adjust to a merger. Employees are often hit by multiple waves of anxiety and need to be supported through the transition. Culture clashes between the two organizations are inevitable, especially between companies with apparently similar approaches. These are the most common causes of merger failure. HR has potentially a key role in anticipating and reducing the impact of those culture clashes.

Mergers and acquisitions, when two organizations are brought together, or are required to collaborate as in a strategic alliance, highlight the need for really effective change management. Indeed, mergers should really be thought of as large and complex change projects. If the merger is to succeed, people have to be supported in integrating working practices. Key employees need to be retained and ways of transferring knowledge across the organization found. HR potentially has a critical role to play in bringing about successful new organizations. HR strategy is vitally important during all stages of M&As and needs to be addressed as early as possible. Yet our research suggested that sometimes HR professionals were not involved until late into the merger process when many decisions had been taken (and sometimes damage caused).

THE GROWTH OF MERGERS

Mergers are on the increase it seems. The drivers for such deals are the changing market conditions which require businesses to regroup their activities, deregulation leading to consolidation and availability of capital. Cross-border deals are becoming commonplace and there is a record number of deals between the USA and the UK. Arguably the increasing focus on the core business is leading to the current trend of horizontal acquisitions and away from opportunistic acquisitions.

These are possibly more problematic than unrelated conglomerate deals. Every merger is different, yet there are certain common factors. Mergers take place for a wide range of reasons. A deal may be opportunistic, such as to refocus on core capabilities and key markets, or defensive, enabling two weaker organizations to compete better together. Typically, mergers occur for a range of the following reasons:

- To increase shareholder value
- Dominate/penetrate new markets
- Develop new products and services
- Defend the organization against a takeover.

In the public housing sector in the UK, for instance, the most common reasons are to extend the geographical spread of Housing Associations' operations, to reduce unit costs and to strengthen the income stream. The rationale for the merger is likely to affect how the merger is managed. Where mergers occur because a company wants to dominate the marketplace with a range of services, such as different fast-food outlets, there is much to be said for leaving the operations broadly separate, with integration only at senior management level. Conversely, if a company wishes to swamp the market with a single brand, full integration may be necessary.

Typically, organizations assume that full merger is required and greater upheaval than is necessary may be caused in some cases. Other possible combinations include considering the acquired company as:

- A separate holding – requiring strategic control
- A managed subsidiary – requiring operational control
- Full integration.

The integration decision should involve assessing the degree of cultural and functional integration required to help the combined company achieve its strategic ambitions. Whatever the rationale for the merger, it seems that the way the process of merging is carried out can have a bearing on whether the organization is able to achieve its business aims. Several cases studied in the Roffey Park research highlight the mistakes made when the acquiring company seeks to impose its procedures onto the acquired company (Devine *et al.*, 1998). Ironically, this often results in the acquirer unwittingly snuffing out the vital spark which made the acquired company seem such an interesting proposition.

In other cases, the uncertainty caused when senior managers of the acquired company are to lose their jobs following a merger can result in the employees of that company feeling especially vulnerable. When one pharmaceutical company acquired another, partly in order to absorb the other company's research capability, there was some surprise among managers of the acquiring company when initially exciting research projects failed to materialize. The phenomenon became known in the organization as 'burying the babies', i.e. employees kept their best projects safe in case they needed to jump ship.

The reason for the merger clearly has a bearing on whether the organization's strategy includes a reduction in headcount, relocation or other issues which have a direct impact on employees. The critical thing seems to be not so much whether there are job losses or whether organizations are renamed but how these processes are carried out. Open and honest communication and fair principles are very important in maintaining employee commitment. Similarly, the degree and speed of integration appears to affect employees, with organizations such as Bristol and West PLC, which had initiated its own acquisition, being able to phase the impact on employees over time. In theory this should help employees cope better with the 'waves of change' described in this chapter. However, other cases, such as the integration of Peter Dominic into Thresher described later in this chapter, suggest that a speedy integration can be highly effective in giving people a clear sense of direction.

WHAT SEPARATES MERGER PARTNERS

The relative size of partners has a bearing on how employees view the merger. It is often assumed that the larger organization swallows up the smaller one. This is not always the case. One relative newcomer to UK DIY retailing acquired a bigger and longer-established competitor. Typically, employees consider issues such as which head office is closed as indicative of which organization is the dominant partner. Similarly, perceptions about the power dynamics between the companies concerned can cause some employees to consider jumping ship.

Some of the main factors which can undermine successful integration are differences in the two organizations' politics, decision-making, cultures, values and leadership styles. Their strategies and structures, including systems and processes, are usually different. Employees are sensitive to those differences which affect them most, especially if they perceive the acquisition to be hostile. Which approaches are adopted and the way in which such decisions are taken can have an effect on employees' morale and willingness to adopt new working practices, especially if the acquired company's employees perceive that these are being imposed on them. One UK building society actively sought a merger partner and was acquired by a large bank. The importance of having a 'fit' at values level between the two organizations was recognized by both sets of senior managers who spent time getting to know one another, and building trust, before the deal was struck. Having taken time to understand each other's skills and attributes, the two organizations found they were complementary businesses and didn't need to fully integrate.

MERGERS NEED MANAGING

Several of the organizations studied by the Roffey Park team draw attention to the need for a skilled team of merger planning experts, and the importance of carrying out an effective human resource due diligence before the merger. Key employees need to be identified and encouraged to stay in the merged organization. The process of recruiting into positions needs to be handled in such a way as to minimize the potential for 'winners and losers'. The role of an influential and skilled Human Resources professional can be critical here.

Each phase of a merger has implications for leadership and for HR. These phases are:

- The 'run-up' or pre-merger
- The immediate transition (the first 100 days or 6 months)
- The integration (the longer-term coming together of the two parties).

Some companies are clearly focused on people issues right from the start of the merger process. They tend to be adept acquirers who have learned from past experience. Some of these companies have succeeded by developing key specialists who handle the merger process. With the full backing of the board, these taskforces are highly adept at getting communications appropriate to the situation and in making sure that the relevant relationships are established early on. The 'run-up' period should be used to carry out an effective HR due diligence and develop an awareness of the likely challenges and pressure points. The 'run-up' team should make a realistic assessment of the probable management workload and find ways of easing the burden somewhat.

The same companies then use a different team to manage the transition, and an effective handover is essential between teams. Typically, as in the Whitbread case study which follows, there is a clear 100-day plan which addresses most of the integration issues at the level of human resource matters, systems and processes. Of course, personnel issues, including policies and procedures, are not the only things which need managing. Other critical issues include integrating:

- IT
- Product ranges
- Supply chains
- Head offices.

Senior managers and directors have a key role in leading the change. In many mergers, the roles of one group of directors simply disappear. Where directors survive the merger, the relative positions which directors occupy in the new organization seems to have an impact on whether other employees consider their organization to be a 'winner' or 'loser' in the merger process. Ideally, at least one or two senior managers from the acquired company should be retained to provide other employees with reassurance. Willing collaboration between management teams before and after the merger also seems to make a positive difference to the way the change is handled.

During the transition period, the pace of change is so fierce that keeping an eye on the business is not easy. The research highlights the importance of managing the integration of the organizations as a critical project alongside keeping the business going and customers satisfied. This conscious management of the integration should carry on for as long a period as is necessary. Some companies manage the longer-term integration by training line managers and making them responsible for the real bedding down of the new organization. In the most successful cases, at least one board member takes responsibility for overseeing the integration for the period of time required for the 'new' organization to have fully emerged.

Even when handled 'professionally', mergers can still backfire. One company closed down its customer support site – when a merger made it obsolete – only to find that a competitor was opening a new facility nearby the very next week. The people whose jobs were made redundant and who had received generous pay-offs went straight into similar jobs with the rival company, taking their expertise and competitor knowledge with them.

COMMUNICATION

The importance of communication cannot be over-emphasized, particularly in the pre-merger phase. For example, a UK manufacturing company agreed to be acquired by a Swiss company in early 1998. The management team were pleased and excited as the firm had been 'on the market' for some time. Then, however, contact between the two companies dwindled, leaving the UK company's management team unclear about the Swiss company's plans and expectations. In a state of limbo, the UK firm was effectively 'off the market'. Some senior managers jumped ship because they had no guarantees for the future. There was no new product development, no investment and customer orders dropped off. Lack of communication led to suspicion, demoralization, and loss of key personnel and business, even before the contract was signed.

Communications are critical throughout, with several management teams learning the hard way that it is better to communicate even when you have nothing to say. HR needs to work alongside or as part of management teams, ensuring that formal communications are effective and that staff are being kept informed. The 1998 Benchmarking survey by PricewaterhouseCoopers, however, suggests the HR department typically does not focus on communication or motivation issues precisely at the very time when they are most needed – during organizational change such as a merger or demerger. Managers may need to be adept at managing rumours and paying attention to the first impressions staff in the acquired organization can form, based on their first encounter with employees from the acquiring company. When a merger is under way, communication mechanisms need to be in place that encourage an upwards flow of information in addition to top-down announcements. Open and frank dialogue between parties brings benefits.

The reaction of employees on both sides of the merger will be conditioned by factors such as the clarity and credibility of the messages given publicly and internally – and by their perception of the 'other party': is this a business they want to work for? The starting point for communication is usually the merger announcement, which is nearly always highly sensitive. The Roffey Park research found that employees sometimes found out first when listening to the radio on their way to work. Often, due to a lack of HR involvement in the run-up phase there is no clear communication plan for employees – all the attention has been paid to other stakeholders.

Early contacts set the tone and arrogance is common. 'Them and us' attitudes can easily result from inappropriate first contacts. The reaction of employees on both sides of the merger/acquisition will be conditioned by factors such as the clarity and credibility of the messages given publicly and internally – and by their general perception of the 'other party': is it a business they want to work with/for?

In one case, employees in both the acquired and acquiring companies were told on day 1 why the merger was happening and it was made clear to employees that 'good' people were in no danger of losing their jobs. People were asked to commit to the new company on the basis that 'we'll see you are alright'. None of the senior management from the acquired company survived the merger. On day 2 a presentation by the new chairman and chief executive conveyed an unfortunate impression to employees in the acquired company. The chairman insisted that the previous management had 'got it all wrong' and that his vision would lead to a successful company. While the message was no doubt meant to be motivational, and many 'acquired' employees agreed that they had been constrained by the previous management, the impression of arrogance created by the chairman's speech was confirmed by early attempts to impose one set of working practices on to another. What made matters worse was that there was in fact no plan of attack to support the chairman's claim and personnel matters such as appointments were left in abeyance. Many employees lost patience and left.

GAINING BUY-IN

Gaining emotional and intellectual buy-in from staff is no easy feat. Employees really need to know why the merger is happening so that they can work out the options for themselves. Issues such as the rationale for the merger, whether it is a proactive or reactive response, how the merger partner was selected, whether this is a merger or a takeover all need addressing. What can help is an early statement about the vision for the merged organization. When the Halifax and Leeds Building Societies merged they decided that their merger would create 'a Yorkshire-based world-class alternative to the clearing banks'. When the Environment Agency was formed out of up to eighty separate bodies, the aim was to provide 'a better environment in England and Wales for present and future generations'.

Typically, mergers are both mechanical/structural and psychological/cultural. All aspects of the merger need managing. In drawing up a checklist of the mechanical aspects of the merger, which tends to be the focus of director attention, care must also be given to being able to provide answers to employee questions which will set the scene for the psychological/cultural merger.

Merger mechanics	Psychological impact
Communication – road shows etc.	What's happening? When will I know if I have a job? Will there be redundancies and if so, when will they be announced?
Business strategy – loose/tight coupling	Why is it happening? Does it make sense? What changes are planned and when will they be announced?
Organizational structure	Where will I be in 6 months? Will there be changes in reporting structure? Who will I be reporting to in future?
Appointments and exits	Will I have a job?
Terms and conditions	Will our terms and conditions change?
Managing performance	Will I lose out? What is expected of me? Will there be Performance Appraisals?
Training and development	Do I have a future?

Fear of the unknown is a major contributor to employee uncertainty. Arguably, finding ways to reduce that uncertainty is a key responsibility of management.

In managing communications around the different phases of a merger, HR should bear in mind the psychological impact on employees of these changes and aim to offer answers to these core questions. While not all of these questions lend themselves to easy answers, people at least need to know when solutions to some of the problems will be worked upon. Some HR processes, such as rationalizing pay and conditions may take time to achieve. While there is no blueprint as to which issues must be tackled in what order, it is important to communicate a broad architecture of the merger process, together with targeted HR and management actions at each stage so that employees and senior managers can be reassured.

WAVES OF CHANGE

Mergers and acquisitions set off 'waves of change' within the organizations concerned. Unless these are managed, business performance can nosedive as a result of employee uncertainty and because senior managers concentrate their time on the merger, to the detriment of the existing business.

In the pre-merger phase, it is essential to explain to employees the strategic business reasons for the merger. Whatever approach is adopted, many organizational cases point to the importance of recognizing and understanding the differences between the organizational cultures as early as possible so that sensitive issues can be carefully handled. Similarly, employee loyalties to their colleagues, ways of working, company brand should not be underestimated. Employees may need to be allowed to 'grieve' the loss brought about by the merger as well as celebrate the new opportunities.

Typically, anxiety is highest at the time of the merger announcement and when the first job losses are announced. The rumour mill is very active at this stage. People wonder how they will be affected, if at all and what their own prospects will look like in the new organization. They are on the alert to signs, such as which company gets the lion's share of the best appointments, which indicate their likely fortune. Employees are hungry for information and this is typically when formal communications are at a standstill (Figure 16.1).

Research suggests that over 40% of the changes take place in the first two months. In the immediate transition, major events include the appointment of a new board of directors and key appointments/redundancies. As the new structure emerges, different groups are affected at different times. Often senior managers have been through their own anxiety and emerged the other end. Their focus may be on the next key business issue and it may be hard for them to appreciate the anxieties of people working in a front-line role who are being affected by restructuring in some cases up to two years after the merger. Other key points at which employee anxiety is high are decisions about which head office will be used, especially where relocation is involved, and when terms and conditions are integrated. Head-office staff are often the first to be affected by an early decision

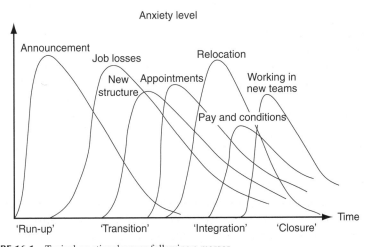

FIGURE 16.1 Typical emotional waves following a merger.

to close down an office. Field staff may wait for some time before the merging companies rationalize their outlets.

Communication alone is not enough – as previously stated, mergers need managing, especially the personnel issues. The way difficult personnel issues such as redundancies are handled will have a long-term effect on the morale of survivors and be a telling indication of the values of the new organization. New appointments must be seen to be fair and employees treated with dignity. Personnel processes should be documented and decisions should be open to scrutiny. The longer-term integration phase is often the period during which sites are closed or merged and staff are informed about relocations. New terms and conditions may be announced. Often a more fundamental revision of working practices and structures takes place.

The case that follows illustrates one approach to managing the pre-merger and transition phases.

The Whitbread Case: The Integration of Peter Dominic with Thresher

Thresher, part of Whitbread PLC, is a well-known UK major chain of off-licences which since a merger with Victoria Wine in 1998 has become known as 'First Quench'. Back in 1991, the Thresher business was doing reasonably well despite strong competition from other major off-licence chains and the supermarkets. Though part of Whitbread, Thresher was effectively run as a stand-alone business, with an experienced board which included Jerry Walton as managing director, Dick Smerdon as sales director, Ralph Hayward as marketing director and David Waters as HR head. The business had been reshaped on the margin side and was run along cost lines.

The Need for Change

In spring 1991 a market strategy analysis suggested that change was inevitable if the business was to continue to be successful. Increasing competition from the major supermarket chains meant that there was pressure to grow bigger in order to survive and thrive. Similarly, for longer-term success it was clear that there needed to be a stronger emphasis on customer focus and on developing brands. There were other drivers for change too. For David Waters, the existing culture of the organization, with its tendency towards Theory X styles of management, was working against the need to retain and grow good people who would be willing and able to provide excellent customer service.

How much people perceived the need for change at that time is questionable. To some extent in 1991, Thresher risked becoming a victim of the success of the two previous years which had been particularly good in terms of business results. Waters believes that this success was largely due to the efforts of a few key people. Thresher really needed to sell more drink and that, to a large extent, depended on the skills and attitudes of staff at shop level. It became apparent that the business could not continue to operate in this way and would need to be reshaped.

The Move towards Restructuring along Brand Lines

The initial move towards reshaping the business came through discussions about how the business could be restructured along brand lines. The business had been developing a segmentation strategy for over a year. A think-tank was set up consisting of key members of the HR team and a consulting group. The group brainstormed how the organization could look two or three years down the line. Though by 1998 Thresher had developed a range of brands including Bottoms Up, back in 1991, the existence of brands such as Wine Rack was embryonic.

The group's recommendations were taken to the board for debate in May 1991. The proposals involved splitting out Wine Rack, Thresher (Wine Stores) and the Drink Stores. This focus on brands implicitly carried with it a greater emphasis on the customer. Initially, the board were reluctant to accept proposals which would so radically shift the organization from being centralized to one which was based on a series of brands, each with its own core functions such as Personnel. The board debated long and hard and finally made the decision to restructure operations only along brand lines in June 1991. Once this decision had been taken, a culture shift became inevitable.

The Decision to Acquire Peter Dominic

As part of Grand Metropolitan, Peter Dominic was effectively available for acquisition. For Thresher, Peter Dominic would be a useful complement to the existing business, resulting in substantially more retail outlets and better geographical coverage. The courtship went on throughout the summer of 1991, with Thresher becoming more confident of acquiring Peter Dominic by September.

During the courtship phase, financial plans were put together as well as a detailed organization plan. The organization plan needed to be reasonably robust and capable of indicating where profit would come from, if not from sales. While it was clear that the Thresher team were leading the process and that this was an acquisition rather than a true merger, the creation of the organization plan was greatly assisted by the general willingness of the Dominic managing director and HRD team to collaborate with the planning team.

They shared detailed information about organization charts, roles, key players, systems and practices within Dominic. The disclosure information included job histories, pay rates, training plans, union agreements and methods of communication such as newsletters. The planning team were able to identify possible synergies, assess the numbers of jobs required, design structures and in other ways carry out an effective human resource due diligence. They were able to identify issues that would need resolving such as those relating to the transfer of undertakings, as well as areas that would need to be negotiated with trades unions, since Peter Dominic was unionized, whereas Whitbread was not. In addition, the planning team were provided with details of the sales histories of each of the stores, together with contracts with outside suppliers. The team were able to identify where the overlaps were and which stores would have to close. A critical decision taken during this time was that some Thresher stores would have to close if they were the less promising option. This subsequently caused some discontent within Thresher employees who found it hard to understand why, if they were on the acquiring or 'winning' side, their sites would have to go.

During this phase, the number of people within Thresher involved in preparing for the merger numbered no more than a dozen. Apart from the board, those actively involved included Chris Johnson the HR controller, the directors of Buying and of Property (estates), people responsible for financial planning, financial services and systems and the security manager. The security manager was considered a vital part of ensuring that business continued as usual during this period of change since it was felt that stock might be lost if management attention was on the merger. In addition, three or four members of Whitbread's corporate team worked closely with the board.

The merger negotiations were well advanced by mid-September. By this time, decisions had been taken about who was going to be on the executive team which made many of the preparations for the transition process much easier. The decision was taken to merge the two organizational cultures as quickly as possible, since the more gradual integration of a previous acquisition had caused significant problems. The board went away for a day to draw up a plan of action and key priorities for the first 100 days following the merger announcement.

The 100-Day Plan

A number of key action areas were identified and intimate, detailed plans drawn up around these. It was obviously important that the businesses should continue to be run effectively during the period of transition and measures were put in place to ensure this. As one board member put it, 'we want the cash in the bucket and no holes'. The board did not underestimate the symbolic significance of some of their earliest acts, one of which was to spend £50 000 changing the locks on all the store front doors in the first week. However, for the first time managers were handed the keys and the implicit message that they were trusted professional retailers carried weight. The plan also made it possible for promises to be made and kept about investing in security to make employees' jobs safer.

Another important area was retaining key employees, especially the planning team, by creating a sense of security around their own futures. Other areas concerned integrating finances, systems, as well as issues relating to employee pay and communications. Perhaps the main feature of the plan concerned the day of the handover itself, and a great deal of preparation was begun to ensure that employees would hear the news first hand as much as possible and have the chance to raise issues with executives. The aim was to ensure that by the end of the first day, all departments would have been seen. Questions and answers were prepared and executives were given a strict schedule of visits.

The Handover

The schedule of visits went ahead on the day of the announcement (31 October). Partnership was very much the order of the day, with senior managers from both companies involved in communicating with staff. Jerry Walton, for instance, saw the clerical teams and, though the day was very emotionally charged, a proper handover took place. The senior Thresher managers met the Peter Dominic staff and all the subgroups had the chance to meet the functional teams. Despite the planning team's best efforts, there were some emotional issues and things that could not be disclosed prior to the merger which now needed to be dealt with. This was an important cultural first step – being open and honest with people.

Communications

The symbolism of senior management actions should not be underestimated during a merger. Some significant positive messages were conveyed to the Peter Dominic staff, who saw themselves as having been acquired. Individual members of the Thresher board spent lots of time visiting the Dominic offices and stores. Board meetings that would normally have been held at Thresher head office were now also taking place at the Dominic head office, though this would shortly close. The effect on Peter Dominic was to acclimatize the organization to change. David Waters describes this as dropping 'open secrets' into the 'collective grapevine'.

Not everything went smoothly, however. Following the announcements, question-and-answer sessions and other active communications of the first few days following merger, information continued to flow for five weeks. The planning team had confidently predicted that the merger would be sorted by 1 December and significant progress had been made. However, knowing that Christmas is the busiest trading period in drinks retailing, the planning team let it be known that active communications on progress would be suspended during the Christmas period in order to allow people to concentrate on doing their jobs – selling drinks. What the team had not envisaged was the effect of suddenly turning off the flow of information, even though warning had been given. People assumed that the merger was going wrong and that bad news was to follow.

Winners and Losers

There were initially people who perceived themselves to be winners and losers. According to David Waters this is inevitable, no matter what you do. The challenge is to ensure that, as much as possible, 'losers' start to find some advantages in the merger situation for themselves.

In the Thresher case, part of this was accomplished by the actions of senior managers. The company kept the board's promise that people would be told the fate of their job within thirty days. The policy was to forge integration in the shortest time possible. The Peter Dominic board all went and a policy for store closures was drawn up under which stores would be given six months' notice of closure and that closure decisions would be reviewed over two years based on profit. This applied to both Dominic and Thresher stores.

Senior managers took the approach that people whose jobs were going would be actively helped to find others and would demonstrate their interest in people who were leaving asking, for instance, whether they were receiving enough help in finding new jobs. It was decided that the Peter Dominic head office in Harlow would be closed down. Employees were told on 1 December that the office would close seven months later. Until closure, staff working in the redundant office still experienced fresh flowers in reception twice a week and the canteen, though expensive to run, was kept open to the end. There were visits from senior management and other small signs were used to ensure that the board could show they were still valued by the company which they would soon be leaving.

The management team tried to show respect to all staff, whether they were going to be part of the future operation or not. Individuals were offered a variety of forms of career counselling and practical support in finding new jobs. There was a party for employees from both of the original organizations when the Dominic head office finally closed.

Not everybody who might have been considered a 'winner' in the merger was pleased with their lot, however. The Thresher team recognized that some of the Dominic team had the kind of skills they were looking for. What the team soon learned was that just because you offer someone a good job, it does not mean that they will accept the job. Some of the Dominic sales and marketing staff were exactly what Thresher wanted – upbeat and bullish. Many of these people left because they were not willing to accept the package offered by Thresher.

One of the main reasons for people leaving, no matter how well a merger is handled, appears to be that people recognize that a merger throws all the job 'balls' into the air. Wherever the job 'balls' land is likely to stay in place for several years. A number of key people who had considered themselves due a promotion and who did not welcome the advent of more competitors for jobs left the company before the job situation had been finalized.

Some of Thresher middle managers also considered that the allocation of jobs turned them from considering themselves to be 'winners' into 'losers' when they found themselves reporting to a more experienced Peter Dominic manager. They could not understand why, if they were part of the dominant group, they were being asked to change role, and people took the matter to heart. They also blamed senior management, complaining that they had not been communicated with enough and that all the attention was being lavished on Dominic staff.

Similarly, there were a number of 'culturally misaligned' people, who, though skilled at their jobs, were effectively undermining the integration process through their cynical behaviour. It was important to confront such behaviour, allow a little time for people to change their ways or part company. There were also strenuous discussions with unions about pay and conditions (Dominic was unionized whereas Thresher was not). A negotiated settlement produced a compromise deal in which there were some, but different benefits and drawbacks for most employees.

Effective communications are clearly critical during and after a merger. Inevitably there will be some things which cannot be disclosed prior to the merger. For David Waters there are some clear fundamentals of good communication which should not be ignored:

> Keep talking with people every day. Questions and answers in week one need to be the foundation of ongoing good communications. You cannot overcommunicate in the early stages of integration. No matter what you do, employees will expect a consistency of approach from you which you may not consider appropriate. By and large they will have less information than you about where the organization is going and may be less able to appreciate the subtleties of your approach. Communications should always be looked at from a variety of employee angles. In particular you have to overcommunicate with the 'home team' in the early stages to secure their commitment as you start to know staff from the other organization.

Integration – Building on the Merger

By Summer 1992 the merger was considered complete. The 100-day plan was completed within 75 days. There were now more brands (four or five were emerging) and the organization structure to support these was in place. Marketing and HR support was aligned to each of the brands. The two cultures were fused with neither having supremacy over the other. This provided a solid platform for changing things further. This was also helped by the injection of talent from outside into key roles that the new structure made possible. This built up the amount of experience within the company of how to run businesses and change processes. This in turn led to a better calibre of management, with the business as a whole benefiting from this blend of approaches from the main two companies and others. Similarly, the merger provided the catalyst for 'releasing' relatively non-performing people.

A significant benefit was that people, including the board, got used to change. The challenge following a successful merger is to introduce yet more change in order to achieve some of the potential of the combined operation. It was at this point that the Operations Development Project (ODP) came into being. The ODP was a strategic, long-term change project which has brought with it new working practices, energized staff and the release of human potential as well as improved business results. More details of the ODP can be found in Holbeche (1997).

Key Learning Points

- Be aware that there are some things you can plan for, and you should make every effort to put plans in place for these. However, some things such as predicting the emotional reaction to the news and dealing appropriately with it are easier to plan for than to cope with. Those on the receiving end of other people's reactions may themselves need support, whether this is from other senior managers, members of the planning team, external mentors or others.
- Senior management teams must stay close to the merger during the period of transition and not become shut off – that is when energy gets dispersed.

- While it is important to use appropriate resources and skills during mergers, make sure that, as far as possible, internal staff lead the integration effort, rather than relying on external consultants. According to David Waters, 'the whole thing is about confidence, not over-confidence, that you can carry people with you'.
- When attempting to integrate cultures, start with the people with the right attitude to people – high energy, prepared to confront things.
- Never make promises you cannot keep.

HOW HR CAN HELP AN ORGANIZATION THROUGH A MERGER

From this and other case studies it is clear that the HR function has a potentially key role to play in a merger. Involvement should begin in the run-up phase. Early identification of sensitive issues can reduce their impact over time. Pay and conditions can become a huge issue and in many cases are dealt with early in the transition period. Without a strategic perspective, the HR team is likely to be overtaken by a host of operational and mechanical issues which must be dealt with. Having said that, time must be set aside to work with directors and individuals on the critical HR issues. Help from consultants may well enable HR teams to focus their energies strategically during a critical period. The research suggests that some of the critical contributions which HR can make are as follows:

Being Involved in Planning, Transition and Integration Teams

- HR professionals need to contribute specific expertise to these teams, enabling the merger to be managed as a project, while keeping the core business going
- Develop effective ways of collaborating with the planning team from the other company in the pre-merger phase, if possible
- Does clear communication exist between members of the negotiating and transition teams? What are the handover issues which will make a difference to the success of the integration?
- If the acquisition is perceived as hostile, identify as early as possible the key information you need to know if a thorough human resource due diligence is not possible. What other ways can the necessary information be obtained?
- What framework is in place for managing the different phases of the merger?
- Find ways in which people from both companies can get to know each other as quickly as possible
- Identify how the emerging organizational vision can best be communicated
- Take a 'best of both' rather than 'equal shares' or 'acquirer dominates' approach to deciding who has which roles, which working practices etc. are adopted
- Decide fair principles on the handling of redundancies.

Identifying the HR Issues and Carrying Out an Effective Human Resource Due Diligence By:

- Comparing terms and conditions of employment and salary scales including the structure of share options and to whom they are available, severance terms in contracts, incentive and bonus schemes in terms of immediate and future commitments
- Gathering information about the management team – how critical are they and will they all remain post-acquisition?
- Gaining perspectives of the management team – their view of the company, employees' view of the senior team
- Understanding the existing skills of the present HR team – are they adequate to coordinate proposed changes to the business?
- Understanding the organization structure
- Identifying what is required in terms of manpower plan to achieve the business strategy
- Identifying key personnel and having initial plans for securing ongoing commitment. To what extent is the necessary knowledge and skill critical to running the business vested in a few staff?
- Identifying the likely level of redundancies involved and prospects for early retirements
- Identifying which job descriptions and/or profiles will need to be changed
- Finding out how communication of the sale has been dealt with so far including the processes used for communication
- Comparing ways of working and identifying major differences that will need to be addressed
- Agreeing the management culture of the combined organization and what will need to be done to achieve it
- Considering the size and location of existing offices. Deciding whether office closures will be necessary and whether the provision of new office accommodation will be appropriate or possible
- Finding out details of any industrial disputes etc. and the number of appeals on job evaluations by the Hay Committee within the last 12 months
- Is the organization unionized or does the staff council or similar employee representation group have any negotiation rights and if so, what do these rights include?
- Being realistic about timescales. Does everything have to be done at once? Many companies attempt to integrate terms and benefits as quickly as possible. If delay is required, there should be a clearly communicated plan so that employees know when key issues will be addressed. Merging cultures may take two years or longer
- Agreeing a clear communication plan for the first 100 days. What clear central message will be sent to all employees?

Carrying Out Effective HR Integration on the Following:

- Remuneration
- Benefits
- Terms and conditions
- Culture and management style
- Career and other development issues
- Communication and climate
- Employee relations.

Ensuring that Management Teams Have the Skills they Need to Manage the Merger Well

Line managers usually play a key role in central project teams. Management teams need to be quickly welded together, with at least a common approach on key Human Resource issues. Some team building may be needed. Management teams need the following:

- Strategic management skills, especially understanding how to add value to the new business
- Integration skills – being able to make decisions about structure, roles and dealing with sensitive situations
- Change management skills – being able to bring people with them through change
- Cultural skills – being able to understand the dynamics of organizational culture, deal with culture clashes and the emergence of a new culture
- People skills – being able to understand the reactions and concerns of employees and support them through change.

Helping Line Managers to Communicate Effectively During the Transition Phase

Managers also have a key role in sustaining communications about the merger process to all employees even when there is 'no news'. Given the symbolic importance of senior management behaviour, managers may need practical help in understanding how to communicate to employees from both companies in the early days. Managers may need to be made aware of the symbolic power of language to help or hinder the merger process. They may need to recognize that a merger is likely always to be an emotional issue for employees and that employees need to be communicated with, and convinced of the benefits at an emotional not simply rational level.

In the first month of a merger between two professional service firms, line managers were given the chance to reflect on how they were going to help implement the organizational changes. For some the main challenge was 'getting staff into confidence mode – our task is to raise staff morale'. Many managers also felt the need to ask questions of their own directors, rather than assuming that they were being kept in the dark. Some managers recognized the importance of sitting down with their team and personalizing the messages which were largely being conveyed via corporate videos. The managers were mainly concerned about the apathy resulting from apparent lack of change following the merger announcement. They recognized that they would need to prepare their colleagues for the ongoing waves of change which would eventually arise from the merger.

Since managers are in the front line for communication, it is essential that they have the ability to develop two-way communications. HR can provide practical help with team briefings and feedback processes. Managers need to communicate why the merger has taken place, what the organization is trying to achieve and how each person's role contributes to achieving this. They need to have a wide range of management styles appropriate to different circumstances and may need help in developing their coaching ability and flexibility.

Managing Individuals with Dignity

Chief executives, often very action-oriented, are keen to get through the difficult business of reorganization and job loss as quickly as possible. Speed is helpful as long as it does not compromise dealing with staff fairly and treating them with dignity. The handling of key changes for individuals – such as job changes, appointments and relocations as well as exits – sets the tone for how staff view the new organization. Handling redundancies inappropriately usually results in a morale backlash among 'survivors'.

Developing and Implementing Actions to Retain Key Employees

Good people have to stay if the two organizations are to learn from each other's strengths. Line managers need to identify and keep close to key staff at all levels and actively involve them in the merger process. If such people are neglected in the early months, they often jump ship. Some organizations develop retention strategies which involve some sort of inducements such as 'golden handcuffs' to encourage people to stay. There appears to be some evidence that, even without financial incentives and firm guarantees, letting people know that they are valued and quickly finding ways of using their talent in the new organization can be sufficient encouragement for some.

Keeping the Top in Touch with the Bottom

HR is uniquely placed to build in upward feedback to keep the boardroom in touch with what is really going on in an organization. In the Roffey Park research senior people described being sucked into the detail of the operational issues and the mechanics of the merger. It was only with the benefit of hindsight that they realized that understanding and managing people's perceptions and expectations were equally vital to promoting a healthy emergent organization. The culture of the new organization begins from day one, not when vision and values statements start to appear.

This is where the special skills of trainers can come into their own. Typically, trainers have good communication skills and are in touch with the 'mood' of employees who are attending courses. Trainers who are able to understand the business dynamics and the sensitivities involved in creating a new culture can provide a useful steer to line managers who are charged with communications in the early days post-merger.

Helping to Clarify Roles

Once the shape of the new organization becomes clearer, people may need help in clarifying their roles, knowing where they fit in the organization's purpose and how to be successful in the new set-up. This may require them to learn new skills or adjust their working practices. Briefings for line managers and some training for individuals may be necessary. Typically, in the early days of a merger a number of temporary policies and short-term priorities are identified. Line managers often need a basic set of 'tool kit' training sessions which are short and focused. These can help build up managers' confidence where responsibility, reporting lines and roles are still ill-defined.

CONCLUSION

Though mergers and acquisitions are tricky territory for organizations, what has become clear from the Roffey and other research is that mergers and alliances are most successful when the 'people' issues are well handled. HR practitioners are uniquely placed to help the organization realize its strategic ambitions – by getting their 'people' strategies right. Trust can be built but this requires a special awareness and influence which HR ought to be able to wield. HR needs to be represented on planning and transition teams and use the opportunity to challenge management thinking about what – and who – is required in the new organization.

Real communication, and for an extended period, may be necessary if employees are to feel committed to the new organization. HR may need to act as the line management 'conscience' on communication once there is a semblance of 'business as usual' returning. Individual transitions need to be handled well and employees should be allowed to deal with their bereavement about departing colleagues – and the changing organization. This does not mean holding formal 'wakes' but celebrating the end of one set of working practices formally can help people integrate the new.

If handled well, mergers and alliances can be a lever for introducing further major change which brings significant business benefits. They are an opportunity to develop a new management style and culture, as well as to manage and improve costs. They are also an ideal opportunity to put the right people in the right jobs. They provide the rationale for putting performance on the map and for measuring the performance of the business and the success of the integration process following the merger. And of course, in an ideal world, they provide the opportunity to do things differently, while adding value to the business; to deliver excellent service to the client while providing a rewarding experience for all employees. To achieve all this, a strategic HR contribution can be pivotal and the HR practitioner who helps his or her organization achieve these benefits can truly be said to have managed change effectively.

CHECKLISTS ON PERSONNEL DECISIONS – MERGERS AND ACQUISITIONS

(Based on Holbeche and Garrow, 2000)

Employment Relationship Issues

- transferring the employment relationship, salary payment etc.
- employment contracts
- employment conditions
- insurances
- corporate security
- employee information
- regulatory/legal issues.

Personnel Policies

It is essential that there is access to personnel handbooks and intranet sites as soon as possible. First decisions with regard to personnel policies require early clarification on the following:

- Acquirer's HR-policy – how applicable is it in foreign subsidiaries and alliances?
- To what extent should HR processes be in common with foreign subsidiaries?

Other policies include:

- Car policy
- Mobile phone policy
- ISDN policy
- Insurance policy
- Travelling policy
- Occupational health services policy
- Occupational safety
- International assignment policy
- Country policies
- Trainee policy.

Tasks and Responsibilities

- What are the skill requirements for the jobs existing in the new entity?
- Assessing the skills of all the people, and possibly reselect people to the jobs. This way the future training needs can also be assessed.
- Job evaluation – provide realistic job reviews.
- Discussion (performance and appraisal discussion) between supervisor and employee to clarify the task and responsibilities and set targets for the future aligned with the goals of the organization.
- Job titles aligned.
- Clear job descriptions defining the objectives of their roles as well as the skills and competencies required for success in the new environment.
- Two-way communication about HR issues. Give people the possibility to discuss the issues that are bothering them. Possibly provide separate orientation sessions for employees.

Compensation and Benefits

- Examine the compensation and benefits systems of both organizations
- Salary frames/grades and levels/competency profiles
- Working hours, practice of the overtime work
- Vacation/holidays, other leaves (parenthood leave, rotation leave)
- What benefits (e.g. car, mobile phone, stable phone, ISDN, rented flat, health-care etc.) and for whom?
- Financial support for sports and leisure
- Examine the performance management systems
- Pension system and conditions
- Performance management system
- Bonuses
- Recruitment reward
- Long-term remuneration, stock options
- Plan how to align the compensation and benefits of two organizations or design a new system
- Financial bonuses/rewards for the integration work.

Development Issues

Current practices:

- Performance and appraisal process
- Training policy
- Career path
- Succession planning
- Induction practices.

Integration

- Induction programme as soon as possible in order to socialize employees of the acquired organization to the acquiring organization. Company presentation right after the announcement of the acquisition would help in creating positive, but realistic image of the acquiring company
- Training for managers on what people are experiencing in acquisitions and suggestions on how to handle and support people
- Separate orientation sessions for managers and supervisors at the acquired organization to explain Human Resource policies and practices
- Find out the training requirements
- Training and development design
- Executive team building
- Provide information about career possibilities
- Provide training possibilities at least to key employees
- Provide ambassador training for members of transition team and their designees who will be spending time at the new facility.

Recruitment

- Recruitment and selection policies
- Employee assessment
- Employee selection (offer the new jobs first to the existing personnel)
- Are relocation or reduction of personnel necessary?
- Improving incentives and compensation schemes. (Plan the appropriate form and timing of the financial rewards for the former management team members and other key employees.)

REFERENCES

Devine, M., Hirsh, W. *et al.* (1998) *Mergers and Acquisitions: Getting the People Bit Right*: Roffey Park Management Institute

Hall, P. and Norburn, D. (1987) The management factor in acquisition performance. *Leadership and Organization Development Journal*, No. 8

Holbeche, L. (1997) *Motivating People in Lean Organizations*. Oxford: Butterworth-Heinemann. Chapter 6

Holbeche, L. and Garrow, V. (2000) *Effective Mergers and Acquisition*. Horsham: Roffey Park Management Institute

Chapter 17

Creating a Learning Culture

If a company has not organized its personnel in a way that allows fast learning and the conditions of 'flocking' (learning in groups), or if it doesn't do, intensively, things like career development, it will be hurt. If it hasn't got the right underlying contract with its people that means, 'I'm interested in your potential, rather than in your immediate output over the next three months', then I think the bell is tolling.

(de Geus, 1997)

Senior managers are now faced with a period of ongoing change and uncertainty given the rate of technological change and global market pressures. The impact of the Information Revolution is now being felt and working patterns are likely to be irrevocably changed. In the knowledge and service economies, factors of production are no longer land, labour or capital, as in the industrial era, but talent, skills and knowledge. At the heart of the Information Revolution is low-cost computing and communication. This is enabling people to communicate externally and internally on a more extensive basis than ever before. The speeding up of communication is changing the rules of business, bringing new opportunities for creating value and the need for new measures to protect existing value.

New measures of value suggest that the market value of a company is based on financial capital and intellectual capital. Intellectual capital represents the intangible assets of an organization. This breaks down into the 'structural' capital, in which some of the knowledge, processes and procedures can be captured by the organization and held there. The other two forms of capital – 'customer', such as the brand, reputation, relationships and 'human' – represent the real competitive advantage since it is the ongoing development of ideas, products and services that meet customer needs which ensures that the organization is sustainable. According to Gareth Morgan (1993), 'an organization has no presence beyond that of the people who bring it to life'. The challenge of managing intellectual capital is ensuring that it does not walk out of the door.

There is a strategic imperative which suggests that managing knowledge is a key priority since the risks of not doing so are high. They include:

- Duplication of effort
- Wasted time (which managers do not even notice because they are too busy)

- Repeated learning curves
- Slower rate of innovation
- Higher threats to the speed and quality of service.

Conversely, it might be argued that having good structural capital, through which new entrants can experience rapid development could make a company an employer of choice.

Few organizations have a blueprint for the future or are able to accurately predict the precise talents and skills needed for future success. However, growing flexible and high-calibre talent does require a long-term view and a strategic approach to talent planning. Preparing an organization for change and learning requires not only tight links between the organization's strategies and training but also an underpinning culture in which learning is valued and encouraged. Developing and exploiting some of the knowledge capability within an organization may be one of the few relatively untapped sources of competitive advantage. Some organizations invest heavily in the latest IT systems and are amazed to find that the systems fail to deliver the desired business advantage. What is becoming increasingly evident is that for information systems to work, human beings must be willing to create and generate useful knowledge which is more than just data. Managing knowledge is essentially a people-related activity.

KNOWLEDGE MANAGEMENT

Knowledge of all forms exists in different parts of an organization, but very few organizations have a 'map' of the knowledge available. The amount and pace of change within businesses today makes it difficult to keep abreast of existing knowledge, let alone identify the knowledge needed for the future. The Chief Executive of Hewlett–Packard, for example, has been quoted as saying 'If HP knew what HP knows, we would be three times as profitable'. Thomas Stewart (1997), writing about intellectual capital, suggests how challenging it can be to try to understand what knowledge resources exist within an organization:

> Trying to identify and manage knowledge is like trying to fish barehanded. It can be done … but the object of the effort is damnably elusive.

Managers may therefore be unaware of the vast potential on offer. Traditional accounting systems for valuing organizations typically fail to register the value of that knowledge since it is notoriously difficult to measure and, by its nature is 'implicit', 'tacit' or inside people's heads. The real value of a company is what acquirers are willing to pay to gain access to staff and their skills and knowledge. In sectors such as advertising, fund management and consultancies, many organizations on the acquisition trail have found that they have bought nothing when key staff walk.

So great has been the staff turnover in some sectors that there are often few people left within the business who really know how things can be done. Arnold Kransdorff (1995) studied organizations that formerly had low rates of staff turnover and now experience a wholesale turnover of staff every four or five years. He coined the term 'corporate amnesia' to describe the loss of learning to the company when staff left. He found that in some cases, expensive mistakes were repeated while in others, systems which had been developed could no longer be used by staff since they were all new and there was no one left with the relevant experience who could teach them. Particularly costly was the loss of customer information which was acquired over years by employees who were invited to retire early.

'Explicit' information, as detailed in databases, staff manuals and process maps shows only a small part of the real knowledge assets of a company. The intangibles, such as know-how, information on stakeholder relationships, experiences and ideas, represent the critical knowledge. Such information tends to stay in the informal system of the organization where it is shared by only a few people. Information alone is not the real asset; it is what people do, or are prepared to do with that information which turns it into valuable, shared knowledge. It is how people convert information into knowledge and the way they use that information to shape decisions which represents the real knowledge asset.

Knowledge tends to generate knowledge when ideas are shared and collaboration is in evidence. Flatter structures, with their emphasis on teamwork and smart ways of working, should be ideally suited to the generation and sharing of knowledge. The challenge is how to capture knowledge in the context of a flexible, mobile workforce. Knowledge management is about harnessing the knowledge and experience that people have; it's about connecting people and creating a culture where senior people think that knowledge sharing is worth investing in. This reinforces the idea that knowledge management is not the exclusive domain of IT specialists but is of direct relevance to line managers and HR professionals. It is fundamentally about creating the conditions in which human beings create and share information, knowledge and learning.

BARRIERS TO SHARING KNOWLEDGE

However, there are a number of important barriers to organizational learning which prevent organizations from making the most of their intellectual capital. One is the rate of change and the increasingly flexible nature of the workforce. Capitalizing on the skills, knowledge and experience is challenging enough, but capturing the knowledge of a flexible workforce, including consultants, contractors and others whose affiliation to the company many be temporary, is even more difficult.

Another barrier is deeply embedded in the old hierarchical structures and related career progression routes. To some extent conventional career development has been based on individuals becoming knowledgeable – about issues, technical and professional bodies of knowledge and about how the organization works – and being able to use that knowledge to get things done. The axiom 'knowledge is power' is evident when skills and knowledge are in short supply, as are certain types of IT skills currently.

Flatter structures too can reinforce the desire to hoard information. People who were once colleagues are now competitors for scarce promotion opportunities. The internal market value of certain types of knowledge is evident in the political battles being waged in many organizations. While Charles Handy (1997) identified knowledge as only one of seven forms of power, knowledge can give individuals career trading power which many people would be unlikely to wish to give up, given the ongoing uncertainty of the jobs market.

Similarly, HR and other systems can undercut people's willingness to share information which might be useful to others. One major UK broking firm was concerned about the ways in which they failed to service clients well because the relevant client information was in the head of one individual. If that individual was sick or left the firm, their knowledge was no longer available. A related problem was that clients were becoming increasingly irritated by the numerous contacts they had with the same firm, while employees at the firm were unaware that other employees were in touch with the same client.

The firm installed expensive hardware and software to enable information about clients to be kept up to date. They were puzzled why employees did not update records and use the new resource. This was not a case of 'technophobia' – another common barrier to knowledge management processes. It was only when they recognized that people were individually rewarded for the 'deals' struck that they realized that there was no incentive for people to share information about the client. It was not until rewards were attached to the quality of the client relationship that people's behaviour, and use of the system began to change. Some of the previous main critics of the new system became its champions when they could see advantages to them in ensuring that the information was kept fresh. Any organization seeking to introduce knowledge management systems needs to be clear about potential obstacles to the sharing of knowledge, and address those obstacles so that people can identify the 'what's in it for me?' factor.

Another common barrier to the sharing of organizational learning is that people often focus rather narrowly on their jobs, rather than the purpose of the organization as a whole. There can be a heavy emphasis on the short term which makes the sharing of knowledge for longer-term gains an impediment to getting the job done now. The new CEO of a major electronics company visited all the decentralized business units and was amazed to find that there were many initiatives under way in separate units which would be useful to the work of other units – but no one apart from the CEO had the full picture. The CEO insisted that interchanges were established so that the organization could benefit more widely from these new approaches.

Making time for reviewing what they have learned can appear an unnecessary luxury. People fail to notice the slight but significant changes in the business environment until it is too late. Teams can engage in 'us and them' mentalities which cause defensive and political behaviour over turf issues. Perhaps the biggest obstacle to shared learning is a blame culture when things go wrong. This is where the tone set by senior management is absolutely critical to the successful implementation of knowledge management strategies.

A key barrier to organizational learning may be embedded in the dominant thought processes in evidence among Western managers. Indeed, some of the leading thinking on knowledge management comes from Japan. Ikujiro Nonaka, co-author with Hirotaka Takeuchi of *The Knowledge-Creating Company* (1995), suggests that Japan is more innovative than the West because the West, with its culture of rationalism, tends to value explicit knowledge. Conversely, the Japanese, with their emphasis on the holistic nature of mind and body, value tacit knowledge, which is both elusive and abstract. Other thinkers agree. Jean Lammiman and Michel Syrett (1999), who carried out Roffey Park research looking at where directors get their ideas from, suggest:

> The foundations on which traditional management is based – rational judgement and decision-making based on sharply expressed definitive ideas – can be counter-intuitive and may shut down all but a fraction of the organization's creative capability.

The interest in recent years in emotional and other forms of intelligence, is starting to percolate through into Western management vocabulary. Roger Leek, Group HR Director at Fujitsu Services, believes that training and development can support a culture change from a relatively hierarchical and inflexible system to a more customer-focused culture, by developing the emotional intelligence of senior managers. Roger recognizes the vital role of line managers in championing knowledge management within the organization in their capacity of leaders.

LEARNING IS ABOUT MUCH MORE THAN TRAINING

It is important to remember, however, that learning is not just another word for training. If we think about personal development, leadership development and organizational development, we know that learning has the capacity to transform people and organizations. The trouble is, according to Sharon Varney (2008), that many established practices around learning (for example, analysing learning needs and articulating desired learning outcomes) are firmly rooted in the training world and may not serve us so well when our goal is to unlock the transformational nature of learning in pursuit of organizational change and transformation.

HOW CAN BARRIERS TO THE SHARING OF KNOWLEDGE BE OVERCOME?

Overcoming all these barriers is a tall order. However, individuals need to be able to identify sharing of knowledge as being in their interest. Sharing knowledge makes existing knowledge more productive and helps to create new knowledge. The more information is used, the more it develops and grows. One of the ways of achieving this is by providing people with the conditions in which information can be shared, and letting them work out the benefits for themselves.

Firms are creating the infrastructure for self-development through online or virtual training. For many organizations this is already well under way. Much of the existing Computer Based Training (CBT) is unit- and text-based, which appeals to some whilst alienating others. Increasingly, organizations provide a mix of learning and development methods that provide opportunities for accelerated self-development by providing a range of interventions from digital learning to team-based collaborative learning.

Employers are trying to stimulate innovation and knowledge sharing and then capture the results – this will help ensure that if key talent leaves the organization, at least some of their knowledge will remain with colleagues. Linking individual growth and progression to knowledge acquisition will assist this process. In broad terms, knowledge management has to address three key activities:

- Motivating people to share information
- Developing a system for managing and storing information
- Motivating people to use the knowledge available to them.

The first step is to find out what knowledge really is important and who has that knowledge. This may involve brainstorming to find out what knowledge is critical to the organization. The next step is making people accountable for managing that critical knowledge. However, some general conditions need to be in place for knowledge management to be effective. Broadly speaking, these are ensuring that top leaders own the knowledge management agenda, creating a culture of trust and teamwork in which collaboration is the norm and building an appropriate infrastructure to facilitate learning. As Morgan suggests:

> You can't create a learning organization ... But you can enhance people's capacities to learn and align their activities in creative ways.

HOW HR CAN CREATE THE CONDITIONS FOR KNOWLEDGE MANAGEMENT

1. *Develop a knowledge management framework*
   - Decide what kinds of data, information and experience is valuable enough to retain and make available
   - Identify what are the strategic management assets and assign someone to manage these
   - Produce guidelines about the kind of information which should be stored so as to avoid the danger of overload
   - Provide appropriate infrastructure in the form of communications technology, systems design and applications tools
   - Decide on a knowledge 'architecture' which gives guidance on what kind of data is valuable enough to retain and make available. This will include not simply product information but also useful knowledge such as lessons learnt from experience with customers, projects etc.
2. *Develop a sharing approach*
   - Experiment with building networks
   - Share 'best practice' via the intranet, Lotus Notes etc.

- Ensure that usable information is catalogued and stored with the relevant technology
- Allow the majority of employees direct customer contacts
- Give free access to all information to all employees
- Disseminate information in a timely and extensive way.

3. *Spot when knowledge assets are being under-utilized and find ways of getting knowledge onto people's agenda*
   - Raise awareness through the use of diagnostics and high-level measurements
   - Create a clear understanding of which knowledge is important for delivering strategic objectives
   - Map knowledge and its integration with other key processes
   - Prioritize important knowledge assets.

4. *Enable people to develop information skills*
   - Provide staff with the appropriate technology – Statoil supplies its employees with PCs and advanced communications equipment at home
   - The UK government, recognizing that a whole new generation who are conversant with cyberspace communication will enter the job market, has equipped secondary school teachers with laptops
   - Universities and business schools are developing various forms of partnerships with business – make appropriate learning links
   - Provide training in IT systems to enable people to acquire and share the information they need
   - Employees need to be skilled at time management in order to use their time effectively for the creation and sharing of knowledge
   - HR can help employees to acquire information skills that will help them to become more employable as well as increasing their value to their employer:
     - Resource investigation skills
     - Networking skills
     - Communication and diagnostic skills
     - A range of learning techniques
     - Team-based problem-solving
     - Flexibility
     - Willingness to try new things, take risks and review learning.

5. *Develop a knowledge-friendly culture*
   - CEOs need to set the style, ensuring that training and educational activities are both short- and long-term oriented
   - Create a clear shared vision and values about the effective creation and dissemination of knowledge
   - Trust is a vital component in the human aspects of knowledge management. Leaders need to encourage the sharing of best practice by recognizing and rewarding people when this happens and by being good role models

- Encourage research and development at all levels
- Actively develop and market new ideas to create new products and services
- Ensure that the formal and informal reward systems reinforce the value of creating and sharing knowledge
- Create a physical work environment which facilitates shared learning and knowledge.

6. *Address the 'what's in it for me?' question*
   - Find synergies between the individual's need for growth and personal development and the company's needs. Effective career development practices are conducive to the sharing of knowledge since people can see that they do not need to hold on to knowledge in order to progress their career
   - For some employees, technophobia prevents them from keeping up in today's workplace. A few years ago, recognizing that some employees needed help, Marks & Spencer declared an IT amnesty for staff so that all employees could get up to speed with computers
   - Employees need to be able to develop key skills for the workplace of tomorrow, which will enhance their employability. These include confidently seeking knowledge from other people, inside and outside the organization, as well as team skills and the willingness to collaborate with others to create new solutions
   - When employees cease to be overloaded with unnecessary data, and start to perceive the benefits of sharing information to their own effectiveness, they are more likely to willingly collaborate in the generation of useful knowledge
   - Employees should respect and value their knowledge and experience as an asset that can add value to the business – and not fear sharing that knowledge
   - Employees can give and receive honest feedback which can help them and others to develop – and at the same time build trusting relationships.

7. *Develop criteria for successful knowledge management projects*
   - Ensure senior management support
   - Link the knowledge project to economic performance
   - Use appropriate technical and organizational infrastructure
   - Develop a standard, flexible knowledge structure
   - Use clear purpose and language
   - Use multiple channels for knowledge transfer.

8. *Communicate knowledge effectively*
   - Communicate at the right level – senior managers often talk at too senior a level to make sense lower down the organization
   - Use the experts to impart information. Involve contractors and flexible workers in communications strategies

- Managers should develop the skills of non-judgemental listening and brainstorming. 'Whacky' ideas should be encouraged
- Make sure that people are rewarded in some way for developing and sharing knowledge.

HOW ORGANIZATIONS ARE DEVELOPING INTELLECTUAL CAPITAL

Knowledge management, or the development of intellectual capital, is very much about the creation of an open, collaborative culture in which learning is valued. This is not simply a question of increasing spend on training. Within this culture, the generation of new knowledge through learning needs to be managed, knowledge needs to be captured, shared and communicated, information needs to be organized for easy retrieval and existing knowledge built upon. To some extent, HR is in a position to take a lead role by agreeing with senior managers what the learning culture would look like, and then agreeing actions to move the culture in the desired direction.

A learning culture will be one in which some risk-taking and a few mistakes are tolerated. They are the opposite of what line managers commonly describe as their experience of the 'blame culture' in their organizations. Leaders are influential and have to understand that they are part of a system which they can shape. This is why leaders at all levels need to be behind moves to create a learning culture, or else ad hoc initiatives will lead nowhere. HR can help leaders to develop to core skills of feedback and how to leverage knowledge and learning.

For many leaders, accepting emergence, learning and the uncertain future that it implies creates anxiety. Managers need to develop ways of openly examining their individual and collective responses to anxiety as a way of avoiding decisions or actions which may be superficial, ineffective or counterproductive for the purpose of the organization. In the same way, managers should be sensitive to the people processes they use and their own tolerance of risk and ambiguity. Particularly important are managers' attitudes to and ability to handle conflict, debate and tension within the organization.

In the West, a number of companies have acknowledged the importance of the management of knowledge by appointing a 'chief knowledge officer'. Though these are currently few in number in the UK, many have grouped together in networks to share learning on a pan-organization basis. This is not considered to be a breach of confidentiality. What works for one organization does not necessarily work for others, but knowledge officers are honing their own insights as to how to create a culture which is supportive of the management of intellectual capital. HR can also help set up networks that bring communities with a common interest in developing and sharing knowledge together.

Other new roles and responsibilities are being created. In some companies, there is a senior-level 'knowledge sponsor' who can ensure board-level attention for knowledge issues. Then there are knowledge managers/facilitators who offer support to client teams. Knowledge owners provide the expert input, and their responsibility is to keep up to date and keep up with the information flow. On the technical side there are information service providers and webmaster roles.

Some sophisticated companies are developing networks to explore issues of knowledge management and to develop strategies for maximizing the value of the organization through knowledge. One such network is the Knowledge Exchange which aims to put a financial measure on an organization's intellectual capital. Another group of companies 3M and Monsanto, have formed a consortium – Strategic Management of Knowledge and Organizational Learning – which acknowledges the need for organizations to collaborate in order to develop and share know-how on knowledge management. This consortium recognizes that these issues must form part of the top management agenda, if more value and sustainable advantage are to be created through the development of knowledge processes. Consortium members understand that the strategic management of knowledge and organizational learning are inextricably interlinked.

The Consortium recognizes that there are key elements and relationships which shape the priorities by which knowledge is selected and focused upon. Without the aligning force of business strategy, knowledge initiatives remain disparate and uncoordinated. However, with strong business drivers, knowledge can take on a purpose and direction. The Consortium members also recognize that while leveraging of knowledge is driven by the value to be created, and guided by the business strategies/strategic imperatives, people are key to success in all elements and relationships in the model. The management challenge is to implement the processes that will support and liberate their capabilities.

So if knowledge underpins every value-added activity that the organization carries out, this body of knowledge must be managed and developed for its full potential to be realized. This requires identifying the processes of creating and sharing knowledge, and supplying the enabling conditions, i.e. developing the organization's capability through its culture and leadership and providing the supporting technology and infrastructure. Starting with existing projects, and involving people is such a way that they begin to understand the benefits to them, leads to employee ownership of the knowledge process.

There are opportunities for sharing and developing knowledge inside the company and with external stakeholders, such as customers. The company needs to learn about its customers and their needs, as well as learn from them. This learning can become reciprocal if there is trust and a partnership. NCR in the UK has developed a Learning Centre which has developed a reputation for thought leadership within the high-technology sector. The facilities are available to clients and leading thinkers address industry gatherings on a range of business and strategic topics. Du Pont supplies customers with a Gold Card which gives them access to Du Pont research.

ICL (now Fujitsu) developed Café VIK (Valuing ICL Knowledge), which is both actual and virtual – 'the global coffee room'. This is both an information service and exchange and a physical location in the UK where employees can meet to share knowledge. Café VIK was developed following extensive staff consultation. Staff were asked 'what kind of information will help you to do your jobs?' so that the knowledge on offer could be made as relevant as possible to the different professional communities within the company. The new service was introduced with roadshows and take-up has been substantial. Information sheets are available on the company intranet. These are both issues sheets and attachments offering solutions based on people's experience. A database on people – their skills/expertise and project experience – facilitates networking. Data warehousing ensures that information is kept up to date.

Moving Towards Organizational Learning

Over and above these knowledge management initiatives, the organization needs to develop its capacity to continuously renew itself in the context of ongoing change. Peter Senge, author of *The Fifth Discipline* (1990), has identified five disciplines that are essential to creating an organization which can learn. These are:

- Systems thinking – which considers the interrelatedness of forces and sees them as part of a common process. 'System dynamics' involves looking for the complex feedback processes which can generate problematic patterns of behaviour within organizations.
- Personal mastery – which acknowledges that we are all a significant part of the systems we work within and 'the most significant leverage may come from changing our own orientation and self-image'. Concepts include personal visioning, treating emotions respectfully and the leader as coach.
- Mental models – which involve the ability to reflect and the theories which make up our current reality. Having the ability to develop and test new mental models will be essential for future-oriented learning and development.
- Shared vision – which involves gaining the commitment and focus which comes when a vision is genuinely shared. The vision should provide clues as to the organization's deep purpose and ways must be found of involving people at every level of the organization to speak and be heard about things that matter to them.
- Team learning – in which collective aspiration gives team members a compelling reason to begin to learn how to learn together. Learning design can incorporate a team, as well as individual development focus. Following a learning activity, people can be encouraged to consider 'who also would benefit from this?' and transfer relevant and helpful learning to others.

Creating a Development Culture in a UK Local Authority

In one local authority many initiatives to support learning, such as lunchtime seminars, are under way. These are complemented by a set of supporting activities, such as linking the seminars to the senior management competencies. These form part of a coherent management development strategy. Self-development is a key part of this strategy, supported by targeted use of Learning Resource Centres. Materials linked to the competencies are networked so that people have ready access to learning materials.

Variations on action learning groups have been established at different levels within the organization. These groups are treated as a legitimate business activity rather than a 'nice to have'. Some are cross-level and are proving helpful in breaking down some of the hierarchical barriers which apparently exist. Learning groups are set up around the different competencies and specific projects. This way learning can be shared between people with different forms of experience. Other learning groups are more open-ended, with people carrying out their own development targets with support from other members of their learning group.

The development team are considering whether learning should be accredited to a recognized qualification such as a Diploma in Management Studies and whether to support individuals selectively in their pursuit of qualifications such as MBAs. These can be a tremendous source of learning and stimulus, especially for relatively high flyers who may feel trapped in their current role. Depending on the course chosen, there can be useful organizational benefits to be gained from business-related project work. However, it is very important that people who benefit from such training have the opportunity to use their enhanced knowledge and skills in some way, even if only to run an in-house seminar on their chosen subject.

In this and other ways, the authority hopes to play to people's strengths. The development team are planning to establish a data bank, showing not only what people's development needs are but also their strengths and areas where they are prepared to be a resource to others. Peer mentoring can be a powerful resource and sometimes needs a little formal help in becoming established. While it is not necessary to go the Investor in People route when creating a development culture, this can often provide the organization with additional kudos for what is happening anyway, if these recommendations are adopted.

Networking

In some companies, networking happens accidentally or as part of the informal system. Smokers' rooms are a good example of where new information circuits have been developed in recent years. Some companies deliberately encourage and enable networking as a means of getting people to share ideas. 3M is well known as a company which encourages innovation. Indeed, every activity revolves around this and individual responsibilities are clear. Networking is the main operating mode and there is a strong culture in which risk-taking is good, innovations can be made by everyone and there is a tolerance of honest mistakes.

Informal working, including working at home, and teamworking are encouraged. In the new corporate headquarters of British Airways, the physical environment has been specifically designed to facilitate employee networking. A 'street' complete with coffee bars is intended to create a community environment in which collaboration will naturally take place. This will enable 'structured' networking in which people with specific forms of knowledge can help one another.

Culture Change at Sainsbury's Logistics Division

The Logistics division of Sainsbury's supermarkets is in the vanguard of a cultural shift which aims to align employee and business development. The cultural shift is away from managers making all the decisions to 'empowerment' of employees to make decisions and to take action. The culture should therefore become more flexible and adaptive to changing business conditions and innovative solutions should be readily found. The process works through a combination of team and personal development – from career planning to corporate vision cultural work – performance management tools such as one-to-ones, and the use of a full range of development techniques including training and flexible/home working. Measures are also used to encourage mutual respect and appreciation, and there's a People's Charter and Staff Council.

Open Access Development Centres at Standard Life

Standard Life has created some very successful learning resource centres, known as Open Access Development Centres (OADCs). These are based in five sites, having been piloted in Edinburgh where the head office is situated. Standard Life has actively encouraged employees to take responsibility for their development but recognizes that the organization must provide resources to make this possible. The OADCs are one of the ways in which Standard Life is investing in its staff.

Employees are encouraged to create a development plan and negotiate their needs with their managers. Having done this, they can have access to a wide range of resources at the OADC where staff are available to provide help and advice. If employees are unable to visit the centre in person, materials are sent out to them. Teams can also use the centres for development purposes. If development is directly linked to a person's role, it is considered legitimate that they spend work time acquiring the new skill or knowledge. Where possible, materials are provided on similar topics in a variety of formats such as videos, books, CD-ROMs, the Internet, self-assessment tools etc. to suit different learning styles. Copies of management development materials from training programmes are also available.

The OADCs are designed to support five operational objectives:

- The development of key role and core organizational competencies
- Training by alternative medium
- Corporate initiatives such as the executive learning programme
- Professional studies in line with the company policy
- Vocational qualifications enabled.

They currently cost around £500000 to run (excluding salaries) and utilization is running at 60%. There have been a number of significant benefits to the business as well as to employees. Staff surveys indicate that there has been a positive impact on retention since employees recognize that Standard Life offers significant opportunities for development. Similarly, there have been cost-benefits in terms of recruitment. In 1998 a modern apprenticeship scheme was launched which has attracted many youngsters who might otherwise have gone to university. A strong selling point to potential recruits was the OADC provision and staff development opportunities. In addition, OADCs provide a tangible demonstration of Standard Life's commitment to developing employees.

Sun Microsystems

All employees are connected through SunWeb, the corporate intranet. Quality staff distribute findings from the Customer Quality Index and the Employee Quality Index, a monthly online survey of 3500 randomly selected employees. This index gauges employee satisfaction and the information it provides is used to target 'performance inhibitors'. Sun University uses the latest technology to train 20000 employees and the workplace has been designed to facilitate learning and knowledge sharing.

Creating a Self-Development Culture at the National Air Traffic Services (NATS)

I am grateful to Dr Jane Yarnall for the following case study which was featured in an earlier edition of this book.

The National Air Traffic Service, a subsidiary of the Civil Aviation Authority, plans, provides and operates safe and efficient air traffic services. NATS is working towards a public/private partnership and has over 5000 staff. The average length of service is 15 years and there is relatively low turnover. Staff skills have a strong technical bias and, given the safety culture, there is an emphasis on critical, problem-identification and problem-solving approaches.

While employees tend to stay with NATS for a long time, a staff survey indicated that career satisfaction was low and highlighted a number of employee concerns with regard to career development. These were:

- Lack of information
- Misconceptions about procedures
- Limited movement across functions
- Uncertainty over the future
- Managers' skills and attitudes were not supportive of career development.

Responding to the survey findings, a new framework was put in place for all staff based on self-development of the organization's 12 core competencies. A number of initiatives were carried out and measures set to establish whether these initiatives would produce improvements in any of the three areas measured, namely:

- Career satisfaction
- Organizational commitment
- Management support for careers.

Among the initiatives introduced were some practical tools to help people to manage their own development. These were all voluntary and the amount of use made of them is roughly in descending order as follows:

- Personal Development Plans
- Development Options Guide (DOG)
- Career workshops
- Coaching training
- Learning Resource Centre
- Secondment policies and guidance
- Career workbook
- NATS Career planning guide.

Interestingly, all the measures improved though there was relatively little impact on career satisfaction. Employees clearly believed that the company should still manage their career. However, management support for development increased as a result of these initiatives. The lessons learned were that extensive communication about career self-development was needed (due to resource constraint at the time, formal communication had been limited) and that line managers were the lynchpin to making a self-development culture work. It was also essential that these learning and career development initiatives had a non-HR senior sponsor who could help tackle some of the issues raised in the next phase.

In addition, the competencies were revised to include a more commercial focus. In a programme for managers, using 360-degree feedback, the findings suggested that there were clear differences of perception between what managers thought they did, and what other people perceived. The major differences of perception were around the following competencies:

- Managing people
- Teamworking
- Challenging complacency.

Clearly work needed to be done to help managers to support people development. NATS recognized that employee satisfaction with regard to career development is important and maintains the strategy of self-development supported by the organization. Therefore to reinforce and support this culture shift, various tools were introduced to help people carry out a realistic self-assessment, such as using 360-degree feedback. A grid of development methods available was developed against the competencies. This allowed people to identify development options which suit them and other tools, such as a computerized Development

Options Guide, provide a steer on training courses and other means of developing the competencies. This also allowed the HR team to understand who needed what type of development, so they were better able to focus resources. Career paths, especially for engineer groups, were developed which should make some development moves possible.

In the move towards a self-development culture, the need for opportunities for people to learn from others, as well as generate new knowledge collaboratively was recognized. A key initiative was the introduction of action learning sets, some of which include managers from other companies. With low turnover, the importance of bringing in new ideas from other organizations was recognized. Other ways in which development was moved outside the organization included the use of cross-company mentoring. Senior manager development focused on leadership, recognizing that if the self-development culture was to become fully embedded, leaders needed to role model learning with and from one another.

CONCLUSION

In today's complex organizations, competitive advantage for the business is likely to depend on the ways in which employees create and share their knowledge in ways that increase the bottom-line. The challenge of knowledge management is to ensure that employees also benefit from developing and sharing knowledge.

But this is not simply a question of helping employees to see 'what's in it for me?', even though the ability to share key knowledge effectively is likely to make employees more truly employable. Just relying on people's goodwill and trust in the organization is unlikely to lead to knowledge sharing and the development of exciting new products and services. To do this, employees need to be provided with the appropriate environment and infrastructure. IT and HR systems need to complement each other, and there needs to be a clear strategy with regard to the types of knowledge the organization wishes to develop, store and be able to retrieve. In addition, employees need to be helped to develop the attitude and skills required for the Information Age.

Managers need to take a lead in developing a culture that is conducive to learning and knowledge creation. Their behaviour and responses to critical incidents, such as when an experimental activity backfires, will speak volumes. They need to both encourage others to learn continuously from one another and be prepared to do so themselves. Managers need to make the time to identify, prioritize and develop knowledge assets that need to be integrated into the main business processes. In large companies tools will need to be developed to enable global sharing.

The accelerating pace of change in the competitive environment now requires organizations not only to move fast to meet market needs but also to leverage their human resources to the maximum if they are to gain and retain competitive advantage. More than that, Human Resources professionals can contribute to value creation in their organizations if they can find ways to help both individuals and teams to play to their strengths and release potential for innovation. Human

Resource development has a critical role to play in identifying and addressing skill gaps. HR is, and will remain, one of the glues that ensure that organizations can operate as a cohesive whole, and can be a key enabler of organizational learning. New roles and responsibilities need to be clarified and ways of connecting people found.

There is a real opportunity for HR to increase its value and visibility within the business, if HR professionals tap into an organization's longer-term strategies and develop an agenda based on meeting the company's future needs. The most powerful opportunity for HR professionals is to develop strategies that build a company's brand through its people. Knowledge management is only one key area where effective line/HR partnership can ensure that the precious human resource can become ever more resourceful.

REFERENCES

de Geus, Arie, in interview with N. Chambers (1997) Does the bell toll for your living company? *HR Focus*, October, 74, No. 10

Handy, C. (1997) *The Hungry Spirit*. London: Hutchinson

Kransdorff, A. (1995) Succession planning in a fast changing world. *Training Officer*, 31, No. 2, 52–53

Lammiman, J. and Syrett, M. (1999) *Innovation at the Top: Where Do Directors Get Their Ideas From?* Horsham: Roffey Park Management Institute

Morgan, G. (1993) *Imaginization: The Art of Creative Management*. London: Sage

Nonaka, I. and Takeuchi, H. (1995) *The Knowledge-Creating Company*. Oxford: Oxford University Press

Senge, P. (1990) *The Fifth Discipline*. New York: Doubleday Currency

Stewart, T.A. (1997) *Intellectual Capital: The New Wealth of Organizations*. London: Nicholas Brealey

Varney, S. (2008) Learning – key to organizational transformation in a complex world, in *Developing HR Strategy (March)*. London: Croner

Conclusion

In the decade since the first edition of this book was published, the field of theory and practice in HR has moved on significantly. The changing business environment has raised awareness of the critical importance of 'human capital' to business success, the search for 'talent' has become a holy grail, 'employee engagement' is seen as synonymous with 'performance', and people management and development are seen as vital levers of competitive advantage in organizations worldwide. This should mean that the people function – HR – is at the forefront of leading exciting and value-adding developments.

In many ways this is happening. The scope of the HR role is expanding and many HR teams have focused on structuring their delivery to address the tactical, operational and strategic needs of their organization in the most efficient and effective ways possible. Dave Ulrich has been pre-eminent among academics in shaping thinking and practice in the field, and his ideas have been widely taken up as the model for structuring HR delivery. Yet though the field of HR theory moves on, the HR function itself still struggles to some extent to be seen as a credible player, especially with respect to the degree to which HR is aligned to business strategy.

So what does the future hold for HR? Will HR remain largely a pragmatic, transactional functional whose value is ever in doubt? Or will HR's function be to provide value-adding leadership, geared to building organizational capacity and capability? Will HR seize the opportunity to bring about culture change conducive to high performance? Will developing leaders at all levels become a central plank of HR strategy? Will skilful use of data enable HR activities to be better targeted to produce employee engagement and better understand the engagement–performance link?

The changing patterns of recent years suggest that the jury is still out. My guess is that as time moves on there will be more, not less need for effective HR contributions. But to be able to operate in ways that truly add value, HR has to lead the way. While no one doubts the importance of Finance as a function, HR still seems to be under the sceptical spotlight, having to prove that it adds value.

In today's organizations, many of these big organizational challenges, such as the need to recruit and retain the right talent, are now being recognized as the strategic issues they are. While HR may have been trying to get these issues on the strategic agenda for years, the irony is that they are often only treated as serious business issues when line managers too see their importance.

That is perhaps one of the key messages of this book. HR can and should be the key interpreter problem-solver and strategic catalyst with regard to people issues, but responsibility for the design and implementation of effective people strategies should be shared between the line and HR. Alignment between business and HR strategies begins with a partnership approach. For this to happen, there needs to be give and take on both sides as well as mutual understanding and respect.

Respect is contingent on delivery. Creating value-adding 'deliverables' that contribute to sustainable performance requires HR professionals to have a thorough understanding of their business and what it is trying to achieve. In the short-term this involves understanding the top two or three current executive priorities and developing actions to implement and track solutions to them. For one focus group of senior HR managers and directors this was about:

- Looking at what the organization needs to deliver (medium and long term)
- Identifying the support needed to implement business decisions across countries and business units
- Supporting the business objectives of the firm by timely, intelligent and commonsensical HR activities and planning.

This requires HR to demonstrate real business acumen and the ability to translate business intentions into the strategies that will deliver the people outcomes required for business success. These outcomes should be measurable so that the relevant value logic for the organization can be tracked through. Mutual understanding requires a common language. The same HRD focus group highlighted the importance of communicating in business language rather than professional jargon:

- Simple rather than sophisticated
- Business focused
- Human!

BECOMING CLEAR ABOUT HR'S PURPOSE

Becoming clear about how HR can add value in your organization is part of the process of making a difference. So first and foremost, as Wayne Brockbank (1997) suggests, HR teams need to define how they are going to contribute unique value to their organizations: 'if HR as a whole is unclear about its purpose, what can be expected from the rest of the company about the purpose of HR'? Brockbank's criteria for developing a departmental point of view include:

- Is it formally stated or is it ad hoc and assumed?
- Does it comprehensively cover the whole organization thereby encouraging the corporate whole to be greater than the sum of the parts?
- Is it linked to issues that are critical to long-term corporate success?
- Does it create explicit and measurable results?
- And it would be a mistake to assume that alignment with business strategy means focusing HR strategy exclusively on short-term requirements, important though these are.

HR teams need to be able to operate strategically, even if their delivery focus is currently operational. Taking time to learn about employee and senior management issues should be a priority, yet it is often driven down the 'to do' list due to the pressure of the daily round of business. Since the HR function is always likely to be thinly resourced, these time pressures may well contain the seeds of functional self-destruction. Team members can be so busy that they do not take time to reflect, to see the 'wood' for the 'trees' and take stock of what needs to be the new focus. Learning how to prioritize their efforts on the deliverables which will make a difference is vital if HR professionals are going to be seen as relevant and adding value.

As I have emphasized throughout this book, the focus of short-term activity should always be informed by a view of what the organization will need to achieve longer-term. That is because as organizations change, what they need from HR, and therefore the scope of the HR role, is expanding. Therefore HR professionals need to think through the implications for their organization of globalization, changing demographics, the more competitive landscape, the changing nature of customer preference, and the changing shape and nature of work and develop their longer-term strategic goals which can inform activity in the here-and-now.

Core Role 1: Attracting and Mobilizing Talent

In today's fast-changing business environment the fortunes of organizations increasingly depend on the quality and output of their talent. This places talent as the key source of competitive advantage and the need to develop organizational capability at the heart of HR's remit. HR's primary role should be to ensure that the organization has the right staff (skills, knowledge, motivations) to deliver. HR can and should be leading thinking and practice about how to secure the talent needed for success, how to motivate and mobilize talent to produce high-quality outputs. They need to ask – and find answers to – the following questions:

- What forms of talent will be needed and where will these be obtained?
- How will the current workforce factor into the future landscape?

- What kinds of leadership and management capabilities, structures and technologies will be required to support work that will be carried out only a few years from now?
- How can the answers to these questions be addressed through the short-term issues and considerations we deal with?

HR needs to develop and implement effective sub-strategies such as workforce planning, building talent pipelines, promoting effective talent management, improving the capability of managers and leaders, enhancing employee engagement, continuously developing skills and providing opportunities for growth, developing more holistic rewards; and building a culture conducive to learning, creativity and knowledge sharing.

Core Role 2: Building Performance Capability

If organizations are to be successful they need high performance from their employees, and the cultural capabilities, such as speed and customer focus, on which future business success will depend. If HR delivers on its mandate – to build successful organizations – then HR will be fulfilling a leadership function.

- A vision for a high-performance organization will provide focus. Components of such a vision include developing the behaviours, systems and processes geared to increasing customer value, leadership throughout the organization to create momentum, decentralized and devolved decision-making, development of people capacities through learning at all levels, and performance, operational and people management processes aligned to organizational objectives.
- HR needs to understand what types of performance are needed in their organization and be able to help line managers get the best out of their teams. So HR can add value by helping line managers manage for performance, working with line managers to create clear accountabilities and performance standards which help employees raise the bar on their own performance.

HR can help line managers create a highly productive work climate. Typically, this is a climate in which people are clear about their roles, have challenging objectives and opportunities for development, access to the information and other resources they need to do their jobs; and receive effective coaching, recognition of achievement and appropriate rewards. Integrated policies and processes can be developed for monitoring and following up results. These processes should follow quality standards, with the customer flow identified end-to-end and the most effective service delivery model agreed and delivered.

These ingredients should not only produce high performance but also higher employee commitment which in turn leads to greater customer satisfaction and better results for investors and other stakeholders. As Dave Ulrich (1997) points out, the proof of effective people management practices is evident when two firms in the same basic industry which have similar results are compared, and where one is considered to have considerably more shareholder value potential than the other.

Core Role 3: Creating Healthy and Successful Organizations

I agree with Hiltrop and Udall (2004) that 'As we move deeper into the 21st century, we can realistically expect that pressures to change the culture, purpose and shape of organizations will intensify as the needs for flexibility, competitiveness, innovation, speed and punctuality improvements become even greater.' In the future, perceptions of improving shareholder value are likely to be based on speed of reaction to opportunity and threat, the quality and volume of profitable new products and services, the capitalization of intellectual capital, the strength and 'reality' of the brand in practice and the quality of leadership and strength of the talent pipeline.

Many organizations are blind-sided about how to build an organization that is in balance. Both organizational design and organizational development are neglected areas. HR can and should be leading the way but to win the mandate to do this, HR needs to be good at the operational personnel processes and practices, however these are delivered, as well as develop a deep understanding of how to bring about change within complex systems. For the HRD focus group this was about:

- Thinking big picture
- Acting as internal change agent – with an eye on strategic business plans and organizational effectiveness
- Making uncertainty manageable
- Making a difference.

HR needs to develop a culture change agenda which is strategic and future-focused, rather than reactive and simply 'picking up the pieces'. HR should anticipate where change will be needed, acting as an enabler and implementer of change, especially when the change is introduced proactively in order to put the organization on the 'front foot' and create new opportunities for the organization. HR should develop expertise in internal communications and ensure that every medium is being used to best effect to create information flows, effective participation and learning. HR should devise structures and ways of working which not only optimize working conditions, especially around knowledge work, but are hard to imitate.

Core Role 4: Building Effective Leadership

HR has a critical role to play in building the leadership of the organization to create shareholder and other stakeholder value. This involves having a global perspective on the business and consciously seeking out global talent. This also means not only developing succession for the medium term but also critically evaluating the quality of current leadership. Again, the changing business requirements should drive the assessment agenda:

- To what extent is the current leadership able to create an adaptable, change-oriented organization in which accountabilities are clear, employees are highly motivated and committed and where the culture is supportive of learning and innovation?

- Are leaders able to provide clarity of direction in ambiguous circumstances so that employees are clear what needs to be done and what is no longer relevant?
- Do leaders develop and manage effective relationships with internal and external stakeholders and are they able to scan the environment for new opportunities for their organization?

Core Role 5: Providing Coherence

The function of HR is that of a key integrator across the organization, acting as organizational 'glue' which ensures that the organization's sum is greater than that of its parts. This is about balancing consistency with flexibility: ensuring both enough consistency that people understand what the company stands for, and how their role contributes to organizational success and what standards are expected, and also creating enough flexibility in structures, roles, skills and mindsets to ensure that the organization can remain agile and innovative. For members of the HRD focus group this was about:

- Creating flexible, broad business people
- Communicating clearly to people about the things that affect them
- Creating a cohesive framework/common company language.

Core Role 6: Ensuring Good Governance

HR also has a growing role to play in good governance, especially the implementation of values-based practices, such as CSR, diversity and environmental policies, and ensuring that the behaviour of leaders at all levels is fair and appropriate. After all, as we have seen in recent years, organizational reputations, once undermined by poor or dishonest practice, tend to be permanently destroyed. But this is not about HR acting merely as company compliance officer, imposing the dead hand of unnecessary policy and over-burdensome scrutiny which produces a risk averse and slow-moving culture. It is much more about leading discussions at all levels which create a shared focus on ethical practice, developing authentic leaders and delivering the reality of what is promised by the employer brand.

IS YOUR ORGANIZATION READY FOR A STRATEGIC APPROACH?

Of course, many practitioners will say that their organization is not ready for a strategic HR approach, that what really counts is delivering the 'pieces' well in the here and now. Other practitioners argue that it is precisely because the function contents itself with administration, hiring and firing, that HR is not valued.

I would argue that this is a false dilemma which can be partly reconciled through the ways in which HR organizes its delivery. While in some organizations HR continues to be organized along generalist lines, the increasingly dominant way of structuring HR, particularly in large organizations, is along the lines of the 'Ulrich' functional role model, whether HR operations are outsourced or insourced using call centres or shared services. Centres of excellence are also becoming repositories of increasing numbers of specialists. Typically, strategic areas such as organization design, succession planning, designing talent recruitment and retention strategies are the remit of a few senior HR staff. While this may be a sensible way of sharing responsibilities, and should allow for both operational and strategic excellence, many HR teams have struggled to make the new HR structure work. It has in some cases created unhelpful role divisions which may make it difficult for the HR team as a whole to develop a strategic approach and may cause problems when it comes to implementation.

However, this approach to HR structures appears here to stay and those organizations who have been early adopters of the model continue to develop and modify the structure as they learn what works, often slimming down the number of business partners to create genuinely strategic roles, while more generally business partnering becomes synonymous with internal consultancy. The ongoing modification of the application of this conceptual framework for HR roles reflects practical experience and feedback about how it is desirable and possible to address both short-term and longer-term needs at the same time.

In yet other organizations, strategic delivery is more hybrid. In Sun Microsystems Europe, for instance, HR service delivery is through 'account managers' who provide consultancy support to specific business units. In addition, these HR account managers each take responsibility for developing expertise in one area of the firm's strategic agenda, such as managing mergers, for instance. This more strategic role requires carrying out effective diagnosis of what is needed to deliver the business strategy and an effective corporate translation into practice of HR strategies. Indeed, some pundits suggest that having a separate 'HR' strategy is a mistake; that HR plans should be seen as so integral to the business strategy that they do not need a separate caption. Perhaps this is the surest way of aligning HR and business strategies – making them one!

To some extent whatever structural model is adopted for HR matters less than the delivery focus it enables. The real challenge, according to the focus group of senior HR managers and directors, is to 'keep the eye on the ball', having worked out what the 'ball' is in the first place. Several comments reveal a common view of what HR needs to focus on:

- 'Anything from not doing "day-to-day" work to looking ahead three years'
- 'Influencing the board and the direction of the company'
- 'Making a difference to the bottom line'

- 'Developing the frameworks, policies and initiatives to move the business forward'
- 'Integrating future business goals/needs with people issues/needs in a plan'
- 'Clear thinking/policies/right direction/motivation of staff'.

What is important is to gauge the actual needs and readiness of your organization for what it intends to do strategically. Does it have the core capabilities, culture, systems and processes, working practices and human skills to accomplish what it wants to do? If not, what does this imply if the strategic aims are to be accomplished? HR should be able to contribute to the strategic planning process inventories of not only the organization's technical capabilities but also its cultural strengths and weaknesses.

How will HR support the development of a high-performance culture, how will work processes need to be managed to achieve high-quality deliverables, how will the core competencies be activated and what aspects of the organization's culture will need to be strengthened, balanced out or changed? HR teams need to develop their own answers which will fit their current organizational context. This means defining the implications of business strategy for organizational capability, such as the firm's ability to learn, and developing measurable actions to build that capability. If, for example, managing costs is a strategic aim, does the organization have the capability to create high productivity, use resources efficiently and become a low-cost provider in its marketplace?

By way of example, the HR team of one organization, which supplies a UK-wide repair service to individual and corporate customers, has analysed the links between business strategy and HR actions as follows:

Business strategy
- Meet customer needs – best service possible – unequalled value for money
- Build on strengths of brand, customer database and IT capability
- Manage for profit and growth

Core values
- Brand
- Courtesy and care
- Stakeholders
- Quality and value for money

Critical success factors
- People
- Financial performance
- Operational performance
- Market share
- Vision and strategy

Translated into Balanced Scorecard
- Customer perspective
- Internal business perspective

- Financial perspective
- People (learning and growth)

Learning and growth measures

- Capability (performance management, succession management)
- Culture and climate (survey measures)
- Skills mix (training and development outputs)
- Capacity for change
- Employee profile (statistics, costs)
- Organization structure.

This organization's HR team has been able to segment the staff population, identify the relevant development needs, establish behavioural standards, business skills and the areas of technical and professional mastery required for the current and future business. HR processes and tools such as recruitment and selection, training and development, performance management and reward, employee relations and management standards are fully integrated to support the learning and growth aims. 'Learning and growth' can then fully enable the organization to achieve its strategic aims.

DEVELOPING HR LEADERSHIP

Earlier in the book I suggested that if HR is to be able to exercise real leadership, this is about more than leading the HR team – it is also about making a full contribution as business professionals with value-adding expertise. The credibility of HR is based partly on being able to deliver results in a business-like way but also by the ability to build trust and influence at all levels, especially at senior levels. Our focus group data suggests that this ability to influence is critical if HR is to be perceived to add value, and that some HR professionals struggle to do this. For instance some HR specialists may not be comfortable selling the business implications of what they are recommending. Conversely, HR generalists may have a good business grounding but may lack confidence in their ability to add specialist value. Again, a way of reconciling this apparent dilemma is by ensuring that specialists develop business and consultancy skills and relationships, and that generalists develop at least one area of expertise.

Similarly, building an image of professionalism through knowing your business allows HR to usefully introduce best practice thinking – but critically and pragmatically rather than falling into the 'initiative of the month' trap. This requires HR to network with other members of the HR profession and line managers from other organizations, picking up ideas and developing a global idea of what externally judged good practice looks like. This will enable HR to more confidently assert what needs to be done with regard to the people implications of business strategies in their own organization and even recommend potential business opportunities.

And in common with members of other professions, in preparing for the future, HR professionals may therefore need to both broaden and deepen their skills in order to keep at the leading edge of their professional knowledge and skill. There is a great deal that can be done by HR teams themselves to ensure that they have the skills needed to develop and deliver people strategies. Prerequisites include business understanding, interpersonal and consultancy skills, planning and implementation skills, and the willingness to learn. Managing change means taking a proactive rather than reactive stance to bringing about change. It involves being able to understand how the organization works as a system, identifying where change needs to occur to enable the organization to achieve its goals, applying project management disciplines and integrating separate initiatives into a change framework. It means working in partnership with line managers and other specialist functions such as Finance and IT to create coherent change execution. It also requires being willing to assess how well the HR team is equipped to manage change and up-skilling the team as appropriate.

Managing culture involves being willing to challenge the status quo and to have the courage of your convictions. It requires having a vision underpinned by humanistic values of what a healthy culture consists of, focused on enabling both high performance and employee well-being. It involves being able to diagnose the kind of culture required to deliver the business strategy and encouraging leaders to 'walk the talk' with regard to the desired culture and values. Challenging senior leaders can be a risky thing to do and will require confidence or 'attitude', as Dave Ulrich once described it, on the part of HR. According to Jeffrey Pfeffer (1996), this is an area that HR needs to develop: 'the comparatively low power of human resources is often further reduced by the reluctance of its executives to engage in organizational politics'.

Of course, strategic business partnership is not a one-way street. If line managers genuinely believe that HR issues have a critical impact on achieving business success, they should insist on involving HR professionals in the business strategy-making process. That way, expensive mistakes can be avoided and potential opportunities can be identified at the optimum time. This partnership approach needs to extend to implementation. HR must be able to understand the practical implications of delivering people-related business strategies and work with line managers to ensure that HR delivery at all levels is professional and effective. The key will be getting the basics right. Line managers need to develop the skills and responsibility to deal effectively with devolved HR responsibilities. Arguably, 'HR' strategies are better called 'People' strategies if they are named at all.

Will HR therefore be the best function to deliver 'people' strategies? Various management thinkers (Hastings, 1993) predict that the changing concept of organization is likely to have a radical impact on the future role of HR – in other words, the evolution may become more revolutionary. The predictions include:

- The average company will become smaller and employ fewer people
- Hierarchical organizations will be replaced by organizations of various forms
- Technicians or 'knowledge workers' will become the worker elite
- Vertical divisions of labour will be replaced by horizontal divisions

- The service economy is here to stay
- Work itself will be redefined by constant training.

Each of these trends has implications for the skills of employees generally, and for HR in particular. The pundits suggest that the HR function of the future will segment into operational, technical roles carried out by a range of specialists whose affinity is to a network rather than the HR function as a whole, and strategists who will take their seats at board tables. I predict that HR will need more real experts and specialists, many of whom will be found in consultancies. Developing HR careers may mean moving around the various structural roles – shared services, centres of excellence and business partnering – working on joint projects with others, ensuring cross-fertilization and development. Business partners will be senior people, who know how to operate profit and loss and are most likely to have a mixture of backgrounds. Increasingly, organizational strategists will be from a range of backgrounds, of which the HR route may be only one: 'The top HR slot is no longer reserved for the career HR professional. Increasingly business experience, coupled with highly developed consulting skills, is the prerequisite for senior HR roles' (SHRM, 2002). This may indeed result in the clearest alignment between HR and business strategies, when the managers involved have similar experiences and understanding of what needs to be done and where professional expertise is a value-add.

So in summary, HR leaders who embrace a change agenda have a key role to play in shaping the future by 'future proofing' their organization. They have many ways to do this, for instance by developing employer brands which are meaningful to current and future employees. They can build employee value propositions which marry up employee needs for work–life balance with employer needs for flexibility. They can create processes through which people development happens both on and off the job. They can support managers in creating line of sight to the organization's purpose and the customer. They can help managers manage change effectively and get the most from talent by up-skilling managers with the skills they need to be effective people managers, such as coaching. They can build employee engagement as the basis of great employee relations by identifying the key drivers of employee engagement in their context and focusing initiatives on these.

HR leaders must embrace the disciplines of HRM, HRD and OD in addition to developing their business understanding and borrowing approaches from other disciplines such as marketing, finance, IT. They can improve the quality of leadership by driving forward leadership selection, succession planning and development processes which result in leadership at all levels. They can design structures, roles and processes which facilitate cross-organizational teamworking and shared learning. They can develop policies that ensure the organization practices what it preaches – on CSR, environment, healthy working. And most of all they can role-model the changes they want to see, becoming capable and authentic deliverers of real value to their organizations.

No HR practitioner would claim that delivering a strategic and value-added contribution is easy. However, I suggest that many of the practitioners featured in this book demonstrate that success is possible, each responding in their own way to the challenges of understanding their organization's changing needs and developing and implementing aligned and integrated HR agendas which equip their organizations for the future.

If Lester Thurow (1992) is right when he asserts that 'In the 21st century, the education and skills of the workforce will end up being the dominant competitive weapon', then the Human Resources function should be the key enabler of organizational success in years to come.

REFERENCES

Brockbank, W. (1997) HR's future on the way to a presence. *Human Resource Management*, Spring 36, No. 1, 65–69

Hastings, C. (1993) *The New Organization: Growing the Culture of Organizational Networking*. New York: McGraw-Hill

Hiltrop, J.M. and Udall, S. (2004) Making the transition from HR manager to HR professional. *Human Resources and Employment Review*, June

Pfeffer, J. (1995) *Competitive Advantage through People*. Cambridge, MA: Harvard Business School Press

Pfeffer, J. (1996) When it comes to 'Best Practices' why do smart organizations occasionally do dumb things? *Organizational Dynamics*, Summer

SHRM (2002) *The Future of the HR Profession*: Society for Human Resource Management

Thurow, L.C. (1992) *Head to Head: The Coming of Economic Battle among Japan, Europe and America*. London: Nicholas Brealey

Ulrich, D. (1997) *Human Resource Champions: The Next Agenda for Adding Value and Delivering Results*. Cambridge, MA: Harvard Business School Press

FURTHER READING

Stroh, L.K. and Caligiuri, P.M. (1998) Increasing global competitiveness through effective people management. *Journal of World Business*, 33, No. 1

Ulrich, D. and Lake, D. (1990) *Organizational Capability: Competing from the Inside/Out*. New York: Wiley

Ulrich, D., Brockbank, W., Yeung, A.K. and Lake, D.G. (1995) Human Resource competencies: an empirical assessment. *Human Resource Management*, Winter

Index